TimeOut

London for Children
timeout.com

Free child entry offer

Save £££s at The Natural History Museum

Dinosaurs, whirlpools, tornadoes, creepy crawlies, meteorites – The Natural History Museum, one of the UK's top visitor attractions, showcases the wonders of nature with fun hands-on exhibits especially for kids to enjoy.

Entrance to the permanent exhibitions in the main galleries is free, but in addition the Museum has a programme of special exhibitions throughout the year to which *Time Out*

London for Children readers can take a child for free. To use this exclusive offer, simply cut out the voucher below and take it with you when you visit the special exhibitions.

Turbulent Landscapes: Play with the Forces of Nature
Until 15 Sept 2002
Whip up a whirlpool, twist through a tornado or erode your own sand dune; Turbulent Landscapes' 19 exhibits put nature's random events in your own hands. Touch and interact with the exhibits to disrupt their peaceful patterns and create natural chaos.

Dino-Birds: The Feathered Dinosaurs of China
18 July 2002-18 May 2003
For more than 140 years scientists have argued that modern birds were linked to dinosaurs. But where was the proof? Solving the puzzle are 15 fossils from China, which show how birds really did evolve from meat-eating dinosaurs. You'll never look at our feathered friends in the same way again.

BG Wildlife Photographer of the Year
19 Oct 2002-Mar 2003
Snow geese in the morning light, pike lying in ambush and a giant bullfrog rescuing his tadpoles were among the winning images of last year's BG Wildlife Photographer of the Year. Capturing the beauty of the natural world, this annual showcase, based on a competition organised by the Museum and *BBC Wildlife Magazine*, presents the best wildlife photography from around the world. Visit and judge this year's results for yourself!

Special exhibition entry: Adults £5; concessions £3; free to under-5s and NHM members.

Cut out the voucher on this page and one child gets in free.

For more information and details of how to get to the museum see pages 71-72.

Edited and designed by
Time Out Guides Limited
Universal House
251 Tottenham Court Road
London W1T 7AB
Tel + 44 (0)20 7813 3000
Fax + 44 (0)20 7813 6001
Email guides@timeout.com
www.timeout.com

Editorial
Editor Ronnie Haydon
Deputy Editor Lesley McCave
Listings Editor Cathy Limb
Listings Assistant Shane Armstrong
Proofreader Tamsin Shelton
Indexer Jackie Brind

Editorial Director Peter Fiennes
Series Editor Sarah Guy
Guides Co-ordinator Anna Norman

Design
Group Art Director John Oakey
Art Director Mandy Martin
Art Editor Scott Moore
Designers Benjamin de Lotz, Sarah Edwards, Lucy Grant
Scanning & Imaging Dan Conway
Ad make-up Glen Impey
Picture Editor Kerri Miles
Deputy Picture Editor Kit Burnet
Picture Librarian Sarah Roberts

Advertising
Group Commercial Director Lesley Gill
Sales Director/Sponsorship Mark Phillips
Sales Manager Alison Gray
Advertisement Sales James Coulbault,
Jason Trotman, Terina Rickit
Copy Controller Oliver Guy
Advertising Assistant Sabrina Ancilleri

Administration
Chairman Tony Elliott
Managing Director Mike Hardwick
Group Financial Director Kevin Ellis
Group General Manager Nichola Coulthard
Circulation Director Jim Heinemann
Production Manager Mark Lamond
Production Controller Samantha Furniss
Group Marketing Director Christine Cort
Marketing Manager Mandy Martinez
Marketing Executives Sandie Tozer, Sammie Squire
Marketing Assistant Claire Hojem
Accountant Sarah Bostock

Features in this guide were written and researched by:
Introduction Ronnie Haydon. **The Story of London** Ronnie Haydon (*The Great Plague, The Great Fire, The Great Stink, The Great Smog* Lesley McCave). **New London** David Littlefield. **By Season** Cathy Limb. **Around Town** *Central London* Rick Jones, Ronnie Haydon; *North London* Dorothy Boswell; *East London* Andrew Shields; *South-east London* Paul Edwards, Ronnie Haydon; *South-west London* Lisa Osborne; *West London* Mary Dohnal. **Eating** Sarah Guy, Ronnie Haydon, Lesley McCave. **Shopping** Héloïse Bergman. **Arts & Entertainment** Sue Webster. **Parties** Sue Webster. **Sport & Leisure** Andrew Shields. **Days Out** Fiona Cumberpatch, Peter Fiennes, Ronnie Haydon, Lisa Osborne, Karen Wolman, Joanna Souter. **Directory** Ronnie Haydon.
The editor would like to thank the following:
Su Blackburn, Sophie Blacksell, Will Fulford-Jones, Ros Sales, Mary McCave, James Mitchell, Dan Conway, Perry, Jack and Carey Miller, Rick, John, Bruce and Jane Jones, Ruth Jarvis, Anna, Natalie, Alexander and Esme Fiennes, William, Hilary, Evan, Jonathan, Huw and Rhiannon Jones, Mary and Teresa Trafford, Celia Wood, Anekin and Edie Telle Nakata, Oliver and Donna Brooks Ham, Gabriella and Francesca Bellavista, Araminta Farquhar.
Thanks to Gap and Jigsaw Junior for clothes featured on cover.

Maps by john@jsgraphics.co.uk.

Illustrations (*The Story of London*) by Lucy Grant.

Cover photography by Matt Carr.

Photography: by pages 10, 14, 19 AKG; 213 Jocelyn Bain Hogg; 219 Sarah Blee; 142 Kit Burnet; 251 Andy Brackenbury; 158 Suzy del Campo; 33, 34, 38, 50, 54, 55, 63, 67, 68, 73, 75, 82, 92, 104, 111, 128, 130, 132, 135, 149, 153, 154, 174, 176, 189, 204, 207, 224, 236, 242, 245, 259 Matt Carr; 39 Michael Carter; 7, 9, 27, 35, 57, 66, 76, 78, 79, 80, 82, 91, 96, 115, 121, 163, 169, 191, 180, 185, 187, 195, 201, 209, 228, 211, 238, 246, 253, 268, 271, 293 Tricia De Courcy Ling; 97, 107, 141 Dominic Dibbs; 49, 61, 86, 131, 144, 170 Amanda Edwards; 181, 262, 263 Michael Franke; 241, 257 Tony Gibson; 215 Mark Guthrie; 18 mirrorpix.com; 275 National Trust Photographic Library/Alasdair Ogilvie; 156 Thomas Pakenham; 21, 30 PA Photos; 37, 43, 123, 136, 138 Natalie Pecht; 64, 83, 85, 101, 102, 105, 112, 116, 119, 127, 145, 165, 166 Jon Perugia; 109 Nichola Levinsky; 150, 178, 186, 192, 196, 265 Alys Tomlinson; 250 Emma Tremlett; 160, 161, 171 James Winspear; 59 Nigel Young/British Museum.
The following images were supplied by the featured establishments/artists pages 22, 25, 32, 45, 52, 58, 71, 84, 93, 94, 125, 216, 223, 227, 231, 232, 248, 273, 279, 281, 283, 286, 289, 292

Repro by Icon Reproduction, Crowne House, 56-58 Southwark Street, London SE1 1UN.

Printed and bound by Southernprint, Factory Road, Upton Industrial Estate, Poole, Dorset BH16 5SN.

ISBN 0 903446 774

Distribution by Seymour Ltd (020 7396 8000)

Combat of the Gladiators

Saturday 20 & Sunday 21 July 2002
Saturday 10 & Sunday 11 August 2002

Book now on 020 7814 5777

www.museumoflondon.org.uk

Contents

Introduction

London, for children, is an awfully big adventure playground. Accompanying adults along for the ride can only marvel at how the city has moved on since their sightseeing days in the square old 20th century. The last few years have seen a change in the capital: it's becoming a more playful place, and our children are reaping the benefits.

What could be more appealing to a child than a giant big wheel? The British Airways London Eye, a towering success on the south bank of the river, dominates the new skyline. How excited are children by the idea of a wobbly walkway, the Millennium Bridge? Once they get over the lack of sway since it reopened, kids love to lark about on the elegant structure. Only their parents tremble as they watch their progeny lean fearlessly over the taut wires that run along the bridge sides to peer at the river below.

For young children used to travelling strapped into the back of the family hatchback, there's joy in London's chugging buses, its screaming tubes and the driverless Docklands Light Railway. To liken the DLR to a rollercoaster might be fanciful, but when children sit up front and experience the swoop of the front carriage trundling down the track into Tower Gateway, they clamour for another ride.

Recently completed river crossings, newly free museums and Mayor Ken Livingstone's traffic-calming measures and shiny buggy-friendly buses have all made the city a more accessible place. This guide takes in all of London town: the trendy bits, from Notting Hill to Docklands, as well as the sights, both famous and obscure. Best of all, it shows you how to make the most of this sprawling playground of a city. The fun starts here.

THE TIME OUT LONDON FOR CHILDREN GUIDE

This is the second edition of the *Time Out London for Children Guide*, produced by the people behind the successful listings magazines, and travel guide series. It is written by resident experts to provide you with all the information you'll need to explore the city or read up on its background, whether you're a local or a first-time visitor.

We hope you enjoy this guide, and we'd like to know what you think. We welcome tips for places that you think we should include in future editions.

THE LOWDOWN ON THE LISTINGS

Addresses, phone numbers, websites, transport information, opening times, admission prices and credit card details are included in the listings.

Details of facilities, services and events were all checked and correct as we went to press. Before you go out of your way, however, we'd advise you to phone and check opening times, ticket prices and other particulars. While every effort has been made to ensure the accuracy of the information contained in this guide, the publishers cannot accept any responsibility for any errors it may contain.

FAMILY-FRIENDLY INFORMATION

Having visited all the places with our own children, we've added what we consider essential information for family groups. In chapters where we think it's particularly important, we've stated whether a building can accommodate pushchairs ('buggy access'), or if there's anywhere you can change a nappy ('nappy-changing facilities'). We've also listed a spot nearby where you can eat your packed lunch ('nearest picnic place'). This is not listed if the sight is a park or garden, an ideal picnic place in itself.

Attractions are required to provide reasonable provision for disabled visitors, although it's always best to ring before setting out to see if people in wheelchairs can get around easily. Disabled visitors requiring more information about getting around the city can call GLAD (Greater London Action on Disability) on 7346 5808 (7326 4554 minicom) or check the website www.glad.org.uk.

PRICES AND PAYMENT

We have noted where venues accept the following credit cards: American Express (AmEx), Diners Club (DC), MasterCard (MC) and Visa (V).

THE LIE OF THE LAND

We've included map references for each venue that falls on our street maps (starting on page 312). However, we recommend that you follow the example of the locals and invest in a standard *A-Z* map of the city.

PHONE NUMBERS

The area code for London is 020. All phone numbers given in this guide take this code unless otherwise stated, so add 020 if calling from outside London; otherwise, simply dial the number as written. The international dialling code for the UK is 44.

Sponsors and advertisers

We would like to thank our sponsor Nickelodeon for its involvement in this guide. However, we would like to stress that no establishment has been included because it has advertised in any of our publications and no payment of any kind has influenced any review. The opinions given in this book are those of *Time Out* writers and editors and are entirely independent.

In Context

Scourge of the Romans, **Boudicca**.

The Story of London

Two thousand years in the making.

ROMAN LONDON

London's story begins in AD 43 when the Roman emperor Claudius and his legions invaded. Whether it was the Romans who built the very first settlement on the banks of the Tamesis (Latin for Thames) or not, we have them to thank for our ancient city wall (built in AD 200), remnants of which survive in the City of London today. The first bridge across the Thames was also a Roman idea.

The wall was erected after the British outpost of the Empire was sacked by warlike Boudicca. She led her armies against the soldiers who had seized her lands and raped her daughters. The settlement was almost destroyed, but the Romans rebuilt and surrounded their town with a two-mile-long, 18-foot-high defensive wall in an attempt to keep out native rebellions. That worked for about 200 years, but continued invasions and internal strife forced the Roman Empire into decline. In 410 the last troops were withdrawn and London became a ghost town. Only the roads and the wall were left, along with the beginnings of Christianity.

SAXON & VIKING LONDON

Saxon settlers, crossing the North Sea to settle in eastern and southern England during the fifth and sixth centuries, appear to have paid little attention to ruins of the Roman creation. They preferred life in the country, and built up farmsteads and trading posts outside the city walls.

The city that became known as 'Lundenwic' stood west of the Roman city, where Covent Garden is today. The name Aldwych comes from the Saxon 'the old wic' (town or port), and the Strand from 'strand', meaning a beach for grounding ships. Gradually, London's status as an international trading post came to the fore.

London's first bishop was Mellitus, a missionary sent by the Pope. He converted the East Saxon King Sebert to Christianity. In 604 Mellitus founded a wooden cathedral, dedicated to St Paul, inside the old city walls. Although his people turned back to paganism after Sebert's death, later generations of Christians rebuilt St Paul's.

In the ninth century there was another threat to London: the Vikings. They crossed the North Sea to ransack London, forcing the king of the time, Alfred of Wessex, to order the reoccupation of the Roman town as its stone walls were still standing and could be defended by his soldiers. While Alfred reigned, churches were built and markets thrived in London, though Winchester was still the capital of England.

As the Saxon city prospered, harassment from the Vikings continued, until in the 11th century, the English had to bow to a Danish king. King Cnut (Canute), who reigned from 1016 to 1040, saw London take over from Winchester as the capital.

Edward the Confessor, an English king, gained the throne in 1042. He devoted almost all his life to building a church. Westminster Abbey, which replaced an old wooden church called St Peter's, took 15 years to build. Edward, who had moved into the new Palace of Westminster, died one week after his abbey was consecrated in December 1065. At least it was ready in time for his burial.

The death caused strife. Edward's cousin William, Duke of Normandy, swore that his kinsman had promised him the crown. But Edward's brother-in-law Harold was favourite with the English people. The two prepared their armies to slug it out at Hastings. On 14 October 1066 William defeated Harold and marched to London. He was crowned in Westminster Abbey on Christmas Day.

MEDIEVAL LONDON

William knew he had to keep the prosperous merchants in the City of London sweet. He decided to give them independent trading rights in return for taxes. The charter that he drew up to state this is kept at the Guildhall. He was still worried about the large, possibly rebellious, population of the city, however, and ordered strongholds to be built alongside its wall. One of these is the White Tower, the tallest building in the Tower of London.

London became a hotbed of political struggle. Fighting for supremacy were three powerful bodies: the king and aristocracy; the Church; and the lord mayor and city guilds.

In the early Middle Ages, the king made all the laws in the country, aided by lords and bishops. During the 14th and 15th centuries, the Palace of Westminster became the seat of law and government, and the king's meetings with the noblemen and clergy – called Parliaments – became increasingly important. As the number of advisors to the king grew, Parliament divided into two groups, called the House of Lords (populated by nobles and members of the clergy chosen by the king) and the House of Commons (full of powerful people elected by rich merchants and landowners).

The privileges of independence and self-regulation granted by the Norman kings to the City merchants were extended by the monarchs. In 1191 the City of London was formally recognised as a self-governing community and won control of the River Thames and lucrative fishing rights, which it kept until 1857. In 1215 King John confirmed the city's right every year to elect a mayor who would have greater

Key events

AD 43 The Roman invasion. Londinium is founded.
61 Boudicca burns the city.
200 A rebuilt Londinium is protected by a city wall.

410 The last Roman troops leave Britain.
c600 Saxon London is built to the west.
604 The first St Paul's Cathedral is built.

authority than the sheriff and the Bishop of London. A month later the new Mayor joined the rebel barons in signing the Magna Carta.

Trade with Europe grew. More imports of spices, cloth, furs, precious metals and wine crowded the wharves by London Bridge and people travelled from miles around to the city's markets, or 'cheaps' around Westcheap (now Cheapside). Foreign traders and craftsmen settled around the port of London. The population grew from about 18,000 in 1100 to more than 50,000 in the 1340s.

Of course, with crowds come hygiene problems: London was incredibly dirty and smelly. In the east, Houndsditch gained its name because people threw dead dogs into the boundary ditch there. At Smithfield, the meat market, butchers dumped animal guts wherever they wanted. Filthy conditions let the Black Death run riot. Around 30 per cent of England's population died during the Black Death's blackest moments (1348-9). The epidemic reoccurred on several occasions over the next three centuries.

With plague killing many of the workers, London was left with a labour shortage, and the working populace found itself greatly overstretched. When the poll tax – a charge of a shilling a head – was introduced, the peasants revolted. In 1381 thousands of them, led by Wat Tyler and Jack Straw, marched on London and rioted. When the young king, Richard II, aged just 14, rode out to face the angry workers, Lord Mayor William Walworth fatally stabbed Wat Tyler. This put a stop to the rioting, and the ringleaders were rounded up and hanged.

The poor sought comfort from the Church. London was full of churches, from the vast, awe-inspiring St Paul's, to little local parish churches where working folk were baptised, married and buried.

Monasteries and convents were founded within and without the city walls. The poor looked to the men and women who inhabited them for help, so the friars were like social workers for the dispossessed. Different orders were known by the colour of their habits: Dominicans were the Blackfriars, Carmelites Whitefriars, Franciscans Greyfriars; such names linger in the city today (Blackfriars Bridge; Greyfriars Passage; Whitefriars Street).

TUDOR & STUART LONDON

In Tudor times, new lands were discovered and new trade brought to London. The city became one of the largest in Europe. Henry VII, who brought an end to the Wars of the Roses by defeating Richard III at the Battle of Bosworth and marrying Elizabeth of York,

The Great Plague

Ring-a-ring o' roses
A pocket full of posies
A-tishoo! A-tishoo!
We all fall down.

Epidemics were common in crowded, insanitary 17th-century London. There had been outbreaks of plague in the city before, in 1636 and 1647, so when a number of Londoners took to their beds in late 1664 – with fever, sneezing (a-tishoo!) and covered in rose-coloured swellings (rings o' roses) – few were greatly disturbed.

A bitingly cold winter (during which the Thames froze over) contained the problem, but with the arrival of spring it became clear that this was not just another minor pestilence. By the end of April hundreds of people were dying. May and June were hot, causing a rapid spread of the disease and mass panic. Charles II discontinued Parliament and everyone who could leave the city did so. By the end of June the weekly death toll was 725, it exceeded 2,000 in August, peaking at 8,000 in the third week of September.

Not since the Black Death three centuries earlier had the city experienced anything like this. The authorities were powerless to resist the plague's progress; the Lord Mayor ordered all dogs and cats to be killed in the belief that they were the plague carriers, but this only led to a surge in deaths as the real villains – rats carrying the fatal fleas – were relieved of their predators.

Houses where plague had been diagnosed were sealed for 40 days, a red cross daubed on their doors. Quacks made fortunes selling potions and 'protective' posies. Graveyards and quicklime pits filled up with the bodies picked up in the streets by patrolling 'dead-carts'. The stench was unimaginable. Businesses collapsed through lack of custom and no ships would dock at the Port of London. Gangs of lawless unemployed workers and abandoned servants roamed the streets.

At the end of September, suddenly and for no obvious reason, the number of deaths dropped. Weekly fatalities fell to 5,000 in the last week of September and two months later they were down to 900. It appeared that the winter cold had finally put paid to the epidemic, which by then had cut the capital's population by nearly 100,000. The return of the king to St James's on 1 February 1666 signalled the beginning of normality. And everyone breathed a sigh of relief, unaware that less than a year later a fire would start in Pudding Lane, unleashing a second catastrophe on the city (*see p15* **The Great Fire**).

841 The first Viking raid.

c871 The Danes occupy London.

886 King Alfred of Wessex retakes London.

1013 The Danes take London; King Cnut reigns.

1042 King Edward builds Westminster Abbey.

1066 William, Duke of Normandy, defeats Harold.

Help Thomas find his shed.

HENRY THOMAS PERCY

A
B
C

There are so many activities on Nick Jr...

How many shells are there for Tula to collect?

1 2 3 4

Colour in Blue's spots.

...the last thing they'll want to do is sit down.

Join-in-tv
09013 800 818
nickjr.co.uk

NICK JR.
A Nickelodeon UK Channel

Queen Elizabeth I, a woman in charge.

left his mark on London by commissioning the building of the Henry VII Chapel in Westminster Abbey, where he and his queen are buried.

His successor was wife collector (and dispatcher) Henry VIII. His first marriage to Catherine of Aragon failed to produce an heir, so the King, in 1527, determined that the union should be annulled. As the Pope refused to co-operate, Henry defied the Catholic Church, demanding that he himself be recognised as Supreme Head of the Church of England and ordering the execution of anyone who refused to go along (including his chancellor Sir Thomas More). Thus England began the transition to Protestantism. The subsequent dissolution of its monasteries changed the face of medieval London: the land sold off as a result was given over to streets and houses. On a more positive note, Henry also founded the Royal Dockyards at Woolwich. The land he kept for hunting purposes became the Royal Parks (Hyde, Regent's, Greenwich and Richmond).

His daughter Queen Mary's five-year reign saw a brief Catholic revival. She was nicknamed 'Bloody Mary' following her order that 300 Protestants be burned at the stake in Smithfield.

Mary's half-sister Elizabeth I oversaw a huge upsurge in commerce: the Royal Exchange was founded by Sir Thomas Gresham in 1566 and London became Europe's leading commercial centre. With Drake, Raleigh and Hawkins sailing to America and beyond, new trading enterprises were developing all the time. By 1600 there were 200,000 people living in London, many in overcrowded, rat-infested conditions. Plague was a constant threat.

It was during the Elizabethan era that London became an important cultural centre, particularly for drama. Two famous theatres, the Rose (1587) and the Globe (1599), were built on the south bank of the Thames, and the plays of William Shakespeare and Christopher Marlowe performed. More earthy drama

1067 Work begins on the Tower of London.
1197 Henry Fitzalwin is the first mayor.
1240 First Parliament sits at Westminster.

1348-9 The Black Death ravages London.
1381 Wat Tyler leads the Peasants' Revolt.
1397 Richard (Dick) Whittington is Lord Mayor.

often took place on the street. Bankside was considered a 'naughty place' where people visited taverns and engaged in popular pursuits of bear-baiting, cockfighting and brothel visiting.

Elizabeth's successor, the Stuart James I, narrowly escaped being blown up. The Gunpowder Plot, remembered every 5 November, was instigated by a group of Catholics led by Guy Fawkes, who planned to protest at their persecution by dynamiting the Palace of Westminster. They were rounded up, and hanged, drawn and quartered.

The City of London's tax-free status was threatened by Charles I, James's son, who stirred up trouble both in the City and in Parliament. Eventually, the supporters of Parliament (later led by Oliver Cromwell) could tolerate the King's interference no longer and a civil war ensued, in which Charles and his Royalists were the losers. Charles was tried for treason and beheaded outside the Banqueting House in Whitehall in 1649. Once the Puritans had declared Britain a Commonwealth, London became a dull place. The theatres were closed down and the drinking and gambling dens of Bankside went with them. When the exiled Charles II was restored to the throne in 1660, the English in general and Londoners in particular were relieved.

The 1660s were a difficult time for the population of London, however. In 1664-5 the bubonic plague killed nearly 100,000 Londoners before cold weather brought an end to its spread (*see p12* **The Great Plague**). The following year, a baker's oven in Pudding Lane started a fire that lasted for three days and destroyed four-fifths of the City (*see right* **The Great Fire**). Today, the Monument (*see p55*) marks the spot where the fire broke out.

London was rebuilt in brick and stone. One of the busiest people at this time was Christopher Wren, who as well as completing his greatest work, the new St Paul's Cathedral, also oversaw the rebuilding of 51 city churches. The Royal Exchange was also rebuilt in the City, but by this time many merchants preferred to conduct their business in coffee houses.

The Great Fire

On 2 September 1666, just seven months after the Great Plague (*see p12*) had ravaged London, a second disaster struck the city. At about 2am in the morning, a fire broke out in Farriner's Baking Shop on Pudding Lane. Fanned by strong winds, the flames rapidly tore through the City's wooden buildings, destroying them in their path. Later that same morning Samuel Pepys noted that 300 houses, half of London Bridge and several churches had already disappeared. Citizens were ordered to pull down houses in an attempt to stop the fire but many refused to do so. The navy were dispatched to blow up houses in Tower Street with gunpowder before the fire reached the Tower of London; luckily, the plan worked.

By the time the fire came under control three days later, four-fifths of the City, including 87 churches, 44 livery company halls and more than 13,000 houses, were destroyed. Only six people were known to have died during the conflagration. Probably many more lives were saved, because most of the rats that had helped to transmit the plague the previous year were killed.

There are conflicting reports about what caused the fire: some claimed that the baker had left an oven unattended, but a Frenchman, Robert Hubert, confessed to setting fire to the shop and was hanged for his alleged crime.

There was a bit of good news to come from the tragedy, however: at least London could be rebuilt as a spacious, rationally planned modern city. Work was started swiftly: though plans by Christopher Wren and John Evelyn for cities of piazzas and wide streets were rejected as impractical for a commercial city, the City authorities were given powers to deal with drainage, water supply and street cleaning. Wooden buildings were replaced with brick and stone ones, and owners began to insure their properties against fire damage. By 1672 most of the private houses had been rebuilt and life and trade in London revived.

The Great Stink

London has always had problems disposing of its waste. For centuries, the unwanted products of households and humans were thrown out of windows to fester in the streets, or tipped into rivers and streams. As early as 1290 the White Friars petitioned Parliament, claiming that the stench from the River Fleet was such that not only could they not mask it with their most powerful incense, but it had actually killed several members of the public.

It took a while before the problem was officially recognised. In 1427 the Commissions for Sewers were founded, but these rapidly gained a reputation for corruption and ineffectiveness. And Londoners, normally quick to complain about the filth, proved remarkably reluctant to abide by restrictions and directives aimed at improving the situation. In the 17th century Samuel Pepys recorded in his diary how his wife stopped in the street 'to do her business'.

As late as the mid-19th century, the city had only 15 miles of sewers; water closets were still only found in the grandest of houses; and the reeking cesspits under most houses would often overflow, their contents seeping through to ground-floor rooms. The authorities finally acted to end this hideous state of affairs by banning cesspits in 1847. But this didn't help matters: the city's raw sewage drained directly into the Thames, causing such an appalling stench and pollution that in 1858 – the year of the so-called Great Stink – the curtains of the Houses of Parliament had to be soaked in chloride of lime to disguise the odour.

Unpleasant as the smell was, the risk of disease was a far more serious problem. Smallpox and typhus regularly decimated overcrowded tenements, and when cholera broke out (as it did most seriously in 1848-9) nothing could be done to combat it.

The person responsible more than any other for forcing the ruling classes out of their apathy was Edwin Chadwick. This tireless reformer investigated the sewers and slums at first hand and produced report after report on the hideous conditions he found. In 1858 Parliament finally acted, passing a bill to purify the Thames. A year later, engineer The Joseph Bazalgette, of the Metropolitan Commissioners of Sewers, began work on a great scheme to construct 1,300 miles of sewers (*see p65*). His work transformed London, cholera died out and people could finally walk the streets without feeling sick.

Charles's brother James II took the throne in 1685, but his Catholicism proved unpopular; he fled the country in 1688. His daughter Mary and her Dutch husband William of Orange were invited to rule in his place. The Bank of England was founded during their reign, in 1694.

GEORGIAN LONDON

When the throne passed to George, the great-grandson of James I, the country had to settle for a German-speaking king who had been brought up in Hanover. In Parliament, the Whig party, led by Sir Robert Walpole, was in power. The opposition were Tories who supported the Stuarts and had never approved of James II's ejection from the throne. Walpole was the first prime minister and was given 10 Downing Street as an official home. This address has been occupied by the serving prime minister ever since.

Streets and squares of attractive Georgian houses around central London are testament to how the city boomed during the Georgian period. It was at this time, too, that crossings over the river were built to increase accessibility. Westminster Bridge (built 1750) and Blackfriars Bridge (1763) joined London Bridge, which until then had been the only bridge to span the river.

While the well-to-do enjoyed their Georgian homes, life for the poor was squalid. Living in slum conditions and grinding poverty, ruined by the cheap and plentiful gin that they drank to escape ghastly reality, it's little wonder people turned to street crime. The writer Henry Fielding and his brother John established a volunteer force of 'thief takers' in 1751 to help the parish constables and watchmen catch the criminals. This force, known as the Bow Street Runners, eventually became the Metropolitan Police (established 1829).

If it hadn't been for the work of enlightened people like Fielding and other philanthropists, life for the poor in London would have been far worse. Attempts to alleviate their suffering included the founding of five major new hospitals. St Bartholomew's and St Thomas's had been established by monks many years before but they were joined by Westminster, Guy's, St George's, London and the Middlesex Hospitals from 1720 to 1745, all of which went on to become world-famous teaching hospitals. Big-hearted sea captain

1664-5 The Great Plague kills thousands.

1666 The Great Fire chars London.

1675 Building starts on a new St Paul's Cathedral.

1694 The Bank of England opens at Cheapside.

1711 St Paul's is completed.

1742 Thomas Coram founds his orphans' home.

Thomas Coram built his Foundling Hospital for abandoned children during this time (the entrance arcades of this hospital, which was demolished in 1926, still remain at the top of Lamb's Conduit Street, in front of Coram's Fields park; *see p60*).

Swelling the ranks of Londoners in the 18th century were thousands of country folk who had lost their land due to the laws of enclosures, which meant that a few farmers had exclusive control of the land. Poor immigrant workers flocked to the East End via the docks. By 1801 London's population had grown to almost a million, the largest in Europe.

VICTORIAN LONDON

By the time Victoria came to the throne in 1837, five more bridges spanned the Thames and the city's first railway line (London Bridge to Greenwich) had been laid. London, the administrative and financial capital of the British Empire, was a huge, grimy industrial town. Fine buildings, posh shops and grand houses made rich living easy, but a few streets away, slums continued to breed misery. Down by the river, life became increasingly malodorous. A less-than-modern sewerage system meant that city dwellers' waste products flowed into the Thames. As there were now millions of Londoners, this resulted in filthy, disease-ridden water. The year of 1858 was famous for its smell: the Great Stink (*see p16*) meant that politicians in the Houses of Parliament could not work with their windows open during the hot summer. Bad smells continued until 1860, when Joseph Bazalgette's drainage system was completed.

Novelist Charles Dickens wrote prolifically about the social problems of this huge metropolis, but as the years rolled by, many improvements were made to ease the lot of Londoners. The new sewerage system made a great difference, and some slum housing was replaced by social housing funded by philanthropists, such as George Peabody.

Building continued apace: streets and streets of houses were constructed for workers, miles upon miles of railway line laid to service the industries.

By the end of the 19th century, London's population stood at over six million. Workers travelling to and from their jobs were transported in horse-drawn buses until 1829; trains came about seven years later and the first underground steam train (which ran between Paddington and Farringdon Road, today part of the Metropolitan Line) opened in 1863. This was an enormous success, attracting 30,000 passengers on its first day. Travellers had to wait till 1890 for the first electric tube to operate; it ran between the City and Stockwell.

In 1851 the Queen's consort Prince Albert helped to organise the Great Exhibition to celebrate the achievements of the Empire. Exhibits from all over the world – jewels, textiles, glass, engines – were proudly displayed in the iron and glass Crystal Palace erected in Hyde Park. The palace was a terrific success; Queen Victoria liked it so much she visited almost every day for three months. When it closed in October six million people had passed through its doors.

20TH-CENTURY LONDON

The last few years of Victoria's reign had been somewhat gloomy, so when Edward VII came to the throne in 1901, a new, fun-filled era began. The luxurious Ritz Hotel on Piccadilly was opened and the Café Royal on Regent Street was the favourite haunt of fashionable people. Department stores, an American idea, made it across to England – the first to open was Selfridges, in 1909, followed two years later by Whiteley's in Bayswater. Horse-drawn buses were finally put out to grass in 1911 – now buses were motorised and electric trams clanked around outer London areas.

World War I saw the first bomb to be dropped on London. It came from a Zeppelin and landed near Guildhall. Nightly raids continued throughout the Great War, killing 650 people. When it was finally over, and those soldiers who had survived were promised 'homes for heroes' on their return, political change was set in motion. Few homes materialised and the mood of the nation was black. In 1924 Lloyd

George's Liberal Party was deposed in favour of a promised fresh start with the Labour Party, under Ramsay MacDonald.

While the upper classes partied their way through the 'Roaring Twenties', the working classes were in the grip of mass unemployment caused by the post-war slump. Dissatisfaction was eventually expressed when all the workers downed tools to support the striking miners. The General Strike of 1926 lasted for nine days: the army was called in to help distribute food and students drove the buses. After the strike, unemployment continued to rise. The New York Stock Exchange crash of 1929 had a devastating knock-on effect; the British economic situation was grim. Nevertheless, the London County Council worked to improve conditions for its people. As the city's population grew (8.7 million in 1939), so did its sprawl. Suburbia expanded, and with it the tube lines. The main entertainment for people was the radio, until 1936 at least, when the first television broadcast went out live from the British Broadcasting Corporation (BBC) at Alexandra Palace studios.

On 3 September 1939 Britain declared war on Germany and Londoners began digging their air raid shelters and sending children and pregnant women to the countryside. In fact, the air raids did not begin until almost a year later. In September 1940 hundreds of German bombers devastated east London and the docks. The raid continued for 57 nights in a row. Londoners under siege became known for their resilience during this time. In 1942 there was a new type of bomb flattening Londoners' homes – the V1 or doodlebug. These caused widespread destruction, as did their successor, the more powerful V2 rocket, 500 of which were dropped on east London. By the end of the war about a third of the city and the East End was in ruins.

Even when the war ended the country was suffering. In the General Election that took place soon after VE Day, Churchill was defeated by the Labour Party under Clement Attlee. Swift changes went ahead to try to improve the life of the nation. The National Health Service was founded in 1948; public transport and communications services were overhauled. But for all these initiatives, life in the city seemed drab and austere. For Londoners facing a terrible housing shortage there were ambitious initiatives to put a roof over their heads. Some of the buildings whisked up for them – prefabricated bungalows – were supposed to be temporary, but many are still inhabited more than 50 years later. High-rise estates, a new concept often put up in a hurry, were consequently rather shoddy.

Take that, Schicklgruber! Small soldiers in **World War II**.

Show me the Monet – London smog, as the artist saw it in 1900.

It was not all doom for Londoners, though. The city hosted the Olympic Games of 1948, and in 1951 the Festival of Britain, which celebrated all that was great about British technology and design. It took place on derelict land on the south bank of the river, and when it ended, the land became the site of the South Bank Centre arts complex.

During the 1950s Britain enjoyed a gradual return to relative prosperity. Families were inspired to buy into the suburban dream, in gleaming new towns away from the filthy city. They had a point: air pollution was a problem. Clean Air Acts, the first in 1956 introduced as a result of the Great Smog (*see p20*) four years later, finally ensured the reduction of noxious gas emissions. With people moving out of town, London was facing a labour shortage. Workers from the country's former colonies, particularly the West Indies, were recruited for London Transport and in the hospitals. Many of these emigrants faced an unfriendly reception from indigenous Londoners: matters came to a head in the Notting Hill race riots of 1958. Some parts of London were more tolerant, though, Soho, with its jazz joints and clubs, for one.

The 1960s belonged to swinging London. It became the fashion capital of the world, and Carnaby Street the hippest street. To find out where the gigs were, young people bought a fold-out weekly guide to London called *Time Out*; the first issue came out in August 1968. People from around the world started flocking to Abbey Road, NW8, because it adorned the cover of the Beatles album of the same name. Hyde Park was the hottest place to be in the summer of '69: the Rolling Stones played a free gig there for half a million fans.

During the 1970s, the lights went out, often literally, on London's glamour. Inflation, unemployment, strikes, IRA bombs and an increasingly fractured Labour government all contributed to an air of gloom. The punk explosion made a few sparks fly, but that fire was shortlived.

Margaret Thatcher came to power in 1979, and the 1980s are generally regarded as her decade. Her Conservative government made sweeping changes, and stood up for 'market forces'. This was the era of the yuppie (Young Urban Professionals), who benefited from the Conservatives' monetarist

1868 The last public execution in Newgate Prison.	**1890** The first electric underground railway opens.
1884 Greenwich Mean Time is established.	**1915-8** Zeppelins bomb London.
1888 Jack the Ripper preys on East End women.	**1940-4** The Blitz devastates much of London.

▶

The Great Smog

In December 1952 London was swathed in a lethal combination of fog and smoke. Over the next four days, an astonishing 4,000 people died, mainly from respiratory and cardiac conditions. Even the livestock at Smithfield Market asphyxiated.

The British capital was no stranger to smog, the main culprit for which was the burning of coal: in 1661 John Evelyn had written of the 'hellish and dismall cloud of sea-coale' that lay over the city. But the authorities ignored him and the choking pollution continued.

In 1813 a persistent fog that cloaked London for a week was so dense it took a mail coach seven hours to reach Uxbridge from the centre of town, just a few miles away. Factories continuously belched gases and huge numbers of particles into the atmosphere, compounding the poisonous cocktail. Acrid-smelling, yellow-tinted fogs – known as 'pea-soupers' – became a common phenomenon, with serious fogs occurring in 1873, 1880, 1882, 1891 and 1892, each of them accompanied by a marked increase in death rate. The worst afflicted areas were invariably in the East End; the fact that it is low-lying also made it difficult for the fog to disperse.

In December 1952 the weather was colder than average. A large high-pressure centre hung over London, forming an 'inversion' – a shallow layer of cool air that trapped the pollution near the ground. On the night of 5-6 December the fog thickened, forming a dense yellow cloud, and visibility dropped to less than half a metre. Cyclists found themselves covered in soot, while pedestrians blundered through the murky darkness. In the Isle of Dogs the fog was so thick that people could not even see their own feet. Choked by acrid fumes, Londoners resorted to face masks and even gas masks. A performance at Sadler's Wells theatre was halted because of choking fog in the auditorium, while films in cinemas had to be cancelled because people couldn't see the screens. Road, rail and air transport was brought to a complete standstill.

Thankfully, the infamous Great Smog of 1952 was the last of its kind – the Clean Air Acts of 1956 and 1968 banned emissions of black smoke, decreeing that residents and factories converted to smokeless fuels, and after several centuries and thousands of human deaths, pea-soupers finally became a thing of the past.

policies and the arrival of the global economy. Meanwhile, the gap between these yuppies and less fortunate people on low pay was only too apparent. It did not take long for the underdogs to start snarling, giving rise to the inner city riots, first in Brixton in 1981, and four years later in Tottenham.

One of the lasting legacies of the Thatcher era is the Docklands redevelopment. This scheme, set up in 1981 to create a new business centre in the docks to the east of the City, was slow to take shape, but is now considered an unqualified success. Businesses and residents are continuing to move into smart office buildings (the smartest so far being Canary Wharf Tower) and apartment blocks around the Isle of Dogs and the whole area exudes prosperity.

In 1986 the Greater London Council (GLC), with its anti-Thatcher outlook (despite being Conservative back in the 1960s), was abolished. (Its leader, Ken Livingstone, 'Red Ken', bided his time, and in 2000 was voted mayor with authority over all the city.)

When a city's economy booms, however, a bust is often just around the corner, and that is what happened to London in the early 1990s. There was a slump in house prices and the reign of the yuppies came to an end. The last straw for Londoners was the introduction of a poll tax. Demonstrations against it led to riots in Trafalgar Square. It marked the loosening of Mrs Thatcher's grip on the nation, and she was replaced by John Major in 1990.

The recession continued and its effects were only too evident in London. The numbers of rough sleepers rose as people continued to lose their homes through unemployment and mortgage rate rises. The IRA stepped up their campaign against the mainland, bombing the City in 1992 and Docklands in 1996. Most of the capital cheered up when Tony Blair's fresh New Labour ousted the Tories in May 1997, but went into shock when, later in the year, Princess Diana was killed in Paris. The gates of Kensington Palace became the focus for the nation's tears and bouquets.

INTO THE 21ST CENTURY

New Labour continued with Conservative plans to celebrate the new millennium with the Millennium Dome, to celebrate the nation's achievements. The spectacular tent shape on the once-derelict Greenwich pensinsula didn't manage to capture the spirit of the nation, however. Its opposers complained loudly about the content and the massive sums of money the enterprise swallowed up. In 2002 the Dome still stands empty.

1948 Olympic Games held in London.

1951 The Festival of Britain takes place.

1952 The last of London's 'pea-souper' smogs.

1953 Queen Elizabeth II is crowned.

1966 England win the World Cup at Wembley.

1982 The last of London's docks close.

London bids the **Queen Mother** farewell.

Nevertheless, despite the expensive Millennium Dome fiasco, and doomy predictions about state education, the National Health Service and traffic chaos in London, there are reasons to be cheerful about being in the capital. You only have to look to the city's skyline to see them – the beautiful London Eye has been a big success, and Tate Modern has turned everyone into art lovers. We have an energetic proponent of quality public transport in Mayor Ken Livingstone. Londoners look forward to a brave new city with trams and reliable tubes and buses with buggy access (while car owners moan about the £5 daily levy Livingstone intends to introduce for driving into central London).

Our general optimism was dealt a blow following the September 11 terrorist attacks in New York and Washington, when London took on an uneasy air similar to that during the IRA's mainland bombing campaigns in previous decades. In the months following the tragedies in the United States, the number of visitors to London went into decline, and though by spring 2002 things had started to pick up again, it was too late to save several West End shows. The impact was not restricted to theatreland: hotels, restaurants and virtually all of the city's tourist attractions saw revenue fall in the latter part of the year. 2002 also marks the Queen's Golden Jubilee, sadly marred already by the deaths of her younger sister Margaret in February, and her mother, at the grand old age of 101, at the end of March. Expect summer-long tributes to Elizabeth's 50 years on the throne, even if there were fewer street parties than when she celebrated her Silver Jubilee back in 1977.

1990 Poll Tax protesters riot.

1992 Canary Wharf opens.

1997 The nation mourns Princess Diana.

2000 Londoners celebrate a new millennium.

2001 Security alerts in the city after US tragedy.

2002 The Queen Mother dies aged 101.

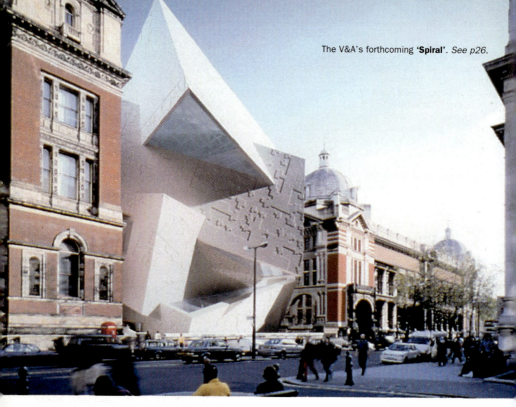

The V&A's forthcoming **'Spiral'**. *See p26.*

New London

The millennium kicked off the greatest building spree in London since the 19th century, with a host of exciting new projects and initiatives.

It is gratifying that the millennial building boom did not stop in 2000. After a monumental construction programme, which saw the completion of the Dome, Somerset House and the British Museum's Great Court, among others, there was always the worry that the enthusiasm to create new public spaces would start to wane. Fortunately, this turned out not to be the case, and two years into the new century, the momentum shows no sign of slowing down. Local authorities have continued to build, rebuild, renew and refurbish. Importantly, this means newer and better facilities for families.

The direction of large capital projects has changed course a little; the arts building programme has been largely completed (the two Tates, the National Portrait Gallery) and most of the new-look museums (National Maritime, Imperial War and Science) are likely to remain unchanged for a generation. Much of the planned building work for the capital is now focused on brownfield-site regeneration and neighbourhood renewal, as well as vast commercial projects. And London Bridge is steeling itself for a redevelopment that includes what could be Europe's tallest tower – a 1,016-foot-high shard of glass more than 200 feet higher than Canary Wharf. The 66-storey building, designed by Pompidou Centre (Paris) architect Renzo Piano, will be a mixed-use development, with shopping and eating facilities for visitors, offices on many of the floors, and, most excitingly, public-access viewing galleries half way up and on the very top. The tower has been granted planning permission by Southwark Council, the project has been given support by Mayor Ken and the GLA and should go ahead pending final approval from the Secretary of State at the Government Office for London.

A NEW LEASE OF LIFE

Planners and developers are also considering dramatic construction programmes to reclaim some of the capital's most neglected places. The enormous area to the north of **King's Cross station**, currently lying empty, is to become a whole new district of London over the next five or six years. Stratford is already being dug up in preparation for the new Eurostar link (which will continue into an extended St Pancras station). King's Cross is also getting a transformed tube station, while talks are ongoing regarding the East London Line's extension beyond Shoreditch. **Battersea Power Station** is scheduled to reopen in a few years' time as a funky new leisure site, complete with hotel, cinemas and a permanent venue for the crowd-pulling Cirque du Soleil circus. By 2012 **Elephant and Castle** could be entirely rebuilt, with traffic passing underground and the '60s tower blocks replaced. Unfortunately, the council is finding it difficult to make a final decision as potential developers are prone to pulling out of the project, so definitive plans have yet to emerge. And, in spite of likely objections from conservation body English Heritage, the **City** is set to spawn a new rash of office towers over the coming years, some of which have been given the go-ahead and are currently works in progress; these include the GLA building and Foster's 'erotic gherkin'.

READY TO ROLL

Aside from these longer-term aims, plenty of new projects have either been recently completed or are due to open soon. The most visible improvements are to the city's open spaces, including **Trafalgar Square**. The partial closure of the square has long been mooted, but work is finally under way and is due for completion by the summer of 2003. This will not only mean the pedestrianisation of the north side of the square, allowing families to walk freely between the National Gallery and Nelson's Column, but there will also be trees and improved crossing points on the remaining three sides. The equestrian statue of King Charles I will also be turned into a proper roundabout with new pedestrian links, meaning that sightseers won't have to run the gauntlet of traffic in order to get to it. Incidentally, the empty plinth on the north-west corner of the square, which has been the site of a series of contemporary artworks in recent years, will remain empty for another ten years. This is probably the highest profile 'shop window' for new sculpture in the capital.

Ken Livingstone's new congestion charge, a £5 fee for driving into the capital's centre that comes into force on 17 February 2003, will in the long run also change the character of the streetscape around Park Lane, Euston Road, Commercial Street and Tower Bridge Road. In the short term, the scheme, which the mayor reckons will raise £130 million a year to spend on public transport (in theory, at least), will merely involve the placement of cameras and creation of parking lots at strategic points around the central zone. But the Greater London Authority (GLA) eventually wants to implement well-designed alteration schemes. We live in hope.

GOING GREEN

Out east, London has acquired a new park that has so far largely gone unnoticed by the public. This is not unexpected, however, due to woefully inadequate public transport links. But the **Thames Barrier Park**, completed in the summer of 2001, is worth a visit – even if you have to negotiate the tricky 20-minute walk from Custom House DLR station or drive down the busy North Woolwich Road (there should be a new DLR station by 2004). The park, right on the river to the north of the barrier, is a strikingly modern place. Running through the flat landscape of lawns and formal flowerbeds is a concrete and granite channel, a giant rut the size of a motorway that dramatically bisects the park. This, too, is filled with hedges and honeysuckle, and leads directly to the riverfront and a 'pavilion of remembrance', commemorating those who lost their lives in the Blitz. The pavilion is a peculiar, flat-roofed structure supported on 23 irregularly spaced columns. There is even a hole cut into the roof, which changes the nature of the place as the sun moves across the sky. Relatively isolated, the park is generally devoid of visitors, but its beautifully manicured lawns make it an excellent spot for a family picnic, and the views of the Thames Barrier are unrivalled, so numbers will undoubtedly increase as word spreads.

Mile End Park, also to the east of the centre, continues to reinvent itself. Distinctive for its two-year-old 'green bridge', which provides a tree-lined foot and cycle path across the busy Mile End Road, the park recently acquired a new underground ecology centre. Fronted by a distinctive procession of curved wooden columns and a series of artificial ponds, the centre is designed to keep itself cool in summer and warm in winter. Although it provided exhibitions and workshops only to schools at the time of writing, the council hopes to open the centre to the general public in the autumn. (Call 7364 4147 for details, or log on to www.towerhamlets.gov.uk and click on Discover Tower Hamlets and then Parks.)

Tree planting is currently de rigueur – even the once-grassy slopes covering the new Canary Wharf station on the Jubilee Line have been dug up and planted with mature trees.

ROYAL FESTIVAL HALL: A NEW START?

Redevelopment plans are not advancing quite so fast at the **South Bank Centre** (SBC), the untidy and increasingly decrepit collection of arts venues between Hungerford and Waterloo bridges. As this guide went to press, Lambeth council had just given the go-ahead to a £50-million refurbishment plan for the **Royal Festival Hall** (RFH), though opposers are threatening to appeal. The future of this building could be very bright – architectural practice Allies & Morrison (who designed the new landscaping around Tate Britain a few years ago) is planning to strip away much of the clutter that has accumulated in the hall since the 1960s, as well as improve the acoustics in the main concert auditorium.

THE SOUTH BANK SITUATION

But while the RFH could be in for a serious makeover (and even if Lambeth refuses planning permission, the hall will continue to be a lively and popular venue), the future for the rest of the South Bank Centre is uncertain. The centre has long been the subject of radical modernisation plans, all of which have come to nothing. Although *Evening Standard* art critic Brian Sewell might have gone a little over the top in condemning the centre as an 'ugly, charmless, inefficient and indefensible relic of cheapjack post-war shoddiness', this complex of brutalist buildings has never been much loved by the public. Its neglected concrete ramparts (a mecca for skateboarders) and confusing walkways are in desperate need of rejuvenation, but managers appear to be at a loss. The most recent plan for the area, by architect Rick Mather, involves constructing a new set of concert halls and a base for the British Film Institute underneath a sloping park on what is currently Jubilee Gardens. But Lambeth planners don't like the idea, and neither does Ken Livingstone.

Tall ideas

At the moment, whenever plans for a new building are proposed in London, it always seems to be a tower. There's a seeming unspoken competitive streak when it comes to topping the last one. But just how tall is tall?

At 773 feet, **Canary Wharf** (the official name is No.1 Canada Square) is currently the capital's tallest building. However, this will be over-shadowed by the 1,016-foot tower planned for London Bridge. Canary Wharf knocked the 600-foot **Tower 42** (the building formerly known as the Natwest Tower) off its perch in the early 1990s. But Tower 42 recently slipped from second to fourth place with the completion of the two 653-foot towers flanking the giant obelisk of Canary Wharf. Next in line is the **BT Tower**, at 540 feet the tallest structure in the West End, followed by the 469-foot **Guy's Hospital** and 442-foot **London Eye**. The three **Barbican** towers follow at 412 feet to complete the top ten. But who knows how long these chart positions will last... Watch this space.

Media magnate Lord Hollick was recently drafted in as chief executive of the SBC to sort out the mess. But whatever the solution finally turns out to be, it's not going to materialise for a few years yet. Separately, developers have also proposed to construct new offices and a shopping complex near the monolithic tower of the Shell building, adjacent to the troubled arts complex. The problem is that Lambeth is unlikely to approve of any development that does not integrate with plans for the SBC – and while that's on hold, so is the Shell scheme. A bit of a mess, really.

BRIDGING THE GAP

On a more positive note, at least the bridge linking Charing Cross to the South Bank is starting to take shape. Although problems have led to construction delays, the two new walkways replacing the inadequate pedestrian link on **Hungerford Bridge** are set to revolutionise this cross-Thames route when they finally open in summer 2002. Apart from replacing one bridge with two, which will ease overcrowding, one of the new links will be on the west side of this Victorian structure, opening up spectacular views of the Houses of Parliament.

No matter how successful the new Hungerford bridges turn out to be, they will always be overshadowed by the more charismatic **Millennium Bridge**, completed in 2000 but closed almost immediately when opening day crowds caused it to develop an alarming wobble. After the fitting of shock absorbers, the bridge reopened successfully in February 2002 and is now an extremely useful and popular pedestrian-only link between St Paul's and Tate Modern. Described by architect Norman Foster as a 'blade of light', this all-metal structure is a tough yet elegant piece of sculpture (artist Anthony Caro was part of the design team). However, you could be forgiven for thinking it's a little too high-tech: timber decking instead of clanking aluminium sheets would have made the bridge feel firmer underfoot, and – call us petty – but it wouldn't glare quite so much in the sun. But that doesn't seem to deter rollerbladers. In fact, the Millennium Bridge could soon be joined by another pedestrian link. Architects are planning to tack a covered footbridge on to the existing Cannon Street Bridge, which carries trains over the Thames. Fundraisers hope that the structure, dubbed the **Jubilee Bridge**, will link into a new 'Jubilee walk' planned for London. Unfortunately, complex negotiations have to be undertaken with the boroughs on either side of the river, as well as the rail companies, and it all seems to have gone rather quiet in this, the Queen's Golden Jubilee year.

WORKS IN PROGRESS

As well as the finished and nearly finished projects in London, there are others that will take a few more years to materialise. Phase 1 of the **Natural History**

Museum's new Darwin Centre is due to open to the public in September 2002. This £27-million glass extension, featuring giant bone-like steel supports, will showcase 22 million zoological specimens that up until now have been kept in storage. This promises to be an Aladdin's cave of wonder for children, who will be able to peer at 300 white-coated researchers through glass walls. This will be the first time that the public has had a glimpse of what goes on behind the scenes at the museum, making the museum staff as much a part of the exhibition as the specimens in the jars. More exciting (or scary, depending on your love of creepy crawlies), is the £50-million Phase 2 of the project. This will house the museum's insects (28 million in all, plus six million botanical samples). But you'll have to wait: this building is not due for completion until 2006.

Next door at the **Victoria & Albert Museum**, curators have even bigger plans. In fact, a ten-year refurbishment and building programme is already partially complete. In November 2001 the museum's British Galleries were unveiled and have proved to be immensely popular – and rightly so. Displaying British arts, crafts and design fashion from 1500-1900, the galleries have something to offer everyone. Books and historical reference material accompany most exhibits, and there are even hands-on areas where you can assemble a Chippendale-style chair or try on a hooped dress. Halfway round this labyrinthine set of galleries is a 'chill-out area' underneath a collection of musical instruments by artist Cornelia Parker. Suspended high in the air on barely visible threads, this collection of trumpets and trombones has been curiously flattened; it looks great, but apparently didn't go down well with the Salvation Army. Here, you can relax, put your feet up and read a magazine or conduct further research on a suite of PCs.

By the summer of 2004 the V&A hopes to open a new architecture gallery. In an attempt to bring this difficult subject to life, the museum intends to combine architectural drawings and models with interactive exhibits showing how buildings are conceived and constructed. Plans are at a preliminary stage, but one idea is to build small walk-in towers that will bombard visitors with sounds and images from different building types – an airport, a monastery and a Japanese temple, for example. As part of this project, the Royal Institute of British Architects (RIBA) plans to move its collection of 600,000 historical drawings over to the V&A and combine it with the museum's own drawing collection. At present RIBA's archive offers only limited access, but the move – branded 'Architecture for All' – will allow the public to get its hands on any drawing, free of charge, on request. In fact, the museum's archive already operates by these

London Bridge Tower: coming soon? *See p22.*

rules – according to curators, whether you're a child or adult, if you've got clean hands you can see any drawing or print you like.

We haven't even mentioned the V&A's most ambitious scheme yet. Designed by architect Daniel Libeskind (designer of the new Jewish Museum in Berlin, which is so intriguing that it attracted thousands of visitors even before the exhibits were put in place), the £75-million 'Spiral' building will provide a new entrance and giant exhibition spaces for the museum. But fundraising for the extraordinary extension, an asymmetrical structure that looks like a house of collapsing cards, is progressing slowly. Trustees have yet to generate even half the sum needed, so the finished building can't be expected until at least 2006.

STATE OF THE ART
There are also plans afoot at **Millbank**, where a new arts campus will combine Tate Britain and Chelsea College of Art & Design. Tate Britain is a far larger and more accessible place now that it has completed its Centenary Project – a largely underground extension that provides a new entrance, extra galleries and better public services. A ramp, around the c orner from the main entrance, takes you down to a new foyer, shop and much-needed toilet facilities. It is wheelchair- and buggy-friendly, and links almost seamlessly into the rest of the gallery. But the café is still crowded and overpriced. Families wishing to visit both Tates in one day will soon have the trip between the two made easier when a connecting river service is finished. At the time of writing, the completion date was uncertain, but the quality of the pier designs are more reliable – the new one by Tate Britain has been designed by Marks Barfield, the same firm that masterminded the London Eye.

The site should become even more interesting towards the autumn of 2003, when Chelsea College vacates its current teaching spaces and moves into the complex of former military buildings just west of the Tate. The heavy gates and fencing are soon due to come down and a new public square will be created for both students and the general public. A new underground entrance is being planned, and student work will be displayed in a maze of subterranean tunnels that will connect the various Victorian buildings.

WEIRD AND WONDERFUL
Further downstream, the egg-shaped **Greater London Authority** (GLA) building is taking shape and is due for completion by the summer. This odd structure will be open to the public, and families will be welcome to look down upon our representatives debating the future of the capital. The top floor is also being reserved for visitors,

who will be able to eat there or just observe the city skyline from a new angle. Kids are as certain to be as puzzled by the building's shape as adults, while the view of the nearby Tower Bridge, as well as the Tower of London opposite, will be a real draw. The architect of the GLA headquarters, Norman Foster, is also constructing the city's most ambitious building yet – the so-called 'erotic gherkin', which is now going up on the site of the old Baltic Exchange in the City. This curvaceous tower, set for completion in 2004, is also a complex piece of engineering and you can get right up close to the construction action. Any child remotely into Bob the Builder will find it fascinating.

BUILDING IN THE 'BURBS
Happily, not all architectural developments are confined to the centre of town. Stoke Newington and Deptford are also appearing on the design map. The former's new **Clissold Leisure Centre** on Clissold Road is already proving popular since it opened in early 2002. A large steel and glass complex with a dramatic roof, the centre is well served with a swimming pool, badminton courts and crèche. Many think it's an impressive place, though not everyone agrees – one letter to *Building Design* magazine complains that community requests for a streetside café have been ignored, and that sharp concrete steps and lack of a buggy park do not make the centre family-friendly.

Deptford Creek is due to make it into the architectural magazines in October with the opening of the new **Laban Dance Centre**. Designed by Herzog & de Meuron, the same architects who were behind the fantastically successful Tate Modern, the multicoloured building could kickstart a regeneration programme that the area so sorely needs.

Talking of sport and leisure, the development of new venues and stadia has transpired to be a catalogue of administrative fudge and incompetence. A spanking new athletics stadium at Picketts Lock has been scrapped, while the futures of the Dome and Wembley continue to be uncertain. What is certain, though, is that Wembley will continue to be the home of English football, although designs and financing have yet to be settled. The Dome looks set to be converted into an indoor sporting arena, hosting events like ice-skating and boxing matches, but designs and dates have yet to emerge. (By the by, there is a rumour that if the Dome plans go ahead, the London Arena will close.) **Arsenal** has a more definitive future: the club has received the go-ahead for a massive redevelopment, which will see a new world-class stadium built near Finsbury Park; the existing ground will be converted into flats, leaving the pitch as open space and a memorial garden to the fans who have had their ashes scattered on the hallowed turf.

London Marathon

By Season

Make a date with glittering, inspiring and downright barking city events.

Being Golden Jubilee year, 2002 has a packed summer programme of public celebrations in London's major venues. But even when the royal jubilations are over, there'll be plenty more special events to relish in the city. There's always something going on, year-round, from big yachts in Earl's Court in January to celebrity fairy-light illuminating in December. We've listed the spectacular, the quirky and the ones we love the best. Don't miss them. To find out about more goings-on, check the Around Town section in *Time Out* magazine every week.

Not all of the events listed below are free, so ring the phone number listed to find out about prices, and also to confirm dates nearer the time.

Spring

Great Spitalfields Pancake Day Race
Spitalfields Market (entrance on Commercial Street or Brushfield Street), E1 (7375 0441). Liverpool Street tube/rail. **Map** p321 R5. **Date** 4 Mar 2003.

On the day before Ash Wednesday and the subsequent 40 days of Lenten fasting comes Shrove Tuesday, aka Pancake Day. This is a fantastically silly and surreal day out: watch the frying pan-wielding teams (often in fancy dress) race up and down Spitalfields Market to raise money for Save the Children. Pancake tossing starts at 12.30pm; would-be competitors should phone the organisers a few days in advance.

London Marathon
Greenwich to Westminster Bridge via the Isle of Dogs, Victoria Embankment & St James's Park (7620 4117/ www.londonmarathon.co.uk). **Date** 13 Apr 2003.
Spectators can choose a vantage point from Greenwich to the Mall to cheer on the thousands of elite and novice competitors, many of whom run the gruelling 26.2 miles in weird and wonderful fancy dress for charities. As well as the main race, there's a wheelchair race and a mini London Marathon for youngsters, and street entertainers and bands. Those intending to take part should apply by the October before the race.

London Harness Horse Parade
Battersea Park, Albert Bridge Road, SW11 (01733 234451). Battersea Park or Queenstown Road rail/ 97, 137 bus. **Date** 21 Apr 2003.
Observe working horses, from huge shaggy Shires to fluffy Shetland ponies, splendidly groomed and harnessed to commercial and private work carts of yesteryear. Judging

takes place from 9.30am, with a grand parade of the winners around noon. Look out for the 'young whips' – carts driven by 7-8-year-olds. The London pearly kings and queens interact by selling programmes and chatting to visitors, and there are books and clothes stalls, ice-cream and fast-food stands, and a funfair in the park.

Covent Garden Festival
Covent Garden, WC2 (7379 0870/0845 601 3600/ www.cgf.co.uk). Covent Garden tube. **Date** May-June 2003.
No festival will be held in 2002, but there are plans for the usual programme of eclectic music, theatre, opera and street performance to take place again in 2003, so check the website or phone nearer the time. Most events are free, family-friendly, and take place in venues around Covent Garden.

Museums & Galleries Month 2002
various venues (7233 9796/www.may2002org.uk).
Date 1 May-1 June 2003.
An annual, national event organised by museums and galleries across the country. Participating venues run creative events and activities for all ages. Classroom projects, open days, exhibitions and interactive activities are all laid on for kids. See the website for a programme.

Canalway Cavalcade
Little Venice, W9 (British Waterways London 7286 6101). Warwick Avenue tube. **Date** early May bank hol 2003.
Organised by the Inland Waterways, this exciting event, combining a boat rally of more than 100 boats and a range of activities for the whole family, is the largest of its kind in London. Other things to look out for over the weekend include craft, trade and food stalls, children's activities such as canal art painting and badge-making and an illuminated procession of boats on the Sunday.

May Fayre & Puppet Festival
Garden of St Paul's Covent Garden, Bedford Street, WC2 (7375 0441). Covent Garden tube. **Map** p319 L7.
Date 11 May 2003.
Commemorating the first sighting of Mr Punch in England by Samuel Pepys in 1662, this free day-long celebration of the art of puppetry makes for a great family day out. Aside from Punch & Judy (and other puppet) shows, booths and stalls, there are workshops, where children can make and take home their own puppets, and dress up in hats and costumes. Bring a picnic to enjoy in the church gardens – you'll need to catch your breath after joining in with the maypole dancing.

Victoria Embankment Gardens Summer Events
Victoria Embankment Gardens, Villiers Street, WC2 (7375 0441/www.alternativearts.co.uk). Embankment tube. **Map** p319 L7. **Date** 26 May-21 July 2002.
Organised by Alternative Arts, these free outdoor events feature global music, dance, poetry and mime by the riverside. Scheduled activities include a Latin American cultural fiesta with music and dance (26 May), dance from diverse UK groups (1-2 June), mime artists (9 June), midsummer performances of contemporary poetry, and lunchtime jazz concerts (23 June). Join the cavalcade on 30 June at Paddington Recreation Ground, where clowns, jugglers, unicyclists, trapeze artists and stilt-walkers will be celebrating the circus and performance arts. African, Caribbean and American programmes take place on Victoria Embankment (7 July), while on 21 July an Eastern flavour takes over, with dance, drama and music from Korea, China and Malaysia. Check the website or phone for further details of the various events.

Summer

Golden Jubilee Celebrations
various locations throughout London (0845 000 2002/ www.goldenjubilee.gov.uk). **Date** 1-4 June 2002.
The weekend of the Golden Jubilee celebrations sees events taking place all over the city, but many special exhibitions in London's major sights will last throughout the summer. Events across town are constantly added to the website, so check for details of what's going on in your area.

Wildlife Week
London Wildlife Trust reserves & centres throughout London (7261 0447/www.wildlondon.org.uk). **Date** 1-9 June 2002.
Every year, the first week in June is the time to celebrate London's greenness. Events in parks, woods and reserves across the city include open days, workshops and children's activities. Ring the LWT or check the website to find out what's going on near you.

Derby Day
Epsom Downs Racecourse, Epsom Downs, Surrey (01372 470047/www.epsomderby.co.uk). Epsom Town Centre/Tattenham Corner rail then shuttle bus. **Date** 7, 8 June 2002.
Stands and spectator enclosures at this prestigious flat race, which starts at 2pm, are open to all, from top-hatted toffs in the grandstand, to families picnicking on the hill in the middle of the course. A market, entertainers, jugglers and funfair all add to the carnival atmosphere, and with the Queen planning to attend on the second day, additional Golden Jubilee celebrations may also be held in 2002. Check the website for updates.

Young Pavement Artists Competition
Colonnade Walk, 123 Buckingham Palace Road, SW1 (7732 1651). Victoria tube/rail. **Map** p318 H10.
Date 8 June 2002.
Part of a national event, this day out for pavement Picassos (just turn up and pay £1 for a pitch and chalk) also includes music, magicians and face painting. Judging categories are for children aged 4-18, and parents can also join in with the 19-plus group. Celebrity guests in the past have included Rolf Harris. This year prizes are presented by Brian Sibley, writer of the official guide to the *Lord of the Rings* film. The fun starts at noon, with judging at 4pm.

Beating Retreat
Horseguards Parade, Whitehall, SW1 (7930 4466). Westminster tube/Charing Cross tube/rail.
Map p319 K8. **Date** 11, 12 June 2002.
A colourful musical ceremony with the Mounted Bands of the Household Cavalry and the Massed Bands of the Guards Division, who beat a spectacular 'Retreat' on drums and pipes. Ring the above number for tickets (for reserved tiered seating) to watch the hour-long march, which starts at 7pm.

Stoke Newington Festival
various venues around Stoke Newington, N16 (8356 6410/www.stokenewingtonfestival.co.uk). Stoke Newington rail/73 bus. **Date** 14-23 June 2002.
A ten-day arts and entertainments-based celebration of Stokey, with many events that appeal to the younger members of the family. A disco for under-10s takes place on 15 June. On the 21st and 22nd there are all-night family events, including children's theatre performances. The box office is at Tana Mana, 150-152 Stoke Newington Church Street.

IT'S TAKEN 900 YEARS
TO MAKE A DAY OUT THIS GOOD

If you thought history was stuck in the past, you are in for a few surprises at
Hampton Court Palace and the Tower of London. There's so much going on throughout the
year, especially for families. At Hampton Court Palace, hear tales of myth and legend from
costumed guides, discover what life was like in the time of Henry VIII and lose yourself in
the famous maze. Visit the Tower and see the legendary ravens, admire the breathtaking
Crown Jewels and learn exciting secrets on a free 'Beefeater' tour. With events and children's
trails, you're guaranteed the best fun in history. See our special offers at the front of this guide.
For details of family events, children's trails, opening hours and admission prices,
please visit our website.

www.hrp.org.uk

The Queen will be greeting thousands of wellwishers during her **Golden Jubilee Celebrations**. *See p28.*

Trooping the Colour

Horseguards Parade, Whitehall, SW1 (7930 4466). Westminster tube/Charing Cross tube/rail. **Map** p319 K8. **Date** 15 June 2002.

The Queen's official birthday is marked each year by this colourful military parade dating back to the early 18th century. The ceremony is watched by members of the Royal Family and invited guests; members of the public may observe from vantage points at either side of the Mall, beginning at 11am on Horseguards Parade. After the ceremony, the Queen rides back to Buckingham Palace at the head of her Guards, before taking the salute at the palace from the balcony, when the Royal Air Force flies past overhead and a 41-Gun Royal Salute is fired in Green Park. At 1pm there's a 62-Gun Royal Salute at the Tower of London.

Wimbledon Lawn Tennis Championships

All England Lawn Tennis Club, PO Box 98, Church Road, Wimbledon, SW19 5AE (8944 1066/recorded info 8946 2244/www.wimbledon.org.uk). Southfields tube/Wimbledon tube/rail. **Date** 24 June-7 July 2002.

To net a seat for the Centre and Number One courts, apply to the All England Lawn Tennis Club for an application form to enter the public ballot for tickets between 1 September and 31 December the year before. If picked, you will be notified in February. The only way to secure a ticket otherwise is to queue on the day of the match. Once you're in, you can wander the outside courts. In the afternoon, returned show-court tickets are available from the resale booth opposite Court One.

City of London Festival

*various venues in the City (7377 0540/www.city-of-london-festival.org.uk). ***Date** 25 June-11 July 2002.

Now in its 40th year, this festival of music, theatre, literature and dance performances is held in some of the most beautiful and historical buildings in the City. The programme for 2002 includes classical concerts from the renowned Hallé Orchestra, South African group Ladysmith Black Mambazo performing gospel songs in St Paul's Cathedral, comedy sketches from the Natural Theatre Group in Broadgate Arena, Asian theatre group Tara Arts in Old Spitalfields Market, and 'commuter jazz' at Liverpool Street station. Visitors to St Edmund King and Martyr Church can observe and chat to Dragan Andjelic in his open studio about his paintings of angels.

Hampton Court Palace Flower Show

East Molesey, Surrey (recorded info 8781 9500/ www.hrp.org.uk). Hampton Court rail/riverboat from Westminster or Richmond to Hampton Court Pier (Apr-Oct). **Date** 1-7 July 2002.

Several of the gardens at this show have been designed with children in mind, in collaboration with the government's Growing Schools Programme, which encourages teachers and pupils to use gardening as an educational tool, so to speak. In 2002, to mark 100 years since Beatrix Potter's *The Tale of Peter Rabbit*, a depiction of Mr MacGregor's vegetable garden will be staged, with a storyteller on site bringing the characters to life.

Henley Royal Regatta

Henley Reach, Henley-on-Thames, Oxon (01491 572153/www.hrr.co.uk). Henley-on-Thames rail. **Date** 3-7 July 2002.

This world-famous event is a well-heeled affair, where fancy hats and blazers are given an outing, though there is, in fact, no dress code, and anyone may attend. Nearly 300 races are held over the five days, with participating crews from around the world. A fireworks display is held on the evening of 6 July, and while picnics are not allowed, catering facilities and a bar are available.

Greenwich & Docklands International Festival

various venues near the Thames (8305 1818/ www.festival.org). **Date** 5-13 July 2002.
The opening night of this festival features an aerial display of daredevil antics from trapeze acts, and fireworks on the Thames. The huge range of international activities and projects include a traditional French market, picnics and an evening of high-wire French circus acts, and a water carnival at Limehouse Cut in Poplar, with barges of floating arts, puppets, dance and music. Canary Wharf, Stratford Circus, the Royal Naval College and Cutty Sark Gardens are among other locations hosting dance, variety, music and theatrical performances, pyrotechnic spectacles, and even a fleet of illuminated sculptural boats. Check the website for details.

London Heathrow Youth Games

Crystal Palace National Sports Centre, Ledrington Road, SE20 (8778 0131). Crystal Palace rail. **Date** 13, 14 July 2002.
2002 is the 25th anniversary of this mini Olympics event, during which 10,000 sporting hopefuls aged under 19 represent 33 London boroughs in sports competitions. The teams are selected through schools and development teams locally, and activities include archery, fencing, canoeing, football, tennis, athletics and show jumping.

Rotherhithe Festival

Time & Talents Centre (7231 7845/ www.timeandtalents.org.uk). **Date** 14th July 2002.
A day-long tribute to this enchanting part of the city, with roadshow, stalls, street performers, sea-shanties, bouncy castles and a whole raft of family fun. Free buses run throughout the day to local attractions and venues on the peninsula, including the Surrey Docks Farm, Watersports Centre and the Brunel Engine House. Contact the above number for information.

Swan Upping on the Thames

various points along the Thames. **Date** 15-19 July 2002.
Today, the Crown still owns all unmarked mute swans in open water, although in practice this means only certain parts

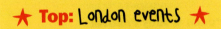

★ Top: London events ★

Canalway Cavalcade
Barge around to Little Venice for this colourful Maytide boat rally. *See p28.*

London Harness Horse Parade
Canter down to Battersea Park to witness impressive equine pulling power. *See p27.*

Marine Week
Be a beach bum in Hammersmith or a pirate in Camden. *See right.*

Regent Street Festival
Go downtown where all the lights are bright, the music's loud and the sideshows magical. *See p32.*

Rotherhithe Festival
Hit the peninsula and get acquainted with this historic riverside settlement. *See above.*

---

of the Thames. Once a year the Queen's Swan Marker and the Swan Uppers of the Vinters' and Dyers' livery companies count, ring and check the health of the swans. The officials wear traditional scarlet uniforms and each traditional Thames rowing skiff flies appropriate flags and pennants. When a brood of cygnets is sighted, a cry of 'All up!' is given to signal that the boats should get into position. On passing Windsor Castle, the rowers stand to attention with oars raised and salute 'Her Majesty the Queen, Seigneur of the Swans'. This archaic ceremony can be seen from the towpaths along the Thames.

Lambeth Country Show

Brockwell Park, SE24 (7926 6200). Brixton tube/ rail then 2, 3, 37, 196 bus/Herne Hill rail. **Date** 20, 21 July 2002.
This annual urban country show fills Brockwell Park with a heady mix of animal attractions (horse show, dog show, farm animals). There's more fun in the form of bouncy castles and fairground rides, food and craft stalls, music and dancing.

Marine Week

various locations throughout the south-east (7261 0447/www.wildlondon.org.uk). **Date** 3-11 Aug 2002.
Marine Week comprises 50 free events to introduce people to marine life, including a beach party at Hammersmith foreshore, Born to be Tidal arts events in front of Tate Modern and pirate boat trips in Camden.

Notting Hill Carnival

Notting Hill, W10, W11 (8964 0544). Ladbroke Grove, Notting Hill or Westbourne Park tube. **Date** 25, 26 Aug 2002.
Europe's biggest street party is staged on the Sunday and Monday of August bank holiday weekend, attracting more than a million revellers. A massive costume parade, live music and plenty of sound systems are among the attractions. The Children's Day starts at noon on Sunday and ends when the last band leaves the carnival route at about 7pm; it has a constantly moving barrier of adult stewards, enclosed in a roped-off band area, and is generally quieter than the main parade. There'll be no avoiding the huge crowds whichever day you visit, however. In recent years, plans to move the carnival to a less residential area have been put forward, so keep an eye on the local press for the latest details.

Autumn

Great River Race

on the Thames, from Richmond, Surrey, to Island Gardens, E14 (8398 9057). **Date** 7 Sept 2002.
More than 250 boats compete in this 22-mile river marathon, aiming to scoop the UK Traditional Boat Championship. Setting off from Ham House in Richmond and passing many historic landmarks until the finish at Island Gardens near Greenwich, the race attracts many fascinating entries from crews from all over the world. Look out for replica Bronze Age Greek galleys, and canvas and tar Irish naomhogs – the type reputed to have crossed the Atlantic in the eighth century.

London Waterways Week

various locations around Grand Union & Regent's Canals, London Docklands & the Rivers Thames & Lee (7286 6101/www.britishwaterwayslondon.co.uk/ lwww). **Date** 7-15 Sept 2002.
A week highlighting the capital's network of waterways. Special events and promotions take place all over London;

boat trips, discounts at waterside attractions and low-cost treats at riverside pubs and restaurants are all part of the fun, which begins with the Great River Race (*see p31*) and ends with the Thames Festival (*see below*).

Thames Festival
on the Thames, between Waterloo Bridge & Blackfriars Bridge (7928 8998). **Map** p320 M7-O7. **Date** 14, 15 Sept 2002.
A celebration of the river, featuring a funfair, food village, street entertainers, floats and an atmospheric night-time procession of over 1,000 people with lanterns, ending with a splendid firework display. There are lantern-making tents during the day for children to craft their own procession lamp, and green-minded kids can join in with environmental workshops and river cleaning on the foreshore.

CBBC Proms in the Park
Hyde Park (booking/info line 0870 899 8001/ www.bbc.co.uk/proms). Hyde Park Corner tube. **Map** p313 F7. **Date** 15 Sept 2002.
Hosted this year by CBBC TV presenters Simon Thomas and Fearne Cotton, this musical party is a light-hearted family afternoon out, featuring bubblegum pop performed by chart-topping acts (2002 will see Gareth Gates, Will Young and S Club Juniors) and accessible classical music from the BBC Philharmonic. Gates open at 12.30pm and the entertainment starts at 2pm. Note that babies are not admitted.

Regent Street Festival
Regent Street, W1 (info 7491 4429). Oxford Circus tube. **Map** p318 J6. **Date** 15 Sept 2002.
Now in its third year, this fun festival starts with a celebrity opening at noon from a stage situated at the junction of Regent Street and New Burlington Street, followed by live music (rock, pop, jazz, classical), which continues until 8pm. Regent Street is closed to traffic and packed with activities; the highlight being a funfair with bumper cars, carousels and big wheel. There are also street entertainers, theatre, story-telling, face painters and magicians, with many stores and restaurants also tempting visitors with special promotions, competitions and al fresco dining.

City Farms & Community Garden Festival
Capel Manor Gardens, Bullsmoor Lane, Enfield, Middx (8366 4442/www.capel.ac.uk). Turkey Street rail. **Date** 21 Sept 2002.
The urban farms we all love have a pleasant day out in the leafy acres of Enfield for this agricultural extravaganza. Events include a farm animal show, milking and shearing demonstrations, vegetable and plant sales, craft stalls and children's activities.

London Open House
various venues throughout London (www.londonopenhouse.org). **Date** 21, 22 Sept 2002.
2002 is the tenth anniversary of this event, held to promote awareness and to celebrate the wealth of magnificent architecture across the city. This is a fantastic chance to gain access to over 500 buildings free of charge, many of which are usually closed to the public, from private homes to civic and industrial institutions, grand historical buildings to pumping stations. Some local boroughs are running architecture-related workshops and activities for children. Check the website for a full list of participating buildings.

Horseman's Sunday
Church of St John & St Michael, Hyde Park Crescent, W2 (7262 1732). Edgware Road tube/Paddington tube/rail. **Map** p313 E6. **Date** 22 Sept 2002.
This ceremony dates back to 1969, when local riding stables fearing closure held an open-air service to protest. A vicar on horseback rides out to bless and present rosettes to a procession of horses and riders, and deliver a short service with hymns and occasional guest speakers. There is little interaction between onlookers and the horses, but it is enjoyable to watch this equine pageant in the lovely setting of Hyde Park.

Punch & Judy Festival
Covent Garden Piazza, WC2 (7836 9136). Covent Garden tube. **Map** p319 L7. **Date** 5, 6 Oct 2002.
With roots deep in folk drama and storytelling, Punch & Judy's brand of knockout nonsense has delighted children for centuries. This festival celebrates the enduring appeal of Old Red Nose and his wife, engaging in mischief and slapstick and providing shout-along fun for kids of all ages. There are over 20 puppeteers dotted around the market building, with performances at set times. That's the way to do it!

Pearly Kings & Queens Harvest Festival
St Martin-in-the-Fields, Trafalgar Square, WC2 (7766 1100/www.pearlies.co.uk). Charing Cross tube/rail. **Map** p319 L7. **Date** 6 Oct 2002.
Arrive early for the 3pm harvest thanksgiving service to watch the arrival of London's pearly kings and queens, splendidly dressed in their pearl button-covered suits. The vicar also wears a pearly stole during attendance, and St Martin's is decorated with fruit and harvest baskets. The crypt downstairs houses a brass-rubbing centre and café, and there's a market on the church grounds, should you wish to only observe the arrivals but not attend the hour-long service.

Trooping the Colour – serious stuff. *See p30.*

The **Thames Festival**, going out with a bang. *See p32.*

Trafalgar Day Parade

Trafalgar Square, WC2 (7928 8978/www.sea-cadets.org).
Charing Cross tube/rail. **Map** p319 K7. **Date** 20 Oct 2002.
This parade of 500 uniformed sea cadets and marching bands
commemorates the 196th anniversary of the Battle of
Trafalgar and the death of Admiral Lord Nelson, ending with
the laying of a wreath at the foot of Nelson's Column in
Trafalgar Square. Kids can board the Sea Cadets mobile
display unit – a 1960s Routemaster bus – converted into the
control room of a Royal Navy submarine, where they can
raise the periscope, stalk enemy ships with sonar contacts,
and try out their skills on dive-dive-dive action stations.

State Opening of Parliament

House of Lords, Palace of Westminster, SW1
(7219 4272/www.parliament.uk). Westminster tube.
Map p319 L9. **Date** early/mid Nov 2002.
The state opening of Parliament by the Queen is a colourful
ceremony that has changed little since the 16th century. Large
crowds gather to watch her arrival and departure from the
Palace of Westminster in the State Coach, attended by the
Household Cavalry. As she enters the House of Lords, a gun
salute is fired. The Queen's Speech in the House of Lords may
only be observed via television.

London to Brighton Veteran Car Run

starting at Serpentine Road, Hyde Park, W2
(01753 681736). Hyde Park Corner tube.
Map p313 E8. **Date** 3 Nov 2002.
Limited to an average speed of 20mph, this motoring spectacle is more of a procession to show off 400 vintage cars
than a race, although bronze medals are awarded to all who
reach Brighton before 4.30pm. The first group of cars are the
older ones, leaving Hyde Park Corner at 7.30am, so set your

alarm clock early if you want to catch the real classics. If
you can't get there, join the crowds lining the rest of the route,
via Parliament Square and Westminster Bridge, then on
through the streets of south London.

Bonfire Night

Date 5 Nov 2002.
Every year Britain celebrates the failure of the Gunpowder
Plot of 1605, when Guy Fawkes attempted to blow up James
I and his Parliament. A 'guy' is burnt on a giant bonfire
and fireworks are let off. Most public displays are held on
the weekend nearest to 5 November; among the best in
London are those at Primrose Hill, Alexandra Palace and
Crystal Palace. It's best to phone your local council nearer the
time for specific details of individual firework displays, as
events have been known to be cancelled (usually due to bad
weather) at the 11th hour.

Lord Mayor's Show

various streets in the City (7606 3030). **Date** 9 Nov 2002.
One of the most colourful and ancient of London traditions,
the Lord Mayor's Show dates back to 1215 and the charter
King John granted the City to elect its own mayor. The charter required the lord mayor to present himself at the Law
Courts for approval and to swear loyalty to the Crown. The
parade has thousands of participants: military personnel,
horses, floats, marching bands and the spectacular State
Coach. Starting at 11am and marked by an aircraft flypast
over the Royal Exchange, Mansion House and St Paul's
Cathedral, it proceeds to the Royal Courts of Justice on the
Strand, pausing as the lord mayor takes his oath, then
sets off on the return journey from Victoria Embankment
to Mansion House. The exact order of the procession is a
closely guarded secret, but you'll be able to get a programme
on the day with details.

Chinese New Year Festival

Regent Street, W1 (7491 4429). Oxford Circus tube.
Map p316 J6.
Bond Street, W1 (7821 5230). Oxford Circus tube.
Map p316 H6.
Trafalgar Square, SW1 (7983 4234). Leicester Square
tube. **Map** p319 K7.
Date all mid Nov-early Dec.
Each year since 1947, a giant fir tree given by Norway takes
up residence in Trafalgar Square, with the decorative lights
being switched on at a ceremony featuring carol singing and
choirs. The main shopping streets boast impressive festive
displays, particularly the larger department stores, with
the lights on Regent Street and Oxford Street invariably
being switched on by some jobbing celebrity. Those on St
Christopher's Place, Bond Street and Kensington High Street
are often more charming.

Winter

International Showjumping Championships
Olympia, Hammersmith Road, W14 (7370 8202/
www.olympiashowjumping.com). Kensington (Olympia)
tube/rail. **Date** 18-22 Dec 2002.
Top-class international showjumping action is interspersed
with dog displays at the Agility Stakes, and the Shetland
Pony Grand National. Trade stands located around the arena
sell equestrian equipment and Christmas gifts. There are also
over 100 exhibitors selling products ranging from clothing
and jewellery to fine foods.

London International Boat Show
Earl's Court Exhibition Centre, Warwick Road, SW5
(info 01784 472222/www.bigblue.org.uk). Earl's Court
tube. **Map** p314 A11. **Date** 9-19 Jan 2003.
All the latest in boating, watersports and holidays in one of
London's most popular shows. All types of seagoing craft are
buffed up for display, with a pool featuring around 20 boats
afloat also being the stage for a daily entertainment programme. Sailing fans can seek out expert advice and peruse
equipment for sale; those without the budget for a new yacht
can simply enjoy a day out watching the aerial acrobatics,
marine fashion shows and impressive vessels.

London International Mime Festival
various venues throughout London (7637 5661/
www.mimefest.co.uk). **Date** 11-26 Jan 2003.
This festival includes children's shows suitable for all ages,
plus performances that are geared for people with hearing
difficulties (they listen to the accompanying music through
a loop system). Expect to see dance-theatre, circus skills, puppetry, animation and mechanical theatre.

Chinese New Year Festival
around Gerrard Street, Chinatown, W1 (7439 3822/
www.chinatown-online.co.uk). Leicester Square
or Piccadilly Circus tube. **Map** p319 K 6/7. **Date**
late Jan/early Feb 2003.
The most important date in the Chinese calendar sees
Chinatown colourfully decorated with red lanterns and paper
dragons, buzzing with street stallholders selling crafts and
delicacies, and restaurants preparing delicious banquets.
Music and drummers accompany lion dances through the
streets, and in 2002 the festivities also spread to Trafalgar
Square, with stage performances and martial arts demonstrations. Check the press for details of 2003's celebrations.

Remembrance Sunday Ceremony
Cenotaph, Whitehall, SW1. Westminster tube/Charing
Cross tube/rail. **Map** p319 L8. **Date** 10 Nov 2002.
An annual ceremony during which the Queen, the Prime
Minister and other dignitaries lay poppy wreaths at the
Cenotaph, Britain's national memorial to fallen heroes
from both world wars, and observe two minutes' silence at
exactly 11am in their honour. Attended by hundreds of ex-
servicemen, a remembrance service is led by the Bishop of
London afterwards.

Discover Dogs
Earl's Court 2 (entrance on Lillie Road), SW6 (7518
1012/www.the-kennel-club.org.uk). West Brompton tube.
Map p314 A11. **Date** 16, 17 Nov 2002.
A canine extravaganza, where you can meet over 180 dogs,
discuss pedigrees with breeders, and gather information on
all matters of the mutt. The Good Citizen Dog Scheme offers
discipline and agility courses, and children can join the
Young Kennel Club, which encourages interest in care and
training, and organises activities, competitions, classes and
camps. Meet husky teams, watch police dog agility demonstrations and witness the doggy dances in the Heelwork to
Music displays.

Christmas Lights & Tree
Covent Garden, WC2 (7836 9136). Covent Garden tube.
Map p317 L6.
Oxford Street, W1 (7629 2738). Oxford Circus tube.
Map p316 G6.

Around Town

Introduction

Capital treasures, many free to see.

Now that so many of London's major museums have done away with their entrance fee, a family day out in town is a far more relaxed affair. You can pop into the Natural History Museum for an eyeful of dinosaurs, wander along to the Science Museum to check out the Launch Pad and still have time to whisk down the Piccadilly Line to the Theatre Museum for a dramatic finale to your day. And all for the price of a family Travelcard.

Our trip around town takes in all the major sights and museums, but travels on north, east, south and west to explore the city's further-flung treasures, and discover what they have to offer children of all ages.

On the buses

See the sights of London and learn the lie of the land from the top of a double-decker bus (the best ones are the boneshaking **Routemasters**, the old-fashioned, open-backed buses that you can hop on and off). Try the excellent and frequent (every four to six minutes) No.12, which trundles from Notting Hill Gate, via Oxford Circus, Marble Arch and Trafalgar Square, over Westminster Bridge and down south to Dulwich. For a dedicated sightseeing bus ride, try the two companies listed below.

Big Bus Company

7233 9533/www.bigbus.co.uk. **Departures** every 10-30mins from Green Park, Marble Arch & Victoria. *Summer* 8.30am-7pm daily. *Winter* 8.30am-4.30pm daily. **Pick-up** Green Park (near the Ritz); Marble Arch (Speakers' Corner); Victoria (outside Royal Westminster Hotel, 48 Buckingham Palace Road, SW1). **Fares** £16; £6 5-15s; free under-5s. **Credit** AmEx, DC, MC, V. Tickets for these informative bus rides, which include guided walking tours and a free river cruise, are interchangeable between the three routes, allowing you to hop on and off the buses at more than 50 different locations. Tour commentaries can be translated into 12 different languages.

Original London Sightseeing Tour

8877 1722/www.theoriginaltour.com. **Departures** *Summer* 9am-6pm daily. *Winter* 9.30am-5pm daily. **Pick-up** Victoria Street, SW1; Marble Arch (Speakers' Corner); Baker Street tube (forecourt); Haymarket (at bus stop L); Embankment station; Coventry Street, WC2; Trafalgar Square (north side). **Fares** £15; £7.50 5-15s; free under-5s. **Credit** MC, V. This tour bus company's five routes allow you to get on and off at over 80 different stops. The yellow English-speaking tour bus includes a live commentary, the red one is multilingual and the Capital Connecters tour picks up from hotels. A free river cruise is included in the price.

USEFUL INFORMATION

Round-ups of notable places to eat are included in each area guide. Some of these restaurants and cafés have their own review in the later Eating chapter (*pp170-191*), but the reviews may be of a different branch. In any case, it's always a good idea to ring to check that a listed place, whether it is a museum, gallery, restaurant or shop, is open before you visit, as some are closed on certain days.

To help you plan your activities, we've included a short, child-friendly walk for each area, as well as the best sights and areas to explore. In this, our second edition of the guide, we've chosen to focus on the River Thames – its bridges, its boats, its fascinating beaches, its glorious history and amazing wildlife. We didn't want to leave out London's canals, either, so a series of 'Water ways' features flows through the guide, to let you in on all the fun you can have on the city's watercourses without getting wet.

PASSPORT TO THE SIGHTS

If you intend a gruelling schedule of sightseeing, it may be worth investing in a **London Pass**. The card, which costs from £22 for one day (£17 for children 5-15) without a Travelcard included, or up to £107 for six days (£56 children) with a Travelcard thrown in, lets you in free to more than 60 attractions. These, naturally, are the sights that aren't free to start with, which many of our best museums now are. It also gives discounts in certain restaurants and theatres. To receive a leaflet about the London Pass, and for information about prices, call 0870 242 9988 or log on to www.londonpass.com.

If we have included the initials 'LP' in brackets before the admission price of a certain place, it means your London Pass will give you either free admission, tours or free entry to exhibitions held there. Likewise, the initials 'EH' means that the sight is an English Heritage property and that members of the organisation can get in free to the special events taking place there. 'NT' means that National Trust members can expect free admission.

Water ways: the Thames

London is a seaside city straddling the mouth of the **River Thames**. Seagulls occupy the air space above the buildings, and tides rise and fall twice a day. In the era before air travel, the capital's proximity to the great oceans of the world accounted for its importance. The British Empire spread by sea and the Thames was crowded with ocean-going vessels bringing goods and people from every part of the vast trade-based Commonwealth. Nowadays, everyone comes to London by plane and the river is much quieter.

At 210 miles, the Thames is the longest river in Great Britain. A large statue of a bearded geriatric – Old Father Thames – marks its source in the Cotswold Hills, near Cirencester on the Welsh border. Flowing east, it drains the nation's most fertile, not to say expensive, region. For its last 30 miles, from Teddington on the outskirts of London to the sea, the river is tidal. As London grew, the tides necessitated the construction of docks, which locked the water in at a constant level so that ships could tie up at the side to be loaded and unloaded, irrespective of the tidal rise and fall. Nowadays the docks mainly accommodate pleasure boats and watersports facilities. The trade in goods has been replaced by trade in money, which does not depend on the river; financial institutions now occupy the sites of former warehouses and the modest homes of stevedores and dockworkers have been bought by wealthy investment bankers and stockbrokers.

Leisure and pleasure are now the Thames's only important functions. Attempts to turn it into a viable commuting route invariably fail because most Londoners cross the river, rather than follow its course, on their journey to work. The majority of boats are tourist vessels offering sightseeing trips with commentaries delivered by boatmen in plausible cockney accents. They sail downstream as far as the Thames Barrier and upstream all the way to Teddington Lock, passing under bridges that are the subjects of song, poetry and postcards.

The river's function as a drainage system used to be applied literally, when the populace of the city tipped their sewage and the effluence from their factories into it. For many years the river was so filthy that the only life-form capable of thriving in it was that staple of the cockney diet, the eel. However, in recent years government regulations have forced a cleaning-up process so that now a hundred different species of fish feel at home in its green-grey waters and as many varieties of bird nest along its banks. Conservationists are fond of referring to the river as a 'wildlife superhighway'. You will be, too, after you see your first heron enjoying a fishing trip on its banks.

Still, it's hardly clean enough yet for human consumption. Indeed, an ancient legend says that whereas to swim in the Nile means you will certainly one day return to Egypt, to swim in the Thames means you will just as certainly never return to London.

Southwark & Bankside

Whether you want a fly in the Eye or a kick up the Bankside,
Southwark is the borough for you.

Around Town

It is remarkable how Southwark has become the city's playground again after four centuries. The **London Eye**, which since January 2000 has added a fun element to the city's silhouette, is already one of the most popular tourist attractions in town. It stands in **Jubilee Gardens**, which have a fenced-off children's playground with apparatus on a squashy safety surface. Whether the Eye continues to gaze down from this point for decades to come is up to Lambeth council, to whom its managers have had to apply for planning permission. Most people believe the wheel will continue to turn here, however, as it has been such a success.

The whole area is a children's paradise. Sharks are the big attraction for parents and children at the **London Aquarium**. The shops, galleries and restaurants at **Gabriel's Wharf** and nearby **Oxo Tower** are also geared towards families. Near the latter, in **Bernie Spain Gardens**, children can enjoy open workshops in a tent as part of the **Thames Festival** in September (*see also p32*). Activities on offer include lantern-making workshops; the lights children create are for use in the after-dark Thames procession.

The art gallery at **Tate Modern** is always full of visitors, many of whom will have crossed the Thames on the beautiful **Millennium Bridge** (*see also p24*). The bridge joins the **South Bank Centre**, including the Royal Festival Hall and the National Theatre, in returning this stretch of riverbank to the entertainment district it was in Shakespeare's day. Nevertheless, while the area has been improved over the years, with the opening of various family-friendly attractions, it lives under the constant threat of redevelopment. Londoners are waiting with baited breath to see if the latest plans – to build new concert halls and a base for the British Film Institute (and perhaps a reprieve for the late, lamented MOMI, Museum of the Moving Image) on the site of Jubilee Gardens – will be given the green light. Even if the project does get the go-ahead, don't expect to see any changes for a while.

Fashion followers should note that the **Zandra Rhodes Fashion & Textile Museum** is soon to open at 83 Bermondsey Street, SE1 (7403 0222). The education department is planning all sorts of children's activities, so call for details. And there's yet more culture in the form of the reconstructed

Book a flight on the **British Airways London Eye**. *See p39.*

Globe theatre, which is an exact replica of Shakespeare's 17th-century playhouse (the original was situated nearby). Shakespeare enthusiasts should also make a bee-line for the nearby **Rose Theatre** (www.rosetheatre.org.uk). There's not much to see for the 'admission' price – just the excavated foundations – although you do get a video presentation of the history of the theatre that staged Christopher Marlowe's plays just as the Globe staged Shakespeare's.

Visitors may also wish to follow our Shakespeare walk (*see p44*), which takes in the ancient streets the Bard trod. It is just as if Elizabeth were on the throne all over again.

Eyes right for **Gabriel's Wharf**. *See p38.*

BFI London IMAX Cinema

1 Charlie Chaplin Walk, SE1 (7902 1234/ www.bfi.org.uk/imax). Waterloo tube/rail. **Open** 12.30-8pm Mon-Thur; 12.30-9.15pm Fri; 11.45am-9.15pm Sat; noon-8pm Sun. **Admission** £7.10; £4.95 4-15s; £5.95 concessions; add-on film costs an extra £4.20 per adult or child; free under-4s. **Credit** AmEx, MC, V. **Map** p320 M8.

IMAX stands for 'image maximum', which is a clue that this tall, circular cinema situated within the roundabout at the southern end of Waterloo Bridge contains the largest screen in Europe. The celluloid itself is the width of a £20 note and the projector the size of a small house. The audience feels that the film is happening all around them, especially when they hear the extraordinary 44-speaker sound system. The 2,000 seats are very steeply banked, so no one, not even tots, has to look over anyone's head to see.

Most of the specially made two- and three-dimensional films shown here are aimed at children. The most popular is *Cyberworld*, a 3-D fantasy animation with a brief appearance by the Simpsons (Homer gets sucked into a black hole – d'oh!). The necessary glasses are provided. *Shackleton* is a 2-D account of the great explorer's Antarctic escapade, narrated by Kevin Spacey. *Beauty and the Beast* is an exclusive IMAX 2-D remake of Disney's original with new sequences and a whole new song. *Haunted Castle* is a 3-D thriller, which is all the scarier for its scale. Note that it carries a PG tag. Leaders of school groups prefer the 2-D documentary *Mysteries of Egypt* as it touches on topics covered by the national curriculum. All shows include a 15-minute Pearl and Dean trailer projected at normal cinema size, which emphasises the vastness of the subsequent IMAX experience. Five different films are scheduled at various times daily – phone to see what's running, or check the website for details. *Café. Nappy-changing facilities. Nearest picnic place: Jubilee Gardens.*

Bramah Museum of Tea & Coffee

40 Southwark Street, SE1 (7403 5650/ www.bramahmuseum.co.uk). London Bridge tube/ rail/381 bus. **Open** 10am-6pm daily. Closed 25, 26 Dec. **Admission** £4; £3.50 concessions; £10 family (2+4). **Credit** AmEx, MC, V. **Map** p310 P8.

The prize exhibit here is the world's largest teapot, which can serve 800 people without a top-up. The museum, which recently moved to this site, was originally set up in the 1990s by former tea taster Edward Bramah to explain the history of tea- and coffee-drinking in the UK from Sir Walter Raleigh's time to the post-war invention of the perforated teabag. The part tea played in the Opium Wars and the Boxer Rebellion is harrowing and shameful from a British perspective. *Buggy access. Café. Shop.*

British Airways London Eye

Riverside Building, next to County Hall, Westminster Bridge Road, SE1 (0870 500 0600/customer services 0870 220 2777/www.ba-londoneye.com). Westminster tube/Waterloo tube/rail. **Open** Feb-Apr, Oct-Dec 9.30am-8pm daily. May-Sept 9.30am-10pm daily. Closed 25 Dec & all Jan. **Admission** Feb-Apr, Oct-Dec £9.50; £7.50 concessions. May-Sept £10.50; £8.50 concessions. All year £5 5-15s; free under-5s. **Credit** AmEx, MC, V. **Map** p319 M8.

The London Eye was constructed by British Airways to mark the year 2000. It has become one of the city's best-loved attractions and the most familiar silhouette on the skyline. It affords stunning views in most weather conditions. A 'flight' on the Eye is one revolution and lasts half an hour, which means you travel at only twice the speed of Big Ben's minute hand. This stately bearing, and the holiday atmosphere inside the all-window pod, makes it a suitably unscary and literally uplifting experience for small children.

When you're on the Eye, you can see right into the Queen's enormous back garden at Buckingham Palace. The trees in the north are Hampstead Heath, in the south Forest Hill. If anyone says they can see France, they're lying. On a night ride, a feast of twinkly lights, the far horizon disappears in the darkness but landmarks in central London are still easy to distinguish, as are the bridges of the Thames. The pods are unmanned. Buy a £2 mini guide, which identifies the landmarks in four main directions. The capsules take 25 people, although the central seat is big enough only for a dozen elbow-to-elbow. All passengers are photographed before the ride and tempted with the Polaroid at the end – £5 for a small picture, £8 large. Advance booking is advised; those who turn up on a whim take pot luck, especially on a clear, sunny day, when the queues may be an hour long. Note that you can take a buggy on board though it must be folded first.

Pods are available for private hire for functions, including civic weddings (it's not cheap at £1,700, but you do get the use of a reception lounge, registrar and champagne for up to 14 guests). Parties may stay on board for more than one revolution but must pay accordingly. *Buggy access. Café. Nappy-changing facilities. Nearest picnic place: Jubilee Gardens.*

Clink Prison Museum

1 Clink Street, SE1 (7378 1558/www.clink.co.uk). London Bridge tube/rail. **Open** 10am-6pm daily. Closed 25 Dec. Tours hourly when available. **Admission** £4; £3 5-15s, concessions; £9 family (2+2); free under-5s. Tours £1. **Credit** AmEx, DC, MC, V. **Map** p320 P8.

In the less tolerant past, children were regarded as miniature adults, which meant that if they broke the law, they often ended up in prison alongside the grown-ups. The museum's

BOO!

several re-creations of prison life between the 12th and 15th centuries feature a number of pre-pubescent dummies cowering in the corners from blank-eyed, older felons, debtors, thieves and murderers. The ironware that kept them bound is displayed round the walls – shackles, ball-and-chains, lockable boots, masks. The stocks seem somewhat harmless until you read that unfortunate miscreants might have been locked up in them for a week and pelted with rotten eggs, fruit and stones by their self-righteous neighbours. The museum is noisy with sound effects, voice-overs and monkish plainchant, which can be heard on the street outside. The glass display cabinet in the small shop contains a death mask of Oliver Cromwell apropos of nothing.
Nearest picnic place: Southwark Cathedral Gardens. Shop.

Dalí Universe

County Hall, Riverside Building, Queen's Walk, SE1 (7620 2720/www.daliuniverse.com). Waterloo tube/rail. **Open** 10am-5.30pm daily. Closed 25 Dec. *Tours* phone for details. **Admission** (LP) £8.95; £6.95 concessions; £4.95 10-16s; free under-10s. **Credit** AmEx, DC, MC, V. **Map** p319 M8.
The world's largest permanent exhibition of the works of the Spanish surrealist painter and sculptor Salvador Dalí now includes a new display of his erotic art, which has obliged the exhibitors to put up warning signs to parents at the gallery entrance. Certainly, some of the positions that Dalí's nudes find themselves in might provoke awkward questions from the innocent. The artist was the most Freudian of all the surrealists. The melting clocks, long-legged elephants, crutches, lobsters, ants and stretched buttocks casting long shadows over his dreamlike sunny plains beg to be interpreted and psychoanalysed. Curated by long-time Dalí friend and collector Benjamin Levi, the exhibition covers Dalí's whole life, although his obsession with Hitler and support for Franco is glossed over. Perhaps it would contrast too unhappily with the memorial to the General's enemies outside in Jubilee Gardens. The exhibition also has a supplementary section devoted to ceramics by Dalí's compatriot Pablo Picasso (never before seen in the UK), for which there is an extra cost (£3.95).
Buggy access. Lift. Nearest picnic place: Jubilee Gardens. Shop.

Design Museum

28 Shad Thames, SE1 (7403 6933/ www.designmuseum.org). Tower Hill tube/London Bridge tube/rail/15, 78, 100 bus. **Open** 10am-5.45pm (last entry 5.15pm) daily. **Admission** £6; £4 5-15s, concessions; £16 family (2+2); free under-5s. **Credit** AmEx, MC, V. **Map** p321 S9.
Chair Alley is the one unchanging feature in this excellent Thameside museum. The top-floor display includes chairs by a score of different designers, from Bauhaus to Charles Rennie Mackintosh. Visitors may touch, feel and sit, but not fall asleep, in them. A basic family trail leaflet has children draw, describe and answer questions about the exhibits.

Apart from Chair Alley, all the exhibitions at the museum are temporary and laid out on the first and second floors of the former dockside warehouse. Forthcoming shows in 2002 include the furniture designer Geo Ponti, an exhibition simply entitled Aluminium, and shoes by Manolo Blahnik. New to the museum is the unbreakable glass display tank on the forecourt outside, which houses a changing exhibit relevant to the displays in the building.

School groups attend two-hour workshops in the museum's Study Centre at which lecturers introduce the principles and theories of design and technology. Practical exercises include a 'mystery objects' game in which students handle

and examine certain exhibits while trying to identify them. These come from the museum's permanent but undisplayed collection of televisions, washing machines, telephones, tableware and other consumer durables. Consumer undurables are available in the pleasant ground-floor café.
Buggy access. Café. Nappy-changing facilities. Nearest picnic place: Butler's Wharf riverside benches. Restaurant. Shop.

Florence Nightingale Museum

St Thomas's Hospital, 2 Lambeth Palace Road, SE1 (7620 0374/www.florence-nightingale.co.uk). Westminster tube/Waterloo tube/rail. **Open** 10am-5pm Mon-Fri; 11.30am-4.30pm Sat, Sun. Last entry 1hr before closing. **Admission** (LP) £4.80; £3.80 5-18s, concessions; £12 family (2+2); free under-5s. **Credit** AmEx, MC, V. **Map** p319 M9.
This exhibition commemorating 'the Lady of the Lamp' is of interest to primary schoolchildren, who come across Florence Nightingale frequently in national curriculum Key Stages 1 and 2. She is the most common subject of study under the heading Victorian Projects. It is also worth visiting by GCSE students taking courses in the History of Medicine. Worksheets encourage children to study pictures of hospitalisation in peace and war before and after Nightingale's career. Objects to handle include examples of soldier food before and after Nightingale's arrival in the Crimea in the 1850s. The museum contains many of her personal effects, including her medicine chest and the lamp that gave rise to her nickname. The Crimea Ward Scene is rather bloody, which will be of interest to small children when they're colouring in worksheets. The exhibition naturally focuses mostly on the army hospital at Scutari (Turkey), but it also draws attention to Nightingale's unparalleled achievements in peacetime health care. She improved living conditions in the army and raised public funds by subscription to set up the Nightingale School for Nurses at St Thomas's – the first of its kind anywhere in the world. The shop sells Florence Nightingale shopping bags, tea towels, teddy bears and stacks of books about nursing.
Buggy access. Café (in hospital). Nearest picnic place: benches by entrance of St Thomas's hospital/Archbishop's Park. Restaurant (in hospital). Shop.

Golden Hinde

St Mary Overie Dock, Cathedral Street, SE1 (0870 011 8700/shop 7403 0123/www.goldenhinde.co.uk). Monument tube/London Bridge tube/rail. **Open** daily, times vary; phone for details. Closed 25 Dec. **Admission** £2.50; £2.10 concessions; £1.75 4-13s; £6.50 family (2+3); free under-4s. **Credit** MC, V. **Map** p321 P8.
This reconstruction of Admiral Sir Francis Drake's 16th-century flagship was built in 1973 to commemorate his 400th birthday. It is open to the public and available for hire. Children's 'pirate parties', aimed at 5-12-year-olds, are popular (see p247). Otherwise, school groups and pre-arranged bookings may take part in workshops, including Living History Days and Overnights, in which participants learn the story of the ship and how men lived on board. On an Overnight children sleep on the gun-deck – not in hammocks, alas, but in sleeping bags on mattresses. Both groups learn to give signals with the bell and how to run the 22 cannons through the portholes.

The ship is open to the public only when no groups are visiting, so call first to check. Tickets are sold in the gift shop nearby. Explanatory leaflets direct visitors on self-guided tours of the five decks. The ship is surprisingly small, yet it spent two decades circumnavigating the globe as a floating museum earlier in its career. Drake spent as long plundering

Around Town

Spanish settlements in the New World in the original – all with the approval of Queen Elizabeth I. The present 'crew' are students and actors who dress up and shout a lot.
Nearest picnic place: Southwark Cathedral Gardens/ riverside benches. Shop.

Hayward Gallery

Belvedere Road, SE1 (box office 7960 4242/ www.hayward-gallery.org.uk). Embankment tube/Waterloo tube/rail. **Open** *During exhibitions* 10am-6pm Mon, Thur-Sun; 10am-8pm Tue, Wed. **Admission** varies; phone for details. **Credit** AmEx, DC, MC, V. **Map** p320 M8.
The Hayward Gallery is one of the most versatile exhibition spaces in Britain. It is part of the South Bank Centre and its frequent exhibitions (they change about every two months) are free to under-16s (check the website to see what's coming up; until 21 June it's the media-friendly Sam Taylor-Wood exhibition, from July to September the work of American photographer Ansel Adams is up for inspection).
On Sundays at 2pm, two of the Hayward's guides take children (and their parents or minders) on a tour of the current exhibition. Debate about the pictures is encouraged. Drawing workshops follow the tour and the afternoon ends at 5pm. All half-terms are filled with fun activities for footloose children. The famous Neon Tower on the roof was created by Philip Vaughan and Roger Dainton and commissioned by the Arts Council in 1970. Its yellow, red, green and blue tubes are controlled by changes in the direction and strength of the wind. Be sure to stop off in the shop, which sells a wide range of art books and merchandise. *See also p217.*
Buggy access. Café. Lifts. Nappy-changing facilities. Nearest picnic place: Jubilee Gardens/riverside benches. Shop.

HMS Belfast

Morgan's Lane, Tooley Street, SE1 (7940 6328/ www.iwm.org.uk). London Bridge tube/rail. **Open** *Mar-Oct* 10am-6pm daily. *Nov-Feb* 10am-5pm daily. Last entry 45mins before closing. **Admission** (LP) £5.80; £4.40 concessions; free under-16s (must be accompanied by an adult). **Credit** MC, V. **Map** p321 R8.
A sense of high adventure beckons children to this 11,500-ton World War II battlecruiser, now floating peacefully on the Thames just upstream from Tower Bridge. Guided tours take in all nine decks, from the bridge to the boiler room, visiting the galley, sick bay, dentist, NAAFI canteen, mess deck and the permanent exhibition entitled HMS Belfast in War and Peace. Films, photos, documents and quiz sheets enhance the experience. Children's birthday parties are available (*see p247*). The new 'kip in a ship' overnight experience is for groups of up to 50 children. Sadly, they do not sleep in hammocks but in sailors' bunks on the original mess deck. Accompanying adults take the officers' separate cabins. The school holidays offer daily study programmes aimed at 7-14-year-olds. Term-time schools' events involve tailor-made workshops and talks using both video and live presentations, but what children really want to see are the three sets of guns that destroyed the German battleship *Scharnhorst* in the Arctic Ocean in 1943. There is usually a queue to climb into the port deck Bofors gun, which young enthusiasts can swivel, elevate, aim, but not, of course, fire.
Café. Nappy-changing facilities. Nearest picnic place: William Curtis Park. Shop.

London Aquarium

County Hall, Riverside Building, Westminster Bridge Road, SE1 (7967 8000/tours 7967 8007/ www.londonaquarium.co.uk). Westminster tube/Waterloo tube/rail. **Open** 10am-6pm (last entry 5pm) daily. Phone for opening times during holidays. Closed 25 Dec. **Tours** (groups of 10 or more) phone for details. **Admission** (LP) £8.75; £6.50 concessions; £5.25 3-14s; £3.50 disabled; £25 family (2+2); free under-3s. **Credit** MC, V. **Map** p319 M9.
'Most fish show no parental care', reads the caption under the Tanganyikan Cichlid's tank. 'But the Cichlid devotes a great deal of energy to protecting its young...' Still, for all the Cichlid's praiseworthy attitude to family life, it is the sleek man-eating sharks in the Pacific tank that children really want to see, especially the new Zebra Shark, which is the only one in the UK. The sharks, which are named after characters on the 1970s children's show *Rainbow*, are fed on Tuesdays, Thursdays and Saturdays at 2.30pm (with Shark Talks at 2pm and 4pm); piranhas get their grub on Mondays, Wednesdays, Fridays and Sundays at 1pm. Divers descend into the Atlantic tank daily at noon to feed the rays, skates, dogfish and conger eels that dwell at the bottom. Children are keen on the two touch-pools where they can stroke the skates and rays as they rise to the surface or pat the crabs if they're careful.
A new adoption scheme raises money to finance the upkeep of the fish. For £30-£80 adopters receive pictures, information and regular bulletins on their ward's progress. An extensive schools' programme attracts enthusiastic groups. Educational tours last an hour and can be designed to focus on any one aspect of marine life such as habitats, the coral reef, the rainforest or defence strategies. A talk aimed at art students looks at the reasons why nature paints her sea creatures the way she does. A constant soundtrack of crashing waves and eerie whale music accompanies visitors as they shuffle from tank to tank. The graceful jellyfish, the nodding sea horses (it's the daddy of this species that does all the childcare), the crustacea scuttling about the rockpools and the black and green hopping mangrove frogs are all of more than passing interest, but nothing quite attracts children (or their parents) like the languid, grinning sharks.
Buggy access. Café. Lifts. Nappy-changing facilities. Nearest picnic place: Jubilee Gardens. Shop.

London Dungeon

28-34 Tooley Street, SE1 (7403 7221/ www.thedungeons.com). London Bridge tube/rail. **Open** *Late Mar-mid July* 10am-5.30pm daily. *Mid July-early Sept* 9.30am-7.30pm daily. *Early Sept-late Oct* 10am-5.30pm daily. *Early Nov-late Mar* 10.30am-5pm daily. Closed 25 Dec. **Admission** (LP) £10.95; £9.50 students; £6.95 5-14s, concessions; £2 reduction wheelchair users, carers free; free under-5s. **Credit** AmEx, MC, V. **Map** p321 Q8.
Set under the gloomy Victorian railway arches of London Bridge, this museum is not recommended for young children. The management says children should be over 8 years old, but one 9-year-old we know fainted at the sight of so much blood. Others lap it up (the atmosphere, not the blood) and revisit so many times they should buy a season ticket.
Even waiting in the ticket queue is part of the experience as hooded figures lurk to startle patient customers. Once inside, the different exhibits, scenes and cameos emphasise the true horror of crime and punishment throughout the ages. Highlights of the visit include a court scene where punters engage in interactive theatre with an utterly unreasonable 'judge', who sends them to Traitor's Gate. The boat journey transports the guilty to fresh heights of terror until they are faced with a firing squad and loud gunfire followed by complete darkness. The Jack the Ripper experience is suitably bloodthirsty, a subtle mixture of gruesome facts and horrors conjured by individual imaginations.
The dark, grimy air, the haunting sounds and the disorientation evoked by weaving your way around different areas all provide the thrill of fear and horror that is a vital part of

Young guns on **HMS Belfast**. *See p42.*

the dungeon's addictive attraction. But do not inflict this on anyone of a nervous or highly sensitive disposition. The shop is raved about by the sort of children who love fake blood, cap cigarette lighters, rubber severed fingers, stick-on warts and edible eyeballs.

Café. Nearest picnic place: Hay's Galleria. Shop.

London Fire Brigade Museum

94A Southwark Bridge Road, SE1 (7587 2894/ www.london-fire.gov.uk). Borough tube. **Tours** 10.30am, 2pm Mon-Fri by appointment only. Closed bank hols, 25 Dec. **Admission** £3; £2 7-14s, concessions; free under-7s. **Credit** MC, V. **Map** p320 O9.

Visitors must book in advance for this museum of firefighting in London. Tours last roughly an hour and take in the appliance bay, where pumps dating back to 1708 stand in tribute to blazes of the past. Small children are given colouring pencils and encouraged to draw the fire engines. This should keep them busy as there are 20 of them, ranging from a hand-drawn, hand-pumped model of the 1750s to the streamlined monsters of today. Older children try on the uni-

forms. There is no pole to slide down but there is a training yard next door where visitors may see recruits learning to rescue people from upper-storey windows. Exhibits in the eight small rooms detail the history of firefighting since the Great Fire in 1666 and include uniforms, equipment and paintings, especially those done by war artists during the Blitz. Plastic fireman's helmets are on sale in the shop.

Nearest picnic place: public park & playground in Marshalsea Road. Shop.

Museum of Garden History

Church of St Mary-at-Lambeth, Lambeth Palace Road, SE1 (7401 8865/www.museumgardenhistory.org). Waterloo tube/rail/C10, 507 bus. **Open** Feb-mid Dec 10.30am-5pm daily. **Admission** free; suggested donations of £2.50 adults, £2 concessions. **Credit** *Shop* (over £10) AmEx, MC, V. **Map** p310 L10.

Three figures important to the history of gardening are buried in the graveyard of this church-turned-museum. Children following activity sheets are invited to investigate the tombs of the Tradescant father and son, international

Walk: Shakespeare's Southwark

▶ Start at the Shakespeare memorial statue inside **Southwark Cathedral**. See how many characters from the Bard's works you can identify in the stained-glass window (*answer below*). Between the choir stalls is the gravestone of the actor Edmund Shakespeare, William's wild younger brother, who died in 1607 aged 26.

▶ Leave the cathedral by the south entrance and the courtyard by the western gate. Turn right along **Cathedral Street** and keep to the cobbles, passing the **Golden Hinde** in St Mary Overie's Dock. Turn left into Clink Street and walk past the ruins of Winchester Palace and the **Clink Prison Museum**. Turn right, then walk left past the refurbished Anchor Tavern, where Samuel Johnson, Samuel Pepys and William Shakespeare himself drank, if the imaginative tourist guides are to be believed. Keeping the river to your right, continue along **Bankside**, which was the address of several of Shakespeare's cast, including Will Kemp the jester.

▶ Follow Bankside under **Southwark Bridge**. Continue past Bear Gardens alley on your left and a quote from Shakespeare's *Henry VIII* inscribed in the handrail by the river on your right. Here you come to the **Globe Theatre**, a working replica of Shakespeare's own playhouse. Gangways lead down to Bankside Jetty, which rises and falls with the tide, from where you can catch a river bus to Westminster or the Tower of London. Facing the river here is a short terrace of houses built in the late 17th century. A plaque on the outside records the fact that Sir Christopher Wren resided here during the building of St Paul's across the river. He took a ferry every morning from the jetty. Nowadays he would have been able to use the pedestrian-only Millennium Bridge. Here, too, on a green patch of land known to Shakespeare's contemporaries as Pye Garden rises the vast red-brick edifice of

Tate Modern. Continue along Bankside towards **Blackfriars Bridge** but don't go beneath it. Instead, turn left and walk away from the river into **Holland Street**. On the left you'll pass the western entrance to Tate Modern. Walk through the gardens behind the museum and emerge at the junction of **Sumner Street**, **Great Guildford Street** (formerly Bandy Leg Walk) and **Park Street** (formerly Maid Lane). Follow the latter to the southern end of New Globe Walk, and a little further on, **Bear Gardens**. Elizabethans loved to gamble on the outcome of fights between dogs and bears or bulls. Later the Hope Theatre stood here and alternated plays with bear-baiting.

▶ Continue along Park Street to **Rose Alley**, where the **Rose Theatre** stood. Pass under the road bridge over Park Street and emerge with the offices of the *Financial Times* newspaper on your left and a cluster of modern council dwellings behind an iron fence on your right. In the fence is a gallery of posters and maps showing the site of the original Globe Theatre. You can see the circular outline of the playhouse in the cobbles.

▶ Follow Park Street, turning right at **Bank End**. In Shakespeare's day this area was known as 'Dead Man's Place' for the bodies that emerged from the Clink Prison. Follow the road round to the left between Georgian terraces. Turn left into **Stoney Street** and walk beside the stalls and aromatic premises of **Borough Market**, eventually turning right into **Winchester Walk**, which has the quaintest views of Southwark Cathedral. This was just the sight that Shakespeare would have enjoyed as he made his way to church or to help his brother out of another hole.

answer: Prospero, Ariel, Caliban, Falstaff, Hamlet, Malvolio, Bottom, Romeo and Juliet, Macbeth, Richard III, King Lear and the Seven Ages of Man as described in As You Like It.

plant-hunters and court gardeners to the Stuart kings, who most famously introduced the pineapple to Britain. This explains the motif in the stonework on nearby Lambeth Bridge. The third is Captain William Bligh of the *Bounty*. His crew complained that he cared more for the plants he was collecting in the South Pacific than he did for their welfare and rose up in mutiny, setting him adrift in a longboat in the middle of the ocean. The story of his survival is a famous film. Various activity sheets introduce children to the lives of these and other great adventurers depicted in the 8m 'Garden of the World' mural as well as to the museum's fascinating collections, whose exhibits include a 4,000-year-old garden hoe and a large number of gnomes. The old graveyard has been redesigned as a Jacobean knot garden with restored 17th-century topiary. Half a dozen Archbishops of Canterbury are buried alongside the gardeners.
Buggy access. Café. Nearest picnic place: Archbishop's Park. Shop.

Namco Station
County Hall (riverfront entrance), Westminster Bridge Road, SE1 (7967 1066/www.namcostation.co.uk). Westminster tube/Waterloo tube/rail. **Open** 10am-midnight daily. Closed 25 Dec. **Admission** (LP) free. *Games* prices vary. **Map** p319 M9.
Children pester hard to be let into this noisy, dark, two-storey amusement arcade within County Hall. Come-hither video games line the walls offering the opportunity to splatter the guts of virtual enemies and hear their repetitive screams or risk death on clifftop car chases. Old-fashioned one-armed bandits and shooting games hold out the prospect of glittering riches. Downstairs there is a 12-lane bowling alley, plus a dodgem arena with reputedly the fastest bumper cars in Europe, dance machines, and seven-table pool hall in an over-18s bar area where a wall of TV screens is permanently tuned to the sports channel. Next door is McDonald's. You could waste hours, and much pocket money, here.
Bar. Lifts. Buggy access. Nappy-changing facilities. Nearest picnic place: Jubilee Gardens.

Old Operating Theatre, Museum & Herb Garret
9A St Thomas's Street, SE1 (7955 4791/ www.thegarret.org.uk). London Bridge tube/rail. **Open** 10.30am-5pm (last entry 4.45pm) daily. Closed mid Dec-early Jan. **Admission** (LP) £3.75; £2.75 concessions; £2.25 6-16s; £9 family (2+4); free under-6s. **No credit cards. Map** p321 Q8.
This genuine Victorian operating theatre attached to St Thomas's Hospital is the centrepiece of a museum whose education staff run talks and demonstrations to young people. Pills and Potions, aimed at 7-11-year-olds, shows the manufacture of medicines from herbs into tablets, infusions, and creams. Victorian Surgery, suitable for less squeamish older students, includes the gruesome enactment of an amputation from around 1850 using a volunteer from the audience and real antique surgical equipment, which sounds appalling but guinea pigs retain all their limbs and no blood is spilled. Students, then as now, watch in nauseated wonder from the tiered observation gallery as the patient is laid on a wooden operating table resembling an old ironing board. The theatre was installed in this ancient church bell-tower in 1821 because the hospital wards abutted it and it was a simple job simply to knock through the walls. The theatre and garret were closed in the 1860s when the hospital moved to its present site at Lambeth opposite the Houses of Parliament. No one thought to look behind its locked doors again until 1956. Exhibits in the herb garret illustrate the history of

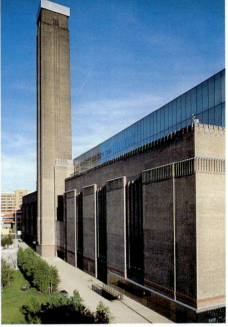

State of the art. **Tate Modern.** *See p47.*

medicine and nursing at Guy's and St Thomas's hospitals. Jars filled with formaldehyde preserve fascinating specimens. Horrifyingly large bladder stones lurk in one; in another a polluted lung shows the debilitating effects of London's famous 'pea-soupers', the thick yellow fogs that caused so much respiratory failure during the last century. Note if you have a child in a pushchair that a spiral staircase of 32 steps leads up to the museum and there are no lifts.
Nearest picnic place: Southwark Cathedral Gardens. Shop.

Royal National Theatre
South Bank, SE1 (info 7452 3400/box office 7452 3400/www.nationaltheatre.org.uk). Waterloo tube/ rail. **Open** Box office 10am-8pm Mon-Sat; 4-8pm bank hols. Closed 24, 25 Dec, Good Friday. **Tickets** *Olivier & Lyttelton* £10-£33. *Loft* £12. *Cottesloe* £10-£27. Standby £8, £16. *Backstage tours* £5; £4.25 concessions. **Credit** AmEx, DC, MC, V. **Map** p320 M8.
Sir Denys Lasdun's blockish concrete theatre complex has three famous stages: the Olivier, the Cottesloe and the Lyttelton. In an effort to draw more under-30s into the theatre, director Trevor Nunn, getting ready to leave in 2003, oversaw the splitting of the Lyttleton Theatre into two separate performance spaces: the Lyttelton and the Loft. The first Loft performance took place in April 2002. Although the new Loft cuts through the old theatre space, the design allows for the traditional proscenium arch to be reverted to in the future.
Thankfully, the spate of building work has not affected the programme available to children. Activities take place in all school holidays. These usually involve bookable workshops or foyer theatre, although the summer months are given over to the annual festival of outdoor theatre.
Backstage tours (not suitable for under-7s) occur three times a day throughout the year, last an hour and may be booked at the information desk. Tours take in the rehearsal rooms, workshops where costumes and props are made, dressing rooms, and the stage, where the guide demonstrates some of the more exciting items of stage machinery like the flying

harnesses. Unfortunately you cannot try them out. Free, informal foyer concerts take place daily at 6pm.

The National Film Theatre, nearby, has its own excellent film club for young people (Movie Magic; *see p219*). *Buggy access. Cafés. Lifts. Nappy-changing facilities. Nearest picnic place: Bernie Spain Gardens. Restaurants. Shop.*

Shakespeare's Globe

21 New Globe Walk, Bankside, SE1 (7902 1500/ www.shakespeares-globe.org). Mansion House or Southwark tube/London Bridge tube/rail. **Open** *Tours & exhibitions* May-Sept 9am-12.30pm daily. Oct-Apr 10am-5pm daily. Closed 24, 25 Dec. *Tours* May-Sept 9am-noon daily. Oct-Apr 10am-5pm daily. *Virtual (video screen) tours* mid May-late Sept 12.30-5pm Tue-Sun. **Admission** *Late Sept-mid May* £8; £5.50 5-15s; £6.50 concessions; £24 family (2+3); free under-5s. *Mid May-late Sept (exhibition only)*£5; £4 concessions; £3.50 5-16s; under-5s free. **Credit** MC, V. **Map** p320 O7.

School students of Shakespeare enhance their researches with organised excursions to this amazing reconstruction of the Bard's own theatre, the 'wooden O' referred to in *Henry V*, built only 100 yards from where the original stood. The project was masterminded and paid for by the American actor Sam Wanamaker, who was astounded that no memorial to Shakespeare existed in the area where he lived and worked. The construction is entirely authentic: the beams are oak, the walls are wattle and daub, the roof is thatched, and wooden pegs hold everything together. Actor-led tours and workshops take place throughout the year and include attendance at staged performances from April to September. The weather precludes winter acting as it did in Shakespeare's day. Tours include backstage visits.

The theatre lies behind iron gates and beyond the administration buildings housing the box office, café, shop and museum on two floors. Exhibits here include few period artefacts but plenty of costumes, props, touch-screen information posts and models of the theatres in Southwark at the end of the 16th century. Sadly, Sam Wanamaker did not live to see his undertaking completed but his name lives on in the Globe.

So do those of the benefactors, which have been etched into the stone paving slabs surrounding the theatre and include many leading thespians of the post-war era. *Buggy access. Café. Nappy-changing facilities. Nearest picnic place: Southwark Cathedral Gardens. Restaurant. Shop.*

South Bank Centre

Belvedere Road, SE1 (box office 7960 4242/Gamelan workshops 7921 0848/poetry workshop info 7921 0953). Waterloo tube/rail. **Open** 10am-10pm daily. Closed 25 Dec. **Admission** free to foyers. **Map** p319 M8.

This haven of art and learning goes out of its way to encourage visits from the young. School groups, youth clubs and playschemes choose between four activities. The most popular is the Gong Club, a Gamelan workshop during which children get acquainted with Indonesian percussion (*see p214*). Ring for details of the poetry workshop.

The Maths Trail is aimed at 5-11-year-olds or candidates for Key Stages 1 and 2 and involves touring the centre while filling in a worksheet available from the information desk on Level 2. Anyone may do this without official supervision, although parents may need to be on hand to explain what several of the terms mean. If that all sounds too educational, children can spend the day surfing the concrete in the skateboarding pit beneath the Queen Elizabeth Hall. *Buggy access. Cafés. Lifts. Nappy-changing facilities. Nearest picnic place: Jubilee Gardens. Restaurants. Shops.*

Southwark Cathedral

Montague Close, SE1 (7367 6700/tours 7367 6734/ www.dswark.org). London Bridge tube/rail. **Open** from 8am daily (closing times vary, depending on religious holidays). *Tours* phone for details. **Services** 8am, 8.15am, 12.30pm, 12.45pm, 5.30pm Mon-Fri; 9am, 9.15am, 4pm Sat; 8.45am, 9am, 11am, 3pm, 6.30pm Sun. **Choral Evensong** 5.30pm Tue (full choir); 5.30pm Thur (girls); 5.30pm Fri (men); 4pm Sat (visiting choir); 3pm Sun (cathedral or visiting choir). **Admission** (LP) *Exhibition* £3; £2.50 concessions; £1.50 1-11s; £12.50 family (5+2); free under-1s. *Audio tour* £2.50; £2 OAPs; £1.25 under-16s, students. **Credit** AmEx, MC, V. **Map** p321 8P.

Water ways: wildlife superhighway

Bankside Pier and Bankside Steps are beside the new Globe Theatre. From the former you can take river boats up and down the Thames. On the latter you can descend to the water's edge. When the tide is out, 'beaches' of alluvial sand and mud are exposed. There are no boundaries to how far you may walk, but you must be careful that you do not get trapped when the tide starts to rise again. These stretches are much used by treasure hunters with metal detectors strapped to their backs. Mostly they just pick up signals from discarded Coke cans but occasionally they find something Saxon or Roman. This may not be so unusual. After all, no one took the ancient city away. It is still there, buried beneath the present metropolis.

Low tide is feeding time for large numbers of birds, which use the Thames as a 'wildlife superhighway', as environmentalists are fond of saying. A billboard at the top of Bankside Steps identifies both predators and prey. Ornithologists

estimate that there are more birds visiting London each year than there are passengers passing through Heathrow Airport. At least 40 species make permanent homes on the river. Seagulls are too obvious to mention although it is still a pleasant surprise to see them and hear their plaintive cries as even locals are wont to forget that London is a seaside city.

Herons roost on upstream Thames islands like Chiswick Eyot (pronounced 'Eight') but are often to be seen stalking their dinner among the 400 species of invertebrates along the banks at Southwark. They stand motionless in the mud so that at first you may think they are driftwood washed up by the tide. Blink and you miss their darting attack. They are executioners with their long beaks of crabs, snails, ragworms, leeches, lice and opossum shrimps. Herons are not alone, although they are the most spectacular, especially if you catch one performing a mating dance.

The ancient cathedral at the heart of Southwark now has beautiful new family-friendly buildings and gardens. The newly landscaped churchyard is a pleasant place to picnic. Inside, the cathedral shows the work of many centuries. There are Roman mosaics in the south aisle and medieval stonework in the transepts, while the nave is Victorian. The contemporary millennium grant buildings include a library, refectory and museum, which displays relics of the centuries found during excavations.

The cathedral commemorates many historic figures and events. The Harvard Chapel recalls John Harvard's baptism in the cathedral. Immortalised in stained glass are Chaucer, who set off for Canterbury from a pub in Borough High Street; John Bunyan who preached in the vicinity; and John Gower, the so-called first English poet. At the east end of the cathedral there is an Aids memorial chapel and at the west a large marble slab inscribed with the names of the people who died in the *Marchioness* boat disaster in 1989.

Southwark has both a boys' and girls' choir, which sing five services a week; applicants are always welcome.
Buggy access. Lifts. Nappy-changing facilities. Restaurant. Shop.

Tate Modern

Bankside, SE1 (7887 8000/www.tate.org.uk). Southwark tube. **Open** 10am-6pm Mon-Thur, Sun; 10am-10pm Fri, Sat. Closed 25, 26 Dec. *Tours* 11am, noon, 2pm, 3pm daily. **Admission** free. *Tours* free. **Map** p320 O7.
The old Bankside Power Station is the home of the Tate's modern art collection. The vastness of the space and the lure of the sloping runway into the Turbine Hall from the west entrance are irresistible to children, who gallop down it in carefree fashion. The whole place is huge and awe-inspiring, and when it's not being used for exhibitions, the hall, with the gantries and pulleys from its past industrial life still hulkingly present, is left as an architectural space.

Galleries run along a slice of the building on its northern face, and are arranged thematically rather than chronologically or by place of origin. The shop should also be explored, for its trendy stationery, fridge magnets, quality books and

Cormorants, black-headed gulls, tufted ducks, teals, widgeons and gedwalls that live on the lakes in London's parks also come to feed at the river. Their presence is evidence of fish. Some 120 species now swim in waters that from 1900 to 1950 from Greenwich to Kew Bridge were so polluted that they were bereft of life. Now even salmon thrive, as well as North Sea flounder and seabass, which swim with the incoming tide.

Besides the fish, the invertebrates and the birds, there is one familiar four-legged Londoner that is occasionally to be seen scavenging at twilight for carrion or whatever it can find on the sandbanks – the fox. One has dug a hole in the bank beneath the MI6 building at Vauxhall. It is really a spy reporting on suspicious new arrivals in the Thames basin from less friendly parts of the world. Another has made a home of the Dome. This cheeky rent-free squatter deserves nothing but admiration.

so on. The top-floor restaurant, with its glorious views across the river, is generally packed at lunchtime; its pastries, sandwiches and drinks in the cafés are good but pricey, so save money and bring your own sandwiches to eat outside on the lawn. There's also an outdoor coffee and ice-cream stall, on the north side of the building, which provides better refreshments than the ice-cream vans along the South Bank.

Shuttle buses and boats wend their way between the Tate Modern and Tate Britain (*see p87*). For more information on art, trails and activities, *see p218*.
Buggy access. Cafés. Lifts. Nappy-changing facilities. Nearest picnic place: Tate Modern grounds. Restaurant. Shops.

Winston Churchill's Britain at War Experience

64-6 Tooley Street, SE1 (7403 3171/ www.britainatwar.co.uk). London Bridge tube/rail. **Open** *Apr-Sept* 10am-5.30pm daily. *Oct-Mar* 10am-4.30pm daily. Last entry 30mins before closing. Closed 25, 26 Dec. **Admission** £6.50; £4.50 concessions; £3.50 5-16s; £15 family (2+2); free under-5s. **Credit** AmEx, MC, V. **Map** p321 Q8.
This is a suitably shabby re-creation of Blitz-time London, with a nostalgic soundtrack of '40s radio broadcasts and showtunes. The highlight of a visit for children is the huge darkened, bombed street, where gruesome images of dummies' legs poking out from under piles of rubble make adults tut and children goggle. There is a lot of fascinating memorabilia, if you care to look for it among the muddled wall displays, a funny display of wartime fashions and economies (witness the cardboard wedding cake) and children also enjoy the atmospheric reproductions of an air raid shelter. During the school holidays, children are given a quiz sheet and the opportunity to dress up in interesting helmets and military workwear.
Buggy access. Nearest picnic place: Southwark Cathedral Gardens/William Curtis Park. Shop.

Where to eat

Two of the smartest restaurants in the area are called **fish!**. There's one just beside Southwark Cathedral (Cathedral Street, SE1, 7234 3333; *see also p171*) and one near County Hall (3B Belvedere Road, SE1, same phone number). **Café 2**, on the second floor of Tate Modern, (7401 5014) has high chairs and is a fabulous place to lunch if you can bag a table. **Southwark Cathedral** has its own refectory (7407 5740), where lunch is served from noon to 2.30pm and the cakes are yummy. High chairs are provided and the atmosphere is sedate. A jolly restaurant around here is **Cantina del Ponte** (Butlers Wharf Building, 36C Shad Thames, SE1, 7403 5403), where a weekend kids' menu includes pizzas, salads, chicken and chips and ice-creams. Over by the Design Museum, which has a useful coffee shop and the expensive **Blue Print Café** (7378 7031), a Conran restaurant, is another outpost of the Conran empire, **Butlers Wharf Chop House** (Butlers Wharf Building, 36E Shad Thames, SE1, 7403 3403; *see also p170*), whose children's brunch menu is available at weekends. There's a **Pizza Express** at Shad Thames (7403 8484) too.

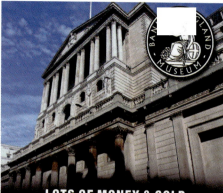

The City

London's heart of gold.

The City is the financial district of the capital, which means that, if you've got children with you, it might not be the most obvious place to visit. Yet to walk up through the ancient streets from Blackfriars station and come upon great **St Paul's Cathedral** looming out of the early morning mists is enough to stir the imagination of any child. There is romance in the winding Dickensian alleys with their quaintly ecclesiastical names – Sermon Lane, Paternoster Row, Amen Corner. There is eerie history in the remnants of the Romans who built the original city, christened it Londinium and lived in it for nearly 600 years. Lengths of the strong defensive wall they built to keep out the barbarians in AD 200 still stand today. The wonderful **Barbican Centre** occupies the site of a Roman fort, and its café tables on the terrace look out over 1,500-year-old battlements. The solid, raven-filled and apparently permanent **Tower of London** has watched over many bloody events in the capital's history since William the Conqueror built it as a city stronghold against the rebels. The wealthy medieval merchants who were attracted to this centre of great power, who bankrolled monarchs and financed wars, have their legacy in the world-famous Stock Exchange and the awesome, glass-sided banks.

The opening of the Millennium (formerly known as Wobbly) Bridge has facilitated the flow of tourist traffic in and out of the City. Visitors no longer loiter around St Paul's once they've visited the cathedral, but circulate, crossing the river, to the many sights along the South Bank of the Thames and back. Teenagers with their skateboards and Rollerblades gather to show off their daredevilry in front of the crowds. The most foolhardy even skate down the steel banisters at the foot of St Peter's Hill. One day they too may grow into merchant bankers (if they haven't broken their necks by then).

Something to call home about. **St Paul's Cathedral.** *See p55.*

Walk: over the rickety bridge

▶ Start at Blackfriars station. Walk along **Queen Victoria Street** and turn left at the Goose at the Castle pub into **St Andrew's Hill**. Follow its narrow winding olde-worlde course past pubs and salad bars. Turn left at **Carter Lane** and immediately right into **Creed Lane**. Emerge into **Ludgate Hill**, where you will be greeted by the dramatic sight of St Paul's Cathedral bearing down on you. If it's before 10am and not too cloudy, the rising sun will make a great halo round the dome. And if it's before 9am you may see the choristers in their flapping black cassocks hurrying to or from their morning rehearsal.

▶ Approach the wide steps at the front of the cathedral but do not mount them unless you want to have a quick look inside. Instead, walk through **St Paul's Churchyard** to the north and east of the cathedral. Pass a statue of John Wesley preaching and a stone mound inscribed with a saying of Churchill – 'In war, resolution; in defeat, defiance; in victory, magnanimity; in peace, goodwill'. Admire the spreading fig trees and opulent laurel bushes in the well-tended gardens. Follow the churchyard path round past the east end of the cathedral between banks of

park benches lining the way like pews. Here you can see the imposing concrete prep school where the choristers board, even on Christmas Day.

▶ Leave the churchyard by the south-east gate and cross the site of **Old Change**, where in the 13th century bullion was changed into coinage. It is now a paved and cultivated sunken garden popular with skateboarders who love the feel of smooth stonework underwheel. Don't stand in one place too long or you'll be mown down by one. They have multiplied greatly since the opening of the **Millennium Bridge**, which you may now see as you look south from St Paul's.

▶ Cross Cannon Street and descend **St Peter's Hill** on the elegant new pavements, with buggy and wheelchair ramps, past the Centre Page pub and offices of anonymous financial institutions. There are plenty of places to sit and study newly installed abstract street sculptures – an eccentric arch, here, a wavy block there – erected arbitrarily on the pavement. Cross **Queen Victoria Street** and continue down past the modern red brick independent City of London School for Boys on your right. Step on to the **Millennium Bridge**, which was closed immediately after opening in 2000 because of its alarming wobble when large numbers of people used it. Many people still refer to it as the 'Wobbly Bridge'. The structure is delicate but sturdy. The walkway hangs from great steel cables stretching between the banks. They in turn are supported by the giant Y-shaped concrete piers resting on the riverbed. Look for the panorama plaques for upstream and downstream views on the railings as you walk across. What a lot of spires there are in the City, and what a lot of churches are named after Mary. Wave at passengers on river cruises passing beneath. On the southern end of the bridge there is a queasy view of the river flowing directly beneath your feet through the grille.

▶ Stepping off the bridge, turn left on to the piazza with its lawns and avenues of silver birches in front of the great **Tate Modern** art gallery (*see p47*). Walk westwards past the Founders Arms pub standing alone on the embankment overlooking the river and the cafés and shops that have opened around Falcon Point to cash in on the increased human traffic that the Tate and the Millennium Bridge now generate.

▶ Walk in a westerly direction toward Blackfriars Bridge but don't walk under it. Instead climb the stone steps up to the road and walk in a northerly direction along the eastern pavement. Arrive at the northern end of the bridge, to get back to the station where you began.

Bank of England Museum

entrance on Bartholomew Lane, EC2 (7601 5545/cinema bookings 7601 3985/www.bankofengland.co.uk). Bank tube/DLR. **Open** 10am-5pm Mon-Fri. Closed bank hols. *Tours by arrangement.* **Admission** *free; £1 audio guide. Tours free.* **Map** p321 Q6.

The Bank of England is not a place to cash travellers' cheques. This fascinating museum is the only part of the historical institution that has any dealings with members of the public. Schoolchildren of all ages come in groups; primaries watch a film, *The Curious History of Money,* about how people engaged in the clumsy act of bartering before money existed. Goods could only be exchanged for other goods, a sheaf of corn for a cudgel, say, or a loaf of bread for an animal skin. At the end of the film the children are invited to dress up as fishmongers, farmers or arms dealers and then to try their own hand at bartering. GCSE scholars, meanwhile, see the film *Ahead of the Game,* which drily explains the functions of the Bank of England and discusses the basics of economics. In the school holidays, staff supply visiting families with various quiz sheets and badges. Screening times vary, so ring in advance for details. Phone, too, for opening times during the holidays.

The museum is housed in several rooms of the original complex of buildings designed by the architect Sir John Soane. One room features a reconstruction of the original modest banking hall, complete with costumed dummies. Everywhere there are ancient heavy-framed pictures showing periwigged Georgians signing documents. Look out for the cheque for a million pounds. There are forgeries for which a 17th-century forger hanged (in the 13th century he would have had his testicles chopped off). But the museum doesn't remain totally in the past: the banking hall runs touchscreen tests on your fiscal know-how. In the central rotunda, a pile of 59 replica gold ingots holds no fascination, but two real ones, each worth £96,000, attract a crowd. In a separate room there is a display in humidified glass boxes of all the banknotes ever designed.

Buggy access. Nearest picnic place: St Paul's Cathedral garden. Nappy-changing facilities. Shop.

Barbican Centre

Silk Street, EC2 (7382 7105/box office 7638 8891/ www.barbican.org.uk). Barbican tube/Moorgate tube/ rail. **Open** 10am-6pm Mon, Tue, Thur; 10am-8pm Wed; noon-6pm Sun. **Admission** *£7; £5 concessions, 12-16s; free under-12s; phone to check.* **Credit** AmEx, MC, V. **Map** p320 P5.

A barbican is a fortified watch-tower and this magnificent arts centre, residence, botanical garden and library was built on the site of the Roman fort in Londinium. Ruined turrets and stretches of the old wall still stand – you can see them if you sit outside at the café tables by the lake of fountains or wander over to St Giles Church, where a plaque on the railings describes their history. The Barbican contains concert halls (it is home to the London Symphony Orchestra, which includes a monthly programme of family fun concerts in its repertoire), a theatre, cinema, art gallery, exhibition space, cafés and restaurants. The complex also incorporates the Museum of London (*see p52*), the Barbican Art Gallery, the Guildhall School of Music and Drama, and the smart City of London School for Girls. The library on Level 2 has an extensive children's section (*see p296*).

Schools in the area are invited to join the 'Adopt the Barbican' scheme, which now includes 12 local schools from Tower Hamlets and Islington. The idea is for teachers and pupils to build up a long-term partnership with the centre. The education department collaborates with teachers in designing and managing cross-arts projects inspired by the main Barbican programme. Schools' work is frequently exhibited in Art Space B, Level O.

LSO Discovery received a lottery grant to partly fund its project to buy and renovate the derelict church of St Luke, just north of the complex. It is hoped that the new education centre, performance and recording space at LSO St Luke's will be up and running by December 2002: a week of activities and performances is planned to celebrate its opening. To join the Family News mailing list and find out more about LSO and Barbican projects for children, call 7382 7049.

Bars. Buggy access. Cafés. Nappy-changing facilities. Nearest picnic place: Barbican Lakeside Terrace. Restaurants. Shops.

Broadgate Arena

Broadgate Circle, EC2 (7505 4068/ www.broadgateestates.co.uk). Liverpool Street tube/ rail. **Open** *Ice rink mid Oct-mid Apr noon-2.30pm, 3.30-6pm Mon-Thur; noon-2.30pm, 3.30-6pm, 7-10pm Fri; 11am-1pm, 2-4pm, 5-8.30pm Sat; 11am-1pm, 2-4pm, 5-7pm Sun. From Apr ring for details.* **No credit cards.** **Map** p321 Q5.

The Broadgate arena becomes an open-air ice rink for six months of the year. Though City workers inevitably like to show off their skills, any adults and children can enjoy the fun – there are even skates for 3-year-olds in the form of blades attached to the child's trainers.

When you've had enough of all that exercise, not to mention falling over, head for the restaurants and cafés in nearby Broadgate Circle or at Liverpool Street station. Alternatively, take a picnic to Finsbury Circus, which is the largest patch of grass in the City and very popular with local office workers. Phone for details of prices in winter 2002-3. The ice is melted in April, after which the arena becomes a venue for other events such as concerts and plays.

Buggy access. Lift. Nearest picnic place: Finsbury Circus.

College of Arms

Queen Victoria Street, EC4 (7248 2762/www.college-of-arms.gov.uk). Blackfriars tube/rail. **Open** 10am-4pm Mon-Fri. Closed bank hols. *Tours by arrangement* 6.30pm Mon-Fri; prices vary. **Admission** *free.* **Map** p320 O7.

This ancient institution dates from 1484, though the present building is from the 17th century. Despite the fact that it is very much concerned with families and their lineage, it's not the sort of place to visit with very young and/or noisy children. Royal heralds work here, granting and designing coats of arms and checking family pedigrees (the old-fashioned form of DNA testing). A large, roped-off throne bears the dark red Queen's Cushion, which has only been sat on three times (at each of the last three coronations) but is starting to look a little tacky. If you wish to trace your roots, ask to see the Officer in Waiting and expect to pay him a fee to look up the information (the price depends on how long it takes; if it's very quick it could be free). It helps to bring a family tree with you, going back as far as possible.

Nearest picnic place: St Paul's Cathedral garden. Shop.

Dr Johnson's House

17 Gough Square, off Fleet Street, EC4 (7353 3745/ www.drjh.dircon.co.uk). Chancery Lane or Temple tube/ Blackfriars tube/rail. **Open** *May-Sept* 11am-5.30pm Mon-Sat. *Oct-Apr* 11am-5pm Mon-Sat. Closed 24-26 Dec, 1 Jan, bank hols. *Tours by arrangement; groups of 10 or more only.* **Admission** *£4; £3 concessions; £1 under-14s; free under-5s; £9 family (2+unlimited children). Tours £3. Evening tours £10 incl refreshments.* **No credit cards.** **Map** p320 N6.

The great lexicographer had 17 homes in the London he never tired of. This is the only one left intact, filled with artefacts and mementoes from the man's life. No special arrangements are made for visiting children, who might find this place a little staid as a result. But instead of visiting the museum, your school could arrange for the curator to visit to present outreach workshop sessions on Johnson and 18th-century life. *Nearest picnic place: Lincoln's Inn Fields/The Temple. Shop.*

Guildhall

Gresham Street, EC2 (7606 3030/tours ext1463/ www.corpoflondon.gov.uk). Bank tube/DLR. **Open** *May-Sept* 10am-5pm daily. *Oct-Apr* 10am-5pm Mon-Sat. Last entry 4.30pm. Closed 25, 26 Dec, 1 Jan. *Tours* by arrangement; groups of 10 or more people only. **Admission** free. **Map** p320 P6.

For more than 800 years, the Guildhall has been the centre of the City's local government. The stunning 15th-century Great Hall was gutted during the Great Fire and again in the Blitz, but has been sensitively restored. It is decorated with the banners and shields of the 100 Livery Companies; the windows record the names of every lord mayor since 1189; and there are monuments to Wellington, Nelson, Churchill and the two Pitts. Look out for the oriental-looking statues of legendary giants Gog and Magog guarding the West Gallery. They are post-war replacements for originals destroyed in the Blitz; the phoenix on Magog's shield symbolises renewal after fire.

Meetings of the Court of Common Council (the governing body for the Corporation of London, presided over by the lord mayor) are held here once a month on a Thursday at 1pm, except during August (visitors are welcome; phone for dates). The hall is also used for banquets and ceremonial events. Below the Guildhall is the largest medieval crypt in London, which can be accessed as part of a guided tour only.

Buildings alongside this one include the Guildhall Library (partly financed by Dick Whittington's estate and the first local authority-funded public library), plus the Clockmakers' Company Museum and a shop with books on London. *Buggy access. Lifts.*

In & around: the Museum of London

These are interesting times for the Museum of London. Since it became free in December 2001, more visitors than ever are bustling along the windswept walkways above the Aldersgate roundabout to trace the history of the city. Having just celebrated its silver jubilee, the museum embarked on an ambitious programme of renovation to make it even more attractive. While the rebuilding and expanding is going on (the first phase should be over by April 2003), the museum will remain open; an exhibition called **Future Dimensions** even lets you in on the plans for improvement.

It's the representations of the past, however, that continue to fascinate people of all ages who wander the galleries. The museum, built on the site of a Roman fort, thoroughly tracks London's

Guildhall Art Gallery

Guildhall Yard, off Gresham Street, EC2 (7332 3700/ www.guildhall-art-gallery.org.uk). Mansion House or St Paul's tube/Bank tube/DLR/Moorgate tube/rail. **Open** 10am-5pm Mon-Sat (last entry 4.30pm); noon-4pm Sun (last entry 3.45pm). Closed 24-26 Dec, 1 Jan. **Admission** £2.50; £1 concessions; free under-16s. Free to all after 3.30pm daily, all day Fri. **Credit** *over £5* MC, V. **Map** p320 P6.

The Guildhall Art Gallery appeals to younger teenagers of an artistic bent. Nonetheless, school groups come not only to admire the art for its own sake, but also for the history and sociology of the capital depicted in the paintings. Teachers, applying in advance, receive a pack that tells them exactly how the exhibits accord with the National Curriculum. The 250 artworks on display are part of a collection of 4,000 owned by the local council, the Corporation of London. A computerised search facility, the Collage System, lets visitors carry out searches of the collections, and is also available online on the website.

The gallery has three floors. John Singleton Copley's *Siege of Gibraltar*, one of the largest paintings in Britain, can be viewed from both the upper and middle levels. It records a naval victory over the Spanish in 1782 and depicts, somewhat improbably, scenes of gentlemanly fair play, common decency and gallantry as the jolly British jacktars generously haul from the water those luckless *marineros* whose ships they have just torched and sunk.

On the top floor are paintings of London, including market, street, river and parliamentary scenes, dozens of cityscapes and portraits of dignitaries and former lord mayors of London. In the middle level (ground floor) there are contemporary paintings, including two new rooms devoted to numerous works of Sir Matthew Smith (1879-1959), a follower of Matisse and the vibrantly colourful Fauvists.

The basement houses the Victorian paintings that formed the bulk of the collection when the gallery was opened in the 19th century. It soon became renowned for daring exhibitions, especially of the Pre-Raphelite Brotherhood, whom Dickens derided and accused of blasphemy. The collection

fortunes, from its prehistoric beginnings among the lush swampy flood plains on which the Romans built the first important settlement. A surprisingly large amount of the Roman city has survived: the ruins of the gate to the fort are even visible in a locked room in the subterranean car park. Viewing is on the second Tuesday of every month at 11am and again at midday. Just turn up at either of those times at the reception desk in the museum.

The Roman Gallery is one of the most popular parts of the museum: a big attraction is the **Princess of the City**, the skeleton of a 20-year-old Roman woman, which was found in a stone sarcophagus at Spitalfields in 1999. School groups jostle with clipboards and pencils to draw the ancient bones, preserved in a glass coffin. A clay facial portrait of the woman has been created by a medical artist, and is displayed above the bones. The combined effect is quite chilling.

Other popular exhibits include the **Cheapside Hoard** (a cache of fine jewels, dating from 1560 to 1640, found in a box under a shop) and the **Great Fire Experience**, an illuminated model with sound effects and commentary depicting the fire that destroyed four-fifths of London in 1666. Reconstructions of Newgate prison cells, the lord mayor's ceremonial coach, and shop/restaurant interiors from Victorian and Edwardian London all help to create an atmospheric and informative experience. The **World City Gallery**, on the lower ground floor, shows how London became a metropolis. Highlights include a Victorian walk-through exhibition comprising original 19th-century shopfronts, and exhibitions on education, the Great Exhibition of 1851, rail travel, entertainments and the lives of the great and good of the period: Wellington, Elizabeth Fry, Queen Victoria and Mary Seacole are all honoured.

It would take a day to fully appreciate the treasures of the Museum of London, but after a couple of hours younger visitors may have had enough. You can break for lunch in the café, where the choices include a hot children's meal, or a sandwich box, or get some air outside.

For a change of scenery, follow the walkway that leads westwards along the north side of the London Wall. When you see the ruined turrets of the old Roman fort below, descend the steps to the **Barber Surgeon's Garden**. Here you can see the medieval turrets and the uneven outline of the old city wall. Barber Surgeons' Tower was built into the wall in the 13th century; its ruins now enclose a fragrant herb garden. In medieval times chaps who cut hair were also considered capable of assisting monks in medical matters. It's a scary thought: imagine Vidal Sassoon whipping out your tonsils while straightening your fringe!

From this garden, you can see the **Barbican Centre** (*see p51*) across the artificial lakes. However, there are no accessible bridges, and to reach the centre; you have to go back up the steps, and follow the signs. The Barbican is a lovely place to stop for lunch, take in an exhibition, browse in the library or catch a free foyer concert. Ring to see what's going on.

Museum of London

150 London Wall, EC2 (7600 3699/24hr info 7600 0807/www.museumoflondon.org.uk). Barbican or St Paul's tube/Moorgate tube/rail. **Open** 10am-5.50pm Mon-Sat; noon-5.50pm Sun. Closed 24-26 Dec, 1 Jan. **Admission** free. **Credit** Shop AmEx, MC, V. **Map** p320 P5. *Buggy access. Café. Lift. Nappy-changing facilities. Nearest picnic place: benches outside museum/grassy area by London Wall. Shop.*

Admire it close up at the **Tower Bridge Experience**.
See p56.

has a large number of Pre-Raphaelite paintings by Dante Gabriel Rossetti, William Holman Hunt and John Everett Millais, the founders of the movement.

The original gallery burned down during World War II, albeit with remarkably little damage to the collection. The excavations that were carried out for the new building in the 1990s revealed the remains of the ancient Roman 11,000-seat amphitheatre. Lines in the new courtyard show the curve of the gladiatorial arena. Plans to allow public access to the ruins are still at the talking stage.

Buggy access. Lift. Shop.

The Monument

Monument Street, EC3 (7626 2717). Monument tube. **Open** 9am-5pm daily. Closed 25-26 Dec, 1 Jan. **Admission** £1.50; 50p 5-15s; free under-5s. **No credit cards. Map** p321 Q7.

Children are quite easily persuaded of the excitement of climbing high towers, and the Monument, with its 311 steps, is the tallest isolated stone tower on earth. It is 200ft tall, the exact distance from the foot of the column to the site of the Pudding Lane Bakery where fire broke out. Here you also get the added benefit of receiving a certificate of accomplishment once you've made it back down again. The tower commemorates the Great Fire of London in 1666. It was built by Sir Christopher Wren, who was the chief architect in the reconstruction of the City after the conflagration. At its head is a flaming urn of gilt bronze. Relief sculptures at the bottom depict souls in hell and enumerate the losses. Because few people came to any harm, the fire was recognised as a hellfire warning from God not, alas, of dodgy building practices but of Roman Catholic Popery. A Latin inscription alleging this was erased in 1860.

Nearest picnic place: riverside by London Bridge.

Museum of Methodism & John Wesley's House

Wesley's Chapel, 49 City Road, EC1 (7253 2262). Old Street or Moorgate tube/rail. **Open** 10am-4pm Mon-Sat. Closed 25 Dec-1 Jan, bank hols. *Tours* ad hoc arrangements on arrival. **Admission** free. *Tours* free. **No credit cards.**

John Wesley opened this chapel for worship in 1778, and in 1981 a museum of his work was unveiled in the crypt. Children who have been booked on a tour in advance are given dressing-up clothes – a preacher's rig for boys and a housekeeper's outfit for girls. Nowadays we might blanch at such gender stereotyping, but in the 18th century things were different. Indeed, the methodical non-conformist religion of prayer and fasting that was founded by John Wesley and his brother Charles was much less child-friendly then than it is now among its 50 million adherents.

Highlights of the museum include the pulpit that John used and a large oil portrait of the tender scene at his deathbed. Guides can give religious, drama and music instruction if desired (the Wesley brothers wrote hymns, many of which are still in use and the chapel here is the actual one that John Wesley built and preached in). Children aged 7-11 are provided with colouring-in worksheets.

Wesley's house next door has been restored to its original Georgian interior design, right down to the paint that he might have chosen. In the kitchen and study you can see his nightcap, preaching gown and, bizarrely, his personal experimental electric shock machine. On the walkway to the Barbican above the southern end of Aldersgate Street stands the petrified tree under which Wesley saw the light. Free tours of the museum and house can be arranged on arrival.

Nearest picnic place: enclosed courtyard at entrance. Shop.

Postman's Park

between King Edward Street & Aldersgate Street, EC2 (7247 8548). St Paul's tube. **Open** 8am-dusk Mon-Fri. **Map** p310 O6.

This well-kept little garden in the heart of the City is famous for its Heroes' Wall, which has nothing to do with the Roman one buried underneath. The wall commemorates fatal acts of bravery. There are plaques to brave men, women and children who leapt in front of trains, entered burning buildings and drowned in treacherous lakes, while trying to save others. It makes touching reading. Postman's Park is a quiet sanctuary away from the traffic noise and endless road drilling that goes on in this part of the City, so it makes a handy spot for a picnic.

St Bartholomew's Hospital Museum

West Smithfield, EC1 (7601 8152/tours 7837 0546). Barbican or St Paul's tube. **Open** 10am-4pm Tue-Fri. Closed over Christmas & Easter periods & bank hols. *Tours* 2pm Fri. **Admission** free. *Tours* £4; £3 concessions; accompanied children free. **No credit cards. Map** p320 O6.

GCSE school groups studying the History of Medicine and Nursing add this small but fascinating museum to the circuit that also includes the Old Operating Theatre (*see p45*) and the Florence Nightingale Museum (*see p41*). It is situated on the ground floor of the north wing of St Bartholomew's Hospital, which, along with the church of St Bartholomew the Great, was built in 1123 by Rahere, a courtier of Henry I. The glass case of old gory instruments holds most fascination for young visitors. It contains a wooden head on which student doctors practised their drilling techniques, along with early stethoscopes, instruments for bleeding patients and restraining trusses. The more squeamish might prefer the display of nursing uniforms, which shows how closely care and femininity were associated in previous decades.

Buggy access. Nearest picnic place: hospital grounds. Shop.

St Paul's Cathedral

Ludgate Hill, EC4 (7236 4128/www.stpauls.co.uk). St Paul's tube. **Open** 8.30am-4.30pm (last entry 4pm) Mon-Sat; services only Sun, 25 Dec. *Galleries, crypt & ambulatory* 9.30am-4pm Mon-Sat. Closed for special services, sometimes at short notice. *Tours* 11am, 11.30am, 1.30pm, 2pm Mon-Sat. **Admission** (LP) *Cathedral, crypt & gallery* £6; £3 6-16s; £5 concessions; free under-6s. *Tours* £2.50; £1 6-16s; £2 concessions; free under-6s. *Audio guide* £3.50; £3 concessions. **Credit** MC, V. **Map** p320 O6.

After the fire. **The Monument.**

This inspiring structure is believed to be built on the site of a Roman temple to Diana. The first Christian church was built by King Ethelbert in AD604. It burned down, as did two more Saxon cathedrals thereafter. The Normans constructed 'Old St Paul's' at the end of the 11th century, and that was the one destroyed in the Great Fire of 1666. The present building was built in 35 years by Sir Christopher Wren, with a bit of help from his master builder, Thomas Strong.

The dome you see on the outside of St Paul's is not the one viewed on the interior: there's a dome inside a dome and the gap in between provides the means to access the galleries. The climb to the Whispering Gallery is the highlight of any trip, for visitors of any age (provided they can make it up the stairs). Two people standing diametrically opposite each other in the gallery will be able to hear each other even if they mumble. The uncomfortable feeling of vertigo is more acute here than it is higher up at the Stone Gallery or even the Golden Gallery, 530 steps above the street, both of which look out on to London spread out below.

The treasures of St Paul's are many. Holman Hunt's famous Pre-Raphaelite painting of the *Light of the World* hangs in the south aisle. So-called 'super-tours' allow visitors access to the choir to see the dark wooden stalls carved by Grinling Gibbons. They are filled most evenings of the year by the choir. Be sure not to miss the crypt, where Lord Nelson is buried in a magnificent tomb, alongside other British war heroes and Wren himself. In the clock tower on the West Front hangs 'Great Paul', the heaviest swinging bell in England. It is tolled daily at 1pm.

Everyone aged over 6 has to pay for the privilege of experiencing Sir Christopher Wren's masterpiece, and for any activities arranged by the education department. A new guidebook, the *St Paul's Cathedral Maths Trail*, aimed at 11-14-year-olds, is available at the cathedral bookshop (£3.99).

It requires children to visit specific locations in the building to count spires, floor tiles and so on, or to identify particular geometric shapes. Also available is the less taxing *St Paul's Explorers' Guide* (£1.99), for kids of all ages. *Café. Restaurant. Lifts. Nearest picnic space: Cathedral garden. Shop.*

Temple of Mithras

on the raised courtyard in front of Sumitomo Mitsui Bank/Legal & General Building, Temple Court, 11 Queen Victoria Street, EC4. Mansion House tube. **Open** 24hrs daily. **Admission** free. **Map** p320 P6.

During the third century AD, the rival cults of Mithraism and Christianity were battling for supremacy. The worship of the macho Persian god Mithras appealed particularly to Roman soldiers, and the troops on the British frontier built the small temple to their champion near this spot. The reconstructed foundations (which haven't changed since they were unearthed in 1954) aren't much to look at, but you can stop and rest awhile on the park bench provided.

Tower Bridge Experience

SE1 (7403 3761/www.towerbridge.org.uk). Tower Hill tube/London Bridge tube/rail. **Open** *Apr-Oct* 10am-6.30pm (last entry 5.15pm) daily. *Nov-Mar* 9.30am-6pm (last entry 4.45pm) daily. Closed 24-25 Dec. **Admission** (incl guided tour) £4.50; £3 5-15s, concessions; £16.50 family (2+3); free under-5s. **Credit** AmEx, MC, V. **Map** p321 R8.

This Gothic triumph of engineering, opened in 1894, was designed by Horace Jones, a City Corporation architect. Mr Jones died shortly afterwards. The 'experience' you pay for is a lift ride up to the top of one tower, along the high-level walkway, then another lift down the second tower. You also

Water ways: beachcombing

Because the Thames is a tidal river, long stretches of its stony beach are exposed at low tide twice a day. At certain points along the north and south banks, steps lead down to the water's edge. If you're wearing sturdy shoes but not your Sunday best, you might fancy a rummage down there. Children, of course, should always be accompanied by an adult.

Find the steps on the north side just to the east of the Millennium Bridge. Hold on tight as you descend, because as the algae-covered, slimy wooden stairs can be slippery. There are strangely inspiring views at the bottom, along the surface of the water under the famous bridges in either direction. Sniff the salty air.

Most of the stones are pebble-sized lumps of red housebrick that have been rounded, smoothed and eroded by the wash. Uninhabited seashells are a common find (inhabited ones are very rare). Walk eastwards over the crunchy ground. You can see how high the tide rises each day by the level of moss and algae on the wharf walls. There are always interesting looking objects to kick over, including bones, some of them disconcertingly large and possibly human. Bits of pottery – a few quite

possibly antique – catch the eye. More contemporary (and mundane) finds include bottle tops, slivers of glass, plastic detergent bottles, warehouse pallets and polystyrene cups. Rusting cables and metal pipes protrude from the shallows like devil's fingers. Surprisingly large lumps of wood lie sunk in sand. Are they the beams of wrecked ships? Sorry looking washed-up shoes and items of clothing are sobering.

If the tide is low enough, you can cross the wide inlet leading to the sign for the Samuel Pepys pub and the red-brick offices beside it. The river pebbles have left uncovered a band of grey, wet mud and silt higher up the beach. Avoid walking on this as it is very squelchy and you are liable to lose your footwear. Continuing past the supporting pillars of grand Vintner's Hall, still dripping with the last high tide, you walk under Southwark Bridge. There are two great hulks of barges resting on the sand. Turn left as soon as you have passed them and you find a set of steps here leading up to the Banker pub in Cousin Lane. Staff admit children as long as they are quiet and there is room for them to sit down. Check that their shoes and yours are not covered in river silt before entering.

Step back in time at the **Tower of London**.

watch a couple of video shows about the history of the bridge during your trip, but the best thing is the view – spectacular.

The tour ends in the engine rooms, which house the steam pump engines that were used to raise the bridge until 1976 (it's all done by electrics now). To find out when the bridge will next be lifted (it's usually at least once a day), and the name and type of vessel passing beneath, phone 7940 3984. There are one or two models of the bridge on the top level walkway and, at the end of the descent, a glass case containing the silver London Marathon cup, because Tower Bridge is where the race ends each year.

Buggy access. Lifts. Nappy-changing facilities. Nearest picnic place: William Curtis Park/Tower of London gardens. Shop.

The Tower of London

Tower Hill, EC3 (7709 0765/www.hrp.org.uk). Tower Hill tube/Fenchurch Street rail. **Open** *Mar-Oct* 9am-5pm Mon-Sat; 10am-5pm Sun. *Nov-Feb* 10am-4pm Mon, Sun; 9am-4pm Tue-Sat. Closed 24-26 Dec, 1 Jan. **Tours** *Beefeater tours* (outside only, weather permitting) free; half-hourly 9.25am-2.50pm daily. *Short talks* given by yeoman warder (40mins) free; advance tickets from kiosk outside Lanthorn Tower 3 times a day. **Admission** (LP) £11.50; £8.75 concessions; £7.50 5-15s; family £34 (2+3); free under-5s. *Audio guide* £3. **Credit** AmEx, MC, V. **Map** p321 R7.

William the Conqueror's stronghold has been the scene of various brutal beheadings in its time. Lady Jane Grey, the nine-day queen, was only 16 when she had her head chopped off on Tower Green in 1554. Indeed, five of the seven people ever dispatched here were women, two of them – Anne Boleyn and Katherine Howard – wives of Henry VIII.

Today, the tower is the UK's top heritage attraction, where the staff, from the 'Beefeaters', or yeoman warders, downward, collude to make a visit a memorable one for children. At half-terms and holidays, Family Trail booklets are available from the tent inside the main entrance at the West Gate. Beefeaters ham it up for the little ones and entertain groups of visitors with facts and anecdotes in booming military voices. A year-round calendar of exhibitions and holiday events

help children enjoy the drama of it all. Summer 2002 sees brave knights a clanking in special activities for children called Arming the Knight, Armed Combat and Archery. It's all about Edward I's knights in the 13th century and involves exhibitions of swordplay throughout the day (ring for details). October half-term events include Escape from the Tower, in which visiting children try to outwit the ghastly gaoler. Special workshops and fun days linked to Bonfire Night, Christmas and Easter are planned every year. At these times, costumed guides, minstrels and storytellers cut an entertaining dash around the medieval buildings: ring up or check *Time Out*'s Around Town listings to find out about events.

Children of a certain age show great interest in the Crown Jewels in the Jewel House, where the crowns and coronets in glass boxes glide by like prizes in a game show. Younger visitors, meanwhile, are more taken with the moving walkways. They're also fascinated by the sentries, who occasionally jerk into life or bellow, 'Make way for the Queen's guard!' at idling tourists who wander into their path.

Café. Nappy-changing facilities. Nearest picnic place: Trinity Square Memorial Gardens. Shop.

Where to eat

If you haven't had time to pack a picnic, any number of sandwich bars, and the ever-enticing **Pret a Manger** (a popular City branch is at 128 Bishopsgate, EC2, 7377 0056), will provide picnic fare to eat in the City's green spaces. These include the gardens of the **Barber Surgeons Hall** (*see p52*), the peaceful churchyard of **St Botolph** (Bishopsgate, EC2), **Postman's Park,** with its wall of moving tributes to individuals who died trying to save others, and the gardens of **St Bartholomew the Great** (*see p55* for both).

There are several branches of **Pizza Express**; the one at 125 London Wall (7600 8880) is a good bet for a decent lunch after a morning at the Museum of

London. The sleek **K-10** (20 Copthall Avenue, EC2, 7562 8510) is a popular and good-value kaiten-sushi bar (the eatables go round on a conveyer belt), with dishes for as little as £1. Children are welcome; they love the grooviness of it all, and most can find something delicious to eat: chicken teriyaki, for example or lovely tuna and salmon plates. **Café Flo** (38-40 Ludgate Hill, EC4, 7329 3900) has a children's menu (simple pasta dishes, sausage and mash, chicken and chips) and high chairs. **Futures** (2 Exchange Square, EC2, 7638 6341) is a pleasant restaurant with an imaginative healthy-eating menu that's open for breakfast and lunch. The great views of the striking Liverpool Street station arch are an added bonus, as are the high chairs if you've got little ones with you. If you're in the Barbican area, pop into **Quiet Revolution** (49 Old Street, EC1, 7253 5556) for a light lunch or coffee and cakes.

Raven mad

The ravens at the Tower of London have a lovely, long life, unlike some of its more famous human inmates. They have a keeper, or raven master, who gives them meat and vitamins, and makes sure his feathered friends are happy. This concern for the sooty birds may be because of the urban legend that states that if the ravens leave the tower, it will fall down and so will the monarchy. Or it may be because these are the only ravens left in the south-east (you can see them in the wild up north and in Wales), so they're quite precious.

The tower staff believe these birds are special. They love the talking one, Thor, who bids them good morning, and feel sorry for the senior citizen, a 21-year-old called Hardy, a large widower raven who lost his mate some time ago (ravens mate for life). The education department has created a workshop for nursery-school children (school groups only) based round the true story of Charlie the Raven. It's about a Welsh boy who rescued a raven, grew up, joined the army, took a posting at the Tower and met again the bird he had saved. There's a book about Charlie in the shop. A nice postscript is that Charlie turned out to be Charlotte, as a clutch of eggs proved later.

Leave the raven-handling to the Master. Children are frequently warned not to touch the birds, but still the Tower Accident Book lists a sorry saga of nipped fingers and bruised pride. Ravens can be vicious. In the days of public execution when the heads of traitors would be impaled on poles outside the gates, the ravens made themselves useful by picking off the flesh and swallowing the eyeballs. This has given them a bad reputation and accounts for the collective term that describes them – an unkindness.

Bloomsbury & Holborn

Best of British.

The **British Museum**'s Great Court.
See p60.

Children rule at **Coram's Fields**. This prince of playgrounds has a notice on its gate permitting the young to bring adults in if they are well behaved and do not embarrass them by shouting at them across the grass or removing food stains from their faces with tongue-moistened hankies. Coram's Fields is the most child-friendly bit of Bloomsbury and Holborn, an area that fills the gap between the City and Westminster. Education is the name of the game here – humanitarianism, philanthropy, learning and self-improvement characterise the institutions in the area. Thomas Coram's playground replaces the sanctuary he built for lost orphans, waifs and strays. Nearby is the Great Ormond Street Hospital. There is something poignant about the toys you can see in the windows of the wards from the street below, just as there is in the elderly teddies and one-eyed dolls destined never to leave **Pollock's Toy Museum**.

Humility possesses the crowd who loiter at the impressive columned portals of the **British Museum**. Even this vast repository contains only the tiniest fraction of the sum of all knowledge. Books struggle to keep up. So many have now been written that they have forced the **British Library** to move to modern new premises where students read computer screens and books are stored as

relics. The collections of Samuel Courtauld, Arthur Gilbert and Tsar Nicholas I fill the rooms around the fountain-filled courtyard at **Somerset House**. Sir John Soane turned his house into the **Sir John Soane's Museum** and William Petrie scoured the cradle of civilisation for mementoes, which he gave to the university as the **Petrie Museum of Egyptian Archaeology**. No one, however, did more for the health of humanity than Sir Joseph Bazalgette, who reorganised the city's plumbing and made our toilets the envy of the world (*see also p65*).

British Library

96 Euston Road, NW1 (7412 7332/education 7412 7797/ www.bl.uk). Euston or King's Cross tube/rail. **Open** 9.30am-6pm Mon, Wed-Fri; 9.30am-8pm Tue; 9.30am-5pm Sat; 11am-5pm Sun, bank hols. Closed 22-26 Dec, 1 Jan. **Admission** free; donations appreciated. **Map** p317 K3. The British Library is a reading room, research centre and repository of the nation's literary treasure. displayed in the John Ritblat Gallery include the Great Charter' of 1215, one of the first dec rights; the Lindisfarne Gospels of machine turning over the pages in glass case); *Alice's Adventures* Carroll; the *Jungle Book* by Rudy of 2002 a 1922 copy of *The Se* Lawrence (Lawrence of Ara' Philatelic Exhibition, recko the world, includes an Indian stamp of 1854 with the Queen's head on upside down, and one of only three 1847 penny orange-reds from Mauritius, worth a £1 million.

The King's Library, in the heart of the building, is the library of George III, and is housed in a six-storey glass tower beside the café. No wonder he went mad. In front of it is a temporary exhibition of letters, photographs and annotated Shakespeare texts belonging to the actor Sir Ralph Richardson, the third and oldest of the great acting triumvirate including Sir Laurence Olivier and Sir John Gielgud. The foyer currently has a further temporary exhibition devoted to the life of Queen Elizabeth the Queen Mother. Exhibits relating to the years 1900-52 are drawn from the British Library's Newspaper Library and National Sound Archive. You can hear her delivering a sturdy speech to the Women of Empire in 1939.

The Education Office has an energetic staff devoted to dreaming up exotic workshops, activities and storytelling sessions for children aged 5-11 and their families to enjoy. The events are usually run during school holidays and half-terms and are always free, run on a drop-in basis. You can have advance notice of these by joining the Education Department's free mailing list: Education Service, British Library, 76 Euston Road, London, NW1 2DB, or by calling 7412 7797 or by logging on to the website.

Buggy access. Café. Nappy-changing facilities. Lift. Nearest picnic place: St James' Gardens. Restaurant. Shop.

British Museum

Great Russell Street, WC1 (7636 1555/textphone 7323 8920/www.thebritishmuseum.ac.uk). Holborn, Russell Square or Tottenham Court Road tube. **Open** *Galleries* 10am-5.30pm Mon-Wed, Sat, Sun; 10am-8.30pm Thur, Fri. *Great Court* 9am-6pm Mon; 9am-9pm Tue, Wed, Sun; 9am-11pm Thur-Sat. Closed 24-26 Dec, 1 Jan. *Highlights tours* 10.30am, 1pm, 3pm daily; phone to check. *EyeOpeners tours* frequently; phone to check. **Admission** (LP) free; donations appreciated. *Temporary exhibitions* prices vary; phone for details. *Highlights tours* £8; £5 concessions, 11-16s; free under-10s. *EyeOpeners tours* free. **Credit** MC, V. **Map** p317 K5.

When visiting this world-famous museum, there are two cardinal rules: go early, and don't try to see everything. A good introduction for novices is the 90-minute Highlights tour of the museum's top treasures (starting from the information desk), and the 50-minute EyeOpeners tours, which concentrate on specific aspects of the collections (such as Europe: Medieval to Modern or Treasures of the Islamic World). Alternatively, there are family themed trail leaflets (£1, available from the information desk) to follow such as the Queen's Trail (May-September 2002), which directs visitors to objects owned by queens past and present in celebration of Elizabeth II's Golden Jubilee. Family backpacks (which you have to give

In & around: Coram's Fields

This wonderful adventure playground was established in 1936 on the site of the 18th-century Foundling Hospital, after a public campaign to save the site from development. The Foundling Hospital was demolished in the 1920s (only the Georgian colonnades remain to enclose the site from the busy streets of Holborn). The site that the hospital occupied is now given over to the kind of play area that any family with young children would love to have in their neighbourhood. There are lawns, huge sandpits, an astroturf football pitch, an asphalt basketball court, a toddlers' gym and fenced-off play areas with a three-storey wooden climbing tower, a helter-skelter chute, swings and an assault-course pulley and quarters for sheep, goats, geese, ducks, rabbits and lots of aviary birds. For the under-3s there's a drop-in centre with messy play on a daily basis and occasional clowns' visits in summer. There's also a café, toilets and shower rooms with full facilities for the disabled, two large halls, a nursery, an under-5s playgroup and after-school and holiday play centres. Within the park an extensive programme of sports and activities is open, all free of charge; ring the office to receive a programme of events.

At the centre of the park a small bandstand is dedicated to the memory of two of Lord Rothermere's sons who died in World War I; in front of it a paddling pool provides welcome relief on hot summer days. Everything is free except the café, which runs to jacket spuds when the weather [is] cold. Adults must be accompanied by a child, [no] dogs, alcohol or glass bottles are allowed.

North of Coram's Fields is Coram Campus, home to Coram Family and other voluntary organisations. Coram Family continues its founder's work by organising adoption schemes, a teenage parents project and a parents' drop-in centre with a crèche where under-5s may spend a morning singing, painting and dancing with their parents in attendance. The Thomas Coram Early Childhood Centre next door is a Camden council nursery.

The Foundling Museum at 40 Brunswick Square reopens in spring 2003. The exhibits are those that attracted the 18th-century public to the Foundling Hospital. The artist Hogarth, who was a friend of the hospital's founder Thomas Coram, thought that it would raise the profile of the hospital and the foundling project if he and other artists including Reynolds and Gainsborough were to establish a gallery there. The idea was a considerable success and the gallery became the first public art exhibition space. Another artist who lent his genius to the cause was the composer Handel, who gave more than 1,000 performances of his *Messiah* for the benefit of the hospital. These were the first charity concerts. Handel donated a copy of *Messiah* to the hospital, which also owns his organ and the manuscript of his Foundling Hospital anthem, which he composed especially for it.

When the museum reopens, it will revive the spirit of child philanthropy by incorporating an education centre to run both schools events and play schemes as well as a new gallery space for the exhibition of paintings by schoolchildren.

back to the museum) relate to various specific exhibitions and contain items for discussion – the Aztec pack includes cocoa beans and a piece of turquoise, for example.

Among other special exhibitions, there is Brief Lives (until 18 September 2002), a reflection on the histories of the currencies of those 12 European nations that adopted the Euro at the start of 2002, and Discovering Ancient Afghanistan: the Masson Collection (12 September 2002-9 January 2003), a study of the troubled past of a country thrust into the news recently. A major temporary display is the Story of the British Museum (June 2002-October 2003), which recounts the history of the collection, from Sir Hans Sloane's sale of artefacts to the government in 1753, to the construction of the beautiful Great Court at a cost of £100 million in December 2000. A turning point in the story was the construction of the neo-classical buildings in 1852, which then also included the British Library (*see p59*) with its magnificent domed Reading Room, which is now a computer-equipped public library focused on the collections of the museum.

One of the museum's most renowned exhibits are the Elgin Marbles, which are on the ground floor, in a gallery to the left as you walk into the Great Court from Great Russell Street. Also very popular are the Egyptian sculpture galleries, also on the ground floor, and the Roxie Walker galleries of Egyptian funerary archaeology on the first floor. Glass cases full of mummies, snatched from their resting places in the desert sand, are at the rear of the building (Montague Place) on the third floor.

The ever-popular sleepovers (based on different themes but children always doss down in the Egyptian sculpture gallery) are open only to Young Friends of the British Museum; the £17.50 annual membership also allows entry to Sunday sessions and receipt of the quarterly magazine *Remus*. If all this is too much for you before you even start, buy a souvenir guide (£6) and scrutinise the highlights, or enjoy one of the tours on the website without even leaving home.

Since December 2001, when various of London's major museums introduced free admission, the museum has seen a downturn in visitors. This is unfortunate for such an important institution as the BM. Make sure you don't miss its treasures. *Buggy access. Cafés. Lifts. Nappy-changing facilities. Nearest picnic place: Russell Square. Restaurant. Shops.*

Courtauld Institute Gallery

Somerset House, Strand, WC2 (7848 2526/education 7848 2922/www.courtauld.ac.uk). Covent Garden or Temple tube (closed Sun)/Charing Cross tube/rail. **Open** 10am-6pm (last entry 5.15pm) daily; *31 Dec* 10am-4pm; *1 Jan* noon-6pm. Closed 24-26 Dec. **Tours** phone for details. **Admission** £5; £4 concessions; free under-18s, students, registered unwaged. Free to all 10am-2pm Mon (not bank hols). *Annual ticket* £10. **Credit** MC, V. **Map** p319 M7. When Somerset House reopened in 2000 it brought with it three of London's most valuable art collections, namely the Courtauld, the Gilbert and the Hermitage (*see p62* for both).

A legacy of caring for children continues at the nearby Great Ormond Street Children's Hospital, which celebrates its 150th birthday in 2002. Until its establishment, children under 10 were simply excluded from medical care. This world-famous children's hospital is a 350-bed National Health Service institution, which means that it is partly funded by the taxpayer, but, as in most hospitals, much of the equipment, research and accommodation are paid for by private benefactors. One of these was the author JM Barrie, who bequeathed the copyright and all film, stage, television and book rights of his children's novel *Peter Pan* to the hospital in 1929.

Coram's Fields

93 Guilford Street, WC1 (7837 6138). Russell Square tube. **Open** *May-Aug* 9am-7pm daily. *Sept-Apr* 9am-dusk daily. Closed 25, 26 Dec. **Admission** free (adults only admitted if accompanied by child under 16). **Map** p317 L4. *Buggy access. Café. Nappy-changing facilities.*

Walk: law & order

This is a stroll among the narrow streets, ancient buildings and lawns of the Inner and Middle Temple, two of the four Inns of Court (the others are Gray's Inn and Lincoln's Inn), where barristers have their chambers.

▶ Start at Temple tube (closed on Sundays). Walk away from the river into **Temple Place** and turn right. Follow the road to its end and enter the grand, grassy courtyard of **Middle Temple**, a small haven of peace and gentility. Cross the courtyard northwards along its length until you come to **Fountain Court**, which Dickens described in *Martin Chuzzlewit*. On the south side is **Middle Temple Hall**, where Elizabeth I watched the world première of Shakespeare's *Twelfth Night* performed by the author and his troupe.

▶ Turn left at the eastern end of Fountain Court into Middle Temple Lane and right into **Pump Court**, one of the oldest parts of the Temple. The pump, which fed from a well, was destroyed in World War II. Turn left into **Inner Temple Lane** and exit into Fleet Street through the half-timbered gateway. Above is **Prince Henry's Room**, named after the elder son of King James I, who died before he could ascend the throne. Walk east along frantic Fleet Street and take a turn around Falcon Court, once the home of publishers. The works of Lord Byron first saw the light of day here. Turn right into Fleet Street and immediately right again into **Old Mitre Court**.

▶ Turn right through a narrow arch into the enclosed yard in front of **Temple Church**. The circular nave is unique and dates from the 12th century when the Knights Templar, the self-appointed vigilantes who set out to protect pilgrims en route to the Holy Land, returned to London and were granted this land by Henry I. When in the 14th century the Knights became too powerful and arrogant they were eventually discredited by the Pope and forced to disband. The lawyers moved in after them and have been here ever since. The east window contains London's finest modern stained glass. Opposite the church is Middle Temple Hall, dating from 1573.

▶ Leave the yard via Pump Court again, turn left at the end into Middle Temple Lane and head south past Fountain Court. Turn left into **Crown Office Row**, where the writer Charles Lamb, who popularised Shakespeare for the young in *Tales from Shakespeare*, spent his happy, bookish childhood. The Middle Temple Gardens stretch away to your right but they are private. At the end enter King's Bench Walk, which is used as a car park by lawyers. Leave the Temple by the barrier into Tudor Street, turn right into Temple Avenue and walk to the end. Turn right on to the Embankment and follow the river upstream back to Temple tube. Full circle, I rest my case.

The bulk of the Courtauld's collection is made up of the Impressionist and post-Impressionist works donated by textile magnate Samuel Courtauld, including Manet's *A Bar at the Folies-Bergère*, Cézanne's *The Card Players* and Gauguin's *Nevermore*. The first Saturday of the month, school holidays and half-terms are given over to family events. For details, *see p216*.

The Courtauld throngs with school groups armed with packed lunches and overalls most days of the week in term time. Those at Key Stages 1, 2 and 3 come from 10.30am until 2pm, enjoy a free guided tour and study paintings in connection with such themes as animals, Bible stories, weather, Greeks and Romans, and light and shade.

Buggy access. Cafés. Lift. Nappy-changing facilities (in Somerset House, near Gilbert Collection entrance). Nearest picnic place: Somerset House courtyard/ Embankment Gardens. Restaurant. Shop.

Gilbert Collection

Somerset House, Strand, WC2 (7240 4080/www.gilbert-collection.org.uk). Covent Garden or Temple tube (closed Sun)/Charing Cross tube/rail. **Open** 10am-6pm (last entry 5.30pm) daily; *31 Dec* 10am-4pm; *1 Jan* noon-6pm. Closed 24-26 Dec. **Tours** phone for details. **Admission** £5; £4 concessions; free under-18s, students, registered unwaged. Free to all after 4.30pm daily. *Annual ticket* £10. **Credit** AmEx, MC, V. **Map** p319 M7.

The second of Somerset House's treasures was the gift of the late Sir Arthur Gilbert, a British-born Californian businessman. It features more than 1,000 exhibits from the world of the decorative arts, including snuff boxes, silverware, mosaics and micro-mosaics from the 16th to 18th centuries. The pride of the collection is a magnificent silver swan, which was Sir Arthur's last acquisition. On temporary loan until December 2002 is King George III's 48-piece silver dinner service. Family events are held regularly throughout the year, with tours of the collection, often with costumed guides. Schoolchildren at Key Stages 1-4 study the artefacts in the collection to explore the history of Somerset House.

Buggy access. Cafés. Lift. Nappy-changing facilities. Nearest picnic place: Somerset House courtyard/ Embankment Gardens. Restaurant. Shop.

Hermitage Rooms

Somerset House, Strand, WC2 (info 7845 4630/ www.hermitagerooms.co.uk). Covent Garden or Temple tube (closed Sun)/Charing Cross tube/rail. **Open** 10am-6pm (last entry 5pm) daily; *31 Dec* 10am-4pm; *1 Jan* noon-6pm. Closed 24-26 Dec. **Admission** £6; £4 concessions; free under-16s. **Credit** MC, V. **Map** p319 M7.

Somerset House's third art collection is a rotating display of objects from the famous State Hermitage Museum in St Petersburg. Displayed in rooms decorated in the style of the original, new exhibitions arrive every six to ten months. Until 18 August 2002 paintings, drawings and sketches by the German artist Caspar David Friedrich (a favourite of Tsar Nicholas I) are on display. This is followed from 28 September 2002 until 9 February 2003 by a collection of Robert Walpole, the first British Prime Minister, which was sold to the Russians after his death. This is the first time it will have returned to the UK. Thereafter, from April to August 2003, the Russians' Rubens collection is in residence. With each exhibition comes a programme of events. To find out about what's going on here, and in the Courtauld and Gilbert collections, get yourself on the Somerset House mailing list (email info@somerset-house.org.uk or write in to request).

Buggy access. Cafés. Lift. Nappy-changing facilities. Nearest picnic place: Somerset House courtyard/ Embankment Gardens. Restaurant. Shop.

Pollock's Toy Museum.

Museum & Library of the Order of St John

St John's Gate, St John's Lane, EC1 (7324 4074/ www.sja.org.uk/history). Farringdon tube/rail. **Open** 10am-5pm Mon-Fri; 10am-4pm Sat. Closed 24 Dec-2 Jan, bank hol weekends; phone to check. **Tours** 11am, 2.30pm Tue, Fri, Sat. **Admission** free; suggested donations for tours £5; £3.50 concessions. **Map** p320 O4.

Though it's more Clerkenwell than Bloomsbury or Holborn, this crusading organisation should not be overlooked – it was out of the Order of St John that the St John Ambulance Brigade rose. Volunteers are trained in first aid and are often to be seen administering it at public events. Child recruits ('Little Badgers' and 'Cadets') are taught the rudiments of first aid and take exams in basic medicine, which, like taxi drivers, they call 'doing the knowledge'. The organisation also runs practical and adventure activities for children. Membership is free, though of course you have to buy the black and white uniform.

The museum traces the history of both the Ambulance Brigade and the Order of St John, which began in the 12th century when the crusading Knights Hospitallers acted as guards and superintendents at the Benedictine hospital next to the Holy Sepulchre in Jerusalem. Exhibits include pharmacy jars from the present-day hospital on the Gaza Strip. The magnificent gateway, which dates from 1504, was once the entrance to the Priory of St John of Jerusalem. The Chapter Hall, Council Chamber, Old Chancery, new church and Norman crypt (the sole survivor from the original building) can only be seen on a guided tour. All that remains of the priory's original circular church is its outline, traced in cobbles, in St John's Square just north of the gate. Note that there's buggy access for the ground-floor galleries only.
Buggy access. Shop.

Petrie Museum of Egyptian Archaeology

University College London, Malet Place, WC1 (7679 2884/www.petrie.ucl.ac.uk). Goodge Street tube. **Open** 1-5pm Tue-Fri; 10am-1pm Sat. Closed 24 Dec-2 Jan, Easter hols. **Admission** free; donations appreciated. **Map** p317 K4.

The late William Flinders Petrie, archaeologist and Egyptologist, donated his private collection to University College London (UCL) in the 1930s. It includes the oldest piece of clothing in the world (from 2,800 BC) and an array of Roman mummy portraits, as well as a dazzling collection of the minutiae of Egyptian life, from jewellery and ceramics to games and grooming accessories. Macabre exhibits include a 4,500-year-old exhumed pot-burial and the coiffured head of a mummy, with eyebrows and lashes still intact. New in 2002 is a 'handling box' of 11 relics from the Roman occupation of Egypt including a beautifully made ceramic jug, bowl and oil lamp, a bone hairpin, a steatite dish and a bronze statuette of a cat, Egypt's sacred animal. Handlers must wear gloves. There are worksheets on clothing, burial and writing to aid personal research, while family backpacks (available in the summer holidays) lead visitors on trails of exploration. Exhibits are relevant to the study of Ancient Egypt in Key Stage 2. Phone for details of guided tours.
Buggy access. Café. Lifts. Nearest picnic place: Gordon Square.

Pollock's Toy Museum

1 Scala Street (entrance on Whitfield Street), W1 (7636 3452/www.pollocksweb.co.uk). Goodge Street tube. **Open** 10am-5pm (last entry 4.30pm) Mon-Sat. Closed bank hols. **Admission** (LP) £3; £1.50 3-18s, students; free under-3s. **Credit** Shop MC, V. **Map** p316 J5.

Eight rooms of this slender four-storey Georgian townhouse contain thousands of children's toys from the last 150 years, from dolls as big as children, old teddy bears (Eric, stuffed and sewn in 1905, is apparently the oldest known surviving teddy in the world) and platoons of Action Men to miniature dolls' houses, clockwork tin railways and games of Pik-a-Styk, Snap!, Ring-My-Nose Quoits and Snakes & Ladders. It doesn't take much to imagine it all coming to life at night. Visitors pay at the old-fashioned till on the ground floor and go up through the house by one narrow, creaky staircase and down by another, finishing in the shop, which sells playing cards, jigsaws, marbles, magic sets and puppets. The toy theatre can be booked for parties (minimum ten children; admission charges as above) and school groups are welcome (call first).
Nearest picnic place: Colville Place Gardens. Shop.

Prince Henry's Room

17 Fleet Street, EC4 (7936 4004). Temple tube (closed Sun). **Open** 11am-2pm Mon-Sat. Closed bank hol weekends. **Admission** free; donations appreciated. **Map** p320 N6.

The eldest son of King James I of England and VI of Scotland, weakling Henry was only 14 when he became Prince of Wales in 1610, the same year the house containing this beautiful oak-panelled room, believed to have been used by the prince's lawyers, was built. Its magnificent plaster ceiling has the Prince of Wales's feathers at its centre, together with the initials PH. Henry died of typhoid at the age of 18, leaving his brother to succeed to the throne as Charles I and eventually have his head chopped off after a quarrel with Parliament.

The rest of the building was once a tavern called the Prince's Arms, which was frequented by the prolific writer Samuel Pepys, who enjoyed remarking upon London events his diary while relaxing down the pub. Various items the diarist left behind in the old tavern, including a letter he wrote, some model boats in glass cases, a number of framed pictures and a quill pen, are housed in Prince Henry's Room. *Nearest picnic place: Temple Gardens.*

Roman Bath

Strand Lane, WC2 (no phone). Temple tube (closed Sun). **Open** 10am-12.30pm Mon-Fri. **Admission** free. **Map** p319 M7.

Despite its name, no one knows the history of this intriguing relic in the basement of a building in an alley off the Strand. Dickens' hero David Copperfield bathes in it, and presumably the novelist did too. No longer used as a bath, it has limited opening hours but is visible at other times through a window and by means of a light switch in the wall outside.

St Clement Danes Church

Strand, WC2 (7242 8282). Temple tube (closed Sun). **Open** 9am-4pm Mon-Fri; 9.30am-3pm Sat, Sun. Closed bank hols. **Admission** free. **Map** p320 M6.

This church is almost certainly not the one that gave rise to the well known nursery rhyme 'Oranges and lemons say the bells of St Clements', (experts reckon that was St Clements, Eastcheap, Clements Lane, EC4, 7626 0210). Nonetheless St Clement Danes behaves as if it were – its bells ring out the famous tune three times a day (9am, noon and 3pm), and an annual Oranges & Lemons service is held in April for the children of St Clement Danes Primary School, Drury Lane, WC2, who perform a short play in exchange for a free orange or lemon. The church's curious name dates back to the time of Alfred the Great, when it was used by Danes married to English wives who were allowed to stay in England after their fellow countrymen were expelled. It's now the central church of the RAF; there's a statue of Arthur 'Bomber' Harris (responsible for the raids on Dresden) outside. *Buggy access. Nearest picnic place: Embankment Gardens.*

St Dunstan in the West

186A Fleet Street, EC4 (7242 6027). Chancery Lane tube. **Open** 10am-2pm Tue; 5-8pm Fri; 2-6pm Sat; 9am-2pm Sun. Closed bank hols. **Admission** free; donations appreciated. **Map** p320 N6.

You don't have to enter this church to see what's most interesting about it – the ancient clock on the outside, which was the first in London to acquire a minute hand, is attached to a great bell. This is struck at a quarter past the hour by two giant clockwork statues that emerge from the background with huge cudgels. Classical music concerts are sometimes held on a Friday, ring for details. *Buggy access.*

Somerset House. *See p65.*

St Etheldreda

14 Ely Place, EC1 (7405 1061). Chancery Lane or Farringdon tube. **Open** 8am-7pm daily; phone to check. Closed 26 Dec. **Admission** free; donations appreciated. **Map** p320 N5.

Britain's oldest Catholic church (built in the 1250s) is the only surviving building of the Bishop of Ely's London residence. Its simple chapel, lined with the statues of local martyrs, is London's sole remaining example (excepting parts of Westminster Abbey; *see p87*) of Gothic architecture from the reign of Edward I. The strawberries once grown in the gardens were said to be the finest in the city, receiving plaudits in Shakespeare's *Richard III*. Every June the church holds a Strawberrie Fayre in Ely Place, which is also the scene of important episodes in Dickens' *David Copperfield. Café (closed Sat, Sun).*

Sir John Soane's Museum

13 Lincoln's Inn Fields, WC2 (7405 2107/education officer 7440 4247/www.soane.org). Holborn tube. **Open** 10am-5pm Tue-Sat; 6-9pm 1st Tue of mth. Closed bank hol weekends. **Tours** 2.30pm Sat. **Admission** free; donations appreciated. *Tours* £3; free concessions, under-16s. **Credit** *Shop* MC, V. **Map** p317 M5.

A house full of the multifarious artefacts amassed by its architect-founder. In among the brilliant chaos, Cantonese chairs sit near vases dating from the fourth century BC; a tiny study is made smaller by the assortment of marble bits and pieces glowering from the walls; another wall is covered by Hogarth's *Rake's Progress* series but then opens up to reveal a stash of Piranesi drawings; and there's a huge 3,300-year-old Egyptian sarcophagus downstairs in the spooky crypt. The overall effect is stunning, especially on the first Tuesday of the month, when the house is lit by candles. Tickets for guided tours go on sale at 2pm in the library dining room, on a first-come first-served basis.

From September 2002 the museum spreads into the house next door, which was also owned by Soane but let to private tenants after his death. It will open to the public at the end of 2003. Although the architecture in the rooms has remained largely untouched, a restoration project is still necessary and the museum is looking for donors to contribute towards the

£3 million needed. The rooms themselves will be the exhibits. Some objects from the main museum will be moved in and a certain amount of space will be used to accommodate schools education programmes, which the museum introduced for the first time in spring 2002.
Nearest picnic place: Lincoln's Inn Fields. Shop.

Somerset House
Strand, WC2 (7845 4600/www.somerset-house.org.uk). Covent Garden or Temple tube (closed Sun)/Charing Cross tube/rail. **Open** 10am-6pm daily; extended opening hours for Courtyard & River Terrace. Closed 25 Dec. **Tours** phone for details. **Admission** *Parts of South Building, Courtyard & River Terrace* free; charge for exhibitions. **Credit** *Shop* MC, V. **Map** p319 M7.
George III, whose statue stands inside the Strand entrance, commissioned this glorious building after its dilapidated predecessor was pulled down. Inside the southern (riverside) building, the information desk has six family trail leaflets directing the inquisitive to the various parts of the mansion and inviting them to make observations about what is to be found. There's also a full programme of free family events, including puppet performances, storytelling, dance masquerades and painting workshops in the various panelled rooms and the fountain courtyard, where children love to splash around in the water jets. In winter it has become customary to turn the courtyard into an ice rink, although no permanent commitment has been made and it would be wise to call for details before setting off with your blades.
The east and west wings are home to the Inland Revenue and are not accessible to the public, but the north and south blocks house three of the most valuable art collections in the capital, the Courtauld Institute Gallery (*see p61*), the Gilbert Collection and the Hermitage Rooms (*see p62* for both). *Buggy access. Cafés. Lift. Nappy-changing facilities. Nearest picnic place: Somerset House courtyard/ River Terrace/Embankment Gardens. Restaurant. Shop.*

Where to eat
The **North Sea Fish Restaurant** (8 Leigh Street, WC1, 7387 5892) is one of the best places to take children for a great British plateful of fish and chips, while pint-sized pasta fans can enjoy reduced-price portions and a cheery atmosphere at **Spaghetti House** (20 Sicilian Avenue, WC1, 7405 5215). **Heal's** homewares shop (196 Tottenham Court Road, WC1, 7636 1666) has an excellent café for those who like to scoff and shop. Huge, noodle-based lunches are available at branches of **Wagamama** (4A Streatham Street, WC1, 7323 9223 and 14A Irving Street, WC1, 7839 2323; *see also p181*) and rather lighter options are served by friendly staff at the local Japanese, **Abeno** (47 Museum Street, WC1, 7405 3211), where little ones are given high chairs. More attractively presented Japanese delicacies are on the menu at the nearby branch of **Yo! Sushi** (myhotel, 11-13 Bayley Street, Bedford Square, WC1, 7636 0076; *see also p179*).

Around Town

Water ways: go with the flow

Although drainage is the primary function of a river, even the mighty Thames was unable to cope with all the effluence that Londoners by the middle of the 19th century were tipping into it and its tributaries. In fact, until it was related to health concerns, this was not considered particularly worrying apart from the terrible smell in hot weather. Indeed, matters worsened when in the 1840s London almost suffocated in what became known as the Great Stink (*see p16*) and Parliament, thinking to right the situation, decreed that the basement cesspits, which existed in almost all London houses, were henceforth prohibited. Unfortunately, this meant that the citizens had no option other than to take their waste and empty it by the barrow-load directly into the city's rivers. In 1800 salmon still spawned in the Thames. By 1850 the only thing you could catch in it was cholera.

Then in 1854 a remarkable discovery was made by Dr John Snow who, by monitoring a Soho water pump and the people who used it, proved that germs were not spread by bad breath as previously thought but by bad sanitation. Although this only minimally widened the circle of a halitosis sufferer's number of friends, it completely put paid to the cholera bacterium and Western civilisation entered the modern hygienic era. Snow's discovery was followed up by the great Sir Joseph Bazalgette, who was given the task of constructing the 1,300 miles of sewers necessary to cope with the daily bowel movements of the six million-strong population of the city. His bust, stuck in a niche in a bit of wall above Victoria Embankment (which he also built; his sewers are underneath), opposite Embankment station, shows a smiling Victorian with a long pointed nose that looks as if it could smell a noxious vapour at a thousand paces.

Bazalgette's scheme involved sewers running alongside the Thames at three levels, which, using pump and gravity, channelled the sewage down towards the sea. There it was treated at special stations and either turned into fertiliser or shipped 50 miles out into the North Sea and dumped where it could not return up the Thames with the tide. The handsome brick-built pumping stations – which can still be seen at Kew Bridge, Pimlico, Deptford and Stratford – were constructed with much romantic Victorian pride. The huge steam-driven machines inside them were examples of 19th-century engineering at its finest. They have since been replaced by 20th-century machines, some powered by methane gas (sewage's most useful by-product) and housed at the former Kew Bridge pumping station, which is now the Kew Bridge Steam Museum (*see p166*). It is worth a visit.

Kensington & Chelsea

Arts and science celebrated in royalty's Never-Never land.

Getting a grip of things in the **Diana, Princess of Wales Memorial Playground**. *See p67.*

Kensington and Chelsea is the only part of London to be designated 'Royal'. It is sometimes referred to as 'RBK & C'. It became the Royal Borough in 1901 following the death of Queen Victoria, to mark the fact that she had spent her happy youth here. There is a statue of her as a slip of a girl outside **Kensington Palace**, where she was born in 1819. She was not the only princess to have loved the area. The **Diana, Princess of Wales Memorial Playground** in **Kensington Gardens** commemorates the residence here of royalty's most tragic princess. The playground was created in her memory after her death in 1997 for the exclusive pleasure of young people. It is full of references to the eternally young Peter Pan, whose creator JM Barrie lived nearby and strolled daily with his dog in the gardens.

Princes also came in carriageloads to this borough of opportunity. They built grand mini palaces, married the princesses, had children and spent their money at the now world-famous department store **Harrods** (*see p198*), which has a toy department to dribble over and an in-house pet shop where you can even order an elephant. Shopping is also a big feature of busy **Kensington High Street**, whose lively but laid-back mix of chain stores and individual shops makes a calmer alternative to the West End's Oxford Street.

Prince Albert, who married Princess Victoria and had nine children with her, brought the Great Exhibition to Hyde Park in 1851 and channelled the profits into schemes that built the famous museums here. The **Science Museum** houses the world's greatest inventions. The **Natural History Museum** celebrates life, much of it fossilised, in all its diversity. The **Victoria & Albert Museum** is a repository of all things beautiful, from sculpted marbles to Victorian playthings. For more on these great centres of learning, *see p70*.

Baden-Powell House

65-7 Queen's Gate, SW7 (7584 7031/www.scoutbase.org. uk). South Kensington tube. **Open** *7am-10pm daily.* Closed 22 Dec-3 Jan. **Admission** free. **Map** p315 D10. Money raised by millions of bob-a-job boy scouts and girl guides all over the world built this memorial hostel to Lord Baden-Powell (1857-1941), the founder of scouting. It was opened in 1961 and provides accommodation for about 300,000 people from 30 different countries each year. A modest exhibition on the ground floor gives an entertaining account of the life of the Chief Scout, as Baden-Powell styled himself. The canteen is open to all (parties of six or more should book in advance).
Buggy access. Café. Nappy-changing facilities. Nearest picnic place: Natural History Museum gardens. Shop.

Chelsea Physic Garden

66 Royal Hospital Road (entrance in Swan Walk), SW3 (7352 5646/www.chelseaphysicgarden.co.uk). Sloane Square tube/11, 19, 22, 239, 319 bus. **Open** *Apr-late Oct* noon-5pm Wed; 2-6pm Sun. *Tours* 1.30pm, 3.30pm (check blackboard to reserve); phone for group tours. **Admission** £4; £2 5-16s, students. *Tours* free. **Credit** *Shop* MC, V. **Map** p315 F12.
This enchanting high-walled garden was established in 1673 and developed by Sir Hans Sloane in the early 18th century. Its 3.5 acres contain healing herbs and rare trees, dye plants and medicinal vegetables; you can even buy some to take home. The garden is primarily a research and education facility, hence the rather limited opening hours. Children, however, are encouraged to visit the garden in school groups or to take part in regular activity days during the holidays. The education department organises craft workshops, wildlife watching and microscopy, reptile displays and storytelling/music sessions. The tea shop sells thick slices of cake with creamy icing served by a man wielding a silver cake-slice and a pair of tongs.
Buggy access. Nappy-changing facilities. Shop.

Diana, Princess of Wales Memorial Playground

near Black Lion Gate, Broad Walk, Kensington Gardens, W8 (7298 2117/recorded info 7298 2141). Bayswater or Queensway tube. **Open** 10am-8pm or 1hr before dusk if earlier, daily. Closed 25 Dec. **Admission** free. All adults must be accompanied by a child. (Adults may view the gardens from 9.30-10am daily.) **Map** p312 C7.

The boy who never grew up commemorates the princess who never grew old in this £1.7-million children's playground. This fenced-off Never-Never Land is situated in the north-west corner of Kensington Gardens and is guarded by rangers who ensure that no unaccompanied grown-ups enter. Peter Pans and Tinkerbells make straight for Captain Hook's pirate ship, moored in a soft sea of fine white sand (shoes fill up with it quickly; let them go barefoot). Older children have fun scaling the rigging to the crow's nest, little ones bring buckets and

Around Town

Walk: Spot the embassy

▶ Start at the southern end of **Kensington Palace Gardens**. It is a private road, so cars may only drive along it with permission. Pedestrians, though, can walk its well-swept pavements with impunity. The buildings in the street look like miniature castles – some have ballrooms and even swimming pools inside. Not surprisingly, they're prohibitively expensive for most people, and today many of them belong to foreign governments.

On the left is the **Israeli Embassy**. It has an armed police guard outside. The next has a red, yellow and blue flag, meaning it belongs to… **Romania**. 'Name the flag' is a good game to play while strolling along beneath the tall, elegant plane trees.

On the right is a broad green polo meadow and beyond it **Kensington Palace**, where a few members of the extensive Royal Family now live. Limousines park in the stable yard.

As you walk, you can often hear a lawnmower in the background. The gardens around the houses are so big that cutting the grass is a never-ending occupation.

The **Netherlands Embassy** has Dutch gables. **Norway**'s has a balcony – handy for making speeches from. The **Finns** keep their windows open and the **Nepalese** their gates. The **Kuwaitis** nestle next to the **Saudi Arabians**, as they do in life, and the **Russian Federation** is so keen on this street that it maintains three buildings here – Residence, Chancery and Consulate.

▶ Pass the green security shed at the north end and turn right into **Bayswater Road**. Pretend to be a consular official to people on buses thundering towards Notting Hill. Admire **Orme Court** and **Orme Square**, whose buildings were erected by Edward Orme, who made his money from Kensington Gravel Pits and sold shiploads of building gravel to Tsar Alexander I when he visited, hence the Russian names of streets round here – Moscow Road and St Petersburgh Place.

At Black Lion Lodge turn right into Kensington Gardens. If anyone needs the loo, there are toilets with baby-changing facilities a little further on. Follow the **Broad Walk** south through the gardens, along with strollers, joggers, rollerskaters, cyclists, dog-walkers and buggy-pushers. On the right are the pirate ship and wigwams of the **Diana, Princess of Wales**

Memorial Playground. The magical elfin oak is enclosed within an iron fence beside the parasol café tables.

The gardens stretch away towards Hyde Park to the left. The ancient sycamores are planted in neat rows. Walk around the **Round Pond**, where swans flock and children try out model boats. Return to and cross the Broad Walk and approach **Kensington Palace**. Admire the statue of young Queen Victoria – see if you can see the join where a new nose was added. She lived in the palace and could see from her bedroom window the future site of the **Albert Memorial**, the gloriously golden monument to her husband. On the south side are the wrought-iron gates made famous by the sea of flowers left there when Diana died. Leave some yourself if you are sentimental in that way.

▶ Return to the Broad Walk and continue south to **Palace Gate**, where there are more loos. The gents has an extract of Beethoven's Choral Symphony in the tiles on the wall. A very upmarket place to pee.

Albert Memorial

...r ways: row your boat

Th... **...rpentine** in Hyde Park is London's oldest and most famous boating lake. In 1730 King George II's wife Caroline, who was very keen on landscape gardening, came up with the idea of damming the River Westbourne, which then flowed through the park and into the Thames. Nowadays, the river trickles through the dam and into the Ranelagh Sewer, a sad fate for a once-proud water course that still provides so much pleasure for Londoners.

Boats are available for hire on the north side of the lake. There are two different types: rowing boats and pedalos. The former are preferable, although slightly harder to operate for the inexperienced. The rower should sit on the middle thwart (bench) with his back to the bow of the boat (the sharp end). Try to maintain a steady rhythm and do not dip the blades too deeply into the water. You can fit as many as five children in with you. Pedalos take a maximum of four persons and are operated by the people in the two front seats, who pedal as if on a bicycle (hence the name).

Charges are the same for either boat – £3.50 per adult and £1 per child for 30 minutes, or £5 per adult and £2 per child for an hour. The season runs from March to October. There is no boating during the winter except on occasional special weekends if the weather is kind (ring first; 7262 1330). You may steer your boat to any part of the quarter-mile lake as long as you think you can get back within the time you have booked for. All children under 12 must wear life jackets provided by the management.

There are lots of rules to obey once you set sail too. You may not: land on the island or any bank; disembark except at the jetty at the end of your ride; play splashing games; smoke on board; fish off the side; play loud music on the lake, or anywhere else in Hyde Park for that matter. The hire company no longer calls out through a megaphone, 'Come in, Number 27, your time is up!' so keep an eye on the clock.

spades for the sand; all adore the ship's wheel, cabins, pulleys and ropes. Equally alluring is the mermaids' fountain and rocky outcrops, beyond which is the Redskins' camp: a trio of wigwams, each large enough to hold a sizeable tribe. The tree house encampment provides walkways, ladders and slides.

The playground's attractions are designed to appeal to the senses: sensitive planting of scented shrubs, whispering willows and bamboo, metal dance chimes (tap your foot and hear the note) and touchy-feely sculpture are all carefully designed to engage visitors on every level. Much of the equipment has been designed for use by children with special needs, as befitting a playground built in Diana's name.

It is well worth coming here, even if you don't live nearby, especially if your children are aged under 10 (older kids after a more physically challenging adventure playground may find this somewhat tame). The food in the café is good, and the loos, housed in a grass-roofed dome, are clean. Drinking water is thoughtfully provided for those long, hot afternoons playing pirates. All in all, a terrific, free day out.
Buggy access. Café. Nappy-changing facilities. Nearest picnic place: Kensington Gardens.

Kensington Palace

W8 (7937 9561/www.hrp.org.uk). Bayswater, High Street Kensington or Queensway tube. **Open** *Mar-Oct* 10am-6pm daily. *Nov-Feb* 10am-5pm daily. Last entry 1hr before closing. Closed 24-26 Dec. **Admission** (LP) *incl audio guide* £10; £6.50 5-15s; £7.50 concessions; £30 family (2+3). **Credit** AmEx, MC, V. **Map** p312 B8.

Living by the river at Whitehall aggravated William III's asthma, so in 1689 he and Mary, looking for a new home, bought this modest Jacobean mansion then known as Nottingham House. Wren and Hawksmoor (and, later, William Kent) were drafted in to redesign the building, which remained the favoured royal residence until the reign of George III (he preferred Buckingham Palace). The future Queen Victoria was born in the palace in 1819, and it has latterly been known as the last home of Princesses Diana and Margaret (one of a number of royal residents). The Duke and Duchess of Kent both have apartments here. The palace is open for tours of the State Apartments, including the ground-floor room where Queen Victoria was baptised, the long King's Gallery, with its Tintoretto nudes and Van Dyck portrait of Charles I, and the Royal Ceremonial Dress Collection, which includes A Century of Queens' Wedding Dresses, 1840-1947. To complete the royal day out, take tea in the Orangery. Remember to protrude the little finger of the hand holding the china cup.
Buggy access. Café. Nappy-changing facilities. Nearest picnic place: palace grounds. Restaurant. Shop.

National Army Museum

Royal Hospital Road, SW3 (7730 0717/www.national-army-museum.ac.uk). Sloane Square tube/11, 19, 239 bus. **Open** 10am-5.30pm daily. Closed 24-26 Dec, Good Friday, 1st bank hol May. **Admission** free. **Map** p315 F12.

Breezily alert old soldiers man the reception desk at this splendidly extensive museum. The several floors exhibit relics from 1,000 years of British military history. The

life-size figures and model battlefields go down well with children, who love to stroke the nose of the full-size horse returning from battle during the English Civil War, then continue the theme by admiring the skeleton of Napoleon's mount, Marengo. Permanent exhibits include Redcoats, a gallery that tells the story of the British soldier from the archers of Agincourt in 1415 to the redcoats of the American Revolution; the Road to Waterloo, which features a huge model of the battle, with 75,000 toy soldiers; and the Nation in Arms, which charts the history of the army in two world wars and includes reconstructions of a trench in Flanders and a landing craft off the coast of Normandy.

School and family groups are given gallery trails to guide them round the various eras at the museum. There are also regular special events days throughout the year, and special events weekends (the first one of each month), which allow children to gain a more hands-on impression of the life of a soldier: they can try on helmets, touch weapons and pity the hapless sappers.

Buggy access. Café. Nappy-changing facilities. Nearest picnic place: benches outside museum/Chelsea Hospital grounds. Shop.

Oratory Catholic Church

Thurloe Place, Brompton Road, SW7 (7808 0900). South Kensington tube. **Open** 6.30am-8pm daily; phone to confirm. **Admission** free; donations appreciated. **Map** p315 E10.

Known to most Londoners as the Brompton Oratory, this huge Roman Catholic church (the second largest Catholic church in the city, after Westminster Cathedral) is full of extravagant marbles and mosaics designed to inspire both reverence and fear in mere mortals. Many of the ornate internal decorations predate the building, including Mazzuoli's late 17th-century statues of the apostles, which previously stood in Siena Cathedral. During the Cold War, the church was used by Russian spies as a dead letter box.

In & around: Albertopolis

The golden statue of Prince Albert in Hyde Park is a memorial to an enlightened patron of the arts and sciences. The husband of Queen Victoria presided over the Great Exhibition of 1851, the profits of which (£356,000, a huge amount of money at the time) built the South Kensington Arts Centre, or Albertopolis, over which the statue gazes. The basis of Albertopolis is the three great free museums – **Natural History**, **Science** and **Victoria & Albert** – which still attract vast numbers of visitors from all over the world.

Science Museum

Some of the world's most famous inventions are held here, including Stephenson's Rocket, one of the first steam engines; Arkwright's spinning machine, which precipitated the industrial revolution; Edison's phonograph (the precursor to the gramophone); Bell's telephone; Whittle's turbo-jet aeroengine; the Vickers Vimy aircraft in which Alcock and Brown crossed the Atlantic in 1919; and the Apollo 10 command module.

Nowadays the museum is less interested in adding to its collections than in designing educative shows and exhibitions. In 2000 the capacity of the building was greatly increased by the opening of the Wellcome Wing, named after the medical charity that contributed to the project, which contains much of specific interest to children. The **Pattern Pod**, for instance, aims to impress upon children under 8 the importance of patterns (the honeycomb, zebra stripes) in nature. The **Launch Pad** is a technological adventure playground where children of all ages can make scientific explorations while having fun. In the basement, the **Garden**, for 3-6-year-olds, involves learning through water play, soft play, construction and dressing up. Kids adore the flight simulator on floor three, which also has a real Cessna light

aircraft to sit in. **Health Matters** is an exploration of the history of medical technology. Waxwork nurses and doctors work to save blood-spattered patients in tableaux displayed upstairs in an exhibition called **Glimpses of Medical History**.

Not everything in the museum is free. The Wellcome Wing's **Virtual Voyages** is a 15-minute simulated motion ride to Mars, which costs £3.50 for adults and £2.50 for children. Tickets for the five-storey **IMAX cinema** costs £6.95 for adults, £5.95 for students, concessions, under-16s and OAPs; and £19.95 for families (2+2). It runs 40-minute 3-D shows. *T-Rex* is a roaring dinosaur movie; *Cyberworld* is a highly animated programme about computer bugs and viruses. *Blue Planet* focuses on geographical features on earth.

If a visit to the Science Museum has fuelled your child's interest in all things scientific, treat them to one of the **Science Night** sleepers (held once a month, except for August, for 8-11-year-olds). They consist of an evening of activities followed by a sleepover among the exhibits. Not surprisingly, they're extremely popular, so book one to two months ahead. But even if you don't make it to one of the sleepovers, there are children's educational events and workshops every half-term and school holidays. These can't be booked in advance, so it's worth turning up early on the day. For details of forthcoming events for children, ask to be put on the mailing list.

Exhibition Road, SW7 (7942 4454/recorded info 0870 870 4868/www.sciencemuseum.org.uk). South Kensington tube. **Open** 10am-6pm daily. Closed 24-26 Dec. **Admission** free; charges apply for special exhibitions. **Credit** IMAX cinema, shops AmEx, MC, V. **Map** p315 D9. *Buggy access. Cafés. Lifts. Nappy-changing facilities. Nearest picnic place: basement of museum/Hyde Park. Restaurant. Shops.*

The 'Brompton' Oratory's Junior Choir sings weekly Mass at 10am on Sundays. Schola, the boys' choir of the London Oratory School, performs Mass on Saturday evenings during term time.
Buggy access. Nearest picnic place: Holy Trinity Brompton churchyard. Shop.

Serpentine Gallery

Kensington Gardens (near Albert Memorial), W2 (7402 6075/www.serpentinegallery.org). Lancaster Gate or South Kensington tube. **Open** 10am-6pm daily. Closed 25 Dec. *Tours* free; 3pm Sat. **Admission** free. **Map** p313 D8.

This light and airy gallery is housed in a tranquil former tea pavilion with french windows looking out on to Hyde Park, imbuing the exhibitions with varying qualities of natural light (depending on our notorious weather, of course). On Saturday mornings, the Children's Art Club offers tours of the artworks on display, plus discussions of the techniques and practical workshops for participants' own creativity and expression. *Buggy access. Nappy-changing facilities. Nearest picnic place: Hyde Park/Kensington Gardens. Shop.*

Where to eat

The restaurants and cafés in the major museums are often crowded and portion sizes have nothing on the platefuls you get for your money at the restaurants around here. **Francofill** (1 Old Brompton Road, SW7, 7584 0087) is a very serviceable French fast-food joint (lovely *biftek* and *frites*), where children are welcomed with high chairs and drawing gear. Head over to Gloucester Road for child-friendly pizza places and burger bars (ASK, Pizza Express, Tootsies).

Victoria & Albert Museum. *See p72.*

Natural History Museum

This 'storehouse for the wonders of creation' was opened in 1881. The collection now runs to 68 million plants, animals, fossils, rocks and minerals. You'd never see them all in a day, of course, but the following gives some ideas about what you should definitely not miss.

For many children, the **Dinosaurs Gallery** is London's best attraction. The initial hysteria generated by the arrival of the animatronic Tyrannosaurus rex in February 2001 may have died down, but his blood-stained teeth and ghastly roar still makes buggy dwellers squawk. The beast will be in his enclosure, especially fragranced for that authentic, prehistoric odour (slightly vegetably, with a tang of the dry ice that makes him yet more scary), until at least spring 2003. To get to the T-rex you walk on a metal walkway above the Dinosaurs Gallery, where three animatronic Deinonychus keep guard.

From 18 July 2002 the **Dinobirds Exhibition** (£5; £3 concessions) brings to Europe for the first time the large quantity of feathered dinosaur fossils that were recently discovered in China. The find greatly enhances our understanding of the transitional lifeforms between declining reptiles and ascendant mammals and birds. Feathers developed from scales and helped to create a temperature-regulation system that enabled cold climates to be colonised. Also from July 2002 **Turbulent Landscapes** (£5; £3 concessions) will feature 19 interactive, press-button and/or hands-on exhibits that are designed to exemplify the effects of certain chaotic weather conditions (tornadoes, droughts, monsoons etc) on our environment.

Other galleries particularly worth checking out if you have kids in tow include **Creepy Crawlies** (gallery 33), which has a live ant colony, as well as plenty of diverting displays of insects' domestic habits. The famous life-size blue whale (three buses long) still hangs in **Discovering Mammals** (Galleries 23 and 24), just as it has done for more than half a century.

The **Earth Galleries** are approached via Exhibition Road. The escalator that takes you in through a suspended, revolving globe is a memorable experience, and that's even before you come across the interactive displays investigating the earth's treasures and natural disasters. **Gallery 61** has a re-creation of the Kobe (Japan) earthquake of 1995. Young visitors will want to relive the floor-shaking supermarket experience more than once.

The Clore Education Centre has **Investigate**, which teaches visitors how to use the equipment available (microscopes, magnifying glasses, computers) to examine and find out about hundreds of specimens on display. There are also activity trails (available from the box office),

In Chelsea there's **Big Easy** (332-4 King's Road, SW3, 7352 4071; *see also p173*), a large-portioned, all-smiling, high chair and children's menu-toting American eaterie, and a more sober, Tex-Mex inspired restaurant, **Cactus Blue** (86 Fulham Road, SW3, 7823 7858), where the chimichangas are excellent and the brownies even better. More American chowing down is possible at the local branch of **Ed's Easy Diner** (362 King's Road, SW3, 7352 1956; *see also p175*). **Benihana** (77 King's Road, SW3, 7376 7799; *see also p174*) is a link in a particularly child-friendly Japanese chain, where food is cooked in front of you on a hibachi grill. Other well-known, welcoming restaurants on the King's Road include Café Rouge and Pizza Express.

Food is plentiful on Kensington High Street and the surrounding area and generally comes in the form of chain restaurants, such as **ASK** for pizzas (No.222, 7937 5540) and **Café Flo** (127 Kensington Church Street, W8, 7727 8142), where children are well catered for with starter pasta portions. **Sticky Fingers** (1A Phillimore Gardens, W8, 7938 5338; *see also p173*), just off the high street, is an American restaurant that has a rock 'n' roll theme, a kids' menu and a magician on Sundays.

A new organic convenience store and café called **Luscious Organic** (240-242 Kensington High Street, W8, 7371 6987) recently opened up next to the Commonwealth Institute. This is a great place to pick up goodies for a picnic in the park.

▶ half-term and school holiday events programmes and weekend workshops for families. The themes of these change frequently so it's best to check the website or ring the booking line (7942 5555) to find out what's on.

The museum is continuing to expand: work progresses on the £100-million Darwin Centre, the first phase of which should be completed as this guide goes to press (*see also p25*).
Cromwell Road, SW7 (7942 5000/www.nhm.ac.uk). South Kensington tube. **Open** 10am-5.50pm Mon-Sat; 11am-5.50pm Sun. Closed 24-25 Dec. *Tours* hourly, 11am-4pm daily; depending on guide availability. **Admission** free; charges apply for special exhibitions. *Tours* free. **Credit** *Shop* AmEx, MC, V. **Map** p315 D10.
Buggy access. Cafés. Nappy-changing facilities. Nearest picnic place: indoor eating area/museum grounds. Restaurant. Shops.

Victoria & Albert Museum

The royal founders' favourite museum was opened in 1857 specifically to house objects representing the application of Fine Arts to manufacturing. Thus the original collection included pottery, porcelain, glass, china, enamel, armour, medals, jewellery, ivories and furniture. However, periodic endowments of paintings and sculpture soon obscured the original well-defined purpose so that now the only common thread linking all the exhibits is aesthetic value.

And the V&A is without doubt a museum of beautiful objects. Nothing exemplifies this better than the current **Tiaras** (until 14 July 2002) exhibition, which features bejewelled headgear owned by princesses, from blue-blooded Victoria Saxe-Coburg to rather less posh Victoria Beckham. The estimated 100,000 diamonds in the show are beautifully complemented by emeralds, sapphires, rubies, pearls, amethysts and topaz.

The **Art & Design** galleries are arranged thematically by place and date, the **Materials & Techniques** galleries by type. The museum is also home to a huge photographic archive, and hosts regular photographic exhibitions. The **British Galleries**, which opened in November 2001 following a massive programme of modernisation, tell the tale of Britain's ascent from a minor offshore island in 1500 to a major world power and cultural authority in 1900.

Exhibits of special interest to children were moved to the Museum of Childhood at Bethnal Green (*see p115*) a few years ago. But there are some remaining ones that will still appeal: the **Ironwork Gallery** (Room 114) has a number of early 20th-century tin toys, while the display of German stained glass (Room 117) includes a panel depicting the Murder of the Innocents in gory detail.

Children's activities take place at weekends. On Saturdays from 1.30pm, 5-11-year-olds may pick up a themed backpack with jigsaws, games, stories and puzzles. On Sundays from 10.30am, under-5s visit the Cart, which contains materials for drawing and model-making and is stationed in a room relevant to the Cart's activities. Half-terms are devoted to daily events such as workshops and fashion displays pertaining to current exhibitions. All children's activities are free.

Be sure to pay a visit to the museum shop, which has a pretty good selection of books, plus ornaments and jewellery.
Cromwell Road, SW7 (7942 2000/ www.vam.ac.uk). South Kensington tube. **Open** 10am-5.45pm Mon, Tue, Thur-Sun; 10am-10pm Wed. Closed 24-26 Dec. *Tours* daily; phone for details. **Admission** free; charges apply for special exhibitions. **Credit** AmEx, MC, V. **Map** p315 E10.
Buggy access. Café. Nappy-changing facilities. Nearest picnic place: Holy Trinity Brompton churchyard. Restaurant. Shop.

West End

Join the throng.

When they talk about going 'up west' in *EastEnders*, they mean the bright lights, big shops and alluring theatricals of the West End. For the purposes of this chapter, the West End includes Soho, Mayfair and Covent Garden.

At the heart of the West End is **Shaftesbury Avenue**. Famous theatres dominate its northern side, and **Chinatown** lies along its southern flank. This road takes its name from the philanthropic 7th Earl of Shaftesbury, aka Anthony Ashley Cooper (1801-85), who was prominent in the Ragged Schools movement (*see p120*), which provided free education and clothing for deprived children. The statue of the boy Cupid, or **Eros**, at Piccadilly Circus at the western end of Shaftesbury Avenue is dedicated to the philanthropic earl. Young people from around the world congregate (not necessarily in his memory) on the steps of the fountain. Many cannot resist the lure of the cavernous, deafening **Trocadero** across the road, as this is the only specifically youth-oriented entertainment site in the West End.

Next to Piccadilly Circus is **Leicester Square**, home of the capital's biggest cinemas. On prestigious opening nights, starstruck autograph hunters strain at the crowd-control barriers screaming to get the attention of celebrities.

Soho is the centre of sleaze. There are sights here from which you may wish to shield innocent eyes. Buzzing **Carnaby Street** poses no great threat as long as you keep a rein on your purse. **Berwick Street Market** is a bit seedy but friendly enough.

Mayfair is best known as the costliest property on the Monopoly board. It's no different in real life. The roads are broad and the trees are tall, and liveried footmen stand at the entrances of its grand hotels. Famously expensive shopping streets feed its reputation. **Regent Street** is home to **Liberty** (*see p199*) and the world-famous toy shop **Hamleys** (*see p208*). Smart **Bond Street** is for quality fashions, antiques, jewellery and fine art. **Savile Row** purveys handmade suits for a bob or two. Not much here for the kids.

Apsley House: The Wellington Museum

Hyde Park Corner, W1 (74995676/ www.apsleyhouse.org.uk). Hyde Park Corner tube. **Open** 11am-5pm Tue-Sun, most bank hol Mons. Closed 1 Jan, 24-26 Dec, Good Friday, 1st bank hol May. **Admission** £4.50 (includes audio guide); £3 concessions; free under-18s, over-60s. **Credit** AmEx, DC, MC, V. **Map** p318 G8.

Once called 'No.1 London,' because it was the first building you came to en route from the village of Kensington to London, Apsley House was built by Robert Adam in the 1770s. It was the London residence of Arthur Wellesley, the Duke of Wellington, from 1817 until his death in 1852. The duke's descendants still live here, but ten rooms, restored to their original state, are open to the public.

Highlights of the collection include the extraordinary 14ft 4in marble statue of Napoleon in the fig-leafed nude by Canova in the main stairwell, the gilt-framed paintings by Velázquez, Caravaggio and Rubens in the Waterloo Room and portraits of kings and popes in the Piccadilly Room. In the China and Plate Room (that is, china crockery and silver plate), the Egyptian dinner service sits around a gigantic plaster model of the Temple at Karnak.

Another impressive statue – this time of Wellington himself – stands outside, on Hyde Park Corner. He sits with his medals and his boots on astride his horse Copenhagen (which died in 1836 at the age of 28 and was buried with full military honours), surrounded by representatives of his regiments, one from each of the United Kingdom's kingdoms – Guards, Royal Highlanders, Inniskilling Dragoons and Welsh Fusiliers.

The museum has popular special events and a keen and busy schools service. In June there's a Waterloo Week, with numerous opportunities for dressing up and messing about with paint and glue, with a few inadvertent history lessons thrown in. The Christmas Festival in December is especially

Mother and baby groups at **Apsley House**.

lovely when the staff organise Victorian themed festivities with storytellers, costumed characters, art workshops and carol singing. For more information about tours, events and workshops, call the administrator on 7495 8525 and ask to be put on the free mailing list.
Buggy access. Lift. Nearest picnic place: Hyde Park. Shop.

Faraday Museum
Royal Institution, 21 Albemarle Street, W1 (7409 2992/ www.rigb.org). Green Park tube. **Open** 9am-5pm Mon-Fri. Closed 24-26 Dec, 1 Jan. *Tours by arrangement.* **Admission** £1; 50p concessions. *Tours* £5. **Map** p318 J7.
This small, eccentric, public museum is part of the Royal Institution, where Michael Faraday (1791-1867), 'father of electricity', worked for 30 years. It is of most interest to those of a scientific/mathematical bent, who can expect a warm welcome and informative tour if they ring up to book a seat at one of the talks or workshops. Exhibits include a re-creation of the lab where Faraday discovered the laws of electromagnetics and identified the compound benzene.

The Royal Institution is responsible for making science a subject of interest to the public. The Christmas lectures have gained wide appeal in recent years. The institution guards its position at the forefront of technology jealously. Over the years, ten chemical elements have been discovered here and 14 Nobel prizes won. The programme of school visits and lectures is extensive and serious. The institution runs a maths masterclass for gifted mathematicians aged 11 and over. For details of these classes and services, ring, check the website or drop in for a brochure.
Buggy access. Lift. Nearest picnic place: Berkeley Square.

Handel House Museum
25 Brook Street (entrance at rear), W1 (7495 1685/ www.handelhouse.org). Bond Street tube. **Open** 10am-6pm Tue, Wed, Fri, Sat; 10am-8pm Thur; noon-6pm Sun; bank hol Mons. Closed 24-26 Dec, 1 Jan. **Admission** £4.50; £3.50 concessions; £2 5-16s; free under-5s. **Credit** MC, V. **Map** p318 H6.
The composer George Frideric Handel lived in this house for nearly 40 years. Now it (and No.23 next door, where the outrageous rock star Jimi Hendrix lived in the 1960s) have been turned into a commemorative museum. In the 18th-century interiors are period paintings, furniture, manuscripts and harpsichords. Live music is played at intervals and tours with a costumed guide can be arranged. Children's events take place at monthly intervals. On special days, and during half-terms, weekends and school holidays, children are given a Handel Bag to rummage through. The bags contain little pots purportedly containing typical 18th-century smells, pieces of fabric to match to paintings, soft furnishings and bedlinen around the house, imaginatively devised puzzles, other items to look for and various cunning challenges to encourage kids' curiosity. There are also individually designed activity packs

and high jinks involving dressing up in 18th-century clothing. Phone for more details of forthcoming activities for children, as well as group tours.
Buggy access. Lifts. Nappy-changing facilities. Nearest picnic place: Hanover Square. Shop.

Royal Academy of Arts
Burlington House, Piccadilly, W1 (7300 8000/ www.royalacademy.org.uk). Green Park or Piccadilly Circus tube. **Open** 10am-6pm Mon-Thur, Sat, Sun; 10am-10pm Fri. *Tours* times vary. **Admission** varies depending on exhibition. *Tours* free. **Credit** AmEx, MC, V. **Map** p318 J7.
Britain's first art school – it opened in 1768 – the Royal Academy also held the country's first annual open exhibitions of living artists. This persists as the Summer Exhibition (June-August each year); anyone of any age or nationality may submit a painting, sculpture or piece of architecture (in model form) for entry. Application forms are available in February each year, and the cost of entry is £18 per item. Only about 10% of the works submitted are chosen for display.

Though there is a permanent collection at the RA, only a few works from it are on show at any one time. But in any case, almost everyone who visits does so to see one of the always popular temporary exhibitions: they're the most visited of any London gallery, so booking for them is sometimes a necessity. Shows to look out for, include, until 14 July 2002, Return of the Buddha, an exhibition of 35 ancient Buddhist statues discovered in China in 1996. The Summer Exhibition runs from 11 June to 19 August 2002. From 16 November until April 2003 the Royal Academy will be hosting a ground-breaking exhibition devoted to the cultural riches of Mexico's Aztec past. One of the most ambitious exhibitions ever staged at the RA, it will bring together a large number of works never previously shown outside Mexico to make the most comprehensive survey of Aztec culture ever mounted. Expect plenty of child-friendly related workshops while this show is on. Check the website for details of all educational activities and exhibitions. *See also p218.*
Buggy access. Café. Nappy-changing facilities. Lift. Nearest picnic place: Green Park/St James's Square. Restaurant. Shop.

St James's Church Piccadilly
197 Piccadilly, W1 (7734 4511/www.st-james-piccadilly.org). Piccadilly Circus tube. **Open** 8am-7pm daily (phone for details of evening events). Closed 24-26 Dec, some bank hols (phone to check). **Map** p318 J7.
The handsome 2,000-seat Christopher Wren church is known for its churchyard market (antiques and collectors' stuff on Tuesdays, arts and crafts Wednesdays to Saturdays) and its lectures and lunchtime concerts (Mon, Wed, Fri); call to see what's on, or pick up a leaflet from the church. Its interior is cool and calm and perfect for silent contemplation; Grinling

Water ways: Thames tales

Head over to **London's Transport Museum** (*see p76*) before 1 September 2002 to have a look at its excellent Thames exhibition. Like most things at the museum, the exhibition is interactive and has a bucketload of associated workshops and craft sessions for children to dabble in. Thames Tales is all about the river's role in the capital, as a source of income to those who work on it, a

leisure centre to those who play on it and in it and as an important (and definitely the most enjoyable) way of travelling across the city. Children who want to go with the flow can dress up as royal bargemasters, load a barge, drive a river bus or have a go at reconstructing the Tower of London. They can even try to build a bridge that doesn't wobble. Now there's a challenge.

London's Transport Museum. *See p76.*

Gibbons carved much of the woodwork (as well as the white marble font) and Henry Purcell tested the organ. The church was badly bombed during World War II but beautifully repaired afterwards. The new spire is made of fibreglass. The on-site Aroma café is good for coffee and cakes.
Buggy access. Café. Nearest picnic place: St James's Square.

Trocadero
1 Piccadilly Circus, W1 (7439 1791/www.troc.co.uk).
Piccadilly Circus tube. **Open** 10am-midnight daily.
Admission free; individual attractions vary. **Credit** varies. **Map** p319 K7.
Funland, a dark and extremely noisy indoor funfair, starts here. Where it ends, we'll never know as once you're in it's extremely hard to find the exit until you've spent all your money. Many parents, if they have any say whatsoever in their offspring's choice of activities, prefer to avoid it. The central attraction is the Pepsi Max Drop Ride (£3), which involves being strapped into a chair and plunging from the top of the building six floors up to the basement in a couple of seconds. Cheaper attractions flash at you from every corner. There are dodgems and a ten-lane, ten-pin bowling alley with a snack bar attached. To release any aggression, there is a small-scale shooting range and various mean fighting machines.

The Pump Pump Feel the Beat International Dance Floor machine, on which the correct steps win points but no prizes, attracts a big audience. Sulky girls watch their boys work off excess energy to hip hop and everyone is suitably impressed when they beat the machine. The Ridge Racer game is played by contestants in life-size red open-top sports cars hurtling round on-screen clifftop bends like amateurish, old-fashioned film effects. Dynamo Hockey is a sort of space age shove-ha'penny, while the Cybersled, a two-seater capsule that spins you up and down, makes you feel queasy just watching. There are also computer games, on Level 1; not surprisingly, they're very popular. The pool hall bar, on Level 2, is available to over-18s only.

The ground floor is dominated by shops, among them HMV, Baskin Robbins, Claire's Accessories and a bunch of tacky novelty and souvenir stores hawking everything from Union Jack towels to fake-blood squirters.
Cafés. Lift. Nappy-changing facilities. Nearest picnic place: Leicester Square/Trafalgar Square. Restaurants. Shops.

Where to eat

The West End is full of excellent restaurants of all price brackets, many of which are reviewed in the Eating chapter on pages 170-191. Two of our favourites are **Ed's Easy Diner** (12 Old Compton Street, W1, 7434 4439; *see also p175*), which is cheap and fun, and **Maison Bertaux** (28 Greek Street, W1, 7437 6007), which sells exquisite French cakes. In Leicester Square, the branch of **Häagen Dazs** (7287 9577) is the place to come for some outrageously good ice-cream combinations.

For lovely light lunches and ice-cream sundaes in the Fountain restaurant, as well as upmarket picnic fare, and even the wicker hampers to put them in, from the legendary ground-floor food hall, it has to be **Fortnum & Mason** (181 Piccadilly, W1, 7734 8040; *see also p175 and p198*). Nearby **Pret a Manger** (163 Piccadilly, W1, 7629 5044) is a cheaper option.

Covent Garden & St Giles's

The arty heart of London, with its tourist-tempting theatres, shops and restaurants and the elegant **Royal Opera House** as the jewel in its crown, has

We all scream for ice-cream in **Leicester Square**. See p80.

always been a stimulating place to visit. It hasn't however, always been a refined one. It's no surprise that the Bow Street Runners of the 18th century, London's first police force, started out here – at the time it was the most dangerous square mile in the capital, with many juveniles among its legions of criminals. Prior to that the area had been Westminster Abbey's convent garden (hence the area's name), and as well as a den of prostitution and lawlessness it went on to become London's main flower and veg market, which later moved south of the river to Vauxhall.

It was the sleaze and general degeneracy of the area that attracted low-lifers of all sorts, and actors in particular. The theatre world shifted here with the restoration of the monarchy in 1662; before that London's theatres had stood next to the brothels and gambling dens of Southwark, but the Puritans shut them down and the playground south of the river went into decline during the Commonwealth. The first playhouse to be built in the area was the **Theatre Royal, Drury Lane** in 1663. It's now the oldest theatre still in use. The title of 'Largest Theatre' goes to the **Coliseum**, home to English National Opera (7632 8300) since 1974, which is currently undergoing a facelift. You can go there to see a show, but the tours of this institution aren't running again until 2004.

The story of London's theatrical heritage is told in an entertaining and interactive way at the **Theatre Museum** in Russell Street. Next door, **London's Transport Museum** allows members of the public to clamber on to buses, trams and trains that have been saved from the scrapheap. When Covent Garden's market moved to Vauxhall in 1973, its place around the piazza was taken over by shops,

bars, cafés, restaurants, craft stalls and licensed street performers, many of whom like to get children involved. It's all very touristy, so expect to pay high prices for snacks and ice-creams.

Away from the piazza, takeaway lunches and picnic fare, alternative remedies and life in the slow lane are all healthily promoted by the good folk of **Neal's Yard**, just off Short's Gardens. Come here, if not to chill out (people queue up here for their wholesome lunches), at least to escape the vast numbers of tourists shuffling around the main market.

London's Transport Museum

Covent Garden Piazza, WC2 (7379 6344/ www.ltmuseum.co.uk). Covent Garden tube. **Open** 10am-6pm Mon-Thur, Sat, Sun; 11am-6pm Fri. Last entry 5.15pm. *Tours* 11am-4pm Sat, Sun. Check at cloakroom for times. **Admission** (LP) £5.95; £4.50 concessions; free under-16s when accompanied by an adult. *Tours* free. **Credit** MC, V. **Map** p319 L7.

With London's transport being something of a joke these days, this splendid museum seems all the more dynamic. As well as harking back to the good old days of reliable ding-dinging trams and steam trains, there are up-to-date displays all about the city's more current travel successes, namely the DLR and Croydon's lovely tram system. Nearly two centuries' worth of London buses stand in crimson splendour in the huge display area. The earliest are harnessed to life-size plastic workhorses that kids like to pat, while the most recent, the driver-only 'hopper', attracts queues of small enthusiasts keen to occupy the driver's seat. Most of the exhibits may be clambered on to, if you don't mind sharing your space with mannequins in period dress.

Call for details of the free guided tours run in the school holidays, which are led by actors in period costume. For 3-5-year-olds there are group sessions, where they can make bus mobiles and take turns to board the well-cushioned Fun Bus. Older kids enjoy the games with bus numbers and timetables and the popular Kidzones, 14 learning stations around the museum at which children complete an interactive challenge

'AN AGELESS PLEASURE AND
A PLEASURE FOR ALL AGES
SHEER THEATRICAL MAGIC'
Nicholas de Jongh Evening Standard

'PETER PAN, EAT YOUR HEART OUT'
Paul Taylor Independent

'This is a fine, four fendered fabulous night.
IT'S CHITTY CHITTY BRILLIANT'
Simon Edge Daily Express

'You hug yourself
with excitement
THIS ONE
WILL FLY
AND FLY
A WINNER'
Simon Edge Daily Express

'A SURE-FIRE HIT'
Kevin O'Sullivan Daily Mirror

'Gasps of
astonished delight
EXHILARATING
FANTASTIC
REMARKABLE'
Michael Billington Guardian

GEN 11

'THE MOST POPULAR
CHILDREN'S SHOW IN TOWN'
Michael Coveney Daily Mail

'BE AMAZED. BE VERY AMAZED'
Warwick Thompson Metro

BOX OFFICE AND 24 HOURS CC WITH BOOKING FEE
0870 890 1108

020 7344 4444 · GROUPS 0870 899 3342
Book on-line www.chittythemusical.co.uk

LONDON PALLADIUM
Vulgarian Splendors not accepted   Argyll Street London W1

Official
hotel partner
Hilton
theatre breaks

and get their free Kidzone card, with a map on the back, which can be stamped at the zones just for fun. In 2001 a learning centre opened in the museum, with hands-on exhibits, computer games and a bumper programme of exciting events for children, whether they're in school groups or with their family. *See also p74.*
Buggy access. Café. Lift. Nappy-changing facilities. Nearest picnic place: picnic area in ground-floor museum gallery/churchyard of St Paul's. Shop.

Phoenix Garden
21 Stacey Street (entrance on St Giles Passage), WC2 (7379 3187). Tottenham Court Road tube. **Open** dawn-dusk daily. **Admission** free. **Map** p317 K6.
This small, shady garden at the north end of Neal Street was established by the Covent Garden Open Spaces Association in 1984. Permanently staffed, it has slides and benches, one of which was contributed by Michael Palin. It's a lovely place to come to escape the nearby bustle of Covent Garden – in the farthest corner willow trees surround a wildlife bog, with the walnut, fig and cherry trees completing the mini Eden feel. A little kiosk sells plants that have been grown here. Tea and coffee are available in exchange for a donation to the garden. *Buggy access.*

Proud Central Gallery
5 Buckingham Street, WC2 (7839 4942/ www.britart.com/proud). Embankment tube/Charing Cross tube/rail. **Open** 10am-7pm Mon-Thur; 11am-6pm Fri-Sun. **Admission** £3; £2 concessions. **Credit** (over £10) MC, V.

When Alex Proud set up this gallery in 1998, his mission was to bring affordable, quality photography to a mainstream market. This was followed three years later by a gallery in Camden (*see p98*). Accessible and fun to visit, the galleries are among the most popular private photographic galleries in Europe. Exhibitions for 2002 include Havana in My Heart, (until 28 July) and Elvis/Marilyn, to mark the anniversaries of their death (1 August-1 September). Check the website for current and future exhibitions.
Buggy access. Nearest picnic place: Embankment Gardens.

Royal Opera House
Bow Street, WC2 (7304 4000/www.royaloperahouse.org). Covent Garden tube. **Open** *Box office* 10am-8pm Mon-Sat. *Tours* 10.30am, 12.30pm, 2.30pm Mon-Sat. **Tickets** £7; £6 under-18s, concessions. **Credit** AmEx, DC, MC, V. **Map** p319 L6.
The House, which has occupied this Bow Street site since 1732, is also home to the Royal Ballet. It's an impressive place to visit, and free to wander around between 10am and 3.30pm when there isn't a show on. The ROH Café is open on the Amphitheatre Level every day and is a smart venue for lunch.
Much has been done to make the place more accessible to all; special events, tours, opportunities to watch the Royal Ballet in class on certain dates and low-price standby tickets for operas and ballets are all cited as reasons why the ROH is no longer just for posh folk. Nonetheless, many of the cheapest tickets are restricted in number, so, in fact, the audience remains largely unchanged. In addition, the ROH's recent bid to intensify its contemporary programme has

In & around: the Theatre Museum

The Theatre Museum, officially the National Museum of the Performing Arts (the thespian arm of the Victoria & Albert), should have its name in lights. Just across the road from London's oldest theatre, Theatre Royal Drury Lane, and right in the heart of 'Theatreland', the museum deserves to pull in the punters. Since it became free, in November 2001, perhaps it will. The museum is a big hit with visiting children, and the education department makes a fuss of those who want to find out more. There are workshops, courses, make-up demonstrations and activities based

around the museum's enormous stock of stage costumes. All of the activities are free, but some must be booked ahead, so call for details.
Children and adults alike are intrigued by the excellent **theatre-rites** exhibition (from the end of May 2002), which celebrates the work of this visionary theatre company founded in 1995 by the late Penny Bernand, whose moving obituary is displayed among the exhibits of the shows she directed and co-wrote. The pudgy-faced puppets, props, videos of work and strange and wonderful characters from the shows create a magical world for children, which is also the effect of Theatre-rites stage shows (*see p223*). The exhibition is expected to continue well into autumn 2002.
As you walk through the museum's sloping corridors down to the permanent exhibitions, look out for the colourful handprints of various flamboyant theatrical stars who dipped their paws in poster paint for posterity.
Among the permanent collection are glass-fronted cases filled with costumes and mementoes from iconic shows and stage icons. You can see the skull/prop Victor Hugo gave Sarah Bernhardt, costumes worn by Diaghelev and Fonteyn, a mock-up of a dressing room, a display about the Royal National Theatre's groundbreaking production of *Wind in the Willows* and one about opera in Britain, with costumes from English National Opera. The Let Paul Robeson Sing! exhibition, about the life

largely been seen as a failure, though the success of Björk's late 2001 appearance mean that attempts to lure in the broader public with a more varied bill of fare are ongoing.

Guided tours start in the pit lobby and include the Vilar Floral Hall, with its bars, restaurants, mirrors, escalators and rooftop garden, the ballet studio, the backstage area, a dressing room and the auditorium (or the crush bar if the latter is inaccessible). Booking is advised, though eight tickets are held each day for last-minute visitors. *See also p221.*
Buggy access. Café. Lift. Nearest picnic place: Covent Garden piazza/churchyard of St Paul's. Restaurant. Shop.

St Giles-in-the-Fields
60 St Giles High Street, WC2 (7240 2532). Tottenham Court Road tube. **Open** *9am-4pm Mon-Fri.* **Open** *for services Sun; phone for details.* **Admission** *free.* **Map** p317 K6.
The shady churchyard was the final resting place of large numbers of Londoners during the plague of 1665 (the contagion is thought to have started in the borough of St Giles's: Sir Thomas Payton is reported to have said 'that one parish of St Giles at London hath done us all this mischief'). Nowadays, it has a jollier role as a family-friendly green patch in the heart of the ci ty. There's a playground with swings, a roundabout, a basketball court, an alphabet frame and a hopscotch court, plus benches to rest on. The church dates back to 1101, when a leper colony stood nearby, and is named after the patron saint of outcasts. Condemned prisoners on the way to the Tyburn gallows at Marble Arch were given a drugged drink known as the St Giles Bowl here, and

A fashion victim in **Covent Garden piazza**.

of the actor/singer, is scheduled to continue until September 2002. Ring for details of new exhibitions, talks, workshops and courses.

After the greasepaint in the museum, the roar of the crowd is only too apparent in **Covent Garden Piazza**, where tourists go for a bit of fresh air, to eat ice-creams and to watch free shows of variable quality. Just up the road from the Theatre Museum is an altogether more rarefied experience, the glamorous **Royal Opera House** (*see p78*), where anyone can go in and admire the stately crush bar, the Vilar Floral Hall or have lunch in the café. From the terrace here you can look down on (in more ways than one) the tourists milling about wondering where on earth to go for lunch.

Theatre Museum
Russell Street, WC2 (7943 4700/group bookings 7943 4806/www.theatremuseum.org). Covent Garden tube. **Open** *10am-6pm (last entry 5.30pm) Tue-Sun. Closed 24-26 Dec, 1 Jan, bank hol Mon. Tours* 11am, 2pm, 4pm Tue-Sun. **Admission** *free. Tours free.* **Credit** *Shop* AmEx, MC, V. **Map** p319 L6.
For details of study sessions and workshops, or to be put on the free mailing list, call 7943 4741. *See also p226.*
Buggy access. Nappy-changing facilities. Nearest picnic place: churchyard of St Paul's. Shop.

many were returned here to be buried. The present building was constructed in 1711 by the architect Henry Flitcroft, whose name is inscribed above the porch. The interior is a cool and calm venue for lunchtime classical music concerts, which take place at 1.10pm for 40 minutes, every Friday (but usually not in the summer holidays). To receive a list of forthcoming concerts, phone to join the mailing list.
Buggy access. Nearest picnic place: Phoenix Garden.

St Paul's Covent Garden
Bedford Street, WC2 (7836 5221/www.spcg.org). Covent Garden tube. **Open** *9am-4.30pm Mon-Fri; 9am-12.30pm Sun. Sunday service 11am. Closed bank hols, 1 Jan.* **Admission** *free; donations appreciated.* **Map** p319 L7.
This squat symmetrical church was built by Francis Russell, Earl of Bedford, in 1638. Nicknamed 'the Actors' Church', St Paul's is linked with the theatre world – the vicar is chaplain to some of the West End theatres. George Bernard Shaw based the opening scene of *Pygmalion* (more commonly known now as the musical with a happy ending tacked on, called *My Fair Lady*) under the portico, and on the walls inside are memorials to Charlie Chaplin, Boris Karloff, Vivien Leigh and others. It is beloved of local workers for its enclosed garden, accessible via either the gates in Bedford Street or the tiny alleys in King Street and Henrietta Street.

There are services on certain days of the week and occasional concerts (phone for details). Facing the Covent Garden piazza, the east end of the church, a bare wall behind a row of columns has always presented itself as a natural stage to those outside. In the 18th century it was the scene of unruly political hustings. Nowadays, musicians, jugglers, acrobats, fire-eaters, monocyclists, tightrope walkers, ventriloquists and magicians book the space to entertain the passing crowds.
Buggy access. Nearest picnic place: churchyard.

Where to eat

Of the many places to eat in the area, the biggest and noisiest must be **TGI Friday's** (6 Bedford Street, WC2, 7379 0585; *see also p179*), whose unfeasibly upbeat staff welcome children with balloons. Also popular with kids is **Belgo Centraal** (50 Earlham Street, WC2, 7813 2233; *see also p174*), where under-12s eat free. **Rock & Sole Plaice** (47 Endell Street, WC2, 7836 3785; *see also p179*) offers excellent fish and chips, while for pizzas there's **Pizza Express** (9-12 Bow Street, WC2, 7240 3443) and **Pizza Paradiso** (31 Catherine Street, WC2, 7836 3609).

If there are vegetarians or vegans in the family, head for **Neal's Yard**, where both the **Neal's Yard Bakery & Tearoom** (No.6, 7836 5199; *see also p178*) and the **World Food Café** (No.14, 7379 0298; *see also p179*) are good for meat-free dining. Nearby, at 31 Neal Street, is the renowned **Food for Thought** (7836 9072/0239; *see also p175*), where the grub is heftily proportioned but always delicious; if the basement restaurant is too crowded, get a takeaway and find a bench to eat it on. The **Great American Bagel Factory** (18 Endell Street, WC2, 7497 1115) is a popular stop-off point for light snacks and ice-cream, perfect fodder for a picnic.

Walk: on stage

▶ Start in **Covent Garden Piazza**, opposite **St Paul's**, aka the Actors' Church. The piazza, next to the pillars of the church, is a stage for street performers of all kinds. On the wall of the church, just by the entrance to the ladies' loos, an inscription reads that the first ever Punch & Judy show took place here, in 1662, in the presence of Samuel Pepys. He was no doubt amused by it, but would have found more of note in the shows that take place today.

One comedian has an act in which he ends up in sequinned boxer shorts and nothing else, even if it's freezing. The crowd are in stitches. Another rides a lofty unicycle. Downstairs, on the lower level of the market, a wild-haired beauty sings arias from Carmen to a taped orchestra. Drop some money into the hat before moving on.

▶ Back over near the church wall, walk past the Doctor Martens shoe shop and down **King Street**. A few metres on your left is the entrance to **St Paul's churchyard**. Go in and admire the beautiful garden. The church is usually open (but closed on Saturday) and you might be lucky enough to catch some sort of recital. Exit the garden via **Inigo Place** and turn right into **Bedford Street**. Cross at the zebra and pass the Tesco on your left into **New Row**. It's quite a narrow street, rarely used by cars. At the end is **St Martin's Lane**. Look left down the road and you see English National Opera, with the Duke of York's Theatre directly opposite. Straight ahead of you, across St Martin's Lane, is the Albery Theatre. Cross the road towards it. **St Martin's Court** flanks the Albery; it's another traffic-free street, lined with quirky bookshops. At the end is **Wyndhams Theatre** on the right, **Gaby's** restaurant (with the best veggie falafel in London) on your left. There's often a *Big Issue* seller in the middle. Buy one before crossing Charing Cross Road into **Leicester Square**.

▶ Now you're in 'Cinemaland' – as opposed to 'Theatreland'. Head for the square. On the side facing the **Swiss Centre**, busking entertainers try to capture the attention of tourists. They have hats

out in front of them, hoping you'll spare them some change, but the calibre of their performance is nothing compared to the Covent Garden pros. You might see one of those 'human statue' performances, which are about as much fun as watching paint dry. Perhaps the 'statue' got the idea from the one of the original funny little man **Charlie Chaplin**, who looks out to the centre of the crowded square, and its Shakespeare Memorial (currently being refurbished).

▶ Leicester Square has four gates: **Reynold's Gate**, **Newton Gate**, **Hunter Gate** and **Hogarth Gate**. Their explanatory notices by the gateposts deliver a curt history lesson. Handprints of the great and the good who have come to London to publicise their films or burger restaurants are pressed into plaques in the paving stones.

▶ Wandering through Theatreland and seeing so much street drama may have put you in the mood for a show with rather more polish. Queue up at the **Tkts** booth in the centre of the square for cut-price tickets – for West End shows, on the day of the performance only. You're guaranteed a bargain (despite the £2.50 service charge).

Tkts

Leicester Square, WC2 (www.tkts.co.uk). Leicester Square tube. **Open** 10am-7pm Mon-Sat; noon-3pm Sun. **Credit** AmEx, DC, MC, V. **Map** p319 K7.

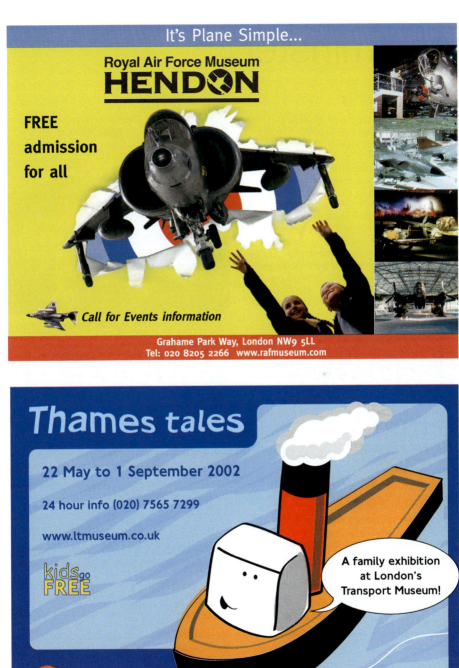

Westminster

Power supply.

The BBC's longest-running programme is a political radio show called the *Week in Westminster*, which started in 1929 as a broadcast aimed specifically and rather condescendingly at housewives to explain the goings-on in the **Houses of Parliament**, which overlook the River Thames by Westminster Bridge.

In fact, the very name Westminster is synonymous with government. It wasn't always the case: the name originally derived from the area's ancient rivalry with the City, which is dominated by St Paul's Cathedral. Westminster literally meant 'the minster (or big church) to the west', that is **Westminster Abbey**, which today is full of the bones of the nation's sovereigns, most of whom have lived nearby with their families at **Buckingham Palace** or the more modest and intimate **St James's Palace**.

Royalty and parliament have always been linked, of course. In centuries past, they came into conflict, fighting each other in the English Civil War. Parliament won and beheaded King Charles I at Whitehall Palace (of which only the **Banqueting Hall** remains), in an act that no other European nation had even contemplated. The resultant early form of republicanism was not entirely successful and eventually the monarchy was re-established on conditions laid down by Parliament, giving rise to Britain's unique brand of democracy. Everyone was subject to the sovereign but the sovereign was subject to Parliament.

The above palaces lie at the very heart of London, which traditionally is **Trafalgar Square**. It is soon to be pedestrianised. Mileposts on the way to the capital always measure to the statue of King Charles I on its southern side. To the north stands the **National Gallery**, storehouse of the nation's greatest works of art. On either side are the embassy buildings of Canada and South Africa. On the north-east corner is the church of St Martin-in-the-Fields, a sanctuary for down-and-outs. In Westminster the poor and the powerful live side by side.

Banqueting Hall

Whitehall, SW1 (7930 4179/www.hrp.org.uk). Westminster tube/Charing Cross tube/rail. **Open** 10am-5pm (last entry 4.30pm) Mon-Sat; sometimes closes at short notice; phone to check. Closed bank hols. **Admission** (LP) £4; £3 concessions; £2.60 5-15s; free under-5s. **Credit** MC, V. **Map** p319 L8.
The two most famous buildings of the architect Inigo Jones (1573-1652) are the Queen's House, Greenwich (*see p131*) and the Banqueting Hall, Whitehall. The latter was built between

Watch out for the tank! **Guards' Museum.** *See p83.*

1619 and 1622 at the request of King James I as an extension to Whitehall Palace where he lived. Its perfect classical proportions were influenced by the Italian architect Palladio and it was celebrated as the first Renaissance building in London. It was decorated by James's son King Charles I, who commissioned the Flemish artist Peter Paul Rubens to paint a representation of the triumph of wisdom and justice over rebellion and falsehood in a swirl of clouds and well-nourished cherubs. Thirteen years later, Charles walked across St James's Park, into the Banqueting Hall and out through one of the tall windows on to a specially erected scaffold where he spoke briefly to a vast throng of his subjects, called himself 'a martyr of the people' and knelt over a chopping block for his execution.

When fire destroyed Whitehall Palace in 1698 the hall was all that was left. From 1700 the hall was used first as a chapel, then as a museum. Nowadays it is primarily a tourist attraction, but classical concerts are performed on Monday lunchtimes at monthly intervals. A visit to the Banqueting Hall is preceded by a video presentation of its history. *Nearest picnic place: St James's Park. Shop.*

Buckingham Palace & Royal Mews

SW1 (7321 2233/www.royal.gov.uk). Green Park or St James's Park tube/Victoria tube or rail. **Open** *State Rooms* early Aug-late Sept 9.30am-4.30pm daily. *Royal Mews* late Mar-Oct 11am-4pm daily. Last entry 30mins before closing. Closed 1, 4, 8, 15 June, 25, 26 Dec. **Admission** (LP) £11.50; £9.50 concessions; £6 5-17s; £29 family (2+2); free under-5s. *Royal Mews* £5; £4 concessions; £2.50 5-17s; £12.50 family (2+2); free under-5s. *Queen's Picture Gallery* £6.50; £5 OAPs; £3 children; £16 family. **Credit** AmEx, MC, V. **Map** p318 H9.
Buck House was originally bought from the Buckingham family by the Queen's ancestor George III, and it was his son, George IV, who commissioned the extensions that constitute the formal parts that the public sees when the palace opens

as a showhome for part of the summer (when Liz and Phil get away from it all in the country). Visitors queue from 9am at the box office on Constitution Hill for tickets to view 18 State Apartments, including the Music Room, which was used for the christenings of Charles, Anne, Andrew and Edward, with water brought from the River Jordan; and the Ballroom, which is occasionally used for sit-down meals and banquets when the number of guests demands (the Queen's great-great grandmother Victoria, who brought up nine children under this roof, used to complain about the lack of space in the palace and insisted that the ballroom at least be able to accommodate the incredibly wide skirts that were fashionable among 19th-century debutantes because they prohibited close dancing).

The Queen's Picture Gallery reopened on 22 May 2002 with a special Golden Jubilee exhibition entitled Royal Treasures. Works of art including sculpture and jewellery have been collected from all the royal residences around the country. Rembrandts and Van Dycks jostle for space alongside some of the Crown Jewels, including the Diadem Crown, as featured on banknotes and postage stamps. Of particular interest is the recently unveiled portrait by Lucian Freud of Her Majesty as a wrinkled old granny. The exhibition runs until 12 January 2003. The shop, on the way out, has special Windsor Family chocs, tea towels, mugs, replica jewellery, jigsaws and tin soldiers modelled on the ones who stamp up and down outside.

Just around the corner from Buckingham Palace, on Buckingham Palace Road, the Royal Mews is home to the royal carriages that are rolled out for the royals to wag their hands from on very important occasions. The family keeps one or two limousines powered by internal combustion engines but otherwise travels around in horse-drawn coaches, of which they have made something of a collection, including the Coronation Coach, the Glass Coach and the fairy-tale golden State Coach built in 1761. The horses, which are beautifully groomed by loving servicemen, have their own exercise and dressage arena. The Mews is closed during Royal Ascot and on state occasions.
Buggy access (Royal Mews). Lift (Buckingham Palace). Nappy-changing facilities (Buckingham Palace). Nearest picnic place: Green Park. Shop.

Cabinet War Rooms
Clive Steps, King Charles Street, SW1 (7930 6961/ www.iwm.org.uk). St James's Park or Westminster tube. **Open** *Oct-Mar* 10am-6pm daily. *Apr-Sept* 9.30am-6pm daily. Last entry 45mins before closing. Closed 24-26 Dec. **Admission** £5.80; £4.20 OAPs, students; £2.10-£2.90 concessions; free under-15s. **Credit** AmEx, MC, V. **Map** p319 K9.

During World War II Prime Minister Winston Churchill, and on occasions even his wife Clementine, actually lived in these bunkers. The labyrinth as it currently exists includes the operations room with the maps, compasses and other paraphernalia left exactly as they were when the war ended. The new rooms will be formally opened to the public in spring 2003. Churchill's famous chamberpot, which is the one exhibit to stay in the minds of the young, will then be returned with his bed to its wartime position. Other rooms will open as a dedicated education suite equipped with internet link-ups to other Churchillian and military sites. A second phase of expansion, which is due to be completed in 2005, will treble the space.

The thorough and wide-ranging schools programmes include a tour, a talk and an educational element focusing on the Home Front, World War II and the subsequent Cold War (in which Churchill but not the bunker was involved). In the workshops (which take place in all school holidays except summer, when the volume of tourist traffic is too high), scouts, guides and students investigate rationing, operate stirrup pumps, wear gas masks, handle items in an evacuee's suitcase or spend an afternoon 'making do and mending'.
Buggy access. Lift. Nappy-changing facilities. Nearest picnic place: St James's Park. Shop.

Guards' Museum
Wellington Barracks, Birdcage Walk, SW1 (7414 3271). St James's Park tube. **Open** 10am-4pm (last entry 3.30pm) daily. Closed 25 Dec, 1 Jan. *Tours* by arrangement; phone for details. **Admission** (LP) £2; £1 concessions; free under-16s. **Credit** *Shop* MC, V. **Map** p318 J9.

A new exhibition to celebrate the Queen's Golden Jubilee focuses specifically on the history since 1656 of the Grenadier Guards of which Her Majesty has been Colonel-in-Chief

Around Town

Big Ben's in the House. *See p85.*

Rubbing shoulders with history at **St Martin-in-the-Fields**. *See p87.*

In & around: Trafalgar Square

Plans to exclude traffic from and pedestrianise the north side of Trafalgar Square by 2004 are well advanced. The move will be of benefit mainly to visitors to the National Gallery and the National Portrait Gallery, who will then have more than the current thin strip of grass to sprawl on while they eat ice-creams, write postcards and have a smoke.

The fountains in the square are wonderful cooling-off paddling pools in the summer. It used to be traditional for New Year revellers to throw themselves in, but the council killjoys now cover them over after Christmas.

Looming over the square is a 145ft column on which a pigeons-only effigy of **Admiral Nelson** stands, guarded by four huge bronze lions that youngsters like to clamber on and pet. Also look for the four statue plinths. Two of them are occupied by empire-building generals, and a third by George IV on horseback. The fourth was empty from 1843 until 1999, when a decision was made to fill it with a succession of modern sculptures, each in residence for about a year. The first was a life-size figure of a shaven-headed Christ by Mark Wallinger, called *Ecce Homo*. Next was a bronze of a tree resting on a head resting on a book called *Regardless of History*, by Bill Woodrow. The most recent was a transparent inverted replica of the plinth beneath it called *Monument*, by Rachel

Whiteread. In spring 2002 the plinth was again empty and awaiting a final decision on whether the policy of temporary sculptures is to continue. A statue of the late Queen Mother has been mooted as a fitting monument.

Behind the National Gallery is the **Westminster Reference Library**, which is useful if you cannot finish your crossword or you need a break from the rain. Behind the church of St Martin-in-the-Fields is a craft market and nearby a large post office with a shop attached selling first-edition stamps. In Craven Street is the Armed Forces Careers Office, where you can sign up for a life of boot-polishing and peace-keeping in strife-torn countries. Northumberland Avenue leads down to the river, where the restaurant ship *Hispaniola* is moored.

The statue of **King Charles I** on the south side of the square stands on the supposed dead centre of London. All mileposts measure to him. He glares down Whitehall, where he met his gruesome end under the axeman's blade. **Downing Street**, where the Prime Minister and his Chancellor are next-door neighbours, is a short walk away. **Admiralty Arch** is now a home for the poor. It straddles the pink asphalt of the **Mall**, which leads grandly down to Buckingham Palace. Cockspur Street is the surprising location of an immensely child-friendly restaurant, the Texas Embassy Cantina (*see p181*).

for the last 60 years. She was but a slip of a girl when they first saluted her. The Grenadiers is the third oldest of the five guards regiments, whose combined stories this splendid museum tells. The others are the Scots (founded 1642), the Coldstream (1650), the Irish (1900) and the Welsh (1915). Among the medals, tunics and weaponry filling most of the display cases is a miniature Guard's uniform tailored for 9-year-old Prince Arthur, son of Queen Victoria. There's also a picture of George II at the Battle of Dettingen in 1743 – this was the last time a British monarch fought in a war. The oldest medal displayed here was awarded by Oliver Cromwell to officers of his New Model Army at the Battle of Dunbar in 1651.

Mementoes collected from the regiments' many actions over the centuries include the gateposts from the farm at Le Caillou where Napoleon encamped the night before Waterloo, and a Nazi propaganda document in English entitled 'Hitler's Last Appeal to Reason' and signed by the Führer himself. There's also a bottle of Iraqi whisky captured in the Gulf War. The Guards can be seen in ceremonial action performing the Changing of the Guard. The toy soldier shop at the museum, the largest of its kind in London, sells all kinds of miniature models, including not-very-military farm animals.
Buggy access. Lift. Nearest picnic place: St James's Park. Shop.

Houses of Parliament

Parliament Square, SW1 (Commons info 7219 4272/Lords info 7219 3107/tours 7344 9966/ www.parliament.uk). Westminster tube. **Open** (when in session) *House of Commons Visitors' Gallery* 2.30-10pm Mon-Wed; 11.30am-7.30pm Thur; 9.30am-3pm Fri. Closed bank hols. *House of Lords Visitors' Gallery* 2.30pm

It stands opposite the National Lottery Office, where you have to go to pick up the cheque when you win a big sum.

Plans to discourage pigeons from Trafalgar Square by excluding vendors of Mary Poppins pigeon food have failed utterly. The vermin of the air still flock there in terrifying numbers. What a shame we do not eat them. Someone could do a roaring trade selling spatchcock pigeon to the lounging culture vultures.

Mon-Wed; from 3pm Thur; from 11am Fri. *Tours* summer recess only; phone for details. **Admission** *Public gallery* free. *Tours* £7; £3.50 concessions, 5-16s; free under-4s. **Map** p319 L9.
For the first time in the history of parliament, members of the public now have the facilities of a cafeteria at their disposal when they visit. The honourable members have agreed to give up one of their own, although they still have five other cafés and eight licensed bars to relax in after going in and out of their 1,000 rooms and up and down their 100 staircases.

The first Parliament was held here in 1275, but Westminster did not become its permanent home until 1532, when Henry VIII made his home at Whitehall Palace. Parliament was originally housed in the choir stalls of St Stephen's Chapel, where members sat facing each other; the tradition continues today. Today, the only remaining parts of the original palace are Westminster Hall, where the body of the Queen Mother lay in state before her funeral in April 2002, and the Jewel Tower (*see below*). The rest burned down in a fire in 1834 and was rebuilt in neo-Gothic style by Charles Barry and Augustus Pugin.

Families can queue up to visit any session of both the Commons and the Lords, though there's such demand for places at Prime Minister's Questions in the Commons (3pm on Wednesdays) that prospective visitors have to apply to their MP in writing. In general, it's easiest to gain access in the evening when even many MPs find it hard to raise the enthusiasm for debate. There's no minimum age for visitors but children must at least be able to sign their name in the visitors' book. Parliament goes into recess at Christmas, Easter and during the summer just as schools do; at these times the galleries are open only for pre-booked guided tours (call for details).

Always phone to check opening times before making a special journey.
Café. Nearest picnic place: Victoria Tower Gardens. Shop.

ICA Gallery

The Mall, SW1 (box office 7930 3647/membership enquiries 7766 1439/www.ica.org.uk). Piccadilly Circus tube/Charing Cross tube/rail. **Open** *Galleries* noon-7.30pm daily. Closed 24-26 Dec, 31 Dec, 1 Jan. **Membership** (LP) *Daily* £1.50, £1 concessions Mon-Fri; £2.50, £1.50 concessions Sat, Sun; free under-14s. *Annual* £30; £20 concessions. **Credit** AmEx, DC, MC, V. **Map** p319 K8.
Though computer screens and digital technology befuddle many parents, kids seem intuitively to know what to do at a terminal. The Institute of Contemporary Arts recognises this, hence its 'Summer University' for 11-16-year-olds, for free fortnightly digital courses in areas such as web design, web movie making and computer game creation. Of a more traditional nature are the sixth-form conferences in which arty teenagers can meet professional artists, and the workshops attended and run by contestants in the annual Beck's Futures exhibition (an art competition sponsored by Beck's beer, won in 2002 by Toby Paterson). Temporary exhibitions provide ready-made subjects for discussion. Half-term breaks are filled with workshops in drawing or sculpture and there are plans for a primary school programme with dance, art appreciation and computer animation strands.
Café. Nappy-changing facilities. Nearest picnic place: St James's Park. Shop.

Jewel Tower

Abingdon Street, SW1 (7222 2219/www.english-heritage.org.uk). Westminster tube. **Open** *Apr-Sept* 10am-6pm daily. *Oct* 10am-5pm daily. *Nov-Mar* 10am-4pm daily. Last entry 30mins before closing. Closed 24-26 Dec, 1 Jan. **Admission** (EH/LP) £1.60; £1.20 concessions; 80p 5-16s; free under-5s. **Credit** MC, V. **Map** p319 L9.

Water ways: bridge spotting

When Westminster Bridge was built in 1750 it was the first new bridge into the capital since the Romans constructed London Bridge. (Putney and Fulham were connected by bridge in 1729 but they were mere country villages, miles from downtown London, in those days.)

Westminster Bridge was a great marvel and opened with a terrific fanfare, followed by a long procession consisting of everyone of rank from King George II down. No dog was allowed on it in case it pooed on the gleaming new pavements, and anyone who defaced the balustrades with graffiti was liable to nothing short of the death penalty. In fact, the idea of a bridge at Westminster had first been mooted 90 years earlier with the return to England of Charles II, but the Thames ferrymen, fearing for their livelihoods, had opposed the plans. In the end, the need for a bridge became so urgent that Parliament debated the matter and commissioned the work but still had to appease the ferrymen with a huge compensatory payment of £25,000.

Today, 21 bridges and only one ferry (at Woolwich, see p134) cross the tidal Thames. Most of the bridges were erected in the 19th century, when London expanded rapidly and enormously to suit its identity as the capital not of a mere nation but of a great empire. Most were pulled down and rebuilt in the 20th century – paradoxically, the newest, **Tower Bridge** (1894), is now one of the oldest, and the oldest, **London Bridge** (AD 100), is now one of the the newest (1972). The latter's predecessor was bought by Americans and transported brick by numbered brick across the Atlantic to be re-erected at Lake Havasu, USA. They say the buyer thought he was purchasing the more famous Tower Bridge and had confused the names, but the story could well be apocryphal.

The Victorians built suspension bridges such as **Hammersmith** (1887) and **Albert** (1873). These are the oldest and prettiest bridges on the Thames. Their supporting towers and cables are covered in fairy lights at night. The present **Chelsea Bridge** (1934) is also suspended. Excavations during its construction unearthed human remains alongside Roman and early British weapons, proving that a costly battle had been fought on the site.

The most stunning bridge is certainly the Queen Elizabeth II modern suspension bridge, which carries the M25 across the Thames estuary to the east of London. It is almost like flying, it is so high. Of course, the newest bridges are all pedestrian ones: the **Millennium**, or 'Wobbly', Bridge and the new **Hungerford Bridges** (see p24 for all).

The bridge of which most photographs are taken remains Tower Bridge, the usual vantage point being City Park on the south bank just in front of the eccentric globular headquarters of the Greater London Assembly. The bridge from which most photographs are taken is Westminster Bridge, since looking west the lens has Big Ben in the background, and east the Millennium Wheel. Even before these attractions were in place, the views of London from its parapets were celebrated: the poet William Wordsworth stood on it one misty early morning in 1802 and concluded that 'earth hath not anything to show more fair'.

The moated Jewel Tower is a survivor from the medieval Palace of Westminster. It was built in 1365-6 to house Edward III's gold and jewels but there are no jewels here now. Instead, the museum, which welcomes school groups, features an exhibition on the past and present of Parliament. Of most interest to children is a Saxon sword that was dug up during excavation of the moat in 1948. But almost as interesting to young visitors is the shop, which stocks tapestries, cushion covers, stationery, toiletries and ice-creams, which might come in handy in this otherwise snack-free area. *Nearest picnic place: Victoria Tower Gardens. Shop.*

National Gallery
Trafalgar Square, WC2 (info line 7747 2885/ www.nationalgallery.org.uk). Leicester Square tube/ Charing Cross tube/rail. **Open** 10am-6pm Mon, Tue, Thur-Sun; 10am-9pm Wed. *Micro Gallery* 10am-5.30pm Mon, Tue, Thur-Sun; 10am-8.30pm Wed. *Sainsbury Wing* 10am-6pm Mon, Tue, Thur-Sun; 10am-9pm Wed. Closed 24, 25 Dec, 1 Jan, Good Friday. *Tours* times vary; check info line. **Admission** (LP) free. *Temporary exhibitions* prices vary. *Tours* free. **Credit** *Shop* MC, V. **Map** p319 K7.

This great collection of Western European painting from the mid 13th century to 1900 started from the 38 pictures that in 1824 constituted the so-called National Collection of Paintings. Hung in light, airy galleries – especially in the Sainsbury Wing – the present vast collection includes famous masterpieces that children, as well as their parents, are bound to recognise: Constable's *Hay-Wain*, Van Gogh's *Sunflowers*, Seurat's *Bathers at Asnières* and Holbein's *The Ambassadors*, which you have to look at sideways to see the skull. Among the temporary exhibitions planned for the near future are Fabric of Vision: Dress and Drapery in Painting

(19 June-8 September 2002); Light (18 July-6 October 2002); and Puvis de Chavannes and the Beheading of John the Baptist (24 July-27 October 2002).

The National's family events are the talk of every cultured family: there are special audio guides, drop-in activities every second Saturday and Sunday of the month and a whole range of creative and educational workshops to encourage a love of art (*see also p217*).

Buggy access. Café. Lift. Nappy-changing facilities. Nearest picnic place: Leicester Square/Trafalgar Square. Restaurant. Shops.

National Portrait Gallery

2 St Martin's Place, WC2 (7306 0055/www.npg.org.uk). Leicester Square tube/Charing Cross tube/rail. **Open** 10am-6pm Mon-Wed, Sat, Sun; 10am-9pm Thur, Fri. Closed 25, 26 Dec, 1 Jan. *Tours* Aug, times vary; phone for details. **Admission** (LP) free. *Temporary exhibitions* prices vary. *Tours* free. **Credit** AmEx, MC, V. **Map** p319 K7.

Before the invention of photography, families who wanted to record their images for posterity had to turn to portraitists for help. You'll find no better evidence of that than at the National Portrait Gallery. All the portraits in the gallery are of people who have contributed in some way to the life of Great Britain over the years.

The main collection hangs in the new Ondaatje Wing (named after a major contributor, Christopher Ondaatje) at the top of a long escalator. Picture 5511, in Room 1, shows the boy-king Edward VI looking serious as he carries the weight of his father Henry VIII's ambitions on his tiny shoulders, while in Room 2 (picture 3914) Walter Raleigh and his son (also named Walter but known as Wat) adopt identical poses, and in Room 5 (picture 4759) Cornelius Johnson immortalises the Royalist Capel family shortly before the father's execution in 1640. Items from the photograph collection change frequently because of their sensitivity to light, which means that Howard Coster's snapshot of AA Milne with his son Christopher Robin and the original Winnie the Pooh may or may not be on display (though you can always buy a postcard of it in the shop). The extension also boasts the Portrait, a swanky restaurant with views beyond Nelson's Column and across a sea of sloping rooftops to Westminster. In the main building, in Room 21 (picture 1833), Henry Jamyn Brooks' painting of the Old Masters Exhibition at the Royal Academy in 1888 focuses on a family visiting an art exhibition, just like you're doing. *See also p217.*

Buggy access. Café. Lift. Nappy-changing facilities. Nearest picnic place: Leicester Square/Trafalgar Square. Restaurant. Shop.

St Martin-in-the-Fields

Trafalgar Square, WC2 (7766 1100/Brass Rubbing Centre 7930 9306/www.stmartin-in-the-fields.org). Leicester Square tube/Charing Cross tube/rail. **Open** *Church* 8am-6pm daily. *Brass Rubbing Centre* 10am-6pm Mon-Sat; noon-6pm Sun. **Admission** free. *Brass rubbing* (LP) £2.90-£15 (special rates for groups and families). *Evening concerts* £6-£16 (7.30pm Thur-Sat). **Credit** MC, V. **Map** p319 L7.

This is Buckingham Palace's local church, and it has a royal box in the gallery, though not many members of the monarchy have visited its beautiful interior since it really was 'in the fields' between Westminster and the City. Nowadays it's chiefly famous for its cheap café in the crypt (*see p89*), its soup kitchen for the homeless and its free lunchtime concerts on Mondays, Tuesdays and Fridays, at 1pm. Its chief attraction as far as children are concerned is the city's only brass rubbing centre, with 90 brasses from all over the world. Many are scaled-down replicas and some have been designed specially for the tourist market. Particularly popular are the

two beautifully ornate Flemish dragons from the late 14th century. Rubbings, which are supervised, take about half an hour to complete. All materials are supplied.

Café. Nearest picnic place: Leicester Square/ Trafalgar Square.

Tate Britain

Millbank, SW1 (7887 8000/www.tate.org.uk). Pimlico tube/C10, 77A, 88 bus. **Open** 10am-5.50pm daily. Closed 24-26 Dec. *Tours* free; 11.30am, 2.30pm, 3.30pm Mon-Fri. **Admission** (LP) free; prices for special exhibitions vary. **Credit** MC, V. **Map** p319 L7.

Since the establishment of Tate Modern downriver in Southwark (*see p47*), Tate Britain has dedicated its galleries to British art from the 16th century to the present, with displays of Blake, Constable, Spencer and Bacon and so on expanded to fit the greater space. To mark 100 years since the Tate opened, the Centenary Development was unveiled on 1 November 2001. The project has created extra space for the collections – new galleries on the main floor plus six new Linbury Galleries on the ground floor. The latter will host temporary exhibitions – look out for Lucian Freud (20 June-15 September 2002) and Gainsborough (17 October 2002-12 January 2003). A grand staircase and increased visitor facilities (another shop, and more talks and conferences) round off the upgrade.

Every Sunday is children's day, with Art Trolley (creative play) for the under-11s and the less messy Art Space for older kids, with jigsaws and other activities. For more on these and on family workshops in the school holidays, *see p218.*

Buggy access. Café. Lift. Nappy-changing facilities. Nearest picnic place: lawns on either side of gallery/Riverside Gardens by Vauxhall Bridge. Shop.

Westminster Abbey

Dean's Yard, SW1 (7222 5152/tours 7222 7110/ www.westminster-abbey.org). St James's Park or Westminster tube. **Open** *Nave & royal chapels* 9.30am-4.45pm Mon-Fri; 9am-2.45pm Sat. *Chapter House* Nov-Mar 10am-4pm daily. Apr-Sept 9.30am-5pm daily. Oct 10am-5pm daily. *Pyx Chamber & Abbey Museum* 10.30am-4pm daily. *College Garden* Apr-Sept 10am-6pm Tue-Thur. Oct-Mar 10am-4pm Tue-Thur. Last entry 1hr before closing. Closed 24, 25 Dec, Good Friday. *Tours* phone for details. **Admission** *Nave & royal chapels* £6; £3 11-15s, concessions; £12 family (2+3); free under-11s with paying adult. *Chapter House, Pyx Chamber & Abbey Museum* (EH/LP) £2.50; £1.90 concessions; £1.30 5-15s; £1 with main entrance ticket; free with £2 audio guide; free under-5s. **Credit** MC, V. **Map** p319 K9.

Visitors to Westminster Abbey are greeted by the boy-king Richard II, whose portrait hangs inside the porch overlooking the Tomb of the Unknown Warrior, the simplest but most haunting memorial in a building full of them. The abbey was consecrated in 1065 by Edward the Confessor, who died in the same year and is buried behind the high altar. On Christmas Day in 1066 his cousin William the Conqueror was crowned King of England. From that time on, the abbey has been linked with royalty – with two exceptions, every English monarch since William the Conqueror (1066) has been crowned here, and many are buried here, too, along with poets, musicians, scientists and many others who have played significant roles in the history of the nation. In April 2002 it witnessed the sombre funeral of the 101-year-old Queen Elizabeth the Queen Mother. Millions around the world tuned in to the broadcast.

Of special interest to children is Innocents' Corner, part of the north aisle of Henry VII's chapel; in it are buried the skeletons of the two small boys found in the Tower of London

Around Town

The Thames Barrier

1 Unity Way, Woolwich, London SE18 5NJ
Telephone 0208 305 4188
Fax 0208 855 2146

'The eighth wonder of the world...'

The Thames Barrier is a major part of the flood defence system protecting London against rising water levels and tidal surges.

INFORMATION CENTRE

This has a working model of the Barrier and a video describing its construction, operation and why we need it. Display boards explain the wildlife and environment of the Thames. Small admission charge. Seasonal opening times apply. Telephone 0208 305 4188 for details.

LEARNING CENTRE

We offer educational activities based around environmental issues and aim to give hands-on learning experiences. They include a river walk and games on flooding and recycling. Teacher-led visits available for school groups.

NEW FOR 2002:

Wetlands Area: this includes a pond for pond dipping activities.
Wildlife Garden: the London Habitat Garden encourages wildlife back into the capital.

ENVIRONMENT AGENCY

www.environment-agency.gov.uk

Walk: goosey gander

This is a walk around the lake in **St James's Park**, home to a huge variety of waterfowl.

▶ Enter the park at the south-west corner. Cross a sign painted on the ground that says 'No Cycling, No Skating'. This is a shame because the path, which you now follow clockwise around the lake, is smooth and good for wheels. Hold on to your pushchairs and prams. Look out for pigeons, which show no shyness of human beings. They like to cadge free rides around the park.

▶ Look up at Buckingham Palace to your left. If the Queen is in, the flag will be flying. If she or a member of her family has just died, the flag will be at half-mast (as it was in April), and there will be television camera crews in the park asking people such as yourself for comments. The swans in the park are extraordinary: special royal birds with black feathers and red bills. If you've brought bread for the birds, you'll be mobbed by Canada geese trying to muscle in on any free scraps of food. There are far too many of them, but they do make a dramatic sight when they fly low in formation and land in the lake with a splash like gunslingers skidding into town.

▶ Pass the bandstand on your left. Stop and listen if there is someone playing. Once only British military bands played here but now wind ensembles from all over the world come and entertain the tourists during the summer. Approach if they are any good and sit in a green-striped deckchair. Pay the attendant £1 for the privilege when he comes by. Snooze in the sun.

▶ Return to the lakeside path. Cross the elegant concrete bridge if you wish – there is an excellent photo opportunity of Buckingham Palace from the middle – but be sure to come back or you'll shorten your walk by half. Continue along the north bank. There is a range of wildfowl swimming where the lake is widest: coots, mallards, mandarins, smews, goldeneyes and shelducks; they all like a handful of crisps if you have any. There are also a number of seagulls, proving that London is really a seaside town. Many of these webfooted bipeds inhabit Duck Island at the eastern end of the lake. Follow the path round the island. On the southern side is a small bungalow where the groundsmen keep their rakes, hoes and wellies. Nearby is a rocky outcrop, where pelicans hold court. If you are lucky, you will catch them at feeding time; their bills go all baggy when they are full of fish. Continue past daffodil plantations and groups of foreign students playing frisbee on the grass. Pass the southern end of the concrete bridge. The walk is nearly over. A little further on you come to a large refreshment kiosk beside a fenced-off children's park. Buy ice-creams all round and lose the kids in the park, which has swings, slides, see-saws and a large soft sandpit.

in the 15th century, believed to be Edward V and his brother Richard, who were thought to have been murdered by their uncle Richard, later Richard III. Here, too, are the tombs of two of the children of James I: the effigy of Princess Sophia, who lived only three days, lies in a stone cradle, and Princess Mary, who died when she was two, reclines on top of a miniature mausoleum.

In 1998 ten niches on the west front of the abbey, which had been empty since the Middle Ages, were filled with new statues of selected 20th-century martyrs, including Archbishop of San Salvador, Oscar Romero; Polish Catholic Maximilian Kolbe; Dietrich Bonhoeffer, who was murdered by the Nazis; and black rights activist Martin Luther King Jr.

The boys' choir, one of the world's most famous, is as old as the abbey itself. Auditions for boys aged 8-10 of any religion take place regularly, with successful applicants educated at Westminster School in Dean's Yard beside the abbey. The luckiest choristers get to sing at coronations (which are admittedly few and far between), royal weddings and other state occasions.

Buggy access. Café. Nearest picnic place: Dean's Yard. Shop.

Westminster Cathedral

Victoria Street, SW1 (7798 9055/tours 7798 9064/ www.westminstercathedral.org.uk). Victoria tube/rail. **Open** 7am-7pm Mon-Fri, Sun; 8am-7pm Sat. *Tours* by arrangement; phone for details. **Admission** free; donations appreciated. *Campanile* £2; £1 concessions; £5 family (2+2). *Audio guide* £2.50; £1.50 concessions. **No credit cards. Map** p318 J10.

Worksheets available at the gift shop familiarise the young with this beautiful late Victorian Roman Catholic cathedral, whose vaulted pitch-black ceiling is still waiting to be decorated. Sheets for the under-10s require kids to study the architecture and spot butterflies in the mosaics; those for the over-10s ask questions on subjects such as the martyrs and saints commemorated in the building. It's worth the climb to the viewing platform at the top of the campanile.

The boys' choir, one of the finest choirs of its type in the world, sings daily Vespers (5pm) and Mass (5.30pm; more on Sundays) all year except August. Roman Catholic boys aged 8-10 can apply to the headmaster of the choir school for auditions, which are held regularly.

Buggy access. Café. Nearest picnic place: Ashley Gardens off Howick Place. Shop.

Where to eat

Try **Texas Embassy Cantina** behind Trafalgar Square (1 Cockspur Street, SW1, 7925 0077; *see also p181*), where there's a childen's menu and sunny staff. The **Cakehouse Café** in St James's Park is good for simple sausages, jacket potato, or soup lunches. There are several internet cafés around Victoria station, including **easyEverything** (9-13 Wilton Road, SW1, 7233 8456) and **Café Internet** (22-4 Buckingham Palace Road, SW1, 7233 5786). There are branches of **ASK** (7630 8228) and **Pizza Express** (7828 1477) on Victoria Street.

Crivelli's Garden (7747 2869), the National Gallery's smart restaurant, has high chairs but a fancy menu. Lunches are cheap and filling in **Café in the Crypt** (St Martin-in-the-Fields, Duncannon Street, WC2, 7839 4342) if all that brass rubbing has worked up an appetite.

Around Town

Marylebone

Universal appeal.

Marylebone is one of the most diverse areas of London. Its attractions are plentiful, and contrasting: it has the cleanest, airiest, most elegant of the capital's green spaces in **Regent's Park**, and the noisiest, most traffic-clogged street in the six-lane **Marylebone Road**. There's wildlife at the world-renowned **London Zoo** and still life at the **Wallace Collection** in Manchester Square, one of the capital's loveliest art galleries.

Marylebone has the nation's most verbose building in the **BBC's Broadcasting House**, which transmits a constant babble of radio voices on many channels to all parts of the world day and night, and a peaceful city space in the serene **Memorial Garden of Rest** at **Marylebone Parish Church**, at the top of Marylebone High Street, where Byron was baptised in 1788.

On the one hand it has a journey through space visiting stars of distant galaxies trillions of light years away at the **London Planetarium**, and on the other it has a journey through time in the waxed effigies of stars of another kind throughout the years at **Madame Tussaud's**.

If you'd rather shop than see sights, you're spoilt for choice. Marylebone is bordered to the south by London's most famous – and busiest – shopping street, **Oxford Street**. There's not much for families here – shops, of course, but try to tackle them on the weekend with the kids and you'll be frazzled in no time. For a more sedate retail experience, it has to be increasingly hip **Marylebone High Street**, with boutiques and brand names but few bargains.

Broadcasting House

Portland Place, W1 (switchboard 7580 4468/shop 7765 0025/www.bbc.co.uk). Oxford Circus tube. **Open** *Shop 9.30am-6pm Mon-Fri; 9.30am-5.30pm Sat; 11am-5pm Sun.* **Credit** *Shop AmEx, MC, V.* **Map** *p316 H5.*
The BBC shop sells books, magazines, CDs, DVDs and audio-tapes of certain radio broadcasts. It also stocks BBC mementoes, souvenirs and toys for junior fans. For backstage tours of the BBC Wood Lane building, *see p163.*

London Central Mosque

146 Park Road, NW8 (7724 3363). Baker Street tube. **Open** *dawn-dusk daily.*
Except on Fridays, this is the most peaceful building in central London. Its golden dome stands out for miles. Anyone may enter, although visitors should remember that they have to remove their shoes and may be embarrassed if their socks are stale. The sexes are still segregated: women upstairs, men down. Inside, the atmosphere is as calm as a good night's sleep. A few people are praying on mats, facing Mecca; others quietly lie about chatting. This is multicultural, multi-faith, multi-tongued London at its most serene, and an inspirational place for schoolchildren studying world religion as part of the National Curriculum.
Buggy access. Nearest picnic place: Regent's Park. Restaurant. Shop.

London Planetarium

Marylebone Road, NW1 (0870 400 3000/www.london-planetarium.com). Baker Street tube. **Open** *June 10am-5.30pm Mon-Fri; 9.30am-5.30pm Sat, Sun. July, Aug 9am-5.30pm daily. Sept-May 10am-5.30pm Mon-Fri; 9.30am-5.30pm Sat, Sun. Closed 25 Dec.* **Admission** *tickets for Planetarium only cannot be pre-booked £2.45; £1.50 5-15s; £1.80 concessions. Under-5s not admitted. Combined ticket with Madame Tussaud's £14.95; £10.50 5-15s; £11.70 concessions; £49 family (2+2 or 1+3).* **Credit** AmEx, MC, V. **Map** p316 G4.

Water ways: canal connections

In 1793 the British government ordained a brilliant new way of getting from London to Birmingham: the Grand Union Canal. Everyone was pleased, except the stagecoach companies and highwaymen. The journey time was about three days (with stops), which isn't much longer than it now takes by car on a bank holiday. Given the small amount of energy required to propel even the hugest narrowboat or barge, canal travel is by far the most efficient form of inland travel ever invented.

The **Regent's Canal**, which runs along the north side of Regent's Park, connects with the **Grand Union Canal**, the main water-artery to the Midlands, at Paddington. From there the Regent's

Canal runs east under Edgware Road and St John's Wood to Camden Town and Islington. A tunnel then links it with the docks in the City Basin, from where it flows to Hackney and Stepney, finally joining the Thames at Limehouse. Forty bridges cross it and a dozen locks regulate its flow.

Even today, there are still 2,000 miles of canals – the length of China's Yangtze River – in Britain. Whole families take their holidays on barges every summer, idling round the country at pre-industrial speeds. And though little commercial traffic now uses this form of transport, London's canal paths provide some of the most interesting walks through the capital.

In a puddle at **Regent's Park**. *See p92.*

The Wonders of the Universe Star Show is a computer-generated 3-D journey through distant galaxies beamed on to the Planetarium's dome by the high-tech Digistar II projector. Choose a seat in one of the back rows, sit back and enjoy an outer-space experience, with meteorite showers and exploding planets and even a re-creation of the Big Bang. The soundtrack delivers the right atmosphere, even if it is a little corny. The 20-minute film plays every 40 minutes; if you just miss one, you have to wait in the lobby area, which is done up to look space age (with models of planets and astronauts, a zero-gravity weighing machine and other gravity-inspired games) but has little to hold the attention of kids. Conveniently, the Planetarium and neighbouring Madame Tussaud's are under the same management and you can buy combined tickets for both. Book ahead to avoid queues.

Café. Lift. Nappy-changing facilities. Nearest picnic place: Regent's Park. Shop.

London Zoo

Regent's Park, NW1 (7722 3333/www.zsl.org). Baker Street or Camden Town tube, then 274 or C2 bus. **Open** *Nov-Mar* 10am-4pm daily. *Apr-Oct* 10am-5.30pm daily. Closed 25 Dec. **Admission** £11; £8 3-15s; £9.30 concessions; free under-3s. **Credit** AmEx, MC, V. **Map** p316 G2.

Good news from the gorilla house. The four females who grieved the death of their solitary male companion in 2001 – one of them developed an eating disorder and started bullying the others – got a new chap in their lives a year later after a worldwide search. Jock, for it is he, may not have been every girl's ideal – he weighs 25 stone, is covered in hair and has smelly breath – but he cheered up his four cage-mates no end. The keepers are now expecting to hear the slap of little feet and the scrape of tiny knuckles on the floor some time in the near future.

The zoo tells daily stories of life and death. On 1 November 2001, just weeks away from the 100th anniversary of the species' discovery, there was general rejoicing over the birth of a baby okapi called Jemima. The same month also saw the arrival of a baby giant anteater, Estrela. Some events are tragic: last year Jim Robson, one of the keepers, was killed by an elephant. The pachyderms have since been moved to Whipsnade Zoo where a plantation of (evergreen) holm oaks, a favourite of elephants for its bark and its leaves, has been established in memory of Jim Robson, who loved the animals. A monument is also to be placed in London Zoo.

Of the large animals that fascinate children, the zoo has lions, tigers, leopards, pygmy hippos, camels, sloth bears, alligators, iguanas and pythons. Whipsnade (see p283) has in addition to these and the elephants, rhinos and wallabies.

The £4.4 million spent on the Web of Life was money well-invested. Set in a light, bright, ecologically aware building called the Millennium Conservation Centre, it is a monument to biodiversity, which is presented, explained and celebrated in a delightful fashion. The cockroaches

Walk: Regent's Park

▶ Start at Baker Street. Walk north towards the trees and open spaces of Regent's Park. Turn right at **Cornwall Terrace** and enter the park through a gate on the left. Follow the course of the boating lake north. Take a pedalo or scull out for half an hour if you have time and energy. Come in when your 30 minutes are up or you will incur a penalty. Continue north along the path until you see the golden dome of the **London Central Mosque**. If it's a Friday, you may hear the muezzin calling the faithful to prayer through a loudspeaker. Turn right and follow the path across the bridge, making for the café, where your boating exertions may demand a rest-stop. Walk on towards the outbuildings of **London Zoo**, where the sights and smells remind adults of childhood, and encourage them to bring their own offspring here.

▶ Regent's Park is more open than London's other green spaces – the oaks and elms of Henry VIII's hunting lands have long since been felled, and only eight of the 56 stuccoed park-covering terraces of the architect John Nash's iced wedding-cake fantasy were ever built – a fact that Londoners are probably grateful for. Still, the layout of the park and many of the beautiful surrounding houses were Nash's design and it is he and his employer the Prince Regent with whom the park is most associated. How the architect came to have such a close relationship with the regent who ruled while his mad father ranted is a matter of conjecture. What is known is that Nash married a girl called Mary Bradley who was already pregnant. She had

another five children, none of whom Nash ever acknowledged as his own. Could they have been the prince's? We'll never know, but historians have their suspicions, because Nash's consultancy as

crawling around in a tank furnished with the detritus of human life is strangely alluring. Much entertainment can be had from the penguins diving and waddling in their cool, white, elegant home (by Tecton and Lubetkin), which shows what a graceful 20th-century substance concrete can be. The Reptile House is another popular haunt, and no child should be denied the pleasure of cuddling goats and sheep in the 'touch paddock' of the renovated Children's Zoo, which has now reopened after closure the previous year due to the foot-and-mouth epidemic. The farm gives practical advice on how to look after hamsters, gerbils, guinea pigs, mice and rats at home. The black rats in the small mammal house are worth a visit. They are the world's hardiest creature, blamed for bringing bubonic plague to Europe. One wonders why they have been afforded space in the zoo, especially when the tag beneath their cage says, 'The rat doesn't need conserving'.

Arachnophobes take note: the zoo's Friendly Spider Programme takes place on several afternoons each year; it's pricey at £110 but said to be very successful. The zoo also has a popular animal adoption scheme, which makes a great gift idea for animal lovers.

The shop, which has been a highlight of any visit for over 30 years, is now even better than ever, with lots of trinkets and mementoes at pocket-money prices.

Buggy access. Café. Restaurant. Nearest picnic-space: zoo grounds. Nappy-changing facilities. Shop.

Postman butterfly, London Zoo. See p92.

See p92.

Around Town

an architect began to prosper alarmingly as he came into possession of an estate on the Isle of Wight, a grand London townhouse and as he was granted royal permission to redesign a large part of central London.

▶ When you reach Nash's **Broad Walk**, turn right and head south, avoiding the rollerbladers and cyclists. At Chester Road, turn right and aim for the **Inner Circle**, which encloses the **Open Air Theatre** and Queen Mary's aromatic **Rose Garden**, where it's so peaceful that the beat of a butterfly wing counts as a loud noise. Enter the garden through elegant black and gold iron gates. Saunter through with the bees and butterflies.

▶ Return to Chester Road and the Broad Walk. Turn right and head south along leafy avenues to the **Outer Circle**. Follow Park Square round the gardens to the thundering thoroughfare of **Marylebone Road**. Cross and enter **Park Crescent**, the most graceful of all Nash's wonderful designs. Perhaps Londoners missed something after all.

Regent's Park

NW1 (7486 7905/tennis courts 7486 4216/www. royalparks.co.uk). Baker Street, Camden Town, Great Portland Street or Regent's Park tube. **Open** *Park & Queen Mary's Gardens 5am-30mins before dusk daily. Tennis courts Mar-Oct 9am-dusk daily. Apr-Sept 7am-dusk daily. Playgrounds 10am-30mins before dusk daily.* **Map** p316 G2.

Madame Tussaud's

Marylebone Road, NW1 (0870 400 3000/www.madame-tussauds.com). Baker Street tube. **Open** *June 10am-5.30pm Mon-Fri; 9.30am-5.30pm Sat, Sun. July, Aug 9am-5.30pm daily. Sept-May 10am-5.30pm Mon-Fri; 9.30am-5.30pm Sat, Sun. Closed 25 Dec.* **Admission** *Combined ticket with Planetarium only £14.95; £10.50 5-15s; £11.70 concessions; £49 family (2+2 or 1+3).* **Credit** *AmEx, MC, V.* **Map** p316 G4.

London's most popular fee-paying attraction, Madame Tussaud's is a shrine to 'personalities'. Trivial information accompanies the dummies. Footballer David Beckham is officially more popular than his wife Victoria, aka Posh Spice, and five-time Olympic gold medallist Steve Redgrave. Actress Catherine Zeta Jones is officially the most beautiful woman in the world.

Celebs stand around in a variety of situations. The first is the Garden Party, where you can meet Babs Windsor and Samuel L Jackson in the crowd. Moving on, you shuffle around Sporting Heroes, and the likes of Mohammed Ali and Linford Christie, into a gallery entitled 200 Years, where Napoleon Bonaparte, who granted Madame Tussaud a sitting in 1801, reclines. The hottest celebrity party is town is one where movie stars stand scowling at each other. World leaders and high achievers fill the Grand Hall, where tourists still sigh around the Princess Diana dummy, which doesn't look a day over 50. Children are usually gagging for the Chamber of Horrors by this time. Here, waxen guts spill out of bloody corpses and royal heads sit on spikes. The horrors are reached through a gloomy passageway, and include a truly horrible Jack the Ripper section and a nasty, screaming soundtrack. They're certainly alarming enough for the under-8s. The finale, a ride in a London 'time taxi', whisks you through significant points in the city's history. If you visit before 30 June 2002, you'll catch the Goal! exhibition for the World Cup.

Buggies aren't allowed but baby carriers are provided.

Café. Lifts. Nappy-changing facilities. Nearest picnic place: Regent's Park.

Becks at **Madame Tussaud's**. See p93.

St James's Spanish Place

*22 George Street, W1 (7935 0943/www.spanishplace.
hemscott.net). Baker Street or Bond Street tube.*
Open 7am-7.30pm daily. **Services** 7.15am, 12.30pm,
6pm Mon-Fri; 10am, 6pm Sat; 10.30am (*sung Latin*)
noon, 6pm Sun. **Admission** free. **Map** p316 G5.
The Spanish connection of this early Gothic Roman Catholic
church dates back to the restoration of Charles II, when a
Spanish Embassy was re-established in London, first in
Ormond Street, then in Manchester Square. In 1791, just after
the repeal of laws affecting Catholic worship, a chapel was built
on the corner of Spanish Place and Charles Street (now George
Street). Most of the holy objects in today's church came from
that older building, although Spanish links officially ceased in
1827. The present church opened in 1890, opposite the first.
Vivian Hartley became Vivien Leigh when she married Leigh
Holman in this church in 1932. The funeral of Russian chore-
ographer Vaslav Nijinsky took place here in 1950.
  Today, the church makes a great place for a spot of silent
contemplation after a day of pounding the pavement.
Confusingly, the church is not actually in Spanish Place –
unlike the original – but on George Street, around the corner
from the Wallace Collection (*see below*).

Wallace Collection

*Hertford House, Manchester Square, W1 (7935 0687/
www.the-wallace-collection.org.uk). Bond Street tube.*
Open 10am-5pm Mon-Sat; noon-5pm Sun. Closed 24, 25
Dec, Good Friday. **Admission** free. **Credit** *Shop* MC, V.
Map p316 G5.
A most handsome house, which once belonged to Sir Richard
Wallace, filled with exquisite pieces of furniture (including a
writing desk owned by Marie Antoinette), paintings and
porcelain, purchased for safekeeping in London after the
French Revolution. Old Masters, including Frans Hals's *The
Laughing Cavalier*, vie for space with magnificent European
and Asian arms and armour and a display of Catherine the
Great's crockery. In the basement space, the Watercolour
Gallery, an interactive Materials and Techniques Gallery and
the entire Reserve Collection, continue to attract art lovers
from all over. The glass-roofed Sculpture Garden is an inspir-
ing setting for the smart Café Bagatelle.
  Families are very welcome and the education department
keeps busy with an imaginative series of trails, workshops
and events to take part in (*see p218*). There's also an
'Eighteenth Century Family Day' every February; partici-
pants dance, take tea, play games and disport themselves in
Georgian style.
*Buggy access. Café. Nappy-changing facilities. Lift.
Nearest picnic place: space in front of museum.
Restaurant. Shop.*

Where to eat

As well as the multitude of cafés in Regent's Park,
Marylebone is pretty well served with the burger and
pizza chains, on Portland Street and Baker Street.
Local parents are fond of the huge and friendly
Pizza Express at the top of Baker Street (7486
0888). For more exotic options, head for Marylebone
High Street – try a cake from **Pâtisserie Valerie
at Maison Sagne** (No.105, 7935 6240) for pudding.
  Substantial meals such as noodles with tomato
sauce and chicken and chips are on the children's
menu at the bright and breezy **Giraffe**

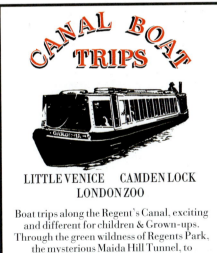

(6-8 Blandford Street, W1, 7935 2333; *see also p182*), which won the *Kids Out* Best Family Restaurant Award in 2001. Reduced-price half portions from the adults' international menu can also be ordered. Noodle joint **Wagamama** (101A Wigmore Street, W1, 7409 0111; *see also p181*) has high chairs, friendly staff and smaller portions for children.

Staff at restaurant-cum-deli **Villandry** (170 Great Portland Street, W1, 7631 3131) are happy to serve well-behaved kids, though child-size portions aren't on the menu. If you're on Baker Street in need of ice-cream, **Baskin Robbins** (No.208, NW1, 7224 6298) has some cool varieties worth investigating.

In & around: the Sherlock Holmes Museum

There is a statue of the world's most famous fictional private detective outside Baker Street tube station, looking towards his home at 221B Baker Street, which does not actually exist. The Sherlock Holmes Museum is at 239 Baker Street, although, confusingly, the number on the door reads 221B, which keeps the millions of Holmes fans around the world happy. The postman delivers their mail to the real No.221, which is now a branch of the Abbey National (a member of staff is deployed to open and answer the letters if necessary).

The **Sherlock Holmes Museum** contains the sleuth's putative deerstalker hat and pipe, leather briefcase, books and toiletries, and mannequins depicting scenes from Conan Doyle's works. Be warned, however: the entrance fee is a little expensive for a fiction.

The Sherlock Holmes Hotel on the other side of Marylebone Road, at 108 Baker Street, has deerstalker hats, magnifying glasses and meerschaum pipes in the foyer to create the right atmosphere. A little shop here displays detective accoutrements: handcuffs, pipes and pens. The **Sherlock Holmes Memorabilia Co** at 230 Baker Street (7486 1426) has a bestselling line in busts

of the much-filmed hero in what looks like his Basil Rathbone incarnation. The stock includes a variety of postcards for 50p, deerstalker hats for £24.95 and first editions of Conan Doyle novels for a cool £500. Upstairs, there's a small exhibition (adults £1.50, children £1) of sets and props from the Granada television series of Sherlock Holmes adventures, starring the late Jeremy Brett. The **Sherlock Holmes Pharmacy** at 80 Baker Street will have been patronised more by Dr Watson, although Holmes also often popped in for his toiletries as he was obviously a Victorian of clean habits. The **Marylebone Library** on the corner of Marylebone Road and Upper Montagu Street contains the Sherlock Holmes Collection and Medical Library from which he will undoubtedly have unravelled a great many mysteries.

The author Sir Arthur Conan Doyle was an eye doctor. He lived in Montagu Place and crossed Baker Street every day on his walk along Paddington Street, passing what is now Sherlock Mews to his surgery at 2 Devonshire Place. Every day he would wait for customers but none ever came, which is why he turned to writing novels instead. Paradoxically, Doyle, who did exist, has no plaque to commemorate him, while Holmes, who did not, is remembered everywhere.

There is always one mystery that periodically bedevils Londoners and those who visit, and that's 'what did I do with my umbrella?' The answer is elementary. You left it on the bus or tube and it has now gone to the **Lost Property Office** at 200 Baker Street, a repository of all the hats, false teeth, briefcases, mobile phones, bags of shopping, snotty hankies, gloves, scarves, caps, violins and umbrellas that end up ownerless on the seats of public transport at the end of the day. The staff here are considered angels of mercy, as shown by the messages of joy and gratitude from the relieved scribbled on the blotters: 'I love England, by Roberta from Italy!'. 'I find me camera, Raffaella!'. 'Thank you Sherlock. Marvin Jones, Colorado, USA.'

Sherlock Holmes Museum

221B Baker Street, NW1 (7935 8866/ www.sherlock-holmes.co.uk). Baker Street tube. **Open** 9.30am-6pm (last entry 5.30pm) daily. Closed 25 Dec. **Admission** £6; £4 6-16s; free under-6s. **Credit** AmEx, DC, MC, V. **Map** p313 F4. *Nearest picnic place: Regent's Park. Shop.*

North London

Join the crush at Camden Market, take the air in Alexandra Park, and breathe in north London's diversity.

Camden

Harry Potter fans may be interested in a detour via grubby old King's Cross station, where regeneration and rerouting for the Channel Tunnel Rail Link is a work in progress. In the station they'll find that platform nine and three quarters, all festooned with HP flags and broomstick emblems, leads you nowhere more romantic than Peterborough. At least, we haven't met anyone who's made it to Hogwarts yet.

A more down-to-earth escape from city grime can be had by a visit to the inspirational **Camley Street Natural Park**. Across York Way from the park is the **London Canal Museum**, which brings to life the history of the local waterways.

Thousands of people come to Camden Town at weekends for the market. If you'd rather avoid the crush, a more civilised attraction comes in the form of the fascinating **Jewish Museum, Camden**, just down Parkway from the tube, or the northern wing of the Proud duo of photography galleries.

But back to the market, said to be London's fourth largest tourist attraction. On fine weekends you can hardly move from the tube station to Camden Lock for crowds of visitors, which is a pretty good reason for avoiding it say exasperated Camden residents and those cynical Londoners who are convinced the stock is hackneyed and a rip-off. We'd say go there for the atmosphere, but don't expect a bargain. And it's not the most relaxing place for people visiting with babies and under-5s. People banging into you, steps and narrow cobbled streets and the proximity of deep water (the Regent's Canal) make small, darting children a liability. But older kids love Camden. As soon as they start being interested in what's cool and fashionable, they clamour for it. Consequently, the crowds are supplemented by gangs of 12-year-old boys and girls on trust to be responsible for their anxious parents.

If it all gets too much, follow the towpath down to Regent's Park (*see p92*), or hop on one of the narrowboats that ply the canal to Paddington.

Camley Street Natural Park
12 Camley Street, NW1 (7833 2311). King's Cross tube/rail. **Open** *May-Sept* 9am-5pm Mon-Thur; 11am-5pm Sat, Sun. *Oct-Apr* 9am-5pm Mon-Thur; 10am-4pm Sat, Sun. Closed 25 Dec-1 Jan. **Admission** free. **Map** p317 L2.

Cock-a-hoop in **Camden Market**.

Come in March for Frog Day, or in May for the festival, but certainly do come to experience this wonderful wildlife oasis. The London Wildlife Trust's flagship reserve, Camley Park has marshlands and flower meadows, ponds and woodland glades. There's a visitors' centre, where you can study the park's history and reserve a place on school holiday playschemes (*see also p233*).
Buggy access. Nappy-changing facilities.

Jewish Museum, Camden
129-31 Albert Street, NW1 (7284 1997/ www.jewmusm.ort.org). Camden Town tube. **Open** 10am-4pm Mon-Thur; 10am-5pm Sun. Closed bank hols, Jewish festivals. **Admission** (LP) £3.50; £2.50 OAPs; £1.50 5-16s, concessions; free under-5s. **Credit** MC, V.
The history of the Jewish population of Britain, from medieval times up to the present day, is set out in an intelligent and colourful way in this renowned museum. Although it's undoubtedly of interest to students of history and world religion, it's not too dry and academic for the young. Children of all ages are welcome, and those aged between 7 and 14 years can take part in art activities, craft workshops and storytelling sessions. Fascinating permanent exhibits pertaining to Jewish life include Hanukkah lamps and an

incredible 16th-century Venetian synagogue ark. Staff take the time to explain the exhibits to visitors. In summer 2002 the museum's exhibition will be Continental Britons: Jewish Refugees from Nazi Europe.

Buggy access. Lift. Nearest picnic place: Regent's Park. Shop.

London Canal Museum
12-13 New Wharf Road, N1 (7713 0836/ www.canalmuseum.org.uk). King's Cross tube/rail. **Open** 10am-4.30pm Tue-Sun, bank hol Mons. Closed 24-26 Dec. **Admission** (LP) £2.50; £1.25 concessions, 8-16s; free under-8s. **Credit** MC, V. **Map** p317 M2.
The warehouse containing this small museum on the Regent Canal's Battlebridge Basin was built in the 1850s by Carlo Gatti, an Italian immigrant who made his fortune importing ice from the frozen lakes of Norway, in the days before refrigeration. The blocks were carried from the docks on canal boats and stored here in huge ice wells. The museum tells the story of Gatti and the families who made their living on the canals, supplementing permanent displays with lectures and temporary exhibitions. Ring for details of any forthcoming school holiday craft and activity sessions, which the dedicated staff try to run during every school holiday.
Nearest picnic place: museum terrace/canal towpath. Shop.

Proud Camden Moss
10 Greenland Street, NW1 (7482 3867/ www.britart.com/proud). Camden Town tube. **Open** 10am-7pm Mon-Fri; 11am-6pm Sat, Sun. **Admission** £3; £2 concessions.
This is the Camden branch of Proud, WC2 (*see p78*). These airy photography galleries have frequently changing exhibitions. Do ring to check the subject covered is suitable for children: the June/July 2002 one entitled Porn? probably isn't,

but there's a good deal of mileage for children in Formula 1 (subtitled: The drivers, the cars, the crashes, the wins, the speed!), which is showing from 26 July to 8 September.

Primrose Hill
One of the most enviable addresses in London, Primrose Hill is the darling of the movie set. Britpack actors live and bring up their children here; location managers are seduced by its villagey charm. Nothing downmarket is allowed to exist here. Primrose Hill's hub is on **Regent's Park Road**, with its cafés and boutiques. It's a small area but its attractions, from kite-flying at the top of the hill to celeb-spotting (100 points for Sadie and Jude!), browsing and latte-drinking, are many.

The Primrose Hill firework display, which takes place on the Saturday closest to 5 November, is too popular for its own good. The pyrotechnic display is enchanting, but horrendous crowds and a mass closing of streets for miles around mean it's essential to bag a good vantage point. Local restaurants are booked solid from two weeks in advance. If you're thinking of going, leave the car at home and walk from Chalk Farm tube; try to arrive well in advance. Small children may be distressed by the crowds, but older ones enjoy the excitement. *See also p33.*

Just over the railway footbridge in Chalk Farm is the **Roundhouse** (7424 9991), a former train turning shed that's now ingeniously used as a circular

---

Water ways: Regent's Canal north

London takes on a different perspective when seen from its canals. These waterways, completed in the 1830s, were dug by armies of labourers, usually Irish 'navvies' (navigators) using only muscle-power, picks and shovels. In the 19th century, when Britain was the centre of the manufacturing world, canals were the main arteries for carrying goods around the country, with London at the hub, linking the industrial centres further north with the Thames, and from there the whole of the globe. In those days casual strollers along their banks would have been assumed to be up to no good, nosing around the warehouse for something to steal. Now that most of the canals are deserted, apart from the occasional pleasure boat, the towpaths are a fascinating way to explore the capital on foot or by bike.

The stretch of the Regent's Canal between Little Venice (*see p161*) and Camden is the best place to take a boat trip. (The canal was originally intended to pass through Regent's Park but affluent local residents objected, concerned that their peace and property would be overrun by unruly 'water gypsies'.) You can start either among the pretty, painted narrowboats of **Little Venice**

(*see p161*), with their flowerpots and ruffled curtains, or amid the mayhem of the market in **Camden** (*see p97*). Boats pass through London Zoo (some allow you to break the trip here). Even if you decide not to stop off, you can glimpse elegant antelopes and giraffe as you glide by.

Narrowboats were pulled by horses before the invention of the internal combustion engine. The animals patiently trudged along the towpaths, but when the boats disappeared into the gloom of the Maida Hill tunnel where the horses couldn't pull them the boatmen would have to 'leg' the boat, lying on their backs and walking the boat along with their feet pressed against the inside of the tunnel. The job had other, more serious, discomforts too. Blow-Up Bridge, just beyond the zoo as you approach from Camden, earned its name when a barge loaded with five tons of gunpowder exploded here in 1874, killing four men, and destroying the bridge and several buildings. The present bridge was rebuilt using the original columns.

On the 45-minute one-way trip you pass elegant terraces with gardens leading down to the canal, willow-fringed towpaths and the converted

theatre. Many of the musical presentations are suitable for older children; the Chinese State Circus usually does a week here when it visits town.

Where to eat

For noodle addicts, there's a **Wagamama** at 11 Jamestown Road, NW1 (7428 0800; *see also p181*). That old standby **Pizza Express** also has a local branch (187 Kentish Town Road, NW5, 7267 0101), housed in a former lecture theatre of the old North London Polytechnic; it's roomy, and popular with local families at weekends.

Almost every other shopfront on Regent's Park Road seems to be a café of some description, and at weekends their pavement tables are an assault course of baby buggies, dogs, chocolate-smeared toddlers and breastfeeding mothers. **Cachao** (140 Regent's Park Road, NW3, 7483 4422) is a friendly pâtisserie and café popular with local stressed-out mothers and children, who take comfort in delicious pastries and enormous lollypops respectively.

There are several good restaurants on the main street of Regent's Park Road, but the biggest, and most popular with families, is **Lemonia** (No.89, 7586 7454), a large, upmarket Greek restaurant, which, with its combinations of delicious starter dishes and great chips, means that even fussy children should find a little of what they'll fancy. It's

annoyingly popular for Sunday lunch, so book well ahead. **Café de Maya** (38 Primrose Hill Road, NW3, 7209 0672) is open only for dinner (from 6pm), but is a sweet little Thai restaurant where you can choose teatime Thai favourites such as fish cakes and satay, at reasonable prices. **Manna** (4 Erskine Road, NW3, 7722 8028), a long-established and excellent vegetarian restaurant, is a lovely place for a family meal. Children like to feed their faces at **Marine Ices** (8 Haverstock Hill, NW3, 7482 9000; *see also p182*) opposite Chalk Farm tube, whose delicious Italian ice-creams and sorbets (take away or eat in) have been refreshing punters since 1913; simple Italian dinner dishes are also on the menu, but many north London children we know say they prefer Pizza Express pizzas. Nearby **Belgo Noord** (72 Chalk Farm Road, NW1, 7267 0718; *see also p174*) is a good bet for great chips, mussels and Belgian beer, although under-5s should go easy on the latter.

St John's Wood

This is a sophisticated neck of the woods, visited by sports fans for the cricket and ladies who lunch for the high street. Expensive clothes shops and interior design studios predominate but there are also cheaper opportunities for consumption in the form of local eateries. Great bagels and other Jewish nosh can be had at **Panzer's** deli (13-19 Circus Road,

---

warehouses of Camden where Jim Henson's Creature Workshop is the birthplace of fantastical successors to his Muppets.

To find out more about London's waterways network visit the **London Canal Museum** (*see p98*) or British Waterways, London (*see p161*).

BOAT TRIPS

The following all run boat excursions along the Regent's Canal. Their seasons are dependent on the weather, so do ring before you set out.

Jason's Trip

Blomfield Road (opposite No.60), Little Venice, W9 (7286 3428/www.jasons.co.uk). Warwick Avenue tube. **Tickets** (LP) *Return* £6.95; £5.50 under-14s. **Credit** AmEx, DC, MC, V. **Map** p312 C4.
A beautifully decorated traditional narrowboat. Light refreshments are available but must be pre-ordered. Trips run from end March to end October. No stops at London Zoo.

Jenny Wren

250 Camden High Street, NW1 (7485 4433/ www.walkersquay.com). Camden Town tube. **Tickets** *Return* £6; £3.50 under-14s. **No credit cards**.

The return trips take roughly 90 minutes. The journeys run only between Easter and October, with weekend trips running into November in the event of an Indian summer. Staff also take private bookings for trips eastwards through the Islington tunnel.

London Waterbus Company

Blomfield Road (corner of Westbourne Terrace Road Bridge), Little Venice, W9, or Camden Lock, off Chalk Farm Road, NW1 (7482 2550/ info line 7482 2660). Camden Town or Warwick Avenue tube. **Tickets** *Return* Little Venice–Camden Lock £5.80; £3.80 3-15s; free under-3s. One-way trip with zoo admission Little Venice–London Zoo £12; £8.50 3-15s; free under-3s. Camden Lock–London Zoo £11.90; £8.50 3-15s; free under-3s. **No credit cards**. **Map** p312 C4.
The London Waterbus Company runs a reliable service, which can be combined with a trip to London Zoo. The company has several painted narrowboats but uses a more practical – and rather more ugly – modern one, the Water Buffalo, in bad weather.

NW8, 7722 8596), or you might prefer to indulge in the coffee and wonderful cake and pastries at **Richoux** (3 Circus Road, NW8, 7483 4001). For fabulous Cantonese cuisine, and a friendly welcome for children, **Royal China** (68 Queen's Grove, NW8, 7586 4280; *see also p176*) is *Time Out*'s restaurant of choice in the area. It has an opulent dining room and an inventive way with dim sum. A short stroll away is the famous **Lord's** cricket ground.

Over on Avenue Road, going up toward Swiss Cottage, **Benihana** (No.100, 7586 9508; *see also p174*) is an exotic restaurant with a special place in many children's hearts; their nutritional and entertainment needs are catered for in a series of dramatic flourishes by the red-hatted chefs. Try to go when there's a promotion on, as a family dining experience here isn't cheap. A little further north is **Abbey Road**, where tourists can often be seen risking life and limb on the zebra crossing to re-enact the cover of the Beatles album of the same name (recorded at the studio here). At No.127 is **Oscar's Den**, one of the best party shops in London; it can provide everything from balloons to a real-life baby elephant (*see also p247*).

Lord's & MCC Museum

St John's Wood Road, NW8 (7432 1033). St John's Wood tube. **Open** *Tours* Oct-Mar noon, 2pm daily. Apr-Sept 10am, noon, 2pm daily. Closed Christmas period, bank hols, all major matches; phone to check. **Admission** *Tours* £6.50; £5 concessions; £4.50 5-15s; free under-5s; £19 family. **Credit** MC, V.
The home of Marylebone Cricket Club has a museum that includes, among the paintings, photos and battered bats, a reconstruction of the shot that killed a passing sparrow in 1936, complete with the stuffed bird and the ball. The Ashes reside here too. The guided tour takes visitors into the Mound stand, the pavilion, the visitors' dressing room and the historic Long Room. As well as cricket-related souvenirs in the shop there's a superior range of kit and equipment, both in adult and child sizes. Given that most high-street sports shops are pretty useless when it comes to shopping for kit, a trip to Lord's may be worth it for the shop alone.
Buggy access. Lifts. Nearest picnic place: St John's churchyard playground. Shop.

Hampstead & around

This area is in many ways the archetypal London 'village', with its pretty cottages and churches strung along a steep hill. Unfortunately, as in many pretty villages, only a lucky few can afford to live here. All the more reason to visit then, and take in the air. Hampstead's roots as a spa, to which Londoners fled for fresh air and health-inducing water, can be seen in the old drinking fountain in Wells Walk near the Wells Tavern.

Smart houses are everywhere. Some of them you can pay to snoop round, such as **Burgh House** (New End Square, NW3, 7431 0144), a small museum

charting the area's history. People of an architectural bent make for **2 Willow Road** (7435 6166), now a National Trust property and a significant example of pre-war modernism. The house was built in 1939 by Ernö Goldfinger (after which the James Bond villain was named, author Ian Fleming hated Goldfinger's work so much) and retains its original fixtures and fittings. Those with an interest in the father of psychoanalysis make a pilgrimage to the **Freud Museum** (20 Maresfield Gardens, NW3, 7435 2002), where the admission charge gets you access to the famous couch, as well as papers, artefacts and frequently changing exhibitions.

Some people come to Hampstead for the chic cafés and great shopping, but the main reason families with young children visit the area is glorious **Hampstead Heath**. There's a chic café on the heath, in Kenwood House: this English Heritage beauty full of art treasures is the picturesque setting for summer concerts.

Just south of the heath, near Gospel Oak, is a different sort of rustic retreat. **Kentish Town City Farm** is one of the capital's oldest and it does a great job of keeping north London urbanites in touch with our agricultural heritage.

Fenton House

3 Hampstead Grove, NW3 (7435 3471/info 01494 755563/www.nationaltrust.org.uk). Hampstead tube/ Hampstead Heath rail. **Open** *Mar* 2-5pm Sat, Sun. *Apr-Oct* 2-5pm Wed-Fri; 11am-5pm Sat, Sun, bank hols. Last entry 4.30pm. *Tours* phone for times. **Admission** (NT) £4.40; £2.20 5-17s; free under-5s. *Tours* £10.
No credit cards.
This gorgeous late 17th-century house is fêted for its award-winning garden, a rural idyll with wonderful scented borders. The priceless collections inside are quirky and appealing: the intriguing Benton Fletcher Collection of early keyboard instruments can be heard in action during the summer at fortnightly baroque concerts (phone for details). Other exhibits include a range of porcelain poodles in the Rockingham Room. The views over London from the attic rooms are most impressive. Entry to the garden (one side is landscaped, the other contains an orchard and vegetable patch) is free. Note that tours are of the instruments and porcelain only.

Hampstead Heath

NW3 (7485 4491). Belsize Park or Hampstead tube/ Gospel Oak or Hampstead Heath rail/24, 46, 168, 214, C2, C11 bus. **Open** 24hrs.
Even in a city blessed with more than its fair share of lovely parks, it's not hard to fathom why Hampstead Heath is one of its most popular green spaces. Fantastic views over London (from Parliament Hill), rolling green slopes, enchanting woodland, several ponds, a couple of good cafés, an art gallery, athletics track, swimming (in the ponds and the lido), kite-flying on Kite Hill, outdoor concerts at Kenwood, model-boating, tennis, angling, boules and bowls are just a few of its attractions. Even on a summer's day it's possible to find peace and quiet in the heath's green acres. On weekday mornings you might hear the mournful swirls of the lone bagpiper who practises on the bandstand, and on a snowy winter's day you might glimpse the lamp-post that is said to have inspired CS Lewis to write *The Lion, the Witch and*

A child's eye view of **Kenwood House**. *See p102.*

the *Wardrobe*. The only disappointments are the rather unimaginative playground at Gospel Oak and the draconian approach to cyclists, who are restricted to a few paths. Pick up a free diary from the office at Parliament Hill to find out more about organised walks and free puppet shows and inflatables in the summer holidays.

Buggy access. Cafés. Nappy-changing facilities.

Keats' House

Keats Grove, NW3 (7435 2062/www.keatshouse.org.uk). Hampstead tube/Hampstead Heath rail/24, 46, 168 bus. **Open** *Easter-Oct* noon-5pm Tue-Sun. *Nov-Easter* noon-4pm Tue-Sun. Closed 25, 26, 31 Dec, 1 Jan. *Tours* 3pm Sat, Sun. **Admission** £3; £1.50 concessions; free under-16s. *Tours* (Sat, Sun only) incl in admission price.

Poet John Keats lived for two years in this romantic Regency cottage before, weakened by TB, he travelled to Italy and died, aged just 24, in 1821. It was in this romantic setting that he fell in love with Fanny Brawne. A plum tree in the garden marks the site of the original tree beneath which he is thought to have penned *Ode to a Nightingale*. Cabinets contain original manuscripts, and visitors can nose round Keats' bedroom, living room and kitchen. On Saturdays and Sundays a tour of the house is included in the admission price. During summer 2002 the house will be undergoing some exterior redecoration; during this time, visitors are welcome in the house and will not be charged an entrance fee.

Buggy access (ground floor only). Nearest picnic place: house gardens. Shop.

Kentish Town City Farm

1 Cressfield Close, off Grafton Road, NW5 (7916 5421). Chalk Farm or Kentish Town tube/Gospel Oak rail. **Open** 9.30am-5.30pm Tue-Sun. Closed 25 Dec. **Admission** free; donations appreciated.

Camden children should count themselves lucky they have their own pony club deep in the urban jungle. Even so, they can only be put on the club's waiting list in September, and just hope a few of the members hit adolescence and exchange a pony obsession with one for Enrique Iglesias. Non-residents can pay £1 for weekend pony rides (1.30pm Sat, Sun, weather permitting). It's only Camdenites who can attend the summer playschemes, too, so popular are these events. The rest of us can enjoy the busy farm's charms, however. These include ducks, chickens, geese, ponies, Wiltshire Horned sheep, goats, cows and a Large Black pig.

Buggy access. Nappy-changing facilities. Nearest picnic place: Hampstead Heath.

Kenwood House/Iveagh Bequest

Kenwood House, Hampstead Lane, NW3 (8348 1286). Archway tube/Golders Green tube then 210 bus. **Open** *Apr-Sept* 10am-6pm Mon, Tue, Thur, Sat, Sun; 10.30am-6pm Wed, Fri. *Oct* 10am-5pm Mon, Tue, Thur, Sat, Sun; 10.30am-5pm Wed, Fri. *Nov-Mar* 10am-4pm Mon, Tue, Thur, Sat, Sun; 10.30am-4pm Wed, Fri. Closed 24-26 Dec, 1 Jan. *Tours* by appointment only. **Admission** (EH) free; donations appreciated. *Tours* £3.50; £2.50 concessions, £1.50 under-16s. **Credit** MC V.

Most north London parents know Kenwood's delectable Brew House Café as a thoroughly classy place to meet for lunch,

Gone fishing on **Hampstead Heath**. *See p100.*

where there's space enough to bring the children without being made to feel uncomfortable. Attached to the café is a sizeable mansion overlooking Hampstead Heath from its northern fringe. Kenwood was rebuilt in the classical style for the Earl of Mansfield by Robert Adam in 1767-9 and bequeathed to the nation in 1927. Today, the building's chief attraction is the Iveagh Bequest, a collection of paintings that takes in works by Reynolds, Turner and Van Dyck, a Rembrandt self-portrait tucked into a darkened corner of the Dining Room and a rare Vermeer (*The Guitar Player*). Botticelli, Guardi and a couple of classic flirtatious Bouchers round out the wonderful collection. The library is vast.

Kenwood has a pretty good education department, whose staff dream up worksheets and organise events such as treasure hunts, dressing-up sessions and family tea parties. The volunteer group, Heath Hands, also has its office here, and it too plans family events throughout the year, mostly to do with improving the look of the heath and the estate gardens. For details of forthcoming events both here and around the heath, pick up a leaflet at the visitors' centre in the Kenwood House Estate Office.

Buggy access (limited in house). Café. Nappy-changing facilities. Shop.

Where to eat

Maxwell's, Pizza Express, **Tootsies** (*see p191*) and other well-known family-friendly restaurants provide the requisite burgers, pizzas, chicken and chips in Hampstead Village. For more exotic dishes, try places like the bizarrely named **dim T Café** (3 Heath Street, NW3, 7435 0024), whose massive platefuls of noodles and trolleys of dim sum are guaranteed child-pleasers. **ZenW3** (83 Hampstead High Street, NW3, 7794 7863) is a classy Chinese restaurant that's popular with local families. Less highbrow but extremely popular with families is **Giraffe** (46 Rosslyn Hill, NW3, 7435 0343; *see also p182*), a stopoff point for smoothies, noodles, stir-fries and the like. Japanese dishes are available at **Hi Sushi** (16 Hampstead High Street, NW3, 7794 2828), or, for a quicker snack, grab a delicious crêpe from the stall by the William IV pub before heading down to the heath for a bracing walk.

If you're heading south from the heath, towards Parliament Hill, you can either stop for coffee and sandwiches at **Polly's** (55 South End Road, NW3, 7794 8144) or push the boat out for a smart Modern European lunch at the superior **Cucina** (45A South End Road, NW3, 7435 7814), where the emphasis is on fish. Children can share their parents' dishes, have a bowl of pasta or dip into the little portions in the vegetarian meze.

Highgate & Archway

One of London's most desirable 'villages', Highgate is fun to visit with children, if only to enjoy **Waterlow Park**, which looks like it's straight out of a story book. Indeed, some locals claim that it inspired the

illustrations for Nick Butterworth's *Percy the Park Keeper* books. Next door, **Highgate Cemetery** (Swains Lane, N6, 8340 1834) is on the visiting list of many a tourist, much to the annoyance of the Friends of Highgate Cemetery, who prefer to play down the visitor attraction aspect of their historic patch. Children are, in fact, discouraged from visiting the place, unless they're coming to see the grave of a relative, but if you're longing to pay respects to Karl Marx, Mary Ann Evans (George Eliot) or Max Wall, or any other admired figure whose monuments are in the Eastern Cemetery, you can bring (well-behaved) children to enjoy the peace and beauty of this delightful boneyard. The Western Cemetery is out of bounds to casual visitors (adults must pay for guided walks) and kids under the age of 8.

A little down the hill from the tube station is Shepherd's Close, from where you can access the Parkland Walk, which runs all the way to Finsbury Park, and **Highgate Wood**, the most delightful woods in London (*see p104*). **Hornsey Lane**, on the other side of Highgate Hill, leads you to the Archway, a Victorian viaduct spanning what is now the A1 and offering views of the City and the East End. **Jackson's Lane Community Centre** (*see p224*) off Archway Road has shows for children on most Saturdays.

Lauderdale House

Waterlow Park, Highgate Hill, N6 (8348 8716/restaurant 8341 4807). Archway tube. **Open** 11am-4pm Tue-Fri; 1.30-5pm Sat; noon-5pm Sun; phone to check weekend openings. *Restaurant* 9am-dusk Tue-Sun. Closed 24 Dec-mid Jan. **Admission** free. **No credit cards.**
This pretty house, the 16th-century former home of Nell Gwynne, is a favoured venue for wedding receptions and other bashes, so it's sometimes closed to the public. Saturdays, however, are sacrosanct, because that's when children come for their morning shows, usually aimed at the 3-8 age group. Ring for details of craft fairs, musical events,

In & around: Highgate Wood

Highgate Wood might not be as famous as its north London neighbour Hampstead Heath but it is a gem all the same, made more precious by its position just yards from the roaring traffic of the Archway Road.

Originally part of the Middlesex Forest, its 70 acres are some of the last remaining ancient woodlands in London. Oak and hornbeam dominate. The wood has been lovingly managed by the Corporation of London and its trusty team of woodsmen and women since 1886, when the Lord Mayor declared the wood 'an open space for ever'. Carpeted with bluebells and wild flowers in spring and with dappled sunlight filtering through the trees, it is hard to believe you are in London at all.

The wood is carefully managed: trees are coppiced in the traditional way, areas are fenced off to encourage new growth, boxes are provided for owls, bats and hedgehogs to nest in, and everything that moves is chronicled. The bird population has increased dramatically in recent years, both in types and numbers – 70 different species of birds have been spotted here, including nesting sparrowhawks and visiting rare golden orioles. Alongside the usual foxes and grey squirrels are five species of bat, more than 20 of butterfly, 100 of spider and a stunning 454 of beetle. Expect much rustling in the undergrowth. Those of us who don't know an oriole from an owl can pick up helpful leaflets in the visitors' information hut beside the café, or join one of the bird identification walks or nature trails. There is always something going on: interactive stories around the Story-Telling Tree in summer, Christmas tree recycling in January, beetle safaris and bat watch evenings (see also p233).

Local families flock to the wood at weekends for the award-winning children's playground, one of the best in the country, which has been carefully planned to allow some integrated play for wheelchair-users and their more mobile friends.

The bridge and tower structure is accessible to buggies and wheelchairs, the swings are designed to be used by children who need more support, and there are braille notice-boards. Children love the flying fox (an aerial runway up in the trees); older folk appreciate the shade and plentiful benches. The playground is supervised and under-5s have their own section. For older children and more sporty types there is a football and cricket field (in front of the café), and exercise equipment for chin-ups, sit-ups and parallel bars work has recently been installed in the wood itself.

The other big draw is the **Oshobasho Café** (8444 1505), a café housed in the old cricket pavilion, where light lunch dishes, such as pasta bakes and ciabatta sandwiches, are on the Italian-influenced menu; in the summer its pretty rose garden is crowded from breakfast to teatime. On summer evenings there are concerts in the garden, so parents can enjoy a glass of wine while their kids play frisbee on the grass. If queues at the café are too long, try **Papa Del's** (see p105) for pizza, pasta and freshly-baked cookies. A few doors up you'll find **Ripping Yarns**, a cracking second-hand bookshop.

Highgate Wood even has its own newspaper, the Treetop News, with details of new sightings of birds and animals, puzzles and crosswords. It can be downloaded from the Corporation of London's website (www.cityoflondon.gov.uk) or picked up free in the visitors' centre.

Across Muswell Hill Road is **Queen's Wood**, which comes under local council management and is an altogether wilder prospect – there are no resident staff and it can be quite deserted, even on summer weekends. From Queen's Wood you can join Parkland Walk, the footpath that follows a disused railway line all the way to Finsbury Park.

Highgate Wood/Queen's Wood
Muswell Hill Road, NW6 (8444 6129). Highgate tube/45 bus. **Open** 7.30am-dusk daily.

exhibitions by local artists and other events held in this busy arts centre (*see also p224*). In the summer, weather permitting, the parkland surrounding the house hosts open-air shows. Whatever's on, it's lovely to sit on the terrace of the café and admire the view over a coffee and ice-cream, or an Italian meal. Make sure to book ahead if you fancy having your Sunday lunch here, because so does half of north London. Waterlow Park, in which the house is set, is beautiful, with several lakes, a toddler's playground, an aviary and gentle grassy slopes that are great for picnicking. *Buggy access (ground floor only). Café. Nearest picnic place: Waterlow Park.*

Where to eat

As well as the cafés in Highgate Wood and at Lauderdale House, Highgate has a branch of **Café Rouge** (6-7 South Grove, N6, 8342 9797), which has a kids' menu and is popular with families at weekends. There's a **Pizza Express** on the High Street (No.30, 8341 3434). **Café Mozart** (17 Swains Lane, N6, 8348 1384; *see also p182*) is recommended for its fabulous East European cakes and laid-back atmosphere.

In Archway, the **St John's** pub (91 Junction Road, N19, 7272 1587) has a restaurant that's popular for Sunday lunch. The interior is a bit dark, but the pub's large rooms mean it's airy enough, and the food is upmarket but generally worth it. **Papa Del's** pizzeria (347 Archway Road, N19, 8347 9797) at the top of the hill is a good alternative.

Islington

It's hard to believe that this modish, wealthy area was once considered rough. Its much-documented gentrification began as far back as the 1960s, but it was the 1980s that made Islington's fortune. **Upper Street** is a hub of trendy culture: a lively mixture of theatres, shops, cafés, pubs and restaurants. Every June the area hosts a two-week festival of music, theatre and art, and there are regular exhibitions at the Business Design Centre. The area has 11 theatres, including the groundbreaking Almeida, and it's also the home of the Anna Scher Theatre School, which has turned many a local working-class kid into classy working actors: Kathy Burke and half of the cast of *EastEnders* learned their trade here. Children who want to emulate their success have to join a five-year waiting list. The **Little Angel Theatre** in Dagmar Passage (*see p228*) is a famous name in London. This purpose-built puppet theatre has a reputation for top-quality shows for children aged from 4, though sadly it's closed until at least September 2002 (if not indefinitely) due to funding problems.

Playground-loving kids rate **Highbury Fields**, where the equipment is challenging, but horribly crowded on sunny days. If weather puts paid to parklife, the Playhouse indoor adventure playground (The Old Gymnasium, Highbury Grove

Around Town

Cooling off in **Highbury Fields**. *See p106.*

School, corner of Highbury Grove and Highbury New Park, N5, 7704 9424; *see also p250*) is where children go to get unfeasibly hot and sweaty. Footie fans of the Gunner variety may like to tour **Arsenal Football Club**.

The borough of Islington shares responsibility for the other big park in the area – **Finsbury Park** – with the boroughs of Haringey and Hackney. It's a great sprawling green space, due north of Arsenal, with many sporting facilities, but it's looking a little run down lately. Fortunately, there's help at hand, in the shape of the Finsbury Park Partnership. This organisation was set up to bid for a slice of the government's Single Regeneration Budget in 1999. The Finsbury Park area, which includes the huge railway and tube station, numerous housing estates and commercial districts, has been awarded £25 million. So the future looks very bright for the park, whose regeneration should be complete by the time the project ends in 2006. Nearby, on Green Lanes, the **Castle Climbing Centre** (*see p253*) is a stately sort of home for London's premier climbing venue. It's a Grade II-listed Victorian folly based on Stirling Castle in Scotland.

Those that crave the smell of the countryside commune with the pigs at **Freightliners City Farm**, or find out about green activities and events at the **Islington Ecology Centre**. A taste of the countryside can be sampled every Sunday from 10am to 2pm at the **Islington Farmers' Market** (Essex Road, opposite Islington Green, N1). **Chapel Market**, N1 (on the street of the same name) is gloriously downmarket, full of bargains, fruit, veg (non-organic), rowdy costers and dodgy durables. Islington's army of estate agents would no doubt like to see that street gentrified too. Long may it prosper.

Arsenal Football Club

Arsenal Stadium, Avenell Road, N5 (7704 4000/ tickets 7413 3366/www.arsenal.co.uk). Arsenal tube/ Finsbury Park tube/rail. **Open** *Gunners Shop* 9.30am-5pm Mon-Fri and before and after all first team home games. *World of Sport Shop* 9.30am-6pm Mon-Sat. *Tours* 11am, 2pm Mon-Fri. **Admission** *Museum* £2; £1 under-16s. *Tours* £4; £2 concessions, under-16s; £1 junior Gunners. **Credit** *Shop* MC, V.

Now that all the powers that be, including Islington council, Ken Livingstone and various government departments, have approved Arsenal's plan for a move, it's full steam ahead to relocate the stadium to Ashburton Grove, on the site of an old dump. Work starts to tidy up Ashburton Grove at the end of 2002, and the Arsenal bosses reckon the new ground will be ready in 2004-5. Meanwhile, keen Gunners fans can pre-book a tour of the ground, changing rooms and museum; the latter has a Gunner-glorifying video, info about the club's early days and memorabilia. The shop stocks replica kit (in all sizes) and souvenirs. *Nearest picnic place: Gillespie Park. Shops.*

Freightliners City Farm

Paradise Park, Sheringham Road, off Liverpool Road, N7 (7609 0467). Holloway Road tube/Highbury & Islington tube/rail. **Open** 10am-1pm, 2-5pm Tue-Sun. Closed 25-26 Dec, 1 Jan. **Admission** free; donations appreciated.

Aptly located in Paradise Park, Freightliners is a big attraction for children in the summer holidays, when the playschemes are booked weeks ahead. There's a varied bunch of animals to pet, including rabbits, chinchillas and guinea pigs, moving on up to less cuddly poultry, pigs, sheep, goats and cows. The farm is gradually becoming known as a rare-breeds centre. It currently has Berkshire and Tamworth porkers, a small, city-friendly breed of cow called a Dexter and – its speciality – a Chilean species of hen whose eggs are green-shelled (a very popular element in the style-conscious Islingtonian's breakfast). Veg from the gardens and best London honey from the farm's hives are sold in season. *Buggy access. Nappy-changing facilities. Nearest picnic place: picnic area in farm. Shop.*

Highbury Fields

Highbury Crescent, N5 (7527 4971). Highbury & Islington tube/rail. **Open** *Park* 24hrs. *Playground* dawn-dusk daily.

A summertime focal point, Highbury Fields is Islington's largest open space. The unusual playground is particularly appreciated by all age groups. The tennis courts have been refurbished and are the outdoor facilities (phone 7226 2334 to book) used by the excellent Islington Tennis Centre, *see also p261*), an all-abilities club that runs all year round (phone 7697 1206 for details of its other venues). Many people make a day of it here, by swimming at Highbury Pool next door, lunching in the café here, then spending a lazy afternoon watching children play. Unfortunately, the fireworks displays no longer take place in November: they became so popular the police became jittery about crowd control and the council cancelled them. *Buggy access. Café.*

Islington Ecology Centre

191 Drayton Park, N5 (7354 5162). Arsenal tube. **Open** *Park* 8am-dusk Mon-Fri; 9am-dusk Sat; 10am-dusk Sun. *Centre* drop-in advice sessions 10am-noon Tue; 2-4pm Thur; for other times phone to check. **Admission** free; donations appreciated.

The place to find out about all things green and pleasant in the area. It's part of the Gillespie Park Local Nature Reserve, which is the largest reserve in the borough, with a range of wildlife habitats (woodland, meadow, wetland and ponds). The café, when it's open, is organic and wholesome, the staff are welcoming and children are encouraged to join in on walks, talks and school holiday activities. The latter this year will include scavenger hunts, herbal potion making, mini beast hunts and sculpture sessions to make recycled artworks. Ring for details or a what's on leaflet. *Buggy access. Café (summer only).*

Where to eat

Cafés, restaurants and bistros, including Pizza Express and Café Flo, abound in Islington; most middle-of-the-road chains seem to have an outlet somewhere along Upper Street. **Frederick's** (106 Islington High Street, N1, 7359 2888) makes a concession to well-heeled parents with a children's menu at Saturday lunchtimes.

Charming poultry at **Freightliners City Farm**. *See p106.*

For cheaper, more relaxed meals, try the Islington branches of the award-winning **Giraffe** (29-31 Essex Road, N1, 7359 5999; *see also p182*) or **Wok Wok** (67 Upper Street, N1, 7288 0333). At **Tiger Lil's** (270 Upper Street, 7226 1118; *see also p187*) children choose the ingredients they want the chefs to stir-fry and at **Santa Fe** (75 Upper Street, 7288 2288; *see also p182*) there's great Tex-Mex food for adults and kids, who can choose from their own menu (£3.95).

Stoke Newington

North-east of Islington, 'Stokey' is an enclave of middle-aged 'alternative' families, a fact that may or may not appeal. It's a pleasantly bohemian, unpolished sort of area, with good independent shops. The heart of the area is **Stoke Newington Church Street**, which hosts a street festival every June.

Stoke Newington is blessed with two fine green spaces – **Clissold Park**, where local families congregate, and the rambling old boneyard of **Abney Park Cemetery & Nature Reserve**.

Abney Park Cemetery & Nature Reserve
Stoke Newington Church Street, N16 (7275 7557). Stoke Newington rail/73 bus. **Open** dawn-dusk daily. Closed 25 Dec. **Admission** free.

Woodpeckers, bats and rare butterflies are known to frequent this magical old cemetery, with its crumbling statues and derelict church, but that's only when the children have cleared off. Local families love to come to walk and picnic here, and the warden is energetic in his attempts to keep them entertained. There are Easter egg hunts, craft workshops, guided walks (ring to find out when the next one takes place) and treasure hunts in school holidays: make sure you don't miss out. The visitors' centre doubles as a shop for guides to Green London and other such environmentally aware literature.
Buggy access. Shop.

Clissold Park
Stoke Newington Church Street, N16 (7923 3660/ tennis courts 7923 3644/café 7923 3703). Stoke Newington rail/73, 149 bus. **Open** *Park* 7.30am-dusk daily.

A much-loved park with ponds for paddling, dipping and duck-feeding, pleasant tree-lined walks with plenty of room for ball games, and a well-equipped playground are all reasons to come here. The mini zoo has fallow deer, a butterfly tunnel and an aviary. Clissold Park is set around a mansion with a café for reasonably priced vegetarian food and snacks. During the Stoke Newington Festival (*see p28*), this delightful park becomes a hive of activity. A stage is set up for bands, there are numerous stalls and face-painted children mill about merrily. The tennis courts here are home to the Hackney wing of the City Tennis Centre (8318 4856; *see p261*). These centres aim to make tennis accessible to the inner-London player, and are particularly active in the search for the new Tim Henmans among young urban players. Ring for details of the busy tennis programme, which includes family tennis evenings, junior clubs and tournaments and

coaching for all levels. The new glass and steel Clissold Leisure Centre, with its popular swimming pool, is just across the road (see p26).
Buggy access in park, steps at café. Café.

Where to eat

Many of the places to eat on **Church Street**, including the acclaimed South Indian vegetarian restaurant **Rasa** (No.55, 7249 0344), are quite small and can't easily accommodate buggies. **Il Bacio** (No.61, 7249 3833) is dependable for good Italian pasta and pizza, or tuck into delicious sandwiches at the **Cooler** (No.67, 7275 7266). **Vortex** (Nos.139-41, 7254 6516) is a grown-up jazz venue that serves excellent, but child-friendly food to cool cats of all ages during the day. **The Prince** (*see p190*) is a converted pub that's swiftly becoming a Stokie family favourite. Away from Church Street, **Itto** (226 Stoke Newington High Street, N16, 7275 8827) is great for a cheap, quick, tasty Thai noodle meal.

Many hip north Londoners give up their swanky central flats and take on spacious family homes in these solidly middle-class areas when they hear the pitter patter. Consequently, Crouch End and Muswell Hill are bristling with classy shops and cafés catering to the exacting tastes of all members of trendy young families. The area's main attraction in the traditional sense has to be **Alexandra Park & Palace**, but there are plenty of green spaces for locals to call their own. **Priory Park** in Middle Lane is great for cycling, rollerskating and football, and has a paddling pool, formal gardens and tennis courts (its Rainbow Café is good for snacks). **Stationers Park**, between Mayfield Road and Denton Road, has a challenging adventure playground, a pre-school children's play area and tennis courts. **Park Road** (8341 3567; *see also p263*) has both indoor and outdoor swimming pools, though the latter can get pretty crowded.

Walk: way up north

▶ It's hard to believe that a babbling brook meanders through the sprawling suburbs of north-west London. Rising near Arkley, not far from Totteridge, Dollis Brook winds its way gently southwards to join Mutton Brook to form the River Brent, which flows south and west before it meets the Thames at Brentford. The **Dollis Valley Walk** links green spaces from Moat Mount, near Mill Hill in the north, to Hampstead Garden Suburb in the south. At ten miles, the walk, which forms part of the London Loop encircling the capital, is probably beyond the range of most children (and their exhausted parents). But it is split into easily manageable sections that can be reached at various points by public transport and is clearly marked for much of the way. The northerly section is recommended as the most peaceful and suitable for young children.

▶ Start from the car park at **Moat Mount Open Space**, accessible and clearly signposted from the southbound carriageway of the A1, just north of **Mill Hill Golf Club** (100 Barnet Way, NW7, 8959 2282). Follow the path into the wood, ignoring the left turn towards the outdoor activity centre. Don't be tempted by the picnic tables by the car park – there are much more peaceful places to stop for a bite. Take the wide tarmac path and after 100 yards follow the first of the green arrows directing you left down some steps and along a narrower (and often muddier) path. From here the roar of the A1 is almost drowned out by birdsong among the towering hornbeams and silver birches interspersed with evergreens such as holly and rhododendrons. There is an informative tree trail

to follow. These woodlands have grown up from ornamental woods planted over two centuries ago for **Moat Mount House**. There are many native species but also some exotic conifers like swamp cypress and giant redwood.

▶ From here you can follow the trail through the wood, past **Leg of Mutton Pond** and beside the fields of **Mote End Farm**. (This is a working farm, so dogs must be kept on a lead.) Unless you are using public transport you will have to return the way you have come so this is probably far enough for little legs, but time, tempers and energy permitting you could carry on through the meadows of **Totteridge Fields** and even continue all the way to **Hampstead Garden Suburb**.

▶ The southern section of this walk from Hendon to Hampstead Garden Suburb is a brave attempt to link hidden green spaces, but too much time is spent on dull residential streets. For a while the path follows the course of Mutton Brook, which sounds bucolic but flows for much of its course within earshot of the busy traffic on the North Circular Road. The walk ends passing through **Little Wood** and **Big Wood**, whose names could have come straight from the pen of AA Milne.

▶ The route is designed to be accessible to buggies but there are occasional steps and several kissing gates, and it can be very muddy in wet weather. Take a picnic to enjoy in one of the many beauty spots, as places to buy refreshments are few and far between, although there are some countryish pubs in nearby **Totteridge**.
For more information, ring 8359 3052 or visit the website: www.londonwalking.com.

Alexandra Park & Palace

Alexandra Palace Way, N22 (park 8444 7696/palace 8365 2121/info 8365 2121/boating 8889 9089/ www.alexandrapalace.com). Wood Green tube/Alexandra Palace rail/W3, W7, 84A, 144, 144A bus. **Open** *Park* 24hrs daily. *Palace* times vary depending on exhibitions. **Admission** free.

On a clear day, the views from the Ally Pally, as the place is fondly known, and the steep slopes of the park it sits atop, are inspirational. Despite being burned down ten days after it was first built in 1873, and again in 1980, the palace still has an entertainment and exhibition centre, where annual events such as Classic Motor Show and the London Gardens Show take place every spring. In the grounds, there's an open-air ice-skating rink (*see p258*), several playgrounds and a pitch & putt course. A recent Lottery windfall has allowed for some much-needed refurbishments in the park: these will take till about 2008 to complete, but the park will stay open throughout the improvements. The animal enclosure (donkeys, fallow deer) will see some changes for the better as the work gets done; the boating lake will also be given a new lease of life. On the Saturday nearest to 5 November (this year it's 2 November) Alexandra Park is the site of one of the biggest firework parties in London, organised by the local council, and funfairs are held on several bank holidays. *Buggy access. Café. Nappy-changing facilities. Nearest picnic place: picnic area by boating lake.*

Where to eat

Restaurants are in plentiful supply in the area – the **World Café** (130 Crouch Hill, N8, 8340 5635) has interesting global food at very reasonable prices; **Banners** (21 Park Road, N8, 8292 0001) is relaxed but crowded, so book in advance. Offering everything from fried breakfasts to exotic fish dishes, it's known for its extensive under-10s menu. **Pizza Bella** (4-6 Park Road, N8, 8342 8541) is also child-friendly, and popular for birthday parties. Terrific chips and super fresh fish are on the menu at **Toff's** (38 Muswell Hill Broadway, N10, 8883 8656). The Broadway is your best bet for family dining in Muswell Hill; there's a well-loved **Pizza Express** at No.290 (8883 5845) and children pay nothing for their favourite Italian dishes at Sunday lunchtimes at the **Caffè Uno** at No.348 (8883 4463). Bear in mind that for every child that chows down free, an adult must order a main meal. Not surprisingly, Sundays are very popular, so do book.

Finchley

Sprawling in three sections (North, East and Central) across the great divide of the North Circular, and served by three tube stations (East, West and Central), this is a difficult area to pin down. The first matter to clear up is that Finchley Road tube station is actually in Hampstead, miles away. Finchley's cosmopolitan background (it has large Jewish and Japanese communities) and air of general prosperity make it attractive, yet it suffers the blight of dull suburbia.

Look out! **Alexandra Park.**

Around Church End, Central Finchley, the true heart of what was once a village, you catch a whiff of Middle England, and can hardly believe you're still in the capital. The attraction here is **Avenue House** and its beautifully landscaped gardens, which were given to the populace in 1918.

Victoria Park, just off Ballards Lane between Finchley Central and North Finchley, has a children's playground, bowling green and tennis courts. In July the Finchley Carnival takes place here.

The **Great North Leisure Park** (Leisure Way, High Road, N12), better known locally as Warner Village, is a US-style entertainment complex built, rather unimaginatively, around its car park. The cinema, **Finchley Warner Village** (0870 240 6020), has a Saturday morning kids' club. There's also an extremely popular swimming pool, with a lido next door, which really comes into its own on warm summer days. The bowling alley (Hollywood Bowl; *see also p266*) has a bar and burger restaurant. Next door is an amusement arcade. A couple of rowdy games here followed by pizza and pop next door at **ASK** (8446 0970) is a tried-and-tested children's party combination in these parts.

Across the North Circular in East Finchley, the **Phoenix Cinema** (8883 2233) has children's films on Saturdays. In East End Road the Old Manor House has been transformed by the Sternberg Centre into a cultural centre, which includes ritual baths, a school and the **Jewish Museum, Finchley**.

To get away from it all, try the **Dollis Valley Green Walk**, which runs for ten miles beside the brook from Hampstead Heath Extension in the south to Moat Mount in the north. *See p108.*

Avenue House

15-17 East End Road, N3 (8346 7812). Finchley Central tube. **Open** *Ink Museum* 2-4.30pm Tue-Thur. Closed 24 Dec-1 Jan, bank hols. **Admission** free; donations appreciated.

The tiny Ink Museum commemorates 'Inky' Stephens, whose father invented ink and once owned Avenue House. Some of the beautiful rooms can be hired out and it's a popular venue for children's parties. Outside the Ink Museum, there's a playground, café and a tree trail accessible to wheelchairs and buggies.

Buggy access. Nappy-changing facilities. Nearest picnic place: Avenue House grounds.

Jewish Museum, Finchley

Sternberg Centre, 80 East End Road, N3 (8349 1143/ www.jewmusm.ort.org). Finchley Central tube/13, 82, 112, 143, 260 bus. **Open** 10.30am-5pm Mon-Thur; 10.30am-4.30pm Sun. Closed bank hols, Jewish hols, Sun in Aug. **Admission** (LP) £2; £1 concessions, 12-16s; free under-12s. **No credit cards.**
The more northerly branch of the affecting and informative Jewish Museum (*see p97* for the Camden branch) focuses on Jewish social history. Reconstructions include a a functional sewing workshop on the ground floor, which gives the feel of sweatshop life at the turn of the 19th century. Upstairs an exhibition traces the life of Leon Greenman, a British Jew who survived Auschwitz (his wife and child both perished). He's in his nineties now, but still comes occasionally to speak to groups of adults and children.

The Holocaust Exhibition may be considered too upsetting for young children, but staff here leave it to the discretion of parents as to whether they let their children venture upstairs. The images are probably best appreciated by young people of at least secondary school age. This branch also has a 12,000-strong photographic archive augmented by 2,000 oral history tapes. Forthcoming exhibitions in 2002 include A Step up the Ladder: Jews in Hackney in the '20s and '30s (from June) and, from September, one about Indian synagogues. Note that the café is open only at lunchtimes, Monday to Thursday.

Café. Nearest picnic place: museum garden/Avenue House gardens. Shop.

Where to eat

Many of Finchley's decent grubstops fall over themselves to please pint-sized customers. **Two Brothers Fish Restaurant** (297-301 Regent's Park Road, N3, 8346 0469) is always full of smart people eating fab fish and chips; grab a takeaway next door if you can't get in. At **Chorak** (122 High Road, N2, 8365 3330) the cakes (including themed party cakes; *see p241*) are baked on the premises.

Rani (7 Long Lane, N3, 8349 4386), a well-known vegetarian Indian, attracts people from a wide area. There's a £4.90 under-12s' menu. The **Old Europeans** (106 High Road, N2, 8883 3964) welcomes kids with open arms, high chairs and half portions of hearty Hungarian grub.

Further north

Keep travelling north up Green Lanes from Finsbury Park and you eventually pass White Hart Lane, the home of **Tottenham Hotspur Football Club**, a tour of which is much easier to arrange than scoring a ticket to a match.

Further west, the North Circular, which thunders out of the city into the somnolent suburbs, is well travelled by Londoners looking for fashion and a handy crèche at **Brent Cross Shopping Centre** (*see p206*). Take the Edgware Road if you have a yen for Japanese goods: **Oriental City** (399 Edgware Road, NW9, 8200 0009) is a Japanese mall with several good places to eat, including a huge self-service buffet. The shops are fascinating, though it's the state-of-the-art amusement arcade that children love – it's a lot less seedy than its counterparts in central London.

Set sail in a westerly direction from Brent Cross to the peace and quiet of the **Welsh Harp Reservoir** (Cool Oak Lane, NW9 8205 1240). This huge open space has been recognised as a site of special scientific interest. The informative environmental centre is a good starting point for nature trips and the reservoir is used for all types of water sports (*see also p267*). The surrounding leafy waterside areas provide space for games pitches, tennis courts, playgrounds and picnicking.

Further north, in Hendon proper, the action-packed **Royal Air Force Museum Hendon** is dedicated to the history of the flying machine.

Royal Air Force Museum Hendon

Grahame Park Way, NW9 (8205 2266/ www.rafmuseum.com). Colindale tube/Mill Hill Broadway rail/32, 226, 292, 303 bus. **Open** 10am-6pm daily. Closed 24-26 Dec, 1 Jan. *Tours* daily; times vary, phone for details. **Admission** (LP) free. *Tours* free. **Credit** MC, V.
It's chocks away at the RAF Museum as it sets about spending its £4.77-million lottery grant. The project aims to make this, the National Museum of Aviation, a true world leader – by the time the new-look museum opens in 2003, it will be three times the size, with many more aircraft on show, special events to show them off and interactive displays and activities to bring in even more children.

Not that the free museum has ever had any trouble attracting crowds to its excellent exhibitions and displays. Of particular note is the spectacular sound and light show Our Finest Hour, which tells the story of the Battle of Britain. There's also a Red Arrows flight simulator, a 'touch and try' Jet Provost cockpit and a walk-through Sunderland flying boat. Activities for children and adults take place year-round: workshops include hot-air balloon making, rocket science, and Search and Rescue role-playing. The workshops are always very popular, so do book ahead. Call for details of special events in the school holidays.

Buggy access. Café. Lift. Nappy-changing facilities. Nearest picnic place: picnic ground on site. Restaurant. Shop.

Tottenham Hotspur Football Club

Bill Nicholson Way, 748 High Road, N17 (8365 5000/ www.spurs.co.uk). White Hart Lane rail. **Open** *Tours* 11am Mon-Fri; 11am, 1pm Sat. **Admission** *Tours* £7.50 adults; £4.50 under-16s, OAPs. **Credit** *only in advance* MC, V.
Tours of the pitchside, the tunnel, changing rooms, board rooms and press rooms take place regularly, but the Saturday ones tend to be booked up well in advance. Note that they cannot take place on a match day, or the day before, more's the pity. Tours last about an hour, depending on how chatty the punters are. Finish in the megastore, where you can blow £50 on a shirt or 50p on a souvenir pencil.

Buggy access. Shop.

East London

From the great East End to the eastern suburbs, via docks, locks and smoking barrels.

Whitechapel & Spitalfields

With its weekend street markets, city farms and one of the most happening art galleries in London (especially where children are concerned), Whitechapel and its trendier sister Spitalfields are definitely worth exploring.

This area has always been lively. As the City's poor neighbour offering cheap rents on slum housing, the heart of the East End has been enriched by waves of immigrants over the centuries. In the 18th century came the Huguenots (French Protestant refugees), whose skill in silk weaving gained the area a reputation for fine cloth and fashionable clothes. Nicholas Hawksmoor's awe-inspiring but rather crumbly **Christ Church** on Commercial Street, E1 (7247 7202) was built in 1714 to provide a place of worship for the weavers. It's currently undergoing restoration to bring it back to its former glory; so ring before you visit in case it's closed.

Irish and German immigrants built communities here in the early 19th century, followed, from 1880

onward, by Jews. Jewish success in the 'rag trade', as it became known, attracted unwanted attention from the British Union of Fascists before World War I, with tension coming to a head in 1936 when a fight broke out between local residents and the police trying to clear a way for Sir Oswald Mosley's Fascists to march through Cable Street, E1. The planned march was cancelled. From the 1950s to the '70s Indians and Bangladeshis took over the textile businesses on Commercial Street and Commercial Road, and the East End is still associated with the Asian clothes trade today.

For some people the mention of the East End brings to mind the unsavoury thought of Jack the Ripper, who stalked and murdered women on these streets more than 100 years ago, but as far as children are concerned the main attractions are quite rightly the farms: **Spitalfields City Farm** and, a short bus or tube journey away, **Stepping Stones Farm**.

Between Commercial Street and Brick Lane runs elegant **Fournier Street**, with its beautifully preserved early Georgian houses, once inhabited

Stepping up for her close-up, at **Stepping Stones Farm**. See p113.

by Huguenot silk barons and now owned by wealthy new East Enders. On nearby Folgate Street is **Dennis Severs' House**, a lovingly recreated Georgian residence, open to adults for tours (ring 7247 4013 for details).

Whitechapel Road has two main points of interest: **Whitechapel Bell Foundry**, where bells have been cast since 1570; and, at No.82, **Whitechapel Art Gallery**, one of London's best exhibition spaces. Hospital-drama fans and connoisseurs of the macabre may be drawn to the **Royal London Hospital Museum**, which is famous for its tragic inhabitant Joseph (or John) Merrick, better known as the 'Elephant Man'. Merrick was a patient here in the late 1800s and part of the museum is devoted to an exhibition about his life.

Royal London Hospital Archives & Museum

St Philip's Church, Newark Street, E1 (7377 7608/ www.brlcf.org.uk or www.bartsandthelondon.org.uk). *Whitechapel tube.* **Open** 10am-4.30pm Mon-Fri. Closed bank hols & adjacent days. **Admission** free.

This little museum, newly refurbished, now has better access for people in wheelchairs or with buggies. Many of the exhibits have also become more user-friendly, especially towards to young people. The sections on Joseph Merrick (popularly, if cruelly, known as the 'Elephant Man'), who was a patient here, includes an edited BBC documentary about his life. Other videos you can select include ones about nursing at the London (1967) and an appeal film made at the Queen's Hospital for Children (1939). A new section on forensic medicine is sponsored by crime writer Patricia Cornwell, and includes original material on the Whitechapel (Jack the Ripper) murders. Rather less ghoulish are the exhibits relating to children and health, as well as Florence Nightingale and 19th-century nursing. Famous nurses who practised here include Edith Cavell, who was executed by the Germans in 1915 for helping Allied soldiers escape from occupied Belgium. Log on to www.medicalmuseums.org for more information.

Buggy access. Café. Nappy-changing facilities. Nearest picnic place: hospital garden. Shop.

Spitalfields City Farm

Weaver Street, off Pedley Street, E1 (7247 8762/ www.spitalfieldscityfarm.org). Whitechapel tube. **Open** 10.30am-5pm Tue-Sun. Closed 24 Dec-2 Jan. **Admission** free; donations appreciated.

Water ways: float & ride

For a DIY sightseeing trip, look no further than the Docklands Light Railway (DLR). Still basking in glory after being named 'Best Rail Operator' of 2001, the DLR can now add 'reliability, punctuality and frequency' to its list of attributes. The rail service has long been marketed as a tourist attraction in itself, and with good reason: sitting at the front of these jolly, driverless, red and blue carriages gives you a window on the delights of Docklands.

It's with the tourist market in mind that the DLR has joined forces with City Cruises sightseeing boats to give fairweather travellers a passport to the capital's most civilised modes of transport. With a Rail & River Rover, you can hop on and off the boats and trains all day long.

Buy your family day pass at either Westminster or Tower Piers, and choose a warm seat in the downstairs cocktail bar (with viewing platform) or a breezier berth upstairs. A chirpy commentator tells you which bridges you're passing under and points out the most important riverside buildings: the British Airways London Eye, the Royal Festival Hall, the Monument, HMS *Belfast*, and finally the Tower of London. Here you can disembark and walk to the DLR station at Tower Gateway for a ride east through the smart Limehouse Basin and on to Beckton. Otherwise, you can stay on the boat until Greenwich (*see p129*) and take a DLR train under the river for further sightseeing on the Isle of Dogs.

Highlights in terms of sights to see include the animals at the farm at **Mudchute City Farm** (*see p117*) and the **National Maritime Museum** and

park at Greenwich (*see p132*). And you can plan to stop for lunch or tour the shops in one of the swish cafés at the Canary Wharf development. Whichever way you do it, you're guaranteed lovely views and relaxed, comfortable and fume-free journeys, and it's not often we can say that about travelling in London.

Docklands Light Railway (DLR)

7363 9700/www.dlr.co.uk. **Rail & River Rover** tickets cost £8.30 for adults; £4.20 children; £22 family ticket (2 + up to 3).

This friendly urban smallholding has chickens, a cow, donkeys, geese, pigs, sheep, goats, guinea pigs and rabbits. Locals come here for free-range eggs and vegetables from the allotments, as well as manure. Staff are keen to deliver an agricultural education of sorts to city-bred young 'uns, and children can enjoy school holiday playschemes and education programmes. Local schools can book into the farm's egg incubation service, which allows children to gaze upon an incubator and watch hatchlings make their way in the world. Ring to find out if there are staff – or donkeys for that matter – able to run donkey rides on the day you visit; they're a great highlight.
Buggy access.

Stepping Stones Farm
Stepney Way (junction with Stepney High Street), E1 (7790 8204). Stepney Green tube. **Open** *Apr-mid Oct* 9.30am-6pm Tue-Sun; bank hol Mon. *Mid Oct-Mar* 9.30am-dusk Tue-Sun; all public hols. **Admission** free; donations appreciated.
A short bus or tube ride away from Spitalfields, this 4.5-acre community farm is run by hard working volunteers. Goats, cows, pigs, donkeys, sheep, poultry and small pets can all be admired. The farmers have devised an educational programme for visiting schools and interested children; young ones enjoy the play area, where a sandpit, bouncy castle and toy tractors and cars all await their attention. Gardeners can buy manure and compost or stock up on eggs, jams and chutneys from the shop; conscientious greens can bring their kitchen waste to the community composting bins. Ring for details of school holiday fun for children: the Easter Egg Hunt is always popular.
Buggy access. Café. Nappy-changing facilities. Shop.

Whitechapel Art Gallery
80-82 Whitechapel High Street, E1 (7522 7888/ www.whitechapel.org). Aldgate East tube/15, 25, 253 bus. **Open** 11am-6pm Tue, Thur, Fri; 11am-8pm Wed; 11am-6pm Sat, Sun. Closed 24-26 Dec, 1 Jan. *Tours* 2.30pm Sun. **Admission** free. *Tours* free. **Map** p321 S6.
The Whitechapel boasts a strong education and community programme, so local schoolchildren have a hand in many of the exhibits. Its founder, a schoolteacher, insisted that every exhibition have its own educational programme for children and as a result its education department is one of the busiest in the gallery world. The large, ground-floor gallery is augmented by an additional sky-lit upper space, providing a beautiful setting for new talent. Summer 2002 (6 July-1 Sept) sees a sculpture show entitled Early One Morning: Sculpture Now, which coincides with the New Generation exhibition at Tate Britain (*see p218*). *See also p219.*
Buggy access. Café. Nappy-changing facilities. Nearest picnic place: grassy area opposite. Shop.

Where to eat

The eating options in the area are traditional, to say the least – though curry, eels and black pudding aren't to everyone's taste these days. But you'll find something for everyone at the 24-hour **Brick Lane Beigel Bake** (159 Brick Lane, E1, 7729 0616), where combinations start at 85p. There are sweet pastries or biscuits for afters.

Alternatively, a traditional Brick Lane curry will set you back less than a tenner at friendly **Preem** (Nos.120-122, 7247 0397), which has high chairs.

Staff here are happy to let children pick the best bits out of the masala dosai. **Café Spice Namaste** (16 Prescot Street, E1, 7488 9242) is somewhat pricier but has a wide range of colourful dishes to entice conservative palates. Those who still insist on plain English grub might fancy meat and two veg at Gilbert & George's favourite local, the **Market Café** at 5 Fournier Street (7247 9470).

The much-fêted **Spitalfields Market**, which takes place in a huge, draughty structure that was once the home of the eastern fruit and veg wholesale market, has become extremely hip with young, ecologically aware parents at weekends, with its ever-expanding range of organic food stalls. It's also a general market during the week, though the buzz is best on Sunday.

Shoreditch & Hoxton

Shoreditch used to be known for its music halls (James Burbage is said to have founded London's first theatre here in 1598, though it was moved to Southwark 20 years later and is now known as Shakespeare's Globe; *see p226*). Trendy Hoxton, the area of Shoreditch north of Old Street and west of Kingsland Road, has a more macabre claim to fame – playwright Ben Jonson fought and killed the actor Gabriel Spencer in Hoxton Fields (now Hoxton Square). Jonson managed to escape the gallows because he was a clergyman, but he had his thumb branded for the crime.

From Victorian times onwards the area was infamous for its slum housing, which was replaced in the 20th century by blocks of flats. Drawn by its rawness and low rents, artists and bohemian types have more recently flocked here and the main attractions are bars and clubs, centred around Hoxton Square. Worth a visit *en famille* are the **Geffrye Museum**, an oasis of loveliness, and **Hoxton Hall** (130 Hoxton Street, N1, 7739 0060/www.hoxtonhall.co.uk), an arts centre and theatre that hosts regular children's crafts and drama classes (*see p229*) and a family-friendly production every Christmas.

Geffrye Museum
Kingsland Road, E2 (7739 9893/recorded info 7739 8543/www.geffrye-museum.org.uk). Liverpool Street tube/rail then 149, 242 bus/Old Street tube/rail then 243 bus. **Open** 10am-5pm Tue-Sat; noon-5pm Sun, bank hol Mon. Closed Good Fri, 24-26 Dec, 1 Jan. **Admission** free; donations appreciated. Under-8s must be accompanied by an adult.
Built in 1715 as an almshouse, the Geffrye was converted into a furniture and interior design museum in 1914, with rooms representing different periods in history from the Elizabethan era to the present day. An imaginative and extremely popular programme of school holiday and weekend events for children reflect the changing exhibitions. Call the museum

for more information about the excellent workshop programme, in which activities for age groups from 3-15 may include cooking, decorative arts, model making and other creative pursuits. All the workshops are free and enormous fun. On summer weekends a jazz band sometimes plays on the lawn, and the airy restaurant is a pleasure to visit year-round. Christmas is also a good time to come – every room is lovingly and evocatively decorated in period festive style, so you can trace the development of the modern Christmas and find out how indebted we are to the Victorians for so many of our yuletide traditions. The lovely herb garden is ten years old in 2002, so staff hope to run some events in celebration. *Buggy access. Café. Lift. Nappy-changing facilities. Nearest picnic place: museum grounds.*

Bethnal Green & Hackney

These once-poor areas, despite the moneyspinning effects of regeneration, gentrification and new-found cool, remain, for the most part, pretty scruffy. Bethnal Green, in Victorian times, held the shameful title of 'poorest district in London' and, despite wholesale slum clearances in the 20th century, there's still a great deal of work needed. The area has its saving graces, however. The most important is the (free) **Museum of Childhood at Bethnal Green**. Also lovely is the **Columbia Road Flower Market** (between Gosset Street and the Royal Oak Pub, 8am-1pm Sun), where horticultural stalls blossom with bedding, shrubs, bulbs, pots and cut flowers for the house. Further north, little gems such as **Sutton House**, the **Hackney Empire** and the **Clowns International Gallery** make faffing with buses around the tube-free bits of Hackney worthwhile.

The beautiful old **Hackney Empire** (291 Mare Street, E8, 8985 2424) was once one of London's great music halls and has seen the best in family entertainment over the years. It's renowned for adults-only comedy nights, but there's a year-round family programme. The Empire is currently closed for refurbishment, but due to open up good as new in winter (ring for details). At present, children's shows take place in the Bullion Room (about once every two months, usually at weekends). The handsome new look of the Empire is part of Hackney's plan to create a 'cultural quarter' around the Town Hall Square (Mare Street), most of which came to fruition in April this year. Central to this is **Hackney Museum**, in a shiny new building with ingeniously interactive ways of charting the last 1,000 years in Hackney. The Central Library has been given lovely new premises in the complex, where shops, restaurants and a gym have joined **Ocean**, a hot local music venue (*see p233*).

There are many places to run wild here: **Hackney Downs** (Downs Park Road, E8, 7923 3644) has three tennis courts, floodlit basketball courts, a bowling green and a playground; **Hackney Marshes**, a large expanse of grassland between Clapton and Leyton

north of Victoria Park (*see p120*), is the muddy home of English Sunday League football. It is the largest space in Europe devoted to the beautiful game, with 88 pitches in all. Teams welcome players of all standards. This windy eastern reach of Hackney Marshes is a favourite unravelling place for kite-fliers, and festivals take place in summer. Further activities include remote-control aircraft shows, American and Gaelic football, rugby and cricket.

London Fields (Westside, E8, 7923 3644) has attracted cricketers since 1802. As well as sports and play facilities, the park has an intriguing sculpture of a seated couple surrounded by pretty, inset mosaic pictures – it's a real favourite with children (and winos), as is a game of pétanque at the Pub on the Park (19 Martello Street, E8, 7275 9586).

Springfield Park (7923 3644) in Clapton is a picturesque green space overlooking the River Lea and Springfield Marina. Its drawing-room café, which opens every day in summer, has huge french windows looking out on to the gardens.

Green space and agriculture come together at the pastoral **Hackney City Farm** (*see below*), next door to which is **Haggerston Park** (7923 3644), with pretty gardens, a softball pitch, a cycle track and astroturf for ball games.

Clowns International Gallery
1 Hillman Street, E8 (7608 0312). Hackney Central rail. **Open** 10am-5pm Mon-Fri. **Admission** free.
The world's oldest established organisation for clowns has had a few financial problems recently but looks to be finding its feet again. That's excellent news as it's a fine place to visit. There's a gallery of famous clowns, and information on the history of madcap acting from the commedia dell'arte of the 16th century to present-day loons in big trousers. Children like the clown car, costumes and audio-visual displays, plus the cases of long-gone clowns' treasures. The shop sells anything with a clown on it, plus tricks, jokes and squirty flowers. The owners are planning on moving to brighter, newly decorated premises nearby in summer 2002, so ring before you set off.

Hackney City Farm
1A Goldsmiths Row, E2 (7729 6381/ www.hackneycityfarm.co.uk). Bus 26, 46, 55. **Open** 10am-4.30pm Tue-Sun. Closed 25, 26 Dec, 1 Jan. **Admission** free; donations appreciated.
This cobbled farmyard is a pleasant place to while away an afternoon in the company of pigs, geese, turkeys, sheep and cattle. Staff run pottery and weaving classes and a popular play-scheme in the summer holidays, and regularly dream up farming-inspired fun days. Parents can appreciate the idyll from the shelter of the café, then stock up on fresh honey and eggs from the shop.
Buggy access. Café. Nappy-changing facilities. Nearest picnic place: Haggerston Park. Shop.

Hackney Museum
Technology & Learning Centre, 1 Reading Lane, off Mare Street, E8 (8356 3500/www.hackney.gov.uk/ hackneymuseum). Hackney Central rail. **Open** 9.30am-5.30pm Mon, Tue, Fri; 9.30am-8pm Thur; 10am-5pm Sat. Closed bank hols. **Admission** free.

Roll up! Roll up! **Spitalfields Market**. *See p113.*

Hackney Museum opened in April 2002 as part of a new smartening-up initiative around Town Hall Square. Housed in a brand-new building, funded through the government's Private Finance Initiative, with exhibitions, resources and hands-on activities financed by the Heritage Lottery Fund, the museum is designed to help visitors find out about the melting pot of Hackney. This area has, we learn here, been culturally diverse for more than 1,000 years, and it's this point the curators want to press. It's all entertaining and educational stuff. There are mock-ups of an Anglo Saxon boat to clamber on board (the real remains of one are on display), a walk-in eel, pie and mash shop and a tower block that visitors can 'blow up'. Computer interactives are in place to reel in the children; ring up to receive a free Hackney Museum Family Pack. Ring for details of the educational programme, which was still in the planning stage at the time of writing.
Buggy access. Café, shops and toilets in Town Hall Square. Nappy-changing facilities. Nearest picnic place: benches in square or London Fields.

Museum of Childhood at Bethnal Green

Cambridge Heath Road, E2 (8983 5200/recorded info 8980 2415/www.museumofchildhood.org.uk). Bethnal Green tube/rail. **Open** 10am-5.50pm Mon-Thur, Sat, Sun. Closed 24-26 Dec, 1 Jan, Good Friday. **Admission** free. Under-8s must be accompanied by an adult.

Nostalgic adults love the Museum of Childhood as much, if not more, than children. Established in 1872 as an east London branch of the V&A, eventually becoming a Museum of Childhood in 1974, this enchanting archive holds the largest collection of toys and childhood paraphernalia in the UK, and one of the largest in the world, with more than 6,000 toys and games.

Among the oldest toys on show is one of only two surviving Nuremberg dolls' houses – part of a wider collection of dolls' houses – dating back to 1673. Young children are entranced by the houses and spend ages spotting tiny details in the rooms. In addition, the museum's permanent displays include dolls, teddy bears, trains, puppets and board games.

The museum also houses a history of children's costume, plus displays of baby and nursery equipment over the years. Though the collection dates from the 16th century, it is kept up to date with Gameboys, a state-of-the-art Kaleidoscope dolls' house and a newly acquired Lego Hogwarts Castle.

The museum has recently expanded its programme of children's activities: the friendly staff hold art workshops and soft play sessions for kids at the weekends and in the school holidays, and a new permanent play area for under-5s makes this an excellent place to bring pre-schoolers. As if that weren't enough fun, there's a giant DIY snakes and ladders game, and tables where children (and adults) can sit and play board games.

Most children come to rest at the shop, where pocket money goes a long way, thanks to an imaginative collection of toys, stationery and gadgets for under £1. The licensed museum

Larking about at the **Docklands Sailing and Watersports Centre**. *See p117.*

café makes for a welcome break from toy-spotting, and has special lunch boxes for children alongside cakes, crisps and sandwiches. If you've been organised enough to bring your own picnic you can eat it outside in the gardens.
Buggy access. Café. Lift. Nappy-changing facilities. Nearest picnic place: museum gardens. Shop.

Sutton House
2 & 4 Homerton High Street, E9 (8986 2264/ www.nationaltrust.org.uk). Bethnal Green tube then 253, 106, D6 bus/Hackney Central rail. **Open** 1.30-5pm Fri, Sat; 11.30am-5pm Sun, bank hol Mon, 4 June (Jubilee Day). *Tours* phone for details. **Admission** (NT) £2.10; 50p 5-16s; £4.70 family (2+2); free under-5s. **Credit** MC, V.
The oldest house in east London, built in 1535 for Henry VIII's secretary of state, Sir Ralph Sadleir. Much more recently, in the late 1980s, this essentially Tudor (but changed over the years) house, with its oak-panelled rooms, was used as a community centre before the National Trust got hold of it. A grand restoration project saved the building's many original charms, as well as elegant Jacobean and Georgian interiors. Don't forget to look in on the 16th-century garderobe, London's oldest loo. There are a few multimedia exhibits, and changing art exhibitions and themed events for children during school holidays, which have included historic cookery workshops, Tudor and Victorian games, dressing-up and ghost story events. Light meals, home-made cakes and drinks are served in the Brick Place Café.
Café. Nappy-changing facilities. Nearest picnic place: St John's churchyard. Shop.

Where to eat

The eating is exotic around Hackney. Turkish and Vietnamese resturants abound, and all welcome children. You have to book at weekends for the popular Vietnamese caff **Hai-Ha** (206 Mare Street, E8, 8985 5388). A favourite for inexpensive fuel food is **Café Alba** (183 Mare Street, E8, 8985 5927), with Indian-inspired dishes and comforting puddings. At **Little Georgia** (2 Broadway Market, E8, 7249 9070), dishes from the meze menu are £1.50 each.

There are plenty of eating opportunities around the Columbia Road end of Bethnal Green: **Jones Dairy Café** (23 Ezra Street, E2, 7739 5372; *see also p185*) is a great weekend drop-in; and, on Columbia Road, there's a brasserie, **Perennial** (No.110, 7739 4556) and **Laxeiro Tapas Bar** (No.93, 7729 1147; *see also p185*).

Docklands

From its heyday in the 18th and 19th centuries, when boats from all over the world unloaded their treasures here, to the breakdown of empire and the modern regeneration of the area into a riverside retreat for the well-off, Docklands has seen it all. Stretching from Tower Bridge to the Isle of Dogs and beyond, it has plenty to keep daytrippers occupied, especially if you buy a Travelcard and hop on and off the driverless Docklands Light Railway (DLR) trains, which is part of the fun (*see also p112*). Now that the Jubilee tube line connects with several DLR stations, Docklands is not such a chore to get to – though an alternative, and amusing, route to the area is the Greenwich foot tunnel, which takes you under the river from the *Cutty Sark* in Greenwich to Island Gardens in Docklands.

The area gained a reputation in the '80s, when the Conservative government set up the London Docklands Development Corporation (LDDC) to regenerate derelict land by building upmarket offices and new homes to attract business to this part of the capital. The dream came to grief when recession came in the '90s. The LDDC ceased operations in 1998. Over the last decade, however, more businesses have moved into the area, and its fascinating history and dramatic architecture attract ever more visitors to Docklands.

The westernmost point to fall under the Docklands heading is **Wapping**, an area brimming with history. Until well into the 19th century, convicted pirates were brought at low tide to Execution Dock (near the river police station, at Wapping New Stairs), hanged and left there in chains until three tides had washed over them. **Captain Kidd**, whose name has been given to a pub, at 108 Wapping High Street, met such a death. The **Town of Ramsgate**, at 62 High Street, is another famous pub, where bloodthirsty Judge Jeffreys, who sent many pirates to their death, was captured. The most famous pub in the area is the **Prospect of Whitby**, built in 1552. It's always full of tourists because Pepys, Dickens, Whistler and Turner all drank here.

Between Wapping and the Isle of Dogs is **Limehouse**, so called because medieval lime kilns once stood here. Like Wapping it has an ancient connection with mariners and in the 17th century was a centre for shipbuilding. The enormous church, **St Anne's Limehouse**, was designed by Hawksmoor between 1712 and 1724, and has the second highest clocktower in Britain (after the one containing Big Ben).

The most visitor-friendly of all Docklands areas, however, is the **Isle of Dogs**. People disagree about the name given to this peninsula sticking out into the deepest loop of the Thames – it's an isle because the stretch of water making up the West India Docks cuts it off from the mainland, but where are, or were, the dogs? Some people think there may once have been royal kennels here, others think 'dog' is a corruption of 'dykes', which were built here by Flemish engineers in the 19th century.

You can explore Docklands' 2,000-year history at the **Museum in Docklands**, scheduled to open late summer 2002. Or you can admire its present-day splendour by hopping on the DLR and disembarking at the astonishing glass and steel Canary Wharf station designed by Lord Foster. Travel on to the southern end of the Isle to discover more rustic pleasures: the honest-to-goodness **Mudchute City Farm**. From Island Gardens at the southernmost tip you can enjoy fantastic views over the river.

The area's reputation as an adventure playground for those with a bit of spare cash is further advanced by action-packed attractions like **Docklands F1 City** kart track (Gate 119, Connaught Bridge, Royal Victoria Dock, E16, 7476 5678; *see also p260*) and **Docklands Sailing and Watersports Centre** (Millwall Docks, 235A Westferry Road, E14, 7537 2626; *see also p267*).

Mudchute City Farm

Pier Street, Isle of Dogs, E14 (7515 5901). Crossharbour or Island Gardens DLR. **Open** 9am-4pm daily. Closed 25 Dec-1 Jan. **Admission** free; donations appreciated.
Ducks, chickens, goats, pigs and llamas, plus a small flock of sheep and a cattle herd all live here, with the Canary Wharf Tower in the background. Local children learn to ride at the British Horse Society-approved school; others come to the Nature Studies resource centre to find out about our green and pleasant land and discover how to shear a sheep. Kids can also join the Young Farmers Club (it's free) and help the farmer with evening livestock feeds, or collect eggs, or even learn to shear a sheep at certain times of year.
Buggy access. Café. Shop.

Museum in Docklands

Warehouse No. 1, West India Quay, Hertsmere Road, E14 (7001 9800/www.museumindocklands.org.uk). Canary Wharf tube/West India Quay DLR. **Open** 10am-6pm Mon-Sat; noon-6pm Sun. **Admission** check website for details.
Housed in Grade I-listed Georgian warehouses right in the shadow of Canary Wharf, this new museum, due to open at the end of the summer, has 13 major galleries relating the story of London's river, its port and its people over the past 2,000 years. This is achieved through multimedia presentations, a children's gallery and artefacts from the Museum of London's collection – from cargo hooks to quayside cranes. The Children's Gallery has been designed for maximum interactive fun and hands-on entertainment; experiences such as the walk-through Victorian sailor's town, which includes atmospheric dockside sights and sounds, the rowdy alehouses, chandlers' shops and busy wharves from the city's life as a port. Check the website for news on the developing educational and children's activity programme. Check the website for more information, such as opening date and admission prices. Or email info@museumindocklands.org.uk and ask to be put on the mailing list.

Water ways: Regent's Canal east

The Regent's Canal (*see also p98*) can be walked in an easterly direction from Victoria Park in Hackney. Follow the canal through Old Ford lock and down to the Thames. You can break the walk at the **Ragged School Museum** (*see p120*), with its Victorian classroom, helpful volunteer guides and Tow Path café, with swans nesting opposite. Continue straight down to Limehouse Basin where the canal joins the Thames. A hundred years ago this was a bustling commercial port where barges unloaded manufactured goods bound for the far-flung corners of the British Empire, and where raw materials were transferred to barges heading to the industrial centres in the Midlands and the north of England. Now it's a marina with luxury yachts and waterside apartments, but you still get a feeling of that time if you sit outside one of the pubs and watch boats passing from the safe harbour of the basin out to the Thames and onward to the open sea.

Walk: Wanstead Park

▶ At first glance, Wanstead looks like just another middle-class suburb on the way out of London. Yet if events during the early 19th century had turned out differently, this area could have been as famous as Blenheim or Versailles.

▶ Take the Central Line to Wanstead and turn left out of the tube station. Walk along George Green and St Mary's Avenue towards the Grade I-listed St Mary's Church, built in the neo-classical style in 1790. This is the first indication that you're in the vicinity of a once-great country house.

▶ Turn left into **Overton Drive**, past the golf club – whose premises occupy the stable block of this former mansion – and right into Warren Road. Walk to the end, with the golf course on both sides left and right. Ahead is an entrance to **Wanstead Park**.

The estate was formed by enclosing part of the royal hunting forest as a deer park in 1545, and the house there was enlarged by Robert Dudley, Earl of Leicester, who used it to entertain Queen Elizabeth in 1578. Almost a century later, the estate was acquired by Sir Josiah Child, governor of the East India Company, who began to plan a large formal garden. The work was carried on by his son, Earl Tylney, whose design echoed that of Versailles. In 1715 he started to build a vast mansion in the new Palladian style, dreamed up by the fashionable architect Colen Campbell. William Hogarth painted a celebrated picture of an 'assembly' held there.

▶ To the left as you enter the park is the '**Long View**', a vista down to the ornamental water and canal that were created in response to changing theories of garden design. You can walk down the hill and, turning left or right, complete a circular route around the lake, with its islands that once housed a sham fort. At the end of the ornamental water to the right is a ruined grotto, built in the early 1760s with a boathouse below and domed, shell-encrusted chamber above.

▶ Alternatively, keep to the main path. This will bring you into an open plain with a classical temple to the left. This is one of the few remaining features of the 'landscape' garden; in front of it is a newly planted avenue of sweet chestnut trees to link the temple to another water feature, the **Heronry Pond**. Here is a great place to throw a ball around, let the dog off its lead or fly a kite. It's also a congregating place for cyclists.

▶ You can follow the trees to the Heronry Pond and, further on, to the pretty **Shoulder of Mutton Pond**, which always has some ducks to feed. The trees in this area towards **Blake Hall Road** are magnificent, many planted by the gardener Humphrey Repton in the 'picturesque' style. Look for small trees placed together in the same hole, which have now grown into a closely packed clump, their trunks intertwining. There are noticeboards with maps showing the park as it is now and as it was in the 1740s.

Where to eat

There are some pretty good eating options nearby, many of them remarkably child-friendly, although in the week family groups have to elbow office workers out of the way between noon and 2pm around Canary Wharf. **Yellow River Café** (10 Cabot Square, E14, 7715 9515) is one of a mini chain of appealing Asian restaurants; here the children's bento boxes can be followed by ice-cream. **Café Rouge** (20 Cabot Square, E14, 7537 9696) has a children's menu with a good line in fuel food and provides high chairs. At the time of writing, a new branch of the American-style chain **Smollensky's** (*see p179*) was about to open at Canary Wharf.

There are pizzas galore at the **Gourmet Pizza Company** (18-20 Mackenzie Walk, E14, 7345 9192). **Hubbub** (269 Westferry Road, E14, 7515 5577) is a quiet place for a light pasta meal, sandwiches and cakes. Another treat is **Baradero** (Glengall Bridge, Turnberry Quay, off Pepper Street, E14, 7537 1666), a tapas bar overlooking the river.

Mile End to West Ham

Mile End – which was mostly common land until the 16th century) – was built on in the 1800s as industrialisation demanded more homes for workers. A confusing sprawl of busy roads and urban housing developments, it would have little charm were it not for its parklife. **Mile End Park** has emerged from an ambitious regeneration project, while **Victoria Park** is even more handsome following a £2-million restoration scheme. The **Ragged School Museum** is also worth heading east for.

Bow, to the east, has a rich industrial heritage dating back to the 11th century. Grain was transported by boat from Hertfordshire and unloaded at mills along the river here. Today, Three Mills, where one of the oldest tidal mills left standing in Britain attracts many visitors, has another claim to fame: *Big Brother* was filmed in a nearby studio. The **Lea Rivers Trust**, a registered charity, also runs a comprehensive and affordable range of activities for organised school groups in six east London boroughs bordering the River Lea.

▶ Across the plain you can discern another building, which looks from a distance like another classical temple. It is, in fact, a modern tea stall.

So what happened to the house? In 1784 the estate passed to a nephew of the second Earl Tylney and then to his daughter Catherine Tylney Long. Her marriage to the Hon. William Pole Tylney Long Wellesley, nephew of the Duke of Wellington, proved a disaster. He spent her fortune, then absconded to Europe. In 1824 the house was demolished and all its contents sold. The park was let for grazing, mature trees were felled for timber and the gardens became overgrown. The site of the house is marked by a large dip in the ground on the golf course; not a single brick survives.

Nowadays the Grade II-listed landscape is managed by the Corporation of London as part of **Epping Forest**. The **Wren** (Waltham Forest, Redbridge, Epping Forest, Newham) Conservation and Wildlife Group is active in its maintenance; the group's website provides a comprehensive history, map and guide to the plants and birds to be found there. A walk around the entire park is about three miles, offering intriguing glimpses of what might have been had history followed another course.

Wanstead Park
Warren Road, E11 (8508 0028). Wanstead tube.
Open daily. **Admission** free.
Wren Conservation and Wildlife Group: Paul Ferris, 8478 4770/www.wrengroup.fsnet.co.uk.

Stratford ('street by the ford') has blossomed since gaining its Jubilee Line tube station, which links it to the West End. The centre is focused around the Broadway, but the real star turn is **Theatre Royal Stratford East** (Gerry Raffles Square, E15, 8534 0310), a delightful old theatre that reopened in December 2001 (just in time for its famously jolly family pantos), after a programme of refurbishment that has added a café-bar, improved disabled access and generally spruced-up the atmospheric Grade II-listed auditorium.

The old theatre has a new neighbour in the state-of-the-art **Stratford Circus Arts Centre** (8279 1000; *see p216*), which runs a full programme of activities, including children's performances and classes and workshops in dance, music and drama for all ages. It has a café, bar and crèche, making it a welcome new resource for families in the area.

There are two good reasons to travel east from Stratford. The first is **West Ham Park**, which was referred to in an 1886 article in *The Times* as 'that blessed oasis West Ham Park'; anyone familiar with the area around it will sympathise entirely.

The other big attraction is **West Ham United Football Club**, London's perennial underachievers, whose famously tight and compact ground has been extensively redeveloped.

Lee Rivers Trust Waterway Discovery Team
Schools Officer, Lea Rivers Trust, Three Mill Lane, E3 (8981 0040 ext 224/Pride of Lee ext 223/ www.leariverstrust.co.uk). Bromley-by-Bow tube.
Open *House Mill* May-Oct 2-4pm Sun. *Funday Sundays* 11am-4pm 1st Sun of mth Apr-Oct.
Admission *Mill tour* £2; free under-16s.
No credit cards.
The House Mill, built in 1776 in the Dutch style and the oldest and largest tidal mill left standing in Britain, was used to grind the grain for gin distilling. Its stones stopped their grinding for good in 1941 and the building was taken over in 1989 as part of a big restoration project by the River Lea Tidal Mill trust.

There's a visitors' centre that provides a history of the area and map-leaflets detailing walks in the area: nearby Riverside Green and Three Mills Green are pleasant for picnicking and strolling. Or wander along the network of the Bow Back rivers and enjoy the wildlife that thrives in this pocket of peace and quiet. Note that there are toilets when the Mill

House is open or in the Tesco superstore nearby, and that those with pushchairs might find the cobbled walkways a little hard-going, though the towpaths are easily accessible. The first Sunday of the month is Funday Sunday, which includes a popular craft market, and children can take part in absorbing workshops with a broadly environmental theme (paper-making, bread-making and willow-weaving are popular). All the activities are free and are run on a first-come first-served basis. One-hour boat trips on the *Pride of Lee* narrowboat to Limehouse Basin and back also run from here (call 8981 0040 for a brochure). Narrowboat enthusiasts flock here for the occasional rally. The Lea Rivers Trust schools programme runs Monday to Friday all year round; call for more information. Note that there is no wheelchair access to the *Pride of Lee*.

Buggy access. Nearest picnic place: Lee Valley Park.

Gone to the dogs

Greyhound racing is Britain's second-most-popular spectator sport (after football, of course) – and there's no better place than **Walthamstow Stadium** to discover the endless fascination of who finishes second behind the hare. Although 'going to the dogs' has a rough and ready image as the favoured pursuit of geezers (both diamond and dodgy), the track has worked hard to promote itself as a lively, friendly destination for all ages. Nor has a little extra publicity from dog-lover Vinnie Jones, who turned up one night with Claudia Schiffer, done any harm.

There's racing at Walthamstow three evenings a week, along with lunchtime meetings, which are staged specifically for broadcast in off-course betting shops. Children's entertainment is usually provided during holidays and half-term, while occasional 'Sunday Fundays' are targeted squarely at a family audience.

The stunning art deco façade is the most famous feature of the 'Stow (cabbie language for Walthamstow), behind which the Paddock and Stowaway Grills offer reasonably priced menus with every table overlooking the track. The Classic Diner is the place for a burger and a beer, and also has a clear view of the play area for those who don't want to follow the canine capers.

However, half the fun of taking kids to the dogs is checking out the animals as they parade up and down before a race, letting them pick a favourite – the waggiest tail, perhaps, or a particular number – then placing a small bet on their behalf. You never know, they might end up paying for the next round of lemonade!

Walthamstow Stadium

Chingford Road, E4 (8531 4255/ www.wsgreyhound.co.uk). Walthamstow Central tube/rail then 97, 357, 215 bus/Highams Park rail. **Racing** 7.30pm Tue, Thur, Sat; 1pm Mon; 11.30am Fri; 2pm Mon, plus occasional Sun. **Admission** £3-£6. **No credit cards.**

Mile End Park

Locksley Street, E3 (8525 9416/www.mileendpark.co.uk). Mile End tube. **Open** 24hrs daily.

This long, thin park is becoming a bit of a legend, thanks to a £25-million makeover. Partly funded by the Millennium Commission, the scheme divides the park into a series of themed areas and adds a state-of-the-art children's playground (to be completed by autumn 2002). The electric go-kart track is probably the biggest draw for older children; those looking for something gentler will enjoy the ecology park with its indoor and outdoor education centres, paddling lake and 850-plus species of plants. New park rangers have been trained to keep the revamped park buzzing, and they're certainly doing their job – there are outdoor sculpture and cutting-edge community art initiatives (which take place in a purpose-built arts pavilion), plus all kinds of events and exhibitions on the theme of 'greening your environment'. Piers Gough's tree-lined Green Bridge spans Mile End Road, providing a link between the two sides of the park. Nearby Mile End Stadium (Rhodeswell Road, E14, 8980 1885) has an athletics track, a multipurpose pitch plus weight training, tennis and cricket facilities.

Buggy access. Nappy-changing facilities.

Ragged School Museum

46-50 Copperfield Road, E3 (8980 6405/ www.raggedschoolmuseum.org.uk). Mile End tube. **Open** 10am-5pm Wed, Thur; 2-5pm 1st Sun of mth; also open 3 June 2002. Closed 24 Dec-1 Jan. *Tours* by arrangement; phone for details. **Admission** free; donations welcome.

Ragged schools were charity schools that provided a basic education for orphaned, poor or down-and-out children. Opened in 1900, this converted warehouse, which was previously used by Dr Barnardo, became the largest ragged school in London. Its fascinatingly sparse Victorian classroom has been recreated and school groups come from all over London to don Victorian togs and sit in it. Their own teachers give the kids old-fashioned names such as Walter and Agatha and hand them over to a hatchet-faced 'schoolmistress' (a museum actress) for some serious learning. There are also exhibitions on local history, temporary exhibitions, plus workshops, treasure hunts and canal walks.

Café. Nappy-changing facilities. Nearest picnic place: Mile End Park. Shop.

Victoria Park

Old Ford Road, E3 (8533 2057). Mile End tube/ Cambridge Heath or Hackney Wick rail/8, 26, 30, 55, 253, 277, S2 bus. **Open** 6am-dusk daily. Closed 25 Dec.

This grand old park, which opened in 1845 after demands for more public space, has a dramatic history. It was the scene of riots during the 19th century, and it contains Bonners Fields, where heretics were burned for daring to speak their mind. Although the park was originally conceived as a Regent's Park of the East End, the poor inhabitants had no carriages to drive through the tree-lined drives or around the park's smart villas. In fact, the slum dwellers, having no running water of their own, used the park's two lakes as baths. Nowadays, they're employed for other purposes – the Western Lake is fished for carp, tench, perch and roach by licensed anglers, and the country's oldest Model Boat Club convenes around the lake near Crown Gate East every second Sunday. Here, model steamboats take to the water, deftly controlled by their captains, young and old.

The park's animal enclosure is cropped by goats and fallow deer. Tennis courts, a bowling green, cricket pitch and athletics track (newly refurbished after a fire ruined it) entice those with a yen for sports, and kids can get stuck into the

Mile End Park – not bad for £25 million. *See p120.*

popular adventure playground in the centre of the park. The Lakeside Pavilion Café is one of the prettiest places for miles around to stop for lunch after a morning in the playground. *Café. Nappy-changing facilities.*

West Ham Park
Upton Lane, E7 (8472 3584/www.cityoflondon.gov.uk). Stratford tube/rail/104, 238, 325 bus. **Open** 7.30am-dusk daily.
This is a Corporation of London-run park, which includes 12 tennis courts, two cricket squares, two football pitches, a running track and a rounders area. Children's sport is taken so seriously at West Ham Park that several schools have their sports days here, and there are organised cricket and tennis coaching courses. The children's playground has a full-time attendant and a full quota of swings, roundabouts and climbing frames. On summer weekday afternoons it has been known for more than 300 children to turn up to see the clowns, ventriloquists and magicians who put on shows around the bandstand. There's also a paddling pool and, at times, a bouncy castle. The rose garden is a beautiful oasis with eight computer-controlled greenhouses. Out of season, staff offer botanical tours to suit both children and adults. *Nappy-changing facilities.*

West Ham United Football Club
Boleyn Ground, Green Street, E13 (8548 2748/ www.westhamunited.co.uk). Upton Park tube. **Open** *Shop* 10am-5pm Mon-Sat. Closed 25 Dec. **Admission** *Tours* phone for details. **Credit** MC, V.

The 'Happy Hammers' may be among the Premiership's also-rans, but a £35-million redevelopment is certainly bringing the Boleyn Ground up to scratch. A West Ham megastore is now up and running, but other attractions, such as a museum telling the story of the club from its origins as Thames Iron Works FC, is not yet open. When it finally does open (ring for details) the museum will exhibit medals, caps and shirts from the late Bobby Moore, Sir Geoff Hurst and Martin Peters, the West Ham trio who helped England win the World Cup in 1966. *Bars. Café. Nappy-changing facilities. Restaurant. Shop.*

Where to eat

The locals of Vicky Park frequent the Lauriston Road duo: Frocks and Mojo. Both restaurants, which are open for lunch and accommodating towards young families, have an international menu and a fairly laid-back vibe. **Frocks** (95 Lauriston Road, E9, 8986 3161; *see also p184*) has gluten-free dishes on its menu, as well as solid comfort food or brunch fare, such as bubble and squeak and sausages. In fact, brunch is a weekend institution, so book. There's a garden, and a delicatessen next door, giving the place a communal feel. **Mojo**, up the road at No.132 (8985 5864), boasts a more ambitious but nonetheless good-value menu, so it often gets packed.

North Woolwich Old Station Museum. *See p125.*

Walthamstow

The last stop north on the Victoria Line, Walthamstow is an intriguing mix: around St Mary's Church there's a quaint, village ambience, which contrasts to the bustle of the famous street market. Listed in the Doomsday Survey as 'Wilcumestou' (when the few scattered farm buildings were valued at £28 and two ounces of gold), today it retains many historic buildings. Picturesque 'Walthamstow village' was designated a conservation area by Waltham Forest Council in 1967.

Walthamstow High Street hosts what is claimed to be the longest daily street market in Europe (it has 450 stalls); its costers wet their whistles at the numerous untrendy pubs and caffs that give the street its genuine East End feel. To the north lies Lloyd Park and the William Morris Gallery while to the west **Walthamstow Marshes** is the perfect location for a picnic or a leisurely stroll through the wilds by the River Lea.

Lloyd Park, on Forest Road, is more than your average park – not only is it the site of the **William Morris Gallery**, and the **Changing Rooms Gallery**, it also contains the **Waltham Forest Theatre** (call 8521 7111 for programme details), which is surrounded by an ornamental moat. There's a children's play area at the far end of the park, attractive gardens throughout and an aviary containing budgies and cockatoos. It's wise to take the car or cycle to **Walthamstow Marshes** at the end of Coppermill Lane (otherwise it's a brisk 15-minute walk from St James Street rail station). There are occasional open days at the old copper mill itself, plus various rambles and boat trips from Springfield Marina. These trips are free but booking is essential with the Lea Rivers Trust Waterway Discovery Team (8981 0040/www.leariverstrust.co.uk; information on other events at the marshes is available from this number).

Five minutes from Walthamstow Central station lies the old village of Walthamstow. Opposite St Mary's Church is the Ancient House – a 15th-century 'hall' house – while nearby the Squire's Almshouses, erected by Mrs Mary Squires in 1795 'for six decayed tradesmen's widows', are still standing. Extensive guides to the village and to other historic buildings in the area are available at the **Vestry House Museum**, which provides an overview of the borough's history.

Across the North Circular Road is a 20th-century landmark, the art deco façade of **Walthamstow Stadium** (*see p120*).

Changing Room Gallery

Lloyd Park, Forest Road, E17 (8496 4563/ www.lbwf.gov.uk/crg). Walthamstow Central tube/rail. **Open** *Exhibitions* Apr-Nov 10am-5pm Sat, Sun; weekdays vary depending on exhibitions. **Admission** free.

The Changing Room is an exhibition space for contemporary arts and crafts, and has a New Agey feel. As well as the changing programme of exhibitions hosted by the gallery, there's studio space for local artists, regular artists' seminars and a popular café.
Buggy access. Café. Nearest picnic place: Lloyd Park.

Hornbeam Environmental Centre

458 Hoe Street, E17 (8558 6880/ www.hornbeamec.co.uk). Walthamstow Central tube/rail. **Open** noon-3.30pm Mon-Thur; noon-3.30pm, 7-10pm Fri; 10am-4.30pm Sat. Closed 25 Dec-1 Jan, bank hols. **Admission** free.

The Hornbeam Environmental Centre is the home of nature studies in the Walthamstow area. It holds frequent exhibitions in the gallery, and has a library and Gannets Café, where a generous plateful of wholefood vegetarian grub costs about a fiver.
Nappy-changing facilities.

Vestry House Museum

Vestry Road, E17 (8509 1917/www.lbwf.gov.uk). Walthamstow Central tube/rail. **Open** 10am-1pm, 2-5.30pm Mon-Fri; 10am-1pm, 2-5pm Sat. Closed 25, 26 Dec, 1 Jan, bank hols. *Tours* groups only, by prior arrangement. **Admission** free.

This museum includes one of the original police cells constructed in 1840, a gallery of toys and games, and the Bremer Car, built by local engineer Frederick Bremer in 1892-4 and said to be one of the first cars ever built in Britain (it was certainly the first in London). The Vestry House museum also holds some archive material on Alfred Hitchcock – he was born in Leytonstone.
Nearest picnic place: museum garden.

William Morris Gallery

Lloyd Park, Forest Road, E17 (8527 3782/ www.lbwf.gov.uk/wmg). Walthamstow Central tube/rail. **Open** 10am-1pm, 2-5pm Tue-Sat; 1st Sun of mth. Closed 25, 26 Dec, 1 Jan, bank hols. *Tours* phone for details. **Admission** free.

The childhood home of the famous designer and socialist, who was born in Walthamstow in 1834, the William Morris gallery is a must-see for anyone interested in design or those who are taking GCSE Art. Examples of Morris's work, ranging from textiles and wallpapers to fine printing, are displayed in four ground-floor rooms alongside work by the pre-Raphaelites.
Nearest picnic place: Lloyd Park. Shop.

Where to eat

There's pie and mash, or there's **Central Kitchen** (226 Hoe Street, E17, 8521 9432) and **Village Kitchen** (41 Orford Road, E17, 8509 2144), which provide ciabattas and baguettes for £2 and hot lunches such as char-grilled chicken and couscous, lasagne or pasta for around £3.75. Village Kitchen becomes a more formal restaurant in the evenings. Dogs dinners (steak, burgers, fish and chips) can be enjoyed in the plushy restaurants of **Walthamstow Stadium** (Chingford Road, E4, 8531 4255) on race-day evenings (ring to book for the Paddock Grill and Stowaway Grill restaurants in advance). *See also p120.*

Further east

South of Walthamstow is its poor relation, Leyton. The largest area of public open space here is **Marsh Lane Fields**, enthusiastically used by local people for picnics, walks, sports activities and nature studies. Part of the Dagenham Brook 'green corridor', the Fields are what remains of the original Lammas Lands (fertile strips of land alongside the River Lea) of the rural village of Leyton, which until 1864 had nothing to do with London at all.

Despite being enveloped by the city, the area is charmingly countrified. More information about its attractions, and those of its near relation, the **Lee Valley Park**, can be obtained by calling the helpful

Lea Rivers Trust Waterway Discovery Team (8981 0040). Next stops out on the Central Line are **Leytonstone**, **Snaresbrook** and **Wanstead**, where urban London ends and greenery becomes more apparent. Like Hackney Marshes, **Wanstead Flats** is transformed into a massive football pitch on Sundays, while Wanstead Park (*see p118*) is a great place for a runaround – with a truly fascinating history.

Heading east along the river to the furthest outpost of the DLR takes you to Beckton. Its legendary 'alp' – or rather, dry ski slope – is now closed but due to reopen in late 2002 as a 'snow dome', with manufactured snow and wide, exciting runs (call the Ski Club of Great Britain on 8410 2000 for details).

In & around: the Royal Gunpowder Mills

Why do fireworks explode? Exactly what was Guy Fawkes using to try and blow up the Houses of Parliament? The story of gunpowder is a thrilling one, and the **Royal Gunpowder Mills**, a new attraction surrounded by 175 acres of natural parkland at Waltham Abbey, tells it well.

The mills were involved in the development of explosives for more than 300 years. Gunpowder came first – production, which relied on water supplied from the nearby River Lea, began in the mid-1660s. The mills were bought by the Crown in 1787, at which time they were the most important in Europe. The site greatly expanded during the Crimean War (1854-6), when large amounts of explosives were needed. Later, the site manufactured guncotton, nitro-glycerine, cordite paste and the highly explosive tetryl. After World War II, the mills were used as a research centre for non-nuclear explosives and propellants before finally closing in 1981.

The site opened to the public in 2001 with funding from the Heritage Lottery Fund and Ministry of Defence and has already won huge acclaim for its sensitive interpretation of industrial history. Few of the buildings have been renovated, in a deliberate attempt to convey their long and complex past.

It's a good idea to start at the visitors' centre, which runs an excellent introductory film full of bangs and flashes, and a hands-on exhibition, which concentrates on the human story behind gunpowder. It's intriguing to see the safety clothing and equipment workers had to wear and use, as, a single spark could have set off a massive explosion.

Much effort has been made by the Royal Gunpowder Mills with the educational programme. On a warm summer's day, rugs are set out on the central grassy area and activity packs suitable for children of all ages are handed out. When you get peckish, there's a basic café; alternatively, bring a

picnic. Special events include an art weekend, military re-enactments, craft fairs and sports days.

The whole site is wonderfully atmospheric, particularly the nature reserve, which can be visited on a trailer ride and includes Essex's largest heronry in among the derelict laboratories, aqueducts and pressing houses.

There's more greenery nearby: the Lee Valley Regional Park (*see p125*) pretty much surrounds Waltham Abbey. The stretch between Waltham Abbey and Broxbourne is known as the **River Lee Country Park**: open countryside dotted with lakes and wildflower meadows attracting a wide range of wildlife including kingfisher, great crested grebe, little winged plover and lots of dragonflies. It's ideal for picnics, walking or fishing. It's all well signposted and is open year-round (01992 702200/www.leevalleypark.org.uk).

If you're feeling energetic, the **Lee Valley Boat Centre** (Old Nazeing Road, Broxbourne, 01992 462085) is the place to hire a motorboat or rowing boat or book a holiday narrowboat. It's from here that the Adventuress River Cruises set off (Mar-Dec, same address, 01992 466111/ www.rivercruises.co.uk). Two enclosed, heated boats cruise up and down the river and are available for parties and other group outings.

Waltham Abbey itself is a small town with plenty of little cafés and shops. History fiends may want to visit the Norman abbey, founded in 1060 by King Harold, who is reputed to be buried there. There's a free exhibition about the abbey and the town in the crypt. Epping Forest (*see p126*) is only a ten-minute drive away.

Royal Gunpowder Mills
Beaulieu Drive, Waltham Abbey (01992 767022/ www.royalgunpowdermills.com). Waltham Cross rail. **Open** *mid Mar-late Oct* 10am-6pm (last entry 5pm) daily. **Admission** £5.90; £5.25 concessions; £3.25 5-16s; £17 family (2+2); free under-5s.

While you're in this part of Newham, you could enjoy country pursuits, such as riding at **Docklands Equestrian Centre** (2 Claps Gate Lane, E6, 7473 4951), rambling at **East Ham Nature Reserve** or visiting livestock at **Newham City Farm**.

South of this lies bleak Silvertown, somewhat less attractive than its name, although it now boasts an exciting piece of modern landscaping, the **Thames Barrier Park** (North Woolwich Road, E16), with its concrete tea pavilion, playground and fountains that kids can't wait to get stripped down to their trunks for (*see p23*). Yet further east, where the Woolwich ferry plies its trade across the northern and southern banks of the river, is **North Woolwich Old Station Museum**, a rather sweet free museum commemorating the good old days of reliable trains that actually kept to a timetable (examples of these rarities are hung about the museum). The **Royal Victoria Gardens**, just across the way, is a well-kept riverside park with plenty of apparatus and a summertime café.

Travel even further east for the bird sanctuaries and open spaces of the Lee Valley Park and Chingford areas. **Epping Forest** (*see p126*) is a gift for walkers, riders and cyclists. The forest is accessible on foot from several underground stations, but to explore fully these areas and the surprisingly pretty Essex villages (and their country pubs) that lie beyond them, a car may be the best option.

East Ham Nature Reserve

Norman Road, E6 (8470 4525). East Ham tube/Beckton DLR. **Open** *Grounds & museum* Mar-Oct 10am-5pm Tue-Fri; 2-5pm Sat, Sun. Nov-Feb 10am-5pm Tue-Fri; 1-4pm Sat, Sun. Closed bank hols. **Admission** free.
Pick up a nature trail, or visit the museum, which combines natural and local history. Current displays include a Victorian schoolroom to terrify the kids and a wartime kitchen showing how people made the most of their rations during the Blitz, but ring before visiting in case the exhibitions have changed. *Buggy access. Shop.*

Newham City Farm

Stansfeld Road, E6 (7476 1170). Royal Albert or Prince Regent DLR. **Open** *Mid Oct-mid Feb* 10am-4pm Tue-Sun. *Mid Feb-mid Oct* 10am-5pm Tue-Sun. Closed 25 Dec, 1 Jan. **Admission** free; donations appreciated.
The farm's visitor centre welcomes families and school groups wanting to find out more about city farming. The Berkshire and Kune Kune pigs are popular residents, but there are also a number of cows, ducks, ferrets, geese, goats and guinea pigs to cuddle as well. Note that there is currently no café so you should bring your own refreshments to eat in the picnic area. *Buggy access.*

North Woolwich Old Station Museum

Pier Road, E16 (7474 7244/www.newham.net/museums). Beckton DLR/North Woolwich rail/Woolwich Dockyard or Woolwich Arsenal rail, then ferry or foot tunnel to North Woolwich Pier. **Open** *Jan-Nov* 1-5pm Sat, Sun. Closed Dec. *School holidays* 1-5pm daily. **Admission** free.

William Morris Gallery – groovy glass. *See p123.*

Sad, rusting hulks of old steam engines can be seen on scrubland as you walk to this museum from the North Woolwich station: it may be wise to keep Thomas the Tank Engine fans' eyes averted from such distressing sights. The Old Station Museum, run by the local authority, is a far jollier option. Carefully preserved old engines, ticket machines, signs and relics from a bygone age of steam travel are all displayed. A station guard, or rather a plastic model, stands at his desk looking suitably busy. The pair of trains on display are Coffee Pot, a Victorian commuter train from the 1890s, and Pickett, from the 1940s. Dudley the Diesel engine lets children climb all over him. There's a small shop, refreshments are provided and, during the school holidays, Wednesday afternoon art and crafts sessions keep small people amused.

Lee Valley Park

Covering a vast area on either side of the River Lee between Waltham Abbey (Essex) and Broxbourne River Lee Country Park (which starts in Hackney and goes all the way into Hertfordshire), this network of lakes, waterways, parks and countryside areas makes a fantastic getaway from east London's concrete acres. There's plenty to do, though a gentle guided walk (call the Lee Valley Park Information Centre for walk information and leaflets) is a good way to set about it. Some walks can easily be tackled with pushchairs.

Lee Valley Park is great for birdwatchers – more than 200 species have been seen here, despite its proximity to London. Of the birds that fly here from thousands of miles away, some come to breed, others to rest and feed, while many stay through the winter, retreating from much harsher weather.

The **Middlesex Filter Beds** on the Hackney side of Lee Valley, not too far from the Lee Valley Ice Centre, are now a nature reserve with great birdwatching potential. The beds, once part of a sewage plant, now have the more savoury purpose of creating valuable marshland for flora and fauna.

Lee Valley Riding Centre (8556 2629), just off Lea Bridge Road, welcomes all ages and abilities and has a floodlit manège for after-work winter riding, as well as an indoor school and a cross-country course (see also p261).

Lee Valley Cycle Circuit (Temple Mill Lane, E15, 8534 6085) is now next to the M11 extension and offers mountain bike, BMX and cyclo-cross courses. The noisiest entertainment comes in the form of the **Lee Valley Ice Centre** (Lea Bridge Road, E10, 8533 3155), which has a frenetic disco soundtrack, a shop and a fast-food café. Children love it, and it's a real boon in wet weather. It also hosts ice ballet shows and competitions throughout the year (see also p258).

Lee Valley Park Farms

Stubbins Hall Lane, Crooked Mile, Waltham Abbey, Essex (01992 892781). Broxbourne or Waltham Cross rail.
Open 10am-4.30pm Mon-Fri; 10am-6pm or dusk if earlier Sat, Sun. **Admission** £3.10; £2.05 concessions, 3-16s; free under-3s. **Credit** MC, V.
Hayes Hill Farm is a rare breeds centre, with a Tudor barn, a restored gypsy caravan and plenty of space in which to play. Nearby **Holyfield Hall** is a commercial farm where visitors can watch the milking of cows (2.45-4pm daily). There are guided tours for school parties, when city children can learn all about agricultural ways.
Buggy access. Café. Nappy-changing facilities. Shop.

Lee Valley Park Information Centre

Abbey Gardens, Waltham Abbey, Essex (01992 702200/ www.leevalleypark.org.uk). Waltham Cross rail. **Open** Nov-Mar 10am-4pm Tue-Sun. Apr-Oct 9.30am-5pm daily. **Admission** free.
This centre has racks of literature about the various activities available to visitors to the park, including messing about on the reservoirs in passenger boats, cruise boats and canoes. Fishing permits can be obtained here, and there are maps for cycle routes and information about scenic riverside pubs.

The old abbey church, parts of which date back to the 14th century, is the centrepiece of Waltham Abbey town. The Augustinian abbey was once one of the largest in the country, with its own farm, fishponds and brewery. Its remains (the gateway, a few walls and a stone bridge) and surrounding parks are now managed by English Heritage and are famous as the reputed burial site of King Harold, who died in 1066. You can still visit the church and the accompanying gardens. The gardens contain a variety of public artworks and there's a 'Sensory trail' (available from the centre) highlighting the natural history of the area. A

short walk away are the Royal Gunpowder Mills, a much-acclaimed attraction that opened to the public in 2001 after years of neglect (see p124).
Buggy access. Nappy-changing facilities. Nearest picnic place: information centre gardens. Shop.

Epping Forest

At 12 miles in length and 22 miles in width, Epping Forest is the biggest public space in London. In 1878 an act was passed giving ownership to the Corporation of London in order to stop development. Today, the forest contains two listed buildings – the restored **Queen Elizabeth's Hunting Lodge** in Chingford (Rangers Road, E4, 8529 6681; under-16s must be accompanied by adults) and the Temple in Wanstead Park (see p118), as well as the remains of two large Iron Age earthworks.

Riders have a huge amount of trekking space, and there are several riding schools in the vicinity (contact the Epping Forest Information Centre to find one to suit your needs). Those who prefer wheels to hooves can hire bikes (it's best to pre-book) at **Top Banana** cycle shop in Woodford Green (7B Johnston Road, 8559 0170) or **Heales Cycles** in Highams Park (477 Hale End Road, E4, 8527 1592). Golfers may fancy a swing at the pitch & putt course at **High Beech** (8508 7323) towards the centre of the forest.

Also at High Beech is a tea hut, which is good for snacks and drinks. For cooked meals there's the **King's Oak** pub, which has children's play areas.

An important wildlife and conservation centre, the forest is home to woodpeckers, nightingales, treecreepers and nuthatches, plus unusual waterfowl such as great crested grebes, goosanders and wigeons. There are also 650 species of flowers and more than 1,000 types of fungi. For a real back-to-nature feeling, there's a campsite at **Debden House** (Debden Green, Loughton, Essex, 8508 3008).

If you're coming to the forest by public transport, Chingford railway station gives access to Queen Elizabeth's Hunting Lodge and some lovely strolls. Loughton and Theydon Bois (Central Line) are the nearest tube stops, though it's an uphill walk from both – which will be a bit of a struggle if you've got small children in tow or buggies to push. Visitors are advised to obtain a map and plan their route around the forest in advance. The *Official Guide to Epping Forest* (£1.50) is available from the Guildhall Library Bookshop (7332 1858).

Epping Forest Information Centre

High Beech, Loughton, Essex (8508 0028/ www.eppingforest.co.uk). Loughton or Theydon Bois tube then 2-mile walk or 5min taxi ride/Chingford rail. **Open** Apr-Oct 10am-5pm Mon-Sat; 11am-5pm Sun. Nov-Mar 11am-3pm Mon-Fri; 10am-4pm Sat; 11am-4pm Sun.
Buggy access. Shop.

South-east London

Millennium money may have helped reinvent Greenwich and Southwark, but regeneration is the watchword further south-east too.

Rotherhithe

Rotherhithe, or Redriff as it used to be called, is where the river loses its attractiveness to tourists and loops up slightly before flowing down to Greenwich Reach and the 'real' visitor attractions. Redriff was a marshy place, inhabited by salty sea dogs, such as shipbuilders and sailors. Its former wharves and warehouses are now desirable riverside flats, but some of the area's ancient streets still maintain an air of mystery.

One of the oldest and most atmospheric pubs in London, the Mayflower, draws the crowds to Rotherhithe. Just across the cobbled street in this Dickensian village, the **Brunel Engine House & Tunnel Exhibition** is a good source of information about the area. A little further west is St Marychurch Street and **St Mary's Rotherhithe**, one of London's most cherished churches. It was built in 1715 by local sailors and watermen. Unwanted attention from vandals over the years has meant that the interior glass doors of the church have to be

locked when not in use, and the inside can only be viewed through glass, under the watchful eye of a video camera. The Lady Chapel contains a communion table and two bishop's chairs made from wood salvaged from the *Fighting Temeraire*, a ship famously painted by Turner. You can see his finished work in the National Gallery (*see p86*). Nearby, housed in a former mortuary, is the excellent **Time & Talents Association** (7231 7845), a community programme set up in 1887 by a group of local women who were appalled by the living conditions of families in the docks area of south London. They were determined to use their time and talents to help the poor (hence the name). Today, the organisation runs a programme of arts and social projects to meet the needs of the whole community. Its drama courses and other activities are outlined on p229.

Inland, the area's green heart reveals itself at sites given over to urban ecology: there's **Lavender Pond Nature Park** (Rotherhithe Street, SE16, 7237 9165), created from an old dock inlet in 1982 and now supporting newts, frogs and dragonflies and

Thames traffic viewed from the peninsula.

attracting herons and tufted ducks to its shores; the
merging greenery of Russia Dock Woodland and
Stave Hill Ecological Park, accessed via Watermans
Walk off Redriff Road, both provide a quiet spot to
walk and contemplate country London.

These wildlife spaces, valued as they are by
the local community, are showing signs of neglect
and are proving to be a headache for Southwark
council's park rangers, whose mobile team are
obliged to tour the woodlands once a day, but
whose work cannot stem the rising tide of vandalism
blighting **Russia Dock Woodland** in particular.
Nonetheless, the willows, birches and ash trees set
around a stream and a series of ponds still provide
homes for fish, eels and various waterbirds (as well
as bricks and supermarket trolleys). **Stave Hill
Ecological Park** is a meadow bordered by wildlife-
rich scrub and trees, providing a haven for birds,
insects and butterflies and a welcome breath of
fresh air for human visitors.

The largest green space in the area is **Southwark
Park**, which was set up 130 years ago and is the
city's oldest municipal park. Having undergone
extensive regeneration in 2001, the park is once
again a valuable local asset and is having a grand
opening to celebrate the fact during the
Rotherhithe Festival (*see also p31*).

Crossing Lower Road from the park brings you
to Canada Water, a watery expanse around which
Surrey Quays is arranged. For trainer-addicts, the
French sports store **Decathlon** (Canada Water
Retail Park, Surrey Quays Road, SE16, 7394 2000),
the biggest shop of its kind in Northern Europe, has
pride of place. Parking is free too.

Hollywood Bowl (Redriff Road, SE16, 7237 3773),
complete with a Burger King next door, is heaven on
earth for many kids. The **Discovery Planet** indoor
adventure playground in the Surrey Quays Shopping
Centre (Redriff Road, SE16, 7237 2388) appeals to a
younger age group. Local parents swear by the
stress-free party service offered here, including a
party room for refreshments and a coach to see fair
play. A toddler group is run here every weekday
morning and there's a four o'clock club for after-
school purposes. The **Surrey Docks Watersports
Centre** (Rope Street, SE16, 7237 5555; *see also p268*)
runs sailing and canoeing courses for children aged
from 8 in school holidays and half-terms.

On the other side of the Rotherhithe peninsula,
looking out across the river at the Isle of Dogs, lies
Surrey Docks Farm, a constant hive of activity
during school holidays.

Brunel Engine House & Tunnel Exhibition

*Brunel Engine House, Railway Avenue, SE16 (7231
3840/www.brunelenginehouse.org.uk). Rotherhithe tube.*
Open *Apr-Oct* 1-5pm Sat, Sun. *Nov-Mar* 1-5pm Sun.

Tours 1st Sun of mth. **Admission** £2; £1 concessions; £5
family (2+2); free under 5s. *Tours* £2 donation requested.
No credit cards.
This exhibition, contained in a Grade-II listed engine house
built in 1852 to house pumping machinery, commemorates
the construction of the Thames Tunnel, the first major underwater thoroughfare in the world, which was conceived by
Marc Isambard Brunel, father of the more famous Kingdom.
Brunel patented a design for a tunnelling shield to protect 36
miners, and his ideas formed the basis of today's tunnelling
methods. The tunnel took from 1825 to 1843 to complete, and
its story, one of ambition, tenacity, tragedy, disease, disaster
and triumph, is all carefully told here. When it was finished
as a foot tunnel (funds having run out before spiral descents
for wheeled vehicles could be built), it was the toast of the
nation, and for years a fair and other festivities took place here.
Over the next decade, however, the tunnel fell out of favour
and turned into a disreputable dosshouse. It is now owned by
London Underground and is used for the east London lines.

Visitors to the building, which was saved from demolition
by local historians who created the museum, admire a J&G
Rennie steam engine, around which the exhibition is arranged.
Children are given quiz sheets and activities based on Brunel's
'Great Bore' (a term coined by *The Times* for the tunnel), so
that they don't find it all too much of a bore. The small souvenir shop is a valuable source of information about this
enchanting part of London.
Shop.

Cutty Sark. *See p130.*

Southwark Park

Gomm Road, SE16 (park rangers 7232 2091/art gallery 7237 1230). Canada Water tube. **Open** *Park* 8am-1hr before dusk daily. *Gallery* (during exhibitions) summer 11am-5pm Wed-Sun; winter 11am-4pm Wed-Sun; phone first to check. **Admission** free.

A £2.75-million lottery grant paid for this historic park's makeover, and now it looks as splendid as it did in its Victorian heyday. The boating lake has been rebuilt and relandscaped and is fully functional throughout the summer. There is a new, attractively rustic-looking children's play area (long overdue), a smart bandstand for summer concerts, a cricket oval and a wildlife garden. The sports stadium, which is not officially part of the park but still an important resource for Southwark's fitness fanatics, is as popular as ever.

Just inside the entrance if you come in from Gomm Road is the gallery, or, to give it its rather windy full name, the Café Gallery Project at the Gallery. Confusingly, there's no café here, although coffee is sometimes offered at quiet times. Instead, this is an important artistic resource for young artists and art lovers who may feel intimidated by big public galleries – access to art for all is the main drive of the project. There has been a gallery here since the 1960s, but it has recently been rebuilt to provide full disabled access and other crowd-pullers, such as nappy-changing facilities.

Upcoming exhibitions during 2002 include a major new photography installation (17 July-4 August), part of a collaboration with local people, and various exhibitions coming out of the gallery's relationship with INOVA (Institute of Visual Art), such as Shona Illingworth's video installation, Drill, based on soldiers on parade (4-29 September) and Andrew Kotting and Mark Lythgoe's video installation about a disabled child (9 October-3 November). The annual open exhibition, from 30 November to 15 December, includes plenty of children's work.

Buggy access.

Surrey Docks Farm

Rotherhithe Street, SE16 (7231 1010). Canada Water or Surrey Quays tube. **Open** 10am-1pm, 2-5pm Tue-Thur, Sat, Sun. **Admission** free (except school parties and play-schemes; phone for details); donations appreciated.

This thriving organic farm has been part of the local community for more than 25 years. It is home to a herd of milking goats, sheep, cows, pigs, poultry, donkeys and bees, and there are also herb, vegetable and willow gardens and an orchard on the site. Holiday playschemes and workshops are very popular with local kids, so book ahead. The splendid riverside location makes the farm a good starting point for a walk along the Thames, and children love playing on the sculptures of farm animals just outside its river exit (see if you can spot the mouse that the cat is chasing).

Where to eat

The riverside walk beside Rotherhithe Street has benches at intervals for walkers to rest and admire the river views. Hope Sufference Wharf and the area near Brandram's Wharf, just along from the Brunel Engine House & Tunnel Exhibition, have little gardens overlooking the water, so on a fine day picnicking around here is a pleasure. Further along Rotherhithe Street, **Spice Island** (163 Rotherhithe Street, SE16, 7394 7108), located in a former spice warehouse, welcomes kids until 8pm, providing high chairs for tots and a chippy, nuggety sort of

children's menu. **Arbuckles** (Mast Leisure Park, Surrey Quays Road, SE16, 7232 1901), which dishes up burgers, fries, pasta and pizza, appeals to those on a budget (the children's menu, £2.95, includes a drink). Much more congenial, if you can fight your way through the American tourists on the heritage trail, is the **Mayflower** (117 Rotherhithe Street, SE16, 7237 4088), with its creaky woodwork, pokey bar area and delightful jetty. This ancient watering hole is where the Pilgrim Fathers' ship was moored before it set off on its fateful journey. Pub grub is served in the restaurant (the only bit that children are allowed in), and although there are no special menus or concessions for children, the chef will provide small portions.

Greenwich

Henry VIII loved Greenwich – his daughters Elizabeth and Mary were born in the palace here, and his hunting ground was **Greenwich Park**. Daniel Defoe described Greenwich as 'the most delightful spot of ground in Great Britain'. You only have to climb one of the hills in Greenwich Park to see what is so special about this place, even in the 21st century, with all the traffic and tourist congestion. The view is stunning. Stretching out before you is the magnificent baroque **Old Royal Naval College**, the palatial **Queen's House**, the **National Maritime Museum**, the masts of the **Cutty Sark**, and the Thames, winding its way through the cityscape.

Maritime Greenwich was designated a UNESCO World Heritage Site in 1997, and since then its various sights and landmarks have been packaged for the tourist trade in a rather more coherent fashion than before. The **Tourist Information Centre** (*see p299*) makes it easier to plan your day out, so you'd be well advised to kick off proceedings there with an armful of free leaflets and maps of the area. The TIC also organises guided walks of Greenwich (phone for details).

The quickest way to reach Greenwich is by train from Charing Cross or via the DLR link through Docklands, but it's relaxing to appreciate Wren's architecture by boat – try **Catamaran Cruises** (7987 1185) or **City Cruises** (7930 9033). For more riverboat companies, *see p299*. It's perfectly pleasant to walk between the various sights at Greenwich, but there is a shuttle bus, useful for little legs that can't make the climb up the hill. The bus runs from Greenwich Pier to the National Maritime Museum and up to the Royal Observatory every 15 minutes or so. Tickets (which last all day) cost £1.50 for adults and 50p for children. The DLR's **Rail & River Rover** (*see p112*) family day pass also takes in the Greenwich river stretch.

The **Royal Observatory**. *See p131.*

Cutty Sark

King William Walk, SE10 (8858 3445/www.cuttysark. org.uk). Cutty Sark DLR/Greenwich DLR/rail. **Open** 10am-5pm (last entry 4.30pm) daily. Closed 24-26 Dec. *Tours* Mon-Fri; depending on availability. **Admission** (LP) £3.90; £2.90 concessions; £9.70 family (2+3); free under-5s. *Tours* free. **Credit** MC, V.

The last surviving tea clipper and the fastest sailing ship of her day, the handsome *Cutty Sark* was first launched in 1869 at Dumbarton on the Clyde. Her cargo changed from China tea to Australian wool before she was decommissioned and set up here in Greenwich, and all her fixtures and fittings restored to their 19th-century perfection, as a museum to the seafaring life. Inside are displays of prints and naval relics, plus the world's largest collection of carved and painted figureheads. Children are intrigued by the hands-on exhibits and the cabins now populated by dummies. On summer weekends there are shanty singers and popular costumed storytelling sessions; school groups can also join in on Sailor for a Day gigs that are part of *Cutty Sark*'s burgeoning education programme. Ring for details of forthcoming events. *Nearest picnic place: Cutty Sark Gardens. Shop.*

Fan Museum

12 Crooms Hill, SE10 (8305 1441/www.fan-museum. org). *Cutty Sark DLR/Greenwich DLR/rail.* **Open** 11am-5pm Tue-Sat; noon-5pm Sun. Closed 25 Dec, Easter, 1 Jan. **Admission** £3.50; £2.50 concessions; free under-7s. Free OAPs, disabled 2-5pm Tue. **Credit** MC, V.

A study in elegance from the days when accessories could make or break a lady, this unique museum is the only one of two dedicated to fans in the entire world (the other one, the Musée de l'Évantail, is in Paris). Needless to say, it is a feminine place, and at the risk of sounding politically incorrect, probably more of a girl thing as far as children are concerned. Students of fashion and the arts love it, too, and young people of either sex intent on a career in fashion and textiles would do well to visit. Only part of the 3,000-strong collection, which dates from the 11th century, is on view at any one time: the fans' elasticity means that they need periodic rest. The fans are displayed by theme, such as design, provenance or social history, and exhibitions change regularly (call for details). There are occasional talks and classes for art students, while the over-12s may be interested in the fan-making workshops on the first Saturday of every month.

The Royal Fans exhibition, in honour of the Queen's Jubilee, runs until 7 July 2002. From 9 July to 11 August 2002 a collection of fan leaves designed by local children who entered a competition to create a fan fit for a queen will be on display. From August until the end of 2002 a lace exhibition will run to other fashionable items of dress as well as fans. *Lift. Shop.*

Greenwich Park

Blackheath Gate, Charlton Way, SE10 (visitors' centre 8293 0703/www.royalparks.co.uk). *Cutty Sark DLR/ Greenwich DLR/rail/Maze Hill rail/1, 53, 177, 180, 188, 286 bus/riverboat to Greenwich Pier.* **Open** 6am-dusk daily.

Recent developments in this, the hilliest and the oldest enclosed royal parkland in London, include the excavations of the site of Queen Caroline Brunswick's bath, which once had its home in the long-gone Montague House. Queen Caroline was a Greenwich Park Ranger, which does not mean she wore a Greenwich council T-shirt and swept the leaves, but rather that she gave her royal connection to the park, and in return lived in a fabulous house and threw lots of parties. The site is now furnished with interpretive panels to give you an idea of what you're looking at. Other refurbishments include the restoration of a 17th-century memorial garden in the south-western corner. Spectacular views across the city from the Wolfe Monument at the top are snapped

Prime Meridian Line.

enthusiastically by tourists, though many prefer to capture their friends and relatives straddling the Prime Meridian Line. Small children like the lower reaches of the park, where the playground and boating lake attract crowds in good weather. Free puppet and theatre shows for children (call the Royal Parks Agency on 8858 2608 for details) take place in the summer holidays.

Now that you have to pay for the parking, the park's hilltop areas aren't as overrun by cars as they used to be, but it's still annoyingly crowded on sunny afternoons. Make sure your walk around this splendid expanse takes in the quieter shrubbery areas and deer enclosure.
Buggy access. Café. Nappy-changing facilities.

Old Royal Naval College
King William Walk, SE10 (8269 4747/www.greenwich foundation.org.uk). Cutty Sark DLR/Greenwich DLR/rail. **Open** 10am-5pm Mon-Sat; 12.30-5pm Sun. Last entry 4.15pm. Closed 25, 26 Dec. **Admission** £3; £2 concessions; free accompanied under-16s. Free for all from 3.30pm daily; free for all Sun. *Tours* £5; £4 concessions; subject to staff availability. **Credit** MC, V.
These spectacular riverside buildings, split in two to give an unimpeded view of Queen's House from the river and vice versa, were designed by Sir Christopher Wren. The site comprises the Chapel of St Peter and St Paul, the Painted Hall and the Greenwich Gateway Visitors Centre, which houses the shops and café. At 11am every Sunday there is a service in the chapel, to which all are welcome.

The Painted Hall was decorated by James Thornhill in 1708-27; this is where the body of Nelson lay in state in 1805. Intended as a palace, then turned into a grand almshouse for former Royal Navy seamen, it was adapted for use as a naval college in 1873. After 125 years in residence, the Navy vacated the buildings in 1998 and the University of Greenwich moved in. Free (or very cheap) events for children take place

at the weekend during the school holidays. Past events include a knot-tying workshop, tours and trips and stories with a teller in costume. For further information on future happenings check the website or ring for details.
Café. Nappy-changing facilities. Nearest picnic place: Naval College grounds. Shops.

Queen's House
Romney Road, SE10 (8312 6565/www.nmm.ac.uk). Cutty Sark DLR/Greenwich DLR/rail. **Open** 10am-5pm daily. Closed 24-26 Dec. **Admission** free; occasional charge for temporary exhibitions. **Credit** *Shop* AmEx, DC, MC, V.
One of the first truly classical buildings in Britain, Queen's House was designed by Inigo Jones in 1616 for James I's wife, Anne of Denmark. Anne died before it was finished and it was completed at the order of Queen Henrietta Maria in 1629. The permanent exhibition about the house, the area and the personalities connected with it is entitled Historical Greenwich. A Sea of Faces, a semi-permanent exhibition (running at least until March 2003), includes 130 portraits of sea captains and shipwrights from the 17th century to the present day, among them works by Reynolds and Hogarth. A summertime contemporary art initiative, entitled New Visions of the Sea, runs from 9 May to 3 October 2002, and includes the briny-themed work of Beth Derbyshire and Tim Brennan, the first specialising in video installation, the second a photographer. Educational hands-on sessions and workshops take place frequently; ring the booking line to find out when you can join in. Face to Face, linked up with the Sea of Faces, is a laugh-a-minute photo session, during which children can learn about portraiture, then dress up for a digital mugshot to take home with them.
Buggy access. Nappy-changing facilities. Nearest picnic place: Greenwich Park.

Ranger's House
Chesterfield Walk, SE10 (8853 0035/www.english-heritage.org.uk). Blackheath rail or Greenwich DLR/rail/53 bus. **Open** *Apr-Sept* 10am-6pm Wed-Sun. *Oct* 10am-5pm Wed-Sun. *Nov-late Dec, Mar* 10am-4pm Wed-Sun. **Admission** (EH) £4.50; £3.40 concessions; £2.30 5-16s; free under-5s. **Credit** AmEx, MC, V.
The Greenwich Park Ranger traditionally lived in this handsome 18th-century red-brick villa. It reopens on 19 June 2002, after a year-long redevelopment programme. On display will be the Wernher Collection of paintings, sculpture, jewellery, furniture and crafts dating from 3 BC to the 19th century. A gate from the side garden takes you out to the park for a range about. English Heritage, the building's keeper, is hoping to launch a programme of family events later in the summer.
Buggy access (garden only). Nearest picnic place: side garden. Shop.

Royal Observatory
Greenwich Park, SE10 (8312 6565/www.rog.nmm.ac.uk). Cutty Sark DLR/Greenwich DLR/rail. **Open** 10am-5pm daily. Closed 24-26 Dec. *Tours* phone for details. **Admission** free.
This observatory was founded when Charles II appointed the first astronomer royal, John Flamsteed, to find out 'the so much desired longitude of places for the perfecting of the art of navigation'. Several of the museum's galleries tell of the search for a means of determining longitude at sea. The rest of the museum includes exhibits on the development of ever-more-accurate timepieces and an extensive history of the buildings as a working observatory, including the Octagon Room, a faithful restoration of Sir Christopher Wren's original interior.

Children enjoy being up inside the dome, which houses the biggest refracting telescope in the world. They also rate the Camera Obscura pretty highly: this is a dark room where an image of London is printed on to a viewing table. There's also the astro web: a website that kids can explore for news and information from the world of astronomy. The planetarium show (£2 adults, £1.50 children), for everyone aged from 4, runs frequently during school holidays and weekends. The school holiday programme of events includes role-playing opportunities, talks, stories and workshops. Ring for details. *Buggy access (not in dome). Nappy-changing facilities. Nearest picnic place: Greenwich Park. Shop.*

Where to eat

With its daily influx of visitors, Greenwich has its fair share of burger, pizza, noodle and fry-up refuelling stations. Salubrious places include **Time** (7A College Approach, SE10, 8305 9767), overlooking the market, which has a friendly attitude to children at weekend lunchtimes. A little further out of the centre, **Inside** (19 Greenwich South Street, SE10, 8265 5060) is a small but popular local restaurant with an excellent brunch

In & around: the National Maritime Museum

The biggest of its kind in the world and refurbished courtesy of the National Lottery, the **National Maritime Museum**, which is set on three floors of an elegant mansion at the foot of rolling Greenwich Park, covers the long history of seafaring.

The museum's most popular areas, for children at least, are the interactive sections on the top floors called **All Hands** and the **Bridge**, where youngsters seem delighted to get to grips with a seaman's chores. They can row in a mock-up of a Viking longboat, practise cannon sharpshooting or hoist flags to send messages. They can also load sacks with a mini crane, try on a deep-sea diver's gloves or even take charge of the ship's wheel and try not to crash the thing.

The rest of the museum provides a more sedate tour of maritime history. Children may enjoy small doses of it, though any visitor would be hard pressed to see it all in one day. In the section

called **Passengers** the feeling of being aboard an ocean liner is well created, while **Rank & Style** is also fun – each door, when opened, reveals a different uniform from the naval hierarchy. Space has been made in the refurbishment to include a number of larger items: a speedboat, a modern submarine and a wonderful gilded royal barge.

The museum has a café with play area, regular weekend and school holiday activities for children, and is currently updating itself to become more ecological in its drift. As part of its Planet Ocean initiative, a permanent interactive exhibit including a wave tank called **Making Waves** explores the power of the ocean and links three main Greenwich attractions – this museum, the **Royal Observatory** and **Queen's House** – through the themes of ships, time and the stars. The huge transparent tank in the museum's central courtyard provides a model of an ocean

menu on Saturdays and Sundays (10am-3pm). **Chibchas** (170 Trafalgar Road, SE9, 8293 0626) has a pan-American menu of tapas and nibbles and a friendly, relaxed atmosphere; it's open for dinner daily from 6pm.

Many local pubs, including the **Trafalgar Tavern** on the river (Park Row, SE10, 8858 2437), have children's menus. The **North Pole** (131 Greenwich High Road, SE10, 8853 3020) is a trendy, clubby place during the week but on

at work, and lets visitors see exactly how a wave develops using a mechanical flume, which they can control.

Running until 30 September 2002 is Skin Deep, an exhibition about the history of tattooing. It traces the beginnings of skin decoration and its use among seamen in the 19th and 20th centuries, from the Pacific tattoo traditions that first fascinated Captain Cook in Tahiti.

But it's probably best not to linger too long on salty sea-dog relics, when after a short walk riverwards, past the splendid **Old Royal Naval College**, the kids can experience the real thing by clambering about on the **Cutty Sark**, the 19th-century tea clipper parked by Greenwich Pier. Kids (and adults) love the planking under their feet and peering into cabins and bunks, some of them populated – by dummies, that is.

An alternative curiosity is provided by a strange brick dome only yards from the *Cutty Sark*. This is the entrance to **Greenwich foot tunnel**. A lift or stairs takes you down to where you can begin (or merely contemplate) a short walk under the river, which is a source of fascination for children.

Greenwich's centre nearby is worth exploring for its covered weekend market, pubs and shops. But even better is **Greenwich Park**, on the other side of the museum. At the top by the observatory you can admire (aided by telescope) one of the best views in London, from the Dome via looming Canary Wharf all the way to St Paul's. This area is probably the best place to begin and end the outing if you're coming by car; there is a pleasant café nearby and ample pay and display parking by the Blackheath Gate, which enables you to avoid the nightmarish traffic of downtown Greenwich, especially at weekends.

National Maritime Museum

Romney Road, SE10 (8858 4422/8312 6565/ tours 8312 6608/www.nmm.ac.uk). Cutty Sark DLR/Greenwich DLR/rail. **Open** *10am-5pm daily. Closed 24-26 Dec. Tours phone for details.* **Admission** *free.* **Credit** *Shop AmEx, MC, V. Buggy access. Café. Nappy-changing facilities. Nearest picnic place: Greenwich Park. Restaurant. Shop.*

Sundays goes mellow, dishing up a family lunch menu encompassing roasts and vegetarian options in the restaurant upstairs (noon-4pm).

Blackheath & Lewisham

Windswept Blackheath, which got its name from the darkness of its soil rather than anything more sinister (no plague victims were buried here, contrary to popular myth), is up Maze Hill from Greenwich Park. Though criss-crossed with often-busy roads, it's a fabulous open space where weekend footballers, kite-fliers and strollers converge (though you should avoid the weekend of the London Marathon, when the area is solid with runners and their families; *see also p27*). Blackheath also plays host to regular kite festivals, bank holiday funfairs and the annual Blackheath Village Fair. After a bit of exercise, 'the Village', as locals quaintly call it, is a good place for a meal or a snack and a nose round the shops.

The **Age Exchange Reminiscence Centre** (11 Blackheath Village, SE3, 8318 9105) is a lovely place to visit. It's a shop and museum with an olde-worlde feel; the shop displays gorgeous old-fashioned sweets and smart wooden toys. The museum hosts about four exhibitions a year: Blackheath Village Remembers is planned for August 2002 onwards, based on stories and recollections of local people about Blackheath. Just through the village past the station, **Blackheath Halls** (23 Lee Road, SE9, 8318 9758) includes Saturday afternoon children's shows in its programming; booking is advisable.

On Sundays Blackheath station car park is home to a farmers' market, where you can usually sample all kinds of cakes and breads before you buy.

Just south-west of the heath and village and now rejoicing in an excellent DLR link to the city, **Lewisham** town centre brings you back to sarf London reality with a bump. Rougher than its neighbour it may be, but the indoor shopping centre yields all the favourites of the high street, including an Early Learning Centre. Even more welcome to buggy-burdened parents is the indoor playground, where little ones can be unstrapped to let off steam while their parents try to tempt them with Marks & Sparks' sandwiches. Lewisham's excellent street market (fruit and veg, fish, clothes, toys, decent, cheap household linen; open Monday-Saturday) is often enlivened by mini roundabouts for the toddler brigade.

The borough of Lewisham has been ticked off about the state of its parks in the past, but one we recommend is **Manor House Gardens**, just off Lee High Road. The manor in question is a lofty-looking place that now houses a library. Its gardens, now the park, form the hub of the local community.

Around Town

Manor House Gardens

Brightfield Road, SE12 (8318 1358). Hither Green rail.
Open *Café & park* 9.30am-dusk daily. **Admission** free.
This delightful, tot-friendly park was once the manor's gardens, and you can walk right up to the back door of the manor. The house, built in 1780 before the invention of fridges, had an egg-shaped ice house on the grounds for keeping game and perishables. The ice was taken from the pond in the gardens and covered with straw to keep it cold. Visitors can enter the ice house down some steps and read up about its history. The manor now houses the library (closed on Wednesdays).

Separate dog-walking areas and a wooden decking overlooking the big pond for duck-feeding purposes make this an extremely popular local park. The park café is a cut above the average; as well as jacket potatoes and sandwiches, the blackboard menu lists pretty exotic daily specials for those after a hot lunch, as well as cakes and hot drinks. On Tuesday morning the café hosts a parent and toddler session, and during fine weather a one o'clock club operates in the playground.

Where to eat

You're spoilt for choice when it comes to eating in Blackheath; there are brasseries and café/bars all over the place. For a special family meal, try **Chapter Two** (43-5 Montpelier Vale, SE3, 8333 2666), with views over the heath, colourful Modern European food and cheery service. Half portions can be arranged for small appetites. There's a local branch of **fish!** (1 Lawn Terrace, SE3, 7234 3333; *see also p171*); its £6.95 children's menu, colouring books and toys keep toddlers fed and entertained.

Lewisham is hardly a culinary hotspot, but the café in Manor House Gardens is a pleasant place to lunch with children. **Green Cabin** (244 Lewisham High Street, SE13, 8852 6666) is a Sri Lankan restaurant with fiery flavours and a reputation for good, authentic curries and snacks. Less exotic, but a local favourite for fish and chips, is **Something Fishy** (117-9 Lewisham High Street, SE13, 8852 7075).

Woolwich

An intriguing riverside settlement whose naval and military associations go back to Tudor times, when Henry VIII established his Royal Dockyard here, Woolwich tends to be overlooked as a visitor attraction. However, the opening of a major new museum here in 2001 has gone some way to bringing the area to the attention of Londoners at large.

During World War I, 72,000 people worked in a weapons-development complex that stretched for three miles down the river. Nowadays the area looks neglected and forlorn. However, plans to regenerate the whole of the former MOD site are evidently going ahead: with swish flats and offices, a multiplex cinema, restaurants and other family facilities, funny old Woolwich won't know itself.

The regeneration will take time, but Woolwich is still a great place to visit. Those into guns and

Ferry good

East of Tower Bridge, there are no bridges spanning the Thames. So if you want to cross to the north bank of the river here, the only way to do so is via tunnels, or the ferry at Woolwich. The free service, which runs about every quarter of an hour throughout the day, takes about four minutes to cross to North Woolwich. Vehicles go on the decks, pedestrians sit below.

If you've never used it before, the ferry is a new and interesting way to make the river's acquaintance, and children think it's great fun. The short journey affords sensational views to the west: the **Thames Barrier**, **Canary Wharf** and the **Dome**. To the east there's the less edifying sight of yet more desirable riverside apartments going up on the north bank, and the vast estates of Lego-like houses filling up the less desirable wasteland of the south. Once you've reached dry land, there are the (free) delights of the **North Woolwich Old Station Museum** (*see p125*) and the rather lovely **Royal Victoria Gardens**, which are excellent for picnics and play. It all adds up to an unusual, and free, day out in London's forgotten backwaters.

interactives based on them love **Firepower**. Riverside walks and ferry rides are free. Woolwich's high street is better than most in the area – highlights include the UK's first ever McDonald's (opened in 1974 and festooned with fascinating Macdo facts) and a bustling market just across the main road from Firepower. The amazing **Woolwich Garrison**, best viewed from the common and Grand Depot Road, has the longest Georgian façade in the country. All around, grand, handsome buildings and decorative cannons are testament to Woolwich's glorious past. Children are far more interested in the hectic **Waterfront Leisure Centre** (Woolwich High Street, SE18, 8317 5000; *see also p266*), of course. With its flume-filled pools and indoor adventure playground, who can blame them?

Downriver, the huge silvery hoods of the **Thames Barrier** glint reassuringly across the water and the views take in industrial units, the Dome and Canary Wharf. The free **Woolwich Ferry**, in operation since the 14th century (when it was a paddle steamer) offers another fascinating view of the river.

Firepower

Royal Arsenal, SE18 (8855 7755/www.firepower.org.uk). Woolwich Arsenal rail. **Open** 10am-5pm (last entry 4pm) daily. Closed 25 Dec. **Admission** (LP) £6.50; £5.50 concessions; £4.50 5-16s; £18 family (2+2 or 1+3); free under-5s. **Credit** MC, V.
The Royal Artillery Experience – aka Firepower – is a noisy one. It's a moving one, too, and that's not just when the floor shakes in time to the sound of gunfire. Charting

the history of the Regiment of Royal Artillery, or the Gunners, this dramatic, interactive and somewhat explosive two-year-old museum has replaced the staid (but free) old Museum of Artillery.

The museum's centrepiece, Field of Fire, shows an introductory film about the Gunners, before herding visitors into the action area, where four screens depict the action seen by the Royal Artillery since World War I. Models of gunners at work, around jeeps, lorries and military equipment, are lit up and obscured by dry ice as the sound effects rain down on bemused spectators and the floor vibrates. Under-5s be warned: it's loud and quite scary. The Real Weapon Gallery lets your trigger finger loose on very small cannons that fire ping-pong balls at targets, and water cannons that do the same, and there are shells you can try to lift. Children are fascinated by the 'do it yourself' indirect firing exhibit, which has one person plotting the target by computer on a huge screen, and a friend lining up a large field gun to blast it. The Gunnery Hall has two floors of weaponry through the ages, from medieval pot cannons to more sophisticated Howitzers and suchlike. There's also a softly lit medals hall and old footage of the Gunners' work at war. Firepower's Monster exhibits – an exhibition of large tanks and artillery vehicles – opened in April 2002.

Half-terms and holidays see the museum staff busy arranging fun events for their young visitors, with activities such as paintballing. The gift shop has all the usual stationery and souvenir stock, with the kind of T-shirts, soldier dog tags, helmets, bullets and water bottles that kids love to spend their pocket money on.
Buggy access. Café. Lift. Nappy-changing facilities. Nearest picnic place: riverside. Shop.

Thames Barrier Information & Learning Centre

1 Unity Way, SE18 (8305 4188/www.environment-agency.gov.uk). North Greenwich tube/Charlton rail/riverboats to & from Greenwich Pier (8305 0300) & Westminster Pier (7930 3373)/177, 180 bus. **Open** *Apr-late Sept* 10.30am-4.30pm daily. *End Sept-Mar* 11am-3.30pm daily. Closed 24 Dec-2 Jan. **Admission** *Exhibition* £1; 75p concessions; 50p 5-16s; free under-5s. **Credit** MC, V.

Precisely how the Thames Barrier protects the capital from flooding is explained by models and videos at this centre. It caters mostly for school parties, though members of the public are also welcome. One of the most popular times to visit is when they set the structure in motion to test it (once a month, usually on a weekday; call for dates and times). The best way to appreciate the barrier, however, is from the water – Campion Cruises (8305 0300) runs trips from Greenwich three times daily. If you're feeling energetic, you could also walk or cycle to the barrier from Greenwich.
Buggy access. Café. Lift. Nappy-changing facilities. Nearest picnic place: riverside. Shop.

Shooters Hill to Eltham

In centuries past, the steep Shooters Hill Road that takes you from Greenwich towards Kent was a lurking place for highwaymen, who were after rich pickings from carriages heading out of town; if they were caught, they were taken straight to the gallows

Around Town

Water ways: safety first

Since 1982 the most impressive structure spanning the river has been the £535-million **Thames Barrier** that protects the city from flooding. The nine silver 'hoods' that line up across the Thames are actually piers anchoring massive steel gates, which can be raised from the riverbed when water levels get too high.

The Great Flood of 1953, which drowned 300 people and submerged farmland, spurred the government of the day to initiate work on a protective barrage across the river. It was a further 12 years before consent to start building was finally given. The winning design was chosen from among 41 submitted. It took some building:
● 500,000 tons of concrete were used.
● the four largest steel gates are 200 feet wide and weigh 1,500 tons.
● when the gates are raised they are as tall as a five-storey building.
● In total, 4,000 men and women worked on the barrier.

The primary reason for building the barrier was to protect London against the surge tides that build up in the Atlantic and make their way round to English waters before speeding up the Thames Estuary, causing a massive rise in the water level. Yet, in addition to the risk from sudden surges, there is another reason we need a barrier: global

warming, say environmentalists, is causing sea levels to rise steadily. The already-high water level at London Bridge is currently rising at a rate of about 75 centimetres each century.

The **Thames Barrier Information & Learning Centre** gives an insight into the history behind the building of the barrier, and the way it works. It's a fascinating place for families to visit, all the more attractive for its riverfront playground and walks, and the romantic bleakness of the industrial wastes and factory views across the Thames.

Hanging about in **Woolwich**. *See p134.*

£6.20; £4.70 concessions; £3.10 5-16s; free under-5s. *Grounds only* £3.60; £2.70 concessions; £1.80 5-16s; free under-5s. **Credit** MC, V.

A crumbling wreck when it was bought by arts patron Stephen Courtauld and his wife Virginia in 1933, Eltham Palace was restored to its former glory by the couple and is now run by English Heritage. Today, it's full of surprises – grafted on to the side of the house is a medieval great hall with a magnificent restored oak roof. The Courtaulds created a dream home, with exotic wood veneers, clean geometric lines and every mod con, including underfloor heating, a centralised vacuum cleaning system and specially designed quarters for their lucky pet lemur.

Now you can tour the palace's rooms while listening to a commentary on handsets. Quiz and information sheets are handed out to children to fill in as they tour the property. Visitors with very young children often eschew the house, however, and stick to touring, playing and picnicking in the fantastic garden. The grounds are beautifully laid out, with views across to the city and out to the greenery of Kent. There's plenty of space to run around and play hide and seek (though be careful of the easily accessible moat). Note that it's closed from 24 December 2002 to 4 March 2003.
Café. Lifts. Nappy-changing facilities. Nearest picnic place: palace grounds. Shop.

at the bottom of the hill. Some say Shooters Hill is so named because of the trigger-happy highwaymen; others reckon it's because the area was used for archery practice by that great sports enthusiast Henry VIII (he was born at Greenwich and spent a lot of time in the area).

Off Shooters Hill is **Hornfair Park**, which is popular among Charlton folk in hot weather for its cool blue lido (8856 7180) and its children's pool (*see also p262*). Further east lies **Oxleas Wood** (*see p143*). Eltham, a suburban enclave surrounded by more woods, parkland and golf courses, is not very interesting in its own right, unless you're bound for **Eltham Palace** for a dose of art deco splendour and a picnic in the grounds.

Charlton House
Charlton Road, SE7 (8856 3951/www.greenwich. gov.uk). Charlton rail/53, 54, 380, 442 bus. **Open** *Library* 2-7pm Mon, Thur; 10am-12.30pm, 1.30-5.30pm Tue, Fri; 10am-12.30pm, 2-5pm Sat. **Admission** free.
Charlton House is, according to experts, the finest Jacobean house in the city. Whatever the case, it's certainly the poshest-looking library in south-east London. It was built in 1612 as a retirement gift for Adam Newton, who was tutor to James I's son Prince Henry. The library section includes an excellent children's section, and is home to Charlton's Toy Library (8319 0055). The house is also a popular venue for weddings and other important gatherings (phone for further information and prices).

Eltham Palace
Court Yard, off Court Road, SE9 (8294 2548/www. english-heritage.org.uk). Eltham rail. **Open** *Apr-Sept* 10am-6pm Wed-Fri, Sun. *Oct* 10am-5pm Wed-Fri, Sun. *Nov-Mar* 10am-4pm Wed-Fri, Sun. Closed 24-26 Dec, Jan. **Admission** (EH) *House & grounds* (incl audio tour)

Kennington & the Elephant

Kennington's proximity to central London and attractive residential squares, including Cleaver Square and Courtney Square, make it a desirable place to live, though Newington Butts, a pretty vile street, and, worse still, the Elephant and Castle – south London's ugliest landmark – are just a walk away. In fact, the Elephant is constantly undergoing cosmetic surgery; although plans for a smart new plaza to replace the depressing roundabout and shabby shopping centre are dogged by setbacks, the word is that the Elephant and Castle will be transformed for the better by 2012.

Also in the area are **Geraldine Mary Harmsworth Park**, with its serene Tibetan peace garden; and a landmark with rather more bombastic origins, the **Imperial War Museum**. If you're a cricket fan, make for the **AMP Oval**, further down Kennington Road.

AMP Oval
Kennington Oval, SE11 (ticket office 7582 7764/6660/ tours 7820 5750/www.surreycricket.com). Oval tube. **Open** *Ticket office* 9.30am-4pm Mon-Fri. Tours by arrangement; phone for details. **Admission** varies; depending on match. **Credit** MC, V.
The home of Surrey County Cricket Club and a famous south London landmark, the Oval traditionally hosts the final test of the summer, as well as county and league matches. There are year-round education projects for keen under-16s (check the website for more information). Tours have to be pre-booked and can be taken on match days; you get a ticket covering both match and tour. They include peeks inside the changing rooms (if not in use!), the broadcast and media studios and the Ken Barrington Centre, an indoor training school. *See also p252.*
Shop.

Imperial War Museum

Lambeth Road, SE1 (7416 5000/www.iwm.org.uk).
Lambeth North tube/Elephant & Castle tube/rail.
Open 10am-6pm daily. Closed 24-26 Dec. **Admission**
free. **Credit** *Shop* MC, V.

The Imperial War Museum is a fascinating, moving and
informative record of the wars of the 20th century. The Large
Exhibits Gallery, the museum's huge ground-floor space,
may have the hardware – weapons, tanks and planes to
admire and climb on – but in the basement, a rotating clock
hand that counts the cost of war in terms of human lives and
the grim Holocaust exhibition serves to banish any thoughts
of war and glory.

The lower ground-floor galleries house the excellent four-
part permanent exhibition of the history of warfare in the
20th century; two of the most popular 'experiences' are the
Blitz and the Trench, which may bring history to life rather
too vividly for some young visitors. Secret War, on the first
floor, looks at espionage from 1909 to the present day;
exhibits range from Brezhnev's uniform to an original
German 'Enigma' encrypting machine. The second floor is
devoted to art collections (paintings from the world wars).

The Holocaust exhibition is a permanent one, housed in a
£17-million, five-storey extension. The documents, artefacts,
photographs and survivors' testimonies make for a moving
display that's suitable only for those aged 14 and above.

The 1940s House, a full-scale re-creation of a typical
wartime home, has proved so popular that its run has been
extended for another year, until 2003. The Trench Exhibition,
which ties in with the BBC2 television series about life in a
World War I trench, continues until 27 October 2002. Hands-
on collections of helmets, uniforms and various props are provided for the kids, and are displayed alongside diaries, letters,
equipment and film footage.

The education department runs a full term-time programme of school-party visits and classes. Youngsters can
be furnished with free quiz sheets, including the popular 'spy
quiz'. During the holidays, children aged 7-11 are treated to
workshops and events, often linked to the temporary exhibitions. These may include wartime cooking sessions (carrot
cookies grab you?), invitingly named 'Do Touch the Exhibits'
sessions, model-making workshops and plenty of opportunities to dress up. Most workshops are free: ring to check
what's on before you visit.
Buggy access. Café. Lifts. Nappy-changing facilities.
Nearest picnic place: Geraldine Mary Harmsworth Park.
Restaurant. Shop.

Where to eat

The streets around the charmless Elephant and
Castle shopping centre yield a couple of venerable
institutions to take refreshment in: **Pizzeria
Castello** (20 Walworth Road, SE1, 7703 2556)
does the best garlic bread in south London (you
can smell it all around the Elephant roundabout)
and welcomes children. If you want a drink with a
difference, the ancient herbalist **Baldwins** (171-3
Walworth Road, SE17, 7703 5550), where an
astounding range of tinctures, potions and remedies
line the shelves, is famous for its sarsaparilla, a tonic
beverage served in half-pint jugs that you drink at
the counter. More pizza, pasta and child-friendliness
is on the menu at the little family-run trat, **La Luna**
(380 Walworth Road, SE17, 7277 1991).

Camberwell & Peckham

Camberwell was the first local authority in London
to own an art gallery, and, despite mounting
gentrification and soaring house prices, the area's
bohemian image persists. Its aura is spreading
to Peckham, which is now basking in a certain
trendiness. This new desirability of the scruffy
old area will be compounded in roughly five years'
time, when Peckham is promised its own tube
station and maybe even a tram.

Camberwell Church Street runs east to Peckham.
Along it are two famous landmarks, the first
of which is **St Giles**, one of the largest parish
churches in London. Further along, on Peckham
Road, is **Camberwell College of Arts** (7514
6300), London's oldest art college, which is worth
visiting for the shop alone, where art materials
and stationery are discounted.

To create the much-needed green lung of Burgess
Park, which stretches from Camberwell Road all the
way to Peckham, a built-up area was bulldozed and
the Grand Surrey Canal was filled in. The canal
disappeared under piles of rubble and earth in 1971,
Burgess Park was named in 1974. Over the decades
the artificial look of the park has been a source of
embarrassment to locals, but these days it seems
to be growing into itself, and the area round
Chumleigh Gardens is a delightful place to be.

You can walk a path that used to be the canal
down to the newly created **Peckham Town
Square**. Here the highly acclaimed and fashionable
architecture of **Peckham Pulse Sports Centre**
(10 Melon Road, SE15, 7525 4999) and Will Alsop's
prize-winning, multicoloured **Peckham Library**
are both symbols of Peckham's regeneration. The
sports centre, with its thoroughly modern pools
and fitness centre, also has a homeopathic drop-in
service, a baby clinic and an excellent café. It was
designed as an all-round healthy living space after
the style of the famously philanthropic Peckham
Experiment, a health programme created to pep
up the community after World War II.

Rye Lane still looks pretty jaded, particularly
after a fire took out one of its indoor markets in
October 2001. **Peckham Rye Common**, at its
top, hasn't much of a playground, but it's a lovely
wide-open space, and the gardens look beautiful
in the summer, thanks to the rangers. Plans for
regeneration are ongoing and locals are holding
out for a café. The pond, soupy as it looks, sustains
perch and waterfowl, the occasional heron and
much of the local rat population, which blatantly
dine out on bread left for their feathered neighbours.

The rampant undergrowth that makes **Nunhead
Cemetery** so lovely ensures that many varieties of
insect, bird and plant enjoy life among the dead.

Around Town

Round and round the extensive gardens of **Eltham Palace**. *See p136.*

Burgess Park

Albany Road, SE5 (park rangers 7525 1066). Elephant & Castle tube/rail, then 12, 42, 63, 68, 171, 343 bus. **Open** 24hrs daily. **Admission** free.

This much-underrated park, which was created from land that was once filled with terraced houses and the Peckham branch of the Grand Surrey Canal, has much to offer visitors of all ages. The Camberwell end, around Wells Way, hosts an intriguing wooden playground, a kart track and a one o'clock club. Call for the opening hours of the go-kart track (7525 1101), which change according to the school terms: regular visitors pay an annual sub and go racing as often as they like. Children's parties (age 8-16) cost £70 for a minimum of ten drivers. Across the park, the boating lake is patrolled by bailiffs who check you have a rod licence (available for adults from post offices at £18 per year). Under-12s fish for free.

The programme of tree planting and cycle-path improving continues: an avenue of different varieties of evergreen tree has been planted along the centre of the park to make the walk or cycle ride from Peckham to Camberwell a positive pleasure. Horticultural delights await at Chumleigh Gardens, where mellow-stoned old almshouses flank a beautiful multicultural gardens collection: five gardens represent different styles, namely English cottage, Mediterranean, Caribbean, oriental and Islamic. The botanical gardens have a café and are the HQ for Southwark's park rangers (call to book).

Nunhead Cemetery

Limesford Road, SE15 (info 7732 9535). Nunhead rail. **Open** *Summer* 8.30am-7pm daily. *Winter* 8.30am-4pm daily. **Admission** free; donations to FONC appreciated. *Guided walks* 2pm last Sun of mth.

As well as being one of the most beautiful final resting places in London, Nunhead also supports an impressive selection of wildlife. It's big on insects, butterflies and small mammals, but there have also been sightings of woodpeckers and owls here. The Friends of the Nunhead Cemetery (FONC) see to it that this old cemetery receives the care it deserves – its woodland paths have been resurfaced, its toppling monuments restored and the central chapel rebuilt (they're awaiting an entertainments licence so that classical music concerts can be staged here). Its wild beauty will never be tamed, but it's good to be able to sit on a sturdy new bench and enjoy views over London unobstructed by rampaging Japanese knotweed and sycamore saplings. The ancient mausoleums and ivy-draped stone angels still exude picturesque neglect.

Peckham Library

122 Peckham Hill Street, SE15 (7525 0200). Peckham Rye or Queen's Road Peckham rail/12, 36, 63, 171 bus. **Open** 9am-8pm Mon, Tue, Thur, Fri; 10am-8pm Wed; 9am-5pm Sat; noon-4pm Sun.

Let's face it: Peckham could do with some positive press, and this fabulous library does the trick. On the fourth floor is a large and lively children's section, much visited by local nursery classes. Kids love pressing their noses against the pink glass, which looks out over developments in progress around Peckham and Camberwell. Children's activities and arts workshops take place during the school holidays, in funny little pod rooms up spiral staircases. Under-5s' activity and storytelling sessions are held on Tuesday mornings, from 10am. Call for details of other activities, including computer clubs and homework clubs.

Buggy access. Nappy-changing facilities.

South London Gallery

65 Peckham Road, SE5 (7703 6120/ www.southlondongallery.org). Bus 12, 36, 171. **Open** 11am-6pm Tue, Wed, Fri; 11am-7pm Thur; 2-6pm Sat, Sun. Closed 25, 26 Dec, bank hols. **Admission** free.

The SLG's director Margot Heller is keen to develop the family and schools' programme at the gallery. Exhibitions, which change every six weeks or so, are usually complemented by children's quiz sheets and community-based activities that revolve around the artist's work. Summer 2002 sees Belgian Joëlle Tuerlinckx playing about with perceptions of space in the gallery's high-ceilinged space (until 7 July 2002), then there's a collaboration with Goldsmith College's MA students until August, followed by a group exhibition called 20 Million Mexicans Can't be Wrong (until 27 October 2002). *Nearest picnic place: Lucas Gardens.*

Where to eat

Interesting eating places in Camberwell include a branch of **Chibchas** (119 Grove Lane, SE5, 7733 7927; *see also p133*), for Spanish and South American tapas that are great to share. **Nando's** (88 Denmark Hill, SE5, 7738 3808) is a popular link in the chicken chain. More colourful flavours can be experienced at the Mexican **Cohiba** (58A Camberwell Church Street, SE5, 7740 6677).

For lunch, **Seymour Brothers** (2-4 Grove Lane, SE5, 7701 4944) is a lovely, but often crowded, deli and sandwich bar. In summer its garden is popular with the pushchair brigade. The **Sun & Doves** (61-3 Coldharbour Lane, SE5, 7733 1525) is a trendy pub and restaurant that doubles as an art gallery. Its half portions and south-facing garden make it a favourite with families.

The newly established arty area of Peckham, Bellenden, has the much-fêted **Peckham Experiment** (168 Bellenden Road, SE15, 7252 9424), where children can enjoy half portions of the smart dishes on the international menu. There's also a right-on, friendly café, **Petitou** (63 Choumert Road, SE15, 07932 508450), with toys and sticky cakes for kids. The **Peckham Pulse Sports Centre** has a pleasant café, with tables outdoors on Peckham Square.

Dulwich & Herne Hill

Villagey Dulwich, its trendy little sister East Dulwich and its near-neighbour Herne Hill are blessed with delightful parks, open spaces and gracious residential roads. At their heart is well-kept **Dulwich Park**, with its acres of playing fields and woodland belonging to the Alleyn estate, and historic Dulwich College. Dividing Herne Hill from sassier Brixton (for which, *see p145*) is **Brockwell Park**.

This is an environmentally sound corner of south-east London. The **London Wildlife Trust Centre for Wildlife Gardening** started life as a derelict bus depot and is now the focus for all wildlife gardeners, while **Sydenham Hill Wood**, just across the South Circular Road from Dulwich Park, is a hangout for bats, hedgehogs, rare hawfinches, tawny owls and all sorts of other birdlife. The wood's London Wildlife Trust warden (who can be

reached on 8699 5698) has his office up the road at the **Horniman Museum** in Forest Hill. The latter is a free museum that's worth crossing town for now that the new extension is finished.

Brockwell Park

Dulwich Road, SE24 (7926 0105/www.brockwellpark. com). Herne Hill rail. **Open** 7am-dusk daily.
Brockwell Hall and the surrounding land were purchased for £117,000 by the local council in 1891 and extended in 1901, when four large houses were demolished (the lido was built where they once stood). The park has a flat area for play (unfortunately not a dog-free zone) and to the west duck ponds, tennis courts (note bookings for courts must be in person) and a bowling green. For older kids there's a basketball court, football pitch and BMX track. The park hosts a big annual festival, the Lambeth Country Show, in July (*see p31*).

At the top of the hill, the attractive old hall houses the family-run First Come First Served café, a cheap and pleasant place for Sunday roasts or weekday lunches. The menu includes all-day fried breakfasts, chips, sarnies, pastries, gingerbread men, ice-cream and pop. It's bright and spacious enough for a birthday tea (staff provide cake and jolly teatime boxes for £4 per child; 8671 5217).

In the summer Brockwell Park comes into its own with families from far and wide scrambling for their own piece of paradise around the picturesque Evian Lido (*see p262*). *Buggy access. Café.*

Dulwich Park

College Road, SE21 (park rangers 8693 5737). North Dulwich or West Dulwich rail. **Open** 8am-dusk daily.
The land that was presented to the people of London by Dulwich College in 1885 is every local's favourite park, not least because its smart playground has a brilliant 'spider web' climbing frame built of taut ropes that children love hanging about in. The newly resurfaced tennis courts are equally popular, together with the steamy little restaurant/café, which is excellent for hot chocolate and chips on chilly afternoons and Slush Puppies and ice-creams on hot ones. The boating lake is open during school holidays and in warm weather, and there's a sand-covered ride for those on horseback. The Rangers Yard is the home of London Recumbents (8299 6636), where you can hire (or buy) bikes and trailers, trikes, tandems and the eponymous horizontal bikes. Its founders run one-to-one safety courses for nervous cyclists of all ages. The rangers are always in evidence, organising rustic activities such as bat-watching and fungus identification walks for urban bumpkins of all ages.
Buggy access. Café.

Dulwich Picture Gallery

Gallery Road, SE21 (8693 5254/www.dulwichpicture gallery.org.uk). North Dulwich or West Dulwich rail/ P4 bus. **Open** 10am-5pm Tue-Fri; 11am-5pm Sat, Sun, bank hol Mon. Closed Good Friday, 24-26 Dec, 1 Jan. *Tours* 3pm Sat, Sun. **Admission** £4; £3 concessions; free under-16s; free to all Fri. *Tours* free. **Credit** MC, V.
This enchanting collection of Old Masters was assembled for the King of Poland in the 1790s. When Poland was partitioned in 1795, the collection was brought to Dulwich, where the clean country air was considered beneficial for the treasures. The attractive and well-to-do village of Dulwich still has a wholesome rural feel even today, and this beautiful building, first designed by Sir John Soane, with a bright and airy new extension added by Rick Mather Architects in 2000, fits into the country scene well indeed.

Around Town

The collection of 17th- and 18th-century paintings includes works by Rembrandt, Van Dyck, Poussin, Canaletto and Gainsborough. Temporary exhibitions boost the core collection: until 26 August 2002 there's Inspired By Italy: Dutch Landscape Painting 1600-1700; a David Wilkie (1785-1841) collection is planned for autumn; and from 18 December the bewitching fairies, goblins and illustrations to folk tales by Arthur Rackham are bound to pull in a family crowd.

The licensed café is an attractive place for lunch or afternoon tea; the staff here have an indulgent attitude toward children and their pushchairs. If it's sunny, though, head to the garden outside. An imaginative educational programme brings art to life for young visitors. For details of school holiday courses for children aged from 5, *see p217*. *Buggy access. Café. Nappy-changing facilities. Nearest picnic place: gallery gardens. Shop.*

Horniman Museum

100 London Road, SE23 (8699 1872/ www.horniman.ac.uk). Forest Hill rail/63, 122, 176, 185, 312, 352, P4 bus. **Open** 10.30am-5.30pm Mon-Sat; 2-5.30pm Sun. Closed 24-26 Dec. **Admission** free; donations appreciated. **Credit** *Shop* MC, V.
Frederick Horniman, who made a fortune from trading tea and founded a museum in his name to celebrate, would no doubt approve of the new-look museum following its extended programme of refurbishment. Now you can walk down through the gardens and enter via a smart, newly refurbished wing, which is the way Frederick always wanted his quirky

museum to be arranged. The £13.4-million extension houses a new series of galleries showcasing a world cultures collection and including an educational activity space. 'Hands-on' is the key word here: a busy programme of workshops and handling sessions, during which visitors can get to grips with African masks, musical instruments, puppets and other specimens from the 7,000-piece collection. The education department also plans to run many more free workshops for children, so ring up and get yourself on the free mailing list.

With all this newness, don't forget to look in on the fantastic stuffed animal gallery and Living Waters, one of the oldest free aquaria in London. It consists of a series of tanks and pools, each recreating a miniature underwater world. There are sea horses and crustaceans, exotic coral reef fish, rockpools and British pond specimens. Tanks of frogs, toads and exotic reptilia have also been added to the museum.

Outside in the gardens, there's a small animal enclosure, where exotic-looking turkeys, ducks and other poultry peck about alongside the barrel-bellied goats, rabbits and guinea pigs. Come here during the summer for free outdoor entertainments, or make your own: bring a packed lunch and admire the views from the picnic tables, but don't feed the goat, however longingly it looks at you.

Autumn 2002 sees the opening of a new Music Gallery, the last stage of the works in progress, which will exhibit instruments from all over the world, brand-new listening stations and a performance space.
Café. Nappy-changing facilities. Nearest picnic place: Horniman Gardens. Shop.

Walk: to Monster island

This two-hour walk links four green areas across the hills of south-east London, starting with exotic poultry and ending with monsters.

▶ Start at the **Horniman Museum** in Forest Hill. Both the museum and its gardens, which offer fine views, are well worth a visit. At the top of the gardens is an animal corner, including rabbits, ducks, goats and some interesting-looking fowl. Cross the busy London Road at the traffic lights at one corner of Horniman Gardens. Just beyond the lights is a lane called **Lapse Wood Walk** – take this road through the small housing estate and across the two service roads. Following the line of lamp-posts will take you upwards into the edge of the wood.

▶ **Sydenham** and **Dulwich Woods** are what's left of ancient woodland, with mainly oak and hornbeam. It's a real oasis of quiet. The Dulwich bit is still owned by Dulwich College, a major landowner in these parts since Edward Alleyn, actor and contemporary of Shakespeare, bequeathed 1,200 acres for the college's foundation as well as the land for Dulwich Village itself.

▶ On entering the woods through a gate, turn right down the hill and cross the footbridge. Beyond the bridge ignore the first gates on the left, and go through a single iron gate to the right. Follow the main path downhill. Here, in the wood's still heart, a man known as the Dulwich Hermit was found murdered in 1802. You will see first a golf course, then allotments, beyond railings to your right. Stay

right at junctions. The path bends round the top of the allotments. At the junction follow the path right, skirting the allotments, and sticking to the main path as it turns deeper into the woods. Ignoring any turnings, you will eventually come to a gate in an iron fence. Here you exit the wood and turn left up a tarmac lane.

▶ The lane ends in **Crescent Wood Road**, opposite the listed 1840-built Dulwich Wood House pub. This has a beer garden and is ideal for a break. Coming out of the south end of Crescent Wood Road, cross **Sydenham Hill** and into **Wells Park Road**. Now the television mast of **Crystal Palace** looms to your right. You are at TV's birthplace: John Logie Baird lived in Crescent Wood Road. There are houses to admire here; the airy heights of Sydenham Hill have attracted the wealthy as well as TV pioneers.

▶ Continuing, take the first entrance into **Sydenham Wells Park**. Bearing right, and downhill, go past a second park entrance and straight on at a crossing until the path leads you down to the lake. The lakes and streams form the centrepiece of this pretty, little-known park. Wildfowl and wild flowers abound. Medicinal springs (hence the park's name) were discovered here in 1640 and the area was saved from development by a public campaign at the end of the 1800s.

▶ After the lake, bear right and exit the park gate. Cross over into Ormanton Road and walk straight ahead. Come out through the pedestrians-only

London Wildlife Trust Centre for Wildlife Gardening

*28 Marsden Road, SE15 (7252 9186/
www.wildlondon.org.uk). East Dulwich rail.* **Open**
10.30am-4.30pm Tue-Thur, Sun. **Admission** free.
The London Wildlife Trust has been persuading citizens for
more than 20 years now that native flora and fauna can thrive
in the Smoke. Its persistence has paid off in recent times: visitor numbers to London's wildlife reserves are increasing all
the time, and LWT flagships, namely this centre and Camley
Street Natural Park in King's Cross (*see p97*), have reported
a massive surge in interest in their work. The Peckham centre, planted on derelict land, inspires wildlife gardeners,
young and old. The central wooden building, with its
balcony, office and tanks full of fish, stick insects and other
specimens, serves as a meeting place for LWT members and
a centre for the many courses and talks that go on throughout the year. The building looks out on to a nursery for native
plants and trees, a pond for dipping (it's the focus for the
centre's annual Frog Day in March) and different styles of
garden: wildlife meadow, woodland, marsh and herb. Add to
this the beehives, the children's play area and sandpit and
the result is a green focal point in an inner city area that needs
one. To join the trust, which also has a junior wing called
Wildlife Watch, enquire at the centre or contact: London
Wildlife Trust, Harling House, 47-51 Great Suffolk Street,
London SE1 0BS (7261 0447/www.wildlondon.org.uk).
Buggy access. Nappy-changing facilities.

Where to eat

Herne Hill has the best fish and chip restaurant
in south London (some say the whole of London) –
Olley's (67-69 Norwood Road, SE24, 8671 8259;
see also p186), and a posh Indian restaurant,
3 Monkeys (136-40 Herne Hill, SE24, 7738 5500),
where children can eat free from 7pm to 7.30pm
(one child per adult reservation).

If you want something for a special family
celebration, particularly at Sunday lunchtime, try
the grand **Belair House** in Dulwich (Gallery Road,
SE21, 8299 9788). It has a children's menu and high
chairs, and you can take fidgets for a runaround in
the park after. Welcoming Dulwich pubs include the
Crown & Greyhound (73 Dulwich Village, SE21,
8299 4976; *see also p189*), which does a children's
teatime menu plus half portions at lunchtime. It has
a garden with play equipment. Other favourites in
the Village include **Pizza Express** (No.94, 8693
9333) and **Le Piaf** (Nos.75-7, 8693 9331).

East Dulwich's trendy centre, North Cross Road,
has a couple of arty cafés where children are part
of the scene: the **Blue Mountain Café** (No.18,

Horniman Museum. *See p140.*

access to Westwood Hill and go straight on into
Charleville Circus. Take either side of the circular
road, then cross **Crystal Palace Park Road** and
turn left. You can now enter **Crystal Palace Park**
through Fisherman's Gate on your right.

▶ This magnificent open space is what is left of a
Victorian grand design: even plonking the National
Sports Centre (*see p265*) in the middle couldn't
ruin it. At the top of the park, to your right, under
the looming tower, a garden now decorates the
empty terraces where Paxton's huge glass palace
once stood. It burnt down in 1936 and you can
revisit it in imagination at the small **Crystal Palace
Museum** over near Crystal Palace station. Turn
left at the gate, then left again. Turning right at
the next junction will lead you down to the lakes,
the 'monsters', and the children's zoo. The
monsters in question are the famous Victorian
dinosaurs (now classed as listed buildings) made
of cement, iron and stone and newly painted in
greys and greens to look even more striking.
The whole area was originally planted with ferns
and designed as an open-air prehistoric museum.
The nearby café, playground and information
centre make this the best destination to round
off this walk.

▶ After you've had refreshments, a short walk up
past the sports complex takes you up to Crystal
Palace station just off Anerley Hill and the buses
on Crystal Palace Parade.

Around Town

8299 6953) also has excellent proper coffee for sale, in ground or bean form. On the main road, Lordship Lane, there are any number of brasseries, spaghetti houses and bistros for families to sample. A branch of **Barcelona Tapas Bar y Restaurante** (No.481, 8693 5111) has a confusingly long but good tapas menu, so everyone in the family should find something they fancy. One of the most basic – and cheapest – cafés is **Café Noodles** (No.159, 8693 4016), which is great for a flavoursome teatime carb fix.

Crystal Palace

The best thing about Crystal Palace is its park – if ever they stop refurbishing it, that is. The worst is the terrible traffic, which makes the streets of Westow Hill, Gipsy Hill and other thoroughfares leading west to Streatham and north to Dulwich hellish at school-run time.

The park was created by the famous Victorian landscape designer Sir Joseph Paxton in 1853-4 as a permanent home for the huge glass and cast-iron building that was used for the Great Exhibition in Hyde Park and then re-erected here. The structure burnt down in 1936 but the stone terraces and many other original features remain, including a unique model dinosaur park (currently under restoration) around the lower lake.

The park contains the National Sports Centre (*see p265*), although a close look at the facilities reveals a rather depressing shabbiness and bodes ill for our beleaguered athletes.

Crystal Palace Museum

Anerley Hill, SE19 (8676 0700). Crystal Palace rail. **Open** 11am-5pm Sun, bank hol Mon. **Admission** free. This little museum is housed in the old engineering school where John Logie Baird invented television and thus changed the lifestyle of mankind forever. It chronicles not the history of the magic rectangle but that of the Crystal Palace and takes about one hour to get round.

Crystal Palace Park

Crystal Palace Information Centre, Thicket Road, SE20 (8778 9496). Crystal Palace rail/2, 3, 63, 108B, 122, 157, 227 bus. **Open** *Information centre* 9am-5pm daily (later in summer). *Park* dawn-dusk daily. **Admission** free. If you're a first-time visitor to Crystal Palace Park, it's best to start off at the main (Penge) entrance at the bottom of the park on Thicket Road – it has free parking and an information centre, where you can get photocopied maps that show kiosks and toilets. There are also more detailed Paxton Heritage Trails that may appeal to older children. Climb the hill to the site of the original Crystal Palace for wonderful views of south London.

The quickest way through the park is straight up the steps through the National Sports Centre (*see p265*), but it's far more interesting to meander round the members-only fishing lake and slightly rusted Concert Bowl, where a variety of open-air concerts take place in summer. The Crystal Palace Park maze, grown of hornbeam, is nearby. It's the biggest

Shy wildlife in **Dulwich Woods**. *See p140.*

maze in London. In fact, it's the only maze in London, Hampton Court (*see p157*) being officially in Surrey.

At the boating lake two to four people can hire a pedal-boat for £3.50 per half hour (though watch out for the timid but fairly energetic rats that congregate here in mild weather). The park's famous model dinosaurs have been repainted and replaced around the lake and a new petting zoo is scheduled to open in July 2002. The authorities are also planning a reptile centre to complement the dinosaur theme, but if you're making a special trip, ring to check it's open before you set out.

Where to eat

The crowded streets around Crystal Palace, Gipsy Hill and West Norwood provide rich pickings for fast-food and pizza fans. Places we like best include **Joanna's** (56 Westow Hill, SE19, 8670 4052; *see also p186*), a friendly brasserie with an undemanding Modern European menu and a good line in hand-made burgers and the down-to-earth vegetarian restaurant **Domali Café** (38 Westow Street, SE19, 8768 0096), whose wonderful soups, pasta dishes and sandwiches fill you up after an energetic walk around the park. There's a garden for al fresco eating.

Further south-east

Oxleas Wood (off Shooters Hill Road, SE18) is an 8,000-year-old area of woodland, which was destined for the developers' bulldozers back in the 1990s. Local residents and conservationists rightly put up a fight, and today, with its wonderful views out towards Kent, it's as big an attraction as ever for families, joggers and cyclists, especially during the bluebell season (May).

The area is a network of footpaths that can be tricky to navigate, especially once you get into the depths of the woods. If you're feeling energetic, some of the paths link up with the **Green Chain Walk**, a 40-mile network of footpaths, which means you can walk from here down to Woolwich and the Thames Barrier as well as to **Crystal Palace Park** and Chislehurst Common. For further information, call the Green Chain Project on 8921 5028, or see its website at www.greenchain.com.

On summer evenings and at weekends many walkers congregate around the café overlooking **Oxleas Meadow** (off Crown Woods Lane). It looks pretty tatty from the outside but is warm and friendly within. There's limited free car parking at Crown Woods Lane and along the Welling Way. Where the Green Chain walk meanders south to Falconwood station, crossing busy **Shooters Hill** (A207), walkers cross the fields of the **Woodlands Farm**, an organic venture where many of the workers are volunteers with a penchant for fresh air.

Croydon and **Bromley**, both prosperous suburbs, are most attractive to families. Sports, shopping and cultural facilities are strong in both places: the Glades Shopping Centre in Bromley and the Whitgift Centre in Croydon are highly rated by shopaholics. But for a real spree it has to be the huge (overwhelming for some) **Bluewater** at Greenhithe, Kent (08456 021021; *see also p206*), whose endless facilities make it as much a family day out as a shopping trip (if you don't have a car, take the train from London Bridge to Greenhithe in Kent). If you can tear yourself away from the shops, pretty **Chislehurst**, another Kentish suburb, is famous for its dark and creepy caves, which have a fascinating history, having been used by druids, wartime evacuees and as a pirate radio station in the past. Tours cost £4 for adults; £2 for children (Wednesday to Sunday; phone 8467 3264/ www.chislehurstcaves.co.uk for details). The caves aren't a suitable venue for young children, who are spooked by the extreme dark, but older kids, especially those into ghost stories, love them.

Croydon deserves recognition for many reasons, among them its £200-million tramlink, its green credentials (it's the third greenest London borough, both in terms of its park space and environmentally friendly initiatives) and the **Croydon Clocktower**. This handsome Victorian building, modernised in 1996 to accommodate three galleries, a library, a theatre space, a cinema and a smart café, is a dream for young families, especially as many of the activities are free and most exhibitions have related events for kids. Visitors of an aeronautical bent may

like to come to Croydon on the first Sunday of each month, when **Croydon Airport Visitor Centre** (Purley Way, 8669 1196) opens to the public from 11am to 4pm. The centre, run by volunteers from the airport society, is housed in the control tower. It's full of hands-on exhibits and information about this old airport's heyday. Purley Way (the other end) is also the home of IKEA's southern outpost, a big Toys 'R' Us and Children's World, and, nearer the airport, the children's friend TGI Friday's: consumer-heaven all round.

Croydon Clocktower

Katharine Street, Croydon, Surrey (info 8760 5400/ box office 8253 1030/shop 8253 1035/tourist info 8253 1009/www.croydon.gov.uk/clocktower). East Croydon or West Croydon rail/George Street tram. **Open** *Clocktower & library* 9am-7pm Mon; 9am-6pm Tue, Wed, Fri; 9.30am-6pm Thur; 9am-5pm Sat; 2-5pm Sun. *Café Opera* 9am-5.30pm Mon-Wed, Fri; 9.30am-5.30pm Thur; 9am-4.30pm Sat; noon-4.30pm Sun, bank hols. *Shop* 10am-7pm Mon; 10am-5pm Tue-Sat. *Tourist Information Centre* 9am-6pm Mon, Wed, Fri; 9.30am-6pm Thur; 9am-5pm Sat; 2-5pm Sun.

Lifetimes is a free interactive exhibition that takes as its subject the history and the future of Croydon. The displays are extremely child-friendly, with touch-screen computer terminals providing additional information about the artefacts and relaying the real-life stories of local people. There's also a dressing-up corner, with shoes, fairy dresses and headgear. On the Move, a transport-through-the-ages exhibition, runs until 24 September 2002. The David Lean Cinema holds the Tick Tock children's club every Saturday (11am), and screens extra family favourites during the school holidays.

The Braithwaite Hall hosts regular weekend and holiday theatre productions for children, while the library holds Bookstart Baby Rhymetime song and rhyme sessions for babies and pre-schoolers and drop-in mornings of stories, music and art for kids of all ages. On Saturday mornings a crèche allows parents to use the library, wander round the displays or slurp double lattes in Café Opera in peace. *Café. Nappy-changing facilities. Nearest picnic place: Queens Gardens. Shop.*

Woodlands Farm

331 Shooters Hill, Welling, Kent (8319 8900/ www.thewoodlandsfarmtrust.org). Falconwood rail/ 89, 486 bus. **Open** 9am-5pm daily. **Admission** free; donations appreciated.

Hardly a city farm – these fields, near Oxleas Wood, do a very good impression of rolling countryside. The Woodlands Farm Trust came into being in 1995 when plans to bulldoze Oxleas Wood to make way for the East London River Crossing were scuppered. The trust, aided by lottery money and funds from the Bridge House Estates Trust, bought the derelict farmhouse and surrounding fields to create an organic farm for everyone to enjoy. Currently home to two shire horses, a 170-strong flock of sheep, 12 cows, geese and hens, the Woodlands Farm has a core staff, but a good deal of the work is done by volunteers from the locality. Anyone can come to visit, and even help out if they want to. Plans for the future include planting a Kentish orchard of the sort that has become almost extinct over past decades, and to get the organic vegetable side of the business up and running. The farm workers are used to visits by school groups and are happy to show visitors around if they're not too busy. *Buggy access. Café (open Sun only). Nearest picnic place: farm grounds.*

South-west London

A green, pleasant, nappy-happy, organic veggie, child-friendly land.

Vauxhall & Stockwell

Though it's primarily famous for the MI6 building that overlooks the Thames beside the ever-clogged bridge, Vauxhall also has a proud history. Known at different times as Fulke's Hall, Faukeshall and Foxhall, it was a village for most of the 18th century and home to the much-admired Vauxhall Gardens, a fashionable park that was used for concerts, shows, displays and general public voyeurism. It closed in 1859 for financial reasons and the only reminder of it now is the mid-sized **Spring Gardens**.

Stockwell's green spaces are few and far between, though **Slade Gardens** on Robsart Street has an adventure playground, play areas and a one o'clock club. Over on Stockwell's west side, **Larkhall Park**, on Larkhall Rise, is quite a peaceful open space, with a one o'clock club, picnic and seating areas, a café, two multipurpose ball-game areas, tennis courts, a walled garden, a playground and nappy-changing facilities.

At the beginning of Stockwell Road as you leave Brixton, the skate park attracts gangs of kids, particularly in summer. The graffitied area, with its graded concrete bumps, allows dextrous skaters and bladers to show off their skills. It's an eyesore to some people, perhaps, but it's popular with spectators nonetheless.

Vauxhall Park (South Lambeth Road, at the junction with Fentiman Road, SW8) has some well-manicured areas for quiet contemplation, as well as tennis courts, a bowling green, a play area, a one o'clock club and a fenced ball-game area. Opposite Spring Gardens is **Vauxhall City Farm**, which is a brilliant place to take kids.

Another nice green space is Bonnington Square's **Pleasure Garden**. The garden started life as a play area during the 1970s but subsequently lay neglected and prey to vandals for years, until local residents pulled away the nettles to form the latest venture, a lovely secret garden with a restored Victorian water wheel.

Vauxhall City Farm
24 St Oswalds Place, Tyers Street, SE11 (7582 4204). Vauxhall tube/rail. **Open** *10.30am-4.30pm Tue-Thur, Sat, Sun.* **Admission** *free.*
Vauxhall City Farm's enthusiastic programme of educational and recreational activities for groups and individuals of all ages is a perfect antidote to this heavily urbanised area. Activities include pony and donkey rides (£2.50); all riders must be farm members and rides aren't every day so phone

for details. Other activities include mosaic-making and mural painting, and music lessons. For those who can't make it to the farm, a lorry carries the animals in comfort and safety to school and nursery groups. Other farm residents include pigs, goats, poultry and small cuddly animals such as rabbits and guinea pigs. *Buggy access.*

Where to eat

A welcome pitstop on Vauxhall's limited culinary scene is **Lavender** (112 Vauxhall Walk, SE11, 7735 4440), which overlooks Spring Gardens; brasserie-style food is served here in adult and child portions.

The experience of eating out in Stockwell is much influenced by its large Portuguese community, whose cafés and bakeries along the Stockwell Road really come alive on summer evenings. Babies and children are welcome at all the following places, and there are usually high chairs available. **O Cantinho de Portugal** (135-7 Stockwell Road, SW9, 7924

Peaceful **Battersea Park**. *See p146.*

0218) is a bar/restaurant where you can spoil yourselves with a long lunch in true Mediterranean style. **Bar Estrela** (113 South Lambeth Road, SW8, 7793 1051) draws families with its well-priced seafood-based snacks and tapas menu. For more tapas head along the road to **Rebatos** (169 South Lambeth Road, SW8, 7735 6388), a long-established Spanish-run bar that attracts everyone from children and students to elderly couples. Yet another Portuguese favourite, tucked away on a quiet backstreet, is **O Barros** (168A Old South Lambeth Road, SW8, 7582 0976), serving tapas and a good range of snacks.

Brixton

The feel of this area has changed over the last decade or so, what with the creeping gentrification estate agents are so pleased to emphasise, but Brixton, liberal Lambeth's capital, is still edgy enough to have a distinctive urban vibe of its own. You only have to go to the market to discover it.

Recent strides in local primary schools' league table performances may be enough to keep young families when the school bell tolls, although the lack of green spaces in the area has traditionally driven them out to the hills (Forest, Gipsy and Herne) in search of some breathing space. Most locals claim **Brockwell Park**, which joins Herne Hill to Brixton, as their own green lung (*see p139*).

Brixton's star turn is the **Ritzy** cinema (Brixton Oval, SW2, 7733 2229; *see also p220*), whose Kids' Club is one of south London's best bargains: children's tickets are only £1 (£2 for accompanying adults) on Saturdays throughout the year and Tuesdays and Thursdays during school holidays. For parents there are free newspapers and tea and coffee in the Ritzy Crush Bar during the show. A recent initiative, Watch with Baby, allows parents to take their under-1s into a film.

Where to eat

Brixton Market is a good place to stop for a meal or a snack: **Eco** (4 Market Row, SW9, 7738 3021) has perfect pizzas, but go early or late to avoid queuing, while the friendly **Jacaranda Garden** (11-13 Station Road, SW9, 7274 8383) serves great focaccia sarnies and big slices of cake. Within the market area are **El Pilón Quindiano**, for both Colombian fare and plainer English food; bright and chirpy **Pangaea** (15 Atlantic Road, SW9, 7737 6777), with its tempting pasta dishes and lovely pizzas; and at 15 Market Row, **Kim's Café**, which is as straightforward as its name

Around Town

and has wide aisles for pushchairs. Older children enjoy the beat at sassy **Bamboula** (12 Acre Lane, SW2, 7737 6633), where 'sudden-fried chicken', rotis, plantains, barbecued fish and other Caribbean delights are served with attitude. Reduced-price portions for youngsters should be requested, as servings are huge.

More than 1,000 years ago Battersea was Badric's Island, a Saxon settlement. Over the centuries it became known for market gardening, but nowadays it's famous for its power station and the dogs' home. The former, built in 1929 and closed in 1983, is destined for a future role as a vast riverside business and entertainment complex. Quite when that project will be completed nobody knows. The latter continues to house unwanted canines and find new, loving homes for them.

Battersea Arts Centre on Lavender Hill (7223 2223; *see also p221*) is one of London's best alternative venues. The BAmC also runs a variety of dance and drama workshops, as well as Saturday afternoon theatre for over-3s. The café is a good pitstop before a show.

Five minutes' walk from the dogs' home is **Battersea Park**, an excellent place to play. Its history is quite bloodstained, however. In 1671 Colonel Blood lay in wait near what is now the boating lake, planning to shoot King Charles II (but he lost his nerve), and in 1829 the Duke of Wellington fought a duel with Lord Winchilsea. Nowadays it's a safe and peaceful place to bring the family, and great for a picnic in summer.

The southern reaches of Battersea, where it meets Clapham, between the two commons of Clapham and Wandsworth, includes the rarefied area nicknamed 'Nappy Valley', because it's said to have the highest population density of under-5s anywhere in Western Europe. It's hard to find the source of this extraordinary statistic, but locals have to put up with it. At the heart of this area is the chi-chi Northcote Road, with its excellent market, delis, upmarket shops and family-friendly cafés, many of which are listed in the Eating chapter (*pp170-191*).

Battersea Dogs' Home

4 Battersea Park Road, SW8 (7622 3626/ www.dogshome.org). Vauxhall tube/rail/Sloane Square tube then 19, 137 bus/Battersea Park or Queenstown Road rail. **Open** *Viewings* 10.30am-4.15pm Mon-Wed, Fri; 10.30am-3.15pm Sat, Sun. **Admission** £1; 50p concessions, under-16s. **Credit** *Shop* MC, V.

If you're looking for a pet, there are around 300 cats and dogs in search of a new home here at any one time, though if you fall madly in love you'll need to be questioned by the rightly circumspect staff before you can take one home. Many of the dogs are unsuitable for homes with young children, but the staff do their best to match up the right pooch with willing adoptive families. It's worth coming for a few visits before reaching any serious adoption conclusions, anyway, and bear in mind that weekends get very busy, so try to visit on a weekday. The shop is also a good source of unusual presents, with its doggy stationery, souvenirs and toys, and there's a café for drinks and snacks.

Buggy access. Café. Nearest picnic place: Battersea Park. Shop.

Battersea Park

SW11 (8871 7530/7531/www.wandsworth.gov.uk). Sloane Square tube then 19, 137 bus/Battersea Park or Queenstown Road rail. **Open** *Adventure playground* School hols 11am-6pm daily. Term time 3.30-5pm Tue-Fri; 11am-6pm Sat, Sun. **Admission** free.

A £12-million restoration programme has transformed Battersea Park's famous Festival Gardens, which were one of the attractions of the 1951 Festival of Britain. The sub-tropical gardens and the riverside promenade are also being given a makeover.

The playground selection includes a one o'clock club (8871 7541) for under-5s, a place for under-8s, and, for 5-15-year-olds, the biggest adventure playground in London. Children will also enjoy the Affordable Art Fair (Tony Hart was a guest in 2001; the next one is 17-20 October 2002) and the fireworks displays for Bonfire Night.

As well as a seasonal boating lake, Battersea Park has 21 tennis courts, three football pitches, four softball pitches, one rugby pitch, three cricket squares, all-weather sports pitches, boules grounds, a bowling green and an athletics track with facilities for all major track and field events. There's also a branch of London Recumbents (next to the athletics track, 7498 6543), from whom you can hire horizontal bikes as well as bikes with trailers for tiddlers. Note that it's normally closed Tuesdays, Thursdays and Fridays.

Certainly one of Battersea Park's most eye-catching and incongruous landmarks is the Peace Pagoda, overlooking the Thames. With its four golden Buddhas, this was built by Buddhist monks in 1985 and donated to the people of London to commemorate Hiroshima Day.

The café by the lake is an essential port of call; it has a licensed bar and a sturdy menu with sandwiches, coffee and cake, plus hot food of the lasagne, curry, and sausage and chips variety, with small portions for children.

Buggy access. Café. Nappy-changing facilities.

Battersea Park Children's Zoo

Battersea Park, SW11 (8871 7540/www.wandsworth. gov.uk). Sloane Square tube then 19, 137 bus/Battersea Park or Queenstown Road rail. **Open** *Apr-Sept* 10am-5pm (last entry 4.30pm) daily. *Oct-Mar* 11am-3pm Sat, Sun. Closed 29, 30 Dec. **Admission** (LP) £2; £1 3-16s; under-2s free. **No credit cards**.

One of the delights of Battersea Park is the Children's Zoo. Established during the Festival of Britain in 1951, it was meant to be a temporary feature, but was such a hit that it's been there ever since. Nowadays it's home to wallabies, meerkats, otters, kookaburras, tortoises, various monkeys and a reclusive Vietnamese pot-bellied pig.

There's something to see all year round, but you're more likely to get your money's worth in the summer, when all the animals are back from their winter quarters. For children there are pony rides, a mini roundabout and a contact area where they can pet and feed the more approachable animals. There's an animal adoption scheme, which for a fee will buy you two tickets to the zoo and a name plaque beside the animal's enclosure. This is a super place to hold children's parties (*see p249*). The exit takes you via the gift shop, which you'll be lucky to leave without a stuffed toy or souvenir pencil sharpener.

Buggy access. Café. Nappy-changing facilities. Nearest picnic place: zoo grounds. Shop.

Where to eat

It's a bit of a culinary hotspot round here, so there's no shortage of places to take the family for a slap-up dinner or a healthy snack. **fish!** (41A Queenstown Road, SW8, 7234 3333; *see also p171*) attracts family groups with its foolproof menu and simple, nutritious fish dishes. On Northcote Road, **Wok Wok** (Nos.51-3, 7978 7181) provides the stir-fries and noodles that make children smile, and the **Gourmet Burger Kitchen** (No.44, 7228 3309; *see also p187*) shows them what a real burger should be. Macdo eat your heart out. **Boiled Egg & Soldiers** at No.63 (7223 4894; *see also p186*) is justly popular for its nursery teas (and lunches and breakfasts). The ubiquitous **Starbucks** at Nos.33-8 (7350 2887) has become an unofficial mother and toddler group that's crammed with babies and pushchairs every weekday morning.

Add a couple of Pizza Expresses and a branch of their Belgian rival, **Strada** (*see p173*), and eating out shouldn't be a problem down Battersea way.

Clapham

In the 18th century, the 'village on the hill' was prized for its clean air and health springs. Nowadays the air is not so clean but the area is still famously desirable, as estate agents will attest. East of the common, **Clapham Old Town** is a precious little cluster of pubs, shops and restaurants around what might resemble a village green if it weren't for all the 88 buses (rather tweely known as the Clapham Omnibus) revving up by the bus terminal.

The **Clapham Picture House** (Venn Street, 7498 3323; *see also p219*), a rep cinema with a busy Saturday morning Kids' Club, is a godsend on a rainy weekend, but most families head for **Clapham Common** for leisure activities, whatever the weather. This flat, windy space has a chequered history. In the 18th century it had a big vermin problem, apparently hedgehogs and polecats were the main offending species and hunters were paid to cull them. During World War I it was turned over to the cultivation of food; and in World War II tunnels and caverns were dug beneath it as training posts for army radio operators (these underground mazes were pressed into service as reception centres for immigrants from the Caribbean in the 1940s). Now the common is south-west London's recreation ground – dozens of sports clubs congregate here, and at weekends you'll see people playing Australian

The green scene

The **Nature Study Centre**, near the bowling green on Wandsworth Common, is a timber cabin that opens regularly throughout the year to promote an interest in urban ecology. Frequent nature-spotting activities are geared to Mother Nature's calendar. Easter holidays, for example, may focus on the stag beetle population or pond dipping. Summer activities may include searching for medicinal herbs. The stately heron is sometimes given a starring role in the centre's Heron Days. Bird spotting is encouraged, and a list of feathered friends to look out for is put up on the noticeboard every month. The pond has a boardwalk all around it for easy dipping and birdwatching, but don't be a coot and fall in.

Nature Study Centre

Dorlcote Road, SW18 (8871 3863/ www.wandsworth.gov.uk). **Open** 3-5pm Wed; 1st Sun of every mth 2.30-4.30pm; ring for school holiday activity days. Ring to be put on the mailing list for forthcoming activities. **Admission** free. *Buggy access.*

rules football, camogie (Gaelic hurling), netball and lacrosse. On Sundays the football pitches on the west side of the common are turned into a London outpost of the South American football league. There are two playgrounds – the one by the corner of Battersea Rise is best for smaller kids, and the one over by the Windmill pub on Clapham South Side, which has more facilities for older children, as well as loos beside the one o'clock club. A rightly popular spot for parents and toddlers is the **Bowling Green Café** beside the tennis courts on the west side of the common (it's here that you book and pay for the tennis courts, in person on the day of play).

The second common that forms the Nappy Valley boundary is Wandsworth. This, too, has a one o'clock club on the corner of Wandsworth Common and Chivalry Road), a small playground for pre-schoolers and an adventure playground with facilities for children with disabilities. Children's football clubs dominate the common along Bolingbroke Grove on Saturday mornings. Railway tracks bisect this great green expanse, where the rangers are particularly well versed in Mother Nature's treasures, even more valuable in London (*see above*).

Bowling Green Café

Clapham Common West Side, corner of Thurleigh Road, SW4 (7801 0904). Clapham South tube. **Open** *Apr-Oct* 9am-6pm daily. *Nov-Mar* 9am-5pm daily. **No credit cards**.

In sunny weather there are slides, playhouses, tractors and bikes to play on near this café, which does a good line in comfort food (bangers 'n' mash, fish fingers, pasta) costing from £1.55 for a child's portion. Sandwiches are fine and fresh, and the cakes go down a treat following an afternoon on the common. Children's parties are catered for in summer. *Buggy access.*

Where to eat

For eating out, the often-frenetic **Eco** (162 Clapham High Street, SW4, 7978 1108) has great pizzas, though it's loud and crowded in the evenings. **Tiger Lil's** (16A Clapham Common South Side, SW4, 7720 5433; *see also p187*) is great fun for kids as they get to choose their own ingredients then hand them to a chef to wok in front of them.

The Pavement is a good place to stop for tea, with the imaginatively named the **Pavement** (No.21, 7622 4944) and **Café Des Res** (No.8, 7622 6602). **Café Wanda** further down the High Street (No.153, 7738 8760) has superior cakes, scones and sandwiches to eat in or take over to the paddling pool on the common for a picnic. Five minutes' walk away beside the boating pond is the **Café on the Common**, a pleasantly hippie-ish hangout serving hot vegetarian food from a converted park building. The outside is fenced in so you can enjoy sitting out knowing that your toddler can't escape – not that he'll want to as the outside is well supplied with enough toys, books and trikes to keep him interested while you finish your coffee. **Pizza Express** (43 Abbeville Road, SW4, 8673 8878) is as solidly child-friendly as ever. For a slightly more exotic dining experience (for parents, at least), **Sash Oriental** (32 Abbeville Road, SW4, 8673 9300) has an extensive children's menu that includes chicken noodles, rice dishes, burgers and fish fingers.

Streatham

It's hard to imagine it these days, but in its heyday Streatham was an upmarket hotbed of intellectual and artistic activity – Edmund Burke, Dr Johnson, Joshua Reynolds, Fanny Burney and David Garrick all lived here. Such exclusivity couldn't last, however, and the advent of the railways saw Streatham expand at a frightening rate at the end of the 19th century. Inter-war development and post-war bombsite infill completed the picture in the 20th century, making Streatham what it is today – a big, sprawling neighbourhood, with good-sized family houses and useful play spaces of Streatham and Tooting Commons, but blighted by the A23, aka Streatham High Road.

The **High Road**, frustratingly jammed with traffic, is nonetheless the gateway to the best that Streatham has to offer families – at the top, near Streatham Hill station, is **Streatham Megabowl**

and further down the High Road, by Streatham Station, is Streatham Ice Rink (No.386, 8769 7771; *see also p258*), for skating (including reasonably priced six-week courses) and spectator ice hockey; it's also a good venue for birthday parties. Speed fiends aged from 8 love karting at Playscape Pro Racing (No.390, 7801 0110; *see also p260*).

To the east, **Streatham Common** is an airy slope, bordered on all sides by busy roads with views south over Thornton Heath to Croydon. Its hidden treasure is the **Rookery** (8679 1635), a beautiful little formal garden. It's a lovely place to picnic and enjoy views over London, and in summer music wafts over from the seasonal open-air theatre. There's also a café. When you've restored your soul and the children are screaming out for something more exciting, let them loose in the woods and commons of **Norwood Grove**, where if you keep your eyes peeled you may even see the celebrated population of ring-necked parakeets.

Where to eat

As on most high streets across the country, the big pizza names line up: **Pizza Hut** (114-8 Streatham Hill, SW2, 8671 7311) and **Pizza Express** (34-6 Streatham High Road, SW16, 8769 0202) are always busy, while the **Waterfront** bar and restaurant (426-8 Streatham High Road, SW16, 8764 3985) offers stone-baked varieties. For more adventurous souls there's **Trini's** (13 High Parade, Streatham High Road, SW16, 8696 9669), where family groups noisily appreciate Trinidadian classics such as goat curry, roti, callaloo and sweet barbecue chicken. Prices are low and high chairs are available.

Tooting & Balham

West Streathamites share **Tooting Common** (Tooting Bec Road, SW17) with the denizens of Balham. It's a wide open space with woods, tennis courts, ponds, football pitches, a couple of good playgrounds for the under-8s, riding, Tooting Bec athletics track and **Tooting Bec Lido** (8871 7198), where up to 2,000 people a day gather in summer to enjoy the pools and the 1930s café (*see p263*).

As Clapham rose stratospherically in the house-price market through the 1990s, Tooting and Balham soaked up the overspill. Nowadays they're as sought after and almost as fantastically expensive as their prettier neighbour, though thanks to their resistance to wholesale gentrification they're more interesting.

Tooting is home to a well-established Asian community, and the annual Diwali Festival of Light (October/November) is celebrated with a street party and lights strung along Tooting High Street and

Royal Botanic (Kew) Gardens.
See p151.

Checking out the goods at **Merton Abbey Mills**. *See p154.*

Upper Tooting Road. The area around and between Tooting Bec and Tooting Broadway has a number of excellent restaurants serving South Asian food, though their proprietors don't go out of their way to encourage diners to bring children along – only **Masaledar** (121 Upper Tooting Road, SW17, 8767 7676), a modern café-style Indian restaurant, supplies high chairs and toys. Babies and children are welcome in most places, however, and smaller portions are available on request.

Up on Balham High Road the **Art of Health & Yoga Centre** (No.280, 8682 1800; *see also p267*) promises serenity, flexibility and muscle tone.

Putney

The river takes on a semi-rural aspect at **Putney Bridge** – looking back down the Thames you can catch glimpses of London's skyline but upstream the Putney treeline is pretty well all you can see. The scene is familiar to many as the starting point of the Oxford and Cambridge Boat Race; indeed, the stretch of river between Putney and Barnes is lined with boathouses belonging to London schools and the university and with various corporate boatclubs. Spring Saturdays are particularly busy as boatloads of strapping punters and rowers take to the water.

Back from the river, Putney has a number of green spaces – **Putney Heath** is the eastern edge of the huge piece of common land that eventually peters out where Wimbledon Common joins Richmond Park. In total, it's three times the size of Hampstead Heath but has much less glamour, and there are no areas set aside for children's play. As with all of London's heath and common land, it's best avoided after dark.

Infinitely tamer, but with more to entertain kids, is **Leaders Gardens**, at the end of Asilone Road. This dainty little riverside park is a delight for all the family, with two play areas and tennis courts. The café (Loo Loo's, 8246 6847, so called because it used to be a loo) enjoys views across the river to Fulham Palace and the football stadium. It's strong on child-friendly meals, which cost from £2.75 to £3.50 with unlimited squash and ice-cream. Children's parties start at £5.75 a head. This also the place to come to book a tennis court (no bookings are taken by phone). In a small open area of the gardens is Beverley Brook, which runs from Putney Heath to Wimbledon.

Where to eat

There are lots of places to eat round here, and even among restaurants that don't cater specifically to junior customers, few will make you feel like a pariah if you bring one or two through the door. The **Phoenix Bar & Grill** (162-4 Lower Richmond Road, SW15, 8780 3131) has Modern European dishes and a special kids' menu that includes old favourites such as chicken and chips or roast beef for £6.50 and up, including ice-cream. Staff provide crayons, comics and high chairs, and there's a lovely sun terrace for summer. Lively Italian **Del Buongustaio** (283 Putney Bridge Road, SW15, 8780 9361) also has high chairs and a children's menu that includes pasta and vegetable dishes and ice-cream. Just before Putney Heath, the **Spencer Arms** (237 Lower Richmond Road, SW15, 8789 5126) allows children in the bar area, where they can feed on nuggets, chips and the like from as little as £1.49.

Barnes, Mortlake & Kew

Fans of '70s supergroup T Rex come to Barnes to pay their respects to Marc Bolan, killed when the Mini driven by his girlfriend crashed into a tree in 1977. Constantly decorated with wilting flowers and tacked-on notes, scarves and little tin hearts, the spindly tree is loathed by most locals. But they are proud of the **WWT (Wildfowl & Wetlands Trust) Wetland Centre**, a unique mosaic of wetland habitats created from scratch from four concrete Thames Water reservoirs. Beyond the Wetland Centre, this entire stretch of Thames-side London is pretty and residential. Mortlake was a fashionable retreat from the 16th century onwards and remains a pleasant backwater on the way to the **Royal Botanic Gardens** at Kew.

Public Record Office
Ruskin Avenue, Richmond, Surrey (8392 5202/ www.pro.gov.uk/events). **Open** 9am-5pm Mon, Wed-Fri; 10am-7pm Tue; 9am-7pm Thur; 9.30am-5.30pm Sat; *Tours* 12.30pm 2nd Fri of mth. **Admission** free. *Tours* free.
The Education & Visitor Centre in the Public Record Office is

an odd hoard of national treasures ranging from the *Domesday Book* to the deed poll that records Reginald Dwight's decision to change his name to Elton John. Regular events in the Visitor Centre include tours by a costumed guide, who tells the stories surrounding various documents in the archive. There are also calligraphy workshops, lectures and poetry readings – call for an events leaflet or see the website for more details. *Buggy access. Nappy-changing facilities. Nearest picnic place: grounds of Public Record Office.*

Royal Botanic Gardens (Kew Gardens)
Richmond, Surrey (switchboard 8332 5000/info 8332 5655/www.rbgkew.org.uk). Kew Gardens tube/rail/ Kew Bridge rail/riverboat to Kew Pier. **Open** *Feb, Mar* 9.30am-5.30pm daily. *Apr-Sept* 9.30am-6.30pm Mon-Fri; 9.30am-7.30pm Sat, Sun. *Oct-Jan* 9.30am-3.45pm daily. **Admission** (LP) £6.50; £4.50 concessions; free under-16s. **Credit** AmEx, DC, MC, V.
The botanical collection at Kew covers a massive 300 acres. Plant hunters established the gardens here in the late 18th century and it's now a world-famous centre for horticultural research. You don't have to be a plant expert to enjoy the wonders it has to offer, but getting around all its highlights is a tall order for small children. First-time visitors, especially those with elderly relatives or small children, would be wise to use the Kew Explorer bus, which takes you round all the main sights. A hop-on hop-off ticket lasts all day and costs £2.50 (adults) and £1.50 (children). Free guided tours leave the Victoria Gate at 11am and 2pm daily.
The colour-coded maps are invaluable for planning your route and locating the nearest food or toilet stops. Of the six places to eat spread through the gardens, none is particularly cheap, though between them they cater for all appetites, providing everything from full hot meals to pizzas, burgers, snacks, cakes and coffee. The various cafés are the best places to go for loos and nappy-changing facilities.
If mobility isn't a problem, pick up one of the self-guided trails at the visitors' centre. 'Kids' Kew' has checklists of plants to find and a timeline of buildings to plot a course round; other trails designed to appeal to families tie in with

Water ways: messing about...

... in Turk Launches
There's been a Turk on the Thames since the 12th century, when an early ancestor was commissioned to build two galleys for the defence of the realm close to the Tower of London. Now the family operates out of its boatyards on the upper reaches of the tidal Thames, running steamers and pleasure boats from Richmond through Kingston to Hampton Court and back. The beautiful steamers are polished and buffed up by their proud crew and provide a romantic river trip on a summer afternoon. You can even hop on for the short trip from Hampton Court's Broad Walk Gate to Hampton Court station.
Turk Launches *Town End Pier, 68 High Street, Kingston-upon-Thames, Surrey (8546 2434). Kingston rail.* **Tickets** *single Kingston–Hampton Court £3.50; Richmond–Kingston £4.50.*

Richmond–Hampton Court £5.50. For children, deduct £1. For return fares, add £1.50. **No credit cards**.

... in rowing boats
Hire a rowing boat on the Thames at Richmond and make like an Edwardian for an hour or a day.
South-west London's riverfront is famous around the world as the course of the annual University Boat Race, which starts at Putney Bridge and ends at Mortlake. If you fancy trying the sport for yourself, a couple of the clubs along this stretch of the Thames have junior sections and are affiliated to Go-Row, the national junior rowing programme, which aims to get more young people involved in the sport (for more information, *see p267*). *Richmond Bridge Boat House (8948 8270).* **Tickets** *£3 per person per hr; accompanied children half price.* **No credit cards**.

seasonal themes. Alternatively, you could construct your own route round some of the reliable children's favourites. For example, you could take a trip back three billion years to experience plant evolution through the Silurian, Carboniferous and Cretaceous periods in the Evolution House, the most entertaining place for children, which contains some ancient species and puts on various special effects (smoking volcano, glowing lava flow, dinosaur footprints and so on).

The elegant Palm House, where the gallery affords an inspiring view of the dense, dripping foliage, contains plants with very early connections with Kew. Beneath the Palm House, the Marine Display's tanks contain fish, corals and primitive algae.

On the other side of the pond, opposite the Palm House, Museum Number 1 houses the Plants & People exhibition, which, through displays and a variety of touch-screens, demonstrates the uses to which people have put plants through the various ages. Nearby, the Princess of Wales Conservatory houses ten climate zones under one glass roof; the collection of carnivorous plants is reliably fascinating. The paths through the conservatory are wide enough for buggies, but when it's very crowded it can be a bit stressful.

If so, take the opportunity to construct a trail round some of the Greek temples and other decorative structures that punctuate these enduringly popular grounds.
Buggy access. Cafés. Nappy-changing facilities. Nearest picnic place: Kew Gardens grounds. Restaurant. Shop.

Where to eat

The best-known place to take afternoon tea in Kew is the **Maids of Honour Tearooms** (288 Kew Road, 8940 2752, closed Sun). Try one of the legendary Maid of Honour (vanilla custard) tarts. If the queues defeat you, buy some cakes from the shop and eat them on the green.

Kew Greenhouse (1 Station Parade, 8940 0183) serves generous portions of comfort food, including cakes, pastries and coffee. Sit outside if you want to leave the buggy up; otherwise, high chairs are provided. The plant-filled back room is a pleasant reminder of the botanical treasures down the road.

In & around: the WWT Wetland Centre

In May 2000 the **WWT Wetland Centre** in Barnes opened to provide 105 acres of habitat for more than 140 bird species, 300-plus species of butterfly and moth, six varieties of bat, four of amphibians and approximately 20 of dragonfly. The following year 200,000 humans came to see them.

Only four miles (as the cormorant flies) from the very centre of London, this extraordinary site provides 14 different wetland habitats for birds from around the world, from New Zealand whitewater to African floodplains, East Asian rice paddies to Hawaiian lavaflow.

Spend a few minutes in the visitors' centre before you kit yourself out with a couple of children's trails and a pair of hired binoculars (£5) if you haven't brought your own. Then stop at the observatory for stunning views across the reserve. The viewing platform is encased in 30-foot high sheets of glass and is flooded with light bouncing off the water below. If you look out beyond the lakes you'll recognise enough London landmarks to ground you in the capital but otherwise it's easy to believe you're an alien in a strange new world. Luckily, there are plenty of guides around to help you tell your sparrow from your sparrowhawk. Because the Wetland Centre is a nature reserve first and a tourist attraction second, what you see will depend on what the birds decide to show you. The attractions change with the seasons – an early evening in summer will reveal bats wheeling over the water, in winter you may see flocks of Russian and Arctic migrants arriving.

At 11am and 2pm knowledgeable rangers take guided tours around the reserve to explain Wildfowl & Wetlands Trust founder Peter Scott's dream of bringing wildlife right into the heart of the city and to regale you with bird facts. Each

walk takes around an hour and a half, so if you think this is too much for the small children under your wing you may prefer to start with a waddle around the farmyard with the ducks and geese or set off on a Great Pond Safari at the thatched Pond Zone. The raised ponds may look like calm patches of water but underneath the surface they are seething cauldrons of life. Dip in and haul up a rich catch of water snails, insect larvae, sticklebacks and water fleas.

A self-guided tour can be arranged using the maps provided at the visitors' centre. From the central cluster of buildings at the entrance to the Wetlands Centre branch two routes around the public bits of the reserve. The southern route is about people and wetlands. From the farmyard follow the path past a series of sustainable gardens into the little thatched house that explains what the wetlands have done for us. Coracles, Fenland stilts and peat creels give a glimpse into a vanishing way of life. At the far end of the southern walk is the Peacock Tower, a three-storey hide with a lift, so people in wheelchairs and buggies have equal access to the spectacular 360° views across the entire reserve.

Retrace your steps to the centre buildings to the large licensed café. In the summer there are tables on the decking outside. Or bring a picnic and eat at one of the tables just outside the visitors' centre. Call in at the Discovery Centre for half an hour's button-pressing and fact-finding in the 'infogrotto'. During half-terms, holidays and weekends children may like to join in one of the arts and crafts activities that take place upstairs.

Back outside, the western walk takes in a whistlestop tour of the world's wetland habitats in a series of minizones. Take your time and find your

The **Depot** (Tideway Yard, Mortlake High Street, SW14, 8878 9462) has sensational views of the Thames and a children's menu; *see p187*. If you're looking for somewhere to eat after a day at the Wetland Centre (*see below*), try the branches of **Browns** (201 Castelnau, SW13, 8748 4486) or **Tootsies** (147 Church Road, SW13, 8748 3630; *see also p191*), both of which have children's menus.

Wimbledon

Just as Kew is synonymous in most people's minds with its gardens, Wimbledon's identity is tightly bound up with the summer fortnight at the All England Lawn Tennis Club. Next door to the museum, **Wimbledon Park** has a lively youth tennis programme at the public courts during the holidays and after school, for those children not

quite up to Henman's standard. Pick up a brochure from the tennis hut from April to September. There's also a paddling pool, a sandpit and a large boating lake. Call 8947 4894 for more information about sports courses and watersports activities.

There may not be any wombles on **Wimbledon Common**, but this huge, partially wooded expanse has cycle paths, five ponds, sites of special scientific interest and riding tracks. For riding lessons, try **Wimbledon Village Stables** (24A-B High Street, SW19, 8946 8579; *see also p264*) or **Ridgway Stables** (93 Ridgway, SW19, 8946 7400).

On a wide open space where the common joins Putney Heath is Britain's last hollow-post flour mill. This is where Baden-Powell began writing *Scouting for Boys* in 1908. Now the **Windmill Museum** (Windmill Road, 8947 2825; £1 adults, 50p children), it is open to visitors on weekends and bank holidays

favourites, from the Australian black swans to the kingfishers flashing out of their purpose-built wall outside the Headley Hide. Acknowledged stars of the WWT breeding programme are the Laysan ducks in the Hawaiian Islands zone. This species once teetered on the brink of extinction, its entire population reduced to a single female in the wild. Luckily (and what are the odds?), the female had eggs to lay and slowly and with infinite care the species was bred back from the edge of oblivion.

Both the walks have plenty of information points along the way, some of them with touch-screen displays. Paths around the reserve are broad, smooth and buggy-friendly and each world zone is separated from the next by a gate with the happy side effect that rampaging toddlers can't charge too far ahead! Beyond the paths are acres of lake, lagoon, grazing marsh and wader scrape.

Away from the Wetland Centre, sights are few and far between, but it's a lovely area to explore nonetheless. Pretty and residential **Mortlake** was fashionable from the 1500s onwards, but is today overshadowed by its more famous neighbour, Kew, known as the home of the world-renowned **Royal Botanic Gardens**. Travelling north up Castelnau from the centre is the great loop of the Thames at Hammersmith Bridge. All the playing fields on this promontory belong to the lucky pupils whose parents can afford St Paul's School. If you walk or take a bus as far as Hammersmith Bridge and cross the river here, you're back in the city, with its bustle, traffic, noise, shops – and public transport, to take your weary legs home.

WWT Wetland Centre

Queen Elizabeth's Walk, SW13 (8409 4400/ www.wetlandcentre.org.uk). Hammersmith tube then 283 bus/Barnes rail/33, 72 bus. **Open** *Mar-Oct* 9.30am-6pm daily. *Nov-Feb* 9.30am-5pm daily. Last entry 1hr before closing. Closed 25 Dec. *Tours* 11am, 2.30pm daily. *Feeding tours* noon, 3.30pm daily. **Admission** £6.75; £5.50 concessions; £4 4-16s; £17.50 family (2+2); free under-4s. *Tours* free. *Feeding tours* free. **Credit** MC, V.
Buggy access. Café. Nappy-changing facilities. Nearest picnic place: picnic area in grounds. Shop.

from April to October (school parties can go at other times by arrangement). The little café that adjoins it has tables outside with plenty of room for smaller children to run around, though beware of cars turning into the (free) car park alongside.

To follow the Windmill Nature Trail, buy a trail guide from the ranger's office (£1.50) or the new information centre – it has areas of special interest marked along the way. If you're visiting in winter, it's advisable to contact the ranger's office beforehand on 8788 7655 (9am-4pm). **Putney Vale Cemetery**, in the north-east corner of the common (accessible from Roehampton Vale), is one of the largest graveyards in London. Lillie Langtry was buried here in 1929. On the east side of the common, the disused Bluegate Gravel Pit forms an idyllic and peaceful lake, barely disturbed by the murmur of traffic on Parkside. You need to cross the road and go down Calonne Road to discover Wimbledon's biggest surprise: set amid prime south London suburbia, the fully fledged **Buddhapadipa Temple**, a Thai Buddhist site, welcomes visitors at weekends (1-6pm Sat; 8.30-10.30am, 12.30-6pm Sun).

To the west side of the common is **Cannizaro Park**, with an ornamental garden, rare trees and plants, a water feature and an open-air theatre that hosts a variety of summer shows (8543 2222).

Wimbledon's cyclists have an organisation that arranges Parks, Playgrounds and Pub rides (PPP; 8946 0912). This is a monthly programme of 10-15 mile cycle rides, along quiet or traffic-free routes with child-friendly stops. The trips start from Wimbledon station on the last Sunday of the month.

Wimbledon Broadway is home to two theatres: the Edwardian **Wimbledon Theatre** (No.93, 8540 0362), which has some family shows and a seasonal panto, and the lovely **Polka Theatre** for kids.

Follow the Morden Road from South Wimbledon tube to visit the animals at **Deen City Farm**, from where you can continue along the River Wandle to **Merton Abbey Mills**, where the waterwheel still turns and a market and the **Colour House Theatre** (*see also p224*) attracts families at weekends.

Deen City Farm

39 Windsor Avenue, SW19 (8543 5300/ www.deencityfarm.co.uk). Colliers Wood tube/200 bus. **Open** 9am-5pm Tue-Sun. **Admission** free; donations welcome.

Home to cows, donkeys, sheep, goats, pigs and fowl, among other animals, Deen has a friendly staff and teams of keen junior volunteers during the school holidays. The latter are young farmers (8-16-year-olds) who sign up for the chance to feed, muck out and look after the animals with the farm staff.

Find out about animal sponsorship schemes as a way of supporting the farm. There's a riding school for both able-bodied and disabled children, and you can hire the party room for birthday parties.

Buggy access. Café. Nappy-changing facilities. Nearest picnic place: Morden Hall Park. Shop.

Scary Boris at **Wimbledon Lawn Tennis Museum**.

Polka Theatre

240 The Broadway, SW19 (8543 4888/ www.polkatheatre.com). South Wimbledon tube/rail. **Open** *Box office phoneline* 9.30am-4.30pm Mon-Fri; 10am-5pm Sat. *Personal callers* 9.30am-4.30pm Tue-Fri. **Tickets** £5-£12.50. **Credit** AmEx, MC, V.

South-west London's dedicated children's arts centre has frequent first-class new shows in two theatres, plus a whole load of workshops and after-school and holiday clubs. There's a playground just outside, lovely rocking horses inside and a jolly café serving own-made cakes, biscuits, fruit and hot lunch dishes. The toy stalls outside the main auditorium, and the smaller Adventure Theatre downstairs (for under-5s), have show-related toys and pocket-money trinkets and stationery. It's easy to spend time here without even seeing a show, but the work receives consistently good reviews so you'd be mad not to. *See also p225.*

Buggy access. Café. Nappy-changing facilities. Nearest picnic place: theatre garden. Shop.

Tiger's Eye

42 Station Road, SW19 (8543 1655). Colliers Wood or South Wimbledon tube. **Open** 10am-6.30pm daily. Closed 25, 26 Dec, 1 Jan. **Admission** *Mon-Fri* £4.50 2-10s; £2 under-2s. *Sat, Sun* £4.50 2-10s; £2.25 under-2s. **No credit cards.**

The Tiger's Eye is an indoor playcentre for children up to the age of 10. It's a vast barn of a place, complete with towering soft play equipment to climb on, slide down and bounce off. In short, good fun.

Buggy access. Café. Nappy-changing facilities. Nearest picnic place: Merton Abbey Park/Merton Park.

Wimbledon Lawn Tennis Museum & Tour

Centre Court, All England Lawn Tennis Club, Church Road, SW19 (8946 6131/www.wimbledon.org/ museum/education). Southfields tube/39, 93, 200 bus. **Open** 10.30am-5pm daily. Closed 24-26 Dec, 1 Jan. *Spectators only* during championships. *Tours* Mar-Oct grounds only £12.75; £11.75 concessions; £10.75 under-16s. **Admission** (LP) £5.50; £4.50 concessions; £3.50 5-16s; free under-5s. **Credit** MC, V.

From the lawns of 19th-century sphairstike (as it was then known) to the multi-million-pound sport of today, more than 150 years of social and sporting history are encapsulated in this well-designed space. Most interesting are the mock-up of an Edwardian tennis party and the section on the history of the game since 1968, with touch-screen commentaries on past and present stars and videos of past championships. The museum is full of unusual information of interest even to those who aren't big fans of the game, and for obsessives there's personal memorabilia aplenty, including some of Pat Cash's headbands and Goran Ivanisevic's 2001 championship winning racket. During the championship fortnight (24 June-7 July 2002), the museum is open only to holders of match tickets; if you come during this time, make sure it's during the first few days to avoid the crowds. Needless to say, the place does particularly brisk business when rain stops play and the covers are drawn over the hallowed lawns. Daily behind-the-scenes tours are also available throughout the summer; call for further details.

The education department is busy all year round planning tennis-based workshops that tie in with the national curriculum for primary-school-aged children. During term time school groups visit for guided tours and tennis history and heritage lessons. During school holidays, children aged 4-11 are well served with fun things to do and see. Easter workshops include egg painting and boater decorating, summer activities number art workshops, museum workshops featuring actors dressed up in Victorian tennis gear and fun and games both outdoors and in. Go to the website to find out more about the school holiday programmes, or ring for booking requirements and prices.

Buggy access. Café. Nappy-changing facilities. Nearest picnic place: benches outside museum/Wimbledon Park. Shop.

Where to eat

Next to Wimbledon Odeon is **Jim Thompson's Flaming Wok** (141 The Broadway, SW19, 8540 5540), which sizzles up Indonesian, Malaysian, Vietnamese, Thai and Burmese dishes. Children can opt for a mini-size bento box.

In the Centre Court shopping centre, **Footlights** (8944 9970) is a café, restaurant and bar offering Mexican, American and European food, plus a special under-12s menu (two courses plus a drink for £4.25). For all parents who adhere to the adage 'you can't go wrong with pasta', **Café Pasta** (8 High Street, SW19, 8944 6893), where children can request small portions, is a lifesaver.

The **Hand in Hand** pub in Wimbledon Village (6 Crooked Billet, SW19, 8946 5720) has a no-smoking family room and a front courtyard. Children's meals are £2.95. Just off the common, the **Fox & Grapes** (Camp Road, SW19, 8946 5599) also welcomes kids; smaller portions at reduced prices can be arranged.

Richmond

Until the early 16th century Richmond was known as Sheen, but its name was changed when Henry VII acquired the local manor house and named it after his earldom in Yorkshire. Elizabeth I spent the last few summers of her life here until she died in 1603. The main reason for braving the heavy traffic that plagues this area is the wide expanse of **Richmond Park**, which, at eight miles across at its widest point, is the biggest city park in Europe and the nearest London gets to wild countryside. It is the last vestige of the great oak forests that surrounded London until medieval times. Most of it is now rough and rolling grassland; on a sunny Sunday the open spaces fill with all-terrain buggies and ring with the sound of fractious toddlers. Herds of red and fallow deer roam freely, much to the fascination of kids, but bear in mind that these wild animals can be fierce in autumn during the rutting season (signs warn you not to get too close to the deer).

The **Old Deer Park**, which you reach if you walk south from Kew Gardens, is home to all things sporty – there's the Royal Mid-Surrey Golf Club, the Richmond Athletic Ground, tennis courts, playgrounds and a wonderful outdoor swimming pool, part of Richmond's **Pools on the Park** complex (*see p263*). On sunny summer weekends, people come from miles around to picnic on the grassy slopes around the pool (there are paddling pools for toddlers) and spend the day dipping deliciously in and out of the cool blue water. To learn more about the area's illustrious royal history, visit the **Museum of Richmond**.

Museum of Richmond
Old Town Hall, Whittaker Avenue, Richmond, Surrey (8332 1141/www.museumofrichmond.com). Richmond tube/rail. **Open** *May-Sept* 11am-5pm Tue-Sat; 1-4pm Sun. *Nov-Apr* 11am-5pm Tue-Sat. Closed 25, 26 Dec, 1 Jan. **Admission** £2; £1 concessions; free under-16s. **No credit cards.**
The Museum of Richmond, as the name suggests, holds a comprehensive collection of information about this most royal of boroughs. Richmond was a seat of kings during the 12th century, when Henry I lived at Sheen Palace on the south-west corner of what is now Richmond Green. Successive monarchs enjoyed its riverside location, until Henry VII redeveloped the entire site and renamed it Richmond after his Yorkshire earldom. The history lesson runs up to life in the town during World War II.
Buggy access. Lift. Nearest picnic place: Richmond Green. Shop.

Where to eat

A number of child-friendly restaurant chains have a Richmond outpost. **Wok Wok** (30 Hill Street, 8332 2646) has an excellent children's menu with oriental basics such as egg-fried rice, chicken satay and noodles any which way. At **Café Flo** (149 Kew Road, 8332 2598) the children's menu includes sausage 'n' mash, chicken and chips, and pasta. If it has to be pizza, there's a **Pizza Express** (20 Hill Street, 8940 8951). There's also a justly successful

Walk: the Thames Path

From Putney to Teddington is a 12-mile walk through all the different landscapes of the Thames. It's a fair old hike, but you can drop in and out of the walk wherever you like along its length – nowhere is far from a bus route or a train station.

Walk 1: Putney Bridge to Hammersmith Bridge

This two-mile walk starts just upstream of Putney Bridge, where the river is bristling with rowers both on the water and carrying their boats to and from the boathouses that line the towpath. **Loo Loo's Café** in Leaders Gardens provides a snacking opportunity and a playground before crossing Beverley Brook and getting back to the towpath. After about a mile, Queen Elizabeth Walk takes you to the entrance to the **WWT Wetland Centre** (*see p152*), where it's perfectly possible to spend the rest of the day among the wildfowl and their global habitats. If you decide instead to press on with the walk along the Thames Path, skirt along the riverside edge of the Wetland Centre, keeping an eye out for the herons, cormorants and watervoles that call this stretch of the river home. Hammersmith Bridge lies just round the bend of the Thames.

Walk 2: Hammersmith Bridge to Chiswick Bridge

This two-and-a-half-mile stretch has a distinct away-from-it-all feel thanks to the watermeadows and playing fields that line the river. It's nature trek country, with lots of different trees to spot. It's

also a popular cycle way for much of its length so be ready to leap into the ditch as the very serious cyclists come steaming along.

Walk 3: Chiswick Bridge to Richmond Bridge

A four-mile walk takes you all the way along to Richmond Bridge. Speed along the **Chiswick** stretch where there isn't much to delay you and under **Kew Bridge** to a wide path with a park and playground to the left. Detour up towards **Kew Green** for **Maids of Honour** (vanilla custard tarts)

Spanish tapas restaurant, **Don Fernando's** (27F The Quadrant, 8948 6447; *see also p187*), where staff make a fuss of children as they tuck into snacky, colourful food. For meaty Californian dinners, **Canyon** (Riverside, near Richmond Bridge, Richmond, Surrey, 8948 2944; *see also p186*) is one of the best spots in London for al fresco dining.

Further south-west

The southern reaches of the river towards Twickenham are beautiful places to ride a bike or walk the Thames Path (*see above*). There are plenty more sights to see along this stretch. **Marble Hill House** overlooking the Thames in Marble Hill Park is a perfect Palladian villa; neighbouring **Orleans House** (Riverside, Twickenham, 8892 0221; free; call for opening times) was built in 1710 for James Johnston, William III's secretary of state for Scotland, and was later home to the exiled Duke of Orléans, hence the name; and **Ham House** is a handsome, red-brick, riverside mansion with a

beautiful garden. Carrying on along the river past Twickenham, you come to the **Museum of Rugby**.

From Twickers, the river passes the busy shopping centre of Kingston-upon-Thames, then curves around to **Hampton Court Palace**. Once Cardinal Wolsey's country seat, this was taken over by Henry VIII, who spent much time and three honeymoons here.

Ham House

Ham Street, Richmond, Surrey (8940 1950/ www.nationaltrust.org.uk). Richmond tube/rail, then 371 bus. **Open** (NT) *House* late Mar-Oct 1-5pm Mon-Wed, Sat, Sun. Closed 25, 26 Dec, 1 Jan. *Tours* pre-booking essential Wed. **Prices** £7.50 non-members; £4 members. Phone for membership details & prices. **Admission** (NT) £6; £3 5-15s; £15 family (2+3); free under-5s. *Garden only* £2; £1 5-15s; free under-5s. **Credit** AmEx, MC, V.
Built in 1610, this enchanting house is lavishly appointed with 17th-century furniture, paintings and decor. From the house, water meadows lead down to the Thames. The part of the grounds known as the wilderness is, in fact, a careful-ly planted, almost maze-like section divided into garden

at the eponymous tearooms. A good ploy is to take them away and eat them on the green, where you're right by the Main Gate for **Kew Gardens**. It takes all day to do the gardens justice, so stick to the towpath for views in and leave a proper visit to the gardens for another day. You can just see over the wall to the Dutch gables of **Kew Palace**, where George III and his enormous brood spent holidays playing farmers. On the other side of the river is **Syon House**, with its child-friendly park and huge adventure playground. You can reach it by the Isleworth ferry on weekends from May to September. From the ferry it's another mile to **Richmond Bridge**.

Walk 4: Richmond Bridge to Teddington

The last two and a half miles of the tidal Thames leads through cow pasture and tidal flood meadows out to the locks at **Teddington**. It's not the most buggy-friendly stretch of the walk since there are a couple of stiles to get over and there's no path across the pastures. But there are refreshment points at the beginning and end, and the view from **Richmond Hill** before you start is awesome. On a clear day, it is alleged, you can see Windsor Castle. The elaborate locking system at Teddington is mesmerising.

For more information about the Thames Path, including a booklist, brochures, events leaflets and maps, contact the National Trails Office (Cultural Services), Holton, Oxford OX33 1QQ (01865 810224).

rooms. The gardens are all now fully restored and charmingly laid out. New for 2002 is the Still House, traditionally used for fermenting rose petals to make scent. Family fun events take place from Easter to autumn: there are egg hunts, teddy bears' picnics, summer Sunday jazz evenings, ghost tours and creepy-crawly hunts. Ring to be put on the mailing list and you'll receive details of all such wacky occasions. *Café. Nappy-changing facilities. Nearest picnic place: Orangery Gardens. Shop.*

Hampton Court Palace

East Molesey, Surrey (8781 9500/www.hampton-court-palace.org.uk). Hampton Court rail/riverboat from Westminster or Richmond to Hampton Court Pier (Apr-Oct). **Open** *Palace* Apr-Oct 10.15am-6pm Mon; 9.30am-6pm Tue-Sun. Nov-Mar 10.15am-4.30pm Mon; 9.30am-4.30pm Tue-Sun (last entry 45mins before closing). *Park* dawn-dusk daily. **Admission** *Palace, courtyard, cloister & maze* £11; £8.25 concessions; £7.25 5-15s; £33 family (max 5 people); free under-5s. *Maze only* £3; £2 5-15s. **Credit** AmEx, MC, V.
The royal palace beside the Thames has more than 600 acres of parkland, including 60 acres of formal gardens with fountains, ponds and the elaborate Privy Garden restored a few years ago. The maze is what most people love here, however. They pay to get lost in it. The west face of the palace is a

Tudor extravaganza, the east face is Christopher Wren's 17th-century remodelling for William and Mary. Tour highlights include Henry VIII's hammer-beam-roofed Great Hall, the Renaissance Picture Gallery, and the huge kitchens, where hundreds toiled to cater for the palace's daily consumption of six oxen, 40 sheep and 1,000-plus larks, pheasants, pigeons and swans. Today, period-dressed minions make 16th-century dishes, turn meat on a spit and talk to visitors.
Every school holiday special events pull in a family crowd. Attractions of summer 2002 include Fool School, at which children receive lessons in juggling, stilt-walking, falling over and general tomfoolery as perfected by the two madcaps who humoured the King himself: Will Somers and Jane the Fool. Musicians wander the formal gardens in period costume in a month-long Music and Majesty special (1 August-1 September). October's half-term event is entitled Pirates at the Palace, so dig out your eye patch and cutlass. The world-famous Great Kitchens at Hampton Court Palace come alive in November and December when a Mastercook and his team prepare a series of feasts fit for a king, using handmade, authentic utensils and dressed for their historical roles. Ring for details of all seasonal events.
Buggy access. Café. Nappy-changing facilities. Nearest picnic place: palace gardens. Shop.

Marble Hill House

Richmond Road, Twickenham, Middx (8892 5115/www.english-heritage.org.uk). Richmond tube/rail/St Margaret's rail/33, 90, 290, H22, R70 bus. **Open** *Apr-Sept* 10am-6pm daily. *Oct* 10am-5pm daily. Closed Nov-Mar, 24-26 Dec, 1-16 Jan. *Tours* by prior arrangement; phone for details. **Admission** (EH, LP) £3.30; £2.50 concessions; £1.70 5-15s; free under-5s. **Credit** MC, V.
Set in acres of parkland beside the Thames, this Palladian villa was built in 1724-9 for Henrietta Howard, the mistress of George II. It was later occupied by Mrs Fitzherbert, George IV's secret wife. The house has been immaculately restored with Georgian furnishings and paintings. There are concerts in the park on Sunday evenings in summer. Send an SAE for an events brochure to find out about family attractions planned throughout the year.
Café (in park). Nearest picnic place: Marble Hill Park. Shop.

Museum of Rugby/ Twickenham Stadium

Gate K, Twickenham Rugby Stadium, Rugby Road, Twickenham, Middx (8892 8877/www.rfu.com). Hounslow East tube then 281 bus/Twickenham rail. **Open** *Museum* 10am-5pm Tue-Sat; 2-5pm Sun. Last entry 30mins before closing. *Tours* 10.30am, noon, 1.30pm, 3pm Tue-Sat; 3pm Sun. **Admission** Combined ticket £6; £4 concessions; £19 family. *Museum only* (match day only) £3; £2 concessions. **Credit** MC, V.
If you want to learn more about the game for ruffians played by gentlefolk, book a stadium tour at Twickers. They take place on non-match days only and are highly entertaining and well organised. Participants are taken round the players' tunnel, the England dressing room, the royal box, pitchside, the top row of the famous stadium and the museum. The museum is open whether there's a match on or not and provides an amusing insight into the history of world rugby. Interactive exhibits include a real scrum machine and have-a-go footage of some of the greatest tries of all time. Nostalgic fans can listen to early radio commentary and muse on the days when players still wore bow ties. The shop has the country's largest cache of England rugby merchandise: call for a catalogue or check out the website.
Buggy access. Nappy-changing facilities. Restaurant. Shop.

West London

Urban chic and suburban cool, west London oozes class.

Float on west to **Little Venice**. *See p161*.

Paddington & Bayswater

When the famous station, with its magnificent Isambard Kingdom Brunel roof, was built in the 19th century, Paddington was the focus of a population boom. The Grand Junction Canal and the railways brought workers and families to live here.

Today, the area is prosperous and cosmopolitan, and becoming more so all the time. High-rises of luxury flats are already being finished on the land just north of the station (officially known as Paddington Central) and to the east (West End Quay), and before long these will be joined by many new shops and restaurants. A new Hilton hotel, complete with swanky bar Steam, recently opened at the front of the station.

Paddington station is the ideal venue for marmalade sandwich eating. A £63-million revamp created the elegant centrepiece of the station, with smart cafés and shops where you can while away the hours waiting for delayed trains. If your children are into spotting them, 10p will buy a pass to admire all the platforms and watch the engines. Before you flee

with your offspring to a different area, it's worth mentioning the **Alexander Fleming Laboratory Museum**, which may be of interest to older children.

In the heart of Bayswater are the bright lights of **Whiteley's** shopping centre. A branch of **Gymboree** (0800 092 0911) has opened here, for music, dance and fun for under-5s and their parents.

Alexander Fleming Laboratory Museum

*St Mary's Hospital, Praed Street, W2 (7725 6528).
Paddington tube/rail/7, 15, 27, 36 bus.* **Open** 10am-1pm Mon-Thur. By appointment 2-5pm Mon-Thur; 10am-5pm Fri. Closed 24 Dec-1 Jan, bank hols. **Admission** (LP) £2; £1 concessions, children. **No credit cards**.
The museum focuses on recreating the environment in which Alexander Fleming discovered penicillin. It all began in 1928, when the scientist discovered a mouldy growth on a Petri dish of bacteria, which prompted him to start research of his own. The staff run special tours for family and school groups (other visitors get a guided tour as part of the entrance fee). The education programme caters to science classes, both in schools and in this lab. Visitors see a video about Fleming's life and the ways in which penicillin has changed global health care.
Nearest picnic place: Hyde Park. Shop.

Where to eat

Whiteley's shopping centre – in particular the second floor – is at the forefront of the Bayswater eating experience. Branches of **ASK** (7792 1977) and **Café Rouge** (7221 1509) keep families happy, and fans of oriental cuisine appreciate **Poons** (7792 2884). The **Great American Bagel Factory** is a spacious, buggy-friendly environment serving a vast range of bagels with different fillings. Just outside Whiteley's is a branch of **TGI Friday's** (96-8 Bishop's Bridge Road, W2, 7229 8600; *see also p179*), where most children will find something appealing on the Sesame Street menu. Diagonally opposite is a **Tiger Lil's** (7221 2622; *see also p187*) for stir-fries.

The area of **Edgware Road** running from Praed Street to Marble Arch has become known as 'Little Mecca' as it's the hub of the Middle Eastern community in London. As a result, this stretch is an ideal spot for a bit of other-worldly dining; most kids will be fascinated by the hubbly-bubbly rituals while enjoying falafels and juices at **Ranoush Juice** (No.43, 7723 5929). The ices at **Regent Milk Bar** (No.362, 7723 8669) are worth the walk.

Maida Vale, Kilburn & Queen's Park

These areas lie north of the Westway (A40), which thunders across Edgware Road. Maida Vale is characterised by wide avenues of mansion blocks, white stucco houses and the canal at **Little Venice**. Much of the activities here surround the **Grand Union Canal** (*see p161*), along which you can walk to London Zoo or Regent's Park in under an hour. If little legs aren't up to it, you could get the Waterbus to Camden Lock (*see p99*).

Just north of Maida Vale is an easily missed entrance to **Paddington Recreation Ground**. This is a huge play area dominated by masses of tennis courts and five-a-side football pitches. It also has a decent café and two excellent play enclosures for young children. Many kids come here for tennis coaching after school and during the summer holidays: ring 7635 4303 for more details.

The next little playful pocket is Queen's Park, where families flock at the first sign of spring.

Kilburn is not really famed for being a place you might go for a day out with your kids. The **Tricycle Theatre** (269 Kilburn High Road, NW6, 7328 1000; *see also p216*) is the area's saving grace.

Queen's Park

Kingswood Avenue, NW6 (info 8969 5661). Queen's Park tube/rail. **Open** 7.30am-dusk daily. **Admission** free.
Come for the paddling pool, the animal enclosure with friendly goats and ducks, the big sandpit play area and the action-packed playground. Added to this, the staff have a

tempting collection of tractors that provides constant preoccupation for most little people. Older children can play pitch & putt or tennis on the beautifully maintained courts and lawns. During the summer holidays, children's magic, puppet and Punch & Judy shows are laid on at the bandstand (3-4pm Mon, Wed, Fri; call for details of future programmes) and bouncy castles are inflated regularly (Tuesday and Thursday throughout the summer). The bandstand is also used by bands on Sundays. Dancing is encouraged.

To round off a day out, there is an excellent café with a children's menu. On weekday mornings the staff at the café run creative workshops, and they also have a few small tables with a permanent collection of crayons and drawing paper for creative teatime urges. There's more jollity in the form of a fun day in September, when the park has its own day of celebration, with funfairs and stalls.
Buggy access. Café. Nappy-changing facilities.

Where to eat

The best spots for child-friendly places to eat are found around Queen's Park. The café in the park is possibly the nicest location to eat with children. Alternatives are found in Salusbury Road where **Baker & Spice** (No.75, 7604 3636) offers high-priced, high-quality goodies ranging from salads and quiches to decadent cakes, all cooked on the premises. Round the corner, **Hugo's Café** (25 Lonsdale Road, NW6, 7372 1232) has a delightful, eclectic menu, beautiful fish dishes and imaginative, brunchy, snacky options for small appetites. The café in the **Salusbury Food Store** (56 Salusbury Road, NW6, 7328 3287) is probably the area's most relaxed eating environment. You can choose anything from the deli, including stews, soups, cakes and coffees, to eat at the informal benched tables. Kids will love the fresh pizza, which comes straight from the oven on huge trays.

Orange, Lemon and Lime has recently opened nearby at 16, College Parade, Salusbury Road (7372 1404; *see also p189*). It serves a lunch for a fiver including coffee, which makes it a cheap alternative to some of the lunchtime spots around Queen's Park.

Red Pepper (8 Formosa Street, W9, 7266 2708; *see also p190*) is the best place to eat near Little Venice, as most kids will find something they enjoy on the pizza/pasta menu.

Notting Hill

However smart and happening Notting Hill claims to be these days, its history is less than illustrious. Until the mid 1800s it was still yokel country, home to pigs and their pigmen. Once the Georgians built their lofty terraces here, the area's fortunes improved, until the last century, when the local working-class population rose up against the West Indian immigrants forced to live in their midst in 1958. Race riots ensued. The streets around

Boyish treasures at **Portobello Market**.

Notting Hill were considered dodgy for years after that, until the yuppies came in the mid 1980s and W11 was considered desirable again. It has never looked back. Every August, the area plays host to Europe's biggest street festival, the **Notting Hill Carnival** (*see p228*).

Notting Hill's main attraction is **Portobello Market**, the world's most famous antiques market. It started life as any other local street market, but it became increasingly fashionable over the decades, and now it's the hip place to stroll and pick up treasures, though bargains aren't really part of the equation round here.

Many Portobello parents find relaxation in nearby Holland Park (*see p164*), although Notting Hill does have a few little-known green spots. The first is **Avondale Park** on Walmer Road, which boasts a small playground, a football pitch and a countryside atmosphere thanks to all the wild plants and flowers in the conservation area. Two other tiny open spaces can be found between Colville Gardens and Powis Square, just off Portobello Road. These two garden squares have decent play equipment and grassy areas for little legs to run around. The other garden squares that you often come across around Notting Hill are usually locked up for the exclusive use of their fortunate residents.

Further up Ladbroke Grove, before you reach Kensal Rise, is the **Making Place** (3 Exmoor Street, W10, 8964 2684; *see also p233*), where an adventurous school-holiday programme of science and technology activities is run for children of an analytical frame of mind.

Over by the thundering Westway, or A40(M), due east from here, is London's best skate park, **Playstation**, where baggy-trousered surfers do impossible things on bits of maple wood with wheels underneath. Less frenetic and frankly scary than this kingdom of callow youth is the little garden tucked under the Westway roundabout, as if to prove a point about urban wildlife. The **Westway Wildlife Garden** (1 Thorpe Close, W8) is tended

by the North Kensington Amenity Trust, and lets locals admire nature under a motorway: there are ponds, a marsh, a wildflower meadow, trees and log piles for overwintering creepy crawlies.

For activities of a more indoorsy nature, little children rate the bouncing and climbing facilities at **Bramley's Big Adventure** (136 Bramley Road, W11, 8960 1515; *see also p249*) extremely highly.

At the edge of Powis Square is the **Tabernacle**, a community centre with a lively programme; it's a perfect place to meet and eat. If you follow the Westway travelling east past Bramley's Big Adventure, you'll reach the Westway Sports Centre. The local authority has obviously made every effort to regenerate what was once an uninviting graffiti-clad underworld. The whole environment under this part of the Westway is surreal, with various odd stone sculptures, a funky concrete climbing wall and a paddock full of urban ponies. Riding lessons can be booked from the **Westway Stables** (8964 2140; *see also p249*) and climbing courses can be booked from the **Sports Centre** (8969 0992; *see also p239*).

Canalside Activity Centre
The Boat House, Canal Close, W10 (8968 4500). Ladbroke Grove tube or Kensal Rise rail. **Open** *Enquiries & bookings 10am-5pm Mon-Fri; 10am-4pm Sat. Closed mid Dec-mid Jan, bank hols. Classes & sessions from £2 members.* **Membership** £50-£120/yr. **No credit cards.**
This unusual watersports centre near Sainsbury's is open to children, families and carers and aims to promote health and education through much hilarious splashing about in the canal. Qualified instructors run courses and one-off sessions in kayaking, canoeing and water activities. Most of the fun takes place all year round – ring for more details. *Buggy access. Nearest picnic place: canalside.*

Emslie Horniman Pleasance Gardens Adventure Playground
Southern Row, W10 (8969 5740). Ladbroke Grove tube. **Open** *Term time 3-7pm Mon-Fri; 11am-5pm Sat. School hols 11am-6pm Mon-Fri. Closed 24 Dec-1 Jan.* **Admission** free.
At this cumbersomely named park you will find a multi-coloured soft-surfaced playground for infants, which is as close to *Tellytubbyland* as you'll get around here. There is also an adventure playground and football pitch for older children. In the spring and summer staff open a small kiosk serving local Disotto's ice-cream, and there are good toilets and nappy-changing facilities. The quiet garden has vine-covered walkways and water features. At the Golborne Road end, below the Trellick Tower, are the Meanwhile Gardens (the subject of an online soap opera) and a wildlife garden. *Buggy access. Nappy-changing facilities.*

Playstation Skate Park
Bay 65-6, Acklam Road, W10 (8969 4669/Pro Shop 8968 8833/www.pssp.co.uk). Ladbroke Grove tube. **Open** noon-4pm, 5-9pm daily. Closed 24-26 Dec, 1 Jan. **Admission** £6 non-members; £4 members. **Membership** £10/yr.
Roll on down to teenage-heaven: one of the best skate parks in the world, where the ramps are challenging, the runways

are fast and the staff seem a little dazed and confused. Check the website to see when supercool visiting professionals are booked in to display their wheely impressive prowess and maybe give a few tips on how low your trousers can go. Many people who practise at Playstation buy their gear at the Pro Shop based at the park, which stocks skateboards, in-lines and all the accessories for the urban roller.
Shop.

The Tabernacle

Powis Square, W11 (7565 7890/www.tabernacle.org.uk). Ladbroke Grove or Westbourne Park tube. **Open** 8.30am-9pm daily; ring for details of late evening activities.

The buzzing community centre in this converted church has a packed programme of family events. There are parent and baby fitness sessions, Tiny Tots dance and music classes, a community education breakdancing project for all ages, salsa and capoeira classes and an over-55s soca school. Music technology and new-media classes are popular, and the 8am yoga classes have captured the imagination of fans of all ages. After all the activity, many dancers and music makers stop for a lunch in the renowned Nectar café (*see also p189*). *Buggy access. Café. Nappy-changing facilities.*

Where to eat

Child-friendly mainstays in the area include a branch of **Café Rouge** (31 Kensington Park Road, W11, 7221 4449) and a **Pizza Express** (137 Notting Hill Gate, W11, 7229 6000), but **Osteria Basilico** (29 Kensington Park Road, W11, 7727 9372) is rather more inviting and irritatingly popular, with divine pasta dishes, fresh focaccia and imaginative pizza choice. **Rotisserie Jules** (133A Notting Hill Gate, W11, 7221 3331) is a high-class sort of fast-food restaurant where the chicken is free range and the fries can be replaced with gratin dauphinois for the more discerning palate. High chairs are provided.

Holland Park

Holland Park is nanny territory, where uniformed carers push large prams along tree-lined avenues to take the air in the park (*see p164*). This is the area's

Water ways: Little Venice

The River Thames may get all the attention, say the navigation experts at **British Waterways, London**, but the pulling power of the capital's 90 miles of canals and smaller rivers and 110 acres of docks in London should not be underestimated.

Little Venice is home to the organisation, which is contracted by the government to keep the canals and waterways safe and well maintained. Over the years, its remit has broadened, and it is now a major player in schemes aimed at regenerating the canals and the areas they run through. At the headquarters, visitors can find out more about the waterways and pick up leaflets and other literature pertaining to the leisure opportunities the canals afford: namely boat trips, angling and walking, and special events throughout the year.

You can walk or cycle over 40 miles along the towpaths of the city's canals, which stretch from Uxbridge in the west to Limehouse Basin in the east, where they join the River Thames. The Grand Union Canal passes through countryside along the Hanwell Flight, a series of six locks that raise the level of the canal over 50 feet in just a third of a mile. The canal continues down to a wooded valley, where it joins the River Brent and passes Osterley Park, before joining the Thames near Kew Gardens.

In the Grand Union's heyday (when it was known as the Grand Junction Canal), canal workers, or 'bargees', lived and learned on their boats. Children brought up on barges were educated in floating schools. A joint initiative between British Waterways, London, the Waterways Trust and the Beauchamp Lodge Settlement has refloated the idea, so to speak. The *Beauchamp*, a 22-metre

boat powered by electricity and containing state-of-the-art educational facilities, has a permanent crew and a teacher, and is available for use as a floating classroom to local schools and community groups. When it's not being used for lessons, the *Beauchamp* is sometimes moored in the Pool of Little Venice, so keep an eye out for it. As many lucky London children can testify, the national curriculum somehow seems a lot more exciting when it's delivered during a cruise.

British Waterways, London

The Toll House, Delamere Terrace, W2 (7286 6101). Warwick Avenue tube. **Open** 8am-6pm Mon-Fri.

main outdoor resource and, due to its size and huge investment from the Royal Borough of Kensington & Chelsea, has plenty to offer everyone, of any age.

Of the lovely houses in the area, the Jacobean **Holland House**, set in the park, is one of the most pleasing, probably because its east wing is a youth hostel and its ballroom a stylish restaurant. **Leighton House** (12 Holland Park Road, 7602 3316), the 19th-century home of the painter Lord Leighton, is free to visit and admire.

Where to eat

The **Holland Park Cafeteria** is the obvious option for a relaxed meal with little ones. It's a typical canteen-style café whose menu lists simple lunches such as pizza slices and spaghetti bolognese. Although the interior is a bit stark, there is ample, picturesque outside seating.

Holland Park Avenue is another popular place to eat as there are a number of posh pâtisseries with outside tables. But the best option has to be **Tootsies** (No.120, 7229 8567; *see also p191*), which becomes a chaotic family venue every weekend, with tables covered in balloons and colouring pads.

Earl's Court & Fulham

From World War I onwards, the imposing houses built in the Earl's Court area for Victorian families were increasingly turned into flats for less-wealthy residents. Eventually, the numerous flats and bedsits became homes for students and travellers passing through. At one time Earl's Court was known as 'Kangaroo Valley' because of all the Australian travellers seeking temporary homes here.

Its slightly scruffy streets and seedy image mean Earl's Court has never established itself as a typical family location, so the resources for children are limited and most parents tend to hang out in neighbouring Hammersmith and Fulham. Earl's Court's distinguishing feature is the vast **Exhibition Centre** (it hosts the Boat Show, the Ideal Home Exhibition and other consumer events).

The **Brompton Cemetery** is the biggest green space in this built-up area. It's quite pleasant to walk in (during the day; it changes character somewhat in the evenings); look out for the grave of Emmeline Pankhurst, the suffragette who founded the Women's Social and Political Union in 1903. Nearby is the **Oratory School**, one of the best state secondary schools in London, favoured by Cherie and Tony Blair for their sons.

Moving south towards the river and Fulham's pleasant aspect, the outlook for children becomes brighter. Bishop's Park is the area's main park, located by a beautiful stretch of the Thames.

Hundreds of runners steam past this stretch of the river each day and the adjacent cycle route is very busy too. This is also a good spot to view the Oxford and Cambridge University Boat Race (the 149th one takes place in March 2003; to find out the exact date check www.theboatrace.org). The park provides fun and frolics for all age groups: there is a small but well-maintained playground, a basketball pitch and a pond. The highlight of the park is the free boating lake, where you can muck about in little rowing boats during the summer months. Next to the lake is the Bishops Rainbow Playhouse, where under-5s can pelt around in the astroturf play area.

Two other attractive green spaces are restricted to members only: the wonderful Hurlingham Sports Club and the Queen's (Tennis and Rackets) Club.

At the end of **Bishop's Avenue** is Fulham Palace, the official residence of the Bishops of London until 1973. At the western end of the park is **Fulham Football Club**, with probably one of the best-located stadiums if you fancy a riverside football match, although next season's games are to be held at QPR's Loftus Road ground while its own is being refurbished.

Just off Fulham Palace Road is **Fulham Road**, where locals shop, eat and socialise in the huge variety of posh boutiques and nice restaurants. At No.735, the **Pottery Café** (7736 2157) has an extensive collection of high-quality plain ceramics and a lovely café where you can while away the days lost in creative expression.

Also at the **Fulham Broadway** end of Fulham Road (which eventually takes you to South Kensington) is **Stamford Bridge**, home to those Surrey favourites, the 'The Blues', aka Chelsea Football Club (7915 2222). The Chelsea Village includes a huge megastore full of Chelsea kit and memorabilia, and fan-filled fast food restaurants.

Fulham Palace

Bishop's Avenue, off Fulham Palace Road, SW6 (7736 3233). Putney Bridge tube/220, 74 bus. **Open** *Museum* Mar-Oct 2-5pm Wed-Sun. Nov-Feb 1-4pm Thur-Sun. Closed 24-31 Dec. *Tours* 2pm 2nd & 4th Sun of mth. **Admission** (LP) *Museum* free. *Tours* £3; free under-16s. This was the official residence of the Bishops of London from 704 until 1973: some of the oldest buildings here date back to 1480, although the main house is 16th century. The most recent addition is William Butterfield's neo-Gothic chapel, from 1866. The museum traces the buildings' history and has some amusing exhibits, not least the mummified rat. Imaginative staff organise children's workshops during the school holidays; a recent workshop series was based on wartime Britain, but most relate to Roman, Tudor and Victorian periods. Ring to check what's coming up. Leave plenty of time to admire the lovely grounds, planted with rare trees, which provide a sanctuary off the busy Fulham Palace Road. The original moat trench can still be found around the grounds. There is also a beautiful walled kitchen garden full of herbs and rare plants.
Buggy access. Café. Nappy-changing facilities. Shop.

Where to eat

Lou Pescadou (241 Old Brompton Road, SW5, 7370 1057), a lively fish restaurant, has a children's menu for £5.50 and tables outdoors. On a similar theme, **Fishnets** (Chelsea Village, Stamford Bridge, SW6, 7565 1430) welcomes youngsters for fish and chips and more fruits of the sea. The well-known **Troubadour** (265 Old Brompton Road, SW5, 7370 1434) still has a laid-back vibe, much as it did in the 1960s, and a very good, homely coffee shop menu: hot daily specials are well priced and there's often entertainment (poetry reading, folk singing) laid on.

No trip to Bishop's Park would be complete without a visit to the **Stevenage Road** ice-cream van, where four generations of the same family have been scooping and serving for more than a century. **Jackie's Cottage Café** is the only café in the park and offers very little except hot drinks and basic snacks. But venturing west along the Thames Path towards Hammersmith takes you to the true gastro stretch of the river: book two weeks ahead for a hallowed table at the **River Café** (7381 8824), or try the **Gate** (7748 6932). The **Crabtree** (7385 3929) has outside tables and a barbecue area in the summer.

On the **Fulham Road**, nearly every other doorway is an eating place, most of which seem to welcome children: there's a **Wok Wok** (140 Fulham Road, SW10, 7370 5355), various pizza joints and any number of tapas bars, brasseries and cafés for snacks and light meals.

Emslie Horniman Pleasance Playground. *See p160*.

Shepherd's Bush & Hammersmith

When you think of these western outposts you immediately envisage roundabouts, which are not the greatest distinguishing feature for an area to be saddled with. **Shepherd's Bush Roundabout** has an interesting arty barometer, which looks like a state-of-the-art toilet cistern, at its centre, while **Hammersmith Roundabout** houses a bus garage, shopping centre and the tube station. Luckily, beyond these traffic-congested road systems are some lovely residential areas, parks and riverside locations to hang out in. It's also a fun and buzzing place to live, with a diverse community, as the many newspaper columnists who have made their home here like to point out.

Just west of Shepherd's Bush is **Loftus Road**, to which dedicated QPR fans may need to make a pilgrimage. The grounds are also close to **Wood Lane**, that famous BBC address that most adults can remember writing on their letters to *Jim'll Fix It*. Most young kids will know it as the home of CBBC, and you are quite likely to spot the odd celebrity if you can be bothered to wait around outside. Even odder celebrities might pop up if you book yourself on a BBC backstage tour (call 0870 603 0304 for details).

Better than hanging around telly-land, ambitious would-be stars would do well to get involved in one of the numerous theatre projects running at Hammersmith's **Lyric Theatre** (King Street, W6, 8741 2311; *see also p225*) or the **Riverside Studios** (Crisp Road, W6, 8237 1111).

Ravenscourt Park is the area's main green space and, as family-friendly parks go, it's one of the best. **Shepherd's Bush Common** is green, and a space, but that's about as much as you can say about it. It forms the centre of yet another roundabout (possibly the biggest in London). It does, however, provide a venue for fairs and circuses throughout the year and there are also some tennis courts here. If you're heading along Shepherd's Bush Road towards Hammersmith, you pass **Brook Green Park**, where there are tennis courts and a playground that has just undergone a major redevelopment, and is now even more chock-full of leaping children than before. Once you reach Hammersmith, you can follow the river back to Fulham where the open spaces are undoubtedly prettier, and the walk is pleasurable in itself.

In & around: Holland Park

With its romantic and magical air, picturesque **Holland Park** is the perfect place for a lazy summer day out. If you enter from Holland Park (the road of the same name), you go through the **Sun Terrace**, an ornate wrought-iron gate set in a high white wall. Nearby is a collection of curved wooden benches under a wooden shelter. This is the most secluded and forested section of the park, where you can enjoy a ramble through the woods heading towards **Holland House**. Along the way, depending on which of the signposted paths you have taken, you will pass either a duck pond or a wildlife area. The paths are named after the trees or plants planted here – look out for **Chestnut Walk** and **Azalea Walk**, among others. Both are best visited in early May, when you can appreciate the blooms fully.

Unusual contemporary sculptures dotted around the park seem to have been selected to appeal to the younger audience because of their quirkiness. They can be found nestled in the lawns or hidden among the trees. Take time to meditate in the **Kyoto Garden**, a Zen garden with rocky waterfalls and little stone bridges over ponds of languid koi carp. Other creatures to look out for are the 12 peacocks, which have a free rein of the park and are most likely to be found wandering the nearby formal rose gardens, where the flowers set off their plumage so nicely. Pass through the cloisters, beyond the formal gardens and fountains, to reach the café. There's a map here, together with information about park activities. This is also the site of the **Ecology Centre**, where a range of activities, from nocturnal bug hunts to orienteering, is organised (call 7471 9802 for details).

If you're hungry and feel like splashing out, Marco Pierre White's **Belvedere** restaurant is housed in the park's Orangery. Babies and children are welcome, but the dishes on the menu seem a bit posh for little mites. The alternative, far less expensive venue is the park café, which has a crowd-pleasing menu of cheap and simple Italian food, including a wide selection of pasta dishes, pizza slices and cakes. In warm weather, the outside tables are a popular spot for chess games and are also a great place to sit and watch the sun set. In summer, a kiosk sells Italian ice-creams.

Just past the café is a playground, where young people like to let off steam. Sporty folk, old and young, make use of the expansive sports field, complete with cricket pitch, tennis courts and football areas. The local **one o'clock club** (7603 2838) is also in the park, just next to the **Abbotsbury Road** entrance. It costs just £1 per child for the whole day (although it's one of the very few such clubs we know of that charges at all). The money is evidently put to good use, however, as the one o'clock club in Holland Park is one of London's best-equipped and definitely the most well-to-do. The adjacent adventure playground was not in use on a recent visit, but a revamp is in the pipeline.

The area outside the park's walls is most entertainingly posh. Well-to-do families and their nannies populate the fine houses around here: this is London at its most attractive. Exploring the area immediately around the park leads you to gracious **Leighton House** and its treasured Victorian paintings. A walk further east brings you to Kensington and the pricey diversions of shops and restaurants. Stay in the park and lunch at the café.

Queen's Park Rangers Football Club

Loftus Road Stadium, South Africa Road, W12 (8743 0262/www.qpr.co.uk). White City tube. **Open** *Shop* 9am-5pm Mon-Fri; 9am-1pm Sat. *Tours* by appointment only. **Admission** *Tours* £4; £2 under-16s. **Credit** MC, V.
Loftus Road, home to QPR and London Wasps rugby, and currently being shared by Fulham FC, is also the hub of community football for young people. The match-day coaching package for children aged 5-16 gives them an exhausting morning of football training, followed by a welcome sit-down to see QPR play at home. The match-day birthday party includes a tour of the ground, two hours of outdoor football training, a £5 lunch voucher to spend in the ground, a ticket to see the match and a goodie bag, all for £16 per head. For more information, phone 8740 2509.
Nappy-changing facilities. Nearest picnic place: Hammersmith Park. Shop.

Ravenscourt Park

Ravenscourt Road, W6 (www.lbhf.gov.uk). Ravenscourt Park tube. **Open** 7.30am-dusk daily. **Admission** free.
In the summer months the packed paddling pool is the most popular spot in this delightful, family-friendly park. It has three play areas, including a challenging wooden adventure playground and a one o'clock club (8748 3180) for under-5s. There's also a big pond, a nature trail and an exotic scented garden designed for the visually impaired. Kids with spare energy can run it off in the large grass pitch area or enjoy a game of tennis on the tennis courts. The café is a useful spot for a family lunch as there is a Kiddies Corner menu (£2.50), listing such dishes as penne with tomato sauce or nuggets and chips; parents tend to go for the imaginative salads and the delicious home-made cakes, which can be eaten outside on the shady lawn. There's an annual flower show with children's fair on the weekend before the August bank holiday (in 2002 it's 17 and 18 August). Fun days with bouncy castles and face painting run throughout the summer holidays.
Buggy access. Café. Nappy-changing facilities.

Where to eat

Shepherd's Bush Market, at the heart of this lively area, has been running since 1918. Its stalls are predominantly loaded with fruit, vegetables and fish with an Afro-Caribbean bias and there are various ethnic food stalls where you can grab a bite to eat.

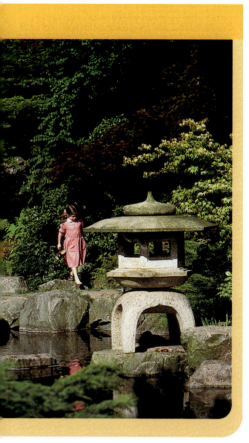

Chiswick

Elegant Chiswick has some of the most beautiful townhouses from the 17th to 19th centuries. It is no surprise that **Chiswick House** is also one of the most magnificent 18th-century houses in London, based on the design of villas found in the suburbs of ancient Rome. This suburb of modern London has inevitably become a popular spot for wealthy families to settle in and as a result the activities available for children are of a particularly high standard.

Duke's Meadows, on the riverfront, is a substantial green space with tennis courts, recreation grounds, boathouses and sports facilities, some belonging to the adjacent Grove Park. You can take a pleasant riverside walk along the length of the **Mall** to the old parish church of St Nicholas, which was mainly rebuilt in 1882-4 but still retains its 15th-century ragstone tower. **Chiswick Common** and **Turnham Green** are more spaces to let off steam than parks with amenities, but make a pleasant enough diversion from the busy Chiswick High Road, and cricket is still played on the green in the summer. **Gunnersbury Park**, on Popes Lane, has plenty of play equipment, a boating lake, mini golf, fishing pond, tennis courts, café and putting greens. The **Gunnersbury Triangle**, a nature reserve on Bollo Lane, was one of the London Wildlife Trust's first nature reserves, saved from the developers' chainsaws by local people in the 1980s.

If poor weather puts an end to frolicking in the park, indoor play opportunities are easy to find. The **Fountain Leisure Centre** (658 Chiswick High Road, W4, 8994 9596) at the Brentford end of Chiswick High Road is home to the Little Tikes activity area, where under-11s can play in a three-storey adventure castle. The centre also has a big pool with a wave machine and a few slides, as well as numerous clubs and classes from karate to badminton. **Art 4 Fun** (444 Chiswick High Road, W4, 8994 4100; *see also p230 and p235*) is a popular spot for children's parties. Alternatively, head out to **Snakes and Ladders**, an incredible indoor play world based at **Syon House**.

The **Kew Bridge Steam Museum** is located in a restored 19th-century pumping station, whose towering chimney is a distinguishing local landmark. Just down the road is the **Musical Museum**, whose selective opening hours ensure it will stay one of London's more obscure treasures. If you're not musically or mechanically minded, the **Gunnersbury Museum** in Gunnersbury Park (8992 1612; open from 1pm only) is less action packed, but offers visitors an insight into life in the Victorian era. The work of local painter William Hogarth, whose portraits and engravings

Much of the eating around Hammersmith is concentrated on **King Street**, which has all the usual fast food chains, in addition to the popular **Polanka** (258 King Street, W6, 8741 8268), a Polish deli where children are given half portions of the filling grub. **Queen Caroline Street** is also lined with fab places to eat: there's a branch of the perennial family favourite, **Smollensky's** (Bradmore House, 8741 8124), and the best vegetarian restaurant in London, the **Gate**, at No.51 (8748 6932).

Shepherd's Bush Road has a fair selection of restaurants, too, including a branch of **Café Rouge** (Nos.98-100, 7602 7732), a popular weekend lunch spot for families. There's a party atmosphere at **Patio** (5 Goldhawk Road, W12, 8743 5194), where family groups are made welcome and children enjoy reduced-price portions of East European delicacies, such as blinis and smoked salmon, plus sausage and roast potatoes.

Chiswick House, perfect for picnics.

constituted sharp social commentary on the state of the nation in the 18th century, are displayed in what was once his country retreat. **Hogarth's House** (Hogarth Lane, Great West Road, W4; 8994 6757), fully restored to its 18th-century condition, is free to get in, but closed in the mornings and on Mondays.

The branch of **London's Transport Museum** at the Depot in Acton opens a few times a year for special transport-related events. It also has exhibitions as this site houses 370,000 London Transport items. (7379 6344 for details of up and coming events. This is the number for the Covent Garden branch – for which *see p76* – but it has all the details of open days.) The museum is located on Gunnersbury Lane opposite Acton Town underground station.

Chiswick House
Burlington Lane, W4 (8995 0508/www.english-heritage.org.uk). Turnham Green tube then E3 bus to Edensor Road/Chiswick rail or Hammersmith tube/rail then 190 bus. **Open** *Apr-Sept* 10am-6pm daily. *Oct* 10am-5pm daily. *Nov-Mar* open only for pre-booked appointments. Last entry 30mins before closing. Closed 24-26 Dec, 1-16 Jan. *Tours* by arrangement; phone for details. **Admission** (EH/LP) *incl audio guide* £3.30; £2.50 concessions; £1.70 5-16s; free under-5s. **Credit** MC, V.
Walking through the picturesque gardens of Chiswick House, you'll come across various delights – obelisks hidden among the trees, a classical temple, a lake and a cascading waterfall. Lots of families come here on summer days and plonk down for a picnic, have lunch at the café (*see p167*) or organise a game of cricket on the well-maintained grounds. In true Chiswick style, a game of afternoon cricket should be followed by a jaunt along the river, which is only a stone's throw away. The Burlington Café, in the grounds, is a splendid place for lunch. English Heritage, which runs the site, sometimes stages family activity days and re-enactments at Chiswick House: see the website for details.
Café. Nearest picnic place: Chiswick Park. Shop.

Gunnersbury Triangle Nature Reserve
Bollo Lane, W4 (8747 3881/www.wildlondon.org.uk). Chiswick Park tube. **Open** *Reserve* open access daily. **Admission** free.
In the late 19th century this area of land was enclosed by railway tracks and unfit for human habitation. As the woodland grew up and the wildlife took over, it became one of the most important sites for urban wildlife in this part of the city. Following the trail, visitors can admire the pond and meadowland and try to spot the 19 species of butterfly that have been recorded fluttering by here. You can visit and have a walk and a picnic any time, but if you want to join in with activities, come when the information cabin is open. The warden, based here full time in the summer, dreams up a wonderful programme of activities (craft workshops, mini beast safaris) for young visitors. They're free and run on a drop-in basis. The reserve's open day is usually held in June: to find out more, call the warden and ask for a programme. There's a small information cabin (open Tuesday and Sunday afternoons), where you can ask the volunteer staff questions of urban ecology, pick up trail leaflets, find out about guided tours (summer only) or hire a net to go pond dipping. You never know what you might find.
Buggy access.

Kew Bridge Steam Museum
Green Dragon Lane, Brentford, Middx (8568 4757/www.kbsm.org). Gunnersbury tube/Kew Bridge rail/65, 237, 267, 391 bus. **Open** 11am-5pm daily. Closed 25 Dec, Good Friday. *Tours* by arrangement; phone for details. **Admission** (LP) *Mon-Fri* £3.50; £2.50 concessions; £1 5-15s; £8 family (2+3); free under-5s. *Sat, Sun* £4.50; £3 concessions; £2 5-15s; £11.50 family (2+3); free under-5s. Free to all after 4pm Mon-Fri. Under-13s must be accompanied by an adult. **Credit** MC, V.
Visit this Victorian riverside pumping station on high days and holidays; it's all sound and fury when the engines are in steam, but this only happens on specific days, so ring before you set out. The Cornish beam engine is fired up at 3pm most weekends and holiday periods, and there are usually a couple of others powering away. During the school holidays and bank holidays, there's a lot of action, because the education department and friendly volunteers run all kinds of activities for family groups. The Water for Life exhibition gives the lowdown on the history of London's vast sewer system and a walk-through section of the city's water ring main, just to show how much water flows around this city all the time. Don't worry about getting wet, though – the section is only for demonstration purposes so there's no water in it. Log on to the website for up-to-date information on special events and exhibitions at the museum. In summer 2002, for instance, the staff hope to have a re-run of the Blacksmith workshops that were so popular a couple of years ago. Such events need to be booked ahead to guarantee joining in the fun.
Nearest picnic place: Kew Green. Shop.

Musical Museum
368 High Street, Brentford, Middx (8560 8108). **Open** *Apr-Oct* 2-5pm Sat, Sun. *Summer hols* 2-4pm Wed; 2-5pm Sat, Sun. **Admission** £3.20; £2.50 concessions; free under-3s. **No credit cards.**
Alive with the sound of music, on just a couple of days of the week, this converted church is full of miraculous automatic instruments of all shapes and sizes. A mighty Wurlitzer cinema organ makes a powerful sound and there are many other treasures whose tones are demonstrated by the staff, including a street barrel piano, a Steinway Duo-Art grand piano and the amazing 'Clarabella', which contains all the instruments of a small band. The 90-minute tour tells you about the origins of this intriguing collection. There are plans to expand the facilities in a new, purpose-built premises in the near future. Ring for details.
Buggy access. Nearest picnic place: riverbank. Shop.

Syon House

Syon Park, Brentford, Middx (8560 0883/London Butterfly House 8560 0378/Aquatic Experience 8847 4730/ Snakes and Ladders 8847 0946/www.syonpark.co.uk). Gunnersbury tube/rail then 237, 267 bus. **Open** *House* Apr-early Nov 11am-5pm Wed, Thur, Sun, bank hol Mon. Last entry 4.15pm. Gardens closed 25, 26 Dec. *Tours* by arrangement; phone for details. **Admission** *House & gardens* (incl audio guide) £6.95; £6.50 concessions; £5.95 5-16s; £15 family (2+2); free under-5s. *Gardens only* £3.50; £2.50 concessions, 5-16s; £8 family (2+2); free under-5s. *Aquatic Experience* £4; £3.50 3-15s; free under-3s; £12.50 family (2+3). *Butterfly House* £4.95; £3.95 3-16s; £4.25 concessions; £15 family (2+3). *Snakes and Ladders* no adults without a child. *Term time* £3.15 under-5s; £4.15 over-5s; free adults. *School hols & weekends* £3.90 under-5s; £4.50 over-5s. **Credit** AmEx, MC, V.

While parents love Syon House for its gracious location, many children find other attractions more enjoyable. The London Butterfly House, for instance, is a memorable experience, where you wander around a tropical plant- and bird-filled conservatory, home to thousands of multicoloured butterflies. A word of advice: be prepared for extreme butterfly bombardment, which some little people may find intimidating. There's also an interesting leaf-cutter ant exhibit, pools of fish and an insect house. Next door is the equally tropical Aquatic Experience, where visitors step gingerly between pools of huge goldfish and tanks of crocodiles. At the back of this house is a pond dipping and identification area with nets for scooping. Both houses have gift shops selling plastic creepy crawlies and souvenir jewellery, and both have ample outside picnic space.

The site that most children head for is Snakes and Ladders. This huge indoor adventure playground is designed like a castle, with three tiers of play areas, which include slides, hanging ropes and masses of huge balls. There's also a good area for under-5s and a café where parents can chill out while viewing the whole scene. There's also an outside area with motorised bikes, which cost £1 a ride. *See also p250.*

In summer you should bring a picnic with you, as the nicest locations to eat are outside. In the winter, when indoor eating is the only real option, the Patio Cafeteria (8758 1175) has a selection of hot meals and a junior menu.

If you do find the time and finances to visit the house and grounds as well as all the child-pleasers above, you can easily spend half a day here. On the weekends, a wooden mini steam railway is operated, which travels through the trees and around the flowerbeds. The house itself is also quite an adventure as each room seems more impressive than the last, from the grand Roman hallway to the Red Drawing Room, with its crimson silk walls and Roman statues.
Café. Nappy-changing facilities. Nearest picnic place: Syon House Gardens/Syon Park. Shop.

Where to eat

The **Burlington Café** in Chiswick House (*see p166*) is good for a light lunch (jacket potatoes, sandwiches and salads), either indoors or outside in the lavish gardens. **Chiswick High Street** has the lion's share of places to eat including child-friendly chains like the **Yellow River Café** (No.12, 8987 9791),

Walk: to Strand-on-the-Green

This walk along the Thames is one of the prettiest west London has to offer, taking in a handful of its quirkiest attractions and any number of welcoming watering holes along the way.

If you're driving, you can park at the free car park at the newly renovated **Watermans Arts Centre** (8232 1010) on the busy Brentford High Street. If you're coming by public transport, catch the 267 bus from either Gunnersbury tube or rail station. If it starts raining the moment you arrive, put Plan B into action and perhaps take in a film or see an event at the centre, or just take refuge in its café.

The walk begins in **Waterman Park**. This is not the world's most beautiful park by any means, but it is on the edge of the river opposite the green open spaces of Kew Gardens and it has a small but well-maintained playground. The **Musical Museum**, directly opposite the park, is fun to visit.

If you walk on along the river path heading towards Kew Bridge, you pass a row of dilapidated houseboats before you have to briefly go on to the High Road again. You now have the option of popping into the **Kew Bridge Steam Museum** on the opposite side of the road or returning to the Thames Path at the next available turning.

This next stretch, before reaching Kew Bridge, is known as the **Hollows**. This is a well-established houseboat community, complete with wrought-iron

walkways, postboxes attached to trees and a cosy *Wind in the Willows* atmosphere. At **Kew Bridge** you can go under or over depending on the height of the tide before reaching the picturesque and popular stretch of the river known as **Strand-on-the-Green**. If tummies are already rumbling, head for **Café Rouge**, opposite a lovely riverside park. Alternatively, follow the path a little way and you'll notice a wide selection of pubs with outdoor terraces. The **Bell and Crown** (8994 4164), in particular, is renowned for its Sunday lunches. Children can feast on a half-size roast with all the trimmings, or opt for sausage or scampi, and chips. It's a good idea to book for Sunday lunch, but it's less busy at other times. Best beers, say boozers, are available at the **Bull's Head** (8994 1204), where children are welcome in the conservatory, and the longish lunch menu features many dishes that appeal to littl'uns (baked potatoes, beef pie, chips, steak, etc). In winter, the tide comes right up and over large stretches of the path around Strand-on-the-Green. This is a good spot to stop and consider turning back if you have to collect a car, or heading inland towards Gunnersbury tube or rail station (about a ten-minute walk). But if you're feeling adventurous, or if you've come by bike, you can carry on along the river enjoying the peace and tranquillity of this relatively unspoilt area.

which boasts a children's menu featuring a free toy bribe for each child. The **High Road** has such wide pavements that during the summer months virtually all the restaurants have tables outside, making them an embarrassment-free option for family meals. If you just fancy an ice-cream, it has to be **Foubert's** (Nos.162-70, 8994 5202), for its huge variety.

Around Town

Further west

To the north of Syon Park, and the horrible M40, is appealing **Ealing**. It is no surprise that the logo for Ealing Borough council is a tree. Ask any local person where the good parks are and they will reel off a list the length of your arm. You are never more than a stone's throw away from one, making it the ideal borough for squirrels and children.

Further west, the imposing **Osterley House**, set in its own parkland, is an excellent choice for a budget day out west (you get quite a lot of house for the entry price and walks and picnics in the park are free).

To the north of the vast park of Osterley, you can follow the pretty River Brent, where it parts company with the Grand Union Canal, to the countrified **Brent Lodge Park**, with its little petting zoo and well-kept maze.

Go to **Southall**, Middlesex, for the market, the closest there is to a proper Indian market outside the country itself. It is an amazing spectacle throughout the week. On Tuesdays live poultry are sold in cages, on Wednesday it's horses, though it may be wise to take a vet with you if you're thinking of buying the children a pony. On Saturdays, it's a rainbow of colour, when saris and salwar kameez, dressmaking materials and trinkets, bangles and sandals are sold.

To the north, there's the stunning **Shri Swaminarayan Mandir Temple**, a building whose delicate beauty is further enhanced by the lumpen tower blocks around it.

The future of **Wembley**'s 78-year-old stadium is still uncertain. As we went to press, the Football Association, which owns the place, was yet to make a decision as to whether to pull it down, sell it off or do it up. Watch those towers.

Brent Lodge Park
Church Road, W7 (8758 5019). Hanwell rail. **Open** 7.30am-dusk. *Maze & animals* Apr-Sept 10.30am-4.45pm daily; Sept-Mar 10.30pm-4pm daily.
Bunny Park is the locals' name for Brent Lodge Park, which is a firm favourite with children, especially since the Millennium Maze was planted in 1999. The maze has had some refurbishment since planting and is bushing out nicely. Now it has a small tower in the centre for children to stand on triumphantly – once they've found their way through – as well as a viewing platform outside for anxious parents to locate their squawking progeny (you can even get lost in it now). The benches surrounding the maze area are all covered in plaques bearing the millennial wishes of vari-

ous people, which are worth reading for inspiration. Leaving the maze and heading up the hill takes you to the hub of the park's activities, where there's a café for ice-cream and sandwiches, a playground and an animal centre. The centre (8758 5019) costs 25p for children and 50p for adults and houses a few squirrel monkeys, a pair of sleepy geckos and some scary spiders, along with a few birds and the odd bunny.
Buggy access. Café. Nappy-changing facilities (in park).

Osterley House
Osterley Park, off Jersey Road, Isleworth, Middx (8232 5050/recorded info 01494 755566/ www.nationaltrust.org.uk). Osterley tube. **Open** *House* late Mar-early Nov 1-4.30pm Wed-Sun. Closed Good Friday. *Park* 9am-dusk daily. *Tours* by arrangement; min 15 people. **Admission** (NT) *House* £4.40; £2.20 5-15s; £11 family (2+2); free under-5s. *Park* free.
Osterley House was built for Sir Thomas Gresham (founder of the Royal Exchange) in 1576 but transformed by Robert Adam in 1761. Adam's revamp is dominated by the imposing colonnade of white pillars before the courtyard of the house's red-brick body. The splendour of the state rooms alone makes the house worth the visit, but the still-used Tudor stables, the vast parkland walks and the ghost said to be lurking in the basement add to Osterley's allure. Children can pick up a house trail from the office to help them explore these delightful surroundings.

Children's activities, such as art and craft workshops and insect safaris, take place every Wednesday in August. These must be booked in advance (01494 755572).
Café. Nappy-changing facilities. Nearest picnic place: front lawn/picnic benches in grounds. Shop.

Pitshanger Manor & Gallery
Walpole Park, Mattock Lane, W5 (8567 1227/ www.ealing.gov.uk/pitshanger). Ealing Broadway tube/rail. **Open** 10am-5pm Tue-Sat. Closed Good Friday, 25, 26 Dec, 1 Jan, bank hols. *Tours* by arrangement; phone for details. **Admission** free.
This beautiful Regency villa is situated in the idyllic surroundings of Walpole Park. Sir John Soane, architect of the Bank of England, rebuilt most of the house in 1801-3 using highly individual ideas in design and decoration. Among the exhibits worth seeing is the Hull Grundy Martinware collection of pottery. There is an art gallery adjacent to the museum (8567 1227), where contemporary exhibitions are held, plus a lecture and workshop programme for all ages.

Walpole Park is home to loads of music festivals in summer. These make great family days out as they usually attract lots of stalls and other entertainment. Phone Ealing council for details (8579 2424). The Walpole Park playground is also up and running with a new range of play equipment.
Buggy access. Lift. Nearest picnic place: Walpole Park.

Shri Swaminarayan Mandir Temple
105-15 Brentfield Road, NW10 (8965 2651). Wembley Park tube then BR2 bus. **Open** 9.30am-6pm daily. **Admission** (LP) free. *Exhibition* £2; £1.50 6-15s; free under-6s.
This Hindu temple is an incredible sight. Built in 1995, it is an extraordinary structure, intricately carved by master sculptors. Much of the stone was sent to India to be carved and then brought back to Neasden at a cost of more than £10 million. It also has a permanent exhibition, with a video, called Understanding Hinduism, presented in a clear and entertaining way (it's particularly useful for those Year Sixes studying world religion). Stock up on incense sticks at the shop and try to recreate the temple's serenity at home.
Nappy-changing facilities. Shop.

Consumer

Eating

Where to enjoy a family feast.

It's surprisingly hard to tell at first glance whether or not a restaurant is going to be child-friendly. There are obvious candidates – places that run the full chicken nugget, high chair, crayons and balloon gamut – but even these establishments can suffer from unhelpful staff and rigid rules. Conversely, some places look a sight too sophisticated to open their doors to toddling gourmets, yet their relaxed attitude to babies and children turns out to be a revelation. Below we've listed the restaurants that have passed the under-14s test, whatever the cuisine, decor or price range. Pubs that make a special effort to keep children occupied and well fed while their parents sup a pint are also included. If you're after a bargain, there are some places where children eat for free – worth bearing in mind if your kids have eyes bigger than their stomachs. We also mention addresses for other branches of restaurants that we list, but note that not all branches will necessarily have the same facilities.

Southwark & Bankside

Butlers Wharf Chop House

Butlers Wharf Building, 36E Shad Thames, SE1 (7403 3403/www.conran.com). Tower Hill tube/London Bridge tube/rail/Tower Gateway DLR/47, 78, 142, 188 bus. Bar **Open** noon-3pm, 6-11pm Mon-Sat; noon-3pm Sun. **Brunch served** noon-3pm Sat, Sun. **Main courses** £6.75-£22. **Set brunch** (Sat, Sun) £12.95 two courses, £15.95 three courses, incl drink. **Set meal** (noon-3pm, 6-11pm Mon-Fri; 6-11pm Sat) £9 two courses, £11 three courses. *Restaurant* **Lunch served** noon-3pm Mon-Fri, Sun. **Dinner served** 6-11pm Mon-Sat. **Main courses** £12-£23. **Set lunch** £19.75 two courses, £23.75 three courses. **Credit** AmEx, DC, MC, V. **Map** p321 R8.

Attracted by the river views and the sights within walking distance, families descend on Conran's Chop House for weekend brunch. The staff are friendly and helpful towards kids, offering spare plates and spoons for sharers and advising them on the finer points of the menu. Young children especially love the square-cut chips arranged like building bricks, the little golden fish cakes and the tomato soup from

Giraffe. *See p182.*

★ Top: brunch venues ★

Bank Aldwych
See p173.

Bluebird
See p173.

Butlers Wharf Chop House
See p170.

Canyon
See p186.

Frocks
See p184.

Jones Dairy Café
See p185.

Quality Chop House
See below.

Smiths of Smithfields
See below.

fish!

the brunch menu's starter list. Main courses from the lunch menu are on the expensive side; stick to the brunch list and enjoy the generous bread basket, those stylish chips and, of course, the views.
Booking advisable (restaurant). Buggy access. High chairs. Tables outdoors (12, terrace).

fish!
Cathedral Street, SE1 (7234 3333/www.fishdiner.co.uk). Waterloo tube/rail. **Meals served** 11.30am-3pm, 5-10.45pm Mon-Fri; 11.30am-11pm Sat; noon-10pm Sun. **Main courses** £8.90-£16.95. **Credit** AmEx, DC, MC, V. **Map** p319 M8.
People coming out of Southwark Cathedral and Borough Market gaze in enviously at the happy diners tucking into their brain food at this aquarium-like restaurant. The bright, airy surroundings and light, healthy dishes are a continuing recipe for success. There's a list of fish available for any given day; you decide how you would like it prepared (for example, steamed, grilled), and order veg, salad and excellent chips (or new potatoes) to go with it. Easy and achieved at seemingly breakneck speed. There are non-fish and vegetarian meals available and anyone who can resist the 'tart of the week' for dessert deserves a medal for self-discipline. The children's menu lists either tuna bolognese, chicken and chips or (outstanding) fish and chips. The price includes a drink and a pud and an intriguing little set of 'sticky sticks': wax strips you can make shapes with. Service is amiable, if brisk. There are branches of fish! throughout town; call 0845 100 4555 for your nearest.
Buggy access. Children's menu (£6.95). High chairs. Tables outdoors (pavement).

The People's Palace
Level 3, Royal Festival Hall, South Bank Centre, SE1 (7928 9999/www.peoplespalace.co.uk). Embankment tube/Charing Cross or Waterloo tube/rail. **Lunch served** noon-3pm, **dinner served** 5.30-11pm daily. **Main courses** £12.50-£17. **Set lunch** £12.50 two courses,

£16.50 three courses. **Set dinner** (5.30-7pm Mon-Sat, all day Sun) £16.50 two courses, £20.50 three courses (£21.50 Sun). **Credit** AmEx, DC, MC, V. **Map** p319 M8.
This restaurant is user friendly, well presented and unintimidating. OK, so the prices are high, but the service – amiable, patient and efficient – cannot be faulted. The views across the river are uplifting, making it a great place for a long, lingering lunch. And the food is as much a draw as everything else – dishes are generously proportioned and prepared with quality ingredients. Fussy eaters might be put off by some of the more adventurous choices, such as rosemary ice-cream with hot chocolate fondant, but there are enough alternatives to keep everyone happy.
Buggy access. Children's menu (£7.50 main, £4 dessert). High chairs. No-smoking tables.

The City

Quality Chop House
92-4 Farringdon Road, EC1 (7837 5093). Farringdon tube/rail. **Lunch served** noon-3pm Mon-Fri; noon-4pm Sun. **Dinner served** 6.30-11.30pm Mon-Sat; 7-11.30pm Sun. **Main courses** £6.75-£22. **Credit** MC, V.
A great place for a brunch treat, or an early supper before a show at Sadler's Wells. The handsome wooden fittings and wipe-down surfaces are pretty much indestructible, and the menu has some real kid-pleasers. Frighten them with the idea of jellied eels, then let them loose on superior versions of eggs, bacon and chips or sausages, mash and onion gravy.
Booking advisable. No-smoking tables.

Smiths of Smithfield
67-77 Charterhouse Street, EC1 (7251 7950/ www.smithsofsmithfield.co.uk). Farringdon tube/rail. Ground floor bar/café **Meals served** 7am-5pm Mon-Fri; 10.30am-5pm Sat, Sun. **Main courses** £2.25-£6. **Credit** AmEx, MC, V. **Map** p320 O5.

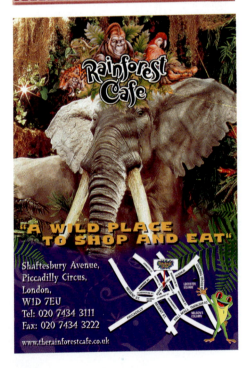

The groovy ground-floor space at Smith's gives children space to roam around in. The menu caters for all tastes (porridge, bacon butties, waffles with maple syrup, BLT, fry-ups, or, for the more health-conscious youngster, fruit salad with yoghurt, muesli and honey) and the gently fashionable folk allow for plenty of people-watching. Worth a journey for a relaxed weekend brunch (when the kitchen serves a mean milkshake).
Buggy access. Reduced-price children's portions. High chairs. Tables outdoors (6, pavement).

Strada
8-10 Exmouth Market, EC1 (7278 0800/ www.strada.co.uk). Farringdon tube/rail. **Meals served** noon-11pm Mon-Sat; noon-10.30pm Sun. **Main courses** £4.95-£12.95. **Credit** AmEx, MC, V. **Map** p317 M4.
Belgo's Italian connection continues to win friends with its wood-fired pizzas. And you can see why: the crusts are extra thin, and loaded with brightly coloured tomatoes, herbs and other goodies. Pasta concoctions are equally impressive, made with top-notch ingredients. Children are made to feel welcome by the friendly staff, and can order half portions of the pasta and risotto dishes or share a pizza. The decor at this branch is a bit drab, so when the sun shines, outside tables on this cheery market street are at a premium.
Buggy access. Tables outdoors (5, patio).
Branches: 15-16 New Burlington Street, W1 (7287 5967); 105-106 Upper Street, N1 (7226 9742); 175 New King's Road, SW6 (7731 6404); 11-13 Battersea Rise, SW11 (7801 0794).

Bloomsbury & Holborn

Bank Aldwych
1 Kingsway, WC2 (7379 9797/ www.bankrestaurants.com). Holborn tube. **Breakfast served** 7-10.30am Mon-Fri. **Brunch served** 11.30am-3.30pm Sat, Sun. **Lunch served** noon-3pm Mon-Fri. **Dinner served** 5-11.30pm Mon-Sat; 5.30-10pm Sun. **Main courses** £8.95-£19.50. **Set meal** (lunch, 5-7pm, 10-11.30pm) £10 two courses, £12.50 three courses. **Credit** AmEx, DC, MC, V. **Map** p317 M6.
Children are welcome in this swish former bank at any time, but particularly on Saturdays and Sundays from 11.30am to 3pm, when they're the stars of the show. Not only do they get a special brunch menu, but the staff also set up a central table with Duplo, books and drawing materials. The kids' menu lists overly generous portions of chipolatas and mash or chips, alongside barbecued chicken, burgers, fish and pasta. They can choose sticky toffee pudding or ice-cream for afters, or forego the pud in favour of a deliciously ice-creamy milkshake. Parents can choose from a two-course set menu, which includes fantastic home-made soups, salads and suchlike.
Booking advisable. Children's brunch menu (£6.95). Crayons. High chairs. Nappy-changing facilities. Toys.

Table Café
Basement of Habitat, 196 Tottenham Court Road, W1 (7636 8330). Goodge Street tube. **Breakfast served** 10am-noon, **lunch served** noon-4pm, **tea served** 4-5.30pm daily. **Main courses** £6.95-£7.90. **Set lunch** £7.50 two courses. **Service** 10% for parties of five or more. **Credit** MC, V. **Map** p316 J4.
It might sound like a cliché, but the Italian staff here genuinely seem pleased to see babies and children. The sturdy wooden tables and chairs can withstand most assaults and there's

room to stretch out in. A short but regularly changing menu has excellent filled ciabattas, pastas, salads and other interesting dishes such as stuffed aubergine with couscous. *Booking advisable (lunch). Nappy-changing facilities. No smoking.*

Kensington & Chelsea

Big Easy
332-4 King's Road, SW3 (7352 4071). Sloane Square tube then 11, 19, 22 bus. **Bar Open** noon-11pm Mon-Sat; noon-10.30pm Sun. **Main courses** £2.75-£15.50. *Restaurant* **Meals served** noon-11.30pm Mon-Thur, Sun; noon-12.30am Fri, Sat. **Main courses** £7.95-£15.50. **Set lunch** (noon-5pm Mon-Fri) £4.95 one course, £7.95 two courses. **Credit** AmEx, MC, V. **Map** p315 E12.
This down-home Louisiana/Texas borderline restaurant is all rustic wood tables with red-chequered tops, rough-hewn wooden wall panelling, fake antique signs with cutesy country sayings. And its American musical hits can be alternately uplifting and excruciating. Nevertheless, the Big Easy is well worth a stop. The menu veers from seafood to steak to barbecue, so there's something for all tastes, and combo plates such as chicken and ribs are huge, making them perfect for bigger appetites. And because of the laid-back mood here, kids are free to roam about without fear of upsetting anybody.
Children's menu (£4.95, dessert £2-£3.95). Crayons. High chairs. Nappy-changing facilities. No-smoking tables. Tables outdoors (5, pavement).

Bluebird
350 King's Road, SW3 (7559 1000/www.conran.co.uk). Sloane Square tube then 11, 19, 22 bus. **Bar Open** noon-12.30am Mon-Sat; noon-10.30pm Sun. *Restaurant* **Brunch served** noon-3.30pm Sat, Sun. **Lunch served** 12.30-3pm Mon-Fri. **Dinner served** 6-11pm Mon-Sat; 6-10pm Sun. **Main courses** £11.50-£19.25. **Set lunch** (Mon-Fri) £12.50 two courses, £17 three courses. **Credit** AmEx, DC, MC, V. **Map** p315 D12.
The restaurant at this veritable Conran village – also home to a food hall, Conran Shop and bar – is an airy, polished space, run by coolly efficient but reassuringly friendly staff. With all this stylishness, you wouldn't think there'd be an open-door policy to children, but like many Conrans, Bluebird does 'em proud. It really comes into its own at weekends, when little ones get their own brunch menu, which lists dishes such as linguini in tomato sauce and fish and chips. Adults can enjoy the set menu, listing such delights as vegetable bruschetta, smoked haddock tart, 'classic' prawn cocktail, roast rabbit and monkfish.
Buggy access. Children's menu (weekends, £4-£5.50). High chairs. Nappy-changing facilities.

Sticky Fingers
1A Phillimore Gardens, W8 (7938 5338/ www.stickyfingers.co.uk). High Street Kensington tube. **Bar Open** noon-8pm Mon-Sat. *Restaurant* **Meals served** noon-11pm Mon-Thur, Sun; noon-11.30pm Fri, Sat. **Main courses** £8.45-£15.95. **Credit** AmEx, DC, MC, V. **Map** p314 A9.
The Rolling Stones are much in evidence at this slick joint. Bill Wyman is part-owner, so the interior is packed with memorabilia such as posters, guitars and gold records. The music blasts out, so it's probably a place to bring older kids and teenagers rather than tiny tots. The food – burgers, steaks, sandwiches and the like – won't win any awards for

Consumer

originality but is just the kind of stuff kids love, and the staff are friendly. The children's menu price buys them an ice-cream for dessert.

Buggy access. Children's menu (£6.95). Entertainment: face painting 1-3pm Sun. High chairs.

Amato Caffè/Pasticceria
14 Old Compton Street, W1 (7734 5733/ www.amato.co.uk). Leicester Square or Tottenham Court Road tube. **Open** 8am-10pm Mon-Sat; 10am-8pm Sun. **Main courses** £5.50-£8.50. **Service** 10% for parties of five or more. **Credit** AmEx, DC, MC, V. **Map** p317 K6.
It's unusual to have to wait for a seat at this Italian café. The menu runs from cooked breakfasts through toasted sandwiches and pasta dishes, to a must-try selection of cakes and pastries from the tempting display. Service comes with a smile. *See also p241.*

Bookings not accepted. Buggy access. High chairs.

Belgo Centraal
50 Earlham Street, WC2 (7813 2233/ www.belgorestaurants.co.uk). Covent Garden tube. **Meals served** noon-10.30pm Mon, Sun; noon-11.30pm Tue-Sat. **Main courses** £8.95-£18.95. **Set lunch** (noon-5pm) £5.75. **Credit** AmEx, DC, MC, V. **Map** p317 L6.
The pride of Belgium continues to thrill the hordes in Covent Garden. There's plenty for diners of all ages to get excited about. Where else in London can you get a main meal with plenty of bread and a glass of wine or beer for just £5.75? It's not just fuel food, either: Belgo grub is well presented, fresh and extremely enjoyable. Mussels are the stars of the show, of course, but kids can also choose from the children's menu, which features chicken nuggets, fish fingers, those gorgeous Belgo frites and a free ice-cream (if they can manage it), and there are fruit juices instead of the usual brown fizz. Tables and benches are a mite claustrophobic – you can almost dip your bread in your neighbour's moules – but the noise level isn't unbearable (it's mostly the rattle of thousands of mussel shells). Children eat free if they bring a paying adult along (one per two children).

Buggy access. Children's menu (£4.95). Crayons. High chairs.
Branches: **Belgo Noord** 72 Chalk Farm Road, NW1 (7267 0718); **Belgo Zuid** 124 Ladbroke Grove, W10 (8982 8400).

Benihana
37 Sackville Street, W1 (7494 2525/www.benihana.co.uk). Piccadilly Circus tube. **Lunch served** noon-2.30pm daily. **Dinner served** 6-10.30pm Mon-Fri, Sun; 6-11pm Sat. **Set meals** *Lunch* £8.75-£30 four courses. *Dinner* £17-£50 six courses. **Credit** AmEx, DC, MC, V. **Map** p318 J7.
Benihana welcomes children with open chopsticks (especially in the Swiss Cottage branch, where a kids' entertainer with balloon-modelling qualifications is brought in to cover Sunday lunch). Even at other times, however, the famously flamboyant red-hatted chefs at the *teppan* (hot plate) juggle their seasonings (over their heads) and indulge in some natty knifework while stir-frying at speed. The children's meals (from £4.75) don't include a drink, but are a light and healthy choice (prawn appetiser, hibachi chicken, ice-cream) for small appetites. Older and/or hungrier children are better off sharing adult-sized dishes, so they can sample more of the menu. Many adore the bento boxes (£8.50), containing prawns, salads, sushi, rice and fruit.

Benihana

Children's menu (lunch Sun, £4.75, £5.25 & £5.50). High chairs.
Branches: 77 King's Road, SW3 (7376 7799); 100 Avenue Road, NW3 (7586 1303).

Busaba Eathai
106-110 Wardour Street, W1 (7255 8686). Piccadilly Circus tube. **Meals served** noon-11pm Mon-Thur; noon-11.30pm Fri, Sat; noon-10pm Sun. **Main courses** £5.50-£8.50. **Service** 10% for parties of five or more. **Credit** MC, V. **Map** p316 J6.
Older children will enjoy the grooviness of this incense-infused, dark-wood restaurant. The shared tables and bench seating (as pioneered by Wagamama) are given a veneer of sophistication by the dim lighting and attractive decor. The long list of tempting Thai dishes (such as ginger beef stir-fry or pumpkin curry) has no desserts, but be virtuous and go for one of the excellent juices instead.

Bookings not accepted. Buggy access. No smoking.

Café Pacifico
5 Langley Street, WC2 (7379 7728/ www.cafepacifico-laperla.com). Covent Garden or Leicester Square tube. **Meals served** noon-11.45pm Mon-Sat; noon-10.45pm Sun. **Main courses** £3-£5.10 (lunch), £6-£14 (dinner). **Credit** AmEx, MC, V. **Map** p317 L6.
The airy, high-ceilinged premises and cheery staff make this Tex-Mex restaurant a no-stress venue, especially in summer, when the sun streams through the open frontage. Provided you have the kind of kids who enjoy nachos, guacamole, tacos and tostadas, there's no arguing with this good-value, central family venue, which celebrated its 25th anniversary in 2001.

Buggy access. Children's menu (£2.75). Crayons. High chairs.

Carluccio's Caffè

8 Market Place, W1 (7636 2228/www.carluccios.co.uk).
Oxford Circus tube. **Meals served** 8am-11pm Mon-Fri;
10am-11pm Sat; 11am-10pm Sun. **Main courses** £4.95-
£8.95. **Credit** AmEx, DC, MC, V. **Map** p316 J6.
A one-menu-fits-all-meals café, where classic Italian dishes
are served alongside savoury and breakfasty-type breads and
pastries. Most ingredients have been sourced from Italy, as
have the waiting staff, it seems, who are very amiable
towards children. Most dishes can be served in small, inexpensive portions for younger diners. Several desserts, such
as the chocolate truffle pudding, seem geared to send chocoholics of all ages into raptures of delight.
Buggy access. High chairs. Reduced-price children's
portions. Tables outdoors (pavement).
Branches: St Christopher's Place, W1 (7935 5927); 2 Nash
Court, E14 (7719 1749); Fenwick, New Bond Street, W1
(7629 0699); Charter Quay, Kingston-upon-Thames, Surrey
(8549 5898).

Down Mexico Way

25 Swallow Street, W1 (7437 9895). Piccadilly Circus tube.
Bar **Open** 5pm-3am Mon-Sat. *Restaurant* **Meals served**
noon-midnight Mon-Sat; noon-10.30pm Sun. **Main**
courses £10-£14. **Credit** AmEx, DC, MC, V. **Map** p318 J7.
Flamboyant dancers and free-flowing cocktails make this
huge but intricately decorated Latin American restaurant a
meal on the wild side for dinner; lunchtimes are far more
sedate. The tapas list is a boon for families: select several items
at £2 a dish and let the children share your main courses.
Young diners love dishes such as crunchy chicken with salad,
golden sticks of inca bread with pumpkin seeds to dip in the
guacamole, and juicy fried mushrooms. The staff are friendly and playful with kids and suggest dishes from the menu
that little palates enjoy. When we visited, they also provided
some old menu lists for them to draw on while the adults lin-
gered over the Latin American spread.
Buggy access. High chairs.

Ed's Easy Diner

Old Compton Street, W1 (7287 1951). Leicester Square
or Tottenham Court Road tube. **Meals served** *Winter*
11.30am-11.30pm Mon-Thur; 11.30am-1am Fri, Sat;
11.30am-11pm Sun. *Summer* 11.30am-midnight Mon-
Thur; 11.30am-1am Fri, Sat; 11.30am-midnight Sun.
Main courses £4.20-£5.90. **Minimum** (peak hours)
£4.20. **Credit** MC, V. **Map** p317 K6.
Ed's was made for kids. But not for babies. The stools are
almost impossible for adults as it is; those holding infants
would be enormously uncomfortable. But if you've come
with teenagers, it's worth teetering for a while when your
reward is a fresh, made-to-order burger, served steaming
from the grill with a selection of cheeses, bacon and so
on, or even with a fried egg on top. Sides like chips and
onion rings are also excellent, and reasonably priced.
Vegetarians can chow down on veggie burgers and hearty
salads. Don't leave without trying a milkshake – flavours
range from traditional, such as chocolate or vanilla, to butterscotch and peanut butter.
Buggy access. Children's menu (£4.95). Crayons.
Branches: Mall 5, Brent Cross Shopping Centre, NW4
(8202 0999); 362 King's Road, SW3 (7352 1956); 19 Rupert
Street, W1 (7287 1951); O2 Centre, 255 Finchley Road,
NW3 (7431 1958); 12 Moor Street, W1 (7434 4439).

Food for Thought

31 Neal Street, WC2 (7836 0239). Covent Garden tube.
Breakfast served 9.30-11.30am Mon-Sat. **Lunch**
served noon-5pm daily. **Dinner served** 5-8.15pm

Mon-Sat. **Main courses** £3.80-£6. **Minimum** (noon-
3pm, 6-7.30pm) £2.50. **No credit cards. Map** p317 L6.
OK, it's a tight squeeze in here during the lunchtime rush, but
after you've queued and snagged a table in the cramped basement, you'll be rewarded by wholesome, vegetarian fare. The
menu of big salads, bakes, hot-pots and quiches is the ideal
counterweight to a burger 'n' fries frenzy. The place is hope-
less for buggies, although you can always grab a takeaway
from the ground floor at busy times.
No smoking.

The Fountain

Ground floor, Fortnum & Mason, 181 Piccadilly, W1
(7734 8040). Piccadilly Circus tube. **Meals served**
8.30am-7.45pm Mon-Sat. **Main courses** £7.95-£19.75.
Credit AmEx, MC, V. **Map** p318 J7.
A posh and very retro treat, at a not-bad price. The ornate
summer room decor sets the scene for a menu of ice-cream
sundaes and high tea savouries. The children's lunch menu
includes Welsh rarebit and sausage and mash.
Buggy access. Children's menu (£4.25-£5.25). Crayons.
Nappy-changing facilities (in shop, until 6.30pm).

Hard Rock Café

150 Old Park Lane, W1 (7629 0382/www.hardrock.com).
Hyde Park Corner tube. **Meals served** 11.30am-12.30am
Mon-Thur, Sun; 11.30am-1am Fri, Sat. **Main courses**
£7.95-£14.95. **Minimum** main course when busy. **Credit**
AmEx, DC, MC, V. **Map** p318 H8.
Hard Rock's only saving grace is that its food is actually pretty damn good. Otherwise, it can be a bit of a nightmare – it's
tacky, the atmosphere is cacophonous, and you inevitably
have to queue to get in. All starters are massive: the nachos
could easily serve four and are smothered with meat, beans,
cheese, salsa, guacamole and sour cream. You might think
you're going healthy with a salad, but even those are piled
high, albeit with healthier ingredients. The famous Hard
Rock hamburger lives up to its reputation, with a half-pound
of meat, cooked to order and served with every imaginable
trimming. With its noise, burgers, chips and sandwiches,
there is no way you'll be able to convince your children they
do not need to come here.
Buggy access. Children's menu (£4.25). Entertainment:
occasional face painting. High chairs. No-smoking tables.
Tables outdoors (10, pavement). Toys.

India Club

2nd floor, Strand Continental Hotel, 143 Strand, WC2
(7836 0650). Temple tube. **Lunch served** noon-2.30pm,
dinner served 6-10.50pm Mon-Sat. **Main courses**
£4.70-£6.80. **Set meal** £11 two courses. **Unlicensed.**
Corkage no charge. **No credit cards. Map** p319 M7.
The decor (lino, formica tables) and the smartly-attired waiters seem stuck in a timewarp, but then so do the prices. The
menu of old favourites lists plenty of vegetarian options (we
swear by the masala dosais) and the most expensive dish at
the India Club hovers around £6. A great choice if you fancy
something different.
Nappy-changing facilities (in hotel). No-smoking.

Masala Zone

9 Marshall Street, W1 (7287 9966/
www.realindianfood.com). Oxford Circus tube.
Lunch served noon-2.30pm daily. **Dinner served** 5.30-
11pm Mon-Sat; 6-10.30pm Sun. **Main courses** £4.25-£9.
Credit MC, V. **Map** p316 J6.
An elegant dining room, simply decorated with tribal art on
the walls, banquette seating with bolsters to support the
lower back, plenty of space to move around in and a

no-smoking policy, this is a comfort zone with a strong feel-good factor. Many of the dishes are based on the street food of Bombay. A vegetarian thali (also available in meat, prawn or child-size portions) includes so many dishes it can be difficult to finish. Other tasty options include curries and noodles. With numerous breads, pastries and crispy things to sample from the intriguing menu, this wonderful place is perfect for a family lunch and the service could not be more helpful. *Buggy access. No smoking.*

Maxwell's

8-9 James Street, WC2 (7836 0303/www.maxwells.co.uk). Covent Garden tube. Bar **Open** *noon-11pm Mon-Sat; noon-10.30pm Sun. Restaurant* **Meals served** *noon-11.30pm daily.* **Main courses** £8.25-£16.95. **Minimum** £7 when busy. **Credit** AmEx, DC, MC, V. **Map** p317 L6. Though the food might not blow you away, the music, noise and rush here will delight youngsters. Especially at lunch, Maxwell's is very child-friendly (raucous office groups tend to fill the place in the evenings). The menu seems tailor-made for kids, listing something for everyone (except dieters, that is): nachos, crab cakes, chicken, burgers, steaks, all available with the requisite chips. Friendly staff add to the equation. *Buggy access. Children's menu (£4.50). Crayons. Entertainment: face painting, lunchtimes Sun (free). High chairs. Nappy-changing facilities. No-smoking tables. Tables outdoors (6, pavement).* **Branch**: 76 Heath Street, NW3 (7794 5450).

Dim sum

The Cantonese habit of families getting together for a dim sum feast at the weekend is one that appeals to many Londoners. The Cantonese term 'dim sum' means something like 'to touch the heart', or 'little pieces so dear to the heart', and it is used to refer to the vast array of dumplings and other titbits that southern Chinese people eat with their tea for breakfast or at lunchtime.

The meal consists of a series of tiny dishes or bamboo steamers, each bearing just two or three dumplings, perhaps, or a small helping of steamed spare ribs or seafood. Modest eaters can ask for a small selection of dishes, while the greedy can keep ordering until the table is laden with snacks. And the really wonderful thing about dim sum is that however wildly and extravagantly you order, it is virtually impossible to run up a bill that is higher than £15 a head, even in the best places in town. Dim sum therefore provides a perfect opportunity for novices to extend an appreciation of Chinese food.

Two London restaurants serve dim sum Hong Kong-style, from circulating trolleys: the cheerful **New World** and the rather less jolly **Chuen Cheng Ku**. The trolley system has the great advantage that you see exactly what you are ordering, but if you go at a quiet lunchtime some of the food may be a little tired by the time it reaches your table. Other places offer dim sum à la carte, so the snacks are usually cooked freshly, to order.

Dim sum lunches at the weekend tend to be noisy, boisterous occasions, so they are great for children. Note, though, that adventurous toddlers and hot dumpling trolleys are not a happy combination, and that strict vegetarians are likely to be very limited in their menu choices, as most snacks contain either meat or seafood.

Dim sum specialists always list the snacks on separate, smaller menus that are roughly divided into steamed dumplings, deep-fried dumplings, sweet dishes and cheung fun (slithery sheets of steamed rice pasta wrapped around meat or fish). Try to order a selection of different types of food, with plenty of light steamed dumplings to counterbalance the heavier deep-fried snacks.

If you are lunching with a large group, make sure you order multiples of everything, as most portions consist of about three dumplings.

Tea is the traditional accompaniment to the feast. Some restaurants offer a selection of different teas, and the musty bo lay (pu'er in Mandarin Chinese) is a delicious alternative to the jasmine blossom tea that is normally served by default to non-Chinese guests. Waiters should keep your teapots filled throughout the meal; just leave the teapot lid tilted at an angle or upside down to signal that you want a top-up.

London's best dim sum are to be found at the **Royal China** restaurants in Bayswater, Baker Street, St John's Wood and Docklands, with the **Golden Dragon** in Chinatown and **Golden Palace** in Harrow close behind. (Be warned that there's a no-bookings policy at the Royal China in Bayswater, and that unless every single member of your party is at the restaurant before the doors open, you're

Mezzonine

*100 Wardour Street, W1 (7314 4000/
www.conran.com). Leicester Square, Piccadilly
Circus or Tottenham Court Road tube.* **Lunch
served** noon-3pm Mon-Fri, Sun; noon-4pm Sat.
Dinner served 5.30pm-1am Mon-Thur; 5.30pm-3am
Fri, Sat; 5.30-10.30pm Sun. **Main courses** £9-£11.
Set meals (noon-2.30pm, 5.30-7pm) £8.90 two courses,
£11.90 three courses. **Service** 12.5%. **Credit** AmEx,
DC, MC, V. **Map** p316 J6.
The cool sophistication of one of Sir Terence Conran's most
famous restaurants can be sampled in this, the upstairs sec-
tion. Here the menu is of an oriental bent, and is a gift for
noodle-friendly children. This being Conran, there is a lot

of polished floorspace in which to spread yourself out, and
the staff's attitude toward fidgety children is indulgent.
Adventurous diners can select various seafood dishes and
delicately seasoned soups and curries. Pad Thai noodles
come in a huge bowl and make a good dish for sharing. But
if all the exoticism is too much, children can have a bowl of
chips, or satay chicken with rice, an excellent compromise.
Make sure they (and you) leave room for one of the wonderful smoothies. All ages also enjoy watching the talented
chefs throwing tantrums in the very visible kitchens. We've
found that service can be slow, but the plus points largely
make up for it.
*Booking advisable, essential weekends. High chairs.
Nappy-changing facilities.*

in for a long wait in the queue.) New World is great
for trolley snacks, and we also enjoy eating at
Harbour City. The greatest concentration of dim
sum restaurants is in Chinatown, but you can also
find the snacks at **Local Friends** in Golders Green,
Royal China in Putney and **Hakkasan** off Tottenham
Court Road.

Chuen Cheng Ku

*17 Wardour Street, W1 (7437 1398/7734 3509).
Leicester Square or Piccadilly Circus tube.* **Meals
served** 11am-11.45pm Mon-Sat; 11am-11.15pm
Sun. **Dim sum** 11am-6pm daily. **Main courses**
£5.50-£13. *Dim sum* £1.95. **Service** 10%. **Credit**
AmEx, DC, MC, V. **Map** p316 J6.
High chairs.

Golden Dragon

*28-9 Gerrard Street, W1 (7734 2763). Leicester
Square or Piccadilly Circus tube.* **Meals served**
noon-11.30pm Mon-Thur; noon-midnight Fri, Sat;
11am-11pm Sun. **Dim sum** noon-5pm Mon-Sat;
11am-5pm Sun. **Main courses** £6.30-£22. *Dim
sum* £1.90-£3.50. **Service** 10%. **Credit** AmEx,
DC, MC, V. **Map** p319 K6/7.
High chairs.

Golden Palace

*146-50 Station Road, Harrow, Middx (8863 2333).
Harrow-on-the-Hill tube/rail.* **Meals served** noon-
11.30pm Mon-Sat; 11am-10.30pm Sun. **Dim sum**
noon-5pm Mon-Sat; 11am-5pm Sun. **Main courses**
£3.50-£9.50. *Dim sum* £2-£3.50. **Service** 10%.
Credit AmEx, DC, MC, V.
High chairs.

Hakkasan

*8 Hanway Place, W1 (7907 1888). Tottenham
Court Road tube.* **Bar Open** noon-1am Mon-
Wed; noon-2am Thur-Sat; noon-12.30am Sun.
Restaurant **Lunch served** noon-2.30pm Mon-Fri;
noon-4.30pm Sat, Sun. **Dinner served** 6-11.30pm
daily. **Main courses** £5.90-£40. *Dim sum* £3.50-
£16. **Service** 13%. **Both Credit** AmEx, MC, V.
Map p317 K5.

Harbour City

*46 Gerrard Street, W1 (7439 7859/7287 1526).
Leicester Square or Piccadilly Circus tube.* **Meals
served** noon-11.30pm Mon-Thur; noon-midnight Fri,
Sat; 11am-10.30pm Sun. **Dim sum** noon-5pm Mon-
Sat; 11am-5pm Sun. **Main courses** £5.50-£20. *Dim
sum* £1.80-£2.80. **Service** 10%. **Credit** AmEx, DC,
MC, V. **Map** p319 K6/7.
High chairs.

Local Friends

*28 North End Road, NW11 (8455 9258). Golders
Green tube/13, 82, 83, 102, 210, 226, 268, 328
bus.* **Meals served** noon-11pm; *dim sum* noon-
4.30pm daily. **Main courses** £4.50-£16. *Dim sum*
£2-£5. **Service** 10%. **Credit** AmEx, MC, V.

New World

*1 Gerrard Place, W1 (7734 0396). Leicester
Square tube.* **Meals served** 11am-11.45pm Mon-
Sat; 11am-11pm Sun. **Dim sum** 11am-6pm daily.
Main courses £4.65-£16. *Dim sum* £1.70-£3.50.
Credit AmEx, DC, MC, V. **Map** p319 K6/7.
Buggy access. High chairs. No-smoking tables.

Royal China

*40 Baker Street, W1 (7487 4688). Baker Street
tube.* **Meals served** noon-11pm Mon-Thur; noon-
11.30pm Fri, Sat; 11am-10pm Sun. **Dim sum** noon-
5pm daily. **Main courses** £8-£30. *Dim sum* £3-£5.
Service 122%. **Credit** AmEx, MC, V. **Map** p316 G5.
High chairs.
Branches: 13 Queensway, W2 (7221 2535); 30
Westferry Circus, E14 (7719 0888); 68 Queen's
Grove, NW8 (7586 4280).

Royal China

*3 Chelverton Road, SW15 (8788 0907). East
Putney tube.* **Lunch served** noon-3.30pm Mon-Sat;
noon-4pm Sun. **Dinner served** 6.30-11pm Mon-
Thur; 6.30-11.30pm Fri, Sat; 6.30-10.30pm Sun.
Dim sum noon-3.30pm daily. **Main courses** £5.50-
£22. *Dim sum* £2-£3.50. **Credit** AmEx.
Note that this restaurant is not part of the Royal
China chain.

Consumer

Belgo Centraal. *See p174.*

Chains

If you've run dry of inspiration, you could do worse than the following chains. The websites will give you a list of branches, so you can find out your nearest one.

Bierodrome *www.belgorestaurants.co.uk.*

Café Pasta *www.pizzaexpress.co.uk.*

Café Rouge *www.caferouge.co.uk.*

Nando's *www.nandos.co.uk.*

Pizza Express *www.pizzaexpress.co.uk.*

Wok Wok *www.wokwok.co.uk.*

Yellow River Café
www.yellowrivercafes.co.uk.

Neal's Yard Bakery & Tearoom
6 Neal's Yard, WC2 (7836 5199). Covent Garden tube. **Meals served** 10.30am-4.30pm Mon-Sat. **Main courses** £3.50-£4. **Minimum** (noon-2pm Mon-Fri; 10.30am-4.30pm Sat) £2.50. **No credit cards. Map** p317 L6.
A more tranquil option than Food for Thought (*see p175*), although equally buggy-unfriendly, as the dining room is on the first floor (with the takeaway counter on the ground). Choose from a daily changing menu that includes the likes of savoury croissants, soup, pizza and a hot dish (mushroom, spinach and cashew biryani, say). A healthy choice.
No smoking.

Neal's Yard Salad Bar
2 Neal's Yard, WC2 (7836 3233). Covent Garden tube. **Meals served** *Summer* 11.30am-8pm Mon-Sat; 11.30am-7.30pm Sun. *Winter* 11.30am-7pm daily. **Main courses** £5.50-£6.50. **No credit cards. Map** p317 L6.
The pedestrian zone of Neal's Yard means that kids can have a worry-free runaround. And, if they eat here (perched outside), a healthy lunch too. Dairy-, yeast- and wheat-free dishes are always available and, despite the name, there are four hot options a day (a stir-fry, for example).
Buggy access. No-smoking tables. Tables outdoors (9, courtyard).

Planet Hollywood
13 Coventry Street, W1 (7287 1000/ www.planethollywood.com). Piccadilly Circus tube. **Meals served** noon-11pm Mon-Thur, Sun; noon-midnight Fri, Sat. **Main courses** £9.95-£16.95. **Credit** AmEx, DC, MC, V. **Map** p319 K7.
This place is a kid's paradise. They get balloons, the staff are markedly indulgent toward them, and all the noise, colours and TV screens are custom-made to distract children. If you think you can handle all that, though, it's worth a trip. Organic ribeye steak, served with perfectly crisp skinny fries and a freshly made béarnaise, seems almost a bargain for the superlative quality, at £14.95. Adults or teenagers with big appetites will be swamped with choice: hamburgers, nachos, pasta, sandwiches, and irresistible desserts like Snickers cheesecake… The kids' menu, featuring similar delights, is shorter but good value.
Balloons. Bookings advisable (weekends). Buggy access. Children's menu (£7.95). Crayons. High chairs. Nappy-changing facilities. No-smoking tables.

Rainforest Café
20 Shaftesbury Avenue, W1 (7434 3111/ www.rainforest.co.uk). Piccadilly Circus tube. **Meals served** noon-10pm Mon-Fri; 11.30am-8pm Sat; 11.30am-10pm Sun. **Credit** AmEx, DC, MC, V. **Map** p319 K7.
Like all overpriced 'pleasures' in life, this place grabs you by the credit card for the sake of it. How they love it. Upstairs it's all merchandising: soft toys, stationery, toys and clothes on a rainforest theme, and all spectacularly expensive. The restaurant downstairs is an experience endured by adults for the sake of their progeny. Animatronic apes, elephants, butterflies lurk in gloomy corners; the light levels are kept low to give a rainforest feel. Freak thunderstorm sound effects occasionally distract you from your meal, much to the delight of most overexcited children. Kids make short work of their special menu, but beware, the price includes crayons and colouring-in material, but not a drink. They're better off ordering plain tap water and saving room for one of the enormously child-pleasing puddings, rather than one of the immensely gooey smoothies.
Buggy access. Children's menu (£8.95). Crayons. High chairs. Nappy-changing facilities. No smoking.

Rock & Sole Plaice

47 Endell Street, WC2 (7836 3785). Covent Garden or Leicester Square tube. **Meals served** 11.30am-10.30pm Mon-Sat; noon-9.30pm Sun. **Main courses** £7-£13. **Credit** MC, V. **Map** p317 L6.

If all else fails, they'll eat chips. This venerable fish and chip shop is a top-notch example of the genre. All the favourites – cod, haddock, rock salmon – are served with chunky chips; extras include excellent mushy peas. The outdoor seating area feels almost Mediterranean come the summer.
Buggy access. High chairs. Tables outdoors (20, pavement).

Smollensky's on the Strand

105 Strand, WC2 (7497 2101/www.smollenskys.co.uk). Covent Garden or Embankment tube/Charing Cross tube/rail. Bar **Open** noon-11pm Mon-Wed; noon-12.30am Thur-Sat; noon-5.30pm, 6.30-10.30pm Sun. *Restaurant* **Meals served** noon-midnight Mon-Wed; noon-12.30am Thur-Sat; noon-5.30pm, 6.30-11pm Sun. **Lunch served** noon-5.30pm, **dinner served** 6.30-10.30pm Sun. **Main courses** £8.85-£19.95. **Set lunch/pre-theatre menu** £10 two courses, £12 three courses. **Credit** AmEx, DC, MC, V. **Map** p319 L7.

With its clubby atmosphere, good food and laid-back feel, Smollensky's excels. The menu lets you be either posh (baked Alaskan salmon with wilted spinach and Puy lentils) or a punter (stuffed bacon busha burger), as you wish. Some dishes tend towards blandness, but if you opt for steak you won't be disappointed. This place tends to get packed on weeknights with heavy-drinking business types, and can be crowded and overwhelming for younger visitors. Parents with kids are likely to feel more comfortable here at lunchtime and on weekends. The children's menu lists a variety of main-course options for £4.95 a throw: macaroni and cheese, chicken breast, fish and chips, spag bol... but bear in mind that drinks and puddings cost extra. At the time of writing, another branch was due to open at Canary Wharf.
Booking advisable. Buggy access. Children's menu (£4.95). Crayons. Entertainment: Punch & Judy show, magic show, Nintendo games, face painting. High chairs. No-smoking tables. Toys.
Branches: Smollensky's 0₂ Centre, 255 Finchley Road, NW3 (7431 5007); **Smollensky's Bar & Grill** Bradmore House, Queen Caroline Street, W6 (8741 8124); **Smollensky's Wapping Riverside** Hermitage Wharf, 22 Wapping High Street, E1 (7680 1818).

Spiga

84-6 Wardour Street, W1 (7734 3444). Leicester Square or Piccadilly Circus tube. **Lunch served** noon-3pm Mon-Sat; 1-4pm Sun. **Dinner served** 6-11pm Mon, Tue, Sun; 6pm-midnight Wed-Sat. **Main courses** £8-£14. **Service** 12½%. **Credit** AmEx, MC, V. **Map** p316 J6.

A lively, sophisticated Italian restaurant where the crowd-pleasing thin-crust pizzas vie for menu space with pastas (including a simple but moreish spaghetti with tomato sauce) and dishes such as sautéd prawns with chilli and garlic or char-grilled ribeye steak with roast potatoes and fennel salad.
Booking advisable. Buggy access. High chairs.

Stanleys

6 Little Portland Street, W1 (7462 0099). Oxford Circus tube. **Meals served** noon-11pm Mon-Sat. **Main courses** £8.50-£10.95. **Credit** AmEx, MC, V. **Map** p316 J5.

Pared-down diner-meets-beer-hall decor, complete with handsome red banquette seating, is the setting for a sausage fest. They come in all guises – straight, game, Thai and vegetar-ian (the Glamorgan), with fries or mash, and cost around £8.50. Further comfort is provided in the form of hearty puds and, for adults, a good range of beers.
Buggy access. High chairs. Nappy-changing facilities. No-smoking tables. Reduced-price children's portions.

TGI Friday's

6 Bedford Street, WC2 (7379 0585/www.tgifridays.co.uk). Covent Garden or Embankment tube/Charing Cross tube/rail. Bar **Open** noon-11pm Mon-Fri; 11am-11pm Sat; noon-10.30pm Sun. *Restaurant* **Meals served** noon-11.30pm Mon-Sat; noon-11pm Sun. **Main courses** £7.15-£15.45. **Credit** AmEx, MC, V. **Map** p319 L7.

With their bright red braces and badges on their uniform, the waiters at TGI's seem stuck in an '80s timewarp. Yet, despite the overall air of generational schizophrenia in terms of the menu (huge, partly devoted to kiddie-friendly foods and part-ly sponsored by Jack Daniels), the food at TGI's is actually quite good. Starters such as nachos are usually big enough to share, though sides of mixed vegetables and a 'loaded' baked potato can seem a bit of an afterthought. The children's menu lists meals for about £4, or they can go the whole hog with the Clubhouse menu, which for £7.25 gets them a main course, dessert and a drink. Service can sometimes seem absurdly friendly, and the pop music's a bit intrusive, which means it's a great place for kids, if not their parents.
Balloons. Buggy access. Children's menu. Crayons. Entertainment: occasional face painting. High chairs. No-smoking tables.
Branches: 702-4 Purley Way, Croydon (8681 1313); Pentavia Retail Park, A41 Watford Way, NW7 (8203 9779); 96-8 Bishop's Bridge Road, W2 (7229 8600); 25-9 Coventry Street, W1 (7839 6262).

World Food Café

Neal's Yard Dining Room, 1st floor, 14 Neal's Yard, WC2 (7379 0298/www.worldfoodcafe.com). Covent Garden or Leicester Square tube. **Meals served** 11.30am-4.30pm Mon-Fri; 11.30am-5pm Sat. **Main courses** £5.95-£7.95. **Minimum** (noon-2pm Mon-Fri; 11.30am-5pm Sat) £5. **Credit** MC, V. **Map** p317 L6.

This clean, white space occasionally resembles a crèche, such is its child-friendly reputation. The vegetarian food is among the best in London, the staff are pleasant and the atmosphere is mellow. Dishes are easy to share – try the Mexican plate (refried beans, melted cheese, guacamole, salsa, sour cream, salads and corn chips).
High chairs. No smoking.

Yo! Sushi

52 Poland Street, W1 (7287 0443/www.yosushi.co.uk). Leicester Square tube. **Meals served** noon-midnight daily. **Credit** AmEx, DC, MC, V. **Map** p316 J6.

This conveyor-belt sushi bar is a big hit with children whose culinary horizons go beyond supernoodles and spring rolls to a rather more authentic Far Eastern menu. Japanese dishes parade past their noses on colour-coded platters: the lime green one costs just £1.50, the most expensive, pink, is £3.50. You eat the delicacies on them and the waiter tots up the bill from your empty plates. Parents should be prepared to finish all the platters that adventurous children have swiped then rejected. Play it safe with the sort of thing you know they'll like: chicken yakitori, prawn rolls and rice in seaweed wraps. Seafood fans love the prawns. Unlimited mineral water is on tap on the counter you sit at; otherwise a robotic drinks trolley, carries juices and soft drinks.
Balloons and stickers. Booster seats. No smoking.
Branches throughout town. Check the phone book for your nearest.

Texas Embassy Cantina.
See p181.

Westminster

Seafresh
80-81 Wilton Road, SW1 (7828 0747). Victoria tube/ rail/24 bus. **Meals served** noon-10.30pm Mon-Sat. **Main courses** £5.55-£15.95. **Credit** AmEx, DC, MC, V. **Map** p318 J10.
There's a slightly wider choice than the norm at this fish and chip restaurant, with fisherman's pie, prawn salad and white-bait bolstering the likes of cod, haddock or plaice and chips. Children will love the nautical trappings.
Buggy access. High chairs.

Texas Embassy Cantina
1 Cockspur Street, SW1 (7925 0077/ www.texasembassy.com). Embankment tube/ Charing Cross tube/rail. **Meals served** noon-11pm Mon-Wed; noon-midnight Thur-Sat; noon-10.30pm Sun. **Main courses** £7.50-£16.95. **Credit** AmEx, DC, MC, V. **Map** p319 K7.
A brightly, busily decorated barn of a place, perfect for refu-elling after visiting the National Gallery or National Portrait Gallery. Large portions of Tex-Mex food keep everyone busy, and staff are niceness personified. Kids get their own menu, which includes tacos, burgers, chicken fingers and dessert, and any child making a noise is easily absorbed into the general hubbub.
Balloons. Buggy access. Children's menu (£4.50). Crayons. High chairs. Tables outdoors (8, pavement). Nappy-changing facilities.

Marylebone

Fairuz
3 Blandford Street, W1 (7486 8108/8182). Baker Street or Bond Street tube. **Meals served** noon-11.30pm Mon-Sat; noon-10.30pm Sun. **Main courses** £9.95-£12. **Set meals** £16.95 meze, £24.95 three courses. **Cover** £1.50. **Credit** AmEx, DC, MC, V. **Map** p316 G5.
Being small, with a vertiginous flight of stairs down to the loos, this is probably not the most accommodating restaurant for babies or toddling children. Older ones, however, especially non-fussy types who like the dippy, picky experience of meze, the sizzle of barbecued meat and stickiest pastries, appreciate the Lebanese classics on the menu. A family could easily go for two orders of the £24.95 set menu: it includes many sizeable dips (houmous, puréed aubergine, yoghurt), along with special little details such as pome-granate kernels, olives and plentiful salad. Then there's a substantial platter of barbecued meat wrapped in flat bread, followed by a flourish of cold fresh fruit for pudding. Round off with a plate of sticky pastries. Your children will thank you for it.
Book dinner. Buggy access. High chairs.
Branch: 27 Westbourne Grove, W2 (7243 8444).

La Galette
56 Paddington Street, W1 (7935 1554/ www.lagalette.com). Baker Street or Bond Street tube. **Breakfast served** 10am-4pm, **meals served** noon-11pm daily. **Main courses** £4.95-£9.50. **Set lunch** (noon-5pm Mon-Fri) £6.95 two courses. **Credit** AmEx, MC, V.
This modern crêperie uses upmarket ingredients (many of them organic). While parents tackle the likes of a paysanne galette (creamed leeks with bacon and parsley) or a salad niçoise, children can get stuck into a crêpe with chocolate

La Galette

Consumer

sauce or a galette with tomato, basil and cheese. From a full list, there's a range of French ciders – and for under-age drinkers, apple juice.
Bookings not accepted. Buggy access. High chairs. Tables outdoors (2, terrace).

Wagamama
101A Wigmore Street, W1 (7409 0111/ www.wagamama.com). Bond Street or Marble Arch tube. **Meals served** noon-11pm Mon-Sat; 12.30-10pm Sun. **Main courses** £4.85-£8.50. **Set meals** £9.95-£10.95. **Credit** AmEx, DC, MC, V. **Map** p316 G6.
It's a shame that Wagamama doesn't do smaller portions of its dishes, as some of them, such as the vast house ramen (a huge soup, with noodles, half a boiled egg, chicken, greens, tofu, prawn and so on), are a bit daunting for kids. Still, everything else at these buzzing sleek canteen-style noodle bars is very child-friendly. Try to avoid peak times, when you often have to queue.
Buggy access. High chairs. Nappy-changing facilities. No smoking.
Branches throughout town. Check the phone book for your nearest.

North London

Afghan Kitchen
35 Islington Green, N1 (7359 8019). Angel tube. **Lunch served** noon-3.30pm Tue-Sat. **Dinner served** 5.30-11pm Tue-Sat. **Main courses** £4.50-£6. **No credit cards.**
A bare, small, Afghan kitchen, really, but a reliable place for a simple, hot meal, where the staff are tolerant and encour-

aging toward young, messy eaters and the food is plentiful and inexpensive. The Kitchen always has the same menu: four meat and four vegetarian dishes, slightly curried, with plenty of vegetables and intriguing seasonings involved. The Afghan-style flatbread is delicious and the sticky baclavas for pudding a gift for sweet teeth.
Buggy access. High chairs.

Banners
83 Hazellville Road, N19 (7686 2944). Bus W5. **Open** 9am-11pm Mon-Fri; 9.30am-11pm Sat; 9.30am-10.30pm Sun. **Meals served** 9am-10.30pm Mon-Sat; 9.30am-10pm Sun. **Main courses** £7.95-£10.95. **Credit** MC, V.
Very family-friendly, but like the original branch in Crouch End, a bit cramped and chaotic. The menu is a list of crowd-pleasers: greasy spoon dishes, a scattering of international mains and a great kids' selection, plus a must-try hot choco-late. On its way to being a local institution, no doubt.
Booking advisable (weekends). Buggy access. Children's menu (until 7pm, £1.50-£3.25). Crayons. High chairs. Tables outdoors (patio). Toys.
Branch: 21 Park Road, N8 (8348 2930).

Café Mozart
17 Swains Lane, N6 (8348 1384). Highgate tube/Gospel Oak rail/214, C2, C11, C12 bus. **Meals served** 9am-10pm daily. **Credit** MC, V.
Although there's no obvious link with Amadeus, this popu-lar local café does have a distinctly mittel-European feel. Beetroot or sour cream often appear on the specials menu, which changes daily and usually includes home-made soup served with a bread basket, and a vegetarian dish, as well as two or three more substantial dishes such as pancetta with grilled vegetables. But it's the unusual selection of compli-cated cakes and pastries that are the draw; they include sachertorte and zwetschkenfleck (plum tart) and can be bought whole to take home (though you're unlikely to be able to pass them off as your own work). Hearty breakfast dishes, sandwiches and freshly squeezed juices ensure there is something to match all levels of hunger and fussiness, which makes it excellent for family eating. Inside can be a bit cramped for buggies but the pavement tables are popular all year round thanks to outdoor heaters. Be prepared to queue at weekends.
Buggy access. Reduced-price children's portions. High chairs. No smoking. Tables outdoors (9, courtyard). Toys.

Giraffe
29-31 Essex Road, N1 (7359 5999). Angel tube. **Open** 8am-4pm, 5-11.30pm Mon-Fri; 9am-11.30pm Sat; 9am-10.30pm Sun. **Drinks only** served 5-6pm Sat, Sun. **Main courses** £7-£10. **Set dinner** (5-7pm Mon-Fri) £6.50 two courses. **Credit** AmEx, MC, V.
Family favourite Giraffe is renowned not only for its funky decor and consistently amiable staff but also for the reliably high standards in the menu department. All dishes on a recent visit got full marks, from house salad to potato wedges (seriously moreish), to slow-grilled organic chicken breast, to Thai green vegetable curry. Come here for an early supper during the week and you choose a starter and main for a piffling £6.50. Similarly, the children's menu scores many points. Dishes are priced individually so you aren't roped into paying for puddings and fizzy drinks that the kids don't want. Instead, small people can choose something as unthreatening as spaghetti hoops on toast, or sample Giraffe's way with poultry (crunchy chicken pieces) or bangers (meaty or guilt-free), all of which are served with fries for £3.95. Young kids, in particular, get thoroughly spoilt by beaming staff.

Buggy access. Children's menu. Crayons. High chairs. No-smoking tables. Tables outdoors.
Branches: 46 Rosslyn Hill, NW3 (7435 0343); 6-8 Blandford Street, W1 (7935 2333); 27 Battersea Rise, SW11 (7223 0933).

Iznik
19 Highbury Park, N5 (7354 5697). Highbury & Islington tube/rail. **Meals served** 10am-4pm Mon-Fri. **Dinner** served 6.30pm-midnight daily. **Main courses** £7.25-£9.50. **Service** 10%. **Credit** MC, V.
The long-suffering staff at this prettily decorated Turkish restaurant see a lot of children at the weekends. But the meze part of the menu lends itself to small appetites, and sharing a range of dishes is always fun; more substantial fare includes a choice of kebabs served with rice and salad. Quality food in a relaxed setting.
Booking advisable (weekends). Buggy access.

Marine Ices
8 Haverstock Hill, NW3 (7482 9003). Chalk Farm tube/31 bus. **Open** 10.30am-10pm daily. **Meals served** *Restaurant* 12.30-3pm, 6-11pm Mon-Fri; 12.30-11pm Sat; 12.30-10pm Sun. **Main courses** *Restaurant* £5.20-£9.60. **Credit** MC, V.
The milkshakes, and Italian ice-cream, served in a kaleido-scope of flavours, are the big draw at this well-known parlour, but the friendly atmosphere and old-style trattoria menu win points too.
Buggy access. High chairs. No-smoking area (restaurant).

Santa Fe
75 Upper Street, N1 (7288 2288/www.santafe.co.uk). Angel tube. Bar **Open** noon-11pm Mon-Sat; noon-10.30pm Sun. *Restaurant* **Meals served** noon-10.30pm Mon-Sat; noon-10.30pm Sun. **Main courses** £6.95-£12.95. **Credit** AmEx, DC, MC, V.
In terms of relatively authentic, New Mexico cuisine, this place is a bit underrated. Part of the problem could be the modern bar out front, with its wiry furniture and trendy young Islington crowd with heads on swivels who stare at everybody who comes in the door. Don't be put off: once you get past the Prada gauntlet, it's all complex sauces and decent cuisine inside. Parents and kids willing to try new tastes will be pleased by the excellent food, including fantastic rellenos and enchiladas. There's a smaller kids' menu, with less spicy items, including 'Spaghetti Santa Fe', 'Roadrunner chicken breast', and… baked beans on toast.
Booking advisable (weekends). Buggy access. Children's menu (£3.95). Crayons. High chairs. Nappy-changing facilities. No-smoking area. Tables outdoors (12, pavement). Toys.

Shish
2-6 Station Parade, NW2 (8208 9290). Willesden Green tube/260, 266 bus. **Meals served** 11.30am-11.45pm Mon-Sat; 11.30am-11.30pm Sun. **Main courses** £4.95-£8.95. **Credit** MC, V.
Shish is no ordinary kebab bar. The extensive wooden bar winds around the kitchen area, providing ringside entertain-ment for would-be grill chefs, and food is simple but effective, involving culinary specialities from the East, which covers Chinese and Indonesian tastes alongside Middle Eastern and Greek dishes. Even the taps are a novelty, supplying as much mineral water as you want for a pound. A children's menu is in the pipeline, but it's easy to find something on the main menu to suit most little people's palates, including fries, bread and dips, juices and ice-creams.
Buggy access. No smoking (downstairs).

- delicious noodles
- fabulous rice dishes
- freshly squeezed juices
- wines • sake • japanese beers

enjoy wagamama in a clean, smoke-free environment • child seating available

wagamama®

www.wagamama.com for locations and menu

(for listing see eating section in this guide)

★ Top: Smoke-free zones ★

Busaba Eathai
See p174.

Café Mozart
See p182.

Food for Thought
See p175.

Giraffe
See p182.

Gourmet Burger Kitchen
See p187.

Jones Dairy Café
See p185.

Masala Zone
See p175.

Neal's Yard Bakery & Tearoom
See p178.

Rainforest Café
See p178.

Table Café
See p173.

Wagamama
See p181.

World Food Café
See p179.

Tartuf

88 Upper Street, N1 (7288 0954). Angel tube.
Dinner served 5-11.30pm Mon-Thur; 5pm-midnight Fri.
Meals served noon-midnight Sat; noon-11.30pm Sun.
Main courses £4.90-£10.80. **Set lunch** £5.90 two
courses. **Set meal** £10.80 eat as much as you like.
Service 12.5%. **Credit** MC, V.
The success of this mellow, kitchen-like café is built around
the tarte flambée. The waiting staff are well versed in introducing first-time tasters to the delicacy, which is best
described as a 'French pizza'. They explain that it's sensible
to order one at a time, to share around the table, and to keep
them coming. This way you can try all kinds of toppings.
The tartes cost from around a fiver and consist of the
thinnest of dough bases, spread with French yoghurt and
onion, then given a topping and baked. We found the classic tarte flambée – the bacon and emmenthal cheese one – to
be the tastiest, while the chicken variety was less successful. The B-side of the menu lists the delightful sweet tartes
flambées; the hot banana and chocolate sauce one goes down
a treat. The down-home, wooden furniture and simple decor
mean there's not much for tiny hands to damage.
*Booking advisable (Fri, Sat). Buggy access. High chairs.
Reduced-price portions for children. Tables outdoors
(10, pavement).*
Branch: 169 Clapham High Street, SW4 (7622 8169).

East London

Arkansas Café

*Unit 12, Old Spitalfields Market, E1 (7377 6999).
Liverpool Street tube/rail.* **Lunch served** noon-
2.30pm Mon-Fri; noon-4pm Sun. **Dinner served**
by arrangement. **Main courses** £4.50-£13.50.
Credit DC, MC, V. **Map** p321 R5.
Located at the fringe of Spitalfields Market, this down-
to-earth café is a carnival for carnivores, dishing up free-range
pork ribs, Irish and US steaks and French corn-fed chicken,
all grilled to perfection. The City crowd has known about
this place for years, and booking is recommended. It's a bit
hectic during the lunchtime rush, and there's no specific children's menu, but the atmosphere is laid-back, the waitresses
are friendly and helpful, and the menu includes hamburgers,
a variety of sandwiches and hot dogs, all likely to please the
little ones. Platters are served with ample helpings of mash,
coleslaw, purple cabbage salad and home-made baked beans,
and desserts are as you might expect – highly calorific and
deeply yummy.
*No-smoking tables. Tables outdoors (30, terrace inside
market).*

Elche

*567-9 Leytonstone High Road, E11 (8558 0008).
Leytonstone tube.* **Lunch served** 12.30-2.30pm Tue-Sat.
Dinner served 6.30-11pm Mon-Thur; 6.30pm-midnight
Fri, Sat. **Meals served** 12.30pm-midnight Sun. **Main
courses** £8.50-£15. **Tapas** £2.50-£5. **Set tapas** (Mon-
Thur, Sun) £10 three dishes. **Set buffet** (12.30-4pm Sun)
£10; £5 children. **Credit** MC, V.
With its cheerful yellow walls, friendly staff and intriguing
suit of armour by the door, Elche is a spacious and sufficiently laid-back place to eat with children at any time of the
day. However, the Sunday lunchtime buffet is a particularly
popular rendezvous for local families. Some 30 dishes are set
out, ranging from simple plates of ham, salads, cold and
smoked salmon to a rich, flavoursome stew of chicken and
olives – plus the house speciality, a high-quality paella. You
can scoff as much as you want and, at £10 for adults (which
includes a half-jug of sangria or wine per person, and a
dessert) and a fiver for kids, it's really excellent value.
*Booking advisable (Fri-Sun). Buggy access. Reduced-price
Sunday buffet. High chairs. Tables outdoors (3, pavement).*

Faulkner's

*424-6 Kingsland Road, E8 (7254 6152). Dalston
Kingsland rail/67, 76, 149, 242, 243 bus.* **Lunch served**
noon-2pm Mon-Fri. **Dinner served** 5-10pm Mon-Thur;
4.15-10pm Fri. **Meals served** 11.30am-10pm Sat; noon-
9pm Sun. **Main courses** £7.50-£13. **Minimum** £4.
Credit MC, V.
An old-fashioned fish and chip restaurant, with busy takeaway attached. Children can choose scampi or chicken
nuggets if they don't fancy cod with their chips, then finish
off with ice-cream. Fish can be poached instead of fried if you
want to go down the healthy route. Deservedly popular.
*Buggy access. Children's menu (£3.95). High chairs. No-
smoking tables.*

Frocks

*95 Lauriston Road, E9 (8986 3161). Mile End tube then
277 bus.* **Brunch served** 11am-4pm Sat, Sun. **Lunch
served** 11am-2.30pm Tue-Fri. **Dinner served** 6.30-
11pm Tue-Sat. Closed Aug. **Main courses** £11-£13.50.
Set lunch £9.50 two courses, £13.50 three courses.
Credit AmEx, DC, MC, V.

Afghan Kitchen.
See p181.

A great brunch venue: it's very close to Victoria Park, staff are friendly and the place has a much-used, second-hand vibe. Sink down with a jug of Bucks Fizz, and choose from a list of fry-ups, filled croissants, eggy bread or fruit compote. The walled garden is the place to be if the weather allows.
Bookings advisable (weekends). Buggy access. High chairs. Tables outdoors (7, walled garden; 4, pavement).

Hadley House
27 High Street, E11 (8989 8855). Snaresbrook or Wanstead tube. **Lunch served** 11.30am-2.30pm Mon-Sat. **Dinner served** 7-10.30pm Mon-Sat. **Meals served** noon-9pm Sun. **Main courses** £8.95-£16.95. **Set dinner** (Mon) £16.50 three courses. **Credit** MC, V.
Attractive and easy going, Hadley House is a popular destination for families, particularly at weekends. A recent Sunday lunch menu included toad in the hole – one portion was ample for two hungry kids – and there's always a pasta dish. Grown-up dishes are based around first-rate meat and fish, while lemon posset and a superb chocolate mousse are examples of the fine desserts. Staff are young, cheery and child-friendly.
Buggy access. High chairs. Reduced-price children's portions. Tables outdoors (6, patio).

Jones Dairy Café
23 Ezra Street, E2 (7739 5372). Bus 26, 48, 55. **Open** 9am-3pm Fri, Sat; 8am-2pm Sun. **No credit cards**.
On Sunday mornings, when the crowds from Columbia Road flower market pour in, Jones operates more as a takeaway for bagels, organic buns or cakes, good coffee and fantastic

orange juice. Otherwise it's a great little local diner, serving brunch-style food (omelettes, scrambled egg and smoked salmon, tomatoes on toast). A pleasantly old-fashioned place, although service is occasionally a bit dour.
Buggy access. High chairs. No smoking.

Laxeiro Tapas Bar
93 Columbia Road, E2 (7729 1147/www.laxeiro.com). Bus 26, 48, 55. **Lunch served** noon-3pm, **dinner served** 7-11pm Tue-Sat. **Meals served** 9am-4pm Sun. **Tapas** £2.95-£7.50. **Credit** DC, MC, V.
An unassuming but very friendly tapas bar. The roll call of barbecue sardines, patatas bravas, chorizo, garlic mushrooms and tomato and mozzarella salad isn't exactly innovative, but is appreciated locally. Prices are very reasonable – tortilla, for instance, is £2.95 a slice.
Booking advisable (dinner). Tables outdoors (2, pavement).

Viet Hoa
70-72 Kingsland Road, E2 (7729 8293). Bus 26, 48, 55, 67, 149, 242, 243. **Lunch served** noon-3.30pm, **dinner served** 5.30-11pm daily. **Main courses** £2.15-£6.90. **Credit** MC, V.
Shoreditch bohos pack in alongside big family groups in this two-floor canteen-style Vietnamese restaurant. The long menu should have something for everyone (there's lots of vegetarian choices) and the noise levels are usually high enough to drown out the noisiest kids.
Buggy access. No-smoking tables.

Boiled Egg & Soldiers

South-east London

Joanna's
56 Westow Hill, SE19 (8670 4052). Crystal Palace rail.
Meals served 10am-11pm Mon-Sat; 10am-10.15pm Sun.
Main courses £7.50-£15.95. **Credit** AmEx, DC, MC, V.
With a keenly priced children's menu and brasserie cooking
that veers from homely roasts and chips to lighter seafood
dishes and imaginative vegetarian options, Joanna's manages
to appeal to its varied south London clientele. It's a restful
place to come during the week with your children, who can
have a delightful home-made burger, or chicken, sausage or
pasta and a bowl of ice-cream from their own menu. At weekends it's far busier, but the staff are still efficient and kindly
disposed toward family groups.
*Buggy access. Children's menu (£3.75). Crayons. High
chairs. No-smoking tables. Tables outdoors (5, pavement).*

Olley's
*67-9 Norwood Road, SE24 (8671 8259/www.olleys.info).
Herne Hill rail/3, 68 bus.* **Meals served** noon-10.30pm
Tue-Sat. **Dinner served** 5-10.30pm Mon, Sun. **Main
courses** £5.75-£18.25. **Credit** AmEx, MC, V.
Surely the best fish and chip shop in London. In addition to
the traditional fried fish and chips, a range of fish is served
(from breaded calamares to swordfish and chips), plus extras
such as own-made pea fritters. There are lighter options too
– seabass is steamed with ginger and spring onions, then
served with broccoli and new potatoes. Staff are friendly and
efficient. Children get dishes such as haddock or scampi, for
about £3 including a drink. You get what you pay for, but if
the prices bother you, get a (cheaper) takeaway and nip across
to Brockwell Park.
*Buggy access. Children's menu. High chairs. No-smoking
tables. Tables outdoors (12, pavement).*

South-west London

Boiled Egg & Soldiers
*63 Northcote Road, SW11 (7223 4894). Clapham
Junction rail.* **Open** 9am-6pm Mon-Sat; 10am-5pm Sun.
No credit cards.
During the week for lunch and tea, this popular café is
the preserve of families. Children's portions are exactly the
right size and there is always something that even the pick-
iest eater will like. Boiled eggs and soldiers obviously, but
also sausages, baked beans, scrambled egg, and staff do a
plate of vegetable sticks, chopped fruit and hula hoops, which
goes down well. There's a good variety of juices, including
apple, orange and cranberry. Plastic plates are provided for
smaller children; chunky hard-to-break glasses are given to
all and spout beakers are available if you haven't brought
your own. There are a number of cartoons around the walls,
which seem to hold kids' attentions for a surprisingly long
time. The puddings and cakes are wonderfully satisfying and
the warm chocolate brownie and ice-cream is just what you
need after a chilly afternoon on the common.
*Buggy access. Children's menu (from £1.75). Crayons.
High chairs. Tables outdoors (3, pavement; 8, garden).
Toys.*

Canyon
*Towpath near Richmond Bridge, Richmond, Surrey
(8948 2944/www.canyonfood.co.uk). Richmond tube/rail.*
Brunch served 11am-4pm Sat, Sun. **Lunch served**
noon-4pm Mon-Fri. **Dinner served** 6-11pm daily.
Main courses £10-£16. **Credit** AmEx, MC, V.
This top-quality restaurant has been going through changes
recently; some worried it had lost its way, but pronounce-
ments of its downward slide appear to have been premature.
It has always had the advantage of its view – at the edge of

the river looking out over the water – and adventurous cooking, with the likes of truffle and pecorino ravioli, and grilled ribeye steak with mashed root vegetables. A separate menu for kids includes more traditional – and less rich – items like crispy cod and chips, macaroni and cheese, and ham and tomato pizza. There is even a separate dessert menu, with familiar banoffee pie and ice-creams. However, realistically speaking, this doesn't seem the kind of place that would have much patience for rambunctious youngsters.
Buggy access. Children's menu (£4, desserts £2). Crayons. High chairs. Nappy-changing facilities. No-smoking tables. Tables outdoors (18, courtyard; 18, terrace).
Branches: **Montana** 125 Dawes Road, SW6 (7385 9500); **Dakota** 127 Ledbury Road, W11 (7792 9191); **Utah** 18 High Street, SW19 (8944 1909).

The Depot
Tideway Yard, Mortlake High Street, SW14 (8878 9462). Mortlake rail/209 bus. **Open** 10am-11pm Mon-Sat; 10am-10.30pm Sun. **Lunch served** noon-3pm, **dinner served** 6-10.30pm Mon-Sat. **Meals served** noon-10pm Sun. **Main courses** £9.95-£13.50. **Set meal** (Mon-Sat lunch) £9.95 two courses. **Credit** AmEx, DC, MC, V.
A local noted for the river views from the picture windows, and a firm favourite for moneyed family groups. This is mostly because the brasserie menu is a huge success, with some perfect vegetarian dishes as well as juicy rib-eye steaks, chargrilled swordfish, cod and crab cakes and rack of lamb. While adults indulge themselves in such dishes, children can work their way through their own simple menu. There's penne with a napolitana or bolognese sauce, or plain with butter and cheese if they prefer, fish goujons and chips, sausage and mash or grilled chicken breast with chips. Service is friendly and encouraging toward young diners.
Buggy access. Children's menu (£3.50, desserts £1.90). Crayons. High chairs. Nappy-changing facilities. No-smoking tables. Tables outdoors (6, courtyard).

Don Fernando's
27F The Quadrant, Richmond, Surrey (8948 6447/ www.donfernando.co.uk). Richmond tube/rail. **Meals served** noon-3pm, 6-11pm Mon, Tue; noon-11pm Wed-Sat; noon-10pm Sun. **Main courses** £8-£13. **Tapas** £3-£5. **Set meals** £14-£18 two courses. **Credit** AmEx, MC, V.
A fine place to lunch after a bracing walk in the Old Deer Park, Don Fernando's, just by Richmond station, is adored locally for its warm welcome and hot dishes. There are 48 dishes on the tapas menu, which means that there's a little plateful to appeal to every palate here. Most of the tapas cost £3-£4, so older children can go all sophisticated with prawns, squid or snails without breaking the bank. Childpleasers such as pincho pollo (barbecued chicken and sausage on a stick) always wins lipsmacking approval, as do the cheese-drenched nachos, jumbo prawns and meatballs. Really unadventurous children can have an enormous bowl of crisp, slim chips.
Buggy access. High chairs. No-smoking tables.

Gourmet Burger Kitchen
44 Northcote Road, SW11 (7228 3309/ www.gbkinfo.co.uk). Clapham Junction rail. **Meals served** noon-11pm Mon-Fri; 11am-11pm Sat; 11am-10pm Sun. **Main courses** £4.95-£6.95. **Credit** AmEx, MC, V.
If you want your kids to appreciate the finer things in life, you could do worse than start them off in Gourmet Burger Kitchen. This new two-link chain takes old-favourite burger and chips to a higher dimension: a Junior Burger, fat-cut chips and a thick creamy milkshake will reliably hit the spot,

although more adventurous budding gourmets may want to try chorizo or chicken satay in their burger buns. Don't worry about the lack of puddings on the menu – with main courses this filling no one will want one. GBK can get busy at weekends, with long queues for a table. Weekday lunchtimes and late afternoons are more relaxed times for a family treat.
Buggy access. Children's menu (£3.80). High chairs. No smoking. Tables outdoors (4, pavement).
Branch: 331 West End Lane, NW6 (7794 5455/5855).

Metrogusto
153 Battersea Park Road, SW8 (7720 0204). Battersea Park rail/44, 344 bus. **Lunch served** 12.30-2.30pm Mon-Thur; noon-2.45pm Fri, Sat. **Dinner served** 6.30-10.30pm Mon-Thur; 6.30-10.45pm Fri, Sat. **Main courses** £7.50-£13.50. **Set lunch** £12.50 two courses. **Service** 10%. **Credit** MC, V.
This airy spacious dining room has rough-plastered walls hung with bold contemporary art that gets children's heads swivelling. Family groups sit around wide, polished tables and choose from a number of quite posh daily specials or stick to the à la carte menu, which lists a number of classic Italian meals that can be served in reduced-price portions. Margerita pizza, spaghetti bolognese, Italian sausage and mash are all firm favourites, while fussier types will be very content with a big bowl of chunky chips. Service is friendly and chatty.
Booking advisable (weekends). Buggy access. High chairs. No-smoking tables.
Branch: 11-13 Theberton Street, N1 (7226 9400).

Tiger Lil's
16A Clapham Common South Side, SW4 (7720 5433/ www.tigerlils.com). Clapham Common tube. **Lunch served** noon-3pm Mon-Fri. **Dinner served** 6-11.30pm Mon-Thur; 6pm-midnight Fri. **Meals served** noon-midnight Sat; noon-11pm Sun. **Unlimited stir-fry** £12.50; £5.50 5-10s; free under-5s. **Credit** AmEx, MC, V.
Stir-fry in industrial-sized quantities is the name of the likeable Tiger Lil's game. You order your starters and drinks at the table, then move on up to the chefs' area to choose your ingredients, which is when the fun starts. With the main course, you pay a set price for your bowl of stir-fry, and you can go back to the wok chef as often as you like. There are loads of chopped veg and leafy greens, cubed white fish, seafood, chicken and turkey to choose from. Resist tempta-

Red Pepper. *See p190.*

Consumer

tion to select too many items: you'll end up with a dog's dinner of a stir-fry. Still, there's always a dessert such as white chocolate cheesecake or ice-cream to make amends. *Buggy access. Crayons. High chairs. Nappy-changing facilities. Toys.*
Branches: 270 Upper Street, N1 (7226 1118); 75 Bishop's Bridge Road, W2 (7221 2622).

West London

Julie's Restaurant

135-7 Portland Road, W11 (7229 8331/ www.juliesrestaurant.com). Holland Park tube. Wine bar **Open** 9am-11pm Mon-Sat; 9am-10pm Sun. **Lunch served** 12.30-2.45pm Mon-Sat; 12.30-3.30pm Sun. **Tea served** 3-7.30pm daily. **Dinner served** 7.30-11pm Mon-Sat; 7.30-10pm Sun. **Main courses** £8.50-£13. *Restaurant* **Lunch served** 12.30-2.45pm Mon-Fri; 12.30-3pm Sun. **Dinner served** 7-11.30pm Mon-Sat; 7-10.30pm Sun. **Set Sunday lunch** £18.95 two courses, £21.95 three courses. **Main courses** £13-£21. **Credit** AmEx, MC, V.

Ladies, with babies, who lunch around Holland Park will probably have Julie's top of their list as it has a relaxed atmosphere despite its austere medieval decor. Kids are well catered for during Sunday lunch with a children's menu, which includes use of the crèche, while adults enjoy Sunday roasts with all the trimmings. The kids' food is served during the starters, which means parents can relax for the rest of meal while their well-fed offspring find entertainment in the crèche upstairs, which has two dedicated staff. The cuisine isn't the best in the world, but the ambience makes amends. *Buggy access. Children's menu (Sun, £9.50). Crèche (noon-3.30pm Sun). High chairs. Tables outdoors (12, pavement).*

Pubs

Parents nowadays expect to be able to spend an afternoon in the pub with their children. High chairs, nappy-changing facilities and kids' menus are just some of the services that pubs now have to offer if they're to cater to the whole family. Groups such as Charlie Chalk, Brewers Fare, Wacky Warehouse, Big Steak and Fullers have fairly generic pubs, but here we have listed some more idiosyncratic choices outside of central London (in the centre of town there are many great restaurants where you can get a drink). But remember: no matter how warm the welcome, families will still have to contend with Britain's archaic licensing laws, of course. Unless a pub has a children's licence (and the majority don't), you'll usually be restricted to certain parts of the pub, such as a family room or restaurant area.

Ashburnham Arms

25 Ashburnham Grove, SE10 (8692 2007). Greenwich rail/DLR. **Open** noon-3.30pm, 6-11pm Mon-Sat; noon-3.30pm, 7-10.30pm Sun. **Food served** noon-2.30pm, 6-8.30pm Tue-Fri. **Credit** (food only) MC, V.

Within walking distance of the rail and DLR station, the Ashburnham is one of the area's best local pubs. Tasty own-cooked pasta dishes are served on four lunchtimes a week and on Tuesday and Friday evenings, alongside jacket spuds, sarnies and the like. Children can order half portions from the standard menu, then burn off any excess energy on the slide outside. The function room is sometimes available for families to spread out in. *Buggy access. Garden. High chairs. Reduced-price children's portions. Tables outdoors (garden). Toys.*

Boaters Inn

Canbury Gardens, Lower Ham Road, Kingston-upon-Thames, Surrey (8541 4672). Kingston rail. **Open** Apr-Sept 11am-11pm Mon-Sat; noon-10.30pm Sun. Oct-Mar noon-3pm, 5.30-11pm Mon-Thur; 11am-11pm Fri, Sat; noon-10.30pm Sun. **Food served** noon-3pm, 6-9pm Mon-Sat; noon-3pm Sun. **Credit** AmEx, MC, V.

Once a café, this modern building occupies a prime spot next to the Thames, north of the town centre. In summer, plenty of outside seating and an elevated front terrace make this a popular spot to watch folk messing about on the water. Kids get to tuck into whale-shaped fish fingers or bug-shaped chicken nuggets, with chips and beans. If you sit by the river, keep a close eye on your kids; otherwise, spread out in the park. *Children's menu (£3.25-£3.95). Nappy-changing facilities. Buggy access. No-smoking area. Restaurant. Tables outdoors (riverside patio, front balcony). TV.*

Bread & Roses

68 Clapham Manor Street, SW4 (7498 1779). Clapham Common or Clapham North tube. **Open** noon-11pm Mon-Fri; 11am-11pm Sat; noon-10.30pm Sun. **Food served** noon-3pm, 7-9.30pm Mon-Fri; noon-4pm (African buffet only), 6-9.30pm Sat, Sun. **Credit** MC, V.

New Age, New Labour, slightly left of centre liberals and organically grown parents have found a home in this brightly coloured, minimalist boozer, which manages to be both traditional pub and arts centre bar. Filling pub food such as sausages and mash or spinach and mushroom burritos help modern workers fend off starvation; children enjoy smaller portions and prices. Music (*see p233* Mwalimu Express), comedy and poetry events, plus Sunday African buffets add to the *Internationalist* flavour. The place is child-friendly to a fault, especially at weekends; toys and high chairs are provided in the spacious conservatory to the rear. *Buggy access. Children's menu (£4). Crayons. Family room. High chairs. Nappy-changing facilities. No-smoking tables. Tables outdoors (patio, rear garden). Toys.*

Nectar

Tabernacle Arts Centre, Powis Square, W11 (7565 7808). Ladbroke Grove, Notting Hill Gate or Westbourne Park tube. **Meals served** 8.30am-11pm Mon-Sat; 10am-5pm Sun. **Main courses** £4-£7.50. **Credit** MC, V. **Map** p312 A6.

This treasure is hidden away in the Tabernacle Arts Centre, a beautiful red-brick building. It's obviously a popular lunchtime retreat for parents and on a recent visit adults were easily outnumbered by kids and babies in buggies. The atmosphere is conducive to relaxed eating as the café is just screened off from the foyer so you feel involved in the bustling arty atmosphere of the centre. The kids' menu is more creative than your average, with mini rotis and cottage pies for around £2. The menu covers all cravings, from healthy breakfasts to hearty mains, and the dishes have a definite Caribbean slant. Desserts range all the way from cream cakes to fresh fruit salad. Such high-quality food for such low prices makes Nectar one of our favourite things in west London.

Buggy access. Children's menu (£2-£2.50). High chairs. Nappy-changing facilities (in centre). No-smoking tables. Tables outdoors (5, pavement).

Orange Lemon & Lime

16 College Parade, Salusbury Road, NW6 (7372 1404). Queen's Park tube/rail/Brondesbury Park rail. **Meals served** 11am-11pm Mon-Sat; 11am-5pm Sun. **Main courses** £8.95-£13.50. **Credit** MC, V.

The only oranges, lemons and limes found at this simply furnished restaurant are stacked in the fireplace, perhaps as a symbolic gesture to its history. When the restaurant originally opened each dish involved something fruity but this idea was obviously shelved in favour of a less restrictive menu. Having been let loose from the shackles of the citrus

Engineer

Crown & Greyhound

73 Dulwich Village, SE21 (8299 4976). North Dulwich rail. **Open** 11am-11pm Mon-Sat; noon-10.30pm Sun. **Food served** noon-2.30pm, 6-10pm Mon-Sat; noon-3pm Sun. **Credit** MC, V.

A historic landmark, this: a vast Victorian mansion of a pub, with a gravel front drive that could grace a prominent country house hotel. The seven wings house a restaurant, conservatory and garden at the back, a separate no-smoking section to one side, and three main bar areas built around an ornate, oval counter. Kids can enjoy chicken nuggets and chips off their own menu (in the evening).

Buggy access. Children's menu (£3.25). Crayons. Family room. Garden. High chairs. Nappy-changing facilities. No-smoking area (restaurant).

Engineer

65 Gloucester Avenue, NW1 (7722 0950). Camden Town or Chalk Farm tube/C2 bus. **Open** 9am-11pm Mon-Sat; 9am-10.30pm Sun. **Food served** 9-11.30am, 12.30-3pm, 7-10.30pm Mon-Sat; 9-11.30am, 12.30-3.30pm, 7-10pm Sun. **Credit** MC, V.

Over the last few years the Engineer has consolidated its reputation as one of London's leading gastropubs. Diners are accommodated in the warren-like rooms off the main bar and (weather permitting) in the attractive back garden. Sunday lunch is hugely popular: arrive early to be sure of a table. Families tend to congregate in the upstairs room, which gives children space to run around. Kids get their own menu for about £4,

fruit, the kitchen is bursting with creativity, with mixed results in terms of main courses, but good, inventive desserts. Other plus points include the collection of toys in the nappy-changing room and the friendly and accommodating staff. Although there isn't a kids' menu yet, the big chips and home-made lemonade will suit most little people's tastes. The wine list is extensive and expensive and from the looks of things booking for lunch will soon be essential.

Booking advisable. High chairs. Nappy-changing facilities. Tables outdoors (4, terrace). Toys.

Red Pepper
8 Formosa Street, W9 (7266 2708). Warwick Avenue tube. **Lunch served** 12.30-3pm Sat; 12.30-3.30pm Sun. **Dinner served** 6.30-11pm Mon-Sat; 6.30-10.30pm Sun. **Main courses** £8-£14. **Credit** MC, V. **Map** p312 C4.
Once upon a time, local customers used to bring their own chairs and sit and eat outside, such was Red Pepper's popu-

larity. On a recent Saturday lunch, things had not really changed and diners were being squashed into every available space while a queue of drooling hopefuls blocked the doorway. The starters are the most creative things on the menu, with the likes of squid with barley and rocket and smoked venison carpaccio. A huge wood-fired oven in the basement churns out extraordinary pizza creations, but there's also home-made pasta in all shapes and styles with everything from clams and pesto to prawns and rocket. The dessert menu is small but perfectly formed, while the wine list offers a substantial collection of Italy's finest. The perfect venue for a cosy family luncheon.

Booking advisable. Tables outdoors (5, pavement).

Sausage & Mash Café
268 Portobello Road, W10 (8968 8898). Ladbroke Grove tube. **Meals served** 11am-10.30pm daily. **Main courses** £2.50-£7. **Credit** MC, V.

with comfort food faves such as fish and chips or healthier options like penne with tomato sauce. Organic ice-cream rounds things off nicely.
Buggy access. Children's menu (noon-3pm daily). Crayons. Garden. High chairs. Nappy-changing facilities. Tables outdoors (10, garden).

Hand in Hand
6 Crooked Billet, SW19 (8946 5720). Wimbledon tube/rail. **Open** 11am-11pm Mon-Sat; noon-10.30pm Sun. **Food served** noon-2.30pm, 7-9.30pm Mon-Sat; noon-4pm Sun. **Credit** MC, V.
Wimbledon Village green is the ideal spot for this charismatic pub full of nooks and crannies, exposed brickwork and settles. There's a family room, or smoke-free zone (depending on your viewpoint), off to the left. Pub grub includes daily specials; the children's menu includes the usual suspects – sausage or chicken nuggets and chips – followed by stodgy but yummy sweets like treacle sponge and chocolate pudding.
Buggy access. Children's menu (£2.95). Family room (no-smoking). Tables outdoors (courtyard).

Jamies
Unit 1, 28 West Ferry Circus, Canary Wharf, E14 (7536 2861/www.jamiesbars.co.uk). Canary Wharf tube/DLR. **Open** 11.30am-11pm Mon-Sat; 11.30am-10.30pm Sun. **Food served** noon-3pm, 6-9pm daily. **Credit** AmEx, DC, MC, V.
One of the new breed of super wine bars, this glamorous half-moon lounge venue has stacks of potential for outdoor summer drinking (100 seats). It is set along a sweeping Thameside promenade of eateries, just ten minutes' walk from Canary Wharf. On a fine summer's day, this place is idyllic. Parents will be content with the well-chosen modern wine list and decent nibbles and snacks (and brunch at weekends). The kids' menu includes sausage and mash, burgers and chips, plus soft drink and ice-

cream. The outside tables are the best for families as inside there's no no-smoking area.
Children's menu (£5.95). Crayons. High chairs. Tables outdoors (riverside terrace).
Branches throughout town. Check the phone book for your nearest.

Old Ship
25 Upper Mall, W6 (8748 2593). Hammersmith tube. **Open** 10am-11pm Mon-Fri; 9am-10.30pm Sat, Sun. **Food served** 10am-10.30pm Mon-Fri; 9am-10pm Sat, Sun. **Credit** AmEx, MC, V.
The most outstanding feature of this riverside pub must be its outside seating areas. A raised front and side terrace and a large first-floor balcony provide punters with an unparalleled view of the river. The waterways theme continues inside with displays of rowing implements, ships' lanterns and other nautical memorabilia. Children have their own menu featuring nuggets, fish fingers, pasta and so on; on Sundays they can have smaller portions of adults' lunches. Home-made ice-creams also go down a treat. They can work it off afterwards in the nearby kids' play area with swings and roundabout, on the green right next to the pub.
Buggy access. Children's menu (£2.95). High chairs. Nappy-changing facilities. Tables outdoors (garden).

The Prince
59 Kynaston Road, N16 (7923 4766). Bus 73. **Open** noon-11pm Mon-Sat; noon-10.30pm Sun. **Food served** 12.30-10pm Mon-Sat; noon-9.30pm Sun. **Credit** MC, V.
Bought and done up a couple of years back by the owner of the highly successful Cooler deli on nearby Church Street, the scruffy old pub that was once the Prince of Wales has come of age. A large part of its new-found popularity also has to do with the reliably delicious food, sourced from the deli and served in a separate little restaurant area at

It's not the location (right underneath the rumbling Westway) or the interior (naff black and white photos) that attracts people to the Sausage & Mash Café. The food is the draw – sausages in many varieties, including various vegetarian options. You choose your own mash and gravy from the ample selection; you'd do well to ask for a bit of advice over what works well together to avoid weird combinations. If you've still got room after all that stodge, consult the specials board for a homely portion of apple pie or bread and butter pudding. Kids love the menu, and the laid-back café atmosphere is perfect for stressed parents who are looking for sustenance and recuperation.

Buggy access. High chairs. Children's menu (£3.50).

Tootsies

120 Holland Park Avenue, W11 (7229 8567). Holland Park tube. **Meals served** 9am-11pm daily. **Main courses** £4.95-£12.50. **Credit** AmEx, MC, V.

Tootsies loves kids. Crayons are available for busy colouring, waiters don't mind working their way around pushchairs, and a kids' menu offers even more options for picky appetites. One of London's most elegant burger bars, Tootsies offers a relaxed, pleasant, sunny environment in which to have a cheery meal. Choices encompass salads, burgers, steaks and fish. The classic hamburger, served simply with a salad, a variety of relishes and chips, is one of the best, most unpretentious burgers you'll find in London. For the diet conscious, there's the junk salad, with sugar snaps, baby corn, avocado and lettuce, with a spicy peanut dressing on the side. While a variety of desserts are offered, we couldn't pass up the dreamy butterscotch shake. If only every lunch could be like this.

Balloons. Buggy access. Children's menu (£3.50). Crayons. High chairs. No-smoking tables. Tables outdoors (4, pavement).

Branches throughout town. Check the phone book for your nearest.

Royal Inn on the Park

Handsome, high-ceilinged and bang next to Victoria Park, the Royal Inn is a comfortable choice for groovy drinkers (although things can get a bit hectic come Saturday night). Come Sunday lunchtime the place is positively brasserie-like, so this is the best time to bring the children. A big blackboard menu runs from light bites and filled ciabattas through to steaks, coq au vin and cottage pie. Food can be eaten anywhere, although there's a small dedicated dining room off to one side, plus a heated tent area out the back. There's no specific children's menu, but youngsters can have smaller portions of sausage and mash for £4, or choose from the normal, wide-ranging menu.

High chairs. Nappy-changing facilities. No-smoking area (restaurant). Tables outdoors (garden).

The Woodman

128 Bourne Hill, N13 (8882 0294). Southgate tube/W9 bus. **Open** 11am-11pm Mon-Sat; noon-10.30pm Sun. **Food served** noon-3pm, 6-9pm Mon-Sat; noon-3pm Sun. **Credit** AmEx, MC, V.

The Woodman is an old-style country pub on the edge of Grovelands Park, blessed with a kids' playground and ample parking. The tiny wood-panelled front bar, with its small fire and little round tables, is popular in the evenings with a quiet group of locals. This is a great choice for families in summer – parents can relax in the beer garden while their offspring make use of the children's playground. A modern extension at the rear of the pub houses another bar, and a conservatory extension to one side provides a sunny no-smoking setting for such 'all time favourites' as chicken curry (£5.95). The children's menu is a bargain, which includes all the usual crowd-pleasers, such as chicken nuggets, pasta and ice-cream.

Children's menu (£2). Garden. No-smoking area. Restaurant. Tables outdoors (garden).

the back. This gives on to a small outside yard that makes a refreshing alternative to the crush at the bar that regularly develops towards the end of the week. There are plans for a dedicated family area, complete with childminder; in the meantime, children can enjoy the kids' menu, with chicken nuggets, fish fingers and pasta.

High chairs. Children's menu (main course £2.95, ice-cream £1.95). Tables outdoors (garden, pavement).

Royal Inn on the Park

111 Lauriston Road, E9 (8985 3321). Mile End tube then 277 bus. **Open** noon-11pm Mon-Sat; noon-10.30pm Sun. **Food served** noon-3pm, 6-9.30pm Mon-Fri; noon-10pm Sat; noon-5pm Sun. **Credit** MC, V.

Consumer

Shopping

From bargains to binges, here are the goodies if you've got the dough.

These days children are a whole consumer industry in their own right – and don't they know it! With the help of targeted advertising, many know exactly what they want, if not where to get it. To help you in the quest for that special outfit, new nursery furniture, shoes, wise pocket-money spending, haircut or first wheels, we've included our favourites in this chapter. Virtually all the places below are geared up for inquisitive, wriggly young visitors; some are so welcoming you can't drag the children away. Note, however, that not all branches of shops have the same opening hours or facilities so you might want to check before you make a special journey.

All-rounders

Daisy & Tom
181-3 King's Road, SW3 (7352 5000/ www.daisyandtom.com). Sloane Square tube then 11, 19, 22, 49 bus. **Open** 10am-6pm Mon, Tue, Thur-Sat; 10am-7pm Wed; noon-6pm Sun. **Credit** AmEx, MC, V. **Map** p315 E12.
A wide range of books is beautifully presented in a large balconied room, from which a central staircase leads up to the clothes and shoes, where the rails yield gorgeous and expensive designer labels such as Petit Bateau, Catimini and Daisy & Tom's own brand. A third room has dolls and a fourth toys, games and baby equipment including the very popular Tripp

Chain reaction

The following essential baby and children's chains have far too many branches for us to list. Their websites have all the information you need to locate your nearest branch, assess the latest crazes and fashions in the hot world of tot commerce and buy online, which, in the case of the vast toy barn Toys 'R' Us and the number of full-scale trolley tantrums its many treasures induce, is a blessing indeed.
Adams (*www.adams.co.uk*)
Workaday children's wear for 0-10s.
Early Learning Centre (*www.elc.co.uk*)
Bright, chunky toys and art materials for babies and young children.
Mothercare (*www.mothercare.com*)
Caring for pregnant mums, new babies and young children in every way.
Toys 'R' Us (*www.toysrus.co.uk*)
A huge range of must-have toys and a useful line in low-priced baby essentials.

Trapp high chair and a large range of three-wheeler buggies from £250. Young shoppers have plenty to occupy them, including rocking horses on the balcony, a colouring table under the big clock and a play train; when that gets too much for them they can settle down in front of a five-minute marionette show of 'Peter and the Wolf' (which runs every half hour). Downstairs, the brightly painted but music-free horse and duck carousel runs at 11am, 1pm, 3pm and 5pm. There's also a hairdressing salon. Staff are friendly and helpful.
Buggy access. Mail order. Nappy-changing facilities. Play area.

Lilliput
255-9 Queenstown Road, SW8 (7720 5554/0800 783 0886/www.lilliput.com). Queenstown Road rail. **Open** 9.30am-5.30pm Mon, Tue, Thur, Fri; 9.30am-7pm Wed; 9am-6pm Sat. **Credit** MC, V.
Lilliput is a one-stop accessory shop for little people. When it comes to prams and buggies, it pretty much stocks the lot, including a large range of three-wheelers (from £250). There are car seats and replacement car seat covers, high chairs (including Tripp Trapp and portable clip-on ones). Also check out the huge toy department, clothes, wooden furniture, plus the new Stokke section. Large items are delivered free and there are tables of Brio to keep the littlies happy.
Buggy access. Mail order. Nappy-changing facilities. Play area.
Branch: 100 Haydons Road, SW19 (8542 3542).

Educational

Books

Bookseller Crow on the Hill
50 Westow Street, SE19 (8771 8831/ www.booksellercrow.com). Gypsy Hill rail. **Open** 9am-7.30pm Mon-Fri; 9am-6.30pm Sat; 11am-5pm Sun. **Credit** AmEx, MC, V.
A general bookshop with a terrific children's section. Local parents come in for a nose (there's a comprehensive range of parenting books), while their children play with toys and read books at tables and chairs provided. Check the website to find out about forthcoming events and author signings.
Buggy access. Mail order. Play area.

Bookworm
1177 Finchley Road, NW11 (8201 9811/ www.thebookworm.uk.com). Golders Green tube. **Open** 9.30am-5.30pm Mon-Sat; 10am-1.30pm Sun. **Credit** MC, V.
This is a warm and friendly children's bookshop, where 2-6 year-olds can enjoy story time at 2pm every Tuesday and Thursday. There's a table full of toys and colouring stuff if the books alone aren't enough to entertain them while their parents browse. Regular events involving favourite authors are listed in the newsletter of the Bookworm Book Club: ring the shop to be put on the mailing list.
Buggy access. Delivery service. Mail order. Nappy-changing facilities.

Swallows & Amazons. *See p205.*

Children's Book Centre
237 Kensington High Street, W8 (7937 7497/
www.childrensbookcentre.co.uk). High Street Kensington
tube. **Open** 9.30am-6.30pm Mon, Wed, Fri, Sat; 9.30am-
6pm Tue; 9.30am-7pm Thur; noon-6pm Sun. **Credit**
AmEx, MC, V. **Map** p314 A9.
Alongside the huge selection of books for babies to teens,
the Children's Book Centre sells CD-Roms, games, puzzles,
jewellery, chocolates, Beanie Babies and Pokémon toys and
videos, all of which can be bought through the website if
it's easier for you to order from home. Every couple of months
the shop hosts a special events day with guest stars such
as Barbie or the Cat in the Hat.
Buggy access. Mail order.

The Children's Book Company
11 The Green, W5 (8567 4324/www.
childrensbookcompany.com). Ealing Broadway
tube. **Open** 9.30am-5.30pm Mon-Sat. **Credit** MC, V.
A huge asset to the local community, this Ealing bookshop
is a pleasure to visit. In addition to books – which cover the
reading needs of all children, from birth to 14 years – there
are book and tape spin-offs as well as character toys. Kids
can take books to the sofa to read; very young children usually prefer to play on the rocking sheep. There are frequent
character events with the likes of Maisy, Percy the Park
Keeper and Preston Pig, with storytelling and activities. You
can sign up for a monthly newsletter, or check the website
for events and information.
Buggy access. Delivery service. Mail order.

Children's Bookshop
*29 Fortis Green Road, N10 (8444 5500). Highgate tube
then 43, 134 bus.* **Open** 9.15am-5.45pm Mon-Sat; 11am-
4pm Sun. **Credit** AmEx, MC, V.
The staff at this jam-packed store demonstrate an impressive
knowledge of children's books and will help kids find their
way round the various sections. Fiction is displayed by age
group: there are board books for babies, early readers for
5-8-year-olds and *Harry Potter* et al for 8-12-year-olds. There's
also a selection of audio tapes. Not surprisingly, the author
events, book signings and the learned atmosphere attract
many teachers and pupils. For solitary bookworms there's a
reading chair in the corner.
Buggy access. Mail order.

The Golden Treasury
*97 Wandsworth Bridge Road, SW6 (7384 1821).
Fulham Broadway tube.* **Open** 10am-6pm Mon; 9.30am-
6pm Tue-Fri; 9.30am-5.30pm Sat. **Credit** MC, V.
This place is as good as a library, allowing children to settle
down with a book without any pressure to buy – although
you'll inevitably want to. Among the goodies are pop-up
books, myths and legends and a board book selection for
under-twos. Downstairs is a comprehensive non-fiction section, including schoolbooks for both teachers and pupils. The
small video stock is growing, while the audio tape collection
is one of the biggest in London.
Buggy access. Delivery service.

Owl Bookshop
*209 Kentish Town Road, NW5 (7485 7793). Kentish
Town tube.* **Open** 9.30am-6pm Mon-Sat; noon-4.30pm
Sun. **Credit** AmEx, MC, V.
A welcoming bookshop with a children's section bigger than
many of the chain stores, the Owl stocks kids' books, story
tapes and videos for babies through to teenagers. The occasional story session or book signing is advertised out front.
Buggy access. Mail order.

Musical instruments

Chappell of Bond Street
*50 New Bond Street, W1 (7491 2777/
www.chappellofbondstreet.co.uk). Bond Street tube.*
Open 9.30am-6pm Mon-Fri; 9.30am-5pm Sat.
Credit AmEx, MC, V. **Map** p318 H6.
London's best-known and most extensive general music store
has an enormously wide range of electric keyboards (useful to
know if you have a piano addict child and a small flat). All
other instruments are represented, as well as the necessary
accessories and sheet music (pop and classical). Children
bitten by the music bug can find beginners' and half-size instruments and sensible advice on renting to buy instruments (you
pay the rental until your child is sure he/she wants to play a
sousaphone and then stump up the difference when you decide
to buy it). A good place to kick off a musical education.
Mail order.

Dot's
*132 St Pancras Way, NW1 (7482 5424/
www.dotsonline.co.uk). Camden Town tube/
Camden Road rail.* **Open** 9am-5.30pm Mon-Sat.
Credit MC, V.
Run by experienced music teacher Dot, this shop has a strong
educational mission: people of all ages who have a yen to
learn about playing and performing would do well to start
off here. Dot sells new instruments, many in the middle-
to-lower price range and therefore just right for beginners.
Instruments are mostly stringed and wind, but those looking
to buy something hefty, say a piano, are given help and contacts. Some second-hand instruments are sold through Dot,
and the full pinboard in the shop has advertisements for
instruments, tuition and services. There's also sheet music
for exam pieces, the classics and pop. Instruments are also
available for hire. Dot runs a recorder club for adult and child
players; her madrigal club attracts mostly adults, though
sweet-voiced, sight-reading young people are welcome.
Buggy access. Delivery service. Mail order.

Dulwich Music Shop
2 Croxted Road, SE21 (8766 0202). Herne Hill rail.
Open 9.30am-5.30pm Mon, Tue, Thur-Sat; 9.30am-
7.30pm Wed. **Credit** AmEx, MC, V.
This is the best dedicated classical music shop south of the
river. The musically trained staff can match a child with the
correct instrument, either a new, beginner's one or, if you're
in luck, something second-hand. They also take in instruments for repair and sell all accessories and sheet music,
including exam pieces and pop tunes. A pinboard advertises
music lessons, instruments for sale and useful contacts in this
sometimes bewildering world. All this plus musical gifts for
the tuneful: stationery, books, CDs and souvenirs.
Delivery service. Mail order.

Northcote Music
*155C Northcote Road, SW11 (7228 0074). Clapham
Junction rail.* **Open** 10.30am-6pm Mon, Wed, Fri; 10am-
6pm Sat. **Credit** AmEx, MC, V.
All the local schools are account customers here at Northcote,
a mine of accessories and expertise for musicians, particularly those young ones just starting out. Stringed instruments
and related accessories are a speciality, although as far as
guitars are concerned, the beginners' end of the market is best
represented – professionals are directed to a specialist guitar
outlet in the area. Northcote is a Yamaha stockist, for begin-
ner-to-mid-range digital pianos, keyboards, woodwind and
brass. Sheet music, both classical and pop, is plentiful and

wider ranging than in most general music shops. A repair workshop at the back deals with string problems; woodwind is sent away for repair. The manager has a teachers' index, so if you're looking for lessons in the locality, consult him. *Buggy access. Delivery service. Mail order.*

Rainbow Violins
16 High Street, Merstham, Surrey (01737 645065/ www.rainbowviolins.com). Merstham rail. **Open** 9.30am-1pm, 2-5pm Tue-Sat. **Credit** MC, V.

Emma Newton's rainbow-coloured violins, violas and cellos are coveted by musicians of all ages, but go down particularly well with children. They are proper violins, however, made of wood and certainly not toys. Many a wee girl scrapes away on a tiny, one-eighth size Barbie-pink instrument thanks to Emma's vision. If the pink doesn't appeal, there are seven other colours to choose from, including Robin Hood green, pillar box red and a limited-edition white (as used on Westlife's 2001 tour). The cost, from £120 for a violin, is reasonable for such a glorious beginner's instrument. This is a general music shop too, where staff can advise on and provide instruments, sheet music, accessories and other essentials, and put customers in touch with teachers. It's worth the trip out of town (take the train from London Bridge). *Buggy access. Mail order.*

Equipment & accessories

Baby Munchkins
186B Hoxton Street, N1 (7684 5994/ www.babymunchkins.com). Old Street tube/rail. **Open** 10am-5pm Mon-Fri; 9.30am-5.30pm Sat. **Credit** MC, V.

Baby Munchkins does a fine line in all-terrain pushchairs, with Mountain Terrain buggies for £530 and Alu-Rax buggies at a more affordable £139. Car seats, Tripp Trapp high chairs, contemporary rocking horses and Stokke cots are also available, along with lamb fleeces and Baby Bjorn carriers for cosy sleeping. While you're here, stock up on wooden toys, Jellycat and Miffy merchandise, organic food, and Sarah Barker shoes for active crawlers. *Buggy access. Delivery service. Mail order. Nappy-changing facilities.*

Baby This 'n' Baby That
359 Forest Road, E17 (8527 4002). Blackhorse Road tube/rail. **Open** 10am-5pm Mon-Sat. **Credit** AmEx, MC, V.

This friendly store with helpful service claims to stock everything but the baby. If you're looking for traditional stuff, you can order Silver Cross prams for £400-£800; if you're after a bargain, there's a three-wheeler for twins, complete with all the accessories, for £220; and if you want a brand name, you'll find Mamas & Papas, Bébécar, Maclaren and the rest. *Buggy access. Delivery service.*

Dragons of Walton Street
23 Walton Street, SW3 (7589 3795/ www.dragonsofwaltonstreet.com). Knightsbridge or South Kensington tube. **Open** 9.30am-5.30pm Mon-Fri; 10am-5pm Sat. **Credit** AmEx, MC, V. **Map** p315 E10.

For those who can both appreciate and afford hand-crafted traditional wooden furniture and toys, this could be your dream shop. Beautifully painted chests of drawers, chairs, toy trains and farm sets line the walls. A child's four-poster bed will set you back around £5,000, while a rocking horse goes for a mere £350. *Buggy access. Delivery service. Mail order.*

Budding bookworms feel right at home at the **Children's Book Centre**. *See p194.*

Family Care

90-94 Kingsland High Street, E8 (7254 8720). Dalston Kingsland rail. **Open** 10am-6pm Mon-Sat. **Credit** MC, V.
Basic designer clothes, toys and nursery items come cheap at this store. Three-piece baby outfits cost from £7, and there's a bargain Chicco Duo pram plus car seat for £199. Among the usual toys by Fisher-Price and Mamas & Papas are fantastic motorised two-seater cars and jeeps for 3-7-year-olds, complete with safety belts (£210). The radio-controlled range is reputedly the biggest in town; prices range from £1.99 for a car to £225 for an aeroplane.
Buggy access. Delivery service. Mail order. Nappy-changing facilities. Play area.

Green Baby

345 Upper Street, N1 (7359 7037/www.greenbabyco.com). Angel tube. **Open** 10am-5pm Mon-Fri; 10am-6pm Sat. **Credit** AmEx, MC, V.
'Earth friendly' and '100% organic' are catchphrases at this friendly eco-store. As might be expected, there are washable nappies by Tushies; Egyptian organic cotton popper nappies are £9.95 and good old terry squares £1.80 each. Look out for the Efie cuddly toys made from chemical-free natural cotton, Green Baby's own brand of creams, organic cradle cap oil, mandarin toothpaste and a goat-hair brush so soft it can be used for baby massage. For stepping out there are strollers, Baby Trekkers and Huggababys. Mums can stock up on toiletries and Bravado nursing bras.
Buggy access. Delivery service. Mail order.

Humla Children's Shop

13 Flask Walk, NW3 (7794 7877). Hampstead tube. **Open** 10.30am-6pm Tue-Sat; noon-6pm Sun. **Credit** AmEx, MC, V.
Kids just love Humla's furniture: chests and wardrobes painted by Heather Spencer and dinky child-sized chairs. There are also attractive biplane bookshelves and toy boxes; tractor bookends and circus bookshelves. But the most amazing items are the Scandinavian bunk beds, which not only have a spare bed in the bottom drawer but also double up as puppet theatres or feature a slide down to the floor (approximately £520). The large traditional wooden toys include some amusing sit 'n' rides. The other branches sell Humla's selection of designer clothes and beautiful own-brand knits.
Buggy access. Delivery service. Play area.
Branches: 9 Flask Walk, NW3 (7794 8449); 23 St Christopher's Place, W1 (7224 1773).

Infantasia

1st Floor, Wood Green Shopping Centre, N22 (8889 1494/www.infantasia.co.uk). Wood Green tube. **Open** 9.30am-6pm Mon-Fri; 9am-6pm Sat; 11am-5pm Sun. **Credit** AmEx, MC, V.
An excellent nursery emporium with friendly service and friendlier prices. Check out the range of casual clothing for 0-6 years, which includes christening gowns for both sexes. There is also furniture and a huge range of prams, plus car seats, cots and cot beds. You can take your damaged buggy in for a service and buy a new set of wheels for £15.
Buggy access. Delivery service. Mail order.

Junior Living

293 Fulham Road, SW10 (7376 5001/www.juniorliving.co.uk). Fulham Broadway tube/14, 211 bus. **Open** 10am-6.30pm Mon-Sat; noon-5pm Sun. **Credit** MC, V. **Map** p315 D12.
If your children's pit is more Rik Mayall than Carol Smillie, take them along to this hip and happening furniture store: the first and only one in London, according to its

Northcote Music, a local fave. *See p194.*

owners. Goodies range from bedroom lamps and bedclothes, work stations and rocking horses, to glorious cabin beds and funky-looking wardrobes. Staff also offer a bespoke design service for a real *Changing Rooms* experience. Visiting the shop is fun, too: while grown-ups examine the woodwork and talk interiors with the staff, children can watch cartoons or play with toys. Complete bedroom sets start at £800 and go all the way up to £3,000.
Delivery service. Nappy-changing facilities.

Little Bridge

56 Battersea Bridge Road, SW11 (7978 5522/www.littlebridge.co.uk). Clapham Junction rail/49, 319, 345 bus. **Open** 9.30am-5.30pm Mon-Fri; 10am-5pm Sat. **Credit** AmEx, MC, V.
Little Bridge's beautiful made-to-measure painted wooden nursery furniture is unique. Prices do reflect this; a lovely Victorian butterfly chest of drawers goes for £595. For those with tighter purse strings, miniature rush chairs start at £49.
Buggy access. Delivery service.

Mini Kin

22 Broadway Parade, N8 (8341 6898). Finsbury Park tube then W7 bus/41 bus. **Open** 9.30am-5.30pm Tue-Sat. **Credit** MC, V.
Anything that makes the business of being a parent more fragrant and calm is fine by us, and at Mini Kin they have everything. There are gifts for newborns: Cacharel vests, dinky bootees, toys and nursery accessories. The aromatherapy ranges for massage and pampering both mother and baby (from the likes of Verde, Weleda, Natalia and Green People) are all hypo-allergenic and therefore safe for sensitive skin. For older children, the Miss Molly make-up range is a fun, understated entrée into the daunting world of cosmetics. The on-site hair salon has a whole menu of services, from a dry style for £12.50 through mini makeovers

Department stores

Though not often known for their individuality, department stores can be a lifesaver when you're in a rush and know what you want to buy. The most central branches of the main ones are listed below, with a list of facilities and services of use to families. Note that facilities may vary from branch to branch. **Harrods** and **John Lewis** also have specific play areas for kids; the former also has theatre and regular children's events (ring for further details).

Bhs
252-8 Oxford Street, W1 (7629 2011/ www.bhs.co.uk). Oxford Circus tube. **Open** 9.30am-7pm Mon-Wed, Fri, Sat; 9.30am-8pm Thur; noon-6pm Sun. **Credit** AmEx, MC, V. **Map** p316 H6.
Children's department (1st floor). Disabled: lift, toilet. Nappy-changing facilities. Restaurant: cold lunch box & hot meals, high chairs. School uniforms.

Debenhams
334-48 Oxford Street, W1 (7580 3000/ www.debenhams.com). Bond Street or Oxford Circus tube. **Open** 9.30am-7pm Mon, Tue; 10am-8pm Wed; 9.30am-9pm Thur; 9.30am-8pm Fri; 9am-8pm Sat; noon-6pm Sun. **Credit** AmEx, V. **Map** p316 H6.
Café. Children's department (3rd floor). Disabled: lift, toilet. Mail order (08456 055044). Nappy-changing facilities. Restaurant: children's menu, high chairs. School uniforms. Toys.

Dickins & Jones
224-44 Regent Street, W1 (7734 7070/ www.houseoffraser.co.uk). Oxford Circus tube. **Open** 10am-7pm Mon-Wed, Fri, Sat; 10am-8pm Thur; noon-6pm Sun. **Credit** AmEx, MC, V. **Map** p316 J6.
Café. Children's department (4th floor). Disabled: lift, toilet. Mail order. Nappy-changing facilities. Restaurant.

Fenwick
63 New Bond Street, W1 (7629 9161/ www.fenwick.co.uk). Bond Street tube. **Open** 10am-6.30pm Mon-Wed, Fri, Sat; 10am-8pm Thur. **Credit** AmEx, MC, V. **Map** p316 H6.
Children's department (babies only, 1st floor). Disabled: lift, toilet. Mail order. Nappy-changing facilities. Restaurant (half portions, high chairs).

Fortnum & Mason
181 Piccadilly, W1 (7734 8040/ www.fortnumandmason.co.uk). Green Park or Piccadilly Circus tube. **Open** 10am-6.30pm Mon-Sat. **Credit** AmEx, MC, V. **Map** p318 J7.
Café. Children's department (ages 0-8, 2nd floor). Disabled: lift, toilet. Mail order. Nappy-changing facilities. Restaurant: children's menu. Toys.

Harrods
87-135 Brompton Road, SW1 (7730 1234/ www.harrods.com). Knightsbridge tube. **Open** 10am-6pm Mon, Sat. **Credit** AmEx, DC, MC, V. **Map** p315 F9.

and the full 'Princess Treatment' for wee girls aged from just 2. The other branch, located at 79 Fortis Green Road (8444 1717), is mainly a salon.
Buggy access. Nappy-changing facilities.

Nursery Window
83 Walton Street, SW3 (7581 3358). South Kensington tube. **Open** 10am-6pm Mon-Sat. **Credit** AmEx, MC, V. **Map** p315 E10.
Nursery Window does its own range of old-fashioned, pastel-coloured nursery fabrics, which come by the metre for curtains, or ready made as matching accessories. There's everything a new mother might need, from Moses sheets and soft toys to changing mats, cot quilts, cushions and sheets.
Buggy access. Delivery service. Mail order.

Fashion

Clothes

Barney's
6 Church Road, SW19 (8944 2915). Wimbledon tube/rail. **Open** 10am-6pm Mon-Sat; noon-5pm Sun. **Credit** MC, V.
French and Italian labels for newborns and children up to 14 years pack the rails. There's Jean Bourget, Les Robes, Petit Bateau, Gasolio and Portofino as well as O'Neill, Paper Moon, Kookai and Oxbow. Stocks of Orchard toys, teddies and other soft animals increase around Christmas, but there's always a good range of christening and new baby gifts, as well as hair accessories for older girls.
Buggy access. Nappy-changing facilities. Play area.

Biff
43 Dulwich Village, SE21 (8299 0911). North Dulwich rail. **Open** 9.30am-5.30pm Mon-Fri; 10am-6pm Sat. **Credit** AmEx, MC, V.
Small children head straight for the toy table here, giving parents time to examine the extensive and eclectic range of clothing, shoes and swimwear. Petit Bateau is a popular line, and the raw silk christening outfits are exquisite. There's also a range of fancy-dress suits for ages 4-6.
Buggy access. Nappy-changing facilities. Play area.

Caramel
291 Brompton Road, SW3 (7589 7001). South Kensington tube. **Open** 10am-6.30pm Mon-Sat; noon-5pm Sun. **Credit** MC, V. **Map** p315 E10.
Caramel is a hip designer boutique for women, babies and children. Highlights of the collection are the adorable little karate-style pyjamas in apricot wool, edged in orange satin (not cheap, at £75) with matching Chinese slippers (£35) for newborns. There are also beautiful ranges by Channe de

Cafés. Children's department (4th floor). Children's hairdressing. Restaurants. Disabled: lift, toilet. Mail order. Nappy-changing facilities. School uniforms. Toys.

Harvey Nichols
109-25 Knightsbridge, SW1 (7235 5000/ www.harveynichols.com). Knightsbridge tube. **Open** 10am-7pm Mon, Tue, Sat; 10am-8pm Wed-Fri; noon-6pm Sun. **Credit** AmEx, MC, V. **Map** p315 F9.
Café. Children's department (designerwear, 2nd floor). Disabled: lift, toilet. Mail order. Nappy-changing facilities. Restaurants (Wagamama has high chairs & children's portions). Toys.

House of Fraser
318 Oxford Street, W1 (7529 4700/ www.houseoffraser.co.uk). Bond Street or Oxford Circus tube. **Open** 10am-7pm Mon, Tue; 10am-8pm Wed, Fri, Sat; 10am-9pm Thur; noon-6pm Sun. **Credit** AmEx, MC, V. **Map** p316 H6.
Café. Children's department (0-8 years, 3rd floor; 9-16 years, lower ground floor). Children's hairdressing. Disabled: lift, toilet. Mail order. Nappy-changing facilities. Restaurants.

John Lewis
278-306 Oxford Street, W1 (7629 7711/ www.johnlewis.co.uk). Bond Street or Oxford Circus tube. **Open** 9.30am-7pm Mon-Wed, Fri; 10am-8pm Thur; 9am-7pm Sat. **Credit** MC, V. **Map** p316 H6.

Children's department (4th floor). Café (children's meals). Disabled: lift, toilet. Mail order. Nappy-changing facilities. Restaurant. School uniforms. Toys.

Liberty
210-20 Regent Street, W1 (7734 1234/ www.liberty-of-london.com). Oxford Circus tube. **Open** 10am-6.30pm Mon-Wed; 10am-8pm Thur; 10am-7pm Fri, Sat; noon-6pm Sun. **Credit** AmEx, MC, V. **Map** p316 J6.
Café. Disabled: lift, toilet. Nappy-changing facilities. Restaurant.

Marks & Spencer
458 Oxford Street, W1 (7935 7954/ www.marksandspencer.co.uk). Marble Arch tube. **Open** 9am-9pm Mon-Fri; 9am-7.30pm Sat; noon-6pm Sun. **Credit** AmEx, MC, V. **Map** p316 G6.
Cafés. Disabled: lift, toilets. Children's department (2nd floor). Mail order. Nappy-changing facilities. Restaurant: lunch boxes. School uniforms.

Selfridges
400 Oxford Street, W1 (7629 1234/ www.selfridges.com). Bond Street or Marble Arch tube. **Open** 10am-7pm Mon-Wed; 10am-8pm Thur, Fri; 9.30am-7pm Sat; noon-6pm Sun. **Credit** AmEx, MC, V. **Map** p316 G6.
Café. Children's department (3rd floor, young children; 1st floor, teenage wear). Disabled: lift, toilet. Mail order. Restaurant: children's menus. Toys.

Biolly and Marni (which are exclusive in London to Caramel), along with Brooklyn handknits, Quincy leather jerkins and Caramel's own stunning range. No wonder Madonna's said to be a fan of the place.
Buggy access. Delivery service.

Catimini
52 South Molton Street, W1 (7629 8099/ www.catimini.com). Bond Street tube. **Open** 10am-6pm Mon-Wed, Fri, Sat; 10am-7pm Thur. **Credit** AmEx, MC, V. **Map** p316 H6.
Catimini has now added shoes for children up to 14 years to match its charming and original range of clothing. Animal motifs dominate, down to the zebra chairs beckoning toddlers to the little colouring table and the wooden rocking hen that peeps out of the changing room.
Buggy access. Delivery service. Mail order. Play area.

Clementine
73 Ledbury Road, W11 (7243 6331). Notting Hill Gate tube. **Open** 10am-6pm Mon-Sat. **Credit** AmEx, MC, V. **Map** p312 A6.
This charming children's clothes and furniture shop occupies a light and airy corner on voguish Ledbury Road. The simple cotton look of Petit Bateau dominates the ground floor, where goods for the newborn up to the teenager are found. Downstairs there are prams (including the sturdy Swedish

Emmaljunga range), simple customised beds (from £300) made of pine and pretty bedlinen and clothing from Damask.
Buggy access. Delivery service. Mail order. Nappy-changing facilities.

Cookie
30 Artesian Road, W2 (7727 1133). Notting Hill Gate tube. **Open** 10am-6pm Mon-Sat. **Credit** MC, V. **Map** p312 A6.
Cookie has recently moved round the corner – look out for the gold door. It no longer does made to measure, but otherwise designer Denise Hurst's glamorous, shiny clothes remain the same. Stock also encompasses Wowo and Zoë and George, along with an ever-changing range of accessories: shoes, soaps, little bags, Russian dolls and jewellery.
Buggy access. Delivery service. Nappy-changing facilities. Play area.

The Cross
141 Portland Road, W11 (7727 6760). Holland Park or Notting Hill Gate tube. **Open** 10.30am-6pm Mon-Sat. **Credit** AmEx, MC, V.
Exclusive labels can now be bagged by mothers and babies at this cool shop. Childrenswear from birth to 6 years includes tiny street fashions from Little Punk and Quincy, babywear from Albetta Creation and tough toddling gear by OshKosh. The gifts and accessories are covetable, and wee girls enjoy

selecting bits and bobs from the hair and make-up stash. There's a room for toys, of the quirky wooden variety, and all visiting children are encouraged to play with them. *Buggy access. Delivery service.*

Early Clothing
79-85 Fortis Green Road, N10 (8444 9309). Highgate tube. **Open** 9.30am-5.30pm Mon-Sat. **Credit** AmEx, MC, V.
This is a friendly, homey kind of shop, which thoughtfully shows kids' videos, allowing mums to sneak a peek at the range of women's clothes and shoes. But the main draw are the shoes by Start-Rite, Buckle My Shoe and O'Neill, plus the cool range of kids' clothes by OshKosh, Quiksilver, Catimini, Oilily, IKKS, Kenzo Jungle and O'Neill.
Buggy access. Delivery service. Play area.

E sharp minor
6 Earlswood Street, SE10 (8858 6648/ www.esharpminor.co.uk). North Greenwich tube. **Open** 10am-3pm Tue-Sat. **Credit** MC, V.
The clever name of this shop suits Ella Sharp's tailored knitwear, which is beautiful and original. Very minimalist, Ella's designs for babies and children up to the age of 10 feature sophisticated colour combinations such as leaf green with turquoise, or cloud blue and raspberry. There is also a range of linen dresses priced at around £70, which is soon to be joined by ranges in cashmere and silk. Ella has recently restarted womenswear too.
Buggy access. Nappy-changing facilities. Play area.

Gotham Angels
23 Islington Green, N1 (7359 8090). Angel tube. **Open** 10.30am-7pm Mon-Fri; 10am-6pm Sat; noon-6pm Sun. **Credit** MC, V.
Children's (and women's) clothes with an eclectic edge are the name of the game at Gotham Angels. Funky labels include Quiksilver, Paper Moon and own brand Gotham Angels, which is girly and glittery with a slight edge. For wee bubs there are babygros by No Added Sugar and Petra Boase.
Buggy access.

Gymboree
198 Regent Street, W1 (7494 1110/www.gymboree.com). Oxford Circus tube. **Open** 10am-7pm Mon-Wed, Fri, Sat; 10am-8pm Thur; 11.30am-5.30pm Sun. **Credit** AmEx, MC, V. **Map** p316 J6.
You can always find a bargain at Gymboree, especially since old stock is sold off at discount prices at the back of the shop every month or so. Cheery designs include pink cotton check trousers, tugboat T-shirts, animal babygros, dungarees, dresses, shirts and leggings for 0-7-year-olds.
Buggy access. Delivery service. Play area.
Branches throughout town. Check the phone book for your nearest.

Hobby Horse Riders
50-52 Crouch End Hill, N8 (8348 9782). Finsbury Park tube then W7 bus. **Open** 10.30am-5.30pm Mon-Fri; 10am-6pm Sat. **Credit** AmEx, MC, V.
Entering this neighbourhood fashion store, with its stock arranged by colour, is like stepping into a retail rainbow. Clothes – for newborns to 8-year-olds – include designs by Marèse, Miniman, Chipie, Confetti and Petit Bateau, and for little feet there are shoes by Kenzo, colourful Buckle My Shoe wellies (and shoes) and Daisy Roots for babes. All ages will enjoy a romp on the Jellycat jungle animal fur rugs (£40-£50). Also check out the new range of car seats, prams (Bébécar £200-£400) and bedroom furniture.
Buggy access.

Jigsaw Junior
190 Westbourne Grove, W11 (7229 8654/www.jigsaw-junior.com). Notting Hill Gate tube. **Open** 10.30am-6.30pm Mon; 10am-6.30pm Tue, Wed, Sat; 10am-7pm Thur, Fri; noon-6pm Sun. **Credit** AmEx, MC, V. **Map** p312 A6.
Jigsaw's children's store fits in plenty of pinks and purples and fluffy jumpers for rock chicks aged up to 13. Baby (girls, aged from 1) can keep warm in beautiful woollen cardigans embroidered with flowers, while sports lovers might choose silver skiwear or turquoise and navy swimwear. There's no ramp down the short flight of stairs to the children's section; instead, there's a silver slide with cushions.
Buggy access. Mail order. Play area.
Branches throughout town. Check the phone book for your nearest.

Little Willie's
16 The Pavement, SW4 (7498 7899). Clapham Common tube. **Open** 11am-5.30pm Tue-Fri; 10am-5pm Sat. **Credit** MC, V.
Offspring of Willie Smart's salon at No.11, Little Willie's is a hairdressing parlour for children, with a few clothes, shoes and accessories for sale. Freshly clipped youngsters can scribble on the blackboard door or try on beautiful shoes by Pom d'Api, Daisy Roots, Elle, Bobux and Naturino. Check out newcomers Chupa Chups – yes, the lollies people have turned to shoes! Resident clothing labels include Nippaz With Attitude, Little Punk, No Added Sugar, and tights by Country Kids.
Buggy access. Nappy-changing facilities. Play area.

M&G Junior Fashions
73 Kingsland High Street, E8 (7249 9728). Dalston Kingsland rail. **Open** 9.30am-6pm Mon-Sat. **Credit** MC, V.
With the most expensive babygro costing £3.99 and the most costly item in the shop £13.99 (a cot bumper and quilt), this East End store certainly offers value for money. Casual clothes for children up to 10 and soft shoes for babies are set out on rails and hooks around the room. If you're dressing a tot on a tight budget, look no further.
Buggy access.

Membery's
1 Church Road, SW13 (8876 2910). Barnes Bridge rail. **Open** 10am-5pm Mon-Sat. **Credit** AmEx, MC, V.
This pretty little shop sells Petit Bateau, Marèse, IKKS, Bluemoon, Berlingot, Kenzo Jungle, Lapin Bleu knitwear and its own classic Sally Membery frocks (£29-£39). There's also a small selection of gifty toys.
Buggy access. Nappy-changing facilities.

MikiHouse
107 Walton Street, SW3 (7838 0006/ www.mikihouse.co.uk). Knightsbridge tube. **Open** 10am-6pm Mon-Sat. **Credit** AmEx, MC, V. **Map** p315 E10.
MikiHouse is a Japanese brand for 0-8-year-olds that is huge in its home country. Its clothes are colourful and made with the attention to quality and detail that Japan is famed for, from summer swimwear to winter skiwear. Toys are also good quality and the accessories are stylish: we love the little house-shaped handbags (£29) and the lunch sets, which come complete with chopsticks.
Buggy access. Delivery service.

Notsobig
31A Highgate High Street, N6 (8340 4455). Archway or Highgate tube. **Open** 9.30am-6pm Mon-Fri; 10am-6pm Sat; 11am-5pm Sun. **Credit** MC, V.

Consumer

Cool Highgate kids are dragging their parents into this small but stylish clothes store, where babywear by Wo Wo and Cacharel make a splash and achingly trendy childrenswear by Bengh and Maharishi will burn a hole in your wallet. The look from LA and NY for children is vintage: the designer clothes cut down from old cashmere originals are stunning. There are a few toys and a small range of funky footwear. *Buggy access. Delivery service. Play area.*

Oilily
9 Sloane Street, SW1 (7823 2505/www.oilily.nl). Knightsbridge tube. **Open** 10am-6pm Mon, Tue, Thur-Sat; 10am-7pm Wed. **Credit** AmEx, DC, MC, V. **Map** p315 F9.
Oilily's spacious white room is flooded by ceiling lights that spotlight the bright colours on sale. Children can flop on the red sofa or play bead games at the round table, while their parents go shopping mad. Clothes for newborns up to the sophisticated tastes of a 14-year-old are cute and hardwearing, but not cheap. Adorable toddler dungarees cost £60; denims for a strapping boy of 10 a whopping £80-£90. *Buggy access. Delivery service. Mail order. Play area.*

Patrizia Wigan
19 Walton Street, SW3 (7823 7080/ www.patriziawigan.com). Knightsbridge or South Kensington tube. **Open** 10.30am-6.30pm Mon-Fri; 10.30am-6pm Sat. **Credit** AmEx, MC, V. **Map** p315 E10.
Classic frocks of the *Alice in Wonderland* type for young girls up to 12 years. Large framed photos of royals wearing Wigan's dresses at various gala occasions adorn the walls. The designs encompass beautiful velvet dresses, moleskin dungarees, plus a wedding collection for page boys and bridesmaids. Don't miss the leather, suede and fur bootees or the old-fashioned leather pilot-style hats.
Buggy access. Delivery service. Nappy-changing facilities. Play area.

Petit Bateau
188 Chiswick High Road, W4 (8987 0288). Turnham Green tube. **Open** 10am-6pm Mon-Sat; 11am-5pm Sun. **Credit** MC, V.
This new shop is dedicated to French label Petit Bateau for 0-18-year-olds. Alongside the signature T-shirts, raincoats and jeans is a wide collection of babywear, including special occasion outfits, nightwear, jeans and dungarees.
Buggy access. Nappy-changing facilities. Play area.
Branch: 106 King's Road, SW3 (7838 0818).

Piccolo Bella
6 Eton Street, Richmond, Surrey (8948 8601). Richmond tube/rail. **Open** 10am-5.30pm Mon-Sat; noon-5pm Sun. **Credit** MC, V.
Two sisters-in-law with five children between them opened Piccolo Bella to cater for distinctly upmarket under-10s. Behind the large glass front you find Baby Pex, Ambitoys and Daisy Roots shoes. There are special things, too: cuddly toys, pyjamas, gifts and a few pieces of baby hardware.
Buggy access. Delivery service.

Rachel Riley
14 Pont Street, SW1 (7259 5969/www.rachelriley.com). Sloane Square tube. **Open** 10am-6pm Mon-Sat. **Credit** AmEx, MC, V. **Map** p315 F10.

Web wise

Once upon a time, piles of catalogues were a common sight in family homes. These days, the internet offers a faster, more efficient and space- (and tree) saving alternative. We're talking instant transactions, constant updating and millions of shopping sites that are available 24 hours a day, reachable from the comfort of your own lounge. Yippee! Here's a round-up of our current faves.

All-rounders

www.nurserygoods.com sells a bit of everything. Delivery is seven days and costs a flat rate of £3.95 in mainland UK.

www.urchin.co.uk A great site with plenty of unusual goodies including the spotty potty (£16.95) and clothes and equipment.

Fancy dress

www.fancydays.com sells 'make your own fancy dress' kit sets. The good news for non-sewers is that the seams are all ironed together so there's no stitching involved at all. Sizes are from 2-7 years and prices start at £10.90.

www.hopscotchmailorder.co.uk has a fab selection of fancy-dress costumes including wizard coats (£33.95) and hats (£9.95), which have no doubt sold like hot cakes since *Harry Potter* came along. There's also a dragon suit (£29.95) and themed hats, from trolls to ants.

Green

www.greenbabyco.com The highlight of this site has got to be the crystal rattles (£10.50), which come in rose quartz or clear crystal. You can also visit the shop in Islington; see p196.

Nearly new

www.kidscloset.co.uk sells nearly new clothes for 0-14 years. An easy-to-navigate site organised by season, sex and age, with colour pics and descriptions of each garment including original price and second-hand one. Brands include O'Neill, Lego, Paul Smith and Quiksilver.

www.kidsnearlynew.com A good selection of nearly new clothes for kids aged 0-12 years. The star item on a recent trawl was a grey, furry hooded Gap top reduced from £22.50 to a mere £7.99.

www.loot.com is a web version of the popular paper, which has sections to buy and sell a wide range of kids' clothes, toys and nursery gear.

Shoes

www.starchildshoes.co.uk. This easy-to-use site sells soft leather shoes for babies and toddlers. Non-toxic dyes are used and designs include Jolly Rogers and rockets. There are two ranges: 0-2 and 2-4 years, from £14 to £16. Postage is free.

www.bobux-baby-shoes.com is a slightly slower site, also selling soft leather baby shoes. Most styles are £16.

This old-fashioned boutique has glass counters displaying Rachel Riley's delicate designs for babies and children up to 10. Soft leather slippers come in pinks and pale blues to match floral Liberty dresses, blue gingham pyjamas and unisex cotton poplin anoraks. Bibs, newborn robes and cotton cardigans are complemented by Petit Bateau baby underwear and babygros. There is also a range of Start-Rite shoes.
Buggy access. Delivery service. Mail order. Play area.
Branch: 82 Marylebone High Street, W1 (7935 7007).

Semmalina

225 Ebury Street, SW1 (7730 9333). Sloane Square tube. **Open** 9.30am-5.30pm Mon-Sat. **Credit** MC, V. **Map** p318 G11.
Step between the two trees and into a small fairytale kingdom complete with drawbridge and castle. Clothes include Cookie T-shirts, stripy knit jumpers from Cinnamon, and other labels such as Kind Hearts and Gerson di Santo, plus Semmalina's own range made from vintage fabrics, many of which are one-offs. We like the range of fantasy tutus (£45), with a variety of appliqué themes. Suede baby bootees (£25), vintage toys and other lovely goodies – some at pocket-money prices – can be gift-wrapped in sequins and tissue.
Buggy access. Delivery service. Mail order. Nappy-changing facilities. Play area.

Stock House

155 Lavender Hill, SW11 (7738 0293). Clapham Junction rail. **Open** 9am-6pm Mon-Sat. **Credit** MC, V.
A spacious shop that stocks an eclectic range of children's clothes (0-12 years) from around the world, including Trois Pommes, Alphabet, Blue Moon plus Sweet Pea and OshKosh from America, Baby Paws (baby shoes) from Tasmania and beautiful hand-painted Balu dresses from South Africa (£25-£40). There is also a hairdresser on the premises, who shows videos while she works.
Buggy access. Play area.

Tartine et Chocolat

66 South Molton Street, W1 (7629 7233). Bond Street tube. **Open** 10am-6pm Mon-Sat. **Credit** AmEx, MC, V. **Map** p316 H6.
One of the most stylish places in London to buy something very French and gorgeous for special new arrivals. A set of tiny babywear, beautifully presented for the newborn, starts at about £80; to have gifts especially presented in a trimmed basket costs over £100. Much of the outerwear is hand-embroidered. The bath stuff and linen fragrances smell divine. Tartine et Chocolat is moving some time in late summer, so ring before you set out.
Mail order. Nappy-changing facilities.

Toe Tho

55 Fortis Green Road, N10 (8442 0419). East Finchley or Highgate tube. **Open** 9.30am-6pm Mon-Sat. **Credit** MC, V.
Pronounced 'tow-tow', the name Toe Tho is Swahili for 'kids'. Clothing for girls in hot colours comes from Germany, France and Italy. There are Mini Claire organza dresses, Stentaler and Sarah Barker fabric shoes for pre-walkers, along with clothes by Alphabet, Abella and Whoopi for under-9s.
Buggy access.

Get spoilt for choice at **Oilily**. See p201.

Tots in the Terrace

39 Turnham Green Terrace, W4 (8995 0520). Turnham Green tube. **Open** *10am-6pm Mon-Sat.* **Credit** *AmEx, MC, V.*

Tots in the Terrace sells everything you need for children under 14, including sweaters and socks, sunglasses and swimwear by Oilily, Catimini, Miniman, Timberland, Kookai, Marèse and Kenzo. A toy box and mini chairs are provided for the amusement of littl'uns.
Buggy access. Delivery service. Mail order. Nappy-changing facilities. Play area.

Trendys

72 Chapel Market, N1 (7837 9070). Angel tube. **Open** *9.30am-6pm Mon-Sat; 9.30am-4pm Sun.* **Credit** *AmEx, MC, V.*

This boutique for 0-16-year-olds has the best of Diesel, Replay, French Connection, Cakewalk, DKNY, Oilily and Timberland. There is a small selection of equally covetable shoes by Moschino, Buckle My Shoe, Kickers and Elle.
Buggy access.

Trotters

34 King's Road, SW3 (7259 9620/www.trotters.co.uk). Sloane Square tube. **Open** *9am-6.30pm Mon, Tue, Thur-Sat; 9am-7pm Wed; 10am-6pm Sun.* **Credit** *AmEx, MC, V.* **Map** *p315 F11.*

Trotters has a stylish range of clothes for under-11s, which includes Baby Dior, Diesel, Oilily, Chelsea Clothing Company, Elle, Chippie and some funky swimsuits. Children can climb aboard the yellow Trotters Express train to have their shoes fitted (the selection includes Start-Rite, Mini Chukka, Dr Martens and pretty gingham sandals) or watch a video while having their hair done in the cool space lab hairdresser's. Also good for funky gift-type toys and accessories.
Buggy access. Delivery service. Nappy-changing facilities. **Branch:** *127 Kensington High Street, W8 (7937 9373).*

What Katy Did

49 Kensington Church Street, W8 (7937 6499). High Street Kensington or Notting Hill Gate tube. **Open** *10.30am-6pm Mon-Fri; 10am-6.30pm Sat.* **Credit** *AmEx, MC, V.* **Map** *p312 B8.*

This small boutique of 'kiddy couture' stocks an eclectic, stylish selection including Bengh Per Principesse, Bunny London, La Princesse Au Petit Pois, Quincy and Belgian label Tree for girls and boys. What Katy Did's pale blue tongue 'n' groove walls and white-washed floors give a seasidey feel enhanced by the retro dolphin on the counter.
Buggy access. Delivery service. Nappy-changing facilities.

Second-hand

Boomerang

69 Blythe Road, W14 (7610 5232). Olympia tube. **Open** *10am-6pm Tue-Sat.* **No credit cards.**

New and nearly new clothes, as well as toys, nursery equipment, maternity wear and buggy boards (£39 for a new one).
Buggy access.

Bunnies

201 Replingham Road, SW18 (8875 1228). Southfields tube. **Open** *9.30am-5.30pm Tue-Fri; 9.30am-4.30pm Sat.* **No credit cards.**

This clothing agency now deals mostly with designerwear for children aged 8 and under. Prams and buggies are a mainstay, although the owner will only take in models less than a year old and in very good condition. New buggies are also sold. Good-quality traditional, wooden toys are sold too.
Buggy access.

Chocolate Crocodile

39 Morpeth Road, E9 (8985 3330). Mile End tube then 277 bus. **Open** *11am-5pm Mon-Sat.* **Credit** *MC, V.*

Chocolate Crocodile benefits from a great location next to Victoria Park. Many a mum delves among the second-hand clothes, new and old toys, books and equipment. New wooden toys by Dutch company Woodware and Charles Toys include ABC puzzles, xylophones and train sets.
Buggy access. Play area.

The Little Trading Company

7 Bedford Corner, The Avenue, W4 (8742 3152). Turnham Green tube. **Open** *9am-5pm Mon-Fri; 9am-4.30pm Sat.* **No credit cards.**

In this small shop there are some great bargains to be had: on our visit we spotted Dragons furniture for less than half price and a Emmaljunga pushchair with toddler seat, rain cover and hood for a mere £150. You'll also find Brio, Lego, Fisher-Price and Early Learning Centre toys, plus books and videos, party shoes and second-hand Rollerblades; all items are taken on a profit-share, sale-or-return basis. There's haircutting on Wednesday and Friday afternoons, costing £9.50 for children aged over 3.
Buggy access. Delivery service. Play area.

Merry-Go-Round
12 Clarence Road, E5 (8985 6308). Hackney Central rail. **Open** 10am-5.30pm Mon-Sat. **Credit** MC, V.
A wide variety of good-quality clothes for babies, children and young adults, with labels ranging from Gap, Next and M&S to OshKosh, Oilily and Bon Bleu. It also stocks casual and maternity wear for women, but the under-3s get the lion's share of the stock, with videos, toys, books and equipment. Buggies, cots and high chairs can be bought at a fraction of the new cost. With nappy-changing facilities and a play area, Merry-Go-Round is fun and practical.
Buggy access. Nappy-changing facilities. Play area.

Pixies
14 Fauconberg Road, W4 (8995 1568/ www.pixiesonline.co.uk). Chiswick Park or Turnham Green tube. **Open** 10am-4.30pm Tue-Fri; 10am-3pm Sat. **Credit** MC, V.
You can find wellies and car seats, board games and tricycles in this well-organised shop. Pixie now stocks the Cosatto pixie buggy, which costs an amazing £49 new and is one of very few buggies with high handles (107cm) for the tall or high heeled. Swimwear and excellent Tripp Trapp high chairs are also new, but there are designer cast-offs for the under-12s if you need to make the pennies stretch further.
Buggy access. Mail order.

Rainbow
249 Archway Road, N6 (8340 8003). Highgate tube. **Open** 10.30am-5.30pm Mon-Sat. **Credit** MC, V.
Anoraks, swimwear, coats and other good-quality second-hand clothes, with labels ranging from M&S to French Connection, Oilily and Moschino. Socks cost just 50p, clothing starts at £2.95 and shoes sell well, especially trainers for babies. There is a play table for trying out the second-hand toys and books, but if you want new ones, pop two doors down to the sister shop (*see p211*).
Buggy access.

Rub-a-Dub-Dub
198 Stroud Green Road, N4 (7263 5577). Finsbury Park tube/rail/Crouch Hill rail. **Open** 10am-5pm Mon-Fri; 9.30am-5.30pm Sat. **No credit cards.**
New and second-hand clothes for the under-6s (including some designer labels) are the treats in this knowledgeably run little store, but you'll also find some second-hand toys (Lego, Brio or Playmobil) and baby hardware. Everything from a Maclaren pushchair to a Baby Bjorn carrier is tested before it goes on sale. New stock includes Tripp Trapp high chairs for £99, plus Groovy Girl toys, accessories and outfits. If you want to sell any goods yourself, bring them along and agree on a price.
Buggy access. Delivery service. Play area.

Swallows & Amazons
91 Nightingale Lane, SW12 (8673 0275). Clapham South tube. **Open** 10am-5.15pm Mon-Sat. **No credit cards.**

Take time to browse the ever-changing rails of second-hand designer and chain-store clothes, toys and equipment for babies and children. Second-hand hardware is also sold here. There is also a hairdresser on the premises.
Buggy access. Play area.

Shoes

Buckle My Shoe
18-19 St Christopher's Place, W1 (7935 5589/ www.bucklemyshoe.com). Bond Street tube. **Open** 10am-6pm Mon-Wed, Fri, Sat; 10am-7pm Thur. **Credit** AmEx, MC, V. **Map** p316 H6.
The HQ of this mini chain is an upbeat black and white shop with a wall of Jellycats and rails of Calvin Klein, Paul Smith, O'Neill and Gasolio.
Buggy access. Delivery service. Mail order.
Branches: Selfridges, 400 Oxford Street, W1 (7629 1234); Harvey Nichols, 109-25 Knightsbridge, SW1 (7235 5000); Brent Cross Shopping Centre, NW4 (8202 4423); Bentalls, Kingston-upon-Thames, Surrey (8546 1001).

Instep
45 St John's Wood High Street, NW8 (7722 7634). St John's Wood tube. **Open** 9.30am-5.30pm Mon-Sat; 11am-5pm Sun. **Credit** AmEx, MC, V.
Instep's own-brand of school, holiday and party shoes and boots are made in Italy. Trained staff will fit mock croc boots, canvas sandals and patent pink shoes on to little or adult feet up to size seven. For babies there are pre-walkers by Timberland and first walking shoes by Start-Rite and Babybotte, while older children can choose from a wide range of Ricosta and Start-Rite shoes, Dunlop wellies, socks and tights by Ergee and Faulke, and school bags. There are toys on hand to keep small shoppers amused.
Buggy access.
Branches throughout town. Check the phone book for your nearest.

Look Who's Walking
78 Heath Street, NW3 (7433 3855). Hampstead tube. **Open** 10am-5.30pm Mon-Sat; noon-6pm Sun. **Credit** AmEx, MC, V.
A tiny, busy gem of a shoe shop, which always seems to be busy, LWW stocks shoes by Pom d'Api, D&G, Mod 8, Naturino and Skechers. There are also a couple of rails of designer kids' gear for the under-12s (Oilily, Diesel, DKNY).
Buggy access.

The Shoe Station
3 Station Approach, Kew, Surrey (8940 9905/ www.theshoestation.co.uk). Kew Gardens tube. **Open** 10am-6pm Mon-Fri; 9.30am-6pm Sat. **Credit** MC, V.
The Shoe Station prides itself on protecting small feet with accurate measuring by trained fitters. Shoes are hardwearing and practical: makes include Babybotte, Start-Rite, Elefanten and Buckle My Shoe cowboy boots. Outside is a shoe recycling bin for cast-offs.
Buggy access. Mail order. Play area.

Stepping Out
106 Pitshanger Lane, W5 (8810 6141). Ealing Broadway tube. **Open** 10am-5.30pm Mon-Fri; 9am-5.30pm Sat. **Credit** AmEx, DC, MC, V.
Staff at Stepping Out aim to find the perfect shoe for every junior customer, whether they're a baby or 14 years old. There are tiny leather pre-walkers, beautifully embroidered bootees and trendy backless trainers. Unusual and exotic shoes by

Mall talk

London's most famous shopping centre is **Brent Cross**. It has everything the sprawling out-of-towners have, with the bonus of a tube station.

Brent Cross can be to tired parents what a life jacket is to the drowning: not exactly super stylish, you might not use it very often, but it can be a life-saver in times of need. In addition to a large, free car park, there are extra-wide spaces to accommodate buggies (level 1 of the John Lewis multi-storey car park). If you'd rather keep your kids with you than use the crèche, you can borrow a buggy from the information desk, for a refundable deposit of £20. For a treat you can rent a Boobaloo children's car for £2.50 per hour (deposit £20). Throughout the complex are toilets and pleasant baby-changing and feeding rooms.

Children's shops at Brent Cross include the ever-popular Early Learning Centre, with a large Brio display for tots to play with, plus a Mothercare, Gap Kids and a separate Baby Gap. At the other end of the complex is a brilliant Fun Learning shop, H&M, Buckle My Shoe and a Disney Store. Otherwise, there are other high-street names as well as designer fashion stores for bigger budgets. Places to eat include numerous burger, pizza and pasta refuelling stations, as well as more refined brasseries for those north London ladies who lunch, this place being their mecca.

Also in town, but for shoppers south of the river, **Centre Court Shopping Centre** has the crèche but fewer shops and less parking space, but it's still a boon for families. Bayswater's **Whiteley's** lacks the crèche but is blessed with a sophisticated range of eateries (Yo! Sushi, ASK, etc), a multi-screen cinema and multifarious shops.

Out-of-town shopping centres most visited by Londoners are **Bluewater** and Lakeside Thurrock, both with more than 300 shops. The former also has a crèche and Welcome Halls, where everything a buggy-pushing shopper might need (loos, feeding rooms and nappy-changing facilities, and pushchairs and toddler reins for hire) is lined up. An atrium houses the Wintergarden, with all the usual fast-food suspects, along with TGI Fridays and Ed's Easy Diner. Bluewater even has its own fishing lake and three miles of cycle paths. Pick up a map on your way in – you'll need one.

On a less bewildering scale but still with more shops than you can get round in a day is **Lakeside Thurrock**, just across the river in Essex. There's also a useful crèche and loads of restaurants and cafés, and a nearby retail park for IKEA and Toys 'R' Us. Children's films shown in the Warner Village cinema at 10.30am every Saturday.

Bluewater
Greenhithe, Kent (08456 021021/ www.bluewater.co.uk). Greenhithe rail/A206 off M25 or A2. **Open** *10am-9pm Mon-Fri; 9am-8pm Sat; 11am-5pm Sun.*

Brent Cross Shopping Centre
Brent Cross, NW4 (8202 8095/www.brentcross-london.com). Brent Cross or Hendon Central tube/North Circular Road (A406). **Open** *9am-8pm Mon-Fri; 9am-7pm Sat; 11am-5pm Sun.*

Centre Court Shopping Centre
4 Queen's Road, SW19 (8944 8323). Wimbledon tube/rail. **Open** *9am-7pm Mon-Wed, Fri; 9am-8pm Thur; 9am-7pm Sat; 11am-5pm Sun.*

Lakeside Thurrock
West Thurrock, Essex (01708 869933/ www.lakeside.uk.com). Lakeside rail/Junction 30/31 off M25. **Open** *10am-10pm Mon-Fri; 9am-7.30pm Sat; 11am-5pm Sun.*

Babybotte, Elle, Catimini, Start-Rite, Mod 8, Ricosta, Naturino and Salamander average at £30, with some models going up to the £50 mark.
Buggy access. Delivery service. Mail order. Play area.

Skate & surf

O'Neill
9-15 Neal Street, WC2 (7836 7686/ www.oneilleurope.com). Covent Garden or Leicester Square tube. **Open** *10am-7pm Mon-Wed, Fri, Sat; 10am-8pm Thur; noon-6pm Sun.* **Credit** *AmEx, MC, V.* **Map** *p317 L6.*
The Californian beach-bum look for pint-sized street surfers can be accessed upstairs here. Those all-important wallets, T-shirts and droopy trousers are expensive but adored by near-teens around the world.
Buggy access.
Branch: 7 Carnaby Street, W1 (7734 3778); Bluewater Shopping Centre, Greenhithe, Kent (01322 623300).

Quiksilver
Units 1 & 23, Thomas Neal Centre, Earlham Street, WC2 (7836 5371/www.quiksilver.com). Covent Garden tube. **Open** *10am-7pm Mon-Sat; noon-6pm Sun.* **Credit** *AmEx, MC, V.* **Map** *p317 L6.*
For many adolescent boys, Quiksilver is the label to crave. This Australian surfwear shop has sporty clothes (for girls and boys aged 2 to adult) that are casual looking but hard-wearing. If the trousers (from about £40) and T-shirts (from around £15) seem too expensive, then check out the accessories – wallets start at less than a tenner and rucksacks can be had from about £18.
Buggy access.
Branch: Unit 7, North Piazza, Covent Garden, WC2 (7240 5886).

Skate of Mind
Unit 26, Thomas Neal Centre, Earlham Street, WC2 (7836 9060). Covent Garden tube. **Open** *10am-7pm Mon-Sat; noon-6pm Sun.* **Credit** *DC, MC, V.* **Map** *p317 L6.*

Young teens come here for the decks as well as the essential look to ride them with. Baggy T-shirts and low-slung trousers are all present and correct.
Branch: 4 Marlborough Court, W1 (7434 0295).

Slam City Skates
16 Neal's Yard, WC2 (7240 0928/www.slamcity.com). Covent Garden tube. **Open** 10am-6.30pm Mon-Sat; 1-5pm Sun. **Credit** AmEx, MC, V. **Map** p317 L6.
Slam City is a mecca for skateboarding adolescents, who flock here for their decks and accessories, and all-important labels by Stüssy, Silas, Fresh Jive, Volcom, Droors and more. Keep an eye out for the great sales, which have people queuing around the block.

Sportswear & trainers

Decathlon
Canada Water Retail Park, Surrey Quays Road, SE16 (7394 2000/www.decathlon.co.uk). Canada Water tube. **Open** 10am-7.30pm Mon-Thur; 10am-8pm Fri; 9am-7pm Sat; 11am-5pm Sun. **Credit** MC, V.
The biggest sports shop in Northern Europe has efficient staff and the wherewithal for 60 types of sport. Children's shoes and equipment are stocked – the store's own brand plus Adidas, Nike et al.
Buggy access. Delivery service. Play area.

First Sport
Whiteley's Shopping Centre, Queensway, W2 (7792 1139/www.firstsport.co.uk). Bayswater or Queensway tube. **Open** 10am-9pm Mon-Sat; noon-6pm Sun. **Credit** AmEx, DC, MC, V. **Map** p312 C6.
This is the biggest London branch of a large chain of sportswear retailers. The trainer selection is impressive, with sizes for children from the age of 4 in the most fashionable brands. If you've got money to burn, kit out your offspring in the coveted Nike Shocks (£90-£129).
Buggy access.
Branches throughout town. Check the phone book for your nearest.

JD Sports
268 Oxford Street, W1 (7491 7677/www.jdsports.co.uk). Oxford Circus tube. **Open** 9am-8pm Mon, Tue; 9am-9pm Wed-Sat; noon-6pm Sun. **Credit** AmEx, MC, V. **Map** p316 H6.
This sportswear chain is renowned for its range of footwear, including teeny tiny trainers for little ones. All the big trainer names are represented, but chaotic service means it may be a while before you get the size you want.
Branches throughout town. Check the phone book for your nearest.

JJB Sports
301-9 Oxford Street, W1 (7409 2619/www.jjb.co.uk). Oxford Circus tube. **Open** 10am-7pm Mon-Wed, Fri, Sat; 10am-8pm Thur; noon-6pm Sun. **Credit** AmEx, MC, V. **Map** p316 H6.
There's a massive range of trainers (Adidas, Nike, Lotto), a good line in reduced-price sportswear, replica kit and end-of-lines at this sports shop. The army of callow youth in JJB T-shirts seem to spend an age discovering whether they have your child's size in the Nikes he's pinned his hopes on. Don't visit at the weekend if you want to stay sane.
Buggy access.
Branches throughout town. Check the phone book for your nearest.

Lillywhite's
24-36 Lower Regent Street, SW1 (7930 3181/ www.lillywhites.com). Piccadilly Circus tube. **Open** 10am-7pm Mon-Wed; 10am-8pm Thur-Sat; noon-6pm Sun. **Credit** AmEx, DC, MC, V. **Map** p319 K7.
The only shop in London where all sports are adequately represented, Lillywhite's is noted for its cricketwear and equipment in season, plus year-round footie kit, swimwear and ski-wear. Its trainer range for young feet is disappointing.
Buggy access.

Niketown
236 Oxford Street, W1 (7612 0800/www.nike.com). Oxford Circus tube. **Open** 10am-7pm Mon-Wed; 10am-8pm Thur-Sat; noon-6pm Sun. **Credit** AmEx, MC, V. **Map** p316 J6.
Though this much-hyped sportswear store has no dedicated children's section, small-size Nikes and leisurewear are on the top floor, with their hefty prices only too evident.
Buggy access. Delivery service. Mail order. Nappy-changing facilities.

Soccerscene
56-7 Carnaby Street, W1 (7439 0778/ www.soccerscene.co.uk). Oxford Circus tube. **Open** 9.30am-7pm Mon-Sat. **Credit** AmEx, MC, V. **Map** p316 J6.
Premier League replica kits, football boots and trainers can all be found in small sizes in this useful central London shop. There's also plenty of merchandising: cups, scarves and hats.
Mail order.
Branch: 156 Oxford Street, W1 (7436 6499).

Toys

Bikes

Chains worth visiting for well-priced children's bikes include **Daycocks** and **Halfords** (check the phone book for branches). We've found Daycocks has the edge when it comes to knowledgeable service, but Halfords has a spectacular range of kids' models.

Action Bikes
23-6 Embankment Place, Northumberland Avenue, WC2 (7930 2525). Embankment tube/Charing Cross or Victoria tube/rail. **Open** 9am-6pm Mon-Wed, Fri; 9am-7pm Thur; 9.30am-5.30pm Sat. **Credit** AmEx, MC, V. **Map** p319 L8.

Top girlie stuff at **Semmalina**. *See p203.*

A well-stocked shop with helpful staff, under the arches at Embankment. Most children's bikes stocked are of the 20- and 24-in wheel variety, but there are a few smaller ones. Main makes include Raleigh and Universal.
Buggy access. Delivery service. Mail order.
Branches: 19 Dacre Street, SW1 (7799 2233); 3 St Bride Street, EC4 (7583 7373).

Bikefix
48 Lamb's Conduit Street, WC1 (7405 4639/ www.bikefix.co.uk). Russell Square tube. **Open** 8.30am-7pm Mon-Fri; 11am-5pm Sat. **Credit** MC, V.
Map p317 M4.
This small, well-established shop specialises in two-wheeled people carriers. If you're after a waterproof pull-along buggy (complete with tall red flag) or a low-slung recumbent bike, this is the place to go.
Buggy access. Delivery service. Mail order.

Chamberlaine & Son
75-7 Kentish Town Road, NW1 (7485 4488/ www.chamberlainecycles.co.uk). Camden Town tube. **Open** 8.30am-6pm Mon-Sat. **Credit** AmEx, MC, V.
This is possibly the best children's bike shop north of the river. Chamberlaine stocks a comprehensive range of two-wheelers from GT, Raleigh and Peugeot and imports an amazingly colourful brand called Cool! Loekie. All bikes are well set up before leaving the shop. An ideal starting point for the novice junior.
Buggy access. Delivery service. Mail order.

Edwardes
221-25 Camberwell Road, SE5 (7703 3676/5720). Elephant & Castle tube/rail then P3, 12, 68, 171, 176 bus. **Open** 8.30am-6pm Mon-Sat. **Credit** AmEx, MC, V.
South-east London's busiest, always full of earnest-looking adults in full Gore-tex regalia, waiting for their smart bikes to be repaired. There's an excellent range of shiny children's bikes by Peugeot, Bronx, Raleigh, BMX and mountain bikes, and trailers and seats for little ones. Repairs are executed quickly, thoroughly and reasonably cheaply.
Buggy access. Delivery service. Mail order.

Crèche out

Dragging your kids around shops or the supermarket can sorely test the patience of both parties. For the days when you can't face anything quite so character building, try an in-store crèche. All the shopping centres featured on p206 have facilities or even dedicated kids' clubs.

Other favourite stop-offs for families that have such services include the following branches: **IKEA** at Brent Park, Drury Way, North Circular Road, NW10 (8208 5600), **Safeway** at Camden Goods Yard, Chalk Farm, NW1 (7267 9151) and **Tesco** – actually a Clown Town next door to its Colney Hatch branch (Deards Corner, North Circular Road, N19 (8361 6600). It's worth phoning for details before you drop by as height restrictions, maximum amount of time you can leave kids there, and whether you have to pay a fee.

FW Evans
111-15 Waterloo Road, SE1 (7928 2208/ www.evanscycles.com). Waterloo tube/rail. **Open** 9am-8pm Mon-Fri; 9am-6pm Sat; 11am-4pm Sun. **Credit** AmEx, MC, V. **Map** p320 N8.
Cyclists will find everything they need in this large, well-stocked emporium. There's nothing in the way of toddler bikes, but it does have the entire Trek range, which is about as good as kids' cycling gets.
Buggy access. Delivery service. Mail order.
Branches: 178 High Holborn, WC1 (7836 5585); 51-52 Rathbone Place, W1 (7580 4107); 77-9 The Cut, SE1 (7928 4785); 127 Wandsworth High Street, SW18 (8877 1878).

Fun & games

Cheeky Monkeys
202 Kensington Park Road, W11 (7792 9022/ www.cheekymonkeys.com). Notting Hill Gate tube. **Open** 9.30am-5.30pm Mon-Fri; 10am-5.30pm Sat; 11am-5pm Sun. **Credit** MC, V. **Map** p312 A6.
London's branches of Cheeky Monkeys may vary in size but all have the same, regularly updated stock of gifts for children. There are some beautiful wooden toys: a blue-shuttered dolls' house and a wooden London bus with removable passengers are popular. Dressing-up treats include a mermaid outfit, fairy wings, dinosaur suits and ladybird raincoats.
Buggy access.
Branches throughout town. Check the phone book for your nearest.

Disney Store
140-144 Regent Street, W1 (7287 6558). Oxford Circus or Piccadilly Circus tube. **Open** 10am-8pm Mon-Sat; noon-6pm Sun. **Credit** AmEx, MC, V. **Map** p316 J6.
Disney merchandise is what this place is all about: toys and clothes, including nightwear, Tigger and Pooh babygros and shiny Tinkerbell and Buzz Lightyear playsuits; you can even dress your baby as one of the seven dwarves. Videos and DVDs of current releases are also on sale.
Buggy access. Delivery service. Mail order.
Branches throughout town. Check the phone book for your nearest.

Fun Learning
Bentall's Centre, Clarence Street, Kingston-upon-Thames, Surrey (8974 8900). Kingston rail. **Open** 9am-6pm Mon-Wed, Fri, Sat; 9am-8pm Thur; 11am-5pm Sun. **Credit** MC, V.
Fun Learning has toys for everyone from 5-15-year-olds, including some brainteasers and puzzles that will even flummox adults. Eager learners try out the educational software at the computer table in the centre, while others head straight to the toys and books arranged around the edges, encompassing themes such as the night sky and the animal kingdom. There's outdoor equipment, including skipping ropes and hula hoops, too, and a large craft area, where kids can make pipe-cleaner figures, tissue flowers or use Hama Beads to make coasters and placemats.
Delivery service. Mail order. Nappy-changing facilities. Play area.

Hamleys
188-96 Regent Street, W1 (8752 2278/ www.hamleys.com). Oxford Circus tube. **Open** 10am-8pm Mon-Fri; 9.30am-8pm Sat; noon-6pm Sun. **Credit** AmEx, MC, V. **Map** p316 J6.

'The world's most famous toyshop' is a dream – or a nightmare – depending on which way you look at it. Upon entering you are bombarded with battery-operated Hoppy Bunnies, magic displays and circling paper gliders in the chaotic demonstration area. Round the corner, three Steiff bears take off in a rocket before you enter a jungle full of soft wild animals. The basement is more peaceful with puzzles and games. Send your child up the Ghost Stair to the giant talking book on the second floor where you'll find everything you need for pre-school and nursery-aged kids. The third floor is stuffed with dolls and a great range of dressing-up clothes, while the fourth houses radio-controlled trains, planes and cars, Action Man and Scalextric. At the top, the Lego Café is an oasis of kiddy portions, high chairs and nappy-changing facilities, watched over by a larger-than-life talking Lego Darth Vadar (£499.99) and circled by an out-size train running round the balcony. To avoid the worst of the crowds, go on a weekday.
Buggy access. Café. Delivery service. Mail order. Nappy-changing facilities.
Branch: 3 The Piazza, WC2 (7210 4646).

Local toyshops

Fagin's Toys
84 Fortis Green Road, N10 (8444 0282). East Finchley tube. **Open** 9am-5.30pm Mon-Sat; 10am-3pm Sun. **Credit** AmEx, MC, V.
Traditional and educational toys aimed firmly at the local clientele. Smart frames, baby walkers and tiny trikes are sold for toddlers, and there are Orchard and Living and Learning games for older kids. The outdoor department shows off the smallest of the TP aluminium climbing frames, while the cheapo section boasts bangles, plastic frogs and whoopee cushions for under a quid. A must for Muswell Hillbillies.
Buggy access. Play area.

Frederick Beck
22-6 Camden Passage, N1 (7226 3403). Angel tube. **Open** 9.30am-5.30pm Mon, Tue, Thur, Fri; 9am-5.30pm Wed, Sat. **Credit** AmEx, MC, V.
The staff in this odd mix of electrical shop and toy emporium pretend not to like kids, but the presence of a Hornby railway set, plus Brio and bead tables suggests they're not as stern as all that. Papo figures (Joan of Arc, pirates, knights and Romans) are all the rage, but there are other exciting goodies in this creaky, wooden-floored space, including marbles, Schleich animals, cap guns and Le Toy Van dolls' houses. It's hard to imagine you'll leave empty-handed, especially given the choice of pocket-money priced goodies.
Buggy access. Play area.

Happy Returns
36 Rosslyn Hill, NW3 (7435 2431). Hampstead tube. **Open** 9.30am-5.30pm Mon-Fri; 10am-6pm Sat; noon-5.30pm Sun. **Credit** MC, V.
You'll return to this toy and party shop again and again to stock up on Christmas and birthday presents. On the top floor are balloons, cards, wrapping paper, Brio trains, Barbie outfits, stickers, finger paints and Miffy boogie bags (£12.99); below you'll find kites and drums, cricket bats and Airfix, Bob the Builder and Cluedo. There's no snobbery about mixing quality with commercial brands here, so you're likely to come across a Tweenies scooter next to Ambi soft toys for newborns, plastic armour, Playmobil, Sylvanian Families, Duplo, Noddy, Plan, Action Man and Tomy.
Buggy access.

Soup Dragon. *See p211.*

Havana's Toy Box
Ground Floor, Putney Exchange Shopping Centre, Putney High Street, SW15 (8780 3722). Putney Bridge tube/Putney rail. **Open** 9am-6pm Mon-Sat; 11am-5pm Sun. **Credit** AmEx, MC, V.
Wooden toys, soft toys, dressing-up clothes and night stuff are all squeezed into this tiny boutique for under-6s. Goodies on show include farms, trucks, push-along animals, Beanies, fairy dresses, Sarah Barker baby shoes, kiddie sleeping bags and night lights with jungle design lampshades. You should find something in that lot.
Buggy access.

Patrick's Toys & Models
107-11 Lillie Road, SW6 (7385 9864/ www.patrickstoys.co.uk). Fulham Broadway tube. **Open** 9.15am-5.45pm Mon-Sat. **Credit** MC, V.
This family-run business has been selling toys and models for over 50 years. Patrick's maintains a balance between traditional faves and latest crazes in the toy department, and stocks models galore upstairs: rockets, planes, cars, military and science fiction figures. Straw bonnets, rubber masks and sheriff's badges will please the small-budget shopper, while old classics like Hornby, Scalextric, toy guns and go-karts will excite active kids. Even the ceiling is covered in tricycles.
Buggy access. Delivery service. Mail order.

Route 73 Kids
92 Stoke Newington Church Street, N16 (7923 7873/ www.route73kids.com). Bus 73. **Open** 10am-5.30pm Tue-Sat; noon-5pm Sun. **Credit** AmEx, MC, V.

The exciting window display at Route 73 Kids is enough to make anyone hop off the 73 bus as they go past. This toy trove is small and cramped, but it's well set out with a central circular table of pocket-money priced delights and a ceiling bedecked with wooden and material mobiles, Jellycat animal rugs and a wooden rocking dolphin. The comprehensive baby range includes Ambi, Lamaze and a wobbly backed Kouvalia snail. The art section sells liquid paint, protective Miffy aprons and marbling, weaving and sponging kits for £8. Performers can try fairy wings and skirt, while puppeteers have a go with the Manhattan Finger Puppet Theatre and Darwin the Wizard marionette.
Buggy access. Delivery service. Mail order. Play area.

Snap Dragon
56 Turnham Green Terrace, W4 (8995 6618). Turnham Green tube. **Open** *9.30am-6pm Mon-Sat; noon-5pm Sun.* **Credit** MC, V.
Colourful, original toys for under-11s occupy this tiny purple outlet. You can excavate dinosaur bones from clay with a Dino Dig or hatch eggs in water to produce shrimp-like 'pets' called Sea-Monkeys (prices from £5.99). Traditional wooden toys – babywalkers, shape sorters, puzzles, rocking horses – are also well represented.
Buggy access. Delivery service. Mail order.

Tiny Set Toys
54 Lower Richmond Road, SW15 (8788 0392). Putney Bridge tube/22 bus. **Open** *9.30am-5.30pm Mon-Sat; 10am-2pm Sun.* **Credit** MC, V.
Britain's major stockist for TP aluminium climbing frames will also help fit them for £25. Swings, slides and paddling pools are piled up at the back of the three-level shop. Sports equipment can be found downstairs, opposite the Barbies, buggies and other dolls. You can snaffle pocket-money bargains such as bubble-blowing kits for 50p and Matchbox cars for 75p on the first floor; here you'll also see traditional wooden sit-and-ride toys, teddy bears and rocking horses. On the top floor are piles of Lego, jigsaws, games and so on.
Buggy access. Delivery service. Mail order.

Toy City
1st Floor, Wood Green Shopping City, N22 (8881 0770). Wood Green tube. **Open** *9am-6pm Mon-Sat; 11am-5pm Sun.* **Credit** AmEx, MC, V.
Everything modern and branded is crammed into this much-needed small local store, with budget tricycles and rocking horses suspended from the ceiling. You can hop into a Batman, Spiderman or Superman outfit or kit Barbie out with a new wardrobe. For imaginative play there are plastic soldiers and animals, and for creativity Galt paints, along with plenty of Lego, Brio and Duplo. If you're planning a kids' party, Toy City's cards, wrapping paper and helium balloons should do the trick.
Buggy access.

The Toy Station
10 Eton Street, Richmond, Surrey (8940 4896/ www.thetoystation.co.uk). Richmond tube/rail. **Open** *10am-6pm Mon-Fri; 9.30am-6pm Sat; noon-5pm Sun.* **Credit** Over £8 MC, V.
This small shop crams its action goods on to two floors; even the stairwell is jam-packed. You can pick up a robotic puppy or a bow and arrow on your way down to the plastic creatures (red-kneed tarantula) and radio-controlled raptor lurking among the games and Airfix kits. The top floor is well stocked with the usual suspects (Lego, Brio, Meccano) and has Scalextric and lots of Beanies.
Buggy access.

Toy Wonderland
10-11 Northways Parade, Finchley Road, NW3 (7722 9821/www.toywonderland.co.uk). Swiss Cottage tube. **Open** *10am-6pm Mon-Sat; 11am-4pm Sun.* **Credit** MC, V.
The plastic wonders you'll find in this chaotic venue are the likes of life-size machine guns, magnifying glasses, boomerangs and Polly Pocket knick-knacks. You can dress a 2-year-old up as Winnie the Pooh or turn an 8-year-old into Spiderman. Other favourite buys include electronic guitars, Hornby trains and Warhammer. Any self-respecting girlie shouldn't miss the glittery stickers.
Buggy access. Delivery service. Mail order.

Traditional toys

Benjamin Pollock's Toyshop
44 The Market, Covent Garden, WC2 (7379 7866/ www.pollocks-coventgarden.co.uk). Covent Garden tube. **Open** *10.30am-6pm Mon-Sat; 11am-4pm Sun.* **Credit** AmEx, MC, V. **Map** p319 L7.
This first-floor shop is famous for its cardboard Victorian theatres. Other toys include British lead soldiers and Beefeaters, Russian dolls, a wooden Noah's Ark, tin toys and cut-out models. Among the appealing traditional pop-up classics are Struwelpeter and Max and Moritz; postcards include commedia dell'arte. There are also Punch & Judy puppets (from £100) and others from the Czech Republic and Bavaria. A colourful alphabet caterpillar with finger puppets costs £35, but there is a shelf of cheaper items for smaller earners.
Mail order.

The Farmyard
63 Barnes High Street, SW13 (8878 7338). Barnes Bridge rail. **Open** *10am-5.30pm Mon-Fri; 9.30am-5.30pm Sat.* **Credit** MC, V.
Despite the name, it's not just beasts you'll find here. The Farmyard is perfect for gifts: one wall is filled with bright wooden toys – a double decker bus, a lorry of building blocks and a Noah's Ark. Opposite are smaller knick-knacks such as glow-in-the-dark stars, games and puzzles, Madeline dolls and pop-up puppets. Kids can dress up as a fairy or a princess for a party, and there's also a gift-wrapping service.
Buggy access. Mail order. Play area.
Branch: 54 Friar's Stile Road, Richmond, Surrey (8332 0038).

Harlequin House
3 Kensington Mall, W8 (7221 8629). High Street Kensington tube. **Open** *11am-5.30pm Tue, Fri, Sat.* **No credit cards. Map** p314 B9.
The longer you look, the more you'll find in this quirky, higgledy-piggledy puppet and mask kingdom. A magnificent Punch & Judy totem pole marks the centre of the store and is surrounded on all sides by intriguing goodies. To the left are glove and finger puppets, from felt dragons to finger mice and pigs in a box. Masks adorn the back wall: Venetian, papier-mâché, commedia dell'arte, party, neutral and cardboard cut-outs. Wooden puppet theatres start at £25 but you can get a nifty material one to hang in a doorway for £35. Even if you don't buy, the gruesome 4ft latex witch and the American ventriloquist dolls are worth a peek anyway.
Mail order.

Kristen Baybars
7 Mansfield Road, NW3 (7267 0934). Belsize Park tube/Gospel Oak rail/C2, C12 bus. **Open** *11am-6pm Tue-Sat.* **No credit cards.**

Craftswoman Kristen Baybars works in the back room painting period dolls' houses to order. One of her specialities is a jigsaw puzzle the size of a thumbnail. You can appreciate the blunt sign 'any unaccompanied children will be sold into slavery' as you slide open the doors of Baybars' exquisitely furnished dolls' houses. Kids just can't be boisterous here. *Buggy access.*

Never Never Land
3 Midhurst Parade, N10 (8883 3997). East Finchley tube.
Open 10am-5pm Tue, Wed, Fri, Sat. **Credit** MC, V.
You can just about squeeze a buggy into this tiny shop specialising in dolls' houses and furniture. Kits of cottages and Georgian townhouses start from £75 and ready-made models begin at £130.
Buggy access. Mail order.

Peter Rabbit & Friends
42 The Market, Covent Garden, WC2 (7497 1777/ www.charactergifts.com). Covent Garden tube/Charing Cross tube/rail. **Open** 10am-8pm Mon-Sat; 10am-6pm Sun. **Credit** AmEx, MC, V. **Map** p319 L7.
Somehow Winnie the Pooh and the Wombles have found their way into Beatrix Potter land. The stock downstairs is largely tacky. Upstairs has the (more covetable) book sets, videos, nightwear, duvet covers, soaps, spoons, postcards, along with a 4ft Peter Rabbit.
Buggy access. Delivery service. Mail order.

Rainbow
253 Archway Road, N6 (8340 8003). Highgate tube.
Open 10.30am-5.30pm Mon-Sat. **Credit** MC, V.
Speciality wooden toys in this quirky shop include farms, fun dolls' houses (£70-£180), pull-along wooden crocodiles and ducks and a push-along terrier. There are also dressing-up clothes and puppet theatres. The sister shop at No.249 (*see p205*) sells second-hand clothing.
Buggy access.

Soup Dragon
27 Topsfield Parade, Tottenham Lane, N8 (8348 0224/www.soup-dragon.co.uk). Finsbury Park tube/ rail then W7 bus. **Open** 9.30am-6pm Mon-Sat; 11am-5pm Sun. **Credit** MC, V.
Soup Dragon has fun clothes and toys for children under 10, to suit every pocket. Bell trees for babies start from £6.90, and beautiful handcrafted sit-and-ride toys for toddlers cost from £27.50. There are forts, farms, castles, airports, garages and all sorts of dolls' houses. Imaginative English-made knitwear sits alongside cool Dracula outfits (from £15.90).
Buggy access. Play area.
Branch: 106 Lordship Lane, SE22 (8693 5575).

Traditional Toys
53 Godfrey Street, SW3 (7352 1718). Sloane Square tube then 11, 19, 22 bus/49 bus. **Open** 10am-5.30pm Mon-Fri; 10am-6pm Sat; 11am-4.30pm Sun. **Credit** AmEx, MC, V. **Map** p315 E11.
This menagerie of toys includes dressable American Muffy VanderBear with his friend Hoppy the Rabbit, bear and cow wooden tricycles (costing £49.99) and entrancing Julip horses. Traditional toys indeed.
Buggy access. Mail order.

Tridias
25 Bute Street, SW7 (7584 2330/www.tridias.co.uk). South Kensington tube/14, 74 bus. **Open** 9.30am-6pm Mon-Fri; 10am-6pm Sat. **Credit** MC, V. **Map** p315 D10.
Children are allowed to play with the traditional toys stocked here, which include Georgian Plan dolls' houses and tasteful dolls, plus prams and double buggies for same. In addition, there's a well-stocked art section and some imaginative dressing-up clothes; we particularly liked the space suits (£19.99).
Buggy access. Delivery service. Mail order.
Branch: 6 Lichfield Terrace, Sheen Road, Richmond, Surrey (8948 3459).

Traditional Toys, full of dolly delights.

Shops by area

Southwark & Bankside
FW Evans (Bikes, *p208*).

Bloomsbury & Holborn
Bikefix (Bikes, *p208*).

Kensington & Chelsea
Caramel (Clothes, *p198*); Daisy & Tom (All-rounders, *p192*); Dragons of Walton Street (Equipment & accessories, *p195*); Harvey Nichols (Department stores, *p199*); MikiHouse (Clothes, *p200*); Nursery Window (Equipment & accessories, *p198*); Oilily (Clothes, *p201*); Patrizia Wigan (Clothes, *p201*); Traditional Toys (Traditional toys, *p211*); Tridias (Traditional toys, *p211*); Trotters (Clothes, *p204*); What Katy Did (Clothes, *p204*).

West End
Action Bikes (Bikes, *p207*); Benjamin Pollock's Toyshop (Traditional toys, *p210*); Bhs (Department stores, *p198*); Buckle My Shoe (Shoes, *p205*); Catimini (Clothes, *p199*); Chappell of Bond Street (Musical instruments, *p194*); Debenhams (Department stores, *p198*); Dickins & Jones (Department stores, *p198*); Disney Store (Fun & games, *p208*); Fenwick (Department stores, *p198*); Fortnum & Mason (Department stores, *p198*); Gymboree (Clothes, *p200*); Hamleys (Fun & games, *p208*); House of Fraser (Department stores, *p199*); JD Sports (Sportswear & trainers, *p207*); JJB Sports (Sportswear & trainers, *p207*); John Lewis (Department stores, *p199*); Liberty (Department stores, *p199*); Lillywhite's (Sportswear & trainers, *p207*); Marks & Spencer (Department stores, *p199*); Niketown (Sportswear & trainers, *p207*); O'Neill (Skate & surf, *p206*); Peter Rabbit & Friends (Traditional toys, *p211*); Quiksilver (Skate & surf, *p206*); Selfridges (Department stores, *p199*); Skate of Mind (Skate & surf, *p206*); Slam City Skates (Skate & surf, *p207*); Soccerscene (Sportswear & trainers, *p207*); Tartine et Chocolat (Clothes, *p203*).

Westminster
Rachel Riley (Clothes, *p201*); Semmalina (Clothes, *p203*).

North London
Baby Munchkins (Equipment & accessories, *p195*); Bookworm (Books, *p192*); Brent Cross Shopping Centre (Mall talk, *p206*); Chamberlaine & Son (Bikes, *p208*); Children's Bookshop (Books, *p194*); Dot's (Musical instruments, *p194*); Early Clothing (Clothes, *p200*); Fagin's Toys (Local toyshops, *p209*); Frederick Beck (Local toyshops, *p209*); Gotham Angels (Clothes, *p200*); Green Baby (Equipment & accessories, *p196*); Happy Returns (Local toyshops, *p209*); Hobby Horse Riders (Clothes, *p200*); Humla Children's Shop (Equipment & accessories, *p196*); Infantasia (Equipment & accessories, *p196*); Instep (Shoes, *p205*); Kristen

Baybars (Traditional toys, *p210*); Look Who's Walking (Shoes, *p205*); Mini Kin (Equipment & accessories, *p196*); Never Never Land (Traditional toys, *p211*); Notsobig (Clothes, *p200*); Owl Bookshop (Books, *p194*); Rainbow (Second-hand, *p205*; Traditional toys, *p211*); Route 73 Kids (Local toyshops, *p209*); Rub-a-Dub-Dub (Second-hand, *p205*); Soup Dragon (Traditional toys, *p211*); Toe Tho (Clothes, *p203*); Toy City (Local toyshops, *p210*); Toy Wonderland (Local toyshops, *p210*); Trendys (Clothes, *p204*).

East London
Baby This 'n' Baby That (Equipment & accessories, *p195*); Chocolate Crocodile (Second-hand, *p204*); Family Care (Equipment & accessories, *p196*); M&G Junior Fashions (Clothes, *p200*); Merry-Go-Round (Second-hand, *p205*).

South-east London
Biff (Clothes, *p198*); Bookseller Crow on the Hill (Books, *p192*); Decathlon (Sportswear & trainers, *p207*); Dulwich Music Shop (Musical instruments, *p194*); Edwardes (Bikes, *p208*); E sharp minor (Clothes, *p200*).

South-west London
Barney's (Clothes, *p198*); Bunnies (Second-hand, *p204*); Centre Court Shopping Centre (Mall talk, *p206*); The Farmyard (Traditional toys, *p210*); Fun Learning (Fun & games, *p208*); Havana's Toy Box (Local toyshops, *p209*); Lilliput (All-rounders, *p192*); Little Bridge (Equipment & accessories, *p196*); Little Willie's (Clothes, *p200*); Membery's (Clothes, *p200*); Northcote Music (Musical instruments, *p194*); Patrick's Toys & Models (Local toyshops, *p209*); Piccolo Bella (Clothes, *p201*); The Shoe Station (Shoes, *p205*); Stock House (Clothes, *p203*); Swallows & Amazons (Second-hand, *p205*); Tiny Set Toys (Local toyshops, *p210*); The Toy Station (Local toyshops, *p210*).

West London
Boomerang (Second-hand, *p204*); Cheeky Monkeys (Fun & games, *p208*); Children's Book Centre (Books, *p194*); The Children's Book Company (Books, *p194*); Clementine (Clothes, *p199*); Cookie (Clothes, *p199*); The Cross (Clothes, *p199*); First Sport (Sportswear & trainers, *p207*); The Golden Treasury (Books, *p194*); Harlequin House (Traditional toys, *p210*); Jigsaw Junior (Clothes, *p200*); Junior Living (Equipment & accessories, *p196*); The Little Trading Company (Second-hand, *p204*); Petit Bateau (Clothes, *p201*); Pixies (Second-hand, *p205*); Snap Dragon (Local toyshops, *p210*); Stepping Out (Shoes, *p205*); Tots in the Terrace (Clothes, *p204*).

Out of town
Bluewater (Mall talk, *p206*); Lakeside Thurrock (Mall talk, *p296*); Rainbow Violins (Musical instruments, *p195*).

Consumer

Activities

Arts & Entertainment

Creativity rules.

Feeling bored? Impossible! The majority of London's children may be chicken coop kids, living in flats and houses on busy roads, but they have some of the best arts and entertainment venues in Europe right on their doorstep. While cultural offerings for adults may be prohibitively expensive (£40 for a ticket to see a West End show? A tenner to go to the cinema in Leicester Square? No wonder video rentals are popular…), the children's equivalents are often surprisingly affordable. Indeed, if you know where to look, they're even free.

Check *Time Out* magazine's children's pages every week for forthcoming family arts events and theatre performances. It also has information about circuses – big-name circuses that come to town annually include **Zippo's** and the **Chinese State Circus**, both of whom spend a week or so in each venue (Blackheath, Peckham Rye, Alexandra Park and Highbury Fields are popular big-top pitching places).

Many of the performance spaces, clubs and workshops included in this chapter cater for children with disabilities and special needs; ask about facilities when you book. Bear in mind, too, that arts workshops and classes change termly, so ring to check your chosen activity is still taking place.

Arts centres

Barbican Centre

Silk Street, EC2 (box office 7638 8891/cinema hotline 7382 7000/textphone 7382 7297/arts education programme 7382 2333/www.barbican.org.uk). Barbican tube/Moorgate tube/rail. **Open** *Box office* 10am-8pm Mon-Sat; noon-8pm Sun, bank hols. **Film Club** *Membership* £5/yr per family. **Gallery** 10am-6pm Mon, Tue, Thur-Sat; 10am-8pm Wed; noon-6pm Sun, bank hols. **Admission** *Library* free. *Exhibitions, films, shows, workshops* phone for details. **Membership** (BarbicanCard) £10/yr. **Credit** AmEx, MC, V. **Map** p320 P5.

The labyrinthine architecture of the Barbican may not be to the taste of many adult visitors, but its vast carpeted halls for running about, glass stairwells to explore and inner courtyard filled with the enticing splashing of fountains in summer suit most kids down to the ground. 2002 sees a turning point in the centre's theatrical focus; since the departure of the RSC in early summer, the two auditoria are being filled with productions by touring companies and a number of family-friendly events are scheduled throughout the year. This year the Barbican is collaborating with the Greenwich and Docklands Festival (*see p31*) in a production by Les Arts Sauts called *Kayassine*, which takes place in east London's Victoria Park in a large inflatable tent. Fun for all the family indeed. Ring the box office for tickets. From 15-20 August 2002, *Telling Tales*, a series of

performances and workshops for children run in the Pit and the Den (the Barbican's more intimate performance spaces). Tickets cost £7 for both show and workshop; £5 for show only and £3 for workshop only. Children are split into two age groups: 3 and over, and 8 and over. To receive more details about all the Barbican's family-friendly theatricals, including the seasonal show from the Generating Company (formed of ex-Millennium Dome acrobats), called *Storm*, ring the 'Family News' mailing list: 7382 7049.

The cinema remains a focal point for children, running a Family Film Club on Saturday mornings for (accompanied) 5-11-year-olds, which combines screenings of films from around the world with workshops and activities.

The children's library is a venue for regular free events for over-3s, featuring storytellers, poets and magicians; phone first to book as numbers are limited and they're extremely popular. School holidays and bank holiday weekends see workshops, puppet-making activities and story sessions, often as part of dedicated Family Festivals complementing productions and concerts in the centre. It's worth scouring the monthly programme for details; some are free foyer events but others are ticketed and must be booked in advance. The BarbicanCard scheme puts you on a mailing list with details of special family events.

South Bank Centre

Belvedere Road, South Bank, SE1 (7960 4242/ www.sbc.org.uk). Waterloo tube/rail. **Open** *Box office phone bookings* 9am-9pm daily. *Personal callers* 10am-9pm daily. **Credit** AmEx, MC, V. **Map** p319 M8.

The South Bank continues to triumph over its brutal concrete setting by providing a vibrant programme of music, dance and visual arts, both in the three concert halls – Royal Festival Hall, Queen Elizabeth Hall and Purcell Room – and in its ample foyer space. Exhibitions in the so-called Ballroom are often family-focused, allowing kids to touch, crawl through and generally interact with contemporary installations. Each weekend there are hands-on drop-in activities and storytelling trails. School term times coincide with the now well-established Gong Club, a weekly class in the RFH for youngsters over 7 and their carers who wish to play Gamelan (prices from £25 per term) – Indonesian percussion instruments – and learn about the accompanying dance forms and shadow puppet theatre. (Anyone unsure of their own aptitude can book a place on a Gamelan Taster Day.)

More musical activities on offer at the centre include regular classical youth concerts on Saturday mornings in the RFH, given by the resident symphony orchestras, the Philharmonia and the London Philharmonic. These London FUNharmonics concerts have been introducing young audiences to classical music for the past four years, and have proved very successful. It's not all Bach, though. Performances have been known to combine African and hip hop styles with baroque and bird tweeting, and in the summer festivals spill on to the river terraces, occasionally sending dancers on to the roof space and stiltwalkers into the crowds. The organisers are keen to provide an interactive sort of show for the yoof, with have-a-go musical instrument sessions and face painting for the very young. For booking and further details call 7960 4203. The Hayward Gallery (*see p217*) is part of the South Bank Centre.

Activities

Every child enjoys **Everyman Cinema** screenings. *See p219.*

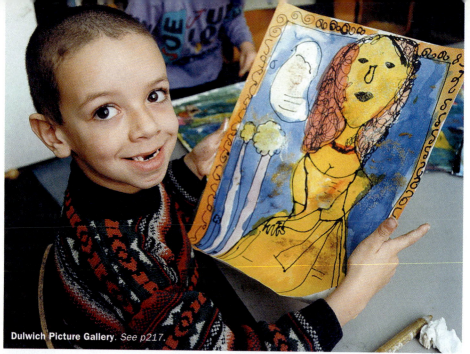
Dulwich Picture Gallery. *See p217.*

Stratford Circus

Theatre Square, E15 (8279 1001/www.stratford-circus.org.uk). Stratford tube/rail/DLR. **Open** *Box office* 11am-6pm or until 15mins after show starts Mon-Sat. **Tickets** £10; £3-£5 concessions, under-16s. *Go-card* £24 (6 shows). **Credit** MC, V.
Since east London's centre for the performing arts opened its doors in June 2001, its directors have developed a quite frenetic programme of dance, theatre, comedy and music events, and garnered a strong commitment to youthful participation in all activities. Courses in DJ-ing, dance, drama, writing, music, choreography and other skills take place in the five studios and performance spaces housed in the building (entitled Circus 1 to Circus 5). Dance and drama groups for older children (14-plus) start at just £1 a session; call for further details and information on courses and performances, and for this season's programme of events.

Tricycle Theatre & Cinema

269 Kilburn High Road, NW6 (7328 1000/ www.tricycle.co.uk). Kilburn tube/Brondesbury rail. **Open** *Box office* 10am-9pm Mon-Sat; 2-9pm Sun. *Children's shows* 11.30am, 2pm Sat. *Children's films* 1pm Sat. **Tickets** *Sat theatre* £4.50; £4 advance bookings. *Sat films* £4; £3 under-16s. **Credit** MC, V.
Behind its narrow, unobtrusive entrance on the High Road, the Tricycle's complex of theatre, art gallery, café and new cinema is an oasis of cultured calm. The theatre space is intimate and offers a variety of children's shows on Saturdays, ranging from conjuring through comedy and puppetry to cannily adapted classics. Also on Saturdays, popular children's films are screened at lunchtime in a laid-back atmosphere of whooping and shrieking. As a big treat, for £150 you can even choose your own family film for a party of up to 50 people.
The Tricycle also has various projects aimed at polishing the creativity of south Kilburn's younger citizens. For example, in 2002 five would-be filmmakers aged between 11 and 25 will be given the wherewithal to produce short features

for public viewing. An Artists Group of 11-18-year-olds meets with the Tricycle's artist-in-residence two nights a week to learn a variety of skills (this is free). In the summer, a group of 30 11-17-year-olds will be given the chance to devise, create and perform their own musical.
In addition to these challenging projects, the Tricycle Theatre runs a busy and intriguing workshop programme for young children with a yen to perform. The teachers here can impart skills in everything from drama to African dance in its popular after-school and half-term workshops. These are intended mainly for 3-9-year-olds (£2.50-£6 per session, £20 per ten-week term). Toddlers can take part in Jumping Jacks, a phenomenally successful daytime playgroup for babies over 18 months and their parents, featuring gentle movement, nursery rhymes and song. All classes are usually oversubscribed, so book early.

Art galleries

Courtauld Institute Gallery

Somerset House, Strand, WC2 (7848 2526/education 7848 2922/www.courtauld.ac.uk). Covent Garden, Holborn or Temple (closed Sun) tube. **Open** *Gallery* 10am-6pm daily (last entry 5.15pm); *31 Dec* 10am-4pm; *1 Jan* noon-6pm. Closed 24-26 Dec. *Tours* pre-booked groups only; phone for details. **Admission** *Gallery* £5; £4 concessions; free under-18s, students. Free to all 10am-2pm Mon (not bank hols). *Annual ticket* £10. **Credit** MC, V. **Map** p319 M7.
You might imagine that the best entertainment for kids at Somerset House is running through the fountains in the courtyard. But the Courtauld Institute Gallery – best known for its world-class collection of Impressionist paintings – offers some great art-oriented activities on the first Saturday of every month from 11am to12.30pm. Children aged 6-12 with an accompanying adult can take part in mask, jewellery-,

costume- and even musical instrument-making sessions after a 45-60-minute talk in front of an exhibit. These events are free. In the summer holidays, morning workshops (10.30am-2.30pm; £12) often involve outdoor painting on Waterloo Bridge. Older students (16-18) can take all-day courses, and sign-interpreted events take place four times a year. *See also p61.*

Dulwich Picture Gallery

Gallery Road, SE21 (8693 5254/www.dulwichpicture gallery.org.uk). North Dulwich or West Dulwich rail/3, 37, 176, P4 bus. **Open** *Gallery* 11am-5pm Tue-Fri; 11am-5pm Sat, Sun, bank hol Mon. Closed Good Friday, 24-26 Dec, 1 Jan. *Tours (incl entry fee)* 3pm Sat, Sun. **Admission** *Gallery* £4; £3 concessions; free under-16s. *Temporary exhibitions* £3; free under-16s. Free to all Fri. **Credit** MC, V.
Never mind dominos; the after-school art club on Thursdays at the Dulwich Picture Gallery teaches kids from 9-12 years how to make paint from earth, green rust and dead beetles; how to construct a pop-up collage or print cards. These are part of the four- or six-week courses (from £30); the gallery's Saturday morning art school (10.30am-1pm, from £40 for four weeks) for 10-14-year-olds offers art and craft techniques such as weaving, embroidery, plate painting and dry point etching. The gallery itself, an architectural gem in the heart of leafy Dulwich Village with its extensive park and playground, is a delight to visit; check the programme or call 8299 8731 for details of summer drop-ins and week-long courses.

Hayward Gallery

Belvedere Road, South Bank Centre, SE1 (box office 7960 4242/www.hayward-gallery.org.uk). Embankment tube/Waterloo tube/rail. **Open** *Gallery* during exhibitions 10am-6pm Mon, Thur-Sun; 10am-8pm Tue, Wed. **Admission** *Gallery* varies; phone for details. **Credit** AmEx, DC, MC, V. **Map** p319 M8.
Specialising in 20th-century art, the Hayward is in danger of being eclipsed by the newer Tate Modern – yet this South Bank gallery is conveniently located and has a permanent education space where free events for children and families cover everything from reading to dressing up. Activities are always themed to tie in with the temporary exhibitions (in 2002, for example, the big summer show is iconic landscape photographer Ansel Adams, followed by wild and wacky Scottish artist Douglas Gordon). Resident artists guide workshop participants in 'drawing on ideas' – imaginative sessions involving storytelling, drawing, painting and photography. Admission to workshops is free for accompanying adults if they buy an exhibition ticket; under-16s have free entry to the Hayward Gallery anyway. *See also p42.*

London International Gallery of Children's Art

O2 Centre, 255 Finchley Road, NW3 (7435 0903/ www.ligca.org). Finchley Road tube. **Open** *Gallery* 4-6pm Tue-Thur; noon-6pm Fri-Sun. **Admission** *Gallery* free; donations requested. **No credit cards**.
This pint-sized gallery is the only one in London dedicated to works of art from children around the world. It holds six exhibitions every year, comprising pictures and sculpture by both local kids and their peers in other countries. The works of art are then used by gallery staff as a basis for educating visitors about the culture, customs and language of the country they came from. Workshops, painting and drawing classes let youngsters draw their response to the art on show and pop it in a box for possible display on the walls. Half-term and school holiday workshops cost £8 per session; art classes £35-£55 per term (six classes).

National Gallery

Trafalgar Square, WC2 (7747 2885/ www.nationalgallery.org.uk). Embankment/Leicester Square tube/Charing Cross tube/rail. **Open** *Gallery* 10am-6pm Mon, Tue, Thur-Sun; 10am-9pm Wed. **Admission** *Gallery* free. *Temporary exhibitions* prices vary; phone for details. **Map** p319 K7.
From gilding to landscape painting and printmaking to portraiture, there is almost no artistic skill that cannot be learned at the National Gallery as part of its wide-ranging education programme – and nearly all of it is free. 'Second Weekend' is a series of artist-led, drop-in drawing events on the second Saturday and Sunday of each month (11.30am and 2.30pm) for accompanied 4-11-year-olds. Sessions explore a different room each month, and combine a gallery talk with an artist-led drawing brief. There are also family talks every Saturday and Sunday at 11.30am, focusing on such themes as light, powder and paint or (especially at Christmas) angels. Half-term and school holiday workshops are aimed at different age groups from 4-15 and feature practical art skills taught in a fun way. Even the gallery trails are guaranteed to get little feet around the building in double-quick time – listening to secret agents decode the paintings on a headset or searching for cats in the pictures. The ultimate consideration for cash-poor parents is a picnic room, complete with sink, bins and nearby drinking fountains – available on Second Weekends and during special holiday activities. To find out more about jolly family events when school's out, ring 7747 2488 or 7747 2424. *See also p86.*

National Portrait Gallery

2 St Martin's Place, WC2 (7306 0055/www.npg.org.uk). Leicester Square tube/Charing Cross tube/rail. **Open** *Gallery* 10am-5.50pm Mon-Wed, Sat, Sun; 10am-8.50pm Thur, Fri. **Admission** *Gallery* free. *Temporary exhibitions* £6; £4 concs. **Map** p319 K7.
Anybody who borrows a free activity rucksack from the information desk (subject to availability) will be amused for hours by the intriguing and imaginative things it contains. Free activities are staged for families with children aged 7-plus during the major holidays; you have to ring to request inclusion on the gallery mailing list to receive details of these events. The interactive IT gallery, complete with 11 terminals and assisting staff, keeps screen-savvy children enthralled with highly visual and word-free activities. The last Saturday of each month features free 'Talk and Draw' activities in the gallery – just ask at the information desk on the day. A highlight for summer 2002 (until 26 August) is a free exhibition, 'From Beatrix Potter to Harry Potter: Portraits of Children's Writers'. Check the website for details of talks and events linked to the exhibition. *See also p87.*

Orleans House Gallery

Riverside, Twickenham, Middx (8892 0221/ www.richmond.gov.uk). St Margaret's or Twickenham rail/33, 90, 290, H22, R68, R70 bus. **Open** *Gallery* Apr-Sept 1-5.30pm Tue-Sat; 2-5.30pm Sun. Oct-Mar 1-4.30pm Tue-Sat; 2-4.30pm Sun. **Admission** *Gallery* free. **No credit cards**.
You might imagine this lovely mansion, standing in six acres of natural woodland and credited with one of the finest baroque interiors in the UK, to be the repository of all things antique. In fact, in addition to its fine collection of 18th-, 19th- and 20th-century art, it hosts exhibitions of sculpture and installations by leading contemporary artists such as Cornelia Parker and Rachel Whiteread. Smaller shows are held in the Stables gallery, ranging in nature from modern tapestry through wood engraving to comic book art. Everything on show is grist to

Activities

the mill of Orleans House's popular after-school clubs (3.45-5pm; £5 per session) on Wednesday and Thursday, as well as holiday and half-term workshops (£6 per session). There are also Sunday Fundays throughout the year and main gallery exhibitions are accompanied by a free activity pack.

Royal Academy

Burlington House, Piccadilly, W1 (7300 8000/ www.royalacademy.org.uk). Green Park or Piccadilly Circus tube. **Open** *Gallery* 10am-6pm Mon-Thur, Sat, Sun; 10am-10pm Fri. **Admission** *Gallery* varies; phone for details. **Credit** AmEx, MC, V. **Map** p318 J7.

Apart from being a gracious pitstop on Piccadilly, with a shop useful for arty gifts and a spacious café with outdoor space in the traffic-free courtyard, the Royal Academy is perfect for young culture vultures, particularly in summer. This is when free art packs, containing a guide to the famous Summer Exhibition, plus creative materials such as collage ingredients, word puzzles, crayons and animal-themed trails can be enjoyed by 3-13-year-olds. There are four workshops planned during this period (phone for details); two of them will be run by musicians from the London Philharmonic, who play music evoked by any of the paintings on show. Other workshops take place during autumn half-term, usually consisting of an introductory slide show, followed by a gallery tour and hands-on activities – painting, pastels, drawing and so on – that may have caught the imagination. All workshops are free with the entrance ticket. *See also p74.*

Tate Britain

Millbank, SW1 (7887 8000/info 7887 8008/ www.tate.org.uk). Pimlico tube/88, 77A, C10 bus. **Open** *Gallery* 10am-5.50pm daily. **Admission** *Gallery* free. *Temporary exhibitions* prices vary; phone for details. **Credit** MC, V. **Map** p319 L11.

Home to Britain's important Turner and Blake collections as well as being a venue for contemporary art exhibitions, the 'old' Tate offers free, family-centred art activities every Sunday afternoon. You're missing some great fun if you have not yet introduced your kids to the famous Art Trolley: two gallery educators supervise cutting, sticking and drawing (no painting), based on activity sheets relating to specific paintings (from noon to 5pm). Create a landscape like Turner; make a collage with layers of fabric to resemble Queen Elizabeth I or use squares of blue and white and white pastels to make your own version of Hockney's *Splash*. From 1pm-5pm, Art Space, a room dedicated to construction and

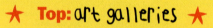

★ Top: art galleries ★

For arty after-schoolers
Dulwich Picture Gallery. *See p217.*

For a day out of town
Orleans House Gallery. *See p217.*

For dressing up
Wallace Collection. *See right.*

For free workshops
National Gallery. *See p217.*

For interactive trails
Tate Modern. *See above.*

sculpture games especially good for under-5s, is open. Dressing up in period costume is also available here. Some Tate Trails will amuse older children, and themed 90-minute workshops take place in the major school holidays (usually £3 or £4; call for dates and prices). Ring to be put on the events mailing list and join in the fun. *See also p87.*

Tate Modern

25 Sumner Street, SE1 (7887 8000/recorded info 7887 8008/www.tate.org.uk). Southwark or St Paul's tube. **Open** *Gallery* 10am-6pm Mon-Thur, Sun; 10am-10pm Fri, Sat. **Admission** *Gallery* free. **Map** p320 O7.

Tate Modern's family programme is energetically committed to turning children on to modern art. Young artists aged from 7 have their own guides, in the form of the Education Department's Viewpoints and Time Capsule games (both family Explorer trails, £1.50 at the box office). Viewpoints takes in the Landscape/Matter/Environment space, where works by Monet, Beuys and Rothko await to inspire. Time Capsule is dedicated to the exploration of the History Suite, and the art of Mondrian, Warhol and Henry Moore. The children's audio tour (£1), with narration by Michael Rosen, also starts with landscape, before moving on to sculpture, cleverly involving the listener in the scene then guiding him/her through a mixture of questions and evocative music. Indeed, Rosen is so engaging that fighting over the handset will be a problem if you only hire one to share. The gallery that children find most intriguing without any tuition is probably Staging Discord, where Rebecca Horn's exploding piano hangs down from the ceiling and mechanical feathered wings flap on the wall.

Families visiting at the weekend can join in with Artmixx (Saturday morning; booking isn't obligatory but it does ensure that there'll be more assistants on hand) – workshops run by the Tate's resident team of artists. Sunday's activity is called Start, for which children are given a map, bag and puzzle kit and sent on a madcap exploration of the galleries. These activities are free, suitable for ages 5 and over (accompanied by an adult) and don't require booking. The Education Department also organises activities, workshops, trails and performances for family fun every half-term and school holiday.

The monthly Tate Tales (every third Sunday of the month, with extra sessions in school holidays) introduce a poet or storyteller who leads role-play and improvised performance based around a work of art. Other activities are organised around individual exhibitions, and a schools' workshop programme runs throughout the year. *See also p47.*

Wallace Collection

Hertford House, Manchester Square, W1 (7563 9500/ education 7563 9551/www.the-wallace-collection.org.uk). Bond Street tube. **Open** *Gallery* 10am-5pm Mon-Sat; noon-5pm Sun. **Admission** *Gallery* free. **Map** p316 G5.

Children love the extensive armoury collection in Manchester Square; their parents love the smart restaurant, set in the beautiful, glassed-over inner courtyard. This impressive house, home to the Wallace family's sizeable art collection, makes a wonderful free outing, whether you pursue one of the quizzes, drift around the galleries or join in one of the imaginative, organised activity sessions. The latter are offered during half-term and other holidays for children aged 5-11 and cost £6 for half a day or £12 all day; they involve a great deal of dressing up (often in real armour) as well as painting, drawing and making things associated with major festivals. Summer 2002 takes the Golden Jubilee as a major theme: there will be opportunities for kids to make a crown or a tiara or dress up as Queen Victoria and have their photo taken in all their finery. Call for a brochure – advance booking is essential. Note that children must be accompanied (adults don't have to pay the workshop fees). *See also p94.*

Whitechapel Art Gallery

80-2 Whitechapel High Street, E1 (7522 7888/ recorded info 7522 7878/education 7522 7855/ www.whitechapel.org). Aldgate East tube. **Open** *Gallery* during exhibitions 11am-6pm Tue, Thur-Sun; 11am-8pm Wed. **Admission** *Gallery* free. **Map** p321 S6.

Canon Samuel Barnett and his wife Henrietta, the Christian Socialists who founded this gallery a century ago, believed that art should be accessible to everyone. As well as being free to see, all the works displayed in this wonderful ground-floor gallery and skylit upper space inspire a whole community education programme for students from primary and secondary schools. The 2002 programme includes a wide variety of schools workshops and family-based activities, as well as continuing the popular Download project, which involves children wedded to their computer screens by exploring drawing and painting in the context of new technologies. In summer 2002, there are occasional workshops with a sound artist; the idea being to investigate the relationship between music and visual art; call the gallery for details. There are also future plans to provide children's activity packs when they visit the exhibitions. *See also p113.*

Cinema in the round. **BFI London IMAX.**

Cinemas

For the ultimate big-screen, big-sound experience, head for the **Empire** (08700 102030/www.uci-cinemas.co.uk), **Warner Village West End** (7437 4347/www.warnervillage.co.uk) or the **Odeon** (0870 505 0007/www.odeon.co.uk) in Leicester Square. These West End giants make big action movies a memorable event, but their prices (about £10 for adults, £5 for children) won't be forgotten in a hurry. Add on all the extras – large vats of popcorn, sweeties and fizzy drinks – and a family trip to the cinema becomes a costly business.

Help is at hand from Saturday morning Kids' Clubs, which run in most multiplexes and one-off local cinemas (unfortunately not available in Leicester Square, where the cinemas are a bit too glamorous). The clubs screen children's favourites (not always very recent) for low admission prices. **UCI** cinemas offer a 'Film Feast' for children, which includes a drink and popcorn at some of its locations (ring 08700 102030/www.uci-cinemas.co.uk for details). Warner cinemas have a Cinemaniacs club, which encompasses Saturday morning films and movie gossip magazines (for more information, log on to www.warnervillage.co.uk).

For more on the **BFI London IMAX**, *see p39 and p247.* For the **Barbican**'s film clubs, *see p214;* for the **Tricycle Theatre**'s, *see p216.*

Clapham Picture House

76 Venn Street, SW4 (7498 3323/www.picturehouse-cinemas.co.uk). Clapham Common tube. **Open** *Box office (telephone bookings)* 10am-8.30pm daily. **Film Club** *Activities* 11.15am Sat. *Screening* 11.45am Sat. **Tickets** £3; members £2. **Membership** £3/yr. **Credit** MC, V.

The Clapham Picture House wins the prize for imagination when it comes to children's activities. An alliance with Battersea Dogs' Home means that six times a year the cinema selects a hound-related film and Battersea handlers bring in a pooch for the children to cuddle. Clapham's Kids' Club runs every Saturday, hosting a crafts workshop before the children's screening. Kids can make an underwater kingdom before *Help! I'm a Fish* or design their own slipper before *Cinderella*. The audience is given three questions to answer after the film, with prizes at stake for correct responses. Birthday boys and girls would do well to choose this cinema for their celebrations, as they not only get to meet the projectionist but start the film rolling too. Note that under-5s must be accompanied by an adult, and under-7s must have an adult with them at screenings of PG films. *See also p248.*

Electric Cinema

191 Portobello Road, W11 (7908 9696/www.electric house.com). Ladbroke Grove or Notting Hill Gate tube. **Open** *Box office* 8am-9pm Mon-Sat; 10am-9pm Sun. **Children's screenings** 1pm Sat. **Tickets** £4.50. **Credit** AmEx, MC, V. **Map** p312 A7.

Children (aged 4-12) enjoy activities and games before the 1.30pm screening of the latest family smash hit, or a less-recent popular classic. Older children (over-5s) can be left to watch without grown-ups fidgeting beside them all the time. Pre-film activities are usually tied in with the screening, and can be anything from a fishing game (*Tintin and the Lake of Sharks*) to assembling body parts in the right order (*Osmosis Jones*). Adult members (who pay £250 per year for the privilege) receive free weekly children's tickets for a special members' screening (phone for details).

Everyman Cinema

5 Holly Bush Vale, NW3 (0870 066 4777/ www.everymancinema.com). Hampstead tube. **Open** *Box office* 6-10pm Mon-Thur; noon-10pm Fri; 10.30am-10pm Sat; 1.30-10pm Sun. **Film Club** 10.45am Sat. **Tickets** £5. **Credit** MC, V.

Founded by local luminaries Eve and Ewan McGregor, Jude Law and Sadie Frost to recreate the atmosphere of Saturday morning film clubs they enjoyed as children, Everyman Kids is now an established feature at north London's favourite independent cinema. Each week a film is shown before an educational workshop. Programming is thoughtful, ranging from Ealing comedies to Beatrix Potter. There's a 45-minute workshop afterwards, involving film discussion, artwork or storyboard making. Laudable – and fun.

Movie Magic at the NFT

National Film Theatre 3, BFI on the South Bank, SE1 (7928 3232/www.bfi.org.uk/moviemagic). Waterloo tube/rail. **Open** *Box office phone bookings* 11.30am-8.30pm daily. *Personal callers* 5-8.30pm Mon-Thur; 11.30am-8.30pm Fri-Sun. **Film Club** *Times vary,* Sat, school hols. **Tickets** £3.50 (children only). **Credit** MC, V. **Map** p319 M8.

The National Film Theatre's reputation for diverse and comprehensive film programming carries through to its repertoire for the under-12s. On Saturday and Sunday afternoons and during school holidays, children and parents at the NFT have the opportunity to enjoy special events and previews of the latest Hollywood releases, well-loved family favourites and an exciting cross-section of shorts, black and white comedy classics and films made for children from around the world (accompanied by earphone commentary for kids who prefer to have the subtitles read to them). On Saturdays and during the holidays, parents and younger siblings can wait in comfort in the Movie Magic Den, fully kitted out with beanbags, videos and crayons, while 6-12-year-olds take part in a workshop related to the day's film, activities ranging from model-making to meeting film industry figures. Phone for the NFT's programme of festivals, family performances of BFI educational touring projects and interactive screening events. No membership fee. Booking in advance is recommended.

Rio Cinema
103-7 Kingsland High Street, E8 (7241 9410/ www.riocinema.co.uk). Dalston Kingsland rail. **Open** *Box office* opening times vary depending on programme. **Film Club** 4.15pm Tue (term time only); 11am Sat. **Tickets** £3; £2 under-15s. **Credit** MC, V.
A wonderfully accessible and friendly place to see a film, the Rio lives up to its pro-community reputation with both an after-school film club on Tuesdays and a repeat performance – of recent Hollywood kids' films – on Saturdays (11am). Membership of this Saturday Morning Picture Club is free, and children receive a special card that gets stamped every time they visit the cinema. Once they've collected ten stamps they get one free entry; 25 stamps warrants a poster.

Ritzy Cinema
Brixton Oval, Coldharbour Lane, SW2 (7733 2229/ www.ritzycinema.com). Brixton tube/rail. **Open** *Box office* bookings 11am-8pm Mon-Sat; 1-8pm Sun. **Film Club** 10.30am Sat. **Tickets** £2; £1 under-16s. **Credit** MC, V.
At last, a cinema that understands parents may be sick of cartoons. Children over 5 may be left to watch either of two films shown every Saturday (one is for under-7s, one for over-7s) while their parents read free newspapers and drink tea and coffee in the Ritzy's café. The Ritzy also has Watch with Baby sessions, when new parents can catch up on latest releases. The school holidays offer more fun, with competitions and special events tied to current movies on Tuesdays and Thursdays. As these are often set up at short notice, it's best to phone for details.

Music venues

See also p214 **South Bank Centre**.

Coliseum
St Martin's Lane, WC2 (box office 7632 8300/fax credit card bookings 7379 1264/textphone 7836 7666/ www.eno.org). Leicester Square tube/Charing Cross tube/rail. **Open** *Box office* 10am-8pm Mon-Sat. **Credit** AmEx, DC, MC, V. **Map** p319 L7.
Hit the high notes with a Saturday family workshop in the Coliseum's Terrace Bar. Each repertory period has two designated Saturdays when 10-year-olds and over can attend a lively introduction to the opera currently being performed by ENO. The company's singers and backstage staff unite to expound on the story, sing excerpts and lead an impromptu chorus or two. All warbling children must be accompanied by an adult (tickets £5 adults; £2.50 children).

London Arena
Limeharbour, Isle of Dogs, E14 (box office 7538 1212/ www.londonarena.co.uk). Crossharbour & London Arena DLR. **Open** *Box office* 9am-7pm Mon-Fri; 10am-3pm Sat. **Credit** AmEx, MC, V.
Entertainment on ice is the main attraction for families at this shed-like venue, with Disney shows every October half-term (*Beauty and the Beast* will grace the ice in 2002) and regular matches of super league ice hockey featuring resident team London Knights. Otherwise, typical highlights include the likes of Destiny's Child and other hot favourites. Ticket prices vary, so phone for details.

Royal Albert Hall
Kensington Gore, SW7 (7589 8212/www.royalalbert hall.com). South Kensington tube. **Open** *Box office* 9am-9pm daily. **Credit** AmEx, MC, V. **Map** p315 D9.
It's a waiting game at the Royal Albert Hall, where a major refurbishment programme is scheduled to be completed in 2004. After this date, a proper education programme is planned, with many more children's events. Meanwhile, it is the prerogative of impresarios such as Raymond Gubbay to stage family-oriented concerts of popular classics with special effects and comic interludes or ice skating. Pre-Christmas carol concerts are always well attended. The summer highlight for children is the Blue Peter concert given as part of the BBC Proms. Prices for the Proms are reasonable, starting at £3 for standing tickets.

Royal College of Music
Prince Consort Road, SW7 (7589 3643/www.rcm.ac.uk). South Kensington tube. **Map** p315 D9.
Budding Alfred Brendels come here to hone their musical skills at prestigious classes for gifted over-8s; entry is by audition on Saturdays. But anyone can be inspired by listening to young players of their own age in the free symphony, chamber and choral concerts given each term (1.05pm Monday-Friday). Call the Junior Department for concert dates and information on tuition.

Royal Opera House
Bow Street, WC2 (7304 4000/www.royaloperahouse.org). Covent Garden tube. **Open** *Box office* 10am-8pm Mon-Sat. *Backstage tours* 10.30am, 12.30pm, 2.30pm Mon-Sat; phone to check. **Credit** AmEx, MC, V. **Map** p319 L6.
Since its renovation a few years back, this gorgeous building has tried to be more inviting to all ages and classes. But despite having an active schools programme, the ROH does not do much to encourage children through its portals except welcome them to matinée performances of opera and ballet and put on the occasional family day. Children who are big fans of these art forms may like to pop in for a programme of productions, or join the information service (£10 per year; ring 7212 9267 to join). For guided tours, *see p78*.

Wigmore Hall
36 Wigmore Street, W1 (7935 2141/education 7258 8240/www.wigmore-hall.org.uk). Bond Street tube. **Open** *Box office* 10am-7pm Mon-Sat; 10.30am-6.30pm Sun. **Credit** AmEx, DC, MC, V. **Map** p316 H5.
A more intimate and certainly prettier venue than most of London's other classical music spaces, the Wigmore holds family concerts throughout the year. More educational initiatives come in the form of Young People's Days (£10), usually at each half-term for children over 11, and jazz and classical 'creative music days' for young musicians of the same age. It's easy enough to get into one of these, whereas the Chamber Tots events for 2-5-year-olds (a gift for ambitious parents), where tiny would-be Mozarts listen to a mini

Activities

concert then participate in a workshop to create their own piece of music, are wildly oversubscribed. Many of the workshops for older kids and their parents mirror the content of the Young People's Days, with lyric writing and composing frequently featured. Except in the case of Chamber Tots and the family concerts, under-5s are not admitted. Log on to the website, or ring, to be put on the free mailing list.

Theatre

Some of the places listed below are dedicated children's theatres, but most are grown-up houses with a strong commitment to family shows. Always ring to find out the age suitability of a show before you book. Most of the show times here are for during the term; call for extra dates during the holidays. Prices below are generally for children's shows.

BAC (Battersea Arts Centre)
Lavender Hill, SW11 (7223 2223/www.bac.org.uk). Clapham Junction rail/77, 77A, 345 bus. **Open** *Box office* 10.30am-9pm Mon-Sat; 3.30-8pm Sun. *Puppet Centre*

2-6pm Mon, Wed, Sat. **Tickets** £5.75; £4.50 under-16s, concessions; £3.50 young BAC club members; £16 family (2+2). **Membership** £10.75/yr; £16.50 family (2+2). **Credit** AmEx, MC, V.

Battersea Arts Centre, self-appointed 'National Theatre of Fringe', is the place to go for new writing and challenging drama. The quality of the productions here remind you why live theatre is so much more exciting than TV. This goes for the programming for children, too. Young people learn to appreciate the art form at Saturday afternoon shows (2.30pm), performed by visiting companies. Both actors and puppets are featured in entertainment usually aimed at the 4-7 age range. The Christmas show tends to be an in-house production of a more interesting nature than panto.

Upstairs, the Puppet Centre (7228 5335) is a resource centre for anyone interested in the ancient art of puppetry. The staff here can tell you all you need to know about the puppets on display and the companies performing around the UK. On Saturday afternoons children are welcome upstairs after the show to workshops where they can make their own puppet (£4; adult carers free). Arts Factory courses in drama, performance and storytelling cater for young people aged 3-15. The courses cost from £45.75 per term (£39.50 concessions; £34.50 Young BAC members). Phone for a brochure.

Famous five

A valuable stimulus for young imagination? A priceless educational resource? Not 'proper' theatre? Whatever you think of children's theatre, it cannot be denied that the companies dedicated to it have enriched the lives of countless children and young adults who love their shows. Five of the best are based in London but tour all over the country: their work is innovative, exciting and enchanting. Check their websites for tour details.

Oily Cart
8672 6329/www.oilycart.org.uk.
Oily Cart has been touring across the capital and nationwide since 1981. Much of its recent, and most acclaimed work, has focused on the creation of 'Wonderlands', interactive spaces where small groups of children can watch and take part in performances.

Recent work has included: **Under Your Hat**, a dressing-up extravaganza for children aged 3-6 and their families; and the **Big Splash** trilogy of work for young people with profound and multiple learning Disabilities which took place in hydrotherapy pools.

Coming up: Boing! (touring June to October 2002) is a bouncy show for young people with learning disabilities, based around trampolines and inflatables. **Jumpin' Beans** (touring December 2002-March 2003) uses the wacky inflatables from **Boing!** to create an imaginative show for under-5s.

Pop-Up Theatre
7609 3339/www.pop-up.net.
Pop-Up is one of Britain's leading touring theatre companies, producing quality drama that is thought-provoking and accessible to young people

and adults. The vitality and relevance of the company's work is informed and enriched by working with young people.

Pop-Up's **Touring Productions**, new writing for different age ranges, respect the intellectual and emotional maturity of the audience. Some plays are presented as OffStreet Productions, a new initiative to attract over-7s to the theatre. **Equal Voice** is a training package for young people, teachers and other adults working with young people that uses drama to encourage self-expression and new approaches to resolve conflicts. **Dramatic Links** is a project involving young people in all aspects of Pop-Up's work. It has been particularly successful in developing new scripts with professional writers that are relevant to children's experiences.

Coming up: The **Nightwatch** by Michael Punter, a new play for over-7s. The national tour is from October to November 2002. Pop-Up is also planning a Christmas show for under-8s in 2002. **Wild Girl, Wild Boy** by David Almond, for over-7s, tours nationally from February 2003.

Quicksilver Theatre
7241 2942/www.quicksilvertheatre.org.
Quicksilver Theatre commissions and produces new plays and performs them to children throughout Britain and abroad. With 24 years of experience, Quicksilver aims to give the highest artistic and production standards to make every play it produces an entertaining and enriching experience, relevant and accessible to children.

Quicksilver's shows for 3-5s are based on the philosophy that young children like small shows for

Activities

Broadway Theatre

Catford Broadway, SE6 (8690 0002/
www.broadwaytheatre.org.uk). Catford or Catford
Bridge rail. **Open** *Box office* 10am-6pm Mon-Sat.
Tickets £3.50-£20. **Credit** MC, V.
It may have taken longer than projected, but the £2.2-million refurbishment of the Broadway (formerly Lewisham) Theatre has restored this listed 1930s building to its former art deco glory. Now, in addition to its well-known traditional and alternative – ie Caribbean – Christmas pantos and mercifully low cost (around £5) teeny bopper pop concerts featuring the likes of 'S Club Heaven' or the music of Robbie Williams, there's a dedicated education department. From September 2002 the staff are aiming to use the 100-seater studio space for Saturday morning shows for children. The plan is to put the Broadway on the children's theatre map, alongside the Half Moon, the Lyric and other well-known venues. South-east London parents are very excited at the prospect.

The Bull

68 High Street, Barnet, Herts (8449 0048/tours
8275 5375/www.thebull.org.uk). High Barnet tube.
Open *Box office* 10am-5.30pm Tue-Sun. **Tickets**
£4.50. **Credit** MC, V.

Astonishing, but true: even babies who can't yet walk can get to grips with drama. The Bull's Learning Ladder features 12 different classes for all ages from 18 months to 19 years, beginning with drama games, storytelling and movement and progressing through to youth theatre via term-time courses (from £40 per term), half-term projects and a two-week professional summer school (from £80). The entertainment factor rates highly. Sundays see performances for 3-12-year-olds and, more recently, for over-8s. During the week plays for the 14-plus age group tend to focus on thought-provoking themes such as mixed marriage, divorce and other issues.

Chicken Shed Theatre

Chase Side, N14 (8292 9222/www.chickenshed.org.uk).
Cockfosters or Oakwood tube. **Open** *Box office* 10am-7pm Mon-Fri; Sat varies. **Tickets** £2-£13.75.
Credit MC, V.
Stars of stage and screen tend to go dewy-eyed over the work of Chicken Shed. And why not, for it has a truly laudable open-access policy, producing excellent shows (mostly with a musical content) for audiences of all ages. The actors are never auditioned, but work their way through the company in all roles, regardless of any disabilities or learning difficulties. The company has 800 members currently, and a

A case in point: **Quicksilver Theatre**. *See p222.*

small people in small places, in small amounts, at the right time of day and based on things that matter to them. Presented in an intimate style, they ensure a gentle introduction to the fun of theatre.

Shows for older kids pursue challenging, thought-provoking themes that are presented with a strong narrative style, bold visuals and original music.

Coming up: In autumn 2002 look out for the tour of Robin Kingsland's new play, **Sea of Silence**, written for everyone over the age of 7.

Theatre Centre

7377 0379/www.theatre-centre.co.uk.
Founded in 1953, Theatre Centre commissions, produces and tours the best new writing for young audiences. The company is committed to intimate, exciting, accessible theatrical work that reflects the diversity of contemporary cultures.

Coming up: In autumn 2002 there will be two new productions for audiences aged from 14: **Listen to Your Parents**, Benjamin Zephaniah's adaptation of his moving play originally written for BBC Radio 4, will do a season at the Lyric Hammersmith (29 November-9 December). **Devotion** by Leo Butler. This is physical theatre created by Liam Steel, collaborating with Leo and designer Louise Ann Wilson. Devotion tours schools and studio venues nationwide from September to December. 2003 is Theatre Centre's Golden Anniversary Year; plans for productions will be announced in due course; see the website for details.

Theatre-rites

8946 2236/www.theatre-rites.co.uk.
Theatre-rites was founded in 1995 by the late Penny Bernand. It is now firmly established at the centre of innovative and challenging work for young people. The company works with artists to create unusual contemporary imagery, made accessible through puppetry and performance.

Theatre-rites is known for site-specific productions, such as **Houseworks**, which took place in a house in Brixton. Touring productions include the **Lost and Moated Land**, which recently finished a tour in Japan, and **Sleep Tight**, which toured in 2000 and 2001. **Taking Shape**, an interactive exhibition of puppetry and installation, mounted by Theatre-rites for the Theatre Museum (*see p78*), runs until autumn 2002.

Coming up: A co-production with the Lyric Theatre Hammersmith, touring in autumn 2002 and ending with a Christmas season at the Lyric. A new site-specific production is planned for spring 2003.

Activities

Sadler's Wells gives you a cultural high. See p225.

waiting list of many more – but its outreach policy ensures that opportunities for would-be actors, writers and directors exist in other boroughs around London (call for details).

The theatre is purpose built and uses its combined space of auditorium, studio, amphitheatre and bar performing area to great effect. There are weekly workshops combining drama, dance and music for over-5s; under-5s are offered puppetry, mime, dance and song in Tales from the Shed. Summer always sees a Children's Shed Week, with outdoor fun and a celebration of books; call for details.

Colour House Theatre
Merton Abbey Mills, Watermill Way, SW19 (box office 8542 6644/theatre school 8648 4180/ www.wheelhouse.org.uk). Colliers Wood tube. **Open** *Box office* 10am-5pm Mon-Fri; 1hr before the start of show. **Tickets** £5. **No credit cards.**
This tiny, independent theatre company, set picturesquely in the midst of the craft market, produces original musicals on weekend afternoons (2pm, 4pm) that are just 60 minutes long and suitable for children aged 3 and over. The shows are invariably crammed with jokes and songs to keep young theatregoers amused. The company also lets space to the Colour House Theatre School, an enterprise designed to foster musical theatre skills in the sort of progeny determined to make it to the West End stage. Classes (every Saturday morning; Monday evenings, or Tuesday evenings) help kids prepare songs and dance, culminating in twice-yearly shows. Courses cost £100.

Edward Alleyn Theatre
Dulwich College, SE21 (8299 9232). West Dulwich rail/ Brixton tube then 3 P4, P13, 115 bus. **Tickets** £5; £3.50 under-16s, concessions. **No credit cards.**
This 180-seater theatre brings in a different children's company about ten times a year, and caters for children aged 3-11. Performances by Dulwich College students are often suitable for older children and families, and include musicals, popular shows and classic theatre. Edward Alleyn is also a good bet for two- to three-week holiday courses in drama and music (from £13 a session, £60 a week). Children aged 7-11 benefit from a relaxed teaching format, where they can turn up when they want to, rather than attend the full course. Activities are based around games, improvisation and roleplay. The senior courses (ages 12-16) are aimed at those with a more serious attitude towards theatre, and tend to be structured around a particular practitioner or text.

Half Moon Young People's Theatre
43 White Horse Road, E1 (77098900/www.halfmoon. org.uk). Stepney Green tube/Limehouse DLR/rail. **Open** *Box office* 10am-5pm Mon-Fri. **Tickets** £4.50; £3.25 under-18s, concessions. **Credit** MC, V.
A main player in London's theatre for children scene, the Half Moon, consisting of a single large black room, is an unpretentious affair, with performances of a consistently high standard. Aside from the Saturday show (for 5-10-year-olds, at 2pm), featuring a mix of storytelling and physical theatre, touring productions make up the majority of the entertainment. The theatre also produces its own shows twice yearly: expect anything from puppetry and traditional shows to interactive installation pieces. In addition, there are weekly Youth Theatre sessions during term time (from £1.50), which teach children and young people how to develop their theatrical, performance and technical skills. Less formal than most theatre schools, the classes allow the youngsters to experiment in a multicultural setting. The Youth Theatre performs regularly here, and is recognised nationally for its high standards. A disability Youth Theatre for 14-18-year-olds also runs once a week. Membership is free.

Jackson's Lane Community Centre
269A Archway Road, N6 (box office 8341 4421/admin 8340 5226/www.jacksonslane.org.uk). Highgate tube. **Tickets** £4. **Credit** AmEx, MC, V.
A converted church with a scruffy, well-used feel, Jackson's Lane is conveniently near Highgate Wood, with its playground and picnic areas in summer and vegetarian café. Lowkey children's shows run most Saturdays, at 11am and 2pm, and are performed by visiting companies, while several different organisations provide a plethora of drama classes for youngsters aged 5-18. The Kaos! Organisation (8442 1413) has Friday evening sessions for 12-18-year-olds (from £3.50), and Debbie Campbell runs drop-in classes on Tuesdays, Wednesdays and Thursdays for different age groups. Phone to grab a place at the after-school club for children aged 5-11, which runs 3.30-6pm at a cost of £5.50 per day (£1.90 concessions). The centre's large auditorium is a venue for a large-scale panto at Christmas, which sells out quickly.

Lauderdale House
Highgate Hill, Waterlow Park, N6 (8348 8716/ www.lauderdale.org.uk). Archway tube. **Open** *Box office* 30mins before performance; bookings not accepted. **Tickets** £3.50; £2.50 concessions. **No credit cards.**
A 16th-century Tudor merchant's house backing on to Waterlow Park is home to this beautiful arts space. A different show each week, ranging from puppetry to music and magicians, is performed by various visiting companies. To ensure your child's seat on the floor, it's advisable to turn up 30 minutes before the performance. Phone for details of dance, drama and art courses for children aged 18 months to 14 years. The termly classes take place both during (from pre-schoolers) and after the school day, with an emphasis on fun learning. There's a pretty good café backing on to the park with a terrace and serene grassy views. Occasional free entertainment takes place in the park during the summer.

London Bubble Theatre Company
5 Elephant Lane, SE16 (7237 4434/ www.londonbubble.org.uk). **Open** *Box office* 10am-6pm Mon-Fri. **Credit** MC, V.
Specialising in promenade productions that require the audience to follow the actors, Pied Piper-style, around London's parks, London Bubble is renowned for its challenging and imaginative approach to theatre in the open air. Puppetry and

Activities

pyrotechnics often feature, illuminating texts such as, this year, *Pericles*, and spanning the intellectual range between children and adults. *Pericles* tours six different outdoor spaces from 16 July to 24 August 2002 and will be of most interest to children aged from 8. For more details on this tour, and the Bubble's Christmas show, *Ali Baba and the Forty Thieves*, running from December 2002 at the Greenwich Theatre, phone or check the website.

Lyric Theatre Hammersmith
King Street, W6 (8741 2311/www.lyric.co.uk).
Hammersmith tube. **Open** Box office 10am-7pm Mon-Sat. **Tickets** £5-£7. **Credit** AmEx, MC.
Despite its modern frontage, the Lyric is a Victorian theatre, so sightlines in the main auditorium are not great for children. This hardly matters, though, if you attend one of the Saturday children's shows, as these are held in the studio. They range from puppetry through magic to clowns and circus performance. The spacious café, with its outside roof terrace, makes a good venue for lunch afterwards. A major children's theatre festival, the Catch, has run for two years since 2000 from February to April and it is hoped it will continue in 2003; call for a brochure. At Christmas, the Lyric puts on its own show, which is always original and challenging, while maintaining appeal for children of all ages.

Nettlefold Theatre
West Norwood Library, 1 Norwood High Street, SE27 (7926 8070/www.lambeth.gov.uk). West Norwood rail.
Open Box office 9am-4pm Mon-Fri. **Tickets** £3.
Credit MC, V (only in advance).
This 200-seater theatre attached to the library is expanding its children's programme with drama and singing workshops that will take place throughout the summer holidays, Bigfoot Theatre Group (8761 2112) and Rise Theatre Arts School (7924 1404) are devising the singing, dance and drama workshops for children and teenagers in summer 2002. Otherwise, there are usually children's shows performed by visiting companies on the first Saturday of every month, and a new artistic policy means 2002-3 will see more traditional fare, such as fairy tales, adapted for the stage.

Open Air Theatre
Inner Circle, Regent's Park, NW1 (box office 7486 2431/ www.open-air-theatre.org.uk). Baker Street tube. **Tickets** £8.50. **Credit** AmEx, MC, V. **Map** p316 G3.
London's only truly open-air theatre (Holland Park, which specialises in opera, has a canopy) is great fun even in mediocre weather, provided you come equipped with a rug (or hire one) and the right spirit. Its staple fare is Shakespeare (from May to September), but a children's show runs every August (in 2002 it will be *Merlin*, in conjunction with Unicorn Theatre; *see p226*). Ample refreshments are available on site, and picnics are encouraged. The theatre also runs a programme of workshops during the summer, covering various themes drawn from the season's plays. There may also be the opportunity to work with choreographers and actors during family 'days out'. Details from the main office on 7935 5756.

Polka Theatre
240 The Broadway, SW19 (8543 4888/ www.polkatheatre.com). Wimbledon South tube/ Wimbledon tube/rail. **Open** Phone bookings 9.30am-4.30pm Mon; 9am-6pm Tue-Fri; 10am-5pm Sat.
Personal callers 9.30am-4.30pm Tue-Fri; 10am-5pm Sat.
Tickets £5-£10. **Credit** AmEx, MC, V.
A dedicated children's theatre, now 22 years old, which stages daily children's shows, plus five major productions for children a year, the majority of which are home-grown (although tour-

ing productions are also received). And entertainment is not limited to the stage: once kids have seen the show and played the games and quizzes in the programme, they can admire past production exhibitions in the foyer. Then there's the outdoor playground, rocking horses and ride-on toys indoors for the little ones. And don't forget the production-related stalls, where children can spend their pocket money. Note that babies and children under 4 aren't allowed in the main theatre; they have their own Adventure Theatre, where parents and carers have proper seating, though in practice they often choose to hunker down with their toddlers to see puppet productions and two-handers, perhaps based on fairy tales.

Clubs and courses (for 3-11-year-olds) every holiday and half-term form the basis of the Polka's education programme. Exploring theatre techniques, voice and characterisation, the participants are often given the opportunity to perform on one of the Polka's stages at the end of the course. Other workshops exploring activities as varied as prop making, origami and puppetry are also available. Children up to the age of 16 can attend similar after-school clubs during term time. Particularly popular are the theatre's 'Polka Days', which combine a morning workshop with an afternoon performance. Phone for details of prices.

The Reading Corner was relaunched at the beginning of 2002; this means an enticing new programme of storytelling afternoons. In addition, a concerted effort to promote new writing for the stage has resulted in adaptations of Roald Dahl's *Boy* and Allen Ahlberg's football poem, *Friendly Matches*, to be shown later in the year.

Royal National Theatre
South Bank, SE1 (box office 7452 3000/info 7452 3400/ www.nationaltheatre.org.uk). Waterloo tube/rail. **Open** Box office 10am-8pm Mon-Sat. **Credit** AmEx, DC, MC, V.
Map p319 M8.
While the three main stages of the National (Olivier, Lyttleton and Cottesloe) usually see more challenging, adult fare, its foyers and recently renovated Theatre Square outside often provide space for family entertainment. Low-cost ticketed events – short performances by well-known visiting children's theatre companies – take place in curtained-off areas of the foyer at half-terms, while early-evening, pre-performance concerts are given free in the ground-floor bar. Summer 2002 (late June to late Agust) will see the fifth *Watch This Space*, a free summer fiesta of street theatre, music, comic turns, acrobatics, music, magic and spectacle from all over the world by the river and in the Square. Even more welcome will be another midwinter (mid November to mid January) celebration of worldwide light festivals. An installation of beautifully lit lanterns and artworks illuminates the National's foyers – a stunning backdrop to a series of five festival Saturdays featuring music, live performance and visual arts. Phone for further details. *See also p45*.

Sadler's Wells
Rosebery Avenue, EC1 (7863 8000/www.sadlers-wells.com). Angel tube. **Open** Box office 10am-8.30pm Mon-Sat. **Tickets** £10-£35. **Credit** AmEx, MC, V. **Map** p317 N4.
Not just for tutu-toting would-be ballerinas, Sadler's Wells' educational programme encompasses free family workshops on Saturdays with drama, mask-making and circus skills alongside dance of all genres (from age 6/7-16). Increasingly, also, visiting companies are being persuaded to adapt their productions to a younger audience in special, shorter Saturday matinées in the main house. While children keen on dance may find the regular presentations of dance from all over the globe sufficiently enthralling, other kids are likely to be better pleased with the programme at Sadler's Wells'

Activities

other home, the Peacock Theatre in Holborn (Portugal Street, WC2, same box office number as above). This is where the work of younger companies and runs of popular children's fare (such as *The Snowman* or Roald Dahl's *BFG*) are shown. Call for more information about forthcoming shows.

Shakespeare's Globe

21 New Globe Walk, Bankside, SE1 (7401 9919/tours 7902 1500/www.shakespeares-globe.org). Mansion House tube/London Bridge tube/rail. **Open** *Box office* (theatre bookings, Feb-Sept 2002) 10am-6pm Mon-Sat; 10am-5pm Sun. **Tickets** £5-£27. **Tours** *Oct-Apr* 10.30am-5pm daily. **Tickets** £8; £6.50 concessions; £5.50 5-15s; free under-5s; £24 family (2+3). **Credit** AmEx, MC, V. **Map** p320 O7.

This beautiful playhouse overlooking the Thames, a reconstruction of Shakespeare's own theatre, is only 100 yards from where the original stood. Productions of William's repertoire are staged here from April to September. The weather precludes winter acting just as it did in his day, but Shakespeare's Globe Exhibition, located in the vast UnderGlobe beneath the theatre, explores theatre in the Bard's time and the London in which he lived and worked using modern technology and traditional crafts.

Phone for details of the Globe's Childsplay Saturdays, when children (7-11) can accompany their parents here, then go off to enjoy a lively storytelling, drama and art workshop (£10 per child) with Globe educators while their parents watch a very authentic, naturally lit, heckling-encouraged performance. The children are invited to join the grown-ups for the last act of the show. Older children may feel they can handle the whole performance, especially if it's on their GCSE reading list. Don't fret that you're skimping by buying the cheaper tickets for groundlings, though: the seating is authentically hard and you may be glad you can wander off at will.

Theatre Museum

Tavistock Street (entrance Russell Street), WC2 (7943 4700/group bookings 7943 4806/ www.theatremuseum.org). Covent Garden tube. **Open** 10am-6pm (last entry 5.30pm) Tue-Sun. Closed 24-26 Dec, 1 Jan, bank hol Mon. *Tours* 11am, 2pm, 4pm Tue-Sun. **Admission** free. *Tours* pre-booked groups £3.50; £2 concessions per person. **Credit** AmEx, MC, V. **Map** p319 L6.

This branch museum of the V&A is a lively and little-discovered resource for young people interested in the theatre. Special exhibitions are usually accompanied by relevant trails; for example, the current focus on Paul Robeson (until September 2002) has given rise to a black theatre history trail. Free drop-in workshops (Stage Truck) on Saturdays (and Thursdays in school holidays) from noon to 5pm are enjoyed most by 7-11-year-olds, who can make masks, finger puppets or even design a set in a model theatre. Professional theatre make-up demonstrations take place throughout the day (11.30am, 1pm, 2.30pm, 3.30pm, 4.30pm) and can centre on ageing, character make-up (eg Cleopatra or a pantomime dame) or special effects such as scars. Then there are costume workshops at 12.30pm and 3pm for those who like to dress up. The one advantage of a group booking is that you can be sure there will be enough costumes and workshop materials. The new Kids Theatre Club for children aged from 8 is a free Saturday workshop, booking is essential.

Unicorn Theatre for Children

Unicorn at the Pleasance Theatre, Carpenters Mews, North Road, N7 (7700 0702/www.unicorntheatre.com). Caledonian Road tube. **Open** *Box office* 10am-6pm Mon-Fri. **Tickets** £5-£10. **Credit** AmEx, MC, V.

Following its allocation of £4.5 million of lottery funding to create a purpose-built, child-centred theatre in Southwark, Unicorn is eagerly awaiting planning permission for its new home close to the river on Tooley Street. The theatre should be finished in 2004. Meanwhile, it continues its exciting programme of original productions for children aged 4-12 in different venues around the capital and on tour all over the country. It's a labour of love – and a huge commitment pursued doggedly in all economic climates since 1947 – to demand the same high standards in writing, directing and producing that the best adult theatre sets itself. Summer 2002, for example, will see *Merlin* at the Open Air Theatre in Regent's Park (7486 2431), followed by an adaptation of *Great Expectations* at the Pleasance (7609 1800) in the autumn and *Beauty and the Beast* (venue to be confirmed) at Christmas. Phone for more information.

Warehouse Theatre

Dingwall Road, Croydon, Surrey (8680 4060/ www.warehousetheatre.co.uk). East Croydon rail. **Open** *Box office* 10am-5pm Mon-Fri; 10am-1pm Sat; extended opening hours during shows. **Tickets** £4.50; £3.50 2-16s. **Credit** AmEx, MC, V.

Children aged 2-9 enjoy the culturally rich offerings of this small and intimate fringe theatre. Visiting companies take centre stage every Saturday morning at 11am, supplemented by an ever-growing holiday programme.

Wimbledon Theatre

The Broadway, SW19 (8540 0362/ www.wimbledontheatre.com). Wimbledon tube/rail. **Open** *Box office* 10am-8pm Mon-Sat; also Sun during shows. **Credit** MC, V.

Children's productions come and go at irregular intervals at this leafy borough's bourgeois theatre; sometimes there are three in a row, then none for months. An enormous venue, with capacity for 1,650 people, the Wimbledon often plays host to teenybopper tribute bands. Despite its size, the theatre manages to retain an intimate atmosphere, occasionally staging drama, dance and music workshops in its smaller studio space. Note that the theatre is dark for a month or so in summer, when the open air theatre festival is staged in Cannizaro Park. Call the theatre for times and prices.

Young Vic

66 The Cut, SE1 (box office 7928 6363/ www.youngvic.org). Waterloo tube/rail. **Open** *Box office* 10am-8pm Mon-Sat. **Tickets** prices vary; phone for details. **Credit** MC, V. **Map** p320 N8.

With its breeze block and steel construction, the Young Vic is a theatre for everybody but, above all, for younger artists and a younger audience. No one sits more than six rows from the stage. The seats are unreserved; each has a perfect view. Family-oriented productions feature mainly at Christmas each year, but a programme of Teaching, Participation and Research (TPR) is aimed at young people aged 7-20 who live or study in Lambeth and Southwark. There are on-stage production workshops and an annual Schools' Theatre Festival. Resource material is also offered free to teachers from the theatre's two local south London boroughs.

West End shows

The long-running plays and musicals listed below are suitable for under-16s. They're all pretty lengthy, however, so children younger than about 7 may find them somewhat hard-going.

The Lion King, a roaring success.

Blood Brothers

Phoenix Theatre, Charing Cross Road, WC2 (7369 1733).
Leicester Square or Tottenham Court Road tube. **Times**
7.45pm Mon-Sat. *Matinée* 3pm Thur; 4pm Sat. **Tickets**
£12-£37. **Credit** AmEx, MC, V. **Map** p317 K6.
Willy Russell's grand, ambitious melodrama has a social con-
science as well as good songs. The story concerns twin brothers, separated at birth and brought up in radically different
economic environments, whose fates are tragically linked.

Chitty Chitty Bang Bang

Palladium, Argyll Street, W1 (0870 890 1108/
www.chittythemusical.co.uk). Oxford Circus tube. **Times**
7.30pm Mon-Sat. *Matinée* 2.30pm Wed, Sat. **Tickets**
£10-£40. **Credit** AmEx, MC, V. **Map** 316 J6.
Said to be the most expensive musical ever staged in the West
End, the new stage version of *Chitty Chitty Bang Bang* will
not disappoint fans of the film or the Ian Fleming novel. This
is a lavish and imaginative adaptation, which works its magic
on people of all ages. All the favourite singalong numbers are
here, including the rousing title song. The entire cast, including the dogs, is excellent.

The Complete Works of William Shakespeare (Abridged)

Criterion Theatre, Piccadilly Circus, WC2 (7413 1437).
Piccadilly Circus tube. **Times** 8pm Tue-Sat. *Matinée* 3pm
Thur; 5pm Sat; 4pm Sun. **Tickets** £8-£29.50. **Credit**
AmEx, MC, V. **Map** p319 K7.
Light relief for schoolchildren trying to get their heads around
the Bard. High-energy and hilarious, 37 plays are condensed
into 1 hour 55 minutes. There's no time to get lost in the plots.
If Shakespeare leaves you cold, try the Complete History of
America (Abridged) on Tuesdays at 8pm.

Fame: The Musical

Cambridge Theatre, Earlham Street, WC2 (7494 5080).
Covent Garden tube. **Times** 7.30pm Mon-Thur, Sat;
8.30pm Fri. *Matinée* 5.30pm Fri; 3pm Sat. **Tickets**
£12.50-£35.
Aspiring little actors will identify with the plot of this song
and dance fest, based on everyday tantrums at the legendary
New York High School of Performing Arts.

The Lion King

Lyceum Theatre, Wellington Street, WC2 (0870 243
9000). Covent Garden tube. **Times** 7.30pm Tue-Sat.
Matinée 2pm Wed, Sat; 3pm Sun. **Tickets** £15-£37.50.
Credit AmEx, DC, MC, V. **Map** p319 L7.
This innovative production uses puppets and live actors and
stays close to the Disney movie's storyline, so children can
wonder at the performance without losing the plot.

Les Misérables

Palace Theatre, Shaftesbury Avenue, W1 (7434 0909).
Leicester Square tube. **Times** 7.30pm Mon-Sat. *Matinée*
2.30pm Thur, Sat. **Tickets** £7-£40. **Credit** AmEx, DC,
MC, V. **Map** p317 K6.
A glossy refit of the Victor Hugo novel, the show has a
fairly complicated plot that might throw some children off
the scent. Nevertheless, the staging is dramatic and effectives.

Mamma Mia!

Prince Edward Theatre, Old Compton Street, W1 (7447
5400). Piccadilly Circus or Leicester Square tube. **Times**
7.30pm Mon-Sat; 8.30pm Fri. *Matinée* 5pm Fri;
3pm Sat. **Tickets** £18.50-£40. **Credit** AmEx, DC, MC, V.
Map p317 K6.
Plot isn't *Mamma Mia!*'s strong point, so children of all ages
enjoy this all-singing, all-dancing Abba extravaganza.

My Fair Lady

Drury Lane Theatre Royal, Catherine Street, WC2 (7494 5060). Covent Garden tube. **Times** 7.30pm Mon-Sat. *Matinée* 2.30pm Wed, Sat. **Tickets** £7.50-£40. **Credit** AmEx, MC, V. **Map** p317 L6.

Martine McCutcheon is no longer treading the boards as Eliza Dolittle, but the show doesn't seem to have suffered a bit, either in terms of popularity or performance quality, since she left. A luvverly evening.

Puppet theatre

Little Angel Theatre

14 Dagmar Passage, off Cross Street, N1 (7226 1787/ www.littleangeltheatre.com). Angel tube/Highbury & Islington tube/rail. **Open** *Box office* 11am-5pm Mon-Fri; 9.30am-5pm Sat, Sun. Closed 24-25 Dec, 1 Jan. **Credit** AmEx, MC, V.

London's only permanent puppet theatre, set in a delightful backwater in the heart of trendy Islington, has become something of an institution since opening in 1961. Seating may be communal padded benches but the theatre is blessed with that rare facility, a proscenium stage complete with bridge. This allows the puppeteers to manipulate traditional, long string marionettes whilst remaining hidden, adding to the magic of a performance. But shows vary hugely, including glove and rod puppets brought to life by comedians on the forestage.

Carnival!

Drama? Singing? Dancing? Sometimes just being part of the performance is enough for young children who have no special affinity for the arts. One of the most accessible ways to be a pageant princess (or prince) is to don a costume and join a Mas (short for masquerade) band for the annual Notting Hill Carnival. The children's carnival takes place every year on the Sunday of August bank holiday and allows 35 costume bands, ten steel bands and up to 25 Soca (a mixture of soul and calypso music) sound systems to fill the air with pulsating colour and rhythm. No special choreography has to be learned; parents simply contact their nearest Mas band club through the carnival office (8964 0544) and buy a costume, which costs between £25 and £55. Clubs are run for every age group, from 0-5, 6-11 and 12-16. Many children enjoy practising their role at meetings held during the summer holidays, but others just turn up on the day of the carnival and fall in line with the other performers.

The children's carnival route is slightly shorter than the adults' one, but at 3.5 miles the smallest of kids will be given places on the floats to help them get around. Those who have tried it say being part of the procession is the best way to enjoy the fun, as participants are protected from any untoward behaviour in the crowds. Older children might like to get involved in the music-making during the year; a junior calypso and pan competition gives them something to aim for.

Productions are mounted both in-house and by visiting companies; even Shakespeare is tackled and folkloric tales from all over the world prove fertile material for puppet drama. A strict no babies policy means you should check the age suitability for each show, as younger children will not be admitted to the auditorium. A children's workshop programme is beginning to flourish, concentrating on making and manipulating different sorts of puppets.

Sadly, the future of this much-loved venue is uncertain due to funding problems. The theatre closed at the end of April 2002 but, as this guide went to press, was aiming to be up and running again by the autumn. In the meantime, children's Saturday clubs and touring shows will continue (prices from £60 for nine sessions).

Puppet Theatre Barge

opposite 35 Blomfield Road, Little Venice, W9 (7249 6876/ www.puppetbarge.com). Warwick Avenue tube. **Open** *Box office* 10am-8pm daily. Closed 25 Dec, 1 Jan. **Children's shows** *Term time* Sat, Sun. *School hols* daily. **Tickets** £7; £6.50 under-16s, concessions. **Credit** MC, V.

As if it were not thrilling enough to walk along the towpath next to Little Venice's canal, with its ducks and echoing tunnels, from November to June such an outing may be combined with a visit to the Puppet Theatre Barge. This unique floating marionette theatre (which travels on the Thames to locations in Henley, Marlow and Richmond in the summer) has a full programme of shows for all ages (note that its ambition to entertain adults means not all shows will appeal to kids.) Often lyrically written or involving narrative poems interspersed with original music and action, the puppet dramas are further enhanced by atmospheric lighting effects. Babies may be admitted, but most shows are unsuitable for under-2s and anyone whimpering is expected to leave the auditorium.

Performance workshops

Centrestage

office: 33 Margaret Street, W1 (7328 0788/ www.centrestage.co.uk). **Classes** Sat mornings, afternoons. **Fees** £200 + VAT 12wk term. **Credit** AmEx, MC, V.

Vicky Woolf's caring drama school for kids has three centres around London (in Hampstead, Harley Street and Holland Park) with a fourth opening in Chelsea in spring 2002. Centrestage's main premise is to get kids hooked on the arts in a fun and non-pressurised environment. The three-hour Saturday sessions are divided into an hour each of acting, dance (everything from salsa to line dancing) and occasional masterclasses incorporating extra activities such as circus skills and percussion. Holiday workshops (from £120 plus VAT per week) run at Easter and in the summer. The youngest children take part in a different activity every day such as face painting or puppetry; the over-7s prepare an original musical and have lots of fun when they perform it on stage at the end of the week; they do all the preparations themselves, including painting the set.

Club Dramatika!

King Alfred School, North End Road, NW11 (8883 1554). Golders Green tube. **Classes** 10-11am Sat; 4-5pm Wed. **Fees** £7 session. **No credit cards**.

Run by Vicky Levy, former head of drama at King Alfred, Club Dramatika! offers weekly sessions that provide children aged 4-10 with the chance to explore improvisation and performance skills, as well as the opportunity to release creative energy. Club Dramatika! also runs themed drama parties; *see p236.*

Activities

Dance Attic

*368 North End Road, SW6 (7610 2055). Fulham
Broadway tube.* **Fees** from £48 11wk term; phone for
individual class prices. **No credit cards.**
In this professional dance and rehearsal studio, Dance Attic's
Saturday morning ballet or tap dancing lessons for 3-12s
come highly recommended; children can work towards their
RAD exams or just aim for fun and flexibility. Street dance
classes on Sundays (1pm) and Fridays (5.30pm) appeal to
aspiring clubbers aged 11-16.

Dramarama

*South Hampstead High School, Maresfield Gardens,
NW3. (8446-0891). Finchley Road tube.*
Fees £65 week 3-4s; £95 5-14s.
The emphasis is on plenty of fun and creativity in these week-
long performing arts courses for boys and girls. Dramarama
course are devised to help children develop their confidence,
learn new skills and, of course, make new friends. Original
shows are devised in just five days and presented to family
and friends at the end of each week during the summer,
Christmas, Easter and half-term holidays. Participants are
taught by a team of professional directors and teachers.
Courses for 3-14 year olds are also held in Totteridge and New
Barnet during the summer holidays. Call Jessica Grant for
more details on the courses, weekly classes in North Finchley
and her popular drama party service for for 6-12 year olds.

Helen O'Grady's Children's Drama Academy

*Headquarters: Garenne House, Rue de la Cache,
St Sampsons, Guernsey GY2 4AF (01481 254419/
www.helenogrady.co.uk).* **Classes** times vary; phone
for details. **Fees** £60 12wk term. **No credit cards.**
Now in its seventh year, Helen O'Grady's Drama Academy has
37 branches catering to children aged 5-17 in the UK, of which
nine are in London. Firmly excluding itself from the talent
school camp, the academy focuses on building up self-esteem
and life skills, welcoming hyperactive, shy, disabled and special needs children. Parents are invited to watch an open lesson
three times a year, as well as a public performance in the summer. The website has comprehensive information.

Hoxton Hall

*130 Hoxton Street, N1 (7739 5431/www.hoxtonhall.
co.uk). Old Street tube/rail.* **Classes** times vary;
phone for details. **Fees** £1 session. **Credit** MC, V.
Hoxton Hall has a refreshingly organic approach to performance art. Not only do the children learn a variety of dramatic techniques and perform twice a year to family and friends –
they actually devise the plays themselves. Through a process
of improvisation, children as young as 8 help to create a storyline that is then performed using techniques as wide-ranging
as digital performance and mime. Hoxton also holds a weekly
craft club for 5-11-year-olds, in which they often make costumes
and musical instruments.

As well as its comprehensive programme of theatre workshops, Hoxton Hall runs an innovative ten-week music course
for 11-15-year-olds. Acting as a band, participants choose their
favourite songs from the radio and learn how to play them,
aided by professional musicians. The children devise choreography to accompany the songs, and then perform them for an
audience. The Christmas shows are especially popular.

Laban Centre

*Laurie Grove, SE14 (8692 4070/www.laban.co.uk). New
Cross tube/rail.* **Classes** Sat. **Fees** from £28 11wk term.
No credit cards.

Get strung up at **Puppet Theatre Barge**. *See p228.*

This higher education college is home to Saturday children's
dance classes. A relaxed, improvisation-based class is held
for toddlers, who work with sound, rhythm and movement.
Sessions for older children are more structured and technique-
based, while those aged 13-18 can leap ahead to join Laban's
Youth Dance Company.

Lewisham Youth Theatre

*Broadway Theatre, Catford Broadway, SE6 (8690
3428/www.broadwaytheatre.org.uk). Catford or
Catford Bridge rail.*
Now it has a new home, in the splendid refurbished Broadway
Theatre (*see p223*), LYT is going all out to entertain London.
Having been selected as one of the youth theatre groups to take
part in the National Theatre's Connections festival of youth
theatre, the project, for young actors aged 14-21 has never been
so busy. Applicants in this age group are welcome to audition
and join the company; there are no fees for the tuition, training and valuable stage experience they gain. LYT also plan to
run performance workshops for younger actors (aged 7-11) in
the school holidays. Again, these activities will be free and will
make full use of the Broadway Theatre's fantastic stage and
studio space in a performance at the end of each small course.
Ring for more details.

Little Actors Theatre Company

*12 Hardy Close, Timber Pond Road, Surrey Quays,
SE16 (7231 6083).* **Classes** times vary; phone for details.
Fees from £40 12wk term. **No credit cards.**
Split between two venues, Little Actors holds classes for
5-12-year-olds at the Time & Talents Centre in Rotherhithe
(*see also p127*), and for 5-11-year-olds at the Open Door
Community Centre in Wimbledon. These drama and movement

Activities

sessions aim to develop self-confidence in the participants and incorporate improvisation, text appreciation and team-building exercises. Public performances are staged once or twice a year, and a new addition for 2002 is the introduction of toddlers' classes at the Time & Talents Centre for 2-4-year-olds (£2.50 per session). Samantha Giblin, the artistic director, also runs a children's party service.

Magic Eye
New Peckham Varieties at Magic Eye Theatre, Havil Street, SE5 (venue 7703 5838/office 7708 5401). Peckham Rye rail/Oval or Elephant & Castle tube/12, 36, 171, 345, 45A, P3 bus. **Classes** times vary; phone for details. **Fees** £1.50-£3. **No credit cards.**
Well known in south east London for its regular, enthusiastic musical shows starring local children, New Peckham Varieties at Magic Eye runs a busy educational programme. An introduction to drama, dance, music and theatre for the young (from 4 years), teaching communication skills, mime, improvisation and group work. Older attendees work on improvised and scripted pieces, developing performance skills. There's also a one-term project for new members and classes for over-16s. Membership costs £6 a term, or £15 per year.

Millfield Theatre School
Silver Street, N18 (box office 8807 6680/courses 8803 8448). Silver Street rail/34, 102, 144, 217, 231, 444 bus. **Classes** Sun. **Fees** *5-7s* £70 12 wk term. *8-16s* £140 12wk term. **Credit** MC, V.
Sunday drama classes are divided into two age groups: children aged 5-7 participate in a general theatre workshop from 10.30am to 12pm, and older youth, aged 8-16, study acting, voice, dance and movement from 11am to 2pm. Both groups put on an end-of-term production in the theatre for friends and family, which is very exciting for all concerned.

Perform
66 Churchway, NW1 (7209 3805/www.perform.org.uk). **Classes** times vary; phone for details. **Fees** £107 weekday 10wk term; £160 weekend 10wk term. **Credit** MC, V.
Perform now has 23 centres all over London, where the teachers run workshops especially suited to young children aged 4-7. The Perform programme of formulated games and exercises is designed to help children increase their four Cs: confidence, concentration, co-ordination and communication. A free trial workshop is offered to each child attending for the first time; ring for more details.

Pineapple Performing Arts School
7 Langley Street, WC2 (8351 8839/www.pineapplearts. com). Covent Garden tube. **Classes** *5-12s* 11am-2pm. *13-14s* 1-4pm. *15-18s* 2-5pm Sun. **Fees** £226 12wk term; trial class £19. **Registration fee** £30. **Map** p317 L6.
Originally designed for energetic, dance-obsessed children from 5-14 years, this fashionable school attached to Pineapple Dance Studio now also runs adult classes to accommodate bored parents waiting for their offspring. There is a diverse range of workshops and classes in dance and drama for all ages, from musical theatre and street theatre technique through to stage make-up and auditioning skills.

The Place
16 Flaxman Terrace, WC1 (box office 7387 0031/ classes 7387 7669/www.theplace.org.uk). Euston tube/ rail. **Fees** from £62 term for 1 weekly class; £10 family discount. **Credit** MC, V.
Newly redeveloped and full of energy and verve, the Place is one of the world's leading centres for dance, and considered by many to be the most cutting-edge one. It's home to Richard Alston Dance Company and London Contemporary Dance school. Classes for children are relaxed and high-spirited, designed to encourage creativity and independent thinking.
Children are further inspired at the Place by OffSpring, a programme of contemporary dance performances running every season. The project was launched by Emma Gladstone, associate producer at the Place, partly because she couldn't find anything she wanted to take her 8-year-old daughter to. Through OffSpring, the Place prides itself on bringing the best in dance to younger audiences. Its performances range in age suitability: there are those for children as young as 3 as well as in the evenings for older teenagers; most shows are accompanied by workshops. For further information, join the OffSpring mailing list by calling the box office.

Stagecoach
Head office: The Courthouse, Elm Grove, Walton-on-Thames, Surrey KT12 1LZ (01932 254333/ www.stagecoach.co.uk). **Fees** £250 (£125 for 4-7-yr-olds) for classes running alongside school term. **No credit cards.**
Britain's largest part-time theatre school offers drama, dance and singing tuition at weekends to young performers. It claims that 'skills for life not just for the stage' are a priority but that's not to say that former students haven't had success on film and TV. There are over 60 Stagecoach schools in the London area for children aged 4-16. End-of-term productions are put on occasionally; practising for this is the priority. Call the head office for prices and details of your nearest school and for information on holiday workshops.

Sylvia Young Theatre School
Rossmore Road, NW1 (7402 0673). Marylebone tube. **Fees** from £4.50 class. **No credit cards.**
The fact that so many of Sylvia's pupils reach the heady heights of the RSC and national theatres is proof that this stage school is one of the best. Whereas the full-time academic school is aimed at children aged 9-16 with a serious vocational interest in drama and dance, children aged from 4 are also catered for, with a range of classes. Week-long summer schools for 10-18-year-olds are led by teachers from the school, with a wider range of activities, is on the menu. Phone for further details.

Workshops

For performance workshops, *see p228.*

Art

Art 4 Fun
Various venues (head office 8994 4800/ www.art4fun.com). **Fees** *Weekend workshops, after-school club* £15. *Half-day course* £25.85. *Full-day course* £38.80. **Credit** AmEx, DC, MC, V.
Art activities of all descriptions are on the agenda here: children of any age can experiment with ceramics, wood, glass, silk, wool, clay and all kinds of other media that parents would rather not have cluttering up their kitchens. Workshops take place at weekends, as well as after school during the week. An extra bonus is the 'Little Artists' club, which gives pre-schoolers the chance to play with clay, salt dough and papier mâché with the help of their parents. Full-and half-day courses are put on during the summer. Art 4 Fun has studios in Notting Hill (7792 4567), Muswell Hill (8444 4333), West Hampstead (7794 0800), Mill Hill (8906 3333) and Chiswick (8994 4100).

Activities

All the floor's a stage. **Perform**. *See p230.*

Ceramics Café

215 King Street, W6 (8741 4140/
www.ceramicscafe.com). Ravenscourt Park tube.
Open 10am-6pm Tue, Wed, Fri, Sat; 10am-10pm
Thur; 11am-6pm Sun. **Fees** £2. **Credit** MC, V.
Functional crocks can be personalised with your own designs
here in the capacious kiln. Children of all ages enjoy decorating their own tableware (for which they pay from £3), and
consuming snacks and drinks from the café to get the creative juices flowing. This branch is a good choice for parties,
too: there's plenty of room, and the special party package (for
children aged from 5) costs £10 per child, for a minimum of
ten children. Ring for details.
Branches: 1A Mortlake Terrace, Kew Green, Richmond,
Surrey (8332 6661); 6 Argyle Road, W5 (8810 4422).

Colour Me Mine

168-70 Randolph Avenue, W9 (7328 5533/
www.colourmemine.com). Maida Vale tube. **Open**
9am-9pm Mon-Thur; 9am-7pm Fri, Sat; 10am-7pm Sun.
Fees *Studio fee* £6.60; £5.50 concessions; £4.40 under-
12s. *After-school club* £20 child (incl materials). **Credit**
AmEx, MC, V.
Anybody can pop into the CMM studios at any time and create mosaics, paint ceramics and daub on glass. If the children
feel they want something a bit more structured, CMM's after-
school club from 4pm to 6pm Tuesdays and Thursdays is suitable for kids aged 6 and up (note that there must be a minimum
of six children for this to run, and you must book in advance).
Mosaic and bead workshops are also available, but the latest
craze is Silver Alchemy, a special clay that turns silver when
fired, which looks very impressive and can be tried for £25 per
session (otherwise, materials start at £3). Parents wanting to
savour their babies' infancy can bring toddlers to create special footprint castings (£39-£70; pre-booking essential).
   The staff cater for parties (*see p235*) and also organise holiday workshops where busy parents can drop their children off
for a few hours to paint pots, make mosaics or design jewellery.
Branch: 452 Muswell Hill Broadway, N10 (8444 6886).

Nellie's Art Classes

179 Arlington Road, NW1 (7428 7600). Camden Town
tube. **Fees** £47 day; £198 wk. **No credit cards.**
The eponymous Nellie (Fenella Shepherd), actress, writer and
artist, began this outfit nine years ago from her kitchen and has
been wildly popular ever since, hiring the best art teachers to
provide imaginative after-school and holiday workshops in
Camden and Notting Hill. The workshops take a theme that
usually involves day trips, such as studying the techniques of
portrait painting at the National Portrait Gallery before embark-
ing on a painterly voyage of self-discovery.
Branch: The Parish Club, St Charles Square, W10
(8964 2710).

Food

The Kids' Cookery School

107 Gunnersbury Lane, W3 (8992 8882/
www.thekidscookeryschool.co.uk). Acton Town tube.
Open *Office* 9am-5.30pm Mon-Fri. **Fees** £15 75mins.
No credit cards.
A registered charity offering children aged 3-14 the chance to
take part in classes in food preparation, cooking and food
therapy. The school welcomes children with eating disorders,
physical disabilities and behavioural problems. Fees include all
the ingredients required for making the delicious meals and a
recipe card to take home. A maximum of eight children per class
is accepted. There are school-holiday workshops for teenagers.

French

Le Club Tricolore

10 Ballingdon Road, SW11 (7924 4649/www.le-club-
tricolore.co.uk). **Fees** vary; £100 10wk term, with
reductions for siblings. **No credit cards.**
C'est fantastique! Le Club Tricolore is probably the oldest
children's language club in London, offering fun French

Activities

Hitting the high notes at the **South Bank Centre**'s Gong Club. *See p214.*

teaching via methods that encourage them to communicate in another tongue without realising it. Games, music and movement are key to the hour-long sessions, which benefit children as young as 2, up to about 12. Juice, biscuits and fun sheets add to the sense of social event. Sessions are held in venues across London, on Saturday mornings in term time and on weekdays in the holidays.

Music

If you're looking for a suitably qualified music teacher, contact the **Incorporated Society of Musicians** (10 Stratford Place, W1C 1AA, 7629 4413), a professional association for musicians and music teachers, for advice and fee information; check out its website at www.ism.org.

Camberwell Choir School
81 Camberwell Church Street SE5, St Giles Church Hall, 161 Benhill Road, SE5 (venue) (7701 2464). Bus 12, 36, 171, 345. **Fees** £1 session. **No credit cards**.
Now music is considered something of a luxury in the general scheme of children's education, places like this are a boon to cultured but less-than-wealthy parents. The Choir School is a community arts project providing high-quality music (including musical instrument tuition and voice work) and arts tuition for local children, aged 8-18. A registered charity, the school aims to provide access to the arts at affordable prices. Classes take place on Saturdays during term time.

London Suzuki Group
Various venues (7386 8006/www.suzukimusic.net). **Fees** vary; phone for details. **No credit cards**.
Designed to draw out inherent musical ability through learning by listening, the Suzuki Method is best adopted by very young children (from age 3) who may then continue with it until their mid-teens. Lessons involve group activities,

parental participation and step-by-step tuition. Founded in 1972, this group now has 16 teachers working in Bayswater and Highgate, and holds residential and non-residential holiday courses as well as the regular weekly classes. Programmes exist for young violin, viola, cello and piano players. Call for times.

Music House for Children
Bush Hall, 310 Uxbridge Road, W12 (8932 2652/ www.musichouseforchildren.co.uk). Shepherd's Bush tube. **Fees** vary; phone for details. **Credit** MC, V.
With over 150 qualified tutors, Music House should have a class and an instrument to suit your child. If you prefer to keep things in-house, Music House teachers will come to your home for individual lessons. Otherwise, regular music and performance arts workshops are held in Bush Hall, as well as masterclasses, group tuition in woodwind, strings, keyboard, dance, drama and voice, plus music and movement classes for the under-5s. Concerts are staged for families and friends at the end of every term, so that fond parents can see how their children are progressing. Music therapy courses have been devised for children with special needs. Call for times.

Music Workshops
The Whippersnapper workshop room, Brockwell Lido, Dulwich Road, SE24 (7738 6633/www.thelido.co.uk). Herne Hill rail/Brixton tube/rail/3, 37, 196 bus. **Fees** from £3.50. **No credit cards**.
A must for fun-loving young musicians, the musical and theatrical workshops at the Whippersnapper workshop at this fantastic outdoor lido take place on a termly and drop-in basis. The sessions are devised for babies, toddlers and pre-schoolers and are a great way of letting off steam and learning about music and dance. African drumming and acrobatics workshops are also held here for children aged 7-11. Music Workshops run by the same company also take place at the Ecology Centre, next to the park's office, in Holland Park (*see p164*) on Tuesdays and Wednesdays. Call the Whippersnapper number for details.

Mwalimu Express

Bread & Roses pub, 68 Clapham Manor Street, SW4 (7498 1779). Clapham Common tube. **Fees** free.
Mwalimu Express, based on the idea of a train stopping off in different places, is a weekly chance for the whole family to go down the pub to investigate the music and cuisine of a particular region of Africa. The musicians invite the young members of the audience to take part in relaxed free workshops, including percussion, singing and storytelling. The sessions are held on Sundays from pm to 5pm. There is also a monthly film club showing African children's films.

Ocean

270 Mare Street, E8 (box office 7314 2800/info 8533 0111/www.ocean.org.uk). Hackney Central or Hackney Downs rail. **Open** 11am-7pm Mon-Fri; noon-4pm Sun. **Fees** vary; phone for details. **Credit** MC, V.
This imaginative £23-million music project in Hackney includes Rising Tide, a training centre for children and adults. There are numerous after-school and evening courses for young musos, covering singing, keyboards, drumming – even music production classes – for kids aged 7 and over. There is also a Saturday school for 11-16-year-olds.

Science & environment

Camley Street Natural Park

12 Camley Street, NW1 (7833 2311/ www.wildlondon.org.uk). King's Cross tube/rail. **Open** *Summer* 9am-5pm Mon-Thur; 11am-5pm Sat, Sun. *Winter* 9am-5pm Mon-Thur; 10am-4pm Sat, Sun. **Admission** free. **Map** p317 L2.
Just around the corner from King's Cross station, nestling behind the buddleias in a rather incongruous setting in the shadow of hulking great gas containers, this nature reserve is a miraculous place. Occasional star visitors include bats and kingfishers, but frequent visitors of the human kind include school and nursery groups, as well as families of nature lovers. Children can indulge in a spot of pond dipping at any point – just ask at the office for a net. Throughout the year, Camley Street also holds special free activity days, which often involve boat trips, barbecues and stalls. In the summer holidays, an environmental drop-in play-scheme means children can turn up and enjoy various craft activities, including clay modelling, tepee-making, trails and quizzes. (Under-8s must be accompanied by an adult.) Note: road access to the park is currently disrupted by works connected with the Channel Tunnel rail link; call for advice on the best entry route.

The Making Place

3 Exmoor Street, W10 (8964 2684/www.the-making-place.co.uk). Ladbroke Grove tube. **Open** 10am-3pm daily. **No credit cards.**
Adventures in science and technology are the order of the day at this place, housed in a purpose-built technology centre, in the grounds of Barlby Scool. During term time, the staff here run workshops for teachers and pupils (costing £5 per child), but it's in half-term that the fun starts. Children aged 5-12 can come along for the day, bringing a packed lunch, and use all the centre's computers, machinery and tools, under the watchful eye of the facilitators. They also have a go at making things, from small explosions, to tooth casts to motorised vehicles. Children must be accompanied by an adult, but adults get in free.

Roots & Shoots

The Vauxhall Centre, Walnut Tree Walk, SE11 (7582 1800). Lambeth North tube. **Open** *July-Apr* 9.30am-5.30pm Mon-Fri. *May, June* 9.30am-5.30pm Mon-Fri; 10am-2pm Sat. Phone before visiting. **Admission** free; donations welcome.
This one-acre site contains a pond (800 newts at last count), a summer meadow for wildflowers and butterflies, a pretty, restful paradise corner and beehives. David, the wildlife outreach worker, runs wildlife study days for school groups, and seasonal family days for everyone, when they can learn more about the flora and fauna here, and take part in honey extraction from the hives (in season), pond dipping, bug-hunting and other activities. Ring for details of the next family day, or for advice on how to encourage more wildlife into your own city patch. Ask to be put on the mailing list for details of open days and activities.

Going batty

A lot of giggling and muted cries of 'Whooo-whooo!' are the inevitable accompaniment to the start of any guided Bat Walk, given that the walks take place at night in the (fairly wild) open spaces of Hampstead Heath, Highgate Wood, Waterlow Park and other woodlands maintained by the Corporation of London and its partners. But after an educational chat about these little creatures (don't expect Hollywood-style vampires; most of the bats that live in the British Isles are pretty tiny), and a tramp through the woods at dusk, the walks settle down to become a magical experience with a serious purpose. Bats are an endangered species, after all: their habitats are threatened by the loss of deciduous woodland, pollution and other modern ills. Hampstead Heath is home to the largest bats in the UK – Noctules – which have a wing span of 35cm, but still weigh no more than a £2 coin. Participants are usually keen enough to do the walk even in wet weather; besides, if there is little to be seen, the 'bat detectors' (electronic boxes that turn bats' inaudible sounds into something humans can hear) ensure their presence is always felt.

The walks are organised free of charge as part of the Corporation's programme of events and take place in July and August on dates advertised locally. Alternatively, call 7482 7073 for information on walks on Hampstead Heath, 8444 6129 for Highgate Wood, or 7272 2825 for Waterlow Park.

Other events on the heath include nature treasure hunts, a creepy-crawly walk in June and a conker championship in autumn. At Waterlow Park, Camden's Nature Conservancy has family bird box-making sessions, frog days and Easter egg hunts. None of the events is bookable and all children aged 6-12 must be accompanied by an adult.

Activities

Parties

Glad rags, bad gags and goody bags.

The children's party business, famously a source of one-upmanship among indulged children and their indulgent parents, is a lucrative industry. We could, in fact, fill a book with all the party people and services available for junior birthday bashes, but we've stuck to the best of the ones we know.

Lots of the people and organisations listed below operate from home – in such cases only phone numbers are listed so you can check all the details by calling. Most of the venues have facilities for disabled visitors, and many of the party people can tailor their package for children with special needs.

Arts & crafts

Art 4 Fun
172 West End Lane, NW6 (8959 7373/
www.art4fun.com). West Hampstead tube/rail.
Open 10am-7pm daily; by appointment until 10pm.
Credit AmEx, DC, MC, V.
Art 4 Fun gives children the chance to do what they do best: make a mess. Tie-dyeing, sculpting, painting ceramics, marbling and cartooning are just some of the activities on offer at this safe, well-supervised creative café. And all this for a bargain price of £3.95 each for an entire day (plus the cost of the items they're decorating, from £1). For details of other branches, call or visit the website. *See also p230.*

The Art Yard
318 Upper Richmond Road West, SW14 (8878 1336). Mortlake rail. **Open** *Classes* 9am-6pm Mon-Fri.
No credit cards.
This hub of artistic activity is meant to be the very antithesis of school art: fun, fun, fun is the key, both for the holiday and term time workshops and the weekend parties. A minimum of eight children is required for a two-hour art party. You bring the food, but all art materials are provided and the guests always make something (papier-mâché mirrors or treasure chests, decorated T-shirts) they can take home. Check prices when you phone (reservations are essential), but as an idea, courses cost from £60 for a ten-week term, holiday workshops are £26.50 per day, and parties £14 per child.

Colour Me Mine
168-70 Randolph Avenue, W9 (7328 5577/
www.colourmemine.com). Maida Vale tube.
Open 9am-9pm Mon-Thur; 9am-7pm Fri, Sat; 10am-7pm Sun. **Credit** AmEx, MC, V.
Friendly staff and a consistently innovative approach continue to put the UK's first ceramics café ahead of the crowd. Several party packages offer different activities to creative kids. At £12 per guest (minimum 12), children are supervised in their own studio as they paint utilitarian items such as plates and mugs. The clay objects, paints, glazes, firing,

invitations and party bags are included in the price; an extra £4 per child gets them an additional logo T-shirt, which can be decorated on the spot. Mosaic parties, where mirror frames are created, cost £15; bead parties are the most expensive at £20, but everyone makes a necklace and a couple of bangles to take home. Catering is often devolved to phone-in pizza or bagel platters, which costs extra. *See also p231.*
Branch: 452 Muswell Hill Broadway, N10 (8444 6886).

Nellie's Art Parties
7428 7600.
'High energy, visually stimulating and very messy' is how Fenella Shepherd (aka Nellie) describes her children's art parties. Held in two studios in Camden and Notting Hill (call for details), the two-hour parties are a spin-off from her popular art classes (*see p231*) and are tailor-made to a theme chosen by the birthday boy or girl. Children spend the first hour painting, glittering and collaging a giant mural, followed by a craft-making session (so all participants go home with a finished product), tea (courtesy of Nellie's mum) and games. The cost is £400 for 22 children, plus food (extra guests £12 each).

Pottery Café
735 Fulham Road, SW6 (7736 2157/www.pottery-cafe.com). Parsons Green tube. **Open** 11am-6pm Mon; 10am-6pm Tue-Sat; 11am-5pm Sun. **Credit** MC, V.
Otter the Potter is the character defining pottery parties here, where £17 per child covers invitations, food, balloons and items of pottery up to £10.50 each – to be decorated by the party guests, of course. A minimum of six children is required for the package.

Cookery

Cookie Crumbles
8876 9912/0845 601 4173/www.cookiecrumbles.net.
Children as young as five can have fun making bread, jammy tarts and crocodile sandwiches in home-cooking parties supervised by Cordon Bleu chefs – who clean up your kitchen afterwards, too. Parties run for two hours, for a minimum of six children (maximum 25). The cooking itself can be themed for 5-15-year-olds; popular motifs are 'disco diva', 'crazy colours' or 'pirates' bounty' for the younger ones, teenagers prefer to fix up a sophisticated dinner party. Prices start at £145 per two hours for a party of six including all ingredients. The Crumbles team can provide party bags and aprons for an extra charge. Ring this number to find out about kids' cookery workshops all over west London.

Fix a Feast
Gayle Wilde (8675 9657) or Lucy Booth (7350 2536).
Clapham-based duo Gayle Wilde and Lucy Booth turn up together at your house, complete with ingredients and utensils, to supervise intimate cookery parties for eight children (£150 per party; extra kids £7.50 a head to a maximum of 12) aged 6-8 or 8-12. In the two hours available, the younger ones can make three dishes, the older ones four. These might include 'stegosaurus pasties', home-made pizza (punching the dough is popular) or 'fantasy' fairy cakes; the menu is agreed

★ **Top:** party ideas ★

For creative hands
Nellie's Art Parties. See p235.

For hearty appetites
Cookie Crumbles. See p235.

For high drama
Marvellous Productions. See below.

For navy larks
HMS Belfast. See p247.

For the trigger-happy
Campaign Paintball. See p239.

in advance. As light relief from the cooking schedule, children are also given chefs' hats to wear and decorate. Light relief for the parents comes in the form of a clean kitchen and the thought that their party has been educational as well as fun.

Drama

Club Dramatika!
8883 1554.
Vicky Levy's performance workshop company (see p228) also offers drama parties, exploring children's favourite themes, such as fairies and magic or heroes and heroines. Parties are workshop based, beginning with drama games involving mime or voice mimicry and progressing to a brief production at the end. It costs £80 for one hour, £130 for two.

Lydie Children's Parties
7622 2540.
Lydie charms children aged 4-9 (and adults) with her lovely French accent and lively themed parties. She turns your living room into a fantasy grotto with decoration and balloons in which the kids become the characters in popular stories, such as Peter Pan or Aladdin. There are tales, activities and Lydie's own games. A two-hour party for up to 26 children including decorations and goody bags costs from £350.

Marvellous Productions
8679 0917/www.marvellous-productions.com.
Fancy a trip on a magic carpet? Call Marvellous Productions, a company of brightly dressed actors (all Equity members), drama therapists and theatre designers. Their interactive, magic carpet rides to Story Land – which take little passengers to the moon, a fairy princess castle, the jungle, a pirate ship or even back in time – are very popular with 3-8-year-olds. Older kids appreciate the drama workshop party in which they choose the destination, or ask for a surprise related to their own interests. Both parties may be followed by a mask-making or prop-making workshop. Face and body painting are also available. Fees start at £85 for face painting, and £135 for a one-hour magic carpet ride.

Miss Sparkle
7684 1745/07939 358854.
The repertoire of former drama tutor Rain Harris includes performances for under-5s, incorporating her visually exciting handmade puppetry. With lots of audience participation, she tells of the prince who lives under the sea, or a

little girl who goes on an amazing adventure. The parties also involve low-key clown-style magic with the birthday child as helper; balloon modelling and parachute games. Art and crafts – making crowns or tiaras, for example – are also a possibility. Older children up to the age of about 14 are offered drama parties – murder mysteries are very popular – culminating in the production of a video or a performance in front of an audience of parents. Prices start at £90 for one hour, £130 for two.

Perform
7209 3805/www.perform.org.uk.
This well-known group of drama schools (see p230) specialising in 4-7-year-olds also supplies drama teachers for interactive, themed parties at a rate of £110 per hour. The Arabian Nights, Thunderbirds and Elizabethan England are popular fantasies to act out through costume, drama games, singing and dancing. Specially written songs to celebrate the child's day can also be organised.

Splodge
7350 1477/www.planetsplodge.com.
Is it drama or is it art? The kids don't seem to care – they have a great time at Splodge interactive parties, where creating a fantasy world with painted backdrop, finger puppets, mobiles, rockets and so on is the build-up to a little song and dance show. Parties for 20 children cost from £275 and all the extras – catering, art materials, party bags – are available by negotiation. The parties are held at Battersea Park Children's Zoo (£10-£15 per session; see p248) and are proving wildly popular.

Tiddleywinks
8964 5490/www.tiddleywinks.co.uk.
What a hoot! Kate Gielgud comes dressed in character for her drama theme parties, which are often fairytales; the party guests take complementary roles (from £195). Murder mysteries such as 'the supermodel murder' turn out to be comedies (from £270), which older children find hilarious. They are dressed by a magazine stylist, complete with hats, bag, jewellery, make-up and props. At the end of the party, they give a performance for the parents.

Face paints & make-up

Magical Makeovers
01932 244347/07957 681824.
This company offers a party service for girls aged 6-15. A team of make-up artists and hairdressers will come to your house and give all the party-goers a 'makeover', with manicure, hair styling (using accessories that are theirs to keep) and make-up. Prices run from £150 for eight children.

Mini Makeovers
8398 0107/www.minimakeovers.com. **No credit cards**.
Girls just wanna have fun, and, according to Mini Makeovers, lots of glitter, make-up and hair accessories to boot. For girls aged 5-12, this popular party firm will come to your house and transform members of a party into princesses, fairies, or, for 8-12-year-olds, mini Steps or S Club stars (bar the costumes). The standard rate, which includes hair accessories and a gift in a bag to take home, is from £130 for a minimum of eight kids; then from £13.50 a head. Optional extras include a limo service to take the little princesses to their favourite pizza eaterie, or a dance instructor, who teaches dance routines to over-8s in a mini disco (this is free for larger groups). Credit card facilities should be up and running soon.

Activities

Having a rubbery time at a **Peter McKenna** party. *See p244.*

Cooking up a storm

Gill Roberts is a home economics teacher and party caterer who took up a suggestion by the parents of her teenage pupils eight years ago to teach cookery to younger children. Initially running an after-school club, she later transposed her workshops (for children aged from 3) to her home in Hampstead Garden Suburb. Two-day workshops for 6-13-year-olds (£80) take place in school holidays; morning sessions for 3-6-year-olds on Saturday mornings (£25). Workshop parties have evolved from these sessions and are available on Saturdays from 9am to 12.45pm or from 2pm to 5.45pm at a cost of £250 (12 children or £5 per additional child up to a maximum of 20).

Parents – who aren't allowed to stay but are assured by Roberts that they'll get all the photos they'll ever need of their child's special day – are invariably impressed by the results. Fresh fruit cocktails, animal bread rolls, pizza faces, raisin crispy cakes, an iced birthday cake and home-made vanilla and chocolate chip ice-cream are always on the menu, and everything is made from scratch. Grown-ups who have attended report that the little guests seem better behaved when their parents are not present and that being encouraged to do things themselves, rather than wait for help, boosts their confidence. What the guests don't eat they take home, but in these days of takeaway snacks and microwave dinners, the pride in being able to cook is often the best present of all.

Gill's Cookery Workshop
10 Sutcliffe Close, NW11 (8458 2608). East Finchley or Golders Green tube. **No credit cards**.

Sport

Alexandra Palace Ice Rink
Wood Green, N22 (8365 2121/ www.alexandrapalace.com). Wood Green tube/ Alexandra Palace rail/W3 bus. **Credit** *Over £10* MC, V.
An ice-skating party here includes a 15-minute lesson before being sent off to slip-slide your way round for 60-90 minutes in a public session. Then comes the food, which costs £6.95 per child for the sandwich menu, £7.95 per child for the hot meal option (there's a minimum of 10 children, and a maximum of 30). *See also p258.*

The Elms Soccer School Parties
The Elms, Pinnacles Close, Stanmore, Middx HA7 4AF (8954 8787/www.the-elms.co.uk). **Open** *Enquiries* 9am-6pm Mon-Fri. **Credit** AmEx, MC, V.
The Elms Soccer School promises that it has the answer for anyone who lives, sleeps and talks football. Children are taught by an FA-qualified coach at a venue of their (or, rather, their parents') choice. One football match later, over-excited partygoers are worn out and ready for their tea. Children are also given football-themed party invitations to send out before the big day. The Elms also provide balloons and goody bags to take home. Football parties last up to 90 minutes, and prices range from £95 to £120.

F1 City

Gate 119, Connaught Bridge, Royal Victoria Dock, E16 (7476 5678/www.f1city.co.uk). **Credit** MC, V.
This go-kart track offers sessions for parties of kids over 5ft 2in tall (ie aged about 12+). The one-hour 'cadet party' costs £250 for eight children and includes instruction, marshalling, races for four karts at a time, a trophy presentation and party food pack. Anyone who's smitten may continue in one of the Sunday cadet clubs (from £10). *See also p260.*

Mallinson Sports Centre

Bishopswood Road, N6 (8342 7272). Highgate tube. **Credit** MC, V.
This sports centre is attached to a famous boys' school and has superb facilities. In addition to school holiday sports camps, two party packages are on offer. The bouncy castle party with games is for 5-6-year-olds and costs £110 for up to 15 children and £130 for a maximum of 25. The sport and swim party for 7-12-year-olds encompasses almost any sport the children would like to play, including basketball, football, hockey, bench and dodge ball, followed by a swim, for £135 for 25 children. Parents supply the grub.

Michael Sobell Leisure Centre

Hornsey Road, N7 (7609 2166/www.aquaterra.org). Finsbury Park tube/rail. **Credit** MC, V.
This concrete block of a place near Holloway Road offers party packages (without catering) in the Pirates Playhouse ball pond (£60 Monday-Wednesday; £120 Thursday-Sunday). At weekends only there are trampolining parties (£75); ice-skating parties (£95); bouncy castle parties (£50) and sports parties (£50). *See also p258.*

Mile End Climbing Wall

Haverfield Road, E3 (8980 0289/ www.mileendwall.org.uk). Mile End tube. **Credit** AmEx, MC, V.
Located in a converted pipe-bending factory, the Mile End Climbing Wall provides strenuous activity for parties of children aged from 8. Children are taught climbing and abseiling techniques by instructors, who cost £28 for an hour (they'll be exhausted after that long), plus £2 for each child. The party room is available free of charge (parents should bring their own trimmings). *See also p252.*

Pro-Active 4 Parties & Entertainment

8440 2682/www.magicalparties.net.
An extensive range of exciting theme-based parties including Gladiators, Circus Skills, Crystal Ball Maze and Mini Olympics is offered by Pro-Active Leisure. Newer departures include makeover parties, discos and karaoke. The company also has a range of entertainers, from clowns and puppeteers to storytellers. Pro-Active's people can set up outside if you have a big garden, but as the activities are so dependent on good weather they recommend you hire a hall for the celebration (their database can point you in the direction of a suitable hall for hire in your area). Prices vary according to venue and the number of children, so call for details.

Playscape Pro Racing

Streatham Kart Raceway, 390 Streatham High Road, SW16 (8677 8677/www.playscape.co.uk/karting). Streatham rail. **Credit** MC, V.
Billed as Europe's foremost karting company, Playscape offers one-hour slots for children aged 8-16 from 10am to 1pm at weekends and 10am to 5pm during the week. The ten drivers in each team are given instructions, race suits, crash helmets and gloves and there is a trophy presentation for the birthday boy or girl.

Westway Sports Centre

1 Crowthorne Road, W10 (8969 0992/www.nkat.org.uk). Latimer Road tube. **Credit** AmEx, MC, V.
Energetic children can choose football, tennis and (particularly popular) climbing as their celebratory activity at this sports centre. All equipment, decorations and invitations are provided, and catering is also available. Prices start from £80 for ten children (maximum 25). *See also p160.*

Young guns

Allied Command

0800 917 0821/www.paintballgames.co.uk. **Credit** MC, V.
Politically correct it ain't, but kids (girls as well as boys) enjoy this rough and tumble, shoot 'em up outing. Allied Command offers children's parties for under-18s at its Effingham (Surrey), Tring (Hertfordshire) and Shoreham (Kent) locations at a cost of £17.50 a child for a full day, including 150 paintballs, and a barbecue lunch. The minimum age is 11, and booking is essential (give at least two weeks' notice). Rest assured, overalls, balaclavas and helmets are provided.

Campaign Paintball

Old Lane, Cobham, Surrey (01932 865999/ www.campaignpaintball.com). Effingham Junction rail. **Credit** MC, V.
Fresh air and gung-ho realism are two of the qualities associated with this place, set in 180 acres of forest, though the owners like to stress that building team spirit is the best reason for coming here. All protective gear is supplied, plus instructors, referees and judges. There's even a presentation of trophies at the end of the day. On Sundays, the range is free of corporate and stag/hen dos, so juniors and adults get to join in the fun. The package costs £17.50 per child (over-11s only) including barbecue lunch and all equipment.

Holmbush Paintball

Holmbush Farm, Faygate, West Sussex (0500 454555/ www.holmbushpaintball.co.uk). Horsham rail then short taxi ride. **Credit** MC, V.
Holmbush has 12 combat arenas set in 250 acres of forest near Gatwick Airport. It's normally only open to over-16s; a full day costs £15 per person, including 100 paintballs, and catering is from £1.50 to £2.50. However, there are special arrangements for younger age groups, namely those children aged from 12 who are fired up by the idea of armed combat. They can be accommodated for private parties, but the minimum number of guests is 20; otherwise, there is a special junior day on the last Sunday of each month (£15 for the whole day or £10 for half a day). Ring for details.

Laserquest

155 Clarence Street, Kingston-upon-Thames, Surrey (8974 8484/www.laserquest.co.uk). Kingston rail. **No credit cards.**
Unlike paintballing, which is mildly painful, shooting your opponents with a laser gun depends merely on coloured lights and computer-linked body armour. Games are played in teams (small groups are matched with any other available groups; larger groups play among themselves). Arguments over who shot whom are a natural feature of the game. Children, particularly competitive ones, love the excitement. Laserquest offers a 90-minute party package at £8.90 per child (minimum 6, maximum 20; over-6s only). You bring the the celebratory tea of your child's choice, including the all-important birthday cake, and set it out in the party area.

Activities

Quasar

13 Junction Road, N19 (7281 5001). Archway tube.
Credit MC, V.
More combat simulation is available at what is billed as 'London's only laser gun range' (others, such as Laserquest, are just out of town). A party package with meal (burgers, chips and the like) costs £9.95 a child. Over-7s only, in parties of up to 20.

Cakes

For those who want to make their own party cakes, there are a couple of step-by-step guides to choose from: Carol Deacon's *No-Time Party Cakes* (£14.99) includes a fairy-tale castle and shows how to model figures and animals quickly and easily, and *New Children's Party Cakes* by Anna Farrell (£9.99) includes 35 cakes aimed at novice cooks. Both are available from bookshops or from the Book People (01942 723333/www.thebookpeople.co.uk).

Ready-made, themed cakes can be bought relatively cheaply at most supermarkets, though you'll need to order special themes in advance. Football pitches, fairies and caterpillars are more likely to be available off the shelf, from around £8.

There is, however, a distinct gap in the market between perfectly decorated but tasteless factory fare and the lovingly home-made sponges with wonky Smarties on top. If your child is young enough not to whine for an entertainer or otherwise expensive party, then you might like to spend your money on a cake that will delight him or her but can also be enjoyed by adult relatives and friends. This is where the handmade cakes from local bakeries come in – see below for our pick of the bunch.

Amato Caffè/Pasticceria

14 Old Compton Street, W1 (7734 5733). Piccadilly Circus tube. **Open** 8am-10pm Mon-Sat; 10am-8pm Sun. **Credit** AmEx, DC, MC, V. **Map** p317 K6.
The craftspeople in this Italian café in Soho produce some of the finest cakes in central London, made with perfect fruits, sparkling glazes and the best chocolate. Ordering a shaped cake – which are made regularly for both adults and children – is a personal, ad hoc affair. You communicate your child's interests to the chef, and he comes up with appropriate ideas. The Starship *Enterprise*, Tower Bridge and Rolly from Bob the Builder have all been made recently. These cakes are pricey one-offs best suited to large parties; a cake serving 80 people might cost £150, but smaller ones still cost £100 because of the hugely time-consuming fine sugarcraft involved. Better value for those with gourmet tastes and a tight budget are regular cakes decorated with delightful, detailed marzipan figures in a theme – say, the jungle or the circus – for around £30. *See also p174.*

Choccywoccydoodah

47 Harrowby Street, W1 (7724 5465/ www.choccywoccydoodah.com). Edgware Road or Marble Arch tube. **Open** 11am-2pm, 3-6pm Tue-Sat. **No credit cards. Map** p313 F5.

A wild confection from **Amato Caffè/Pasticceria**.

Chocolate cake heaven for any posh party, these lavish creations are layered with fresh Belgian truffles and coated in solid white, milk or plain chocolate, and are sized from eight to ten portions for £18, to £80 for up to 70 portions. Hand-crafted bespoke cakes and moulded figures (designed to your imagination's limits) are a speciality; the chocolate can even be dyed to match your colour scheme.

Chorak

122 High Road, East Finchley (8365 3330). East Finchley tube. **Open** 8.30am-6pm daily. **Credit** MC, V.
Cakes for all occasions are made on the premises with themed and very ornate party cakes made to order. Ideas range from the well known – Pooh Bear or Beauty and the Beast – to the inventive – such as a miniaturised merry-go-round. Prices are from £38 to £46.

Dunn's

6 The Broadway, N8 (8340 1614/www.dunns-bakery.co.uk). Finsbury Park tube/rail, then W7 bus/ Crouch Hill rail. **Open** 7am-6pm Mon-Sat. **Credit** MC, V.
This very English – and locally revered – bakery can make almost any cake you dream about, with wholesome ingredients, on the premises. (Half) footballs, open books, teddy bears et al are supplemented by grinning Disney characters and edible photo-imaging. Prices start at £19.50 for an 8in round cake, rising to over £35 for a generously proportioned creation to feed 20 children.

Jane Asher Party Cakes

22-4 Cale Street, SW3 (7584 6177/www.jane-asher.co.uk). South Kensington tube. **Open** 9.30am-5.30pm Mon-Sat. **Credit** AmEx, MC, V. **Map** p315 E11.
Come to Ms Asher's cake kingdom in South Kensington to look at the catalogue and have a cake decorated to order. There are 3,000 designs to choose from; prices start at about £55 for, say, a square cake made into a parcel with ribbons and message-bearing gift tag. The average 3-D cake costs £150 and might comprise a cowboy hat or a ranch with figures, a tank, castle or bunch of fairies in the garden, adorned with glitter. At least you can be sure what is under the sugar paste is yummy: chocolate, vanilla or lemon sponge made

Elms Soccer School. *See p238.*

fresh on the premises with praline-flavoured buttercream, perhaps. Fruit cakes are also available. Note that you should give at least ten days' notice. If you like making your own, this is also a sugarcraft and baking equipment shop, and Jane Asher cake mixes are sold too.

Maison Blanc

102 Holland Park Avenue, W11 (7221 2494/ www.maisonblanc.co.uk). Holland Park tube. **Open** 8am-7pm Mon-Thur, Sat; 8am-7.30pm Fri; 8.30am-6pm Sun. **Credit** MC, V.
This resolutely French pâtisserie chain will customise any of its delicious gâteaux with handwritten birthday greetings for £2.10. The vanilla and strawberry *fraisier* (ten-portion size, £23.55) is popular with young children; chocoholics go for the chocolate mousse cake (£21.95) to which cute marzipan animal figures can be added (£1.20 each). For once, that chocolate moustache seems worthwhile.
Branches throughout town. Check the phone book.

Pierre Péchon

127 Queensway, W2 (7229 0746). Bayswater or Queensway tube. **Open** 7am-7pm Mon-Wed; 7am-8pm Thur-Sat; 8am-7pm Sun. **Credit** MC, V. **Map** p312 C6.
Trains, fairytale cottages, sporting motifs, cartoon characters – you name it, and this successful chain of west London pâtisseries will create it for you in vanilla or chocolate sponge with fresh or butter cream. A 6in cake costs from £9.85; a 12in cake giving 30 portions costs £53.60. If you're fresh out of ideas, flick through the shop's catalogue of past designs.
Branch: 4 Chepstow Road, W2 (7229 5289).

Purple Planet

318-20 Portobello Road, W10 (8969 4119/ www.purpleplanet.co.uk). Ladbroke Grove tube. **Open** 10am-5pm Mon-Fri; 10am-2pm Sat. **Credit** AmEx, MC, V. **Map** p312 A6.

This party supply shop also has a sugarcraft and cake baking section for people who want to decorate their own cakes. The fabulous range of party candles is an inexpensive way of impressing small children: try the fountain ones (£2.50); or if you're feeling creative, choose the gold, silver and glittery edible paints. In terms of general party wares, there are streamers, balloons, tableware and banners. For dressing up, there are masks, theatrical make-up and bad-taste jokes.

Costumes

Gone are the days when parents would sit up into the small hours sewing sequins on their offspring's party costume. Nowadays, you're spoilt for choice when it comes to buying or hiring outfits. Several of the shops in the Shopping chapter (*pp192-212*) sell or rent out party costumes. You don't even need to brave the high street: many have mail-order facilities (in addition to the specialist companies below), and those on p203 also do online ordering.

Mail order

Hill Toy Company

Unit 6, Studlands Business Centre, Newmarket, Suffolk CB8 7SS (0870 607 1248/www.hilltoy.co.uk). **Open** *Phone orders* 9am-5.30pm Mon-Fri. **Credit** MC, V.
Bestselling costumes from this well-established toy company include lusciously furry leopards and dotty Dalmatians (from £21.95), a jolly gingham clown outfit (£23.95), white and black knights (£21.95), a nurse uniform (£21.95) and fringed suedette Indian brave (£24.95). You can order a wigwam while you're about it.

Parties

Hopscotch
61 Palace Road, SW2 3LB (8674 9853/ www.hopscotchmailorder.co.uk). **Open** *Phone orders* 9.30am-5.30pm Mon-Fri. **Credit** MC, V.
A huge range of outfits to get boys and girls in the party mood, from the ever-popular angels and fairies and disco queen costumes to futuristic astronauts. Prices range from £9.95 for the ready-made Christmas nativity robes to £33.95 for a spectacular wizard's coat covered with stars and moons. All have been tested for ease of use and comfort by Hopscotch's team of mini testers (lucky them). There's also a selection of animal hats, from cats and pigs to zebras and even a dragon, which make quick dressing-up solutions for £12.95. Accessories include wands, halos, hats and wigs.

J&M Toys
46 Finsbury Drive, Wrose, Bradford, W Yorks BD2 1QA (01274 599314/fax 01274 591887/ www.jandmtoys.co.uk). **Credit** MC, V.
Frazzled at the thought of yet another stage costume to sew, or planning a theme party? This catalogue is bound to have the outfit you need, since its range is vast and catalogued in groups. There are not merely nurse outfits, but gear for a whole medical team; policemen are supported by lollipop ladies and firefighters; chefs by waiters and cooks. They are all great value, too, with discounts on sets of costumes, so that a single dinosaur might cost £17.50, but a pack of six animals outfits costs £95 (less than £16 each). Note that orders are taken by post and fax only, not by phone.

Make Believe
PO Box 343, Guildford, Surrey GU5 9YW (01483 203437/www.make-believe.co.uk). **Open** *Enquiries & orders* 9am-3pm Mon-Fri. **Credit** MC, V.
Outfits in this catalogue may seem expensive, but they turn out to be good value when you consider that most accessories are included in the price. A cowboy, for example, will come with a hat, neckerchief, shirt, waistcoat, badge, gun and a holster for £29.99, while a pirate sashays about in a bodysuit, belt, buckle, striped socks and hat with feather for £37.99. Some accessories are available separately – for example, a red wig (£9.99) to turn a mermaid (£39.99) into Ariel.

Shops

Escapade
150 Camden High Street, NW1 (7485 7384/ www.escapade.co.uk). Camden Town tube. **Open** 10am-7pm Mon-Fri; 10am-6pm Sat; noon-5pm Sun. **Credit** AmEx, MC, V.
There are 2,000 costumes for hire here, a small proportion of which fit children. For a bear costume or full Buzz Lightyear regalia, you pay £18 for three days' hire (deposit £30). To hire a wizard costume, morph into a squirrel or step out as a Tudor queen it's also £18 for three days, plus a £50 deposit.

Harlequin
254 Lee High Road, SE13 (8852 0193). Hither Green rail/Lewisham rail/DLR. **Open** 10am-5.30pm Mon, Tue, Thur-Sat; 10am-1pm Wed. **Credit** MC, V.
A colourful little dressing-up shop with a selection of children's costumes on sale, from GI Joes and Samurai to princesses and Indian squaws. Cheapest of all are the £3.50 'kits', such as a bandanna, eye patch, earring and moustache, to turn any kid in T-shirt and tracksuit pants into a pirate in a flash. The average all-inclusive costume is £14; animals in plush fur fabric cost £20-£25; medieval robes around £30.

Deals on wheels

The Party Bus
07836 605032/www.childrenspartybus.co.uk.
This converted bus, which will park in your drive (or nearby), holds up to 24 children at a time. Each party is pitched according to the age group: games, magic and puppets for small children, or a disco for older ones. Prices are from £300 and include all catering except a cake. Party bags cost an extra £2.25 per child. For ages 4-9.

The Wonderbus
8968 3798/www.wonderbus.co.uk.
This team will travel anywhere within the Greater London area to get to you. Coming complete with José, a friendly uniformed driver, Jessica Christie-Miller's funky blue double-decker allows up to 30 children at a time to run riot on the two imaginatively designed floors, which are decked out with soft flooring for dancing and playing, chill-out sections for reading and snacking, a ball pond for letting off steam, and music ranging from poptastic treats to jazz. The starting price is £250 for up to 15 children, which includes staff and face painter, food, pass the parcel and other games. Ages are from 2-7 years, with sessions organised for set age groups.

The Wonder Years
07000 123455/www.network7.com.
Children with a taste for stardom can don their dark glasses and film star clothes and cruise London in a limo. Book a tour or take trips to and from, say, Planet Hollywood (*see p178*). Soft drinks are supplied. Car hire costs from £160 for the first three hours. Cars seat from six to eight people.

Entertainers

See also p245 **Organisers**.

Ali Do Lali
01494 774300.
After 30 years in the business, magician and illusionist Ali Do Lali has built up a distinguished clientele and remains as popular as ever. Levitation, chopping off dads' heads with a French guillotine, breathing fire and twisting balloons into animals are his stock-in-trade. Just lately he has been joined by his son, Ali Da Noodle, whose repertoire mirrors his own. Ali Senior also does shows and discos for older kids and traditional parties for ages 2 and up. Party bags, helium balloons and fireworks can also be supplied.

Blueberry Playsongs Parties
8677 6871/www.blueberry.clara.co.uk.
This is the party arm of an established musical group with mother and toddler classes all over London. The entertainer turns up with a guitar to do a 45-minute slot (from £75) for up to 20 kids. Highlights include hopping and circle games, pop-up puppets and dancing through a cloud of bubbles.

Boo Boo
7727 3817/www.mr-booboo.co.uk.
Lots of laughter and prizes are the order of the day at Boo Boo's parties. He has extensive experience with children of all ages and his winning ways work with the shy ones. Boo Boo's repertoire runs from magic tricks, games, silly juggling, balloon modelling and puppet shows, through to teenage discos with the latest music, flashing lights, dancing competitions, group games and – hilarious – limbo dancing.

Activities

Time Out London for Children **243**

Chris Howell

7376 1083.

Self-taught American magician Chris Howell is well known for his fun, colourful, fast-moving show, which takes the form of a narrative in the first half and a balloon modelling session in the second. Children aged 4-8 participate by acting out characters in the magical story and are also taught certain tricks – strange how they always seem to go comically wrong before they go right. Parties last one hour and cost from £85. Magic workshops for over-11s are also available.

Foxy the Funky Magic Genie

8769 3370/www.foxythefunkygenie.com.

Bald-headed Foxy, with his trademark ponytail, glittery costume and curly-toed shoes, goes down well with children, who enjoy lighting his magic lamp or being turned into a Harry Potter character. The 45-minute act is £85; prices rise in stages to £155 for longer parties with puppets, balloons, discos and karaoke. He can also supply catering and marquees.

Jolly Dolly

01932 786023/07855 768986.

Madcap, magical comedy is provided by this aptly named entertainer, who is active in south London and keeps children unflaggingly entertained for two hours (£150). Her act includes a mini disco, games and prizes; parents have to do the food and party bags. A one-hour show is available by negotiation, in which balloon modelling, juggling and a furry, spring-loaded puppet, Rocky Raccoon, all feature. Little kids think he's alive.

Jugglers Etc

8672 8468/www.jugglingjohn.com.

The success of Juggling John has inspired him to assemble a team of entertainers, each of whom has a repertoire that may include juggling, clowning, fire-eating, storytelling, balloon modelling and even escapology. Children should be able to find something among this lot to inspire them. Parties are tailored to suit the guests' tender ages (from 3 upwards) and cost from £90 to £250.

Lee Warren

8670 2729/www.sorcery.org.uk.

Affable magician Lee has been entertaining children (and adults) for 18 years now. His act, which comes highly recommended, lasts about an hour and is ideal for 4-8-year-olds. The classic shows are full of colour and fun and involve plenty of joining in – children come up and help, often dressing up as pirates, princesses and wizards, and earn a certificate. His young audiences find it especially hilarious when tricks appear to be going wrong. Lee can deal with from eight to 600 kids and charges £100.

Little Blisters

8948 3874.

This drama-based show by multi-talented actress Eva features such characters as Flossie the Fairy, Sea Lily the Mermaid and Kitty Willow the Cat. Their adventures are punctuated by conjuring tricks, singing, dancing and lots of audience participation – not to mention balloons, games and face painting. Phone for prices.

Merlin Entertainments

tel/fax 8866 6327.

This children's entertainment service has more than 40 entertainers on its books, from jugglers, magicians and clowns to stilt-walkers and fire-eaters, for children aged from 3 upwards. Junior discos are another speciality. A one-hour magic show costs from £100.

Pekko's Puppets

8579 7651/www.pekkospuppets.co.uk.

Stephen Novy's puppet shows come highly recommended. His party service can be adapted for children from 3 right up to the grand old age of 12. For very little ones, an hour-long set involving a couple of well-known stories (*Three Little Pigs* is a favourite), games and songs, goes down very well. Older children see a whole play unfold from Pekko's booth. The cost is from £100 for one hour. Pekko's Puppets can perform in your home, or, for larger audiences, in a hired hall. You can often catch this show on the children's theatre circuit (Polka Theatre, Jackson's Lane, and the Lyric Hammersmith, for which *see also p222*).

Peter McKenna

7703 2254/07956 200572/www.childrensentertainer.net.

Magic Circle member Peter McKenna appears as Bimbo the Clown, Mezmo the Wizard or Peter the Balloon Man to entertain children of all ages for one- or two-hour shows including magic, balloon modelling and a mini disco. McKenna is super efficient, too: he models the balloons while the kids are dancing, so the process doesn't slow down the entertainment. Prices start at £90 for one hour, £145 for two.

Professor Fumble

01395 579523.

Described by adult fans as 'especially endearing', Prof Fumble is a master of slapstick, sitting in his own custard pies, falling off a unicycle and, well, fumbling with juggling balls. He charges £90 for one hour or £130 for two, including games.

Equipment hire

Disco

Jukebox Junction

12 Toneborough, Abbey Road, NW8 (7328 6206). St John's Wood tube. **Open** *by appointment only* 9am-5pm Mon-Fri. **No credit cards**.

Hire one of two Seeburg 1970s jukeboxes and up to 50 singles from a choice of 3,500 at Jukebox Junction. The cost is £275 a night, plus £50 deposit.

Young's Disco Centre

20 Malden Road, NW5 (0800 980 2321/7485 1115/ www.youngsdisco.com). Chalk Farm tube. **Open** 11am-6pm Mon-Sat. **Credit** MC, V.

Sound systems and DJs for children's parties cost from £100 for a two-hour weekday party, and from £130 at weekends, depending on venue and type. Hire a karaoke machine for around £80, plus another £80 for a disco. Popcorn and candyfloss machines are also available.

Fairground

PK Entertainments

07771 546676.

It's Pinocchio's dream: a fairground just for you and your friends, set up in your garden if it's big enough, or even indoors. You'd need a sizeable party room for the basic indoor package, which at £200 includes a toboggan run, 'unridable horse', small bouncy castle and so on. Prices start at £400 for the full-blown private fair with roundabout, swingboats, bouncy castle, coconut shy, hoop-la and other delights. Phone for more details about what PK can provide for the party.

Hot party gear from **Escapade**. *See p243.*

Marquees

Minimarkee
20 Bradmore Park Road, W6 (8741 2777/ www.minimarkee.co.uk). Hammersmith tube.
Open 9am-5pm Mon-Fri. **Credit** MC, V.
If you've got the garden to pitch them in, you can keep the chaos out of the house with a Minimarkee – available in all shapes and sizes. Frame tents cost from £90 to £290; multi-pavilions cost from £130 for a for a neat, complete 3x3ft one; for a real treat for those with spacious acres hire a big top tent (from £325). Trestle tables, dancefloors, heating, matting and lights are all available.

Organisers

Action Station
7263 8468/www.theactionstation.co.uk.
Leave it to Action Station if inspiration has run out and the big day is looming. This organisation has something for everyone, from drama, storytelling and theme parties to mini sports days. Children aged 4-6 will love the magical interactive storytelling parties, when they are encouraged to act out the roles of wizards and witches, mermaids or cowboys (£110 for one hour). Games workshops have an ebullient game leader who could wear out the most energetic group, while film make-up parties teach children to recreate grisly cuts, bruises and other horrors with putty (not surprisingly, these are very popular). Alternatively, go for a party workshop involving face painting, balloon modelling, drama or even circus skills (from £130).

Adam Ant's
8959 1045/www.adamantsparties.com.
One-man entertainment powerhouse Adam Ant supplies the kit and the performers for magic shows, puppet theatre, balloon modelling and fun and games for the under-8s. Hireable equipment runs from furniture to ball ponds and bouncy castles. Rates are from £75 an hour depending on location. For £85 you can get a 'kidogram' in the shape of a Snow White, Barbie, Batman or other character, who stays to sing, dance, or – in the case of Sporting Barbie – run a keep-fit session.

Laurie Temple & the Party Wizard Company
8840 5293.
Highly recommended Laurie Temple has 15 years experience in film, TV, circus and cabaret. His variety show is full of magic, comedy, juggling, storytelling and balloon modelling, and his junior disco is popular with teenyboppers. Laurie's parties can be tailored to suit children of all ages. The Party Wizard Company can also conjure up various entertainers who organise themed parties according to your brief. Tables, chairs, inflatables, catering, balloons and other party essentials can be hired and bought as part of the party organisation service. Ring for details.

Puddleduck Parties
8893 8998/www.puddleduckparties.co.uk.
This company claims to come up with 'stress-free' themed parties for children of all ages, and can package everything from entertainers, tableware and goody bags to home-made food and cake. Themes include Batman, Teddy Bear's Picnic, Pirate, Fairy Princess, Circus or your own choice. Also available are drama parties, art and crafts, sport and discos.

Activities

Twizzle Parties

8392 6788/www.twizzle.co.uk.
Twizzle Parties is a one-stop shop offering traditional parties complete with character visits, mini discos, proper discos with smoke and bubble machines (from £220), cowboy and sports parties (from £180). A creepy crawly party (from £250) allows junior naturalists to cuddle up to a boa constrictor (ages 5 and over), while a circus party for over-3s (from £220) features clowns, slapstick comedy, juggling, magic and games.

Paraphernalia

Mail order

Baker Ross

Unit 53, Millmead Industrial Estate, Millmead Road, N17 9QU (enquiries 8808 6948/orders 0870 241 1867/www.bakerross.co.uk). **Credit** MC, V.
Originally aimed at schools and scout groups as a means of fundraising via tombolas and the like, this catalogue of toys, art materials and novelties is a brilliant source of low-cost ideas for children's parties. Bendy animals, bird gliders, stampers and tattoos are among the possible goody bag fillers; face paints and animal party boxes could be prizes or lucky dip items. A jar of 120 lollipops costs £5.99; a tub of 3,000 assorted beads £3.95. The art materials are inspiring: why hire an entertainer when kids can entertain themselves with modelling, painting and sticking?

Party Directory

29 Spruce Drive, Lightwater, Surrey GU18 5YU (01276 850501/www.partydirectory4kids.co.uk).
Open *Phone orders* 9.30am-6pm Mon-Fri; 9am-noon Sat.
Credit MC, V.
This mail-order catalogue has a small, carefully chosen range of party tableware, goody bag fillers and so on. Its best feature is a range of food and drink carriers shaped, for instance, like Barbie's pink Cadillac, a pick-up truck or pirate galleon (58p each). Other themes include Harry Potter, Thunderbirds, Pokémon, Cinderella, football and the emergency services.

Party Pieces

Child's Court Farm, Ashampstead Common, Berks RG8 8QT (01635 201844). **Credit** MC, V.
This attractively produced catalogue with personal service comes as a blessed relief from computerised ordering systems. Themes for tableware, gifts and dressing-up clothes include pirates (check out the inflatable parrot, £1.85), a dolphin-oriented seaworld, cowboys and Indians with brave-style party hats (£1.45), scary dinosaurs and and twinkly fairies. Birthday medals (£1.95) are good fun, and some products are designated suitable for under-3s.

Partyworks

The Buffer Depot, Badminton Road, Acton Turville, Glos GL9 1HE (0870 240 2103/www.partybypost.co.uk). **Open** *Enquiries & orders* 9am-5.30pm Mon-Fri. **Credit** MC, V.
Dinosaurs and bugs, construction and vehicles or ballet and butterflies are just three themes in this handy catalogue of co-ordinated, themed party tableware, stationery and gifts. Reading through it gives potential party-throwers delusions of grandeur. For cake bakers there are cookie cutters and castle-shaped cake tins; arty types love the dyed feathers or pom-poms (£3.95 for 90). There is even a book featuring 12 treasure hunts and a set of sturdy nylon bags (£44.50 for six) for sack races. A must-have directory.

Just popping into **Just Balloons**. *See p247.*

Shops

Balloon and Kite Company

613 Garratt Lane, SW18 (8946 5962/www.balloonandkite.com). Tooting Broadway tube/Earlsfield rail. **Open** 9am-5.30pm Mon-Sat.
Credit AmEx, MC, V.
London's widest variety of balloons, from foil cartoon character shapes to balloon canopies. Helium gas can be hired, or balloons can be helium-filled in the shop. Filled latex balloons are £1 each; foil balloons £2.99. Delivery and decoration service available.

Balloonland

12 Hale Lane, NW7 (8906 3302/www.balloonland.co.uk). Edgware tube/Mill Hill Broadway rail. **Open** 9.30am-5.30pm Mon-Fri; 10am-5.30pm Sat. **Credit** MC, V.
These balloon and party specialists offer a seven-day delivery service. Helium party packs, helium gas rental and balloon clusters guarantee a swinging party.

Circus Circus

176 Wandsworth Bridge Road, SW6 (7731 4128/www.partysource.co.uk). Fulham Broadway tube.
Open 10am-6pm Mon-Sat. **Credit** AmEx, MC, V.
Especially useful for its child-size tables and chairs rental service, this shop also stocks party tableware, cards, costumes (from £9), toys, novelties for party bags, decorations and cakes. Ring Circus Circus if you need to hire an entertainers, any kind of inflatable (bouncy castle) and catering.

Just Balloons
127 Wilton Road, SW1 (7434 3039/
www.justballoons.com). Victoria tube/rail. **Open** 9am-6pm
Mon-Fri; 10am-5pm Sat. **Credit** MC, V. **Map** p318 J10.
Every kind of balloon you could possibly want, especially
novelty ones, from inflatable giraffes to bananas and globes.
If you need to hire a small helium gas cylinder to inflate, say,
150 balloons, the cost is £46.41 for the week (£100 deposit).

Mexicolore
28 Warriner Gardens, SW11 (7622 9577/
www.pinata.co.uk). Battersea Park or Queenstown Road
rail. **Open** by appointment only. **No credit cards**.
Once tried, never forgotten: a Mexican *piñata* is a papier-
mâché container shaped liked a ship, star, flower, fish, bird
or other animal. It is filled with small gifts – usually sweets,
fruit, nuts and small toys – then hung up for blindfolded
party guests to take turns at smashing with a stick. This
is surprisingly difficult to do, especially if wily parents
keep raising and lowering the *piñata*, thus tormenting the
over-excited children bent on destruction. Call this friendly
company, which sells them either pre-filled or for you to put
your own goodies in. Prices from £14.95.

The Non-Stop Party Shop
214-16 Kensington High Street, W8 (7937 7200).
High Street Kensington tube. **Open** 9.30am-6pm
Mon-Sat; 11am-5pm Sun. **Credit** AmEx, MC, V.
Map p314 A9.
As the name implies, this shop is all about having a good
time. Stock up on goodies from the year-round displays of
fireworks, wrapping paper, cards, helium balloons, party
hats, wigs, false noses, masks, streamers and more.

Oscar's Den
127-9 Abbey Road, NW6 (7328 6683/
www.oscarsden.com). Swiss Cottage tube/West
Hampstead tube/rail. **Open** 9.30am-5.30pm Mon-Sat;
10am-2pm Sun. **Credit** AmEx, MC, V.
Local celebs are known to get their party paraphernalia here,
and it's hardly surprising given the company's boast that it
can procure just about anything you want; you only need ask.
Everything is available, from entertainers, fireworks (year-
round), soft play areas, inflatables and ball ponds (from £40
plus VAT). Bouncy castles cost from £40 plus VAT and entertainers start at £125 for one hour, £150 for two. Worth a visit
for ideas alone, though you're bound to make a purchase.

Party Party
11 Southampton Road, NW5 (7267 9084/
www.partypartyuk.com). Chalk Farm tube/Gospel Oak rail.
Open 9.30am-5.30pm Mon-Sat. **Credit** MC, V.
Party Party is packed with bright ideas for children's and
teenage parties. Choose from Mexican *piñatas*, fancy dress
costumes (from £8.50 to £22.99), party bags, novelty cakes,
helium-filled balloons, paper plates, cake tins and party pop-
pers. Table and chair hire is available.

Party Superstore
268 Lavender Hill, SW11 (7924 3210/
www.partysuperstore.co.uk). **Open** 9am-6pm Mon-
Wed, Fri, Sat; 9am-7pm Thur; 10.30am-4.30pm Sun.
Credit AmEx, MC, V.
London's biggest party shop, with a whole floor devoted to
children's jollifications, including a huge range of decorated
balloons, napkins, paper plates, cups and tablecloths. All your
child's favourite celebrities, from Winnie the Pooh to the
Tweenies, Spiderman to Monsters Inc, are represented on the
paperware. Fancy dress costumes and fireworks are also sold.

Venues

All aboard

Golden Hinde
St Mary Overie Dock, Cathedral Street, SE1 (0870 011
8700/www.goldenhinde.co.uk). London Bridge tube/rail.
Credit MC, V. **Map** p320 P8.
Thankfully, the menu on board the 16th-century *Golden
Hinde* has changed slightly since days of hard tack biscuits,
maggoty meat and rancid water, and nowadays kids aged 4-
11 who come to a party here get to tuck into sandwiches,
crisps, sausage rolls and biscuits. Before tea comes the action
– a treasure hunt, games and tales of stormy seas with a costumed crew. All you need bring is the birthday cake. Parties
cost from £165 for 15 children, plus £9 for every extra guest
(maximum 35). Party bags can also be supplied. Rarely has
messing about been quite so educational. *See also p41.*

HMS Belfast
Morgan's Lane, Tooley Street, SE1 (7940 6328/
www.iwm.org.uk). London Bridge tube/rail. **Credit** MC, V.
Map p321 R8.
Entrance to the ship is free for children up to 16, so you could
organise a trip as part of your own party (for opening times
and admission, *see p42*), but for £5 per child you can have
the use of a room for the day, goody bags, quiz sheets, a baseball cap and a birthday card. For every five children one adult
goes free. If you want the catering staff to rig up a party tea
for the celebrations, the cost is £5 extra per child and for £100
you get the services of the ship's party organiser Captain
Corky for two hours – kids can climb in hammocks and dress
up in costume. Available for up to 26 children.

London Waterbus Company
*58 Camden Lock Place, NW1 (7482 2550). Camden
Town tube.* **No credit cards.**
Have your child's party on a canal boat going down the river
from Camden Lock or Little Venice (Warwick Avenue tube),
a perfect treat for a sunny summer birthday. You can hire the
boat during the day (£155 for the two-hour minimum); bring
your own refreshments, games, balloons, entertainer or whatever you like. The maximum number of children is about 20.
Alternatively, if you have a small number of people to entertain, you could just take the regular tour (50 minutes), with
return tickets costing £3.80 (children) or £5.80 (adults) and
break up the trip with a special picnic in Little Venice by the
playground. Combination tickets with London Zoo are also
available, ring for details. Note: services only run at weekends in winter. *See also p99.*

Cinemas

BFI London IMAX Cinema
*1 Charlie Chaplin Walk, South Bank, Waterloo, SE1
(7902 1234/group bookings 7960 3120/www.bfi.org.uk).
Waterloo tube/rail.* **Credit** AmEx, MC, V. **Map** p320 M8.
This is the ultimate film party trip. If you book in a party of
ten or more children, tickets cost £4.20 per child and £6.20
per adult. There are usually four or five screenings to choose
from, all are suitable for children. Films here usually last
about an hour. If you have sufficient funds, repair to the Film
Café (7960 3118) for tea. Staff here prepare party packages
for children aged 5-10. For £5.95 each child can tuck into
sausage rolls, mini pizzas, trifle, crisps, assorted sandwiches
and a carton of juice. *See also p39.*

Activities

Animal man

Nick Spellman must be a glutton for punishment. He works with both animals and children, employing the first to amuse and entertain the second. His show is deservedly popular, combining magical illusions with a varied chorus of exotic animals, including a barn owl, bird-eating spider, turtles, lizards, snakes, chinchillas and, most famously, Marky the meerkat.

Like many entertainers, Spellman grew up wanting to be an actor and served his time as a bluecoat at Pontin's before graduating to seaside panto star. But the slot he has now on the Playhouse Disney channel evolved out of his party act with animals, and it's clear he still really enjoys performing live for children.

There is, however, another side to Spellman's work: part of the income generated from his act is used to fund captive breeding programmes for endangered species, in conjunction with the naturalist Charles Mason. Indeed, it was Mason who first introduced Spellman to performing with animals as a teenager, suggesting to the young would-be thespian that although acting was fine, some gainful employment would have to be found for the periods when he was out of work. Spellman took to it like a, ahem, duck to water – even roping in his long-suffering mother to transport him and his delightful 11-foot python to parties when he was still too young to drive.

These days Spellman offers two different shows for age groups 4-7 and over-7s. Little ones are treated to his star turn – levitating the birthday boy or girl, often to the astonishment of all the adults present. Older children learn more about the animals and are allowed to handle them 'in a quiet and respectful way'. Spellman feels an important bonus for clients is the way party guests get a better understanding of the animals; many of them find that their irrational fears or prejudices are reduced when they see the animals up close.

In case you are wondering about the possibility of a spider escaping in your house, don't worry – this has never occurred, although Spellman says he does carry full public liability insurance. The worst that can happen, then, is that the meerkat pees on your rug and nobody sympathises – they'll all be laughing too hard.

The Nick Spellman Show

Impeyan Productions (01992 446211/ www.impeyan.co.uk). **Prices** £150-£280; phone for details. **No credit cards**.

Kids Club

Clapham Picture House, 76 Venn Street, SW4 (7627 7555/www.picturehouse-cinemas.co.uk). Clapham Common tube. **Credit** MC, V.
Kids Club parties take place in a specially decorated upstairs room at the Clapham Picture House. For £8 each, children get entry to the film at 11.45am, popcorn and a drink plus a goody bag following an hour of games with prizes. The birthday child also gets to visit the projection box and start the film. If you're after a special birthday treat, book at least two months in advance for a themed party with a specific film that the cinema will do its best to arrange (no Disney). There's no catering but parents are welcome to arrange their own. Adults pay £2 to see the film. *See also p219.*

Screen West

The New Boat House, 136-42 Bramley Road, W10 (7565 3030/bookings 7565 3102/www.screenwest.co.uk). Latimer Road tube. **Credit** MC, V.
A state-of-the-art preview cinema that offers an hour in an air-conditioned 74-seat screening room followed by an hour and a half in an adjoining function room (prices start at £280). Staff will try and source favourite films, or you can take along a video of your choice to watch instead. The function room is big enough for plenty of running around on a child-friendly wooden floor. Four large sofas, five tables, 20 chairs and a CD player are available and you can take in your own food and snacks. There's just one catch: you have to do the clearing up yourself.

Meet the animals

Aka Rampage/London Zoo
*London Zoo, Regent's Park, NW1 (7722 5909/
www.londonzoo.co.uk). Baker Street or Camden Town
tube then 274, C2 bus.* **No credit cards. Map** p316 G2.
There are more than 600 species, including invertebrates, reptiles, fish, birds, gorillas, tigers and bears, in this landmark
zoo (*see p92*), which makes a fab day out in itself if your
offspring are intent on bonding with wildlife. However, the
affiliated aka Rampage, a company that offers various children's activities here, can make a birthday visit extra special.
It runs two parties, both of which supplement zoo tours, food
and general party paraphernalia with extra activities: for £18
a head, the Doctor Squiggles puppet party for younger
children, which features a safari with 'the crazy cartoonist
explorer and his puppet friends', and for £19.50, an art activity party. Parties are held on Friday afternoons, Saturdays
and Sundays and there is a minimum of 15 and a maximum
of 25 children. Call for details of Easter and summer holiday
workshops for the over-5s (£130 per week plus VAT).

Battersea Park Children's Zoo
*Battersea Park, SW11 (zoo 7924 5826/Splodge 7350
1477). Sloane Square tube then 19, 137 bus/Battersea
Park or Queenstown Road rail.* **No credit cards.**
This splendid little zoo is home to some of the smallest monkeys in the world (marmosets), the loveable pot-bellied pig
Tum Tum, otters, reptiles and meerkats. Parties, run by the
Splodge (*see p236*) company, are held daily in a two-hour slot
between 10am and 5pm. (Although the zoo is closed to the
general public on weekdays in winter, it opens for these party
bookings, so the experience is quite special as children have
the run of the place.) There's lots of touchy-feely animal stuff
along with art activities, treasure hunts and puppet shows,
in tailored packages (from £200). The capacity is ten to 30
children. *See also p146.*

London Aquarium
*County Hall, Riverside Building, Westminster Bridge
Road, SE1 (7967 8000/children's tour enquiries 7967
8007/www.londonaquarium.co.uk). Westminster tube/
Waterloo tube/rail.* **Open** 10am-6pm (last entry 5pm)
daily. Phone for opening times during hols. **Credit** MC, V.
Map p319 M9.
Go wallow in waterworld at the aquarium if you have
between ten and 20 over-6s to entertain. The entrance fee is
£5.25 per child aged 3-14 (£8.75 for accompanying adults;
free for under-3s). The partygoers enjoy an hour-long tour of
the tanks, where friendly rays and snooty sharks wish them
many happy returns and the piranhas just look daggers.
After this, they have the opportunity to feed certain fish. This
is a privilege denied the average visitor. *See also p42.*

Nature Study Centre
*Wandsworth Common, Dorlcote Road, SW18 (8871
3863). Wandsworth Common rail.* **Open** 3-5pm Wed;
2.30-4.30pm 1st Sun of mth. **Admission** free; occasional
charge for activities. **No credit cards.**
This well equipped and spacious log cabin on the common is
a little-known centre of mini-beast safaris and environmental education. It may be hired for private parties and also doubles as a second venue for Splodge (*see p236*). A mini monster
party features puppet Desmond the Dragonfly and his fishy
friends, followed by tea, games and a nature treasure trail
outside, when guests use nets to catch their party gifts. The
package costs from £225 and may be substituted with any
other theme of your choice. *See also p147.*

Westway Stables
*20 Stable Way, W10 (8964 2140). Ladbroke Grove or
Latimer Road tube.* **Open** 9am-9pm Tue-Fri; 9am-5pm
Sat, Sun. **No credit cards.**
This place is party-heaven for the pony-mad, offering over-
5s gymkhana games in a newly refurbished arena, followed
by the chance to brush the ponies and plait their manes.
Novices can be led. There's a minimum number of six guests
required for the party package (maximum 20) at £35 each,
including food chosen from a range of menus. *See also p160.*

Museums

Museum of Childhood at Bethnal Green
*Cambridge Heath Road, E2 (8983 5200/recorded info
8980 2415/www.museumofchildhood.org.uk). Bethnal
Green tube/rail.*
Parties at the museum are informal and allow parents to cater
for the most finickity of tastebuds. The adults bring the food,
cake, drinks, paper plates, cups, tablecloth, music and entertainment and the museum supplies the party room, kitchen
facilities and cleaning up. There's also optional and exclusive
use of the soft play area. You can set up the party room from
1pm, with soft play available from 2.25pm. Throughout the
whole afternoon (until 5.50pm), the group has free access to
all the galleries, exhibitions, shop and other play areas (so it's
best if the food is left till later). Prices, for a maximum of 12
kids, are £50 for the party room and £30 for a 40-minute soft
play session. *See also p115.*

Science Museum
*Exhibition Road, SW7 (7942 4747/www.nmsi.ac.uk). South
Kensington tube.* **Credit** AmEx, MC, V. **Map** p315 D9.
There are no specific party facilities at the Science Museum,
but the thrilling prospect of staying up late and dossing down
within its hallowed portals makes the monthly science sleepovers a favourite birthday treat for children aged 8-11.
There's a minimum of five children (£25 each), plus one adult
(£20). Book early (three months ahead is usual). *See also p70.*

Playgrounds & games

Bramley's Big Adventure
*136 Bramley Road, W10 (8960 1515/
www.bramleysbig.co.uk). Latimer Road tube.* **Open** 10am-
6pm Mon-Fri; 10am-6.30pm Sat, Sun. Closed 25 Dec, 1 Jan,
Aug bank hol. **Credit** AmEx, MC, V.
An indoor adventure playground complete with slides, inflatable balls, monkey swings and much more, where 75 minutes
of play, a party meal, goody bags and balloons cost from £7
per child for ages 0-11 (£9.50 at weekends). Up to 40 children
can be seated in the party room; larger parties can hire the
whole playground. There are extras available, such as a 20-
minute visit by Bramley the Brontosaur (£12.50). There are
separate play areas for under-5s and a café for parents.

Clown Town
222 Green Lanes, N13 (8886 7520). Southgate tube.
Open 10am-7pm daily. **No credit cards.**
This immensely popular, somewhat steamy play centre has
a monkey treehouse, tarzan ropes, net climbs and ball ponds.
Supervised parties cost £7.50 per guest. Included in the price
are invites, an hour of play, a meal and a party bag per child.
There is a height limit of 4ft 9in, and a minimum of ten children in the week, 12 at weekends.

Activities

Glittering prizes at **Party Party**. *See p247.*

Coram's Fields

93 Guilford Street, WC1 (7837 6138). Russell Square tube. **Open** *9am-dusk daily.* **Admission** *free (adults admitted only if accompanied by child under 16).* **No credit cards. Map** p317 L4.

A famous, shady playground and a lovely place for a party. Coram's Fields has a paddling pool, sand pit, play equipment, sports areas and a small pets' corner with sheep, goats and rabbits. You can hire out a party room for £25 – the smaller room seats up to 60 – and there are kitchen facilities, so bring your own party food. *See also p59 and p60.*

Discovery Planet

Surrey Quays Shopping Centre, Redriff Road, SE16 (7237 2388/www.discovery-planet.co.uk). Surrey Quays tube. **Open** *10am-6pm Mon-Sat; 11am-5pm Sun.* **Credit** *(over £10) MC, V.*

This indoor adventure playground has kids all hot and sticky before cooling them off with ice-creams and fizz. Choose from bronze, silver or gold parties for a minimum of eight children (£5.99-£10.99 per head, significant discounts apply Monday-Thursday), which include your own party room and host. Gold and silver parties include Burger King food, soft drinks and ice-cream, plus goody bags. The gold gets you further extras, such as birthday cake and extra-large goody bags.

Kidzmania

28 Powell Road, E5 (8533 5556). Clapton rail. **Open** *10am-6.30pm daily.* **No credit cards.*

An indoor adventure playground with ball ponds, chutes, slides, ropes, bouncy things and climbing things. For £7.50 a child (in a group of ten to 40) you get 90 minutes of play followed by 40 minutes of scoff, with a host. Ages 1-12.

Namco Station

County Hall (riverfront entrance), Westminster Bridge Road, SE1 (7967 1066/www.namcostation.co.uk). Westminster tube/Waterloo tube/rail. **Open** *10am-midnight daily. Closed 25 Dec.* **Admission** *free.* **Map** p319 M9.

A potentially bank-breaking, but enduringly popular, option for a young dudes' party, this vast arena of sound and light is home to more than 200 video games and simulators, the fastest dodgems in Europe and a high-tech mini bowling alley. Games cost from 30p to £2. *See also p45.*

The Playhouse

The Old Gymnasium, Highbury Grove School, corner of Highbury Grove & Highbury New Park, N5 (7704 9424). Highbury & Islington tube/rail/4, 19, 236 bus. **Open** *10am-6pm Mon-Thur; 10am-7pm Fri-Sun.* **No credit cards.*

This indoor play centre with ball pond, climbing ropes, slides and so on is housed in a Victorian school building with lofty ceilings, natural light and extended seating area for adults. It's quite cheap, too: you pay £2.50 per child, plus £25 for the hire of an enclosed table with benches. The noisy fun goes on all around during your two-hour slot, or for £95 you can have exclusive use of the place (from 7pm to 9pm only). You do the catering or accept the usual junk food at £6.95 per head.

Snakes and Ladders

Syon Park, Brentford, Middx (8847 0946/ www.syonpark.co.uk). Gunnersbury tube then 237, 267 bus. **Open** *10am-6pm (last entry 5.15pm) daily.* **Credit** *MC, V.*

Hire of the party room at Snakes and Ladders, together with a host, 90 minutes on a play frame, party bags and invitations, is a popular party option. Prices per head are £9.65 with a hot meal, £8.65 for cold. *See also p167.*

Take in a show

Jackson's Lane

269A Archway Road, N6 (8340 5226/ www.jacksonslane.org.uk). Highgate tube. **Credit** *MC, V.*

There are three rooms for parties, available at weekends at a rate of £50 per room or £75 for two rooms for up to three hours. Party groups taking in a kids' show (11am and 2pm Saturday, for 3-8-year-olds) get £1 off the £4 tickets. Catering – of the pizza, chips, ice-cream variety – is done by the Jackson's Lane café, called Veggie House (8348 7666), for £3.50 a head. *See also p224.*

Lyric Hammersmith

King Street, W6 (8741 2311/www.lyric.co.uk). Hammersmith tube. **Open** *Enquiries 10am-7pm Mon-Sat.* **Tickets** *£7 adults; £5 under-16s, concessions.* **Credit** *AmEx, DC, MC, V.*

Children's shows aimed at 3-7-year-olds take place here at 11am and 1am on Saturdays. Young theatre-goers can make use of a dedicated no-smoking area and terrace next to the café to eat a hot or cold meal (£5.50/£4.50). *See also p225.*

Puppet Theatre Barge

opposite 35 Blomfield Road, Little Venice, W9 (07836 202745/www.puppetbarge.com). Warwick Avenue tube. **Credit** *MC, V.* **Map** p312 C4.

Waterborne puppet shows at weekends and daily during school holidays, usually at 3pm, cost £7 for adults and £6.50 for children and £50 for the hire of the space. Private performances can also be booked at other times at a rate of £295, including the chance to conduct a self-catered tea party afterwards. The barge is here from November to June; the rest of the year it tours the river to other locations such as Henley, Richmond and Marlow. *See also p228.*

▶ For more **theatre** and **workshop** venues, *see p222, p228 and p230*; for more **cinemas**, *see p219*; and for **restaurant** venues, *see p170*. Parties can also be held at many of the venues reviewed in **Sport** *(pp251-270).*

Sport & Leisure

London is a fit place for sports players and watchers of all ages.

The capital is home to dozens of sports at hundreds of venues, to suit all budgets. Whether you have the cash to finance your child's pony obsession, or are more inclined to take advantage of a free dip in an outdoor swimming pool, it's easy to get fit and active in London. The city is well served when it comes to instruction and courses designed for kids, with child-friendly facilities and qualified instructors.

Note that exact details of classes and opening times are given where possible, but it's still always best to phone to check such information first. For many classes and most courses you need to book in advance. Larger establishments accept at least Visa and MasterCard as methods of payment.

Participation Sports

Athletics

The high profile enjoyed by athletes like Denise Lewis, Dean Macey and Jonathan Edwards has pushed British athletics into the spotlight. Track and field is a vibrant sport at grass-roots level, too, with most clubs running a junior section for children aged 9 and over.

There are 18 different disciplines in athletics, and most children, no matter their physical dimensions, will find at least one they're good at.

If your kids are interested in honing their skills during the school holidays, get in touch with **Maureen Jones** (8224 7579/07956 807689), a senior UK athletics coach who organises regular courses during the Easter and summer holidays at tracks around London for children aged 8-15. Courses run from 10am until 3pm and cost £11 per day.

South of England Athletics Association
Suite 1, 23 Mitcham Lane, SW16 (8664 7244/ www.seaa.org.uk).
The SEAA has details of local clubs. There's also a comprehensive national directory at www.british-athletics.co.uk.
Belgrave Harriers *Contact Carl Lawton (8669 0971/ www.belgraveharriers.com).*
Ealing, Southall & Middlesex *Perivale Park Track, Stockdove Way, Greenford, Middx. South Greenford rail. Contact Alan Keeler (www.esm.org.uk).*
Herne Hill Harriers *Tooting Bec Track, Tooting Bec Road, SW17. Tooting Bec tube. Contact Steve Bosley (8687 0386/www.hernehillharriers.co.uk).*
Thames Valley Harriers *Linford Christie Stadium, Du Cane Road, W12. White City tube. Contact Kathy Davidson (01895 676513/ www.thamesvalleyharriers.com).*

Off track at **Herne Hill Stadium**. *See p255.*

Victoria Park Harriers *Victoria Park Track, St Mark's Gate, off Cadogan Terrace, E9. Hackney Wick rail. Contact Richard Newbold (7254 4546/ www.vph.org.uk).*
Woodford Green & Essex Ladies *Ashton Track, Chigwell Road, Woodford Bridge. Woodford tube. Contact Keith Hopson (8524 1959).*

Badminton & Squash

Both sports have excellent junior development programmes and most clubs welcome children on court. To find your nearest venue, contact the **Badminton Association of England** (01908 268400) or the **Squash Rackets Association** (01752 560900). The following all have junior squash classes; phone for prices and times.
Dulwich Sports Club *Burbage Road, SE21 (7274 1242). Herne Hill rail.*
New Grampian Squash Club *Shepherd's Bush Road, W6 (7603 4255). Hammersmith tube.*
Wimbledon Racquets & Fitness Club *Cranbrook Road, SW19 (8947 5806). Wimbledon tube/rail.*

Baseball & softball

These two sports have joined forces to create a single agency, **BaseballSoftballUK** (7453 7000). With the weight of America's Major League Baseball behind it, the organisation has put together impressive packages to teach the basics to children aged 6 upwards.

Windsor is already an established centre for junior baseball. Based at Windsor Boys School, the **Little League** run by the Windsor Bears club attracts some 500 players. Children aged from 6-9 are known as 'PeeWees'; they then move on to the 'Bronco' class until they're 12. Under-16s play in 'Pony' competitions. This progression has taken players right to the top: two of the current GB squad began playing with the Bears as 12-year-olds.

To find a club with junior teams, contact Geoff Ellingham (*see below*) or one of the following:

Essex Darts *Phil Chesterton (01376 551254).*
London Baseball Association
(www.londonsports.com).
London Meteorites Baseball & Softball
Geoff Ellingham (0870 238 2134).
South London Ravens *Robin Webb (8251 7050).*
Thames Valley Softball Club *John Middlemist (0118 962 8469/www.tvsoftball.com).*
Windsor Baseball & Softball *John Boyd (07769 655496).*

Basketball

Hoops has a cool image, whether you're watching (*see p269*) or playing, and London is a great place to learn how to dribble, slam and dunk. There are clubs all over the capital playing in local leagues, and the sport is extremely well organised at junior level, with competitions right up to national standard. To find your nearest, call the **English Basketball Association** (0113 236 1166).

Climbing

Most of the world's best climbers first discovered the delights of getting high when they were in their early teens, and London's indoor centres all cater for children aged around 8-plus with safe, structured sessions that are run by qualified instructors. To have a go, try one of the climbing centres below.

For general information on climbing, contact the **British Mountaineering Council** (0870 010 4878).

Castle Climbing Centre
See p253.

Mile End Climbing Wall
Haverfield Road, E3 (8980 0289/ www.mileendwall.org.uk). Mile End tube.
Open noon-9.30pm Mon-Thur; noon-9pm Fri;

10am-6pm Sat, Sun. **Admission** *Registration* £4, then £5.50/session. *Children's introduction* £6 Fri; £5 Sat, Sun. Located in a converted pipe-bending factory, the centre runs children's sessions every Friday evening and Saturday morning, as well as birthday parties (*see p239*) and a summer holiday programme. Booking for the Mile End Climbing Wall is essential.

Westway Climbing Complex
Westway Sports Centre, 1 Crowthorne Road, W10 (8969 0992). Latimer Road tube. **Open** 10.30am-10pm Mon-Fri; 10am-8pm Sat, Sun. **Prices** *Off-peak* £5; £3 children. *Peak* £6; £4 children; £2 sessions with instructors.
Spectacular new indoor climbing facilities to inspire the novice and challenge the very best have recently been unveiled at this community sports centre under the Westway. There are also more tennis courts than before, plus football pitches and, uniquely, a fives court. Phone for details of sessions and prices. For parties at the Westway Sports Centre, *see p239.*

Cricket

There may be a decline in cricket in state schools, but clubs all around the capital have stepped in to develop the game for boys and girls aged 7 and up. Many run junior sections, with 11-year-olds and under playing an adapted form of the game called 'Terrier Cricket', in which everyone gets an equal chance to bat, bowl and field. Safety is to the fore, with all under-16s required to wear a helmet when batting, wicket-keeping or fielding close to the wicket against a hard ball. Most clubs will provide this, along with the other essential protective equipment, until a youngster decides whether they want to play regularly.

Surrey County Cricket Club, based at the AMP Oval (*see p136*), has an enthusiastic programme designed to tempt under-16s into the sport, with summer courses, training facilities for schools and outreach projects. Under-16s can watch all Surrey's Championship games for free.

There are hundreds of clubs around London. To find your nearest, contact the relevant County Board office:

Essex *Tony Debenham (01245 252420).*
Hertfordshire *Derek Dredge (01707 658377).*
Kent *Paul Millman (01227 456886).*
Middlesex *David Holland (7266 1650).*
Surrey *Karen Meaney (7582 6660).*

London Community Cricket Association
PO Box 17, Wallington, Surrey SM6 8YA (8669 2177).
More than 400,000 people live in Islington, Hackney and Tower Hamlets, yet these boroughs have just two grass cricket pitches between them. The London Community Cricket Association was founded in 1984 and helps to promote the game in some of the most recreationally disadvantaged parts of the capital. The Association is also involved in developing cricket projects with inner-city schools and youth organisations.

Cycling

In Denmark, 60 per cent of children cycle to school. In the UK, a mere two per cent do. This feeble statistic, when combined with the fact that a cyclist is 12 times more likely to be killed or injured in the UK than in Denmark, raises questions about our attitude to both green transport policies and safety on the road.

In response, Safe Routes to Schools supports projects throughout the country that encourage children to cycle and walk to school by improving street design, calming traffic and linking with the 5,000-mile National Cycle Network, which opened in 2000. For more information, see the *Official Guide to the National Cycle Network* by Nick Cotton and John Grimshaw (Sustrans, £9.99). **Sustrans** is the pressure group working to create a safer environment for cycling: check out www.sustrans.org.uk. The **London Cycling Campaign** (7928 7220) acts as an umbrella organisation for local groups while working to create a cycle-friendly city.

By far the best guide to family rides around the capital is the *London Cycle Guide* (Haynes, £8.99), published in association with the London Cycling Campaign. The book contains 25 outings of varying difficulty, with maps and route planners.

Activities

Head for heights

Whatever your age, few sports are more instantly addictive than climbing. It demands a unique combination of physical and mental agility, which explains why reaching the top of a wall brings such enormous satisfaction. For some youngsters, a well-structured session with a nurturing instructor can help them overcome a fear of heights.

The **Castle Climbing Centre** in Manor House is an atmospheric Grade II-listed Victorian pumping station, originally designed to look like Scotland's Stirling Castle. But it's as if the folly was built with its future use in mind, since it offers a 120ft drop ideal for aspiring spiderboys and girls. The centre has its own children's club called the Geckos on Friday evenings and weekend mornings, and on midweek afternoons during school holidays. A two-hour session costs £16.

Teamwork, self-confidence, trust, motivation, increased levels of fitness and responsibility for others are among the benefits of climbing for kids, say staff at the Castle. The minimum age is 8 for unaccompanied children; if accompanied by a climbing adult, the children can be any age (the centre has harnesses for kids aged from about 4). A birthday party at the centre costs £100 for six children, with additional kids charged at £15 a head.

Castle Climbing Centre

Green Lanes, N4 (8211 7000/www.castle-climbing.co.uk). Manor House tube. **Open** 2-10pm Mon-Fri; 10am-7pm Sat, Sun. **Admission** *Registration* £4 (adults only). *Visits* £7.50; £3.50 children (accompanied by climbing adult/instructor).

Cycle Training

15B Dryden Court, Renfrew Road, SE11 (7564 5990/
www.cycletraining.co.uk). Elephant & Castle tube/rail.
Cost £25/1st hr (hr); £22/hr thereafter.
Established in 1998 to promote cycling and emphasise the
freedom it gives to riders of all ages, Cycle Training offers
tuition for everyone aged 5 and over. Older children who have
mastered riding the bike are given lessons in road safety and
assertive cycling.

Cycle sport

There are three main cycling venues in London, all
offering a range of activities for cyclists of every
age. **Herne Hill Stadium** (see p255) is the
capital's only purpose-built velodrome for racing.
Hillingdon is a tarmac track for racing and tuition.
Lee Valley Cycle Circuit has a tarmac track, a
mountain bike/BMX circuit and Saturday morning
sessions for children aged 4-16. All the above have
kids' clubs; phone the venues for details of times
and prices.
Hillingdon Cycle Circuit Springfield Road,
Hillingdon (Stewart Benstead, 8570 3230). Hayes
& Harlington rail.
Lee Valley Cycle Circuit Quarter Mile Lane, E15
(8534 6085/www.leevalleypark.com). Leyton tube.

Dance

A useful resource is the **London Dance Network**
(www.londondance.com), which has an extensive
directory of dance venues and organisations.
    The following centres around town offer a range
of dance classes for children; phone for details. For
details of dance workshops, see p228.
Chisenhale Dance Space 64-84 Chisenhale Road,
E3 (8981 6617/www.chisenhaledancespace.co.uk).
Mile End tube.
Danceworks 16 Balderton Street, W1 (7629 6183/
www.danceworks.co.uk). Bond Street tube.
Map p316 G6.
Drill Hall 16 Chenies Street, WC1 (7307 5060/
www.drillhall.co.uk). Goodge Street tube.
Map p317 K5.
Greenwich Dance Agency Borough Hall, Royal Hill,
SE10 (8293 9741). Greenwich rail.
The Place 17 Duke's Road, WC1 (7387 7669/
www.theplace.org.uk). Euston or King's Cross tube/rail.
Map p317 K3.
Ravenscourt Theatre School 30-40 Dalling Road,
W6 (8741 0707). Hammersmith tube.
Rona Hart School of Dance Rosslyn Hall, Willoughby
Road, NW3 (7435 7073). Hampstead tube.
Tricycle Theatre 269 Kilburn High Road, NW6
(7328 1000). Kilburn tube.

Dance techniques

Some children love the formality and rigidity of
ballet, but many more prefer the freedom of the
following, more unusual, techniques:

Biodanza The facets of Biodanza emphasised in children's
classes (for 6-year-olds upwards) are vitality, creativity and
'affectivity' (the capacity to care for and relate to each
other). Marita Sanguinetti (7485 2369) runs occasional
Biodanza courses for children in Camden and Hampstead.
Call her to be put on the mailing list for her next course.
Capoeira The dynamic leaps, cartwheels and
handstands of this exciting Brazilian martial art-cum-
dance help to develop agility, flexibility, self-expression
and freedom. Youngsters from the age of 8 can take part
in classes, which are held on Saturdays at the Place (see
above); and for 8-12-year-olds at 4.30pm on Fridays at the
Art of Health & Yoga Centre (see p267).
Chantraine Described as a 'development of the whole
person', Chantraine was created in France more than 40
years ago. No formal training is needed to take part and
its free-spirited approach is ideal for children. There are
two centres in the London area; classes are for children
aged from 4 and take place every day in central London
(ring Patricia Woodall, 7435 4247) and Wanstead (Kate
Green, 8989 8604).

Disability sport

A number of organisations have responsibilities in
this area, which, as the success of the Paralympic
movement and personalities like Tanni Grey-
Thompson have shown, is finally being given
the recognition and funding it deserves.
    An interesting development is between Wimbledon
Football Club, the Limbless Association and the
One2One Ability Counts programme operated by
the English Federation of Disability Sport. The
partnership provides regular training sessions
with qualified coaches and opportunities to play
in tournaments, plus free kit and match tickets.
Training takes place every week at the **Furzedown
Recreation Centre**, Ramsdale Road, SW17, and
the junior squad welcomes players aged 7-14. For
more details, phone 8767 6542.
    In addition to the organisations listed below, the
following offer sports programmes: **British Blind
Sport** (01926 424247); **British Deaf Sports
Council** (01943 850214); **English Sports
Association for People with Learning
Disabilities** (01924 267555); **Limbless
Association** (8788 1777).

British Wheelchair Sports Foundation

01296 395995/www.britishwheelchairsports.org.
This is the umbrella body for 17 wheelchair sports, from
archery to rugby. It organises a number of major events each
year at the National Wheelchair Sports Centre in Stoke
Mandeville in Buckinghamshire, provides a comprehensive
information service and is currently developing regional
sports camps for disabled children aged 6-plus.

English Federation of Disability Sport

0161 247 5294/www.efds.co.uk.
This is the umbrella organisation for disability sport. Its local
office is the London Sports Forum for Disabled People (7354
8666/textphone 7354 9554/www.londonsportsforum.org.uk).

Football

Football dominates the sporting scene in this country – and with good reason. At the top level, it's a billion-pound industry, with 13 professional clubs in London. Lower down the pyramid, more than 45,000 clubs in the country cater for all standards and ages, and both sexes.

Finding a club

Most local newspapers have a column of classified ads placed by clubs looking for players. When helping your child to find a team to play for, make sure that he/she is of the appropriate standard.

Also ask about:

● Whether the club coaches hold FA qualifications. If possible, watch a session to see how well organised it is.

● The number of children in each age group. Some clubs have large memberships, which may mean only the best get to play regularly.

● The atmosphere and ethos: is it a club where winning is all that matters, or is 'sport for all' the priority? Are parents and supporters encouraged to lend a hand, and is their contribution valued?

To find a girls' team, contact the **Football Association** (01707 651840) or Ann Mason, secretary of the **Greater London Women's League** (8977 3658). Fulham, which is the country's first professional women's team, runs an extensive girls' development programme: details from Natalia Lodge (8336 7481).

Coaching

All the professional clubs in London run 'Football in the Community' coaching courses, fun days and skills clinics. These are suitable for boys and girls of all standards aged from about 6 upwards. They usually take place within the club's immediate locality and are staffed by FA-qualified coaches. Phone for details and dates (for addresses, *see p269*): **Arsenal** (7704 4140); **Brentford** (8758 9430); **Charlton Athletic** (8850 2866); **Chelsea** (7385 5545); **Crystal Palace** (8768 6000); **Fulham** (7384 4759); **Leyton Orient** (8556 5973); **Millwall** (7740 0503); **Queen's Park Rangers** (8740 2509); **Tottenham Hotspur** (8365 5000); **Watford** (01923 440449); **West Ham United** (8548 2707); **Wimbledon** (8785 3155).

Similar schemes operate through the County FAs. Call the following offices for details: **Essex** (01245 357727); **Hertfordshire** (01462 677622); **Kent** (01634 843824); **London** (8690 9626); **Middlesex** (8424 8524); **Surrey** (01372 373543).

On your bike

Despite the optimistic daubing of cycle lanes all over the tarmac, London's congested streets are not pleasant cycleways. Many parents would rather strap their couch potato children into the people carrier than have them risk their necks out there in the rush hour. The result? Bikes stay in the shed year-round and children forget what their legs are for. Keen pedallers, therefore, love purpose-built, car-free cycle tracks, and the one at Herne Hill Stadium is one of the best.

The stadium was first opened in 1892 for all those Victorian pedal pushers. During World War II, it was used as a barrage balloon station by the RAF. Its finest hour was when it hosted the cycling events of the 1948 Olympics. Its next great moment came in 1992, when its well-used track was redeveloped and modernised. It now has a magnificent 450-metre banked, oval, all-weather concrete track, which cyclists say is the fastest in the country. If the children prefer a bit of dirt to chin-down speeding, there's a new mountain bike track for dramatic bunny hopping and berm-riding without bailing (these are all cycling terms). Pedal Posse mountain bike camps run in the school holidays, along with cycling proficiency and skills courses. A programme of wider sports activities includes football (Arsenal and Millwall are just two of the League clubs that run football training courses for children on the grass pitch). Ring for details of sports events.

Herne Hill Stadium
Burbage Road, SE24 (7737 4647). Herne Hill rail.

Finally, there are plenty of commercial football clinics to choose from, some of which dangle the promise of visits from Premiership stars. An **Ian St John Soccer Camp** (0151 707 9300), for example, costs £65 for five days (10am-3.45pm) and caters for children aged 8-15, who all receive a goody bag.

Golf

Too many golfers still want their clubhouses to be a refuge from children (and, in some cases, women) for the sport to offer a uniformly warm welcome to would-be juvenile thwackers. But youngsters – and those who care about the future of golf – should take heart because the **English Golf Union** (01526 354500) has developed 'Tri-Golf' for 6-12-year-olds and is aiming to introduce the game to 3,000 primary schools by the end of 2002.

Activities

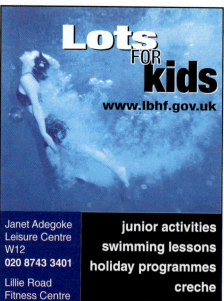

The Golf School

Regent's Park, NW1 (7724 0643). Baker Street tube/Marylebone tube/rail. **Open** 8am-9pm daily. **Map** p316 G2.

Staff at the Golf School welcome children who are 'old enough to take instruction' (in the past the coaches have taught golf-mad kids as young as 5). The membership fee for juniors is £30; the Saturday afternoon clinic for young golfers costs £5 per hour (note that you must book in advance). Club hire is £1.

Gymnastics & trampolining

Although still dominated at elite level by Eastern Europe, British competitive gymnastics is steadily improving. It's a lovely sport both to watch and take part in, which explains why the governing body, the **British Amateur Gymnastics Association** (01952 820330), has around 100,000 members.

En garde!

If you're seeking a sport with real cut and thrust, why not have a go at fencing? It's physically demanding, very skilful and a cool alternative for children who don't enjoy team games. What's more, it offers instant gratification. Unlike, say, cricket or rugby, where an inability to hit the ball or make a tackle can leave some kids shivering on the sidelines, anyone can don a mask and quickly learn to deliver a good thwack.

Dashing tales of the *Three Musketeers* have given the sport a glamorous and sophisticated image that it retains to this day. You can begin learning it young, too: at the Finchley Foil Fencing Club, youngsters aged 8-16 turn up every Saturday afternoon for two hours of enthusiastic swishing.

Three types of sword are used in the sport. The foil is the oldest, a flexible weapon with which only thrusts using the point of the blade to the trunk of an opponent are valid. The sabre is a lighter version. Hits are made by 'cutting' with the edge or 'thrusting' with the point to any part of the body above the waist. The épée is a development of the duelling rapier, and you can hit with the point to any part of the body, arms, legs and head. Experts reckon this is as close as safety will permit to a real sword fight. Most junior classes comprise warm-up activities to develop co-ordination, flexibility and balance, formal work towards the nine fencing grades, and finally the bit that everyone enjoys best: free fighting. The sport has a strong safety ethic, and no one is ever allowed to participate without full protective clothing, a mask and the supervision of a qualified instructor.

For details of clubs and regional organisers around London, contact the British Fencing Association (8742 3032; www.britishfencing.com). Here's a selection that offer regular junior sessions:

Egham Fencing Club

Egham Sports Centre, Vicarage Road, Egham, Surrey (Terry Albano, 01784 243518). Egham rail.

Finchley Foil Fencing Club

Christ's College, East End Road, N2 (Clare Halsted, 7485 1498). East Finchley tube.

Haverstock Fencing Club

Haverstock School, Haverstock Hill, NW1 (7267 0975). Belsize Park tube.

King's College School & Wimbledon High School Joint Fencing Club

Southside Common, SW19 (8255 5300). Wimbledon tube/rail.

Kingston Fencing Club

Beverley School, Blakes Lane, New Malden, Surrey (Karen Vinson, 8943 2157). Motspur Park rail.

Richmond & Twickenham Fencing Club

Clifden Centre, Clifden Road, Twickenham, Middx (Nick Mort, 8892 0692). Twickenham rail.

Salle Paul Fencing Club

Highgate School, The Old Gym, Hampstead Road, N6 (Tony Coton, 8640 4702). Highgate tube.

Streatham Fencing Club

Dunraven Lower School, Mount Nod Road, SW16 (Roger Barnes, 8677 6207). Streatham Hill rail.

Activities

Through its clubs and schools, sessions for 4-year-olds and under are based around soft play equipment and simple games. After that, there's a series of proficiency awards. As well as a general scheme for boys and girls, there are separate awards for rhythmic gymnastics and sports acrobatics. The **British Trampoline Federation** (01952 820330) offers a similar structure.

In response to the issue of how and when to teach small children using adult equipment, Bill Cosgrove, a former national gymnastics coach, created **TumbleTots** and, later, **Gymbabes** and **Gymbobs**. Gymbabes is for babies from 6 months to the crawling stage, TumbleTots is for walkers, and Gymbobs from school age up to 7. For details of centres around the country, call 0121 585 7003 or see www.tumbletots.com.

The following clubs offer a range of age-appropriate activities, most offering trampolining as well. Both sports are available at many public sports centres.

Avondale Gymnastics Club *Hollyfield Road, Surbiton, Surrey (8399 3386). Surbiton rail.*

Enfield Girls Gymnastics Club *Aylward School, Silver Street, N18 (8807 4736). Silver Street rail.*

Hillingdon School of Gymnastics *Victoria Road, South Ruislip, Middx (8841 6666). South Ruislip tube.*

Islington Gym Club, Arts & Media School *Turle Road, N4 (8983 6799). Finsbury Park tube/rail.*

North-East London Gymnastics Club *Carpenters & Dockland Centre, 98 Gibbins Road, E15 (8534 4151). Stratford tube/rail/DLR.*

Plumstead Leisure Centre *Speranza Street, SE18 (8855 8289). Plumstead rail.*

Redbridge School of Gymnastics *Pulteney Road, E18 (8530 3810). South Woodford tube.*

Richmond Gymnastics Centre *Townmead Road, Kew, Surrey (8878 8682). Kew Gardens rail.*

Ice skating

London's ice rinks offer an ideal combination of free skating, formal instruction and discos, where children can strut their stuff and show off the skills they've learned in classes. Session times vary from day to day as the ice needs regular refreezing and sweeping, but venues are generally open from 10am until 10pm. The prices below include skate hire.

For more information about the sport, contact the **National Ice Skating Association** (0115 853 3100).

Alexandra Palace Ice Rink
Alexandra Palace Way, N22 (8365 4386). Wood Green tube/Alexandra Palace rail/W3 bus. **Open** 11am-1.30pm, 2-5pm Mon-Thur; 11am-1.30pm, 2-5.30pm, 8.30-11pm Fri; 10.30am-12.30pm, 2-4.30pm, 8.30-11pm Sat, Sun. **Admission** Mon-Fri £4.20; £3.50 under-15s; Sat, Sun £5.50; £4.50 under-15s. Fri, Sat evening £5.50/person.
A six-week course of lessons at this international-size rink costs from £44. For parties at the centre, *see p238.*

Broadgate Ice Arena
Broadgate Circle, Eldon Street, EC2 (7505 4068/ www.broadgateestates.co.uk). Liverpool Street tube/rail. **Open** *Late Oct-Apr* noon-2.30pm, 3.30-6pm Mon-Thur; noon-2.30pm, 3.30-6pm,6-10pm Fri; 11am-1pm, 2-4pm, 5-8pm Sat; 2-4pm, 5-7pm Sun **Admission** £7; £4 under-16s. **Map** p321 Q5.
This tiny outdoor rink is a wonderful discovery amid the high-tech offices of the City. *See also p51.*

Lee Valley Ice Centre
Lea Bridge Road, E10 (8533 3154). Clapton rail. **Open** noon-4pm Mon; noon-4pm, 6.30-9pm Tue, Wed; noon-4pm, 8.30-10.30pm Thur; noon-4pm, 8.30-11pm Fri, Sat; noon-4pm, 7-9.30pm Sun. **Admission** Mon-Thur £5.70 adult, £4.70 under-15s; Fri-Sun £5.90 adult, £4.90 under-15s.
The disco nights are popular at this large, well-maintained rink, but because it's hard to get here by public transport, it's never too busy. Rink management says Lee Valley has high-quality ice (it certainly feels hard enough when you land on it) and the warmest skating environment in the UK.

Leisurebox
First Bowl, 17 Queensway, W2 (7229 0172). Bayswater or Queensway tube. **Open** 10am-1.45pm, 2-4.45pm, 5-6.45pm, 8-10.45pm Mon-Thur; 10am-1.45pm, 2-4.45pm, 5-6.45pm, 7.30-10.45pm Fri, Sat; 10am-1.45pm, 2-4.45pm, 5-6.45pm, 8-10pm Sun. **Admission** £6; £6.50 after 7.30pm Fri, Sat. **Map** 312 C7.
Once known as Queens, this is the most famous rink in London, where countless top skaters have learned their moves before becoming famous. The disco nights with DJs on Fridays and Saturdays are legendary, but beginners and families are also well looked after.

Michael Sobell Leisure Centre
Hornsey Road, N7 (7609 2166/www.aquaterra.org). Finsbury Park tube/rail. **Open** 10.30am-2pm Sat; 10.30am-4pm Sun. **Classes** *Beginners* 6.45-8pm Mon. *After school* term time 4-5.30pm Wed, Fri. *Parent & Toddlers* term time 1-2pm Mon. *Beat on Ice* 7.30-10pm Wed, Fri; 7.30-9.30pm Sun. **Admission** £3/person; £2.70 parent & toddler session.
Children from 4 upwards are welcome at this small rink, which runs popular after-school sessions. A six-week course of lessons costs £29. For parties at the centre, *see also p239.*

Somerset House
Strand, WC2 (7845 4600/www.somerset-house.org.uk). Covent Garden, Holborn or Temple tube (closed Sun). **Open** 10am-6pm daily; extended opening hours for courtyard and terrace. Closed 25 Dec. **Tours** phone for details. **Admission** *Courtyard & terrace* free. **Skating** phone for prices. **Credit** *Shop* MC, V. **Map** p319 M7.
Every December (ring for the exact date), the beautiful courtyard here is iced over to become the most attractive rink in London. It's a limited skating season, however, as the ice is melted usually by mid January. It is hoped the area of ice will be bigger in winter 2002, to fit in more keen skaters.

Streatham Ice Rink
386 Streatham High Road, SW16 (8769 7771/ www.streathamicearena.co.uk). Streatham rail. **Open** 10am-4pm, 4.15-7pm, 7.30-10pm Mon-Fri; 10.30am-5pm, 5.30-7.30pm, 8-11pm Sat; 10.30am-5pm Sun. **Admission** £6.80; £5.50 under-12s; £2.50 under-4s.
Another of London's best-known rinks, where a six-week course of lessons costs £39 for adults, £30 for children and £23 for 'toddlers' aged up to 4.

Somerset House ice rink. *See p258.*

Karting

Many of the world's top Formula One racers discovered life in the fast lane as children on a kart circuit. Kids love it as they zip around in their little buggies. Safety is always uppermost, however. Drivers receive a full briefing before they begin and anyone disobeying the marshals is removed from the track. The venues listed below welcome children and can be booked for exciting, if expensive, parties; some of the others are more geared towards the corporate market. Phone for more details – some tracks have a minimum age or height limit. All the following provide the necessary safety gear including helmet and gloves.

Daytona Raceway
Atlas Road, NW10 (8961 3616/www.daytona.co.uk). North Acton tube. **Open** *9am-10pm daily.*
Children aged 8-13 can enjoy ten-minute trials for £15 on Sunday mornings. Over-13s are eligible to race with adults: £20 for a 15-minute practice session, while the standard entry fee for a meeting starts at £40. Booking is essential for the Junior Club on the first and third Sunday of the month. Parties can also be held here. This track is indoors; the branch at Milton Keynes (01908 695694) is outdoors.

F1 City
Gate 119, Connaught Bridge, Royal Victoria Dock, E16 (7476 5678). Royal Albert DLR. **Open** *(LP)* 10am-6pm daily. **Admission** from £20/person.
This go-kart track is the widest in London (beginners will be pleased to hear) and 800m in length. Children (only those who meet the height requirement of 5ft 2in) are given their own track times during which to play. The Cadet Club is the place to learn how to kart safely, with the assistance of the F1 City racing team. Phone for details of sessions.

Playscape Pro Racing
390 Streatham High Road, SW16 (8677 8677/ www.playscape.co.uk). Streatham rail. **Open** 10am-10pm daily. *Children's practice* 10am-5pm Mon-Fri. **Admission** £42.50/2hrs adults. *Test sessions* from £20 per 30min session/person.
The raceway can be booked for children's parties (aged 8-plus) or for half-hour taster sessions. Those who become addicted can find out about the Playscape Cadet School, a founder member of the RAC's Association of Racing Kart Schools. The school operates on the first and third Saturday of each month (9.30am-12.30pm) and students are put through their paces before gaining an RAC racing licence.

Martial arts

Most local sports centres will be home to at least one martial arts club; others are based in church halls and community centres. Look for evidence of a lively but disciplined atmosphere, with well-organised and age-appropriate teaching. Ask the instructor about his/her qualifications, and for proof of insurance cover. However, few community facilities extend their insurance to the instructors who rent them.

For more information, contact the **Amateur Martial Association** (07973 507716). The association can give details of your nearest classes. The **National College of Martial Arts** (7278 5608) offers various classes for children, with the emphasis on self-discipline rather than combat.

Call the following for information on classes.

Academy Health & Fitness Centre
16 Hoxton Square, N1 (7729 5789/www.bobbreen.co.uk). Old Street tube/rail.
Kung fu is an ancient art that the Chinese regard as part of the historical tapestry of their lives. This excellent centre offers Saturday morning classes for children aged 7 upwards.

The Budokwai
4 Gilston Road, SW10 (7370 1000). Gloucester Road tube. **Map** p314 C12.
This is one of Britain's premier martial arts clubs, offering judo tuition for children aged 6-12.

Hwarang Academy
(07740 192336/www.hwarangacademy.com). Sunday Club: The Armoury, 25 Pond Street, NW3. Belsize Park tube. Tuesday Club: St Saviour's Hall, Eton Road, NW3. Chalk Farm tube.
The Korean martial art of tae kwondo is now an Olympic sport, and youngsters aged 8-18 can learn its spectacular kicks on Sunday afternoons (3-4pm beginners and tinies; 3.30-4.30pm juniors aged 10 and over) and Tuesday evenings (4.30-5.30pm juniors).

School of Japanese Karate (Shotokan International)
Various venues (8368 6249).
Karate is the most popular Japanese martial art in this country. There are no holds or grappling, just strikes and kicks. David and Lilian Alleyn, who run this well-established and highly respected school, teach children aged from 5. Call the above number to find out about venues.

Netball

For those who enjoy its combination of speed, skill and sleight of hand, London is a strong netball area with plenty of clubs around the capital – most running junior sections for girls aged 11 and up. To find your nearest, contact the **All-England Netball Association** (01462 442344).

Orienteering

For many adults, orienteering is like tackling the *Times* crossword while out on a run. The aim is to navigate around a course, which can vary in length from two to 12km, moving from one control point to the next using a specially drawn map. For children, though, orienteering is all about hidden targets and adventure. Few sports are more family-friendly, and it's a great way to make country walks fun. Some of the permanent courses are suitable for buggies, while many events include a special route for very young children with or without mum and dad, where a line of string takes them round a set of controls marked by the likes of Postman Pat or Rupert Bear.

London's permanent courses offer an excellent introduction to the sport. There are 45 around the city, some in remarkably urban locations. A leaflet giving a complete list of courses is available from the **British Orienteering Federation**, 'Riversdale', Dale Road North, Darley Dale, Matlock, Derbyshire DE4 2HX (01629 734042).

For details of events held regularly around London, contact the **South Eastern Orienteering Association** (8948 6056).

Riding

London has a surprisingly large number of riding schools. The following are by no means all of them, just our favourites. They are all BHS (British Horse Society) approved.

Some schools run 'Own a Pony' days and weeks, which involve some lucky rider's parents paying about £40 (for a day) or over £100 (for a week) for the privilege of looking after their favourite pony in the school: mucking out, grooming, feeding and watering, exercising and schooling. Riding is usually included. Many places also offer birthday party packages, based around a ride and a party tea with equine friends looking on. Many also have facilities for disabled riders.

Riding lessons and hacks must all be booked in advance: ask the management whether its run 'taster' sessions for new young riders. Riders, whatever their age, should always wear a hard hat (establishments can usually lend one if you don't have your own, sometimes for a small fee) and boots with a small heel, not trainers or gumboots. Your bottom will thank you for wearing sturdy jeans or jodhpurs.

Most rates below are for children and per hour.

Aldersbrook Riding School
Empress Avenue, E12 (8530 4648). Manor Park rail/ Wanstead tube. **Lessons** from £14.
Aldersbrook is a small, friendly riding school with a countryside feel to it. There are eight ponies and four horses working here. Lessons take place in an outdoor manège, hacking on Wanstead Flats.

Ealing Riding School
Gunnersbury Avenue, W5 (8992 3808). Ealing Common tube. **Lessons** £17.
This riding school has a benevolent attitude towards children. Riders aged from 5 can take part in many activities, including the occasional gymkhana. Lessons are held in an outdoor manège.

Hyde Park & Kensington Stables
Hyde Park Stables, 63 Bathurst Mews, W2 (7723 2813/ www.hydeparkstables.com). Lancaster Gate tube. **Lessons** *Individual* £35 Mon-Fri; £39 Sat, Sun. *Course of 10* from £280. **Map** p313 D6.

Clissold Park
Home to the Hackney wing of the City Tennis Club, whose mission it is to make the game accessible to young inner-London players. *See p107.*

Highbury Fields
As used by the excellent Islington Tennis Centre, another invaluable City Tennis Club. *See p106.*

Hyde Park
A smart tennis club for adults and children. *See p66.*

Paddington Recreation Ground
Lively after-school tennis sessions and summer camps. *See p159.*

Regent's Park
Great location; great tuition. *See p266.*

Wimbledon Park
OK, it's not the Wimbledon, but still an ace place for school holiday tennis. *See p153.*

Children aged from 5 can enjoy an hour-long instruction of patient, streetwise ponies in the glamorous surroundings of Hyde Park. All rides must be booked in advance.
Branch: Kensington Stables 11 Elvaston Mews, SW7 (7589 2299).

Lee Valley Riding Centre
Lea Bridge Road, Leyton, E10 (8556 2629). Clapton rail/ 48, 55, 56 bus. **Lessons** £15.50 4-6.30pm Mon-Fri, all day Sat, Sun. £9 beginners 30mins Sat, Sun.
Local children love to help at this well-appointed riding school, where 28 extremely placid horses and ponies enjoy the breezy open spaces of Walthamstow Marshes. During hot weather some hacking out is available to regulars.

London Equestrian Centre
Lullington Garth, N12 (8349 1345). Mill Hill East tube. **Lessons** from £18.
This busy yard in North Finchley has 30 assorted horses and ponies; some are delightfully placid and deservedly popular with local children (minimum age 4). There's a junior members club for regulars, who may be able to take part in occasional informal gymkhanas. There's a restaurant on site.

Ross Nye's
8 Bathurst Mews, W2 (7262 3791). Lancaster Gate tube. **Lessons** £30; £25 Pony Club members. *Pony Club Membership* £30/yr. **Map** p313 D6.
If your kids are serious about ponies, it makes sense to join the Hyde Park branch of the Pony Club, as membership gives many privileges, such as reduced prices (ten lessons for £250 or £25 each); newsletters, and the chance for members to do their Pony Club achievement tests at the centre. Children aged from 6 can learn to ride here (instructional rides take place in Hyde Park). Club members can join in on good-value Pony Club Days in the Christmas holidays (£30/day) and take part in week-long pony camps in the stables' Surrey farm.

Activities

Lidos of the gang

Outdoor swimming pools, or lidos, always seem to be under threat of closure. London is blessed with a number of quite beautiful lidos, many of which date from the 1930s, when all public baths meant goosepimples and blue lips. People must've been tougher then. Nowadays, the pools only attract a crowd during a heatwave, which means the last few summers have been lean times for many. Note that Hampstead Ponds, where you really can enjoy the Iris Murdoch experience of swimming at one with nature, are only suitable for strong swimmers.

Charlton Lido

Hornfair Park, Shooters Hill Road (corner of Charlton Park Lane), SE18 (8856 7180). Charlton or Kidbrooke rail. **Open** *May-Sept 10.30am-6pm daily.* **Admission** *£2.50; £1.60 children; £5.70 family.*
South-east London's other lido is not as glamorous as the Evian one (*see below*), but is still a godsend on a hot day. Its 2-foot-deep children's pool is wonderful for very young kids.

Evian Lido

Dulwich Road, SE24 (7274 3088/www.thelido.co.uk). Herne Hill rail. **Open** *May 10am-7pm Sat, Sun. June-Sept 6.45am-10am Mon-Fri; 10am-6pm Sat,* Sun. **Admission** *6.45-10am £2.50; £2 concessions, £1.50 under-16s. 10am-7pm £4-£5; £3 under-16s; free under-5s.*
With Evian as its sponsor (you can't miss the logo on the pool bottom), this wonderful 1930s lido will hopefully stay open. As well as the swimming pool, there are paddling pools and sunbathing terraces, though these, naturally, have an uncomfortable lack of shade. Phone for details of activities.

Finchley Lido

High Road, N12 (8343 9830). West Finchley tube. **Open** *May-Sept 9am-9.30pm Mon-Fri; 9am-4.30pm Sat, Sun.* **Admission** *£2.80; £1.60 5-17s; free under-5s.*
There are two indoor pools here, as well as the outdoor pool and terrace.

Hampstead Heath Swimming Ponds

(7485 4491). Men's & women's ponds, Millfield Lane, N6. Gospel Oak rail. Mixed pond, East Heath Road, NW3. Hampstead Heath rail. **Open** *7am-dusk daily, all year round.* **Admission** *free.*
Children need to be aged 8-plus, able to swim at least 25 metres and accompanied by an adult in the water. Note that the authorities close the pool in times of ice and algal bloom, so call first.

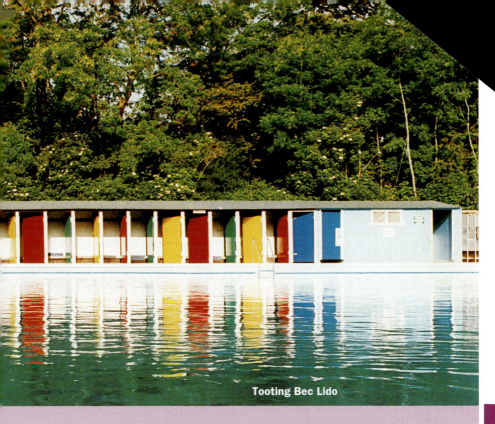
Tooting Bec Lido

Oasis Sports Centre

32 Endell Street, WC2 (7831 1804). Covent Garden tube. **Open** *7.30am-8.30pm Mon-Wed; 7.30am-8pm Thur; 9.30am-5pm Sat, Sun.* **Map** *p317 L6.*
The 28-metre outdoor pool is open all year round and used by hardy office workers. In the summer, less hardy types emerge, so the pool is packed at lunchtime in hot weather. There's also an indoor pool if it gets too cold or crowded. Call for details of prices.

Park Road Pools

Park Road, N8 (8341 3567). Hornsey or Alexandra Palace rail then bus W7. **Open** *Lido* May-Sept 11am-7pm (last entry 6.30pm) daily. *Indoor pools* 7am-7.30pm Mon, Fri; 7am-8pm Tue-Thur; 7.15am-7.30pm Sat; 7.15am-4.30pm Sun. **Admission** *Lido* £4.20; £2.70 concessions; £2.10 3-15s. *Indoor pools* £3; £1.25 concessions; £1.40 3-15s. Free under-3s.
Outdoors, on sunny days, it's difficult to find a patch of grass to put your towel down at Park Road Pools. The water in the outdoor pool is heated, which means that swimming in the rain is an almost attractive option.

Parliament Hill Lido

Gordon House Road, NW3 (7485 3873). Gospel Oak rail. **Open** *Sept-Feb* 7am-10.30am daily. *May-Sept* 7-9am, 10am-6pm daily. Closed for maintenance early spring (phone for details). **Admission** £3.50; £1.50 children.
A lovely 1930s lido, teeming on hot days.

Richmond Pools on the Park

Old Deer Park, Twickenham Road, Richmond, Surrey (8940 0561). Richmond tube/rail. **Open** *Mar-Sept* 6.30am-7.45pm Mon; 6.30am-9pm Tue, Thur, Fri; 6.30am-9.30pm Wed; 8am-6pm Sat; 7am-6pm Sun. **Admission** £3.50; £2.50 5-16s; free under-5s.
A 33-metre indoor pool and the same size outside, plus a sunbathing area.

Tooting Bec Lido

Tooting Bec Road, SW17 (8871 7198). Tooting Bec tube/Streatham rail. **Open** *Late May-Sept* 10am-8pm daily. *Oct-May* closed except for club members. **Admission** £2.60-£3.10; £2.10-£2.25 5-15s; free under-5s. **Membership** £15; £80 season ticket for members.
At 94 metres by 25 metres, this is the second largest open-air pool in Europe. Popular in summer.

...ing School

...row Weald, Middx (8954 3618).
...e rail. **Lessons** from £15.
...res of rolling Harrow Weald for horses
...chool is an important local social centre,
...é and a separate junior riding school.

Willowtree Riding Establishment
The Stables, Ronver Road, SE12 (8857 6438). Grove Park or Lee rail. **Lessons** from £7.70/30mins.
Captain the one-eyed Shetland is great for small children to learn to ride on at this friendly local riding school. This is the only riding school we know of that has enchanting pure-bred Arab ponies in its riding school stock.

Wimbledon Village Stables
24A/B High Street, SW19 (8946 8579/ www.wvstables.com). Wimbledon tube/rail. **Lessons** from £25.
Wimbledon's riding club (phone for membership details) allows children all sorts of perks to feed their pony habit: gymkhanas, newsletters, special events. Riding is on Wimbledon Common.

Rugby union

Most rugby union clubs have a junior section, playing 'mini rugby' on Sunday mornings in front of hordes of screaming parents. In the younger age groups – some clubs take children as young as 6 – the aim is to encourage handling, passing and running, with tackling outlawed. Female rugby has made rapid progress in recent years, and there are more than 100 girls' teams in this country, feeding in to a well-established network of women's clubs.

The governing bodies, **Rugby Football Union** (8892 2000) and **Rugby Football Union for Women** (8831 7478), can direct you towards a club offering junior rugby, although you only need turn to the sports pages of a local newspaper to find out what's available. The RFU for Women website (www.rfu-women.co.uk) also has interesting material on future plans.

Skateboarding

Although the names of stunts like hot-dogging, double deckers and hanging tens may not mean much to most parents, there's no denying skateboarding's popularity with the kids. On the one hand, the sport has retained its cool and radical edge, with children still skating for free at traditional haunts like the South Bank, Shell Centre and beneath the Westway. On the other, there's **PlayStation Skate Park** (_see also p160_), which runs classes for beginners and is reckoned to be one of the best skateparks in Europe, with superb ramps, vert and street course. Have a look at its website at www.roadrunner.co.uk/pssp.

Skiing & snowboarding

There's nothing quite like the feel of proper snow, but a few practice turns on a dry slope make excellent preparation for the real thing. Gloves, long sleeves and trousers are compulsory as the surface can deliver a nasty burn should you fall. Also note that if you're thinking of taking a mixed-ability group out for an open recreational session, perhaps as a birthday party activity, the minimum requirement is to be able to perform a controlled snowplough turn and use the ski lift.

The feel of real snow can be yours from winter 2002 at the former Beckton Alpine Centre in east London, whose old slope and mogul field is currently being converted into a snow dome (with the genuine cold stuff).

For more information, both about Beckton and skiing in general, contact the **Ski Club of Great Britain** (8410 2000).

Bromley Ski Centre
Sandy Lane, St Paul's Cray, Orpington, Kent (01689 876812). St Mary Cray rail. **Open** noon-10pm Mon-Thur; 10am-10pm Fri; 9am-6pm Sat; 10am-6pm Sun.
Three lifts serve the 120m slope with mogul field and nursery slope. Skiing and snowboarding taster sessions cost £12 and £13 respectively. Booking is a must.

Sandown Sports Club
More Lane, Esher, Surrey (01372 467132/ www.sandownsports.co.uk). Esher rail. **Open** 10am-10pm Mon-Fri; 1-8pm Sat.
The 120m main slope, 80m nursery area and 90m snowboarding slope are closed during horse racing meetings. Tuition is available for 7-year-olds upwards, although special half-hour lessons can be arranged for children as young as 4. You can do taster sessions if you're unsure. Call for details of the Junior Ski Club. Advance booking a must.

Swimming

Most local authority pools run lessons for children aged from around 3 upwards, plus parent and baby sessions to develop water confidence from as young as three months. However, these can be over-subscribed and have long waiting lists. Ask at your local pool for a timetable and booking details.

When children are past the lesson stage, joining a club is the best way to improve, meet like-minded friends and, perhaps, swim competitively. Again, look on the noticeboards, ask at your local pool or contact the **Amateur Swimming Association** (01509 618700).

Dolphin Swimming Club
University of London, Malet Street, WC1 (8349 1844). Goodge Street tube. **Classes** 9.15am-2.45pm Sat.
Admission £209 for 11 individual 30min lessons; £67.10 for 11 30min small-group sessions (max 5 per group).

Islington Tennis Centre. *See p266.*

There are some children whose fear of the water needs more specialised help than even a caring parent can provide. The Dolphin Swimming Club teaches aquaphobic youngsters (and adults) to overcome their fear. Ring for details.

Swimming pools

Most swimming pools are 25 metre-long rectangles. We haven't the space to list them all in this guide, but the pools below are a bit special. Please note that opening times and admission prices change seasonally. Ring to check times and prices before you visit. For outdoor swimming, *see pp262-3.*

Barnet Copthall Pools
Great North Way, NW4 (8457 9900). Mill Hill East tube. **Open** 6.45am-8am, 9am-9.30pm Mon-Fri; 9am-4.30pm Sat, Sun. **Admission** £2.80; £1.60 5-17s; free under-5s.
Three pools and a diving area, with coaching and clubs.

Brentford Fountain Leisure Centre
658 Chiswick High Road, Brentford, Middx (8994 6901). Gunnersbury tube. **Open** 9am-7pm Mon; 10am-9.45pm Tue; noon-6pm Wed; 10am-8pm Thur; noon-9pm Fri; 9am-5.30pm Sat, Sun. **Admission** £3.20; £1.30 5-11s; £1.50 12-17s; free under-5s.
Leisure pool with 40m aquaslide, underwater lighting and wave machine alongside a conventional teaching pool.

Crystal Palace National Sports Centre
Ledrington Road, SE19 (8778 0131/diving courses 8659 4561). Crystal Palace rail. **Open** 8am-5pm Mon-Wed, Fri; noon-7pm Thur; 10am-7.45pm Sat; 10am-1pm, 2-5.45pm Sun. **Admission** £2.35; £1.30 3-16s; free under-3s.
One of London's two 50m Olympic-size pools, plus fabulous diving facilities.

Goresbrook Leisure Centre
Ripple Road, Becontree, Essex (8593 3570). Becontree tube. **Open** 12.15-10pm Mon; 9am-6.30pm Tue; 9am-12.15pm, 1.15-8.30pm Wed; 10am-10pm Fri; 10am-4pm Sat; 9am-6.30pm Sun. **Admission** £3.30; £1.75 3-16s; free under-3s.
Fountains, cascades and a 60m flume.

Gurnell Leisure Centre
Ruislip Road East, W13 (8998 3241). Perivale tube. **Open** 7am-7pm Mon, Fri; 7am-9pm Tue-Thur; 8am-4.45pm Sat, Sun. **Admission** £2.75; £1.55 5-16s; free under-5s.
The capital's other 50m Olympic-size pool.

Ironmonger Row Baths
Ironmonger Row, EC1 (7253 4011). Old Street tube/rail. **Open** 6.30am-9pm Mon; 6.30am-8pm Tue-Thur; 6.30am-7pm Fri; noon-6pm Sat; noon-5pm Sun. **Admission** £2.80; £1.20 3-16s; £7.50 family (2+2), or £6 (2+1); free under-3s.
Take a trip back in time at this 1930s 30m pool and Turkish baths (one of only three remaining in London).

Latchmere Leisure Centre
Burns Road, SW11 (7207 8004). Clapham Junction rail. **Open** 7am-9.30pm Mon, Wed, Sat, Sun; 7am-7pm Tue; 7am-7.30pm Thur; 7am-8pm Fri. **Admission** £2.95; £2.05 5-16s; free under-5s.
Lane swimming main pool, teaching pool and a beach area with palm trees. The main pool shelves on a shallow slope, and the wave machine springs into action on the hour.

Leyton Leisure Lagoon
763 High Road, E10 (8558 4860). Walthamstow Central tube/rail. **Open** 7am-10pm Mon-Fri; 8am-6pm Sat, Sun. **Admission** *Peak* £3.50, £1.55 5-15s; free under-5s. *Off-peak* £2.25; 70p 5-15s; free under-5s.
Flume, slides, fountains, rapids and cascades in a tropical island setting.

Northolt Swimarama
Eastcote Lane North, Northolt, Middx (8422 1176). Northolt tube. **Open** 7am-7pm Mon, Fri; 7am-10pm Tue; 9am-10pm Wed; 7am-7.30pm Thur; 8am-4pm Sat, Sun. **Admission** £2.60; £1.45 5-15s; free under-5s.
Three pools, a 60m slide and diving boards.

Pavilion Leisure Centre
Kentish Way, Bromley, Kent (8313 9911). Bromley South rail. **Open** 11am-2pm, 4-7pm Mon-Thur; 10am-7pm Fri; 8am-9pm Sat, Sun. **Admission** *Peak* £3.30; £2.10 3-18s; free under-3s. *Off-peak* £2.80; £1.85 3-18s; free under-3s.
Large leisure pool with gentle shallows, flumes and a wave machine at weekends (plus a separate toddlers' pool).

Activities

...entre
...30 5522). Victoria
...30am-8pm Tue;
...Sat, Sun. **Admission**
...p318 J10.
...rate diving area in this
...hoolchildren.

...entre
...Woolwich Arsenal rail.
...ri; 9am-5pm Sat, Sun.
...ree under-3s.
Three pools, a ~~...~~ slide, five-lane multi-slide,
waves, jets and a water 'volcano.

Wavelength Leisure Centre
Giffin Street, SE8 (8694 1134). Deptford rail. **Open**
session times change regularly, ring for details.
Admission £2.80; £1.45 5-16s; free under-5s.
Flumes, waves, wild water and cannons.

York Hall Leisure Centre
Old Ford Road, E2 (8980 2243). Bethnal Green tube/rail.
Open 7.15am-8.30pm Mon, Sat; 7.15am-9.30pm Tue,
Thur; 7.15am-5.30pm Wed, Fri; 7.15am-3.45pm Sun.
Admission £2.35; £1.05 3-16s; free under-3s.
Built as a bath house in the 1920s and still housing Turkish
and Russian baths, the 33m main pool and separate children's
pool here provide real East End character.

Water polo

'Aquagoal' is a version of this fast and furious
game with amended rules for 10-year-olds upwards.
Like handball, the aim is to score goals in your
opponent's net – but without touching the side or
bottom of the pool. It's a great challenge, then,
for good swimmers. Contact the **Amateur
Swimming Association** (01509 618700) for
general information about the sport or check out
the website: www.swimming.org. The **National
Water Polo League** website (www.nwpl.co.uk)
has useful club contacts.

Tennis

Public courts offer easy access at cheap prices,
but may be of poor quality and lack a coaching
programme. Private clubs, on the other hand,
require the commitment of an annual fee, which
can be anything from £10 to £500-plus per person.
But for families who plan to play the game together
or want access to qualified instruction for a young
beginner, they're often worth it. Look for a club
that values children rather than sees them as an
inconvenience: are times set aside for kids to play
casually? Is equipment available for first-timers?
If not, go elsewhere.

Most London boroughs run holiday courses
at Easter and in the summer: contact your local
sports development team or nearest public library
for the latest details.

Lawn Tennis Association *7381 7000.*
The LTA's information department publishes free, comprehensive county guides giving contacts for hundreds of
private clubs and public courts listed by borough, and the
name and address of the County Development Officer. Details
of tennis holidays are also available.
David Lloyd Leisure *0870 888 3015.*
Phone for your nearest venue.
Islington Tennis Centre *Market Road, N7 (7700
1370/www.aquaterra.org). Caledonian Road tube.*
Redbridge Sports Centre *Forest Road, Barkingside
(8498 1026). Fairlop tube.*
Regent's Park Tennis Centre *York Bridge Road,
NW1 (7486 4216/www.rptc.co.uk).*
Individual coaching can be arranged through contacting one
of the centre's coaches; prices from £8 per session.
Westway Tennis Centre *1 Crowthorne Road, W10
(8969 0992/www.westwaysportscentre.com). Latimer
Road tube.*

Tenpin bowling

'Bowling is for everyone, from the age of 4 to 84,'
says the **British Tenpin Bowling Association**.
A trip to a local centre makes for a fun (and
relatively cheap) birthday party or family day out.
Computerised scoring has made the game less
complicated – but for youngsters keen to progress
towards the magical 'perfect score' of 300, there's a
network of regional and national youth tournaments
and leagues (for more information, contact the
association on 8478 1745).

All the centres listed here are open seven days a
week, typically from 10am to 11pm. Admission
prices vary according to the time of day, but average
around £3 per game, with the hire of soft-soled
bowling shoes £1 extra. Phone for details of parties.
Acton Super Bowl *Royale Leisure Park, Western
Avenue, W3 (8896 0707). Park Royal tube.*
Airport Bowl *Bath Road, Harlington, Middx (8759
1396). Hatton Cross tube.*
GX Superbowl *15-17 Alpine Way, E6 (7511 4440).
Beckton DLR.*
Harrow Super Bowl *Pinner Road, North Harrow,
Middx (8863 3491). North Harrow tube.*
Hollywood Bowl Finchley *Leisure Way, High Road,
N12 (8446 6667). Woodside Park tube.*
Leisurebox *First Bowl, 17 Queensway, W2 (7229
0172). Bayswater tube.* **Map** p312 C7.
Lewisham Bowl *11-29 Belmont Hill, SE13 (8318
9691). Lewisham rail/DLR.*
Rowans Bowl *10 Stroud Green Road, N4 (8800 1950).
Finsbury Park tube/rail.*
Streatham Megabowl *142 Streatham Hill, SW2
(8678 6007/www.megabowl.co.uk). Streatham Hill rail.*

Volleyball

Though it's a minor sport in this country, volleyball
is great fun to play for children aged 9 upwards.
Many clubs around the capital run junior teams,
with 9-14-year-old beginners playing three-a-side

Activities

'mini volley' on a badminton-sized court with a lower net. To find your nearest club, contact **London Volleyball Association** development officer Gary Beckford (8539 5276/07904 586359) or see www.whiteeaglesvc.org.uk/london, a website in association with the White Eagles Volleyball Club based in Balham (contact David Jenkinson on 8715 7358 for further details on the team).

Watersports

London has more than 430 acres of briny in Docklands, plus numerous reservoirs and the vast natural resource of the Thames. Some of the best watersports venues in Europe are accessible by tube. Many are very family-friendly (most cater for ages 8 and over) – indeed, watersports are ideal activities for parents and children to enjoy together. Phone for details of courses and sessions at the following clubs and you'll be gratified to learn how affordable a hobby sailing can be.

The **Welsh Harp**, or Brent, Reservoir, is one of the busiest London venues for sailing, windsurfing and canoeing. A number of London clubs run their courses on this 70-acre expanse of water, which is also a nature reserve. The **Welsh Harp Sailing Association** can be contacted on 8205 1240. The only licensed activity centre to use the reservoir is the **Youth Sailing Base**, which runs sailing courses for school groups, as well as child-friendly weekend activities. Contact it on 8202 6672.

The **Royal Yachting Association** (023 8062 7400) operates a Young Sailors' scheme, and its website, at www.rya.org.uk, lists numerous training courses. **Capital Sailing** (07050 223817) has details of RYA courses and marine activities around London. There's a vast online resource at www.uksail.com.

Amateur Rowing Association Ltd *6 Lower Mall, W6 (8748 3632/www.ara-rowing.org).*
The governing body of rowing has over 600 clubs affiliated to it. It also endorses a scheme called Go-Row, run by the National Junior Rowing Programme, which aims to encourage more junior members to its ranks. Clubs that have the Go-Row seal of approval have been deemed friendly, safe and suitable for junior rowing activities. To find out about a Go-Row scheme in your area, check the website.
Broadwater Sailing Club *Moorhall Road, Harefield, Middx (info 01494 436314). Denham rail.*
A very family-friendly club based at Broadwater Lake, close to the Grand Union Canal. Casual sailing is available every day, and there's an annual 'junior fun week'. Phone for details of prices.
BTYC Sailsports *Birchen Grove, NW9 (8731 8083/www.btycsailsports.org.uk). Neasden or Wembley Park tube/83, 182, 245, 297, 302, N98 bus.*
Among its members, the initials stand for Better Than Your Club, although they really date from the 1950s, when private companies had their own sailing interests. This one started life as the British Transport Yacht Club, before becoming a public club years ago. The initials stuck, however. Dinghy-

Catching the bug

Madonna and other celebrities may have transformed yoga from a pursuit viewed as hippie-ish and retrospective into an everyday recreation, but parents across the capital are also beginning to see its potential as a family pursuit. Yoga Bugs™ classes, held at the **Art of Health & Yoga Centre**, are designed to inspire children to use their imagination while teaching them how to maintain their natural physical flexibility and to relax their body. Participants – both children and adults – find the classes gently stimulating yet relaxing.

Fenella Lindsell and Vicky Oliver run regular teacher training sessions at the centre and there are already more than 100 Yoga Bugs™ teachers giving classes in over 20 London schools. If you're keen to get your children exploring their stretching potential, you needn't wait long: Baby Music classes at the centre are a gentle introduction to the world of music through songs, rhythm, stories, movement and musical instruments.

The therapeutic aspect of yoga is also being developed at the **Yoga Therapy Centre**, which runs weekly classes for children with asthma and other medical needs.

Art of Health & Yoga Centre
280 Balham High Road, SW17 (8682 1800/ www.artofhealth.co.uk). Tooting Bec tube.

Yoga Therapy Centre
Royal London Homeopathic Hospital, 60 Great Ormond Street, WC1 (7419 7195). Holborn tube. **Map** p317 L5.

racing, windsurfing, basic training and Royal Yachting Association courses are offered to BTYC members. Family membership is available.
Capital Rowing Centre *(07973 314199).*
This is a rowing school, where adults and children can receive expert tuition before going off and joining a club. Groups and school parties are also catered for.
Docklands Sailing & Watersports Centre *Millwall Dock, 235A Westferry Road, E14 (7537 2626/ www.dswc.org). Crossharbour DLR.*
Kids (aged from 8) and adults can choose from canoeing to dragonboat racing, windsurfing and dingy sailing. All levels are catered for, although youngsters are required to be confident in the water before they have a go at anything: give the centre a call prior to visiting. The Dock has a restaurant and bar, plus facilities and sailing courses for the disabled.
Lea Rowing Club *Spring Hill, E5 (8806 3097). Stamford Hill or South Tottenham rail.*
Rowing and sculling for all young people aged from 10 who can swim at least 50m. The Lea also runs intensive school holiday rowing courses.
Lee Valley Watersports Centre *Banbury Reservoir, Harbet Road, E4 (8531 1129). Angel Road rail.*
Sailing courses, plus canoeing and waterskiing, on 94 acres of water for 8-year-olds upwards.

Activities

Westminster Boating Base

London Corinthian Sailing Club *Linden House,
Upper Mall, W6 (8748 3280/www.lcsc.org.uk).
Hammersmith tube.*
Dinghy sailing courses for beginners.
Royal Victoria Dock Watersports Centre *Gate 5,
Tidal Basin Road, off Silvertown Way, E16 (7511 2326).
Royal Victoria DLR.*
The Royal Victoria Dock Watersports Centre offers low-cost
summer sailing, canoeing and rowing for children aged from
8 years and up.
Shadwell Basin Project *Glamis Road, E1 (7481
4210). Shadwell DLR.*
Downriver from Tower Bridge and run on a voluntary basis,
this multi-activity centre offers affordable summer sailing,
canoeing and dragonboat racing. The Shadwell Basin
Project takes children aged 9 and over.
Surrey Docks Watersports Centre *Greenland Dock,
Rope Street, SE16 (7237 4009). Surrey Quays tube.*
Sailing, windsurfing and canoeing for 8-year-olds upwards
takes place in the sheltered dock throughout the school
holidays and half-terms. Children take part in the Royal
Yachting Association's structured sailing courses, which
require three days to complete. Once the juniors have their
certificates, they take part in Thursday and Friday
'Splashday' events.
Westminster Boating Base *136 Grosvenor Road,
SW1 (7821 7389). Pimlico tube.*
Right in the heart of London, the Westminster Boating
Base is a charitable training centre that offers low-cost sail-
ing and canoeing on the tidal Thames for children aged 10
and over.

Yoga

Just as yoga is booming among adults, so
imaginative teachers are exploring its potential
for children. Though often characterised as an
inward-looking pursuit, it's actually an expressive
art that uses the whole body. *See also p267.*
Holistic Health *64 Broadway Market, E8 (7275
8434/www.holistic-health-hackney.co.uk). Cambridge
Heath rail.*
This centre runs the Yoga Babes class (age 3-6) on
Thursdays, 4-4.30pm.
Iyengar Institute *223A Randolph Avenue, W9 (7624
3080/www.iyi.org.uk). Maida Vale tube.*
Ring the Iyengar Institute for an information pack on
classes and courses.
Sivananda Yoga Vedanta Centre *51 Felsham Road,
SW12 (8780 0160/www.sivanandayoga.org/london).
Putney rail.*
Children's classes are held at the Sivananda Yoga Vedanta
Centre from noon to 1.30pm on Sundays. Here, admission is
by donation.
Triyoga *6 Erskine Road, NW3 (7483 3344/
www.triyoga.co.uk). Camden Town or Chalk Farm
tube/31 bus.*
Europe's largest dedicated yoga centre runs children's
clubs for 6-10-year-olds and 11-plus, costing £5. Children's
classes are held from 4pm Monday and Wednesday; ring
Triyoga for details.

Spectator Sports

Football continues to be the sport children most want to watch. However, almost all Premiership matches are now off-limits to the casual spectator – it's club members and season-ticket holders only (and even they're not guaranteed a seat). Other sports are far more accessible and just as exciting, especially if you go as a group for a party treat.

Basketball

London Towers
Crystal Palace National Sports Centre, Ledrington Road, SE19 (8776 7755/www.london-towers.co.uk). Crystal Palace rail. **Admission** £8; £6 under-16s.
The Towers are not only the best team in Britain, they're among the leading clubs in the whole of the Northern Hemisphere and compete in the Euroleague just to prove it. There's a game most weeks from October to April and the atmosphere is loud, street-cool and very family-friendly.

Cricket

Both these grounds stage at least one Test match each summer. Tickets for these games require advance booking (unlike county matches, where you can pay on the gate) and information is usually released during the preceding winter. Call or check the websites for details.

Middlesex
Lord's, St John's Wood Road, NW8 (7289 1300/ www.middlesexccc.com). St John's Wood tube. **Admission** £9-£10; £4.50-£5 6-16s; free under-6s.
Middlesex are in the Second Division of both the County Championship and National League, and going through lean times. That said, Lord's is a magnificent venue to watch a game and any child interested in cricket will be thrilled to attend. The season runs from mid April to mid September.

Surrey
AMP Oval, SE11 (7582 7764/www.surreyccc.co.uk). Oval tube. **Admission** £7-£10; free under-17s if accompanied by adult; if unaccompanied, £10 membership/yr charge.
The Oval is an excellent ground with fewer airs and graces than Lord's. What's more, Surrey are the best in the country in the County Championship (though less of a force in Division Two of the National League). Their team is crammed with internationals, although the likes of Alec Stewart and Graham Thorpe turn out for their county only rarely. For information on youth cricket activities and courses ring 7820 5719/5762.

Football

Any mad-keen young football fan will enjoy being given 'membership' of the team they support. But if that team plays in the Premiership, it certainly doesn't mean a steady supply of match tickets. A top club may have three or four times as many members

as the capacity of its ground, while the likes of Arsenal even have a waiting list for season tickets. In the Nationwide League, it's far easier to get in to games. Indeed, lower-division clubs positively encourage youngsters and families with cheap tickets and special deals: at Leyton Orient, a children's season ticket costs just £40, less than £2 a match. Listed below are London's big-league noises. At the time of going to press, Millwall were hoping to win a place in the Premiership, while Brentford had their sights fixed on Division One. Ticket prices and membership packages are too numerous to list for each club: call for details or check out the website. As a rule, a seat at a Premiership match will cost £25-£30 for an adult, half that for children, with a discount for club members. Nationwide League prices are around £15-£25, again with reductions for children and club members. The season runs from August to May.

FA Carling Premiership

Arsenal *Arsenal Stadium, Avenell Road, N5 (7413 3366/www.arsenal.co.uk). Arsenal tube.*
Charlton Athletic *The Valley, Floyd Road, SE7 (8333 4010/www.cafc.co.uk). Charlton rail.*
Chelsea *Stamford Bridge, Fulham Road, SW6 (7386 7799/www.chelseafc.co.uk). Fulham Broadway tube.* **Map** p314 B13.
Fulham *(7893 8383/www.fulhamfc.co.uk).* Playing at Queen's Park Rangers' grounds for the next two seasons.
Tottenham Hotspur *White Hart Lane, High Road, N17 (08700 112222/www.spurs.co.uk). White Hart Lane rail.*
West Ham United *Boleyn Ground, Green Street, E13 (8548 2700/www.westhamunited.co.uk). Upton Park tube.*

Nationwide League

Brentford *Griffin Park, Braemar Road, Brentford, Middx (8847 2511/www.brentfordfc.co.uk). Brentford rail.*
Crystal Palace *Selhurst Park, Park Road, SE25 (8771 8841/www.cpfc.co.uk). Selhurst rail.*
Leyton Orient *Matchroom Stadium, Brisbane Road, E10 (8926 1111/www.leytonorient.com). Leyton tube.*
Millwall *The Den, Zampa Road, SE16 (7231 9999/ www.millwallfc.co.uk). South Bermondsey rail.*
Queen's Park Rangers *Rangers Stadium, South Africa Road, W12 (8740 2575/www.qpr.co.uk). White City tube.*
Watford *Vicarage Road, Watford, Herts (01923 496010/www.watfordfc.com). Watford High Street rail.*
Wimbledon *Selhurst Park, Park Road, SE25 (7413 3388/www.wimbledon-fc.co.uk). Selhurst rail.*
'The Dons' currently share Crystal Palace's ground.

Horse racing

Although the image of exotic headgear perpetuated by Royal Ascot might suggest that a day at the races is an entirely adult activity, all 59 courses around the UK offer a warm welcome to children too. Admission for under-16s is free at the majority of

Activities

meetings, and most racecourses stage special 'family days'. Children love the hubbub of the parade ring where the magnificent thoroughbreds can be seen at close quarters, and there are plenty of places to eat and drink – or you could take a picnic.

The Racecourse Association publishes an excellent free guide, *Come Racing*, available by calling 01344 625912. The RCA website at www.comeracing.co.uk has details of (and links to) all the British courses, a full calendar and previews of major meetings.

Admission prices stated below are for adults attending regular meetings; children go free.

Ascot *High Street, Ascot, Berks (01344 622211/ www.ascot.co.uk). Ascot rail.* **Admission** £5-£15.
Epsom Downs *Racecourse Paddock, Epsom, Surrey (01372 726311/www.epsomderby.co.uk). Epsom Downs rail.* **Admission** £5-£16.
Kempton Park *Staines Road East, Sunbury-on-Thames, Surrey (01932 782292/www.kempton.co.uk). Kempton Park rail.* **Admission** £6-£17.
Lingfield Park *Racecourse Road, Lingfield, Surrey (01342 834800/www.lingfield-racecourse.co.uk). Lingfield rail.* **Admission** £12-£15.
Sandown Park *Portsmouth Road, Esher, Surrey (01372 463072/www.sandown.co.uk). Esher rail.* **Admission** £5-£17.
Windsor *Maidenhead Road, Windsor, Berks (0870 220 0024/www.windsor-racecourse.co.uk). Windsor & Eton Riverside rail.* **Admission** £5-£16.

Ice hockey

London Knights
London Arena, Limeharbour, E14 (7538 1212/ www.knightice.co.uk). Crossharbour DLR. **Admission** £12-£18; £7 under-14s.
British ice hockey has enjoyed a resurgence in recent years, and the Knights have certainly played their part. Match night at London Arena is an upbeat, family-oriented affair, with plenty of rough, tough action to relish. Children love it. The season runs from September to April.

Rugby league

London Broncos
Griffin Park, Braemar Road, Brentford, Essex (8853 8800/www.londonbroncos.co.uk). Brentford rail. **Admission** £10-£15; £4-£6 under-16s.
The Broncos are still determined to prove that rugby league can succeed outside its northern heartland, although it's a tough task to win over the southerners. Still, the club tries hard and there's always a host of family-oriented entertainment to enjoy if the action in the Tetley's Bitter Super League fails to inspire. The season runs from March to October.

Rugby union

While England continue to dominate the international oval-ball scene in this part of the world, the club game finds it harder to make ends meet. The move to professionalism has brought ongoing financial problems, as exemplified by the half-empty grounds for most matches. Nevertheless, the three top London clubs all have a slew of internationals in their line-ups, and a trip to a match is an absolute bargain compared to football. The season runs from September to May and admission is about £10-£25 for adults, £2-£10 for children.

Harlequins *Stoop Memorial Ground, Langhorn Drive, Twickenham, Middx (0870 887 0230/www.quins.co.uk). Twickenham rail.*
London Wasps *Rangers Stadium, South Africa Road, W12 (8740 2545/www.wasps.co.uk). White City tube.*
Saracens *Vicarage Road, Watford, Herts (01923 475222/www.saracens.com). Watford High Street rail.*

Twickenham Stadium
Rugby Road, Twickenham, Middx (8892 2000/ www.rfu.com). Twickenham rail.
This superb ground plays host to England international matches and a full programme of club, county and representative games. While tickets for the Six Nations Championship (held Feb-Apr) are almost impossible to obtain unless you're a member of a rugby club, the others are more accessible and also less expensive.

Bangers & crash

Expect more pile-ups around Plough Lane on a typical Sunday night than occur in an entire year on the M25. That's because the racing at **Wimbledon Stadium** is a mere sideshow to this most basic form of gladiatorial entertainment – what really matters are the crashes.

Bangers are the final stop on the highway for vehicles that were once someone's pride and joy but failed to squeak through the last MOT. Contact is not only legal, it's actually encouraged – leading to some spectacular collisions as soon as the green flag drops. Stock car racing is also a contact sport, although the motors are protected by plenty of exterior ironwork. They're

no less exciting than the bangers, it's just that there isn't as much loose metal hanging off...

And what happens to the cars after these shunts, scrapes and acts of premeditated mechanical violence? They all end up the same way in a no-holds-barred demolition derby.

Wimbledon Stadium
Plough Lane, SW17 (8946 8000/ www.spedeworth.co.uk). Wimbledon Park tube. **Admission** £10; £5 5-15s; free under-5s.
The season runs from August through to May. Meetings held around twice a month – phone for more details.

Activities

Days Out

...y confines of the M25 ...r than the hills and valleys of the Home Counties. The treasures they hold are numerous, so we've listed our favourite day trips from the Smoke, including seaside resorts, ancient monuments, farms, zoos, country parks and those child magnets – theme parks. They're all great places to picnic, so bring a packed lunch with you.

None of the places listed below is more than a two-hour train ride from the capital. If you want to find out about more attractions, visit the website, or the offices, of the Britain Visitor Centre (1 Regent Street, SW1, www.visitbritain.com). For opening hours for personal callers to the offices, *see p299*.

TICKETS & INFORMATION

For main entries in this chapter we include details of opening times and admission prices, but be aware that these can change without notice. If you're planning a trip around one particular sight, always phone first to check that it's open. Most places have informative websites for events and special dates.

Though we've given basic directions for sights (the nearest rail station, and which motorway and junction you should take if you're coming by car; most sights are signposted from there on), it's always best to check on a detailed map first when coming by car. Better still, work out your route with the Automobile Association (AA), whose routeplanner service is available on www.theaa.co.uk. The Royal Automobile Association (RAC) also has one, available on www.rac.co.uk. Likewise, to check train times and get details for national rail enquiries, call 08457 484950 or visit www.nationalrail.co.uk. The website has a journey-planning facility that is particularly helpful.

As coach travel becomes increasingly comfortable and reliable, National Express at London Victoria (08705 808080, www.gobycoach.com) is worth considering for trips out of town.

Castles

The castles below are the most family-friendly ones we know.

Bodiam Castle

nr Robertsbridge, East Sussex (01580 830436/ www.nationaltrust.org.uk). By train Robertsbridge rail then taxi. By car M25 (Junction 5). **Open** *mid Feb-Oct* 10am-6pm/dusk daily. *Nov-mid Feb* 10am-4pm/dusk Sat, Sun. Last entry 1hr before closing. Closed 25 Dec. *Tours* groups of 10 or more people only,

by arrangement; phone for details. **Admission** (NT) £3.90; £1.95 5-16s; £9.75 family (2+3); free under-5s. **Credit** AmEx, MC, V.

Bodiam, now owned by the National Trust, was built in 1385. It looks like a fantasy castle, with its four round towers and ramparts reflected romantically in the moat. Children love it for its drama, and the fact that they can tear around the grounds playing knights and don't have to worry about shuffling meekly from room to room admiring interiors, because there aren't any. It's a wreck inside.

The layout of the castle is very straightforward and easy to grasp. Wondering about the nitty gritty of castle life is part of the fun here. Vague hints of domesticity, such as the 28 fireplaces suspended in the walls, help you rebuild the place in your imagination. The staircases leading up to the two towers are extremely steep, but the climb is well worth it. Views of the surrounding countryside are breathtaking, as is the sheer drop down into the moat.

A £10 refundable deposit buys you a Bat Pack, which provides children with a tabard to wear, a trail to follow and various interesting activities to get stuck into while they're here. Moreover, a summer programme of family weekends in August brings the castle to life. During this time, a selection of characters wander the ruins in period costume. There are representatives of the kinds of people who would have lived at the castle in its heyday, from the so-called 'gong farmer' who cleaned up sewage, to the leather worker and his wife, and the various lords and ladies. Check the website for exact dates of such fun. The castle has a National Trust café in renovated quarters and the gift shop stocks a children's guidebook, priced £1.95.

School visits (pre-booking required) are a frequent feature at the castle. Pupils and teachers are allowed into the corner towers, where there is a room containing armour, chain mail, longbows and crossbows, and one with medieval-style games, costumes and musical instruments. Schools also have sole access to a covered picnic area. Bodiam can be bleak in the rain, though the castle has enough rooms intact for visitors to duck into during a downpour.
Car park. Nappy-changing facilities. Restaurant. Shop.

Hever Castle

nr Edenbridge, Kent (01732 865224/www.hevercastle. co.uk). By train Edenbridge Town rail then taxi, or Hever rail then 1-mile walk. By car M25 (Junction 5) or M25 (Junction 6). **Open** *Gardens* Apr-Oct 11am-6pm (last entry 5pm) daily. Mar, Nov 11am-4pm daily. *Castle* Mar-Nov noon-6pm (last entry 5pm daily). Mar, Nov noon-4pm daily. *Tours* groups (min 20 people) by prior arrangement. **Admission** *Castle & gardens* £8.20; £7 concessions; £4.50 5-14s; £20.90 family (2+2); free under-5s. *Gardens only* £6.50; £5.60 concessions; £4.30 5-14s; £17.30 family (2+2); free under-5s. **Credit** MC, V.

Anne Boleyn's childhood home, and an idyllic setting for Henry VIII' s wooing of the ill-fated maid, Hever is an elaborate and romantic Tudor palace, surrounded by a double moat. The castle was lavishly restored in the early 20th century by the American millionaire Waldorf Astor, and filled with treasures. He also built the pretty 'Tudor' village that lies behind the castle grounds, as well as restoring the gardens and lake.

Uprising at **Hever Castle**. *See p272.*

The castle now contains precious collections of paintings and furniture, in addition to two rare historic *Books of Hours*, beautifully illuminated manuscripts that were inscribed by Anne Boleyn. The well-tended gardens contain an elaborate yew maze, along with an adventure playground and a water maze set on Sixteen Acre Island. The water maze is a refreshing piece of nonsense on a hot day, but a nightmare in chill spring sunshine, when children gambol among the water spouts, get soaked, then shiver like whippets for the rest of the day. A change of clothes is highly recommended.

Hever is known for its re-enactments of Tudor revelry and regularly stages jousting tournaments and medieval archery among its special events at half-terms and holidays. In May there is the Merrie England weekend, involving foot soldier combat, medieval music and crafts. At Easter there is a traditional Easter egg trail. In summer the lake is the venue for a festival of music and plays.

Buggy access (grounds only). Cafés. Car park. Nappy-changing facilities. Restaurant. Shop.

Leeds Castle

Maidstone, Kent (01622 765400/www.leeds-castle.com). By train Bearsted rail then coach service. By car M20 (Junction 8). **Open** *Castle* Mar-Oct 11am-6pm daily. *Nov-Feb* 10am-4pm daily. Last entry 1hr before closing. *Gardens* Nov-Feb 10am-3pm daily. *Mar-Oct* 10am-5pm daily. Closed 25 Dec, open-air concert days in June, July (29 June, 6 July 2002). *Tours* pre-booked groups only. **Admission** *Castle, gardens & Dog Collar Museum* Mar-Oct £11; £6-£9.50 concessions; £7.50 4-15s; £32 family (2+3); free under-4s. Nov-Feb £9.50; £5.50-£8 concessions; £6 4-15s; £27 family (2+3); free under-4s. **Credit** MC, V.

Leeds Castle, built just after the Norman Conquest in 1066, rises dreamily from a lake in Kentish parkland. Over the centuries, it was fortified and enhanced by various royal householders, including Henrys V and VIII. Leeds was once known as the Queen's Castle because so many kings gave it to their wives. On a darker note, two women, a duchess and Queen Joan of Navarre, were imprisoned at Leeds long ago for witchcraft. Nowadays, the castle is maintained purely by the private Leeds Castle Foundation and no one gets shut in, although children occasionally get lost in the maze.

Inside the castle, the Heraldry Room is lined with portraits of the royal owners of the castle. You admire coats of arms while listening to a simplified explanation of heraldry. The modernised quarters upstairs have a formidable view over the lake, in which you can see reflected the twisted shapes of the Judas trees. As you're leaving the main island, just before going through the gate tower, you come to the quirky Dog Collar Museum, with its collection of exhibits spanning four centuries.

Head for the gardens: the outdoor attractions are many and various. There's the delightful Culpeper cottage garden and the Mediterranean formality of the Lady Baillie garden, as well as a vineyard and greenhouses. The aviary is home to a colourful collection of rare and endangered bird species. Grown of tightly packed yews, the maze has at its centre a leafy secret grotto, decorated with mythical beasts fashioned with stone and shell mosaics.

Ring for an events leaflet to find out about children's classical concerts and open-air theatre events in summer. The castle hosts other special year-round events, too, including an annual Easter Egg hunt and a hot-air balloon festival. Note that pushchairs can be used on the ground floor of the castle only with special permission from the duty guard.

Nearby, only about five miles up the road on the M20, is the Museum of Kent Life (Lock Lane, Sandling, Maidstone, 01622 763936, www.museum-kentlife.co.uk). Here, children

can stroke farm animals in the courtyard, admire the birds in the aviary and learn about various aspects of farming life through the hands-on exhibits.

Cafés. Car park. Nappy-changing facilities. Restaurants. Shop.

Mountfitchet Castle & Norman Village

Stansted Mountfichet, Essex (01279 813237/ 24hr info line 0906 470 0898/www.gold.enta.net). By train Stansted Mountfichet rail. By car M11 (Junction 8). **Open** *2nd Sun in Mar-2nd Sun in Nov* 10am-5pm daily. **Admission** £5; £4.50 OAPs; £4 2-14s; free under-2s. **Credit** MC, V.

The House on the Hill Toy Museum *(address, phone & website as above).* **Open** 10am-5pm daily. Closed 24-26 Dec. **Admission** £3.80; £3.50 OAPs; £3 2-14s; free under-2s. 10% discount on prices if visiting both sites on same day. **Credit** MC, V.

It's only a 40-minute hop from Liverpool Street station, and a further two-minute walk from Stansted Mountfitchet station, but this motte and bailey castle and Norman village, reconstructed on an original site, whisks you back 900 years to give an evocative picture of life in 1066. The approach to the castle compound is pastoral (nearby Stansted airport doesn't intrude). Once inside, there's no shying away from the fact that life in Norman times was nasty, brutish and short (the severed head of an invader is stuck on a spike at the entrance). Lifelike figures in the castle dungeon demonstrate the grisly punishments meted out for the mildest misdemeanours. But it's not all gore: you can peer into a timber and thatch peasant home, where a family huddles around the cooking pot on a real fire, admire the everyday artistry of the potter, basket maker and weaver, beautifully reconstructed with the tools of their trade, or witness a feast in the baronial hall. The smell of drifting wood smoke adds to the ambience, while snippets of recorded information set the scene.

The layout is a manageable size for toddlers, but for older kids there are twisting paths to be explored, open grassy areas, and lookout posts to climb. Tame fallow deer, goats, guinea fowl, sheep, chickens and peacocks, breeds that the Normans kept for food and fur, wander everywhere and you can buy food for them at the ticket office. Picnic in the outdoor area, eat at the on-site café, or fuel up at the chippie across the road. After lunch, drop into the House on the Hill Toy Museum next door, which has 70,000 exhibits, from end-of-the-pier games to play, and a working Meccano fairground.

Buggy access. Café. Nappy-changing facilities. Shops.

Windsor Castle

Windsor, Berks (7321 2233/bookings & info 7321 2233/ www.royal.gov.uk). By train Windsor & Eton Riverside rail. By car M4 (Junction 6). **Open** *Mar-Oct* 9.45am-5.15pm (last entry 4pm) daily. *Nov-Feb* 9.45am-4.15pm (last entry 3pm) daily. Closed 25, 26 Dec. **Admission** (LP) £11.50; £9.50 concessions; £6 5-16s; £29 family (2+2); free under-5s. *Audio guide* £2.95. **Credit** AmEx, MC, V.

One of the Queen's official residences, Windsor is the largest and oldest occupied castle in the world. The site covers 13 acres and contains many treasures. The beautiful St George's Chapel is the final resting place of Queen Elizabeth the Queen Mother, who died on 30 March 2002.

The North Terrace, which has a dramatic view of the surrounding countryside below, is the entrance to the State Apartments and Queen Mary's Dolls' House. Queues for the latter's tiny delights can last for 30 minutes at busy times, but it is an amazing piece of craftsmanship. All the furnishings, crockery and household effects are perfect in every detail. The engineering equipment – lights and plumbing –

Bodiam Castle, looming dramatically over its moat. *See p272.*

were made to work when it was given to Queen Mary in 1924. The miniature casks actually contain vintage wines. There's a car collection stored in the garages and the crown jewels locked up behind tiny bars. In the adjoining hallway, twin French dolls named Marianne and France, are all dolled up ready to go out, in tiny leather gloves, garden party gowns with matching shoes and hat and an ermine evening cloak.

Up the Grand Staircase is the highlight of the rest of the apartments: the fabulous Windsor collection of medieval weaponry. This is contained in the Grand Vestibule, the Queen's Guard Chamber and the restored St George's Hall. Trophy swords, pairs of pistols and even an Ethiopian crown are displayed. You can also gaze at Napoleon's scarlet cloak, which was captured at Waterloo, or the bullet that killed Lord Nelson at Trafalgar in 1805. The sequel to the Grand Vestibule is the Queen's Guard Chamber: floor to ceiling weapons here again. Carved eagles and lions adorn the ivory Indian throne.

If you're planning your trip to coincide with the Changing of the Guard, note that it takes place from April to July outside the Guardroom in the Lower Ward, at 11am Monday to Saturday, and on alternate days the remainder of the year. (The sentries are changed throughout the day.)

Many of the families descending on Windsor during the school holidays are hanging the expense and going for the whole Berkshire experience by combining a trip to the castle with one to nearby Legoland (*see p292*). Consequently, there's a shuttle service connecting the two attractions.
Nappy-changing facilities. Shop.

Bewl Water

nr Lamberhurst, Tunbridge Wells, Kent (01892 890661/ www.bewl.co.uk). By train Wadhurst rail then taxi, or Tunbridge Wells rail then Heritage Hopper bus. By car M25 (Junction 5). **Open** 9am-dusk daily. Closed 25 Dec,

Concert Day (13 July 2002). **Admission** *per vehicle* Apr-Oct £3.50 Mon-Fri; £4.50 Sat, Sun. Nov-Mar £2.50 daily. *Concert tickets* phone for details. **No credit cards**.

This reservoir is the largest lake in the South-east, with 450 acres of green fields and woodland all around it. Bewl Water is noted for its romantic Wealden scenery and the bike riding, walking and watersports opportunities laid on for sporting bodies of all ages. It also hosts a summer concert and fireworks extravaganza in July (ring for details of this and other family events, such as treasure hunts and car rallies).

The lake has 15 miles of shoreline and is 97ft at its deepest, which, as there are no lifeguards, prohibits swimming. However, fly-fishing for trout (the only fish in the reservoir) is available and very popular, as the many little fishing boats strewn along the lake demonstrate. You're obliged to take any fish you catch home with you. In order to fish you need an Environment Agency licence, which are sometimes available at Bewl, or from a post office. You also need a fishing permit for the day, which you can buy when you get here (available from the fishing lodge, 01892 890352). This costs £15 for adults for eight fish and £9.50 for two fish (£4 for under-15s). The staff at Bewl suggest that under-8s don't fish as they're probably not strong enough to cast the line, but they're happy for parents who know how to fly fish to teach their kids on the premises. Note that the tackle shop sells flies but you must bring your own fishing rod and appropriate clothing.

In summer you can hire bikes and ride, or just hike, around the reservoir on the recommended 12.5-mile walk. This takes about six hours to complete. If you don't fancy that much exercise, jump on the ferry boat that leaves every hour from 11am to 4pm (£3 for adults, £2 kids) and either cruise around the lake or stop off halfway round and go the rest of the way on foot. Several picnic spots and shelters are dotted along the route, allowing the less athletic to gaze at the views.

RYA (Royal Yachting Association) instructors will teach keen windsurfers over the age of 8 to windsurf within a two-hour lesson. The £25 fee includes the board, rig, wetsuit,

Days Out

spray-top (which acts as a wind shield in chilly weather), buoyancy aid and safety cover. Alternatively, there's rowing or powerboat instruction available nearby. Younger children love the woodland playground, with its wooden forts, towers, bridges, swings, a huge slide and House of the Three Bears.

For Bewl Water Outdoor Centre (canoeing, sailing, climbing, rowing, powerboat instruction, etc) call 01892 890716 or log on to www.bewlwater.org.
Car park. Nappy-changing facilities. Restaurant. Shop.

Painshill Landscape Garden

Painshill Park Trust, Portsmouth Road, Cobham, Surrey (01932 864674/Camp Hamilton 01932 866743/www.painshill.co.uk). By train Cobham or Weybridge rail. By car M25 (Junction 10). **Open** *Apr-Oct* 10.30am-6pm (last entry 4.30pm) Tue-Sun, bank hols. *Nov-Mar* 11am-4pm (last entry 3pm) Tue-Thur, Sat, Sun, bank hols. Closed 25, 26 Dec. *Tours* groups of 10 or more only, by arrangement; phone for details. **Admission** £4.50; £4 concessions; £12 family (2+3); £2 5-16s; free under-5s. *Season ticket* £20; £40 family (2+3). **Credit** MC, V.

These beautiful gardens, created by Charles Hamilton between 1738 and 1773, were designed as a country retreat for fashionable London society. They still attract Londoners in search of greensward today, who enjoy the lovely vistas.

Children love Painshill for reasons a little more energetic than the views. Outward bounders run day Camp Hamilton courses here for children aged 7-11 during the Easter, summer and Christmas holidays (£20 per day). The activities are similar each year, with three main structures: an outdoor trail, an indoor activity and a creative one, where children make something to take home with them. The most popular activity is the woodland quest, where the children go to a pre-selected part of the woods and create a camp from scratch, before being treated to a barbecue cooked by the staff.

With a little planning, you can make your child's activities coincide with some cultural ones of your own. Painshill holds study days for adults throughout the year. The programme varies annually, but popular topics include lectures on art and history, with many discussions on botany. You can attend the lectures and occasional guided tours; expect to pay about £20 for the lecture and tour, or around £15 just for the lecture.

The Painshill Park gardens are also splendid enough to keep parents busy while their children get the pioneering spirit. They were lavishly landscaped in the 18th century, but subsequently allowed to run wild; now they have been spectacularly restored (although it's very much a work in progress). Highlights of a hike round the grounds include a series of follies (a Turkish tent, a Gothic temple, a grotto and a huge water wheel) as well as some lovely lakes and views.
Buggy access. Car park. Nappy-changing facilities. Restaurant. Shop.

Wildwood Wildlife Park

Herne Common, Herne Bay, Kent (01227 712111/www.wildwood.gb.com). By train Herne Bay then bus. By car M2 (Junction 7). **Open** 10am-5pm daily. Last admission 4pm. **Admission** £5.75; £4.25 disabled, 3-15s; £3.25 disabled child; £18 family (2+2); free under-3s. **Credit** MC, V.

These 30 acres of wonderful wilderness give children the opportunity to commune with the animals. Not that they'd want to commune with all the animals – the 350-400 on the site include wolves and wild boars. Thankfully, the wildlife is contained in huge enclosures that blend into the woodland. The friendly deer are attention seekers and come to the fence; other animals are shy and retiring. Among the 50 species kept here are beavers, wild cats, red squirrels, otters, owls,

badgers and pine martens. When you enter the woodland, check the board for the feeding times. This is when you can join the various keepers for a Feed and Talk time, when you see the animals have their tea and find out more about them. The park has a strong conservation commitment; one recent coup has been the successful breeding programme for water voles, one of many endangered species under protection here.

Family visitors who come here for a day's woodland walking and wildlife safari can bring a picnic to enjoy in the areas inside and outside the park, or partake of the lunch menu in the restaurant. Children should not miss the impressively challenging adventure playpark, with its ropes, platforms and ramparts. Wildwood isn't far from Herne Bay, so if you fancy a dip in the sea after your wildlife watching, head coastward.
Buggy access. Car park. Nappy-changing facilities. Restaurant. Shop.

Down on the farm

2001 was a bad year for animal attractions all over the UK. The foot and mouth outbreak took its toll on most establishments at the beginning of the year and it was months before they could open again. With the crisis over, 2002 looks like being a better year for London's local farms, where diversification is taken to ever more imaginative extremes. Playgrounds and tractor rides are standard, but some places even have theatres for puppet shows and animal demonstrations to pull in the buggy brigade. Farming's future, it seems, lies in the hands of tiny tourists, all eager for chick-cuddling, pig-feeding and sheep-shearing hands-on experiences.

Remember to wash your hands after touching animals. You could hardly forget to: every farmyard is peppered with 'Now Wash Your Hands' notices, because of the danger of enteritis and potentially deadly E coli infection from handling animals.

Days Out

Barleylands Farm

Barleylands Road, Billericay, Essex (01268 532253/ 290029/www.barleylandsfarm.co.uk). By train Billericay or Basildon rail. By car M25 (Junction 29). **Open** *end Mar-Oct* 10am-5pm daily. **Admission** £4.50; £2.50 3-12s; free under-3s. **Credit** MC, V.

The country's agricultural heritage is preserved in aspic and celebrated in a hands-on way at this farm museum and animal centre in Essex. Farm equipment and machinery through the ages are housed inside a series of barns. Tractors take pride of place; Fergy (the tractors, not the royal redhead) fanatics will have a field day here. There are also steam-operated engines parked outside. On Sundays and bank holidays from March to October (and daily during August) a miniature railway pootles around the fields to give a broader view of the farm. Once you've admired all the machinery, make for the animals. There are ponies, sheep, pigs, geese, ducks, chickens and rabbits, many of which can

---

Dahl-ing Roald

Roald Dahl may have penned his imaginative stories in a dilapidated hut at the bottom of his Buckinghamshire garden, but his legions of devoted fans can expect a more lavish experience inside this converted coach house, an extension of the child-friendly Bucks County Museum. Five areas, decorated with colourful frescoes by Quentin Blake, introduce different themes based on Dahl's stories.

Encounter James and his mini beast friends inside the Giant Peach and examine the insect world with the aid of a video microscope. Explore sound with the BFG by playing on his giant pipe organ. Or crawl along Fantastic Mr Fox's tunnel, spotting buried treasure as you go. The Imagination Gallery upstairs is a chance to experience Roald Dahl's anarchic world with some fun experiments. Freeze your own shadow in the dark room and watch it fade before your eyes. Or see the Twits' upside-down room and touch the things hidden in their wall. Younger children will enjoy meeting Tim Burr the wooden man and loading his train for market, or riding in the Great Glass Elevator, part of a new extension to the gallery. Oh yes, and there are even some books, in Matilda's Library, where you can discover more about Dahl's life and work. It's a popular place for families, with prime appeal for the under-10s, but it only holds 85 people, so it's worth pre-booking in the school holidays. Picnic in the walled garden or snack in the reasonably priced museum café.

Roald Dahl Children's Gallery

Church Street, Aylesbury, Bucks (01296 331441/ www.buckscc.gov.uk/museum). By train Aylesbury rail. By car M25 (Junction 8). **Open** 10am-5pm Sat; 2-5pm Sun. *Term time* 3-5pm Mon-Fri. *School hols* 10am-5pm Mon-Sat. **Admission** £3.50; £2.75 3-16s; free under-3s. **Credit** MC, V.
Buggy access. Nappy-changing facilities.

---

be petted and fed. A chick hatchery shows children what a piece of magic an egg can be. The adventure playground, picnic area and tearoom make spending the entire day here a possibility. The September Steam Rally (14 and 15 September 2002; check the website for details of next year's) is a lovely event, when the farm is taken over by all sorts of artisans and entertainers; there are craft workshops, glass-blowing demonstrations and fairground rides to enjoy.
Buggy access. Café. Car park. Nappy-changing facilities.

Bocketts Farm Park

Young Street, Fetcham, nr Leatherhead, Surrey (01372 363764/www.bockettsfarm.co.uk). By train Leatherhead rail then taxi. By car M25/26 (Junction 9). **Open** 10am-5.30pm daily. Closed 25, 26 Dec, 1 Jan. **Admission** £3.95; £3.75 3-17s; £2.95 2s; free under-2s. **Credit** MC, V.

An idyllic English farm with a red-brick farmhouse, a yard with chickens and ducks, surrounded by rolling acres of crops and grazing, all tucked into a fold of the North Downs. Bocketts has been farmed continuously since the 18th century. Now that truly mixed farms are the exception rather than the rule, Bocketts is a relic of a bygone age, and, of course, a popular visitor attraction.

The first thing visitors see at the farm is the large covered area, where some of the friendlier animals are kept. Goats are here with their kids, as are Haggis the Aberdeen Angus and his round-horned pals, chewing pensively on their haynets; Ernie the barn owl, whose contract demands he stays up during the day to let visitors stroke his soft back; and a menagerie of rabbits and other rodents that are up for a bit of a cuddle. The covered barn also ensures a good time on wet winter days. Beyond the barn past the stables you'll find the race track: one of the highlights of a day at Bocketts Farm is the pig race, which takes place twice a day and involves seven piglets racing hell for leather up a hill to reach the pig nuts provided for them at the top. Choose your colours and roar your chosen piglet on. Race times vary, so phone for details.

New for 2002 in the large and well-equipped play area is a 70ft, four-lane waveslide. A pedal-tractor circuit provides amusement for younger kids and there are some endearing-ly old-fashioned games such as Bowling for a Pig (not a live one…) and a giant wooden jigsaw to complete. Tractor and trailer rides allow small children to reach more of the farm before their legs give out, and pony rides are available too.
Buggy access. Café. Car park. Shop.

Fishers Farm

New Pound Lane, Wisborough Green, West Sussex (01403 700063/www.fishersfarmpark.co.uk). By train Billingshurst rail then taxi. By car M25 (Junction 10). **Open** 10am-5pm daily; ring for details of opening times of special events. **Admission** *Oct half-term-Feb half-term* £5.75; £5.25 3-16s; £4.25 OAPs; £20-£29.50 family (2+3); free under-3s. *Feb half-term, Easter hols-start summer hols, Oct half-term, Christmas hols* £6.75, £6.25 3-16s; £24-£35.50 family. *Summer hols* £7.75; £7.25 3-16s; £28-£41.50 family. **Credit** MC, V.

Part farm, part outdoor adventure centre, Fishers Farm has plenty of animals to pet, cuddle, feed and ride, as well as an enormous range of peripheral activities to keep children active and amused. The Farm Theatre has a daily programme of events, including animal feeding (such as feeding spring lambs with bottles), veterinary demonstrations, magic shows and farm animal displays. Children can admire the poultry pecking around the farmyard, enjoy a pony ride, or commune with the goats in their pen. As well as the multifarious livestock, there's an adventure playground, a climbing wall,

Getting a handle on the hens at **Odds Farm Park**.

tractor and combine harvester rides, a giant paddling pool with beachy sand for the summer, and an indoor playzone for wet weather, with trampolines and bouncy castles. Pick up an itinerary when you arrive and plan your day around the fun. Fishers also organises children's birthday parties; go to the website for prices and to print off invitations.
Buggy access. Cafés. Car park. Nappy-changing facilities. Restaurants. Shops.

Godstone Farm

Tilburstow Hill Road, Godstone, Surrey (01883 742546/ www.godstonefarm.co.uk). By train Caterham rail then 409, 410, 411 bus. By car M25 (Junction 6). **Open** *Mar-Oct* 10am-6pm daily. *Nov-Feb* 10am-5pm daily. Closed 25 Dec. **Admission** £4.10 2-16s, incl one adult; free under-2s. **Credit** AmEx, MC, V.
Nice and close to London, like its sister Horton (*see below*), this 40-acre Surrey farm has been tramped by millions since it opened to the public in 1980. The cows, goats, sheep, hens, ducks, geese and small animals of Godstone are an obvious draw. For some of them, namely the sheep and poultry, their role in the rural education of pre-school urbanites goes beyond merely ambling about in pastures and pens: the sheep are used in shearing displays in spring, while the fowl provide eggs for the incubators, where the hatching process is carried out in the public gaze. On wet days small children make an undignified rush for the huge covered area, where an assortment of rides on tractors, trucks, bikes and trolleys can be trundled about at speed. The play barn (30 minutes, 80p) has tubes, cubes, bridges, ball pools and walkways for children aged under 9 to play on. If the weather's fair, the adventure playground, on the top field, is terrific, with its wooden walkways, ropes, tyres, tunnels, slides and a set of ropes on pulleys, which children love to do their best Tarzan impersonations on.
Café. Car park. Nappy-changing facilities. Shop.

Horton Park Children's Farm

Horton Lane, Epsom, Surrey (01372 743984/ www.hortonpark.co.uk). By train Epsom rail then bus. By car M25 (Junction 9). **Open** *Summer* 10am-6pm daily. *Winter* 10am-5pm daily. Last entry 1hr before closing. **Admission** £4.10 over-2s (accompanying adult free). **Credit** MC, V.
Bigger than a city farm, but conveniently close to the city, Horton is sister to Godstone (*see above*) but has a more simple bill of fare. It's a petting farm for the very young, carefully laid out so as not to stress buggy-toting parents out for a bit of fresh air. There's plenty for little children to get involved in, but nothing too challenging. They can meet Jack the Llama, a legend in his own paddock, sheep, pigs, cows, ponies and goats. In the pet animals section there are a few non-threatening reptiles (lizards and small snakes); hamsters, gerbils and chipmunks, baby rabbits and chicks to hold very carefully. The maze, the soft play barn (70p) and a climbing structure called Fort Horton helps children work up an appetite for a nuggety meal or sandwich box in the tearoom, or something from their rucksack in the picnic area.
Buggy access. Car park. Nappy-changing facilities. Shop.

Odds Farm Park

Wooburn Common, nr High Wycombe, Bucks (01628 520188/www.oddsfarm.co.uk). By train Beaconsfield rail. By car M40 (Junction 2) or M4 (Junction 7). **Open** *early Feb-May, early Sept-late Oct* 10am-5.30pm daily. *June-early Sept* 10am-6.30pm daily. *Late Oct-mid Feb* 10am-4.30pm daily. **Admission** *Summer* £4.75; £3.75 2-16s; free under-2s. *Winter* £4.25; £3.25 2-16s; free under-2s. **Credit** MC, V.
Jolly events change with the seasons, but there's always something going on at Odds, where farming is all fun and games. Feed rabbits from babies' bottles, or collect eggs from

the chickens at this friendly hands-on farm. Regular activities change throughout the year – feed the lambs between February and April, watch the shearing from May to July, and carve pumpkins in October. Tractor and trailer rides are available daily through the summer (weather permitting). Milling and orienteering around the farm take place year round. You can even hold your child's birthday party here – there are two private rooms to choose from: 'Bunnies Burrow' or 'Piggies Playpen', which can be hired from 10.30am to 12.30pm or 1.30pm to 3.30pm (half an hour later in the summer) at a cost of £8.95 per child over 2 years (under-2s £5.20), which includes entrance to the farm park, a bag of special animal food for each child, free admission for four adults, party food and goody bags.

Buggy access. Car park. Nappy-changing facilities. Shop.

South of England Rare Breeds Centre

Highlands Farm, Woodchurch, nr Ashford, Kent (01233 861493/www.rarebreeds.org.uk). By train Ashford rail. By car M20 (Junction 10). **Open** *Apr-Sept* 10.30am-5.30pm daily. *Oct-Mar* 10.30am-4.30pm Tue-Sun. Closed 24, 25 Dec. **Admission** £4; £2.50 3-15s; free under-3s. **Credit** MC, V.

British breeds that were once common, such as cows with handlebar horns, sheep with long, curly fleeces and spotty pigs, ginger pigs and tall ducks, all parade around the acreage enjoying their exclusivity. The 'Tamworth Two' (little piggies that escaped the market), who shot to fame thanks to the *Daily Mail*'s in-depth coverage, live out their days here. Children can get hands-on with the animals, enjoy beautiful woodland walks and trailer rides and get the coolbox out and tuck into its contents in the picnic areas. Throughout the year there's a host of special events for both kids and their parents, including, in June 2002, a Classic Car Rally and on the summer bank holiday a save-the-planet Green Roadshow. Some carol singing in the barn rounds the year off in traditional style. Check the website for more events.

Buggy access. Café. Car park. Nappy-changing facilities. Shop.

Wimpole Hall Home Farm & Garden

Arrington, Royston, Cambs (01223 207257/ www.wimpole.org). By train Royston rail. By car M11 (Junction 12). **Open** *late Mar-June, Sept-early Nov* Tue-Thur, Sat, Sun, bank hol Mon, Good Friday. *July, Aug* Tue-Sun. *Nov-Mar* Sat, Sun (*open Feb half term*). **Times** *late Mar-early Nov* 10.30am-5pm Tue-Thur, Sat, Sun. *July Farm* also open Fri. *Aug* Farm & hall open Fri. *Nov-Mar* Farm only 11am-4pm Sat, Sun. **Admission** (NT members: free Hall & Garden, reduced admission to farm £2.60 adults, £1.60 3-17s; free under-3s). *Farm & gardens* £4.90; £2.80 3-17s; free under-3s. **Credit** AmEx, MC, V.

This open working farm (with baffling opening times) near Cambridge is a small part of the Wimpole Estate, which includes 350 acres of landscaped and wooded parkland and an impressive country house, now owned by the National Trust. It's a real oasis in the mainly arable Cambridgeshire countryside, so the place can get overcrowded – go off-peak if possible. The farm, which was designed in the late 18th century by Sir John Soane, is the largest rare breeds centre in East Anglia. Enjoy the sight of a majestic Suffolk Punch shire horse and the enormous White Park cattle, thought to be the most ancient breed in the UK. There's a collection of pigs, sheep, donkeys, ponies and poultry of all shapes, sizes and colours, and a suitably rustic playground with wooden toys and a large fleet of pedal tractors. Older children, on the other hand, enjoy the more challenging

Beautiful blooms, **RHS Gardens, Wisley**. *See p281.*

adventure playground, which is hidden among the trees. If the heavens open, repair to the Farm Kitchen restaurant, which has indoor play facilities.

A wide programme of family activities operates throughout the year, including lambing weekends in spring, a Tractor day in June, and visits from Father Christmas in December. Gravel paths make the going tough with a lightweight buggy, and if you venture out of this kiddie ghetto into the gardens, do make sure your children obey the intermittent 'keep off the grass' signs – or face the wrath of an irate gardener.

Buggy access. Car park. Nappy-changing facilities. Shop.

Gardens

Bedgebury, the National Pinetum

nr Cranbrook, Kent (01580 211044/www.forestry.gov. uk). By train Etchingham or Tunbridge Wells rail then Heritage Hopper bus (Sat, Sun, bank hols May-Sept). By car M25 (Junction 5). **Open** *Summer* 10am-6pm daily. *End Oct-end Jan* 10am-4pm daily. *End Jan-late Mar* 10am-5pm daily. Last entry 1hr before closing. **Admission** £3; £2.50 concessions; £1.20 5-16s; free under-5s. **Credit** MC, V.

There aren't many opportunities for children to go on a real woodland walk these days, but Bedgebury gives them the freedom to romp around huge trees, a lake and wildflower glades with impunity. Bring a picnic to make a day of it (note the café is closed on Mondays). The Pinetum comprises one of the finest collections of conifers in the world. Originally planted by Viscount Marshall Beresford of Bedgebury, an officer of Wellington at Waterloo, the pinetum was founded as a joint venture between the Forestry Commission and the Royal Botanic Gardens at Kew, with the first plants (having been raised at Kew) planted here in 1925. The pinetum is a year-round attraction: spring sees the rhododendrons and azaleas ablaze with colour; in summer the place is alive with birds (the RSPB counts the pinetum as one of the country's most important habitats) and a staggering 19 species of dragonfly; in autumn the deciduous trees go russet and gold,

and in winter the rare and stately conifers come into their own. On a frosty morning Bedgebury is a picture. Choose a fine December morning to come here for your Christmas tree (they're on sale from 1 December). The Pinetum has an education officer, who organises all the school field trips and team-building exercises. During the holidays she runs twice-weekly events for children (£5 per child; accompanying adult free), when they go bug hunting, for example, or learn all about fungi (there are more than 900 species of them here). Ring the shop (01580 211781) to book your place, or check the website for details.
Buggy access. Car park. Shop.

Capel Manor
Bullsmoor Lane, Enfield (8366 4442/www.capel.ac.uk). By train Turkey Street rail. By car M25 (Junction 25). **Open** *Mar-Oct* 10am-6pm (last entry 4.30pm) daily. *Nov-Feb* 10am-5pm (last entry 4pm) Mon-Fri. **Admission** £4; £3.50 concessions; £2 3-16s; free under-3s; £10 family. **Credit** MC, V.
Just off the M25, Capel Manor is one of outer London's undiscovered secrets. It's a college specialising in horticulture, landscape and garden design, floristry and animal care, but it's also home to dozens of demonstration, themed and historic mini gardens, a lovely collection of animals, a Victorian stableyard and numerous special events throughout the summer.

Children usually hate being dragged around nurseries, in which plants are often set out in boring old rows with little sensory appeal. But if there's any place that will help kids to develop an interest in the colour, smell and feel of plants,

this is it. There are few ropes or 'keep off the grass' signs, and many of the gardens have little gates to open and sheds to hide behind. Disability access is excellent, and there are special areas for those with physical handicaps or visual impairment. When the children are tired of sniffing roses, they can meet the college's Galloway cattle, Kune Kune pigs, Soay sheep, ponies, goats, rabbits, chickens, guinea pigs and magnificent Clydesdale horses.
Buggy access. Café. Car park. Nappy-changing facilities. Shop.

RHS Gardens, Wisley
nr Woking, Surrey (01483 224234/www.rhs.org.uk). By train West Byfleet or Woking rail then taxi or bus. Wisley Bus runs from Woking to Wisley May-Sept (call 01483 224234 for times). By car M25 (Junction 10). **Open** *Mar-Oct* 9am-6pm Mon-Sat. *Nov-Feb* 9am-4.30pm Mon-Sat. Last entry 1hr before closing. Closed 25 Dec. *Tours* by arrangement; phone for details. **Admission** £6; £2 6-16s; free under-6s. **Credit** MC, V.
More than just a pretty garden, Wisley's delightful Surrey acres make up the flagship garden of the Royal Horticultural Society, where horticultural techniques are investigated, gardening courses are run and new cultivars are field tested. However, for all this grown-up horticultural detail, Wisley is a delightful place to take all members of the family. The formal central pond and its koi carp and ducks attract young children, who also love the bigger duck pond across the lawn from the restaurant and smaller froggy pools throughout the garden. Others love to run around the huge apple orchards,

Run, piggy, run!

The sheer gorgeousness of **Groombridge Place Gardens** is as good a reason as any for making the trip to the Kent Weald, but children generally expect more than perfect planting. Luckily, there's plenty of fun laid on for them here.

The land was medieval pig pasture before being sold on to Norman barons, who built a moated castle here. This was destroyed in the 17th century and a manor house, Groombridge Place, built in its stead. It passed through the hands of various people and in 1992 was bought by a businessman, who started the restoration programme. Beautifully tended formal gardens (but not the private manor house) were opened to the public in 1994.

Since then the site has changed owners once more and the renovation and enhancement continues, along with the creation of more visitor attractions. The formal gardens have peacocks strutting and floral bowers, a delightful secret garden, giant chessboards, a knot garden and rose gardens. The Enchanted Forest, a favourite with children, has giant swings, rainforest planting, Indian camps with teepees, Dinosaur Valley, Romany camps and a spooky place called the Serpent's Lair. Equally fascinating in this woodland is the Valley of the Groms, with its Dark Walk Adventure Trail – all very *Lord of the Rings*. Check the website for details of a 2002 programme of special events.

In line with the gardens' humble beginnings as pig grazing land, there are twice-daily porker races during the high season. This summer's athletes are six little snorters called Super-, Liver-, German-, Spicy-, Rocket- and Intercontinental Ballistic-Sausage. The races take place on a proper circuit (with fences) every day at 12.30pm and 4.30pm.

As well as the pigs, there are the Harris hawks and falcons of Eddie's Raptor Centre, who give swooping demonstrations three times a day. Check the website (www.raptorcentre.co.uk) for details. The biggest rabbits in the world (probably) lounge about in purpose-built houses, designed for them by *Gardeners' World* eccentric Ivan Hicks. The rabbits are British Giants and have been known to weigh 25 pounds (more than some of the children who pet them). Kune Kune pigs, attractive swine from New Zealand, wander about in Grom Village (near the Enchanted Wood). They're too right-on to race.

Groombridge Place Gardens
Groombridge Place, Groombridge, nr Tunbridge Wells, Kent (01892 861444/recorded info 01892 863999/www.groombridge.co.uk). By train Tunbridge Wells then taxi. By car A264 off A21. **Open** *Easter-early Nov* 9am-6pm (dusk if earlier) daily. **Admission** £8; £7 OAPs; £6.50 3-12s; free under-3s; £26 family (2+2). **Credit** MC, V.
Buggy access. Café. Car park. Nappy-changing facilities. Shop.

explore the woodland gardens, gallop down the grassy slopes and marvel at the orchid house and cactus collection. Bring a picnic – there are tables to eat them at. Special events, and occasional children's trails, are organised on a regular basis. Apple Days in October include some serious tasting and apple-based events for all the family. This year's Family Fortnight, with specific activities laid on for children, takes place 27 July-11 August. For more details check the website or send an SAE to Nicky Pickett, Education Department, RHS Garden Wisley, Woking, Surrey GU23 6QB.
Buggy access. Car park. Nappy-changing facilities. Restaurant. Shop.

Go wild in the country

Birdworld

Holt Pound, Farnham, Surrey (01420 22140/ www.birdworld.co.uk). By train Aldershot, Bentley or Farnham rail then taxi. By car A3 then A31 or M3. **Open** *mid Feb-Oct* 9.30am-6pm daily. *Nov-mid Feb* 9.30am-4.30pm daily. Closed 25, 26 Dec. **Admission** £9.25; £6.95 concessions; £6.25 3-14s; £27.95 family (2+2); free under-3s. **Credit** MC, V.

Bird-spotting is easy here in this 26-acre landscaped park, where a huge variety of avian species shake their tail feathers in aviaries and enclosures. A daily highlight is watching the penguins cluster round their keeper to be fed – if you book in advance (there's a £6.50 fee, which goes towards penguin research) you can even feed them yourself. Penguin Island is the park's most popular attraction; you can see them diving and playing underwater from the viewing enclosure. Bird enclosures and aviaries are organised according to habitat, so the seabirds all hang out on a route called the Seashore Walk, and native birds can be seen in the woodland part. The place for exotics and parrots is hot and sticky. Heron Theatre is an amusing idea: the young, haughty birds can be persuaded by their keeper to perform the tricks they would in the wild. Keepers of the large species, such as vultures, emus and ostriches, can take you on a land train ride to show you their charges and tell you all about each species. Children enjoy the Jenny Wren farm, where sheep, lambs, goats, rabbits and other animals can be handled. Other attractions include Underwater World (fish and alligators) and birds of prey tours. The restaurant overlooks the wildfowl pond, but on a fine day the picnic areas allow for a pleasant lunch to the sound of birdsong.
Buggy access. Café. Car park. Nappy-changing facilities. Restaurant. Shop.

Drusillas Park

Alfriston, East Sussex (01323 874100/www.drusillas. co.uk). By train Polegate rail. By car M23 then A23 then A27. **Open** *Summer* 10am-6pm daily. *Winter* 10am-5pm daily. Last entry 1hr before closing. Closed 24-26 Dec. **Admission** £8.99; £6.99 concessions; £7.99 1m tall up to 12 years old; free less than 1m tall. **Credit** MC, V.

Residents at Drusillas include monkeys, penguins, rats, meerkats, mongooses, porcupines, beavers, otters, owls, ring-tailed lemurs, ruffed lemurs, cervals, llamas, maras (which look like a cross between a hare and a guinea pig), snakes, spiders, crocodiles, iguanas, fish, mice, birds, pigs, wallabies, emus, cows, sheep, goats, Shetland ponies – all of them small, most of them friendly, and with imaginatively designed enclosures to allow maximum interaction with their visitors. The viewing bubbles in the meerkats' enclosure, for example, allow visitors to get very close to the curious creatures.

The park isn't huge so it's kind to shorter legs and there's nowhere you can't get to with a buggy. One of the three picnic areas is under cover, and the restaurant is a friendly jungle-themed place that sells all the usual child favourites, plus baby jars. Drusillas also recognises that children need to let off steam and it has set aside well-equipped areas for the purpose. The acre-square playground incorporates swings, slides, ropes and climbing frames and there's an indoor play barn for wet weather. New for 2002 are Monkey Kingdom, an SAS-style assault course with bridges, ropes and chutes for 8s and up to pit their muscles against, and Explorers Lagoon, a paddling pool and sandpit for younger kids. End the day with a trip to the wacky workshop, where you can get involved in mask-making and other arty activities with an animal theme.
Buggy access. Cafés. Car park. Nappy-changing facilities. Restaurant. Shops.

Howletts

Bekesbourne, nr Canterbury, Kent (01227 721286/ www.howletts.net). By train Bekesbourne rail. By car M2 then A2. **Open** *Nov-Mar* 10am-dusk (last entry 2.30pm) daily. *Apr-Oct* 10am-6pm (last entry 4.30pm) daily. Closed 25 Dec. **Admission** £11.95; £8.95 concessions, 4-14s; £34 family (2+2), £39 (2+3); free under-4s. **Credit** MC, V.

Right on the edge of the Cathedral City, the 70-acre Howletts Parkland is home to elephants, tigers, Atlas lions, gorillas, antelopes and many more beautiful and dangerous creatures besides, housed in conditions as close to their natural habitat as possible. The late John Aspinall, who founded the wild animal park in 1958, believed that animals need to bond with their keepers, and that through contact with an animal, a keeper can enjoy a closer understanding with his charge. The practice continues today, and has extraordinary results. The breeding programme accounts for many successes. Howletts now lays claim to the largest family group of gorillas in captivity, and a 16-strong breeding herd of African elephants.

Visitors can bring a picnic to one of the designated areas in this beautiful, wooded park, or eat at the Conservatory Restaurant. The gift shop sells soft toys, pocket-money toys and T-shirts among other animal-themed merchandise. The whole park is buggy-friendly. Check the website to see the gorillas and elephants live via webcam. Note that you get a discount on tickets if you book online (allow five working days for processing).
Buggy access. Car park. Nappy-changing facilities. Restaurant. Shop.

Marwell Zoological Park

Colden Common, Winchester, Hants (01962 777407/ www.marwell.org.uk). By train Eastleigh rail then bus. By car M3 (Junction 11). **Open** *Summer* 10am-6pm (last entry 4.30pm) daily. *Winter* 10am-4pm (last entry 2.30pm) daily. **Admission** £10; £9 concessions; £7.50 3-14s; free under-3s; £32 family (2+2). **Credit** MC, V.

Noted in zoological circles for its breeding programme for endangered species, especially ungulates (antelopes), felids (cats) and primates, Marwell's 40 acres are put to good use, being home to more than 200 species. The warm atmosphere of Tropical World is a rainforest in microcosm with exotic plants, frogs, butterflies, chameleons and Malayan mouse deer (the smallest hoofed animal in the world), one of which gave birth to a tiny fawn in spring. Penguin World is an award-winning enclosure with Humboldt penguins, where the birds can be seen underwater through three large viewing windows. World of Lemurs is a pretty walled garden setting for rare primates from Madagascar. Outside in the paddocks, zebras and giraffes kick up their heels. A young newcomer, Isabella the giraffe calf, was born in 2002. A new breeding bull called Christopher has settled down nicely with his new harem.

Rhino love... **Port Lympne Wild Animal Park**.

The beautiful Hampshire parkland is a delight to explore; there are playgrounds for children, as well as a new incubation and rearing unit in Encounter Village (halfway through refurbishment as we go to press, so ring for details to see how the building work is going). Eventually, it will be a sort of farm/pets corner, with guinea pigs, ferrets and chinchillas, and goats, deer, sheep and poultry wandering around in a paddock. *Buggy access. Café. Car park. Nappy-changing facilities. Restaurant. Shop.*

Port Lympne Wild Animal Park

Lympne, nr Hythe, Kent (01303 264647/www.howletts. net). By train Ashford rail then link bus. By car M20 (Junction 11). **Open** *Oct-Mar 10am-dusk (last entry 2.30pm) daily. Apr-Sept 10am-6pm daily. Last entry 4pm. Closed 25 Dec.* **Admission** £11.95; £8.95 3-14s; £8.95 disabled; £6.95 disabled child; £34 family (2+2), £39 (2+3). **Credit** AmEx, DC, MC, V.

Bigger (350 acres) and more of a safari park than its sister Howletts (*see p282*), Port Lympne is vast, set on a dramatic escarpment overlooking Romney Marsh. The wild beasts have plenty of room to take the air, which may explain why the park has such a successful breeding record. The black rhinos have done particularly well this year: there are now 22 in the herd and three new babies to look out for. Another enormously successful animal attraction is the Palace of the Apes, the largest family gorilla house in the world. Other species with room to stretch their legs include tigers, lions, wolves and elephants. Find out on admission about the regular animal feeding and encounter sessions. As well as the animals there's the Port Lympne mansion, a beautiful old stately home, whose ground floor is open to visitors (ring to

check it isn't being used for a function before you visit). The grounds are magnificent and include chessboard gardens, terraces and a vineyard. Don't be wimpy about climbing the 125 Trojan Steps for one of the most awesome views in the Southeast. The huge size of the safari park may tempt you to invest in a trailer ride around the acreage (£2 adults; £1 children). Check the website for seasonal and special children's events here and at Howletts, for which visitors here receive a £4 voucher on paying their entrance fee. *Buggy access. Café. Car park. Nappy-changing facilities. Shop.*

Whipsnade Wild Animal Park

Whipsnade, Dunstable, Beds (01582 872171/ www.whipsnade.co.uk). By train Luton or Hemel Hempstead rail then taxi or bus. By car M25 (Junction 21) or M1 (Junction 10). **Open** *Mid Feb-mid Mar 10am-5pm daily. Mid Mar-early Oct 10am-6pm daily. Early-late Oct 10am-5pm daily. End Oct-mid Feb 10am-4pm daily.* Last entry 1hr before closing. Times subject to change, so phone to check. *Tours* free tour bus around the park; phone for times. *Cars* Car entry into the park £8.50 (£4.25 for members), or use £2 car park opposite main gate. **Admission** £11.50; £8.50 3-15s; free under-3s. **Credit** AmEx, MC, V.

The provincial outpost of the Zoological Society of London was bought by the society as a derelict farm in 1926. In 1931 it opened as Whipsnade Zoo with a modest animal collection. Today, the 600-acre park has 2,500 beasts, including the three elephants, Mya, Lyang Lyang and Dilberta, moved from London Zoo last year. The three seem much happier now they've been integrated into the herd. As well as the elephants, there's a huge variety of wild animals, including many species endangered in the wild: giraffes, bears, tigers, rhinos and hippos. Arrive early in peak times to make the most of the place. *Buggy access. Café. Car park. Nappy-changing facilities. Restaurant. Shop.*

Woburn Safari Park

Woburn Park, Beds (01525 290407/www.woburnsafari. co.uk). By car M1 (Junction 13) or M11 (Junction 13). **Open** *Mar-Oct* 10am-5pm daily. *Nov-Feb* 11am-3pm Sat, Sun. Closed 25 Dec. **Admission** *Early Mar-late May, mid June-mid July, early Sept-late Oct* £12.50; £9 3-15s; free under-3s. *Early-mid June, late July-early Sept* £13.50; £10 3-15s; free under-3s. Family tickets 2 adults and 2 or more paying children: £2 off second and subsequent children. 1 adult and more than 2 paying children: £2 off third and subsequent children. **Credit** MC, V.

The Safari Drive around the Duke of Bedford's vast grounds is the main event. Lions, Siberian tigers, bears, wolves, monkeys, elephants, rhinos, giraffes and many more animals roam free here. The idea is to drive your car (as many times as you like in a day; it takes about an hour) around the park, getting up close to the various beasts who'll either ignore you or maybe nibble at your car aerial. After that full-on experience, you can take a swan boat out to the lake, or repair on foot to see squirrel monkeys, penguins, lorikeets and, from 2002, sealions in their new pool. From April to August, at weekends and during school holidays, there are birds of prey demonstrations. The Woburn Deer Park, thought to be first enclosed in Henry VIII's reign, contains 1,200 animals of ten different species, including Père David, saved from extinction by Woburn's breeding programme. There are plenty of play areas for children (older ones love the Treetop Action Trail, like an army assault course; tots like Badger Valley) and a railway line that chunters around the safer parts of the park. Once finished with the animals, adults may like to visit the spectacular Woburn Abbey with its stunning Tudor portraits and antiques centre, but their children probably won't let them. *Buggy access. Café. Nappy-changing facilities. Restaurant. Shop.*

Seaside

A day-return train ticket from the Smoke to the coast buys you a whiff of ozone, a stick of rock, pleasure beaches, cockles, mussels, promenades, piers and playgrounds. Seasides accessible for a day trip from London have all this and coastal walks, crabs and oysters, sand and a gentle sort of surf. They may not be wild and rocky, more mild and cocky, really, but we love them for all their glorious tackiness.

Brighton

Tourist information centre 10 Bartholomew Square, Brighton, East Sussex BN1 1JS (0906 711 2255/ www.visitbrighton.com). By train Brighton rail. By car M23/A23, follow A23/A27 into Brighton.

Brighton is phenomenally busy, and its eight million annual visitors all seem to descend on the punishingly pebbly beach during hot summer weekends. People come here to enjoy the buzz, and for families that means a trip to glittering, tacky Brighton Pier (01273 609361, www.brightonpier.co.uk), where archetypal seaside fun awaits.

A huge amount of money has recently been spent on redeveloping the seafront, and the meandering promenade running between the piers provides constant entertainment.

The beach has been decorated with large sculptures, some of which make great climbing frames for the little ones. They also enjoy stopping off to watch the action on the beach basketball court and neighbouring volleyball court (which also makes a fantastic sandpit). In season you'll often find free music, theatre and dance events at the Ellipse performance area. There are always flocks of exotic street performers, and also fairground rides, the most splendid of which is an 1888 carousel. The children's free play area by the West Pier has proved a boon to visiting parents. Colourfully themed on pirates and tropical seas, it boasts three interlocking play areas, including a paddling pool, sandpits and dry play equipment. The latter is especially useful as it provides something to do year-round. East of the pier, the beach is more expansive and quieter, but also rather rundown and drab. Here, the Volks Electric Railway (01273 292718) is the oldest electric passenger-carrying train in the world: most of its carriages are over 100 years old. It takes you on a ride along the beach from the Palace Pier to Blackwater.

On bad weather days you can happily spend a few hours at the Sea Life Centre (01273 604234, www.sealife.co.uk), a large underground aquarium. There's a ball pond facility attached to the café, which you can use without paying admission if you are eating there. Or for a bit of culture, take the kids to the Royal Pavilion (01273 290900, www. royalpavilion.brighton.co.uk), where they can learn all about this most exotic royal palace commissioned by the Prince Regent in 1811. Or you could wander around the Lanes and North Laine, a maze of little shops to rival Covent Garden.

Broadstairs

Tourist information centre 6B High Street, Broadstairs, Kent CT10 1LH (01843 583334/www.tourism. thanet.gov.uk). By train Broadstairs rail. By car M25 (Junction 5).

Charles Dickens called this Thanet resort 'our English Watering Place' and that rather staid image that goes with crusty old Victorian writers still holds today. Broadstairs is very different to flashy Margate (*see p287*). The Dickens connection is its main claim to fame; the writer spent some years here, and used it as a base when writing *David Copperfield*. The Dickens House Museum (01843 861232), with its beautiful views over Viking Bay, tells you the whole story if you have time to take in a little English culture after paddling and buying your 'Kiss me Quick' hat.

Broadstairs' beaches – it has seven to its credit – are busy and sheltered. Viking Bay is a hugely popular one, and is near the town centre. It's a traditional seaside resort, with donkey rides and deckchairs, and a sweet, quite safe children's playground (Kiddies Corner) at the southern end of the bay. There's an annual water gala at Viking Bay every August, with fireworks and crashing music at its finale. Between Viking Bay and its neighbour Louisa Bay there's a tidal paddling pool, which is lovely for tinies to splash about in when the tide is out. Joss Bay is said to have inspired a famous 18th-century smuggler to change his name. Today, surfers enjoy its long shallow beach and decent (for Kent) waves. Joss Bay hasn't all the noisy attractions of other Thanet resorts, but you can find an ice-cream and a café or two. It lies at the bottom of Elmwood Farm Valley, and is a nature conservation area. Broadstairs also has a lighthouse, at the North Foreland headland, which is the oldest working lighthouse in England (1691), the best view of which is seen from Joss Bay.

The Dickens Festival runs for eight days every June (ring 01843 861 1827 for details). During this cultured event you can see Dickens fans dressed up in costume, enjoy a country fair, watch a play, take part in a cricket or croquet match and generally laugh at people being new Victorians by the seaside.

Eastbourne

Tourist information centre Cornfield Road, Eastbourne, East Sussex BN21 4QL (01323 411400/www.eastbourne. org). By train Eastbourne rail. By car M25 (Junction 7).

Reputed to be one of the sunniest resorts in the United Kingdom, Eastbourne is a busy yet famously sedate seaside town and a cheerful place to bring the family for a day out. The coastline here, where the white chalk hills of the South Downs meet the sea in spectacular style – a sheer, chilling drop of 575ft – is the famous cliff known as Beachy Head, a known leaping place for suicides. The coastal path, a heritage site with spectacular views out to sea, can be followed all the way to Seaford.

In the shelter of the cliffs, the beaches are shingly but good for rockpools and crabs. The most family-friendly one is Holywell Beach, at the end of the promenade, which has a lifeguard watching out for intrepid bathers from May to September. Eastbourne Pier, a venerable, Victorian structure, is an understated attraction. It is a lovely place to wander seaward, have an ice-cream, a meal in the café/bar, sit and take the air on a deckchair (there's a small hire charge) or pop along to the family entertainments. A glass-blowing workshop is one of these; you can pick up a just blown vase or ornament as a souvenir along with your rock and box of fudge.

Eastbourne's promenade runs for five miles along the beachside, and proves an easier tramp than the more strenuous clifftop trail several hundred feet above it. Also on the seafront is Fort Fun (01323 642833), an indoor and outdoor play area with a café and miniature carnival area – a godsend if it rains.

Eastbourne's other attractions number canoeing, sailing and windsurfing clubs, mini golf, bowling greens and acres of well-tended gardens, the most famous of which is the Carpet Gardens: a symphony of colours in peak season and the pride of the town. Speedboat trips on the nippy 007

boat can be arranged at the end of the pier. The speedboat operates daily from Whitsun to the end of September (ring 01323 765559 for more details).

If you want a change from beachside fun, take the children up Lottbridge Drove to the Railway Adventure Park (01323 520229), where visitors travel behind one-eighth scale miniature locomotives as they bowl along for about a mile around a country park. Young children may be impressed by the treasures inside the cunningly named Thomas the Tank Engine gift shop. There's also a little village for them to play in, an adventure playground for their older siblings and a maze to lose the lot of them in.

Littlehampton

Tourist information centre Windmill Complex, Coastguard Road, Littlehampton, East Sussex BN17 5LH (01903 713480/www.sussexbythesea.com). By train Littlehampton rail. By car M25 (Junction 6).

Another Sussex beach, not so far from Brighton, but soft sandy and traditional where its trendy sister is shingly and edgy. Littlehampton is a beach, bucket and spade day out, with not nearly as many other attractions as Brighton and Eastbourne, but absorbing and lovely for all that.

At low tide the sandy beach is sprinkled with shells, pebbles and other beached treasures ready for collection. The western end is the mouth of the River Arun and this is where Littlehampton's more resorty attractions lie. There are fish and chip shops and cafés, and shops selling rubber rings, buckets and spades, flip flops and other essentials you may have forgotten. A small funfair with an indoor section for arcade games and ride-on toys, as well as a tot area with ball pool, is useful in the rain. Outside there are mini (ie certainly not white-knuckle) fairground rides, dodgems and crazy golf. This western end is where the little fishing boats can be

Board silly at **Brighton**. *See p284.*

Ship ahoy! Due west

The home of the Royal Navy at Portsmouth Harbour has a full day's worth of activities for the sporty and the studious. Aim to arrive at opening time (10am). Nine dockyard attractions are available. These can be paid for individually but more economically with a Passport ticket, which gives access to everything.

The main purpose of most people's visit is to see HMS *Victory*. This is the ship in which Admiral Nelson won the Battle of Trafalgar, although he died doing so. You can only go aboard the ship as part of a 40-minute guided tour at a specific time, which is stated on the ticket. Don't be late: the guides are naval officers who expect punctuality.

Mind your heads! Men were shorter in Nelson's day. The tidy, cramped decks smell of wood polish and tar. All the brasses gleam. Nelson's quarters are spacious and elegant but the lowly crew ate, slept and fired their cannons all in the same tiny space. Some gunners were only boys. The guide ushers youngsters in the party to the front to tell them this. He sees himself as the ancient mariner, spinning yarns and romanticising the sea.

The harbour tour also has a specific start time. The catamaran *Solent Cat* has a bar, comfy seats and a windy top deck. The helmsman gives a running commentary on the passing frigates, destroyers and minesweepers as the vessel trawls the perimeter of this beautiful natural harbour. The Romans were the first to recognise its potential; their fort still stands on the western shore.

Back at the dockyard, children press ahead for Action Stations, which has a simulated helicopter ride, ski machine, kayak machine, shooting, rock-climbing and computer games in which those who do well are invited to sign up. There is also a screening of the Royal Navy film *Command Approved*, which depicts Brits of both genders tackling a band of murderous hostage-takers of swarthy complexion but non-specific nationality.

There are two other ships to visit. The *Mary Rose* was the finest galleon in Henry VIII's navy until it sank to the bottom of Portsmouth Harbour in 1530. Her rotting hull was hauled to the surface in 1980 and kept in the humid conditions of Mary Rose Ship Hall. More interesting still are the dining plates, bowls, leather shoes and bags, weapons, books and musical instruments that were salvaged at the same time and now kept in the Mary Rose Museum. HMS *Warrior* was a fighting ship in Queen Victoria's navy and now lies moored just outside the entrance to the dockyard. She was built for speed and was in her day one of the fastest military ships afloat. She could make the USA in four days with a following wind. Now you can do it in four hours on Concorde but you don't get as many meals on the journey.

Portsmouth Historic Dockyard

HM Naval Base Portsmouth, Hants (0239 286 1533/www.historic dockyard.co.uk). By train Portsmouth. By car M27 (Junction 11). **Open** *Apr-Oct* 10am-5.30pm daily. *Nov-Mar* 10am-5pm daily. Last entry 1hr before closing. Closed 24-26 Dec (phone to check). **Admission** £17; £12.50 children. *Passport* (valid for 1yr) £18; £14.50 OAPs; £14.50 children; £57 family. *Saver Ticket* (any 3 attractions) £13.75; £11 under-16s; £44 family. Separate prices for individual attractions, from £2.50-£7. **Credit** MC, V.
Buggy access (not on ships). Cafés. Nappy-changing facilities. Restaurant. Shop.

spotted arriving with their catch. There are also boat trips to nearby Arundel. At high tide children enjoy crabbing off the river wall, where you have beach on one side and the river on the other. There's a little lighthouse here too. The seaside shop sells crab lines, which you can bait with bacon, limpets or remnants of your packed lunch and dangle into the water. It is customary, not to mention humane, to throw the crabs back in once you have collected a few in a bucket of water and counted your haul. Do not be tempted to keep them as pets; they don't make very good ones.

The promenade is lovely for ice-cream breaks and a ten-minute land train ride to the eastern reaches of the beach. This is the quieter side of Littlehampton, where grassy slopes and formal gardens make space for a small play area for children and a shady break from sun, sand and sea. The Sussex by-the-Sea website above is worth checking if you fancy a really raucous seaside day out, at lovely Bognor Regis and its ever-ready Butlins (call Bognor Tourist Office on 01243 823140 for more information).

Margate
Tourist information centre 12-13 The Parade, Margate, Kent CT9 1EY (01843 220241/583334/www.tourism. thanet.gov.uk). By train Margate rail. By car M2 then A2.

Saucy Margate enjoyed a brief period in the limelight in 2001, thanks to positive publicity from old Margatian Tracy Emin and various 'bad taste is good'-type articles in the *Observer* and the like. But whatever the style monitors say, this historic old town, with its uncouth attractions and sandy beach, is a lovely day out – when the sun shines, that is.

One of Margate's best points is its practically beachside station. You can struggle off the Victoria train, laden with buckets and spades, cross the main road, past the reasonably well-kept loos, down some steps and you're ankle deep in golden sand.

Unless you're down on a particularly hot bank holiday weekend, you can usually find a patch of sand to call your own on Margate's main beach. It's easy to spend the whole day on the beach, especially if you hire a windbreak and parasol from the many beach-furniture providers operating from huts on the sands. You only have to part with £1 to ride on one of the beach's four donkeys, which amble up and down the sands doing their best, mournful Eeyore impressions and enduring passionate hugs from their diminutive jockeys. The donkeys start out from the beach playground, which is a rather sweet mini funfair for small children. Older children and teenagers prefer to discover Dreamland Fun Park, open from Easter through the summer season (01843 227011),

Ship ahoy! Due east

The anchorage known as Chatham became the dockyard that launched many vessels from the 16th century over 400 years until its shipbuilding activities came to an end in 1984. Since then, thanks to the Chatham Historic Dockyard Trust, its ancient buildings and other nautical attractions have been keeping Britain's maritime history alive.

There is a huge number of things to see and do on the 80-acre site – too many really to get round in a day, although you'll enjoy having a good crack at it. People who find walking difficult may want to make use of the two heritage buses, all done up in vintage 'Maidstone & District' livery, to take them to the far-flung areas around the dockyard.

Children enjoy the enthusiastic guided tours around both a 40-year-old submarine, HMS *Ocelot*, during which you can marvel at the tiny amount of space the sailors had to put up with; and a World War II destroyer, HMS *Cavalier*. Wooden Walls is a walk-through exhibit for a full-on experience of the sights, sounds and smells of the 18th-century dockyard. Evidence of life in the dockyard that produced HMS *Victory*, now at Portsmouth (*see p286*), comes from the diary of an apprentice called William Crockwell. From the exhibition, you learn how the oak was seasoned, how the templates for the hull in the mould loft were fashioned, how the wood was bent and how it was made water-tight. Well over 1,000 oaks were cut down to supply the wood for one ship such as HMS *Valiant*. The mind boggles at the acreage of forest sacrificed to construct the British naval fleet.

A major attraction at Chatham is the huge ropery. Here you can watch craftsmen making rope, and even have a go at doing it yourself.

On a smaller scale, but nonetheless absorbing to children, are the new interactive displays. There's a radio-controlled boat and ship-docking exercise, cannon-aiming fun in a shipfight mock-up and a new improved interactive history trail. If all these ships leave children at sea, they can throw themselves about in the soft play area with a ball pool. Adults and older kids who love the spooky atmosphere of the old place may be interested in the autumn and winter ghost walks (sponsored by a funeral parlour, no less). Ring the number below for details.

Various cosmetic improvements have been made to the site over the past year. The newly restored dockyard bell-tower is striking, but equally arresting is the 100-foot cast-iron mast at the entrance, which is over 120 years old. Beyond it is a huge car park and, in the Mast House, a ship-shape new visitors' reception area, with the inevitable gift shop.

Ring for details of Chatham's annual Navy Days, (this year's, 2-4 June 2002) honours the Golden Jubilee). The family fun includes visiting warships, air displays and military bands. Check the website for all the latest on children's holiday activities, at Easter, half-term and during the summer holidays.

Historic Dockyard Chatham
Dock Road, Chatham, Kent (01634 823800/ www.chdt.org.uk). By train Chatham rail. By car M2 (Junctions 1-4). **Open** *Early Feb-late Mar, early Nov-early Dec 10am-4pm Wed, Sat, Sun. Feb half-term 10am-4pm (last entry 3pm) daily. Late Mar-early Nov 10am-4pm (last entry 4pm) daily. Closed Dec, Jan.* **Admission** *£9.50; £7 concessions; £6 5-15; £25 family (2+2; £3 per additional child).* **Credit** *MC, V. Buggy access. Café. Car park. Shop.*

a fabulously trashy theme park where entrance is free but rides cost. A special wristband (£6.99-£11.99) can be bought if you want to spend hours on the rides.

If you can wrest the children away from Margate's number-one visitor attraction, there are other, much more quirky places to explore. Margate Caves (01843 220139), hewn from the town's less famous rock, were once used by smugglers. The strange Shell Grotto (01843 220008) was discovered by Victorian schoolboys, digging in a field. It's a series of underground tunnels lined with 2,000sq ft of shell mosaics. Opinion is still divided as to who created them. Are they pagan (as HG Wells thought), or are they a more recent folly? Whatever, they're worth seeking out. But call both places first; the Grotto, in particular, has erratic opening hours.

Southend

Tourist information centre 19 High Street, Southend-on-Sea, Essex SS1 1JE (01702 215120/www.southend.gov.uk). By train Southend Central or Southend Victoria rail. By car M25 (Junction 30).

The closest seaside resort to London really is chirpy Cockney country. The brevity of the train ride here, and the variety of attractions that have built up around the seven miles of gentle estuary coastline, make it a Big Treat option for children of all ages.

Southend is the largest town in Essex and one of the main providers of that great tooth-rotting seaside essential: rock. Southend's rock factory provides the sweeties for Brighton and many other southern resorts, and its ice-cream plant keeps holidaymakers across the country refreshed. The only thing that Southend lacks is decent sand, but the powers-that-be have sorted that little problem: they ship it in, tons of the stuff, to provide the sort of golden sand that everyone demands for their castles. Estuary mud does not feel right between the toes. If the tide's out, there's a long walk to a decent swim, although each of Southend's beaches have outdoor paddling pools (as well as showers and loos) to keep mini bathing beauties happy till the tide comes in. The beaches have Tidy Britain Group Seaside Award Flags and the favourite with children is the one at the Three Shells.

You can walk along the pier (01702 215622), which juts 1.33 miles out to sea (be warned: on a windy day your face will take a bit of a battering), or take the train (Southend is the only resort to have a pier train). Children enjoy the end-of-the-pier fun: there are rides, ice-creams and arcades. Admission to Southend Pier Museum (open in summer only 01702 611214/614553) is 50p and accompanied children under 12 go free. The museum explores the history of the pier since its beginnings, with an old pier train and interesting temporary exhibitions. Adventure Island (01702 468023) is Southend's theme park, which no parent worthy of the name can deny their little darlings.

If the weather's dodgy, holidaymakers make a beeline for the Sea Life Adventure (01702 601834), not far from the pier, where a Little Tikes Play Centre is an added attraction and cheers up little tikes when the new piranhas look at them funny.

Whitstable

Tourist information centre 7 Oxford Street, Whitstable, Kent CT5 1DB (01227 275482/www.canterbury.co.uk). By train Whitstable. By car M2 (Junction 7).

A picturesque old sea port on the Thames estuary, Whitstable is about as far from your average seaside resort as you can get. But that's not to say its singular charms do not appeal to family day trippers. It's easily accessible by train, and though its shell and shingle beaches might lack the golden stuff for sandcastles, they have a singular charm. Walk along to the beach at Tankerton Slopes for more space to play. The beach, with groynes to play on, grassy slopes to fly kites on and play hide

and seek in, and enormous potential for exploring, are big pluses for young children. If you want to wander further, there are beach walks all the way to Margate (*see p287*).

Once the beach possibilities have been exhausted, there's the ramshackle harbour to admire, with all its fishing boats, cranes and machinery. Along Beach Walk, and back up to the town, past picture-box cottages, sailmakers and fishermen's huts, there are numerous cafés, pubs and restaurants to sample. Whitstable is known for its oysters, and has plenty of places to eat them. The fascinating Oyster & Fishery Exhibition, where you used to be able to find out about their lifecycle and watch them grow in their special pools, is currently closed pending planning permission. The new management would love the attraction, housed in the harbour's oldest building, to be reopened later in 2002, but it's best to ring the tourist information centre to find out the latest news. More oyster information can be gleaned from the Whitstable Museum & Gallery (01227 276998). Regular art exhibitions take place here, and there's a display about Whitstable's oyster heritage, the old railway that used to run here and the little town's heyday as a Victorian leisure centre. The Peter Cushing exhibitions honour the town's most famous and devoted resident.

If you want something more challenging than excellent fish and chips, try the much-loved Whitstable Oyster Fishery Company (01227 276856), where a variety of fishy dinners are on the menu, alongside the all-important shellfish. Phone to book first as it's very popular.

Steam trains

Note that steam train timetables change month to month, but most lines run special trains to accommodate the half-term hordes. Ticket prices given are for round trips only; most prices are due to rise in January 2003.

Bluebell Railway

Sheffield Park Station, on A275 between Lewes & East Grinstead, Sussex (01825 723777/talking timetable 01825 722370/www.bluebell-railway.co.uk). By train East Grinstead rail then 473 bus. By car M23 (Junction 10). **Open** *Easter-Sept* daily. *Oct-Apr* Sat, Sun, school hols, bank hols. **Admission** £8; £4 3-15s; £21.50 family (2+3); £6.40 OAPs; free under-3s. **Credit** MC, V.

This is one of the biggest success stories in Sussex. Train enthusiasts, from those still in nappies to those in their dotage, love the Bluebell. The line was the UK's first preserved standard gauge passenger railway; it reopened part of the Lewes to East Grinstead line of the old London Brighton & South Coast Railway in 1960. Each station the line passes through is restored according to a different era: Victorian, the 1930s and the 1950s. Apart from the occasional Thomas the Tank Engine extravaganzas (check the website), there are all kinds of specials in steam for children. Their favourite train is Stepney, a lovely old engine that pulls his special train between Sheffield Park and Kingscote. The Stepney Specials run during the school holidays. Fans aged 3-8 can join the Stepney Club (from £4.50 per year) through which they receive a newsletter, birthday cards, reduced-price train tickets and other perks. Other childish delights include a bedtime story service on summer evenings, and teatime specials on Saturday afternoons, when you can scoff tea and cake while steaming through the verdant Sussex landscape. Ring for details of such fun, and the Sheffield Park special tickets, which combine a train ride with free entry to the National Trust's lovely 120 acres.

Steam on down to **Didcot Railway Centre**, where the trains run on time.

From October until Christmas Eve, there are a series of Santa Specials, which run from Sheffield Park to Kingscote, a nine-mile journey, which takes you through the atmospheric Sharpthorne tunnel, on the way to Kingscote. The ticket price includes a meeting with Santa as you board the train, a gift for your child, mince pies for the adults (a glass of wine is extra), a children's entertainer and a free ride on the children's roundabout. The Santa Special tickets start at £3 for children (rising to £9 in the observation car) and £10 for adults; all children under 1 go free. If all of this is bringing out the trainspotter in you, why not sign up for a one-day course (8am-4.30pm) on driving a steam engine (there are eight people on each course and after one hour's briefing you can use the controls, driving under instruction). There is also a five-day course, during which you'll get to fire the engine too. Call Clive Groome for details on 01273 731873.
Buggy access. Café. Car park. Nappy-changing facilities. Shop.

Didcot Railway Centre
Didcot, Oxon (01235 817200/www.didcotrailwaycentre. org.uk). By train Didcot Parkway rail. By car M4 (Junction 13). **Open** 10am-5pm (last entry 4.30pm) daily. *Tours* bank hols (times depend on events; phone for details). **Admission** *Steam days, incl tour* £6.50; £5.50 concessions; £4.50 3-16s; £19 family (2+2); free under-3s. *Non-steam days* £4; £3.50 concessions; £3 3-16s; £12 family; free under-3s. **Credit** MC, V.
This is the home of the Great Western Railway, staffed by enthusiasts and visited by train lovers of all ages. At the Railway Centre you can enjoy the smell, sound and smoke of the steam engines, and see the activities of a steam locomotive depot, including engines being coaled, watered and turned on the turntable. The admission price includes unlimited travel on the trains during your visit. The trains travel around the museum complex, but on special event days can

run along the main line. Thomas the Tank Engine is a big draw here on certain dates during the holidays – there are rides behind Thomas as well as lots of children's activities. It is always best to ring the centre before you set out, as the engines are not always in steam. The informative website lists an up-to-date programme of special events, and staff will send you a current timetable if you ask them nicely.
Buggy access. Café. Car park. Nappy-changing facilities. Shop.

Kent & East Sussex Railway
Tenterden, Northiam & Bodiam stations (01580 765155/ www.kesr.org.uk). By train Headcorn rail then link bus to Tenterden. By car M20 Junction 9. **Open** *May-Sept* trains run 10.30am-4.40pm daily; weekends only at other times of year; ring for details of Easter and half-term services. **Admission** £8; £4 3-15s; £20 family; free under-3s. **Credit** MC, V.
Trains, carriages and line that are the stars of this increasingly popular Kentish nostalgia trip have been scavenged and rebuilt by a band of enthusiasts. On high days and holidays the volunteers here dress up in period costume and drive their steam and diesel engines through ten or so miles of exquisite English countryside. The main base is at the market town of Tenterden, but you can also join this fabulous old steam railway line at Northiam or Bodiam. If you stop at the latter, you can visit the medieval castle (*see p272*); otherwise, the round trip takes about two hours. There's a reduced service in winter, but the trains run all year: at Christmas you can board the Santa Express for mince pies and mulled wine; Thomas the Tank Engine is a predictable year-round visitor. For details of train times for the rest of 2002 and 2003, or to receive a timetable and dates of special events, ring the above number.
Buggy access. Café (Tenterden and Northiam stations). Car park. Shop.

Chocks away!

Duxford is a Big Day Out, with five vast themed hangars of exhibits, as well as the futuristic glass-fronted American Air Museum, designed by Lord Foster, and the Land Warfare Hall, filled up with tanks and military vehicles. The complex is so huge that a convenient, free 'road train' operates all day, dropping off at the major attractions. The air shows are superb (there are about four each year), but you'll still see plenty of thrilling flying action if you opt for a less crowded weekend or midweek visit.

There's plenty of hands-on activity too. Take a walk through Concorde's cabin in Hangar 1 or experience the sounds and smells of the Blitz in the Land Warfare Hall. Here, tanks, military vehicles and artillery pieces are on show in dramatic battlefield scenes. You may even see them rolling over the turf, too, as dedicated enthusiasts work to restore them.

Kids can let off steam in two excellent play areas, including an adventure playground. There are cafés on site; alternatively, eat your own picnic while watching the action. And if the temptation is too much, you too can take to the skies in an elegant 1930s biplane airliner (call Classic Wings on 0870 902 6146/www.classic-wings.uk.com).

Duxford Imperial War Museum

Duxford, Cambs (01223 835000/www.iwm.org.uk). By train Cambridge rail then free bus. By car M11 (Junction 10). **Open** *Mid Mar-late Oct* 10am-6pm daily. *Late Oct-mid Mar* 10am-4pm daily. Last admission 1hr before closing. Closed 24-26 Dec. **Admission** £8; free under-16s. **Credit** MC, V. *Buggy access. Café. Car park. Nappy-changing facilities. Restaurant.*

Romney, Hythe & Dymchurch Railway

New Romney Station, Kent (01797 362353/ www.rhdr.demon.co.uk). By train Folkestone Central rail then 711 bus to Hythe. By car M20 (Junction 11). **Open** *Mar-Oct* Sat, Sun. *Easter-Sept* daily. Ring for train timetable info as times change monthly. **Admission** £9.50; £4.25 children. **Credit** MC, V.
A miniature railway barrels merrily from the Nuclear Power Station in Dungeness (a weird, wild promontory that's also home to an RSPB Nature Reserve – for information, call 01797 320588 – and a desolate pebble beach) all the way to Hythe in the east. Along the way it stops at New Romney and the coastal village of Dymchurch, the self-proclaimed 'Children's Paradise', which boasts an amusement park and a fine sandy beach. It also passes some beautiful, flat scenery and seems to sweep through any number of back gardens. The railway was built by the millionaire racing driver Captain Howey in 1927 and everything (track, engines, the sweetest carriages) is one-third actual size. It's a real treat – on a warm day. *Buggy access. Cafés. Car park. Nappy-changing facilities. Shops.*

Watercress Line

The Station, Alresford, Hants (01962 733810/talking timetable 01962 734866/www.watercressline.co.uk). By train Alton rail. By car A133 then B1027. **Open** changes monthly; ring for details. Closed Jan. **Admission** £9; £2 3-16s; £20 family; free under-3s; ring for prices during special events. **Credit** MC, V.
The line is run by keen volunteers, who finally fulfilled their dream of resurrecting the old trains in 1977. The trains run throughout the year, and their route takes in rolling Home Counties countryside at its most alluring.

Although the mid-Hants Watercress Line is based in Alresford, it's easier to catch one of its puffing stars from the market town of Alton, which has a direct rail link with London's Waterloo. The ten-mile, two-hour round trip to Alresford can be broken up by stopping at the smart village stations of Ropley, or Medstead & Four Marks between the two main stations. Both places provide some pretty picnic places: Ropley has a children's picnic play area as well as the engine shed and yard to look over. Alresford, slightly less busy, is a touch more upmarket, and has some beautiful places to walk, smart shops to visit, and friendly inns to lunch in. The information office here can furnish you with leaflets and friendly advice about what to do in and around the town. On certain days during the school holidays the blue train dresses up and makes like Thomas the Tank Engine. Ring to request a timetable and to find out about the next TT day, in addition to other themed children's days, such as the teddy bears day or Santa specials at Christmas. *Buggy access (footbridge at Alton). Shop.*

Theme parks

Chessington World of Adventures

Leatherhead Road, Chessington, Surrey (0870 444 7777/ www.chessington.com). By train Chessington South rail. By car M25/M26 (Junction 9). **Open** *Late Mar-end Nov* 10am-5/6pm daily. *Late July-early Sept* 10am-7pm daily; times may vary according to special events, check website or phone for details. **Admission** *on the day* £17-£21; £14.50-£17 4-12s, concessions; from £52 family (2+2); check the website for online advance bookings that give fast-track entry. **Credit** MC, V.
Thrill-seekers find enough to whiten their knuckles here, but connoisseurs of gut-wrenching rides know the real thrills are at sister park Thorpe (*see p292*). Nonetheless, the family appeal of Chessington is that it has something to please children of all age groups. Tinies like the Safari Skyride, a good bet because it helps you to get an overview of the park before you choose where to home in on, and you get a bird's-eye view of Animal Land, where you can be a whisker away from some big cats or whoop it up with the gorillas. Visitors can learn more about animals like Persian leopards, Sumatran tigers, Asian lions and gorillas. There are many other species to encounter, too, spread out over the vast 65-acre park. Be sure not to miss feeding time for the seals and discover the habits of insects down in the Creepy Caves. Under-10s like Beanoland, with Dennis's Madhouse, a new foam-ball firing arena, stunt shows and Bash Street themed rides. For intrepid children and sulky adolescents, the 'hot three' are still Samurai, with its gyrating rotor arms that spin you through 360 degrees, Rameses Revenge, another vicious spinner, which has the added attraction of soaking its

Another wet weekend at **Thorpe Park**

is still the nearest thing to a white knuckle, but all the rides are a pretty tame by Thorpe Park (*see below*) standards. The Dragon Knight's Castle and Dragon rollercoaster is another hot favourite. Tinies adore the Duplo gardens and their water jets.

Legoland is more popular than ever, and as usual the main drawback is that the rest of the world seems to be there whenever you visit. Avoiding state school holiday periods is one way of beating the crowds, but that's easier said than done. If you're bringing pre-schoolers only, do come during term-time. Coming in the rain isn't a bad idea, either. Yet Legoland is mostly a delightful place to be, especially if you're organised enough to bring a picnic to eat in the extensive grounds, thus avoiding the punishing prices in the restaurants. Log on to the website for news of special children's events throughout the season, but rest assured that at peak times there's usually a show to enjoy in the Imagination Theatre; this year it's a film based on Lego racers, with 4-D effect such as smoke and water. Shows for little ones take place in the Puppet Theatre regularly too. With so much to suit children of all ages, as well as adult Lego fans, this remains our favourite theme park, irritating queues notwithstanding.

Buggy access. Cafés. Car park. Nappy-changing facilities. Restaurants. Shops.

Thorpe Park

Staines Road, Chertsey, Surrey (0870 444 4466/ www.thorpepark.com). By train Staines rail then bus. By car M25 (Junction 11 or 13). **Open** *Late Mar-early Nov 9/10am-5/6pm daily. Late July-early Sept 9/10pm-7.30pm daily.* **Height restrictions** vary, depending on rides. **Admission** *on the day* £17-£23; £14.50-£18 4-12s, concessions; £52-£65 family (2+2 or 1+3); free under-4s. Check the website or phone for details of online & phone advance bookings. Allow min 2 days to process advance ticket purchases. **Credit** AmEx, MC, V.

Many of the biggest star rides at Thorpe leave you a soggy, rumpled, gibbering wreck, for not just white-knuckle but wet-knicker experiences await you here. It is the thrill-seeker's park and the one recommended for older children and teenagers. Parents with young children to amuse are better off at Chessington (*see p290*), another Tussaud's Group theme park. In Amity Cove the newest, wettest attraction is the 85ft Tidal Wave – set in a New England village about to be hit by a huge wall of water – coming your way. New this year is Colossus, a rollercoaster that climbs to 100ft then hurtles riders through ten loops stretching over 2,789ft of twisting tracks at speeds of 40mph. Back again for another sickening season is the gut-clenching Detonator, in which hapless saps are winched up 100ft in the air then hurled back to earth at 75mph. The G-force in this experience is 5.5, which sounds hideous. That's probably not one you could share with a pre-schooler. Never fear, there are gentler forms of fun for them, away from the screaming adolescents.

A trip to Thorpe Farm helps reduce your heart rate. Families can make the trip either by waterbus or via the railway to this turn-of-the-century working farm with duck pond, rare breeds and children's petting area. Younger visitors might also like Ranger County, between Canada Creek and the central area, with its jungle boats, attractive banana swingboats and the ranger's carousel, where kids can track down and tame their own big game.

Eating places include big-name fast-food outlets and themed restaurants, such as Sleepy Joe's Rib Shack, which can get very crowded in peak season. There are plenty of places to eat a picnic, buy an ice-cream or recover from the shock of the mighty Colossus with a hot, sweet tea.

Buggy access. Cafés. Car park. Nappy-changing facilities. Restaurants. Shops.

riders (they must be over 4ft 7in), and the big coaster Vampire, spruced up for 2002, which swings and suspends riders over the tree tops. Also new this year is the interactive adventure ride known as Tomb Blaster; trigger-happy participants ride in cars armed with laser guns, to be ambushed by a variety of moving targets. For the less combative, Toadie's crazy cars and the pink knuckle delights of the Berry Bouncers can be found in the gentle Toytown zone. For pitstops there's Pizza Hut, KFC, McDonald's and a whole host of themed restaurants including the Mexican Diner and the Krazy Keg family inn.

Buggy access. Café. Car park. Nappy-changing facilities. Shops.

Legoland

Winkfield Road, Windsor, Berks (08705 040404/ www.legoland.co.uk). By train Windsor & Eton Riverside or Windsor Central rail. By car M3 (Junction 3) or M4 (Junction 6). **Open** *Mid Mar-early Nov 10am-5pm or 6pm daily (until 7pm during school summer hols).* **Admission** *Peak season (school hols)* £22.95; £19.95 3-15s; £16.95 concessions. *Off-peak season* £18.95; £15.95 3-15s; £12.95 concessions. **Credit** AmEx, MC, V.

This is the theme park parents approve of, because of the creativity suggested by all those astonishingly detailed Lego brick buildings in Miniland. They really are fantastic. Miniland London now has the London Eye and Buckingham Palace; there's also a brick-built interactive racing circuit, where you can have a go at racing at Le Mans. In the Lego Creation Centre, the Hall of Fame contains ranks of models of the rich and famous, including the Queen. New rides include the Adventurers Express, a train ride that allows passengers to go on a Lego safari, spotting model animals. Pirate Falls

Directory

Directory

The following pages should come in useful when it comes to getting around, seeking help and learning more about the city. Where necessary, we've included full contact details.

Councils

Barnet 8359 2000/www.barnet.gov.uk.
Brent 8937 1234/www.brent.gov.uk.
Camden 7278 4444/www.camden.gov.uk.
Corporation of London
7606 3030/www.cityoflondon.gov.uk.
Ealing 8579 2424/www.ealing.gov.uk.
Greenwich 8854 8888/
www.greenwich.gov.uk.
Hackney 8356 5000/
www.hackney.gov.uk.
Hammersmith & Fulham
8748 3020/www.lbhf.gov.uk.
Haringey 8489 0000/
www.haringey.gov.uk.
Hounslow 8583 2000/
www.hounslow.gov.uk.
Islington 7527 2000/
www.islington.gov.uk.
Kensington & Chelsea
7937 5464/www.rbkc.gov.uk.
Lambeth 7926 1000/
www.lambeth.gov.uk.
Lewisham 8314 6000/
www.lewisham.gov.uk.
Merton 8543 2222/
www.merton.gov.uk.
Newham 8430 2000/
www.newham.gov.uk.
Richmond-upon-Thames 8891 1411/
www.richmond.gov.uk.
Southwark 7525 5000/
www.southwark.gov.uk.
Tower Hamlets 7364 5000/
www.towerhamlets.gov.uk.
Waltham Forest 8527 5544/
www.walthamforest.gov.uk.
Wandsworth 8871 6000/
www.wandsworth.gov.uk.
Westminster 7641 6000/
www.westminster.gov.uk.

Education

To find out more about the state schools and nurseries in your area, contact the education department of your local council.

Advisory Centre on Education (ACE)
0808 800 5793/Exclusion advice line
0808 800 0327/www.ace-ed.org.uk. **Open**
Exclusion advice line 2-5pm Mon-Fri.
Ring the Advisory Centre on Education for advice pertaining to your child's schooling.

The advice line is for worried parents whose children have been excluded from their school.

Anti-Bullying Campaign
7378 1446.
If school bullies are making your child's life a misery, contact the Anti-Bullying Campaign for practical advice.

British Association for Early Childhood Education
136 Cavell Street, E1 2JA (7539 5400/www.early-education.org.uk).
Open 9am-5pm Mon-Fri.
Ring the British Association for Early Childhood Education for information on education from birth to 8 years. Send an SAE for extra information.

Gabbitas Educational Consultants
Carrington House, 126-30 Regent Street, W1B 5EE (7734 0161/www.gabbitas.net or www.gabbitas.co.uk). **Open** 9am-5pm Mon-Fri.
Write to or ring Gabbitas, the independent schools consultants, for advice on choosing the right independent school for your child.

Home Education Advisory Service
PO Box 98, Welwyn Garden City, Herts AL8 6AN (01707 371854/www.heas.org.uk). **Open** 9am-5pm Mon-Fri.
Call the service for information if you are thinking of educating your child at home, and to order information packs and leaflets. An introductory pack costs £2.50, and a year's subscription to the Home Education Advisory Service £11.

ISC Information Service
London & South-east 7798 1560/www.iscis.uk.net.
The Independent Schools Council information service works to help parents find out about independent schools in their area.

National Association for Gifted Children
Suite 14, Challenge House, Sherwood Drive, Bletchley, Milton Keynes, Bucks MK3 6DP (0870 770 3217/www.nagcbritain.org.uk).
Help and support for the parents of gifted children.

Parenting Education & Support Forum
Unit 431, Highgate Studios, 53-79 Highgate Road, NW5 1TL (7284 8389/www.parent-forum.org.uk). **Open**
10.30am-5.30pm Mon-Thur.
Information about parenting classes and support for parents.

Pre-School Learning Alliance
69 King's Cross Road, WC1X 9LL (7833 0991/www.pre-school.org.uk).
Open 9am-5pm Mon-Fri.
The Pre-School Learning Alliance runs courses and workshops for parents of children under the age of 5 in pre-schools around the country. It also offers a pack for pre-school leaders wishing to run courses, called 'Looking at Learning Together'.

Fun & games

Indoor play

Crechendo
1 George Mills Weir Road, SW12 (0800 092 0911/www.crechendo.com).
Open phoneline 9am-5pm daily.
Crechendo runs active play classes throughout London. Children aged from 3 months to 4 years can take part in the programme. Ring the above number for your nearest class.

Gymboree Play & Music
0800 092 0911/
www.gymboreePlayUK.com.
A parent and child play organisation, based on music and movement, for children aged 16 months to 4 and a half years. New recruits receive a free trial session.

National Association of Toy & Leisure Libraries (NATLL)
7387 9592/www.natll.org.uk. **Open**
phoneline 9.30am-5.30pm Mon-Fri.
Provides information on the more than 1,000 toy libraries across Britain. It's also a good source of useful publications on related subjects.

Tumble Tots
0121 585 7003/www.tumbletots.com.
Tumble Tots is a parent and baby play class for children from 6 months up to school age. The children play on a range of equipment to help build co-ordination and social skills. They also take part in music and singing sessions. Ring this central number to find out about Tumble Tot play centres in your area.

One o'clock clubs

These weekday clubs, which generally open around lunchtime (12.30-1.30pm) and go on until school's out, are a meeting place within a park for parents and carers of pre-school children.

North London

Barnard Park *Copenhagen Street, N1 (7278 9494). Angel tube.*
Clissold Park *Stoke Newington Church Street, N16 (8809 6700). Bus 73.*
Finsbury Park *Young Children & Family Drop-in Community Centre, Jamboree Playhuts, Seven Sisters Road, N4 (8802 1301). Finsbury Park tube/ rail.*
Highbury Fields *The Bandstand, Highbury Fields, N5 (7704 9337). Highbury & Islington tube/rail.*
Islands Club at the Grove *Alexandra Park, Muswell Hill, N22 (8883 7173). Bus 134, 144, 144A, W3, W7.*
Peggy Jay Centre *Parliament Hill Fields, NW5 (7485 6907). Gospel Oak rail.*

East London

Haggerston Park *Queensbridge Road, E2 (7729 6662). Bus 26, 48, 55.*
Millwall Park *Stebondale Street, E14 (7515 6807). Mudchute DLR.*
Springfield Park *Springfield Lane, E5 (8806 0970). Clapton rail/253 bus. Just outside the park.*
Victoria Park *Cadogan Terrace, E9 (8986 6150). Bus 277, S2.*
Wapping Park *opposite St Patrick's Church, off High Street, E1 (7481 9321). Wapping tube.*

South-east London

Crystal Palace Park *Crystal Palace Park Road, SE20 (8659 6554). Crystal Palace, Penge East or Penge West rail.*
Geraldine Mary Harmsworth Park *St George's Road, SE1 (7820 9724). Lambeth North tube.*
Kennington Park *Bolton Crescent, SE5 (7735 7186). Oval tube/36, 45, 131, 159 bus.*
Leyton Square *Peckham Park Road, SE15 (7639 1812). Bus 53, 78, 172, 381.*
Myatts Fields *Cormont Road, SE5 (7733 3609). Bus P5.*
Norwood Park *Salters Hill, SE19 (8761 1752). Gipsy Hill rail.*
Peckham Rye *Peckham Rye Road, SE15 (8693 0481). Bus 12, 63, 312.*
Ruskin Park *Denmark Hill, SE5 (7733 6659). Denmark Hill rail.*
Southwark Park *Hawkstone Road, SE16 (7231 3755). Canada Water tube/ Surrey Quays DLR.*

South-west London

Agnes Riley Gardens *corner of Clarence Avenue & Poynders Road, SW4 (8673 1277). Clapham South tube.*
Bishops Park *Rainbow Playroom, Stevenage Road, SW6 (7731 4572). Putney tube/14, 74, 220 bus.*
Brockwell Park *Arlingford Road, SW9 (8671 4883). Herne Hill rail.*
Clapham Common *Windmill Drive, SW4 (8673 5736). Clapham Common or Clapham South tube.*
Streatham Vale Park *Abercairn Road, SW16 (8764 3688). Streatham Common rail/60, 118 bus.*
Vauxhall Park *Fentiman Road, SW8 (7582 3209). Vauxhall tube/rail.*
Windmill Gardens *Blenheim Gardens, SW2 (8671 5587). Brixton tube/rail/ 3, 45, 109, 159 bus.*

West London

Acton Park *East Acton Lane, W3 (8743 6133). East Acton tube.*
Lammas Park *Playcentre, Elers Road, W13 (8810 0240). South Ealing/ Northfields tube.*
Meanwhile Gardens *Elkstone Road, W10 (8960 7894). Westbourne Park tube.*
Ravenscourt Park *Under-5s centre, Ravenscourt Park, W6 (8748 3180). Ravenscourt Park tube.*

Support

Contact-A-Family

7383 3555/helpline 0808 808 3555/ www.cafamily.org.uk. **Open** 10am-4pm Mon-Fri.
If you're a parent of a child with disabilities, ring the number to find out about local support groups.

National Asthma Campaign

helpline 0845 701 0203/www.asthma. org.uk. **Open** 9am-7pm Mon-Fri.
Contact the campaign for advice and help if you or your child has asthma.

NHS Direct

helpline 0845 4647/www.nhsdrect.nhs.uk. **Open** 24hrs daily.
Staffed by nurses and health information advisors, NHS Direct provides confidential health advice and information. Calls are charged at the local rate and all are recorded.

Serene

7404 5011/www.our-space.co.uk/ serene.htm. **Open** 8am-11pm daily.
If a constantly crying baby has you at the end of your tether, get in touch with Serene for advice and support.

Childcare

Academy Childcare

Family Zone, Victoria station forecourt (7983 7219). **Open** 8am-6pm Mon-Fri; 10am-6pm Sat; 11am-5pm Sun. **Map** p318 H10.
Academy runs crèches in lots of places; this one, in Victoria station, welcomes children aged 3 months to 4 years weekdays and 2-12 years weekends for up to four hours. There are all-day nursery places too. Phone for details of fees.

Bestbear

8675 3131/www.bestbear.co.uk. **Open** 24hr answerphone.
Log on to the website for information about tried, tested and recommended childcare agencies and everything you need to know about hiring, or becoming, a child carer.

Childcare Link

0800 096 0296/www.childcarelink.gov.uk. **Open** 9am-9pm Mon-Fri; 9am-noon Sat.
Parents can ring up, or log on to the website, for information on childcare options open to them, and request leaflets on same. Where possible, callers will be given a list of childcare organisations in their area.

Childminders

6 Nottingham Street, W1 (7935 3000/ www.childminders.co.uk). **Open** 8.45am-5.30pm Mon-Thur; 8.45am-5pm Fri; 9am-4.30pm Sat.
Childminders is a long-established babysitting agency. Sitters on its books are locally based nurses, teachers and nannies.

Daycare Trust

21 St George's Road, SE1 6ES (7840 3350/www.daycaretrust.org.uk). **Open** 9.30am-5.30pm Mon-Fri.
National childcare charity promoting high-quality and affordable childcare. It publishes useful booklets, including *No More Nine to Five: Childcare in a changing world* (£5).

Kids' Club Network

7512 2100/7512 2112/www.kidsclubs. org.uk. **Open** 9.30am-5.30pm Mon-Fri. Information on after-school clubs.

Nannytax

PO Box 988, Brighton, East Sussex BN2 1BY (01273 626256/www.nannytax.co.uk). **Open** 9am-5pm Mon-Fri.
For £164.50 a year Nannytax will register your nanny with the Inland Revenue, issue his or her payslips and organise National Insurance payments. There's employment advice on the website for nannies too.

National Family & Parenting Institute

430 Highgate Studios, 53-79 Highgate Road, NW5 1TL (7424 3460/ www.nfpi.org/www.e-parents.org). Kentish Town tube/rail. **Open** 9.30am-5.30pm Mon-Fri/24hr answerphone.
An excellent resource centre for all families, with factsheets and booklets on all aspects of parenting.

Night Nannies

7731 6168/www.night-nannies.com.
A useful service for parents whose children are denying them sleep, Night Nannies can be contacted for professional, reliable, night-time childcare. After the initial phone call, when the parent's needs are discussed (how many nights the nanny will be needed, for example, and from what time), Night Nannies provides a list of suitable, qualified carers, who the parent can then get in touch with.

The Parent Company

6 Jacob's Well Mews, W1 (7935 0123/ www.theparentcompany.co.uk). **Open** 9am-5pm Mon-Fri.
Information and seminars on employing nannies. *See also p297.*

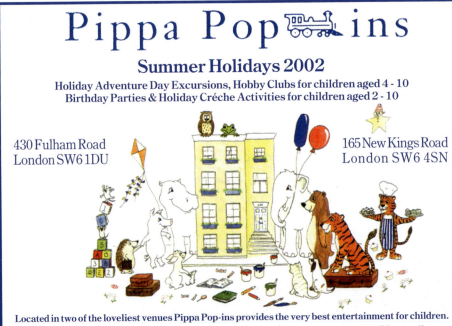

Simply Childcare

*16 Bushey Hill Road, SE5 (7701 6111/
www.simplychildcare.com).* **Open** 9am-
5.30pm Mon-Fri.
As the company has expanded, so the
name has changed, but the service of
the organisation formerly known as the
Register is the same. If you are seeking a
nanny to work in or near London, you can
pay £22 for inclusion in three issues of this
32-page printed list, or £30 for five issues.
Entry on the list is free for prospective
nannies looking for full- or part-time work.

Parent courses

Holy Trinity Brompton

*Ennismore Gardens Mews, SW7
(7581 8255/www.htb.org.uk).* South
Kensington tube. **Open** Office 9.30am-
4.30pm Mon, Wed-Fri; 10.30am-4.30pm Tue.
Runs 'The Parenting Course' for parents
with kids under the age of 12. The price
of admission is £15. 'Parenting Teenagers',
for parents of children aged 13-18,
costs £20. Both courses involve four
two-hour sessions, and prices include
supper and materials.

The Parent Company

See p295.
Runs seminars on weekday evenings on
diverse subjects, from time management
to discipline. Seminars cost £45 per session
per person, or £60 for two people. Ring for
further details.

Parent Network

*Parentline Plus 0808 800 2222/
www.parentlineplus.org.uk.* **Open**
8am-10pm Mon-Fri; 9.30am-5pm Sat;
10am-3pm Sun.
Organises nationwide courses on how to
cope with being a parent. For more details
phone the free helpline, Parentline Plus.

Parent Support Group

helpline 8469 0205/www.psg.org.uk.
Open 24hrs.
As well as the helpline, staff run one-
to-one support sessions and courses in
parenting skills to parents and carers
of adolescents who are acting in an
antisocial or criminal manner.

Parents for Inclusion

7735 7735/www.parentsforinclusion.org.
Organises a series of workshops for
parents of disabled children. A helpline
(7582 5008) operates 10am-noon, 1-3pm
Tue-Thur.

Information

Literature

Families magazine

Families North *PO Box 14965,
NW3 5WA (7794 5690);* **Families
East** *Enterprise House 113-115 George
Lane, E18 1AB (8694 8694);* **Families
South East** *PO Box 11591, SE26 6WB
(8699 7240);* **Families South West** *PO*

Box 4302, SW16 1ZS (8696 1680);
Families West *PO Box 32231,
W5 1JR (8930 4707);* **Families North
West** *PO Box 32358, HA1 1GF (8810
5388);* **Families Upon Thames** *PO Box
425 Walton-on-Thames, KT12 5AG
(01932 254584).* **All:** *www.familiesmagazine.co.uk.*
All areas of London are covered by this
informative freesheet, available in libraries,
nurseries and selected children's shops,
which lists places to visit, things to do,
independent health practitioners and a
wealth of information for anyone bringing
up a child in London.

Time Out magazine

7813 3000/www.timeout.com.
For up-to-the-minute information about
where to go and what to see in London,
check out the Around Town and Children
sections. Available from most London
newsagents.

Libraries

Every local borough has a string
of libraries to its name. We don't
have the space to list them all,
but below we have included a
selection of large, central London
libraries with good children's
sections.

Barbican Library

*Barbican Centre, Silk Street, EC2 (7638
0569/www.cityoflondon.gov.uk/libraries).*
Barbican tube/rail. **Open** 9.30am-5.30pm Mon, Wed-Fri;
9.30am-7.30pm Tue; 9.30am-12.30pm
Sat. **Map** p320 P5.
The children's library here has comfortable,
raked seating and a big, well-organised
choice of titles. Occasional events are
laid on for the under-5s, but space is
limited and admission is on a first come,
first served basis.

Commonwealth Resource Centre (CRC)

*Commonwealth Institute, Kensington
High Street, W8 (7603 4535/www.
commonwealth.org.uk).* High Street
Kensington tube. **Open** 10am-4pm
Mon-Sat. **Map** p314 A9.
The CRC is a comprehensive focal point for
material about Commonwealth countries.
It is ideally suited to children studying
for school projects, with more than 20,000
books, atlases, periodicals, travel guides,
plus a wealth of multimedia resources. The
institute hosts temporary exhibitions by
contemporary artists throughout the year,
which focus on the Commonwealth and
related themes. Visit the website to find out
what's on; it may help with your homework.

Kensington & Chelsea Central Library

Phillimore Walk, W8 (7937 2542). High
Street Kensington tube. **Open** 9.30am-8pm
Mon, Tue, Thur; 9.30am-5pm Wed, Fri, Sat.
Map p314 A9.

Under-5s are treated to a story session
10.30-11am every Tuesday. It's a popular
slot, and as numbers are limited to 30, it's
worth picking up your free ticket earlier
in the week. On Mondays, Tuesdays and
Thursdays there's a homework club from
3.30pm to 6.30pm. The Children's Library
is a pleasant place to be, with little chairs
in the under-5s section and window seats
to sit and read in.

Marylebone Library

*109-17 Marylebone Road, NW1 (7641
1041/www.westminster.gov.uk/libraries).*
Baker Street tube/Marylebone tube/rail.
Open Children's Library 9.30am-5.30pm
Mon, Tue, Thur, Fri; 10am-5.30pm Wed;
9.30am-1pm, 2-5pm Sat. **Map** p313 F4.
This children's library has a huge selection
of books and educational resources for
young people of all ages. There are two
under-5s sessions every week: at 10.30-
11.30am on Tuesdays children enjoy a story
session and craft activities; at 2.15-3.15pm
on Thursdays the play is more toy-based.

Victoria Library

*160 Buckingham Palace Road, SW1 (7641
4289/www.westminster.gov.uk/libraries).*
Victoria tube/rail. **Open** 9.30am-7pm Mon,
Tue, Thur, Fri; 10am-7pm Wed; 9.30am-
5pm Sat. **Map** p318 H10.
The Children's Library has under-5s
sessions, with toys and stories, every
Wednesday at 10-11.30am, as well as a
special event every month. The cheerful
library staff also organise events and
activities for young children up to the age
of 8 throughout the year.

Travel

The prices we've listed for
transport and services were
correct at the time of going to
press, but bear in mind that
some prices (especially those
of tube tickets) are subject to
a price hike each January.

Public transport information

All the information below
can be accessed online at
www.transportforlondon.gov.uk
and www.thetube.com, or by
phoning 7222 1234. Transport
for London (TfL) also runs
Travel Information Centres,
which provide maps and
information about the tube, buses,
Tramlink, riverboat, Docklands
Light Railway (DLR) and national
rail services within the London
area. You can find them in the
following stations: Brent Cross

bus station, Euston station, Hammersmith bus station, all Heathrow Airport terminals, Liverpool Street station, Oxford Circus station, Paddington station, Piccadilly Circus station, St James's Park station and West Croydon bus station.

To find out more about Mayor Ken Livingstone's **Transport Strategy for London**, log on to the Greater London Authority website, www.london.gov.uk.

Transport for London's Accessibility Unit
7491 4600.
Ring this number to find out which tube stations are buggy friendly and which bus routes use low-floor buses.

London Transport Users' Committee
Clements House, 14-18 Gresham Street, EC2V 7PR (7505 9000). **Open** 9.30am-5.30pm Mon-Fri.
This is the official watchdog monitoring customer satisfaction with transport in London; it campaigns for a better deal for the city's travellers.

Fares & tickets

Adult fares
The single underground fare for adults within Zone 1 is £1.60, or £1.90 for Zones 1 and 2, rising to £3.60 for an all-zones (1-6) single fare. Single bus fares are 70p for a journey outside Zone 1 and £1 for a journey within Zone 1 or one that crosses the Zone 1 boundary.

If you are staying in London for more than a day, it's always better value to buy a Travelcard (*see below*).

Child fares
On all buses, tubes and local trains, under-16s are classified as children; under-5s travel free. Under-16s pay a child fare until 10pm; after 10pm (buses only) they pay an adult fare. Fourteen- and 15-year-olds must carry Child photocards, available from any post office – take a passport-size photo and proof of age (passport or birth certificate) with you. The single Underground fare for children in Zone 1 is 60p, or 80p covering Zones 1 and 2; rising to £1.50 for an all-zone (1-6) ticket. Single child bus fares cost 40p to anywhere in London.

One-Day LT Cards
One-Day LT Cards will only be of interest if you intend to travel during peak times (ie before 9.30am on weekdays) and make several journeys during the day. They are valid on buses (including night buses), Underground services (except those running to and from Bakerloo Line stations north of Queen's Park; this

section of track is not run by London Underground) and Docklands Light Railway (DLR) services, but not on overland rail services or airbuses. The cards are only available as an All Zones (1-6) ticket, and cost £7.90 (£3.40 child). If you are travelling within Zones 1-4 only, a Peak Day Travelcard would be cheaper.

Travelcards
These can be used on the tube system, buses, rail services within London, Docklands Light Railway and some Green Line buses, and can be bought at all tube and rail stations as well as appointed newsagents. Travelcards also entitle you to one-third off the cost of travel on scheduled riverboat services. The most convenient cards for short-term visitors are the Day or One-Week Travelcards, while monthly and yearly tickets are also available for longer stays.

Day Travelcards are valid in the selected zones on bus, tube, Tramlink, DLR and national rail services.

The **Peak Day Travelcard** can be used from 12.01am Monday to Friday on the day of validity and for any journey that starts from 4.30am the following day. Prices are as follows: Zones 1 and 2 £5.30/£2.60 children; Zones 1-3 £6.20/£3.10 children; Zones 1-4 £6.80/£3.40 children; Zones 1-5 £8.70/£4.30 children; Zones 1-6 £10.50/£5.20 children.

Off-Peak Day Travelcards can be used from 9.30am Monday to Friday (12.01am Saturday, Sunday and bank holidays) on the day of validity and for any journey that starts before 4.30am on the following day. Prices are as follows: Zones 1 and 2 £4.10; Zones 1-4 £4.40; Zones 1-6 £5; child £2.

Family Travelcards are available for families and groups of one or two adults travelling with between one and four children. Like regular Day Travelcards, they are valid after 9.30am Monday to Friday and all day on weekends and bank holidays, and can be used until 4.30am; they cost £2.70 for Zones 1 and 2, £2.90 Zones 1-4 or £3.30 Zones 1-6 (set child price 80p Zones 1-6).

If you'll be travelling on consecutive weekend days, it's probably worth getting a **Weekend Travelcard**, which allows travel on consecutive weekend days or bank holidays, and are valid on N-prefixed night buses. They cost £6.10 for Zones 1 and 2, £6.60 Zones 1-4 and £7.50 Zones 1-6 (child £3 Zones 1-6).

One-Week Travelcards offer unlimited journeys throughout the selected zones for seven days, including use of N-prefixed night buses, and are valid around the clock. Weekly Travelcards cost £16.20 for Zone 1; £19.30 for Zones 1 and 2; £22.50 for Zones 1-3; £28.10 for Zones 1-4; £33.80 for Zones 1-5; £36.90 for all zones (Child Weekly Travelcard rates: £6.70 Zone 1; £7.90 Zones 1 and 2; £10.50 Zones 1-3; £13 Zones 1-4; £14.40 Zones 1-5; £15.70 Zones 1-6).

Carnet
If you're planning on making a lot of short-hop tube journeys within Zone 1 over a period of several days, it makes sense to buy a carnet of ten tickets for £11.50 (£5 for children). This brings

down the cost of each journey to £1.15 rather than the standard £1.60. Note that if you exit a station outside of Zone 1 and are caught with only a carnet ticket, you are liable to a £10 penalty fare.

'Saver' tickets
If you make a number of single journeys by bus, buy a book of six single bus tickets from Travel Information Centres or selected newsagents in advance of travel, to be used on all bus services, including night buses. A book of adult tickets costs £3.90, while the children's rate is £2.10.

Photocards
Photocards are required for all bus passes and Travelcards except the Day and Weekend versions. Child photocards are required for 5-15-year-olds using child Travelcards and bus passes. Fourteen- and 15-year-olds need a Child photocard in order to buy any ticket at the discounted rate.

London Underground

Timetable
Tube trains run daily, starting at around 5.30am every day except Sunday, when they start an hour to two hours later depending on the line. The only exception is Christmas Day, when there is no service. Generally, you won't have to wait more than ten minutes for a train, and during peak times the service should (in theory) run every two or three minutes. Times of last trains vary, though they're usually around 11.30pm-1am every day except Sunday, when they finish 30 minutes to an hour earlier.

The only all-night public transport is by night bus (*see p299*).

Docklands Light Railway (DLR)
7363 9700/www.dlr.co.uk.
The DLR is administered as part of the London Underground network, so Travelcards and Underground tickets are valid. DLR's driverless trains run on a raised track, so grab the front seats for the best views, from Bank (Central, Northern or Waterloo & City Lines) or Tower Gateway, close to Tower Hill tube (Circle and District Lines), to Stratford, Beckton and down the Isle of Dogs to Island Gardens, then under the Thames to Greenwich and on to Lewisham. Trains run from 5.30am to around 12.30am Monday to Saturday and 7am-11.30pm Sunday.

The DLR is keen to promote itself as a tourist attraction as much as a transport system. To this end, it offers Rail & River Rover tickets, which combine unlimited travel on the DLR with a riverboat trip between Greenwich, Tower and Westminster Piers (boats depart from 10.30am to 6.30pm; *see also p112*). Starting at Tower Gateway, selected trains leave with a DLR guide giving passengers the low-down on the area as the train glides along. Tickets cost £8.30 for adults, £4.20 for children, or £22 for a family ticket (two adults and up to three children).

Buses

Travelling on London's extensive bus network is one of the most pleasurable ways of getting to know the city. However, allow plenty of time for your journey: progress through the traffic can be very slow, especially during the morning and evening rush hours.

Night buses

Night buses are the only form of public transport in London that runs through the night. They operate from around 11pm to 6am, about once an hour on most routes (more frequently on Fridays and Saturdays). All pass through central London and the majority stop at Trafalgar Square, so head there if you're not sure which bus to get. All types of Travelcard are accepted on night buses. Pick up a free map and timetable from one of the LT Travel Information Centres.

Night bus fares from central London are the same as daytime fares, but there are no child fares.

For information, call the London Buses helpline on 7918 4300.

Rail services

National rail enquiries

0845 748 4950/www.nationalrail.co.uk. Ring this number to find out how the trains are running on your route, and for timetable information.

Independently owned commuter services run out of all the city's main line rail stations. Travelcards are valid on these services within the relevant zones. **Silverlink** (0845 601 4868/ www.silverlinktrains.co.uk) is a handy and underused overground service that carves a huge arc through the north of the city, running from Richmond (in the south-west) to North Woolwich (in the east), via London City Airport. The line connects with the tube network at several stations.

Families who frequently travel by rail together may consider investing in a **Family Railcard**, which for £20 gives two named adults, two other adults, and up to four children discounted fares on most off-peak journeys. Adults save a third of the ticket price; children 60%.

Tramlink

Croydon's tram service links you to the tube network at Wimbledon and national rail services at Mitcham Junction, East and West Croydon, Beckenham Junction, Elmers End and Birkbeck stations, and to the south London bus network. The single adult fare is 90p in one zone (zones 3 or 4) and £1.30 for travel in both. There is a flat fare of 40p for children. You can also buy a one-day bus and tram pass (price £2.80 for an adult, or £1.20 for children). Weekly tram passes cost from £8 (£4 for children).

Water transport

The times of services vary, but, as a rule, most operate every 20 minutes to an hour between about 10.30am and 5pm. Services may be more frequent and run later in summer. Call the individual operators below for details of schedules and fares. The names in bold below are the names of piers: the central ones are on the maps at the back of this guide.
Westminster–Greenwich (50mins) *Westminster Passenger Services (7930 4097/www.westminsterpier.co.uk).*
Westminster–Tower (30mins) *City Cruises (7740 0400/ www.citycruises.com).*
Westminster–Festival (5mins) – **London Bridge City** (20mins) – **St Katharine's** (5mins) *Crown River Cruises (7936 2033).*
Westminster–(Thames) Barrier Gardens (1hr 10mins). Note that this service is only available as a group booking and not as a public service. *Thames Cruises (7930 3373).*
Westminster–Kew (1hr 30mins) – **Richmond** (30mins)–**Hampton Court** (1hr 30mins) *Westminster Passenger Service Association (7930 2062).*
Embankment–Tower (30mins) – **St Katharine's** (5mins)–**Greenwich** (25mins) *Catamaran Cruises (7987 1185).*
Greenland Dock–Canary Wharf (2mins)–**St Katharine's** (5mins) – **London Bridge City** (2mins)–**Blackfriars** (4mins)–**Savoy** (2mins) *Collins River Enterprises (7237 9538).*
Savoy–Cadogan (18mins) – **Chelsea** (2mins) *Riverside Launches (0831 574774).*
Waterloo/Westminster – Tower (30mins) *City Cruises (7740 0400/ www.citycruises.com).*
Greenwich–(Thames) Barrier Gardens (25mins) *Thames River Services (7930 4097).*

Taxis

Black cabs

Two useful numbers are those for **Radio Taxis** (7272 0272) and **Dial-a-Cab** (7253 5000), which both run 24hr services for black cabs (with a pick-up charge). Any enquiries or complaints about black cabs should be made to the Public Carriage Office (7230 1631; 9am-4pm Mon-Fri).

Minicabs

Minicabs (saloon cars) are generally cheaper than black cabs, especially at night and weekends. **Addison Lee** (7387 8888) is one of the bigger companies, and claims to do pick-ups from all areas. Women and children travelling alone may prefer to use **Lady Cabs** (7254 3501), which employs only women drivers. **London Taxis International** (www.london-taxis.co.uk) is notable in that it has child seats available for younger passengers. Whoever you use, ask the price when you book and confirm it with the driver when the car arrives.

Tourist information

London Tourist Board & Convention Bureau

Admin line 7932 2000/London Line 0906 866 3344/www.londontouristboard.com. Call the LTB for information about where to stay and sights to see in the capital. Its London line (60p per minute) has information for families planning a trip to London. The website has a fun for kids section on the home page. You can ring or write to LTBCB at Glenn House, Stag Place, London SW1 5LT to ask for a special London Information Pack before your visit.

Tourist information centres, listed below, can provide free maps of central London and advice on visitor attractions in and around the city.
Camden Direct Information Centre *Town Hall, Argyle Street, WC1 (7974 5974).* **Open** 9am-5pm Mon-Fri.
Greenwich TIC *Pepys House, 2 Cutty Sark Gardens, SE10 (0870 608 2000/ 8858 6376).* **Open** 10am-5pm daily.
Heathrow Terminals 1, 2, 3 *Tube station concourse, Heathrow Airport.* **Open** 8am-6pm daily.
Liverpool Street Station *tube station concourse, EC2.* **Open** 8am-6pm Mon-Fri; 8.45am-5.30pm Sat, Sun.
Richmond TIC *Old Town Hall, Whittaker Avenue, Richmond TW9 1TP (8940 9125).* **Open** 10am-5pm Mon-Sat. *Easter-Sept* 10am-5pm Mon-Sat; 10am-1.30pm Sun.
Southwark Information Centre *London Bridge, corner of Tooley Street, SE1 (7403 8299).* **Open** *Winter* 10am-4pm Mon-Sat; 11am-4pm Sun. *Summer* 10am-6pm Mon-Sat; 11am-4pm Sun.
Waterloo International Terminal *Arrivals Hall, South Bank, SE1.* **Open** 8.30am-10.30pm daily.
For information on travel in the rest of Britain, try the **Britain Visitor Centre**:
1 Regent Street (south of Piccadilly Circus), SW1 (no phone/www.visitbritain.com). *Piccadilly Circus tube.* **Open** *Jan-July, Oct-Dec* 9am-6.30pm Mon-Fri; 10am-4pm Sat, Sun. *Aug, Sept* 9am-6.30pm Mon-Fri; 9am-5pm Sat; 10am-4pm Sun. **Map** p319 K7.
Personal callers only.

Advertisers' Index

Please refer to relevant pages for
addresses and telephone numbers

Around Town

Eating

Shopping

Arts & Entertainment

Parties

Sport & Leisure

Days Out

Directory

Index

Index

Index

Place of interest and/or entertainment	■■
Railway station	■■
Park	■■
Hospital	■■
Neighbourhood	**SOHO**
Tube station.	⊖
Church	✚
Synagogue	✿
Casuatly unit	✚
Toilet	wc

Maps

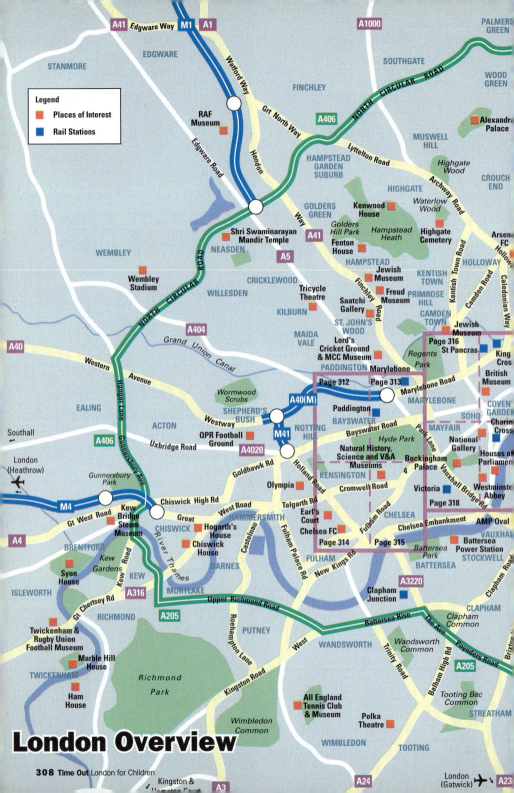

London Overview

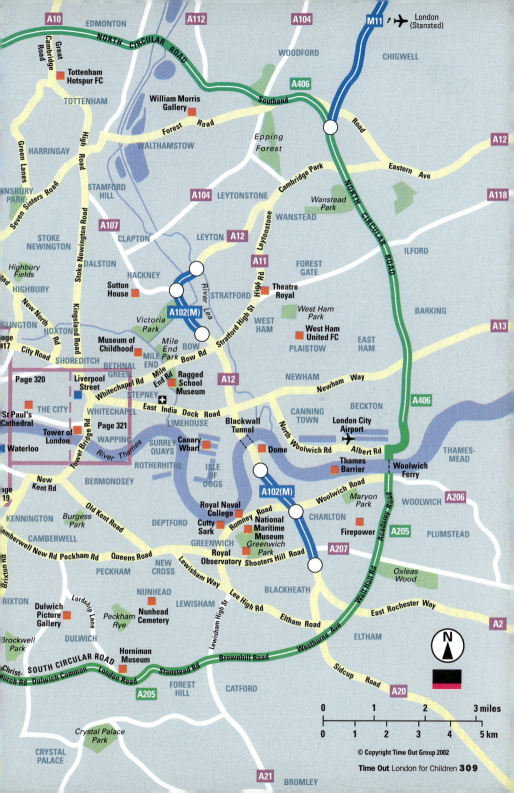

Central London
by Area

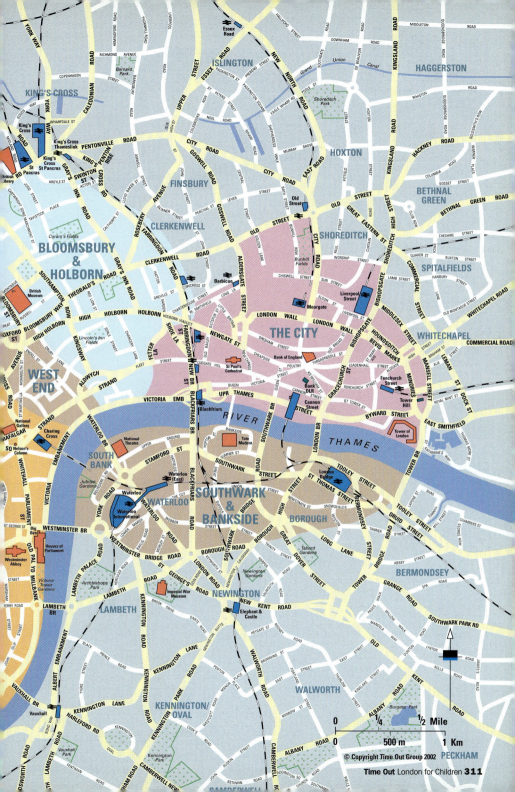

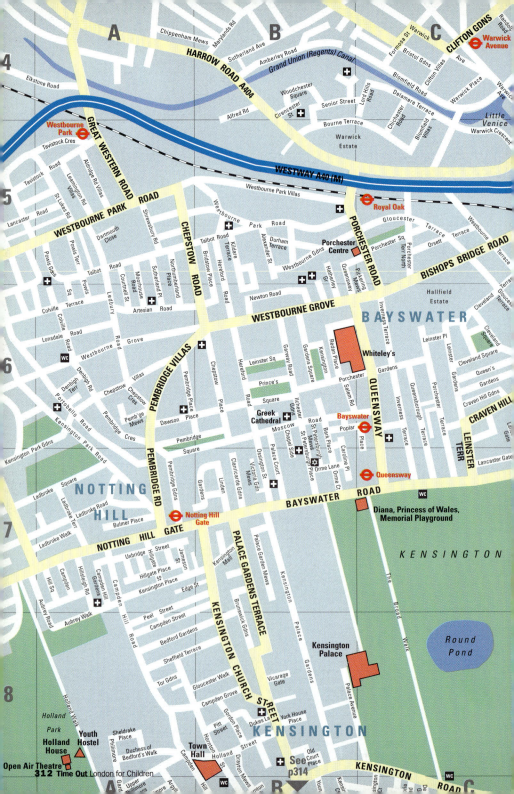

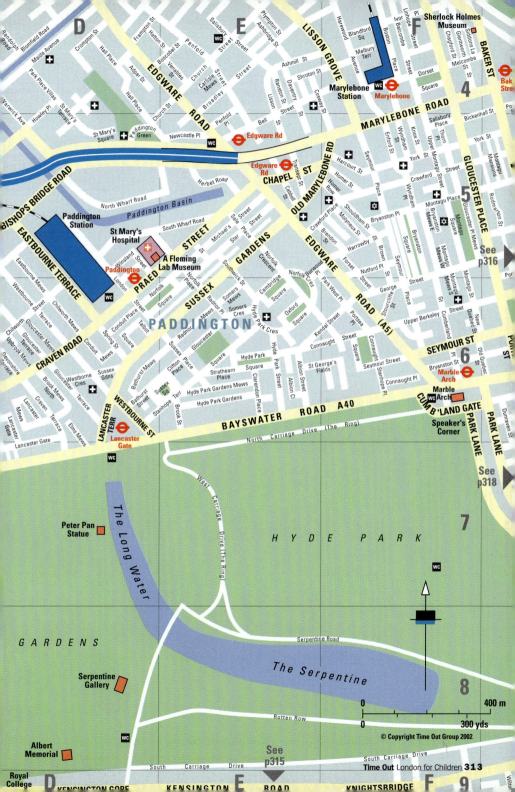

D

Randolph
Road
Blomfield Road
Maida Avenue
Park Place Villas
Warwick Ave
St Mary's Terrace
Howley Pl
St Mary's Square
Crompton St
Hall Place
Adpar St
Church St
Hall Place
Venables St
Church St
Penfold St
St Mary's Square
Paddington Green
Newcastle Pl
Penfold Pl
Bell St

EDGWARE ROAD

Carlisle Mews
Broadley St

E

Plympton St
Salisbury St
Ashbridge St
Frampton St
Hatton St
Boscobel St
Penfold Street
Street
Street
Ashmill St
Ranston St
Daventry St
Shroton St
Lisson St
Street
Cosway St
Transept St

LISSON GROVE

Harewood
Blandford Sq
Boston Pl
Linhope St
Ivor
Balcombe St
Melbury Terr
Melcombe
Place

Marylebone Station
WC
⊖ Marylebone

MARYLEBONE ROAD

Chapel St
Dorset
Square

Harcourt St
Seymour
Homer St
Homer Row
Shouldham St
Crawford Place
Molyneux St
Brendon St
Crawford St
Nutford Pl
York St
Upper Montagu St
Montagu Place
Montagu Square
Bryanston Square
George
Seymour

Salisbury
Place
Bickenhall St
York St

Knox St
Wyndham Pl
Enford St
Wyndham St
Thorn St

⊖ Edgware Rd

Herbet Road
North Wharf Road
Paddington Basin
South Wharf Road

Paddington Station
St Mary's Hospital
⊕
A Fleming Lab Museum
⊖ Paddington
Winsland Street
London St
WC

BISHOPS BRIDGE ROAD

EASTBOURNE TERRACE

Eastbourne Mews
Westbourne Street
Chilworth Mews
Gloucester Terrace
Upbrook Mews
Devonshire Terrace

CRAVEN ROAD
Gloucester Mews
Brook Mews
Craven Terrace
Elms Mews
Lancaster Mews
Lancaster Gate

PRAED STREET
GARDENS

St Michael's St
Sale Street
Star St
Norfolk Cres
Southwick St
Cambridge
Square

Norfolk Place
Norfolk Crescent
Radnor
Place
Oxford
Square
Cambridge
Square

Hyde Park Cres
Somers Cres
Kendal Street
Connaught
St George's
Fields

Oxford
Square
Hyde Park
Square
Connaught
Square
Connaught Place
Seymour Street
Stanhope Pl

PADDINGTON

Conduit Place
Talbot
Square
Spring St
Conduit
Mews
Gloucester
Square
Sussex Gdns
Bathurst Mews
Sussex Sq
Bathurst Street
Clifton Place
Strathearn
Place
Hyde Park
Street
Hyde Park
Square
Albion Street
Albion Cl
Clarendon Place

SUSSEX

WESTBOURNE ST
LANCASTER TERR
⊖ Lancaster Gate
WC
Stanhope Terr
Brook St
Hyde Park Gardens Mews
Hyde Park Gardens

F

Sherlock Holmes Museum

BAKER ST
Siddons La
Glentworth
Chagford St
Chiltern St
Dorset
Square

⊖ Bak Stre

4

Gloucester Place
Rodmarton St
Montagu Mansions
York St

Montagu
Square
Montagu
Mews W
Montagu
Mews
Montagu
Place E
Gloucester Pl Mews

See p316

5

New Quebec St
Old Quebec St
Upper Berkeley Street
Seymour
Street
Cumberland
Street

SEYMOUR ST
⊖ Marble Arch

Marble
Arch
WC
Speaker's Corner

CUMB'LAND GATE
PARK LANE
PARK LANE

6

Port
ST

Dunraven St

See p318

7

BAYSWATER ROAD A40
North Carriage Drive (The Ring)

Peter Pan Statue

The Long Water

West Carriage Drive (The Ring)

H Y D E   P A R K

WC

G A R D E N S

Serpentine Road

Serpentine Gallery

The Serpentine

8

Rotten Row

0 .... 400 m
0 .... 300 yds

Albert Memorial
WC

© Copyright Time Out Group 2002

Royal College

Time Out London for Children 313

9

D
KENSINGTON GORE
KENSINGTON ROAD
E
See p315
ROAD
F
South Carriage Drive
KNIGHTSBRIDGE

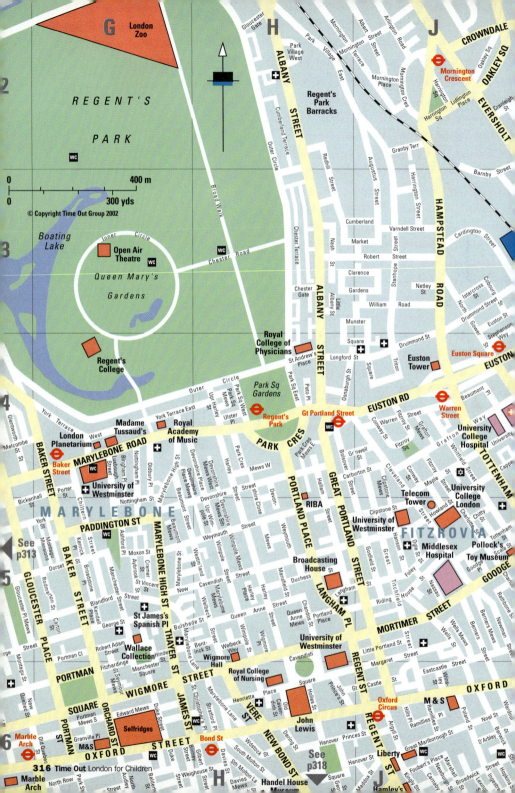

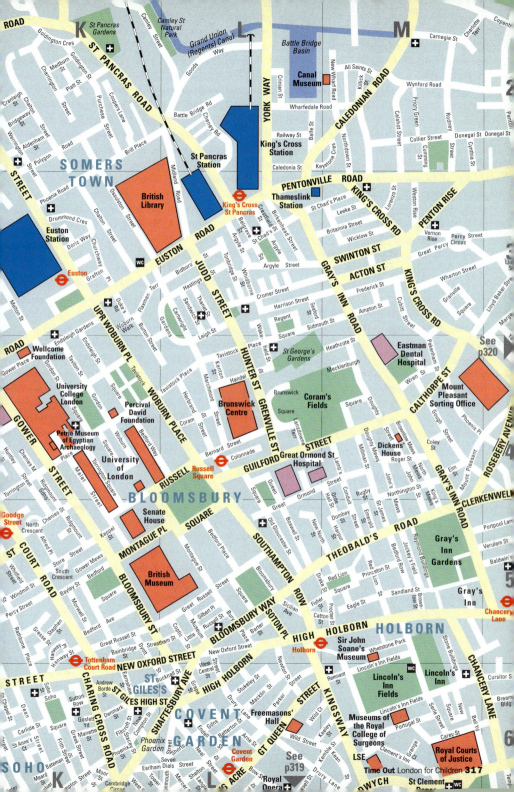

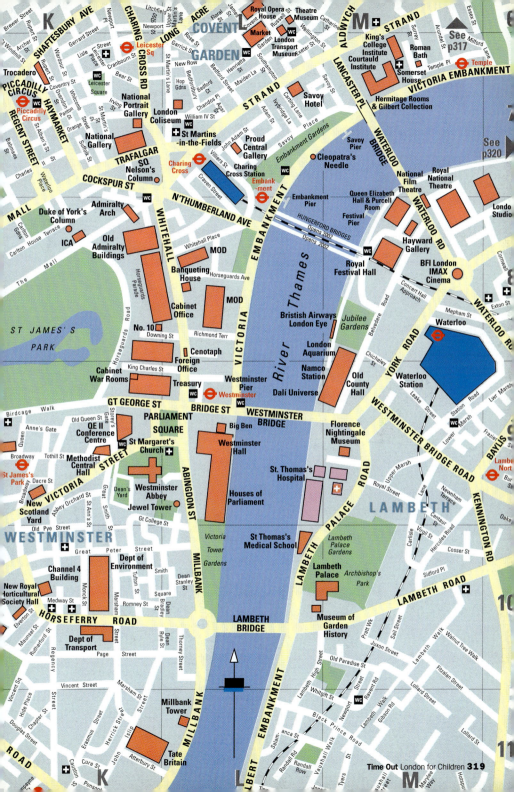

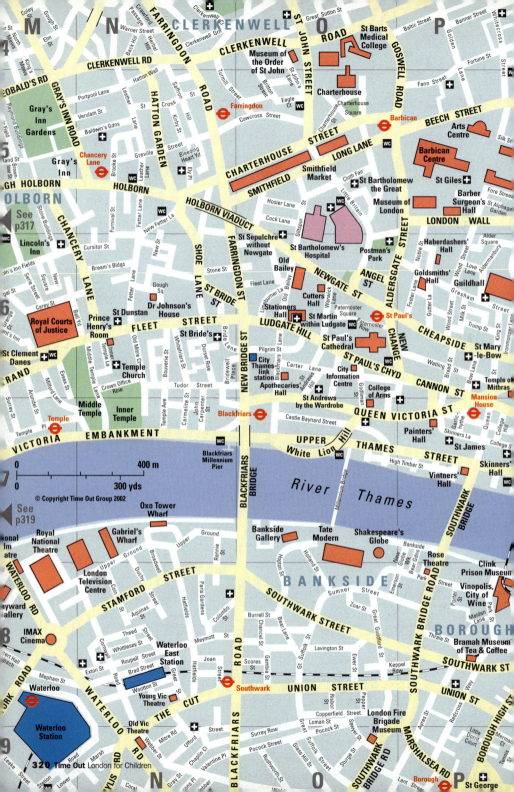

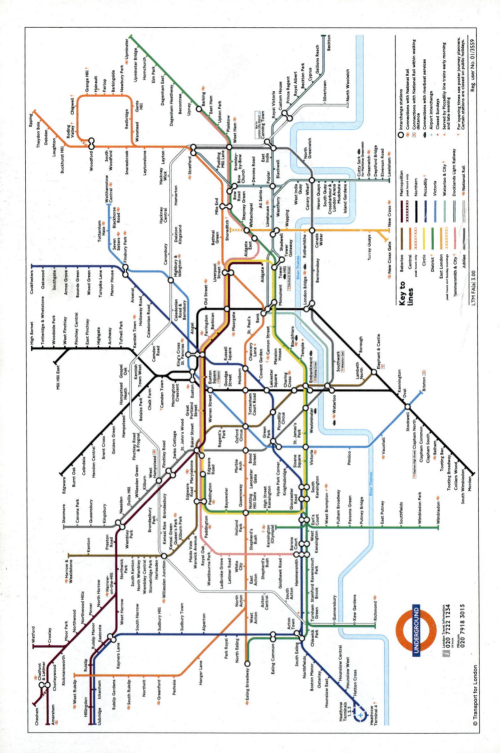